1500 AD

THE MARK TWAIN PAPERS

THE MARK TWAIN PAPERS

Of the projected fifteen volumes of this edition of
Mark Twain's previously unpublished works
the following have been issued to date:

THE MARK TWAIN PAPERS

Editorial Board

WALTER BLAIR
DONALD CONEY
HENRY NASH SMITH

Series Editor of The Mark Twain Papers

FREDERICK ANDERSON

THE MARK TWAIN PAPERS

Of the projected fifteen volumes of this edition of
Mark Twain's previously unpublished works
the following have been issued to date:

MARK TWAIN'S LETTERS TO HIS PUBLISHERS, 1867–1894
edited by Hamlin Hill

MARK TWAIN'S SATIRES & BURLESQUES
edited by Franklin R. Rogers

MARK TWAIN'S WHICH WAS THE DREAM?
edited by John S. Tuckey

MARK TWAIN'S HANNIBAL, HUCK & TOM
edited by Walter Blair

MARK TWAIN'S MYSTERIOUS STRANGER MANUSCRIPTS
edited by William M. Gibson

MARK TWAIN'S CORRESPONDENCE WITH HENRY HUTTLESTON ROGERS
edited by Lewis Leary

MARK TWAIN'S CORRESPONDENCE WITH HENRY HUTTLESTON ROGERS

1893-1909

Edited with an Introduction by Lewis Leary

UNIVERSITY OF CALIFORNIA PRESS
Berkeley and Los Angeles   1969

CENTER FOR EDITIONS OF
AMERICAN AUTHORS

AN APPROVED TEXT

MODERN LANGUAGE
ASSOCIATION OF AMERICA

UNIVERSITY OF CALIFORNIA PRESS
Berkeley and Los Angeles, California

UNIVERSITY OF CALIFORNIA PRESS, LTD.
London, England

© 1969 The Mark Twain Company
Library of Congress Catalog Card Number: 68–23900

Designed by Adrian Wilson
in collaboration with James Mennick

Manufactured in the United States of America

Editor's Preface

THIS COLLECTION of correspondence between Clemens and Rogers may be thought of as a continuation of *Mark Twain's Letters to His Publishers, 1867–1894*, edited by Hamlin Hill. It completes the story begun there of Samuel Clemens's business affairs, especially insofar as they concern dealings with publishers; and it documents Clemens's progress from financial disaster, with the Paige typesetter and Webster & Company, to renewed prosperity under the steady, skillful hand of H. H. Rogers.

But Clemens's correspondence with Rogers reveals more than a business relationship. It illuminates a friendship which Clemens came to value above all others, and it suggests a profound change in his patterns of living. He who during the Hartford years had been a devoted family man, content with a discrete circle of intimates, now became again (as he had been during the Nevada and California years) a man among sporting men, enjoying prizefights and professional billiard matches in public, and—in private—long days of poker, gruff jest, and good Scotch whisky aboard Rogers's magnificent yacht.

Their friendship tended not to include the Clemens family, for in those years, when the Clemenses were traveling or living abroad, the family was frequently separated. Olivia Clemens was seriously ill for much of this period, and both Rogers and Clemens survived her by some five years. Mrs. Clemens's acquaintance with both Mr. Rogers's first and second wives seems to have been cordial but distant. And except for occasional brief meetings in Europe, the Clemens daughters seem not to have known the Rogers daughters.

Clemens himself was always welcome at Rogers's town house in New York and at his country home in Fairhaven, Massachusetts. The whole Rogers clan—including Benjamins, Broughtons, and Coes—welcomed him to their homes, offering companionship in otherwise lonely years; and each of Mr. Rogers's wives treated him with indulgent affection. Clemens responded by becoming both surrogate parent and playmate of the Rogers children, especially young Harry. Clemens's relationship with Harry—a kind of fellowship between young rogues—stands as the unique instance of a boy who was admitted to his close friendship.

This book contains the complete texts of all known correspondence between Clemens and Rogers, as well as relevant letters to and from their wives and secretaries. The texts have been transcribed from the letters the authors originally sent whenever these were available. Several of Rogers's letters, however, had to be taken from office copies, typewritten duplicates apparently kept for his own records. Photocopy or printed sources have supplied the text only when no original could be located. Clemens's letters are customarily in his own handwriting, although some are in that of an amanuensis. Most of Rogers's letters are typewritten and were sent from his business office, where they were apparently dictated to his secretary, Katharine I. Harrison. The Calendar of Letters gives the location and nature of the source used for each letter text. Enclosures or letters mentioned by the correspondents but not reproduced or described here have not been discovered.

The date and place of each letter are given in standard form. Additional significant information in the heading—"At Sea" or "(In bed—noon)"—is, however, presented as written. Details such as street addresses, firm names, and the names of hotels, clubs, and residences given in printed letterheads have been silently dropped unless they provide useful information, in which case they are described or quoted in footnotes. Brackets enclose places and dates which are conjectural; where there is sufficient uncertainty to warrant further warning to the reader, a question mark has been supplied as well.

Various silent emendations have been made to clear the text of insignificant errors—particularly those which appear in letters typed by Rogers's secretaries. Inadvertent omissions of letters or punctuation have been corrected. Thus, the final *s* is added to "Sincerely your"; and "solictous," "ide," and "osteopah" are printed as "solicitous," "idea," and "osteopath" (letters 171, 218, and 253). Necessary accents are added to foreign words; needed terminal punctuation and opening and closing quotation marks or parentheses are added to sentences. Silent deletions have been kept to a minimum, but minor errors have been rectified; where Clemens wrote "P. of. W." (for Prince of Wales), the second period has been dropped (letter 230). Clemens normally punctuated possessives accurately; the other correspondents were less consistent, The apostrophe has been added or deleted when necessary.

All of Clemens's idiosyncratic spellings ("recal," "envelop," "negociation") have been retained, and proper names have been emended only where it is evident that the misspelling resulted from a slip of the pen or a typing error. But unintentional misspellings like Clemens's "laryngual" or "sieze" are silently corrected.

In all cases where misspelling is suspected but not certain, the correct form has been printed. And in doubtful cases, especially hyphenated compound words ("hand-shake"), Clemens's dominant usage has been assumed. Where possible compounds hyphenated by Clemens break at the end of a line in this volume, Clemens's hyphen is represented by a double hyphen ("hand=shake"). Telegrams and cablegrams have been printed without emendation.

Necessary capitalization is supplied, and a standard relationship between punctuation and closing quotation marks or parentheses is imposed. Accidental conflation of two words ("hast lost"), when no suspicion of dialect or intentional misspelling is present, has been corrected (letter 313).

Certain kinds of emendations have been enclosed in square brackets. When Clemens wrote "hoping a" or "first & June," a conjecture has been substituted for the error: "hoping [I]" and "first [of] June." And where a correspondent has inadvertently omitted a word, or where the manuscript has been partly destroyed, editorial conjecture is again supplied in square brackets.

To avoid cluttering the text, complete evidence of revision in the manuscripts is not presented. Insertions, marginal comments, and interlinear additions are printed in their logical order without editorial comment. All postscripts are paragraphed and printed at the ends of letters, no matter where they were originally placed. When a writer failed to change a capital letter to lower case after inserting a word at the beginning of a sentence, or after changing a final period to a comma, the necessary change has been silently made. If Clemens wrote "There's" and then changed his verb to "are," the apostrophe and *s* are silently dropped.

Cancellations appear within angle brackets, thus: "Yet I ⟨will⟩ *would* make it." As far as possible, they are printed in the order of their composition. Those cancellations which cannot be recovered, or which are fragmentary and therefore doubtful, have been silently omitted. Canceled false starts and slips of the pen have also been dropped without comment.

Certain additional conventions have been adopted. Positioning of signatures and complimentary closes, as well as that of most salutations, has been standardized. Clemens's carelessly written complimentary closes, which can be read as "Ys" or "Yr," have been uniformly rendered as "Yrs." Flourishes and devices to separate portions of the text have been dropped or conventionalized as a short, centered rule. Superscript letters and numerals have been lowered to the line and accompanying punctuation supplied when needed; "%" (meaning "care of") is rendered as c/o; ampersands, except in formal business titles (Harper & Brothers) or in quotations from previously published texts, have been expanded to "and"; "&c" is rendered as "etc."; and Clemens's square brackets are given as parentheses. Clemens indicated emphasis by single, double, or even triple underlining. Except where distinction of emphasis is required (as in *"Phe*-e-u," letter 338), all underlined words are simply italicized. Similarly, such directions as "over" at the bottom of a page have been dropped, since these become meaningless in a continuous text.

Despite these necessary exceptions, every effort has been made to obey Clemens's injunction to "follow my copy EXACTLY, in every minute detail of *punctuation, grammar, construction* and (in the case of proper names) *spelling*" (SLC to Mr. Harper, 11 September 1894, CWB).

Acknowledgments

So MUCH assistance has been received in editing these letters that in plain justice the title page should be filled with collaborators' names. First thanks go to Peter A. Salm, to the late Henry Rogers Benjamin, to William Rogers Coe, Dallas Pratt, and Paul Peralto-Ramos, descendants of Henry Huttleston Rogers, who have been generous in contributing both materials from their collections of Mark Twain memorabilia and important information about the Rogers family. Next, thanks go to the librarians and curators of manuscripts at the Clifton Waller Barrett Library of the University of Virginia Library; the Henry W. and Albert A. Berg Collection of the New York Public Library and the Astor, Lenox and Tilden Foundations; the University of California Library at Berkeley; the Benjamin Collection at Columbia University; the Morse Collection at Yale University; the Laurence Hutton Collection of Mark Twain Papers at Princeton University; the Millicent Library in Fairhaven, Massachusetts; the Estelle Doheny Collection at St. John's Seminary, Camarillo, California; Manuscript Collections, Carnegie Library, Syracuse University; and the Enoch Pratt Free Library, Baltimore, Maryland, who have permitted the use of materials from their collections. The American Council of Learned Societies, the

Center for Editions of American Authors sponsored by the Modern Language Association of America, and the Council for Research in the Humanities at Columbia University have been generous in providing funds for research and travel. Serie Lawson Larson, Acting Director of the Mark Twain Memorial in Hartford; Rita E. Steele, Librarian of the Millicent Library in Fairhaven, Massachusetts; Dorothy Plourde of Pratt & Whitney Company, Inc.; Sheldon H. Harris of San Fernando State College; Marguerite Pettet, Vice-President of the Coe Foundation; Ruth Borel and Erika Oliver, Mr. Salm's secretaries; F. D. Murray, of the Henry Rogers Benjamin Fund; and Mrs. Charles E. Ives, who gave permission for examination of the papers of her father, the Reverend Joseph Twichell, have all been of important assistance. Rheita Zeitlin, Barbara Martineau, Martha Leary Combi, Heather von Manowski, Rhoda St. James, Theodore Guberman, Victor Fischer, Mark Miller, and Mariam Kagan have been invaluable in necessary dull tasks of typing, filing, and copy reading.

Henry Nash Smith, of the University of California at Berkeley, Claude M. Simpson, Jr., of Stanford University, and Judith Kartman of the University of California Press have made the collection more sound through close reading and helpful criticism of the manuscript; Howard G. Baetzhold, of Butler University, John S. Tuckey, of Purdue University, Mark Wilson, of the University of North Carolina, and Horace S. Peck have saved it from several errors.

Frederick Anderson, Editor of the Mark Twain Papers, has provided throughout a generous but demanding example of what the good editor must be—chief gratitude goes to him and to the group of graduate students from the University of California at Berkeley who have worked under his supervision, and also to Esther Hyneman, a graduate assistant from Columbia University, who in early stages broke ground which all the others have since cultivated. The companionable and selfless labors of Michael Frank, George P. Germany, Alan D. Gribben, Robert Hirst, and Bernard L. Stein are responsible for most of the excellences of this volume; its shortcomings are the editor's. The hours on hours which members of this group, assisted briefly but importantly by Thomas Beeler of Columbia University, have devoted to deciphering what had seemed to the editor undecipherable cancellations, to ascertaining dates for what he had thought to be undatable letters, in running down hints and allusions until they became documented facts, checking and rechecking, and pulling their sometimes erring elders up short, provide heartening evidence that the future of literary scholarship among us is in good hands.

LEWIS LEARY

January 1968

Contents

Abbreviations

THE FOLLOWING abbreviations and location symbols have been used in annotations. Unless otherwise indicated, all materials quoted in the documentation are transcribed from originals in the Mark Twain Papers (MTP). Transcriptions from typescript copies are identified as TS, from Office Copies as OC, from photocopies as PH.

COLLECTIONS

Benjamin	The Henry Rogers Benjamin Fund New York City
Berg	Henry W. and Albert A. Berg Collection New York Public Library
Coe	The Collection of William Rogers Coe New York City
Columbia	Columbia University Library New York City
CWB	The Clifton Waller Barrett Library University of Virginia Charlottesville
Fairhaven	The Millicent Library Fairhaven, Massachusetts
MTP	Mark Twain Papers University of California Library Berkeley

Pratt   The Collection of Dr. Dallas Pratt
                 New York City

Princeton   Mark Twain Collection
                 Princeton University Library

Salm   The Collection of Peter A. Salm
                 New York City

Syracuse   Manuscript Collection, Carnegie Library
                 Syracuse University

Yale   Mark Twain Collections
                 Yale University Library

CORRESPONDENTS

ERR   Emilie Randel Rogers
HHR   Henry Huttleston Rogers
IVL   Isabel V. Lyon
KIH   Katharine I. Harrison
OLC   Olivia Langdon Clemens
SLC   Samuel Langhorne Clemens

PREVIOUSLY PUBLISHED TEXTS

LLMT   *The Love Letters of Mark Twain,* ed. Dixon Wecter
         (New York: Harper & Brothers, 1949).

MTA   *Mark Twain's Autobiography,* ed. Albert Bigelow Paine
         (New York: Harper & Brothers, 1924).

MTB   Albert Bigelow Paine, *Mark Twain: A Biography* (New
         York: Harper & Brothers, 1912).

MTBus   *Mark Twain, Business Man,* ed. Samuel C. Webster
         (Boston: Little, Brown, 1946).

MTE   *Mark Twain in Eruption,* ed. Bernard DeVoto (New
         York: Harper & Brothers, 1940).

MTHL   *Mark Twain–Howells Letters,* ed. Henry Nash Smith
         and William M. Gibson (Cambridge: Harvard Univer-
         sity Press, 1960).

MTL   *Mark Twain's Letters,* ed. Albert Bigelow Paine (New
         York: Harper & Brothers, 1917).

MTLC   Paul Fatout, *Mark Twain on the Lecture Circuit* (Bloomington: Indiana University Press, 1960).

MTLM   *Mark Twain's Letters to Mary*, ed. Lewis Leary (New York: Columbia University Press, 1961).

MTLP   *Mark Twain's Letters to His Publishers, 1867–1894*, ed. Hamlin Hill (Berkeley and Los Angeles: University of California Press, 1967).

MTS (1910) *Mark Twain's Speeches*, ed. Albert Bigelow Paine (New York: Harper & Brothers, 1910).

MTS (1923) *Mark Twain's Speeches*, ed. Albert Bigelow Paine (New York: Harper & Brothers, 1923).

MTSatan   John S. Tuckey, *Mark Twain and Little Satan* (West Lafayette: Purdue University Studies, 1963).

MTW   *Mark Twain at Work*, ed. Bernard DeVoto (Cambridge: Harvard University Press, 1942).

S&B   *Mark Twain's Satires & Burlesques*, ed. Franklin R. Rogers (Berkeley and Los Angeles: University of California Press, 1967).

SCH   Dixon Wecter, *Sam Clemens of Hannibal* (Boston: Houghton Mifflin, 1952).

WWD   *Mark Twain's Which Was the Dream?*, ed. John S. Tuckey (Berkeley and Los Angeles: University of California Press, 1967).

INTRODUCTION

This is to make you acquainted with Mr. H. H. Rogers,
who is a friend of mine and yet is not damaged by that,
but survives it and is all the better for it. . . .
I do not need to explain to you who Mr. Rogers is,
since whoever knows the Standard Oil knows *him*.
                                SLC to T. K. Webster, 31 October 1893

A LATER generation may not recognize Henry Huttleston
Rogers as instantly as Clemens's generation did. The magnitude of
his wealth, the ruthlessness with which he was said to have gained
and controlled it, and his occasional benefactions were envied,
feared, or applauded by his contemporaries. But he was among the
last of his kind: "the astonishing career of Mr. Rogers," explained
an editorial in the New York *Times* on the day after his death on
19 May 1909, "can never be repeated in this country." [1] It was the

---

[1] No full biography of Rogers exists, and one which can present all details of
his mercurial rise is not likely to be written. Allan Nevins, who in 1936 and 1937
applied for access to Rogers's papers, reports that he was told by an attorney
connected with the Rogers estate that the business papers were then being
destroyed (*Study in Power: John D. Rockefeller* [New York, 1953], I, 413–414,
n. 5), and subsequent inquiries have not indicated that they are now available.
Materials for the present sketch are drawn from sources few of which are
unbiased: Nevins's biography of Rogers's principal associate; Ida M. Tarbell's
The History of the Standard Oil Company (New York, 1904) and her autobio-
graphical *All in the Day's Work* (New York, 1939); Thomas W. Lawson's
Frenzied Finance (New York, 1905); John S. Gregory's, "Henry H. Rogers—
Monopolist," in *World's Work*, X (May 1905), 6127–30; "The Engaging
Personal Side of Henry Rogers," *Current Literature*, XLVII (July 1909), 34–37;
Harper's Weekly, LIII (29 May 1909), 5, 9; *The Nation*, LXXXVIII (27 May

1

familiar pattern of Benjamin Franklin's or Abraham Lincoln's life story, and Samuel Clemens's also—the poor boy who works hard and achieves phenomenal success—but with a difference. Rogers became a speculator with a Midas touch, such as Colonel Sellers or Samuel Clemens might well admire, but he had an iron fist which they could not, or would not, have wielded with such devastating vigor.

Born in Mattapoisett, Massachusetts, on 29 January 1840, Rogers grew up in nearby Fairhaven, where he was graduated from high school in 1856. He clerked in a grocery store, peddled newspapers, and worked as a brakeman and baggage master on a local railroad for $1.16 a day. By the time he was twenty-one, he had saved $600, enough for him and another equally frugal young man from Fairhaven, Charles P. Ellis, to set off for the newly opened oil fields of Pennsylvania. There they pooled their savings to establish a small refining plant at McClintocksville on the outskirts of Oil City. By 1862 the firm of Rogers & Ellis was sufficiently prosperous to allow Rogers to return briefly to Fairhaven to marry Abbie Palmer Gifford. Vigorous and authoritative, Rogers advanced so fast in the new industry that in 1866 he was invited to join Charles Pratt & Company, which owned one of the largest refineries of crude oil in the Allegheny valley. From its Brooklyn offices the company controlled the distribution of oil in New York City, Long Island, and northern New Jersey. When in 1872 the Rockefellers in Cleveland attempted to form an alliance among the leading refineries of that city, Pittsburgh, Philadelphia, and New York, Rogers returned to Pennsylvania in an attempt to organize small refineries there in opposition to the merger. But in October 1874, when the coalition Standard Oil Company was formed, he and Pratt became part of the emerging alliance which Allan Nevins has called "perhaps the ablest in the history of American business." Nevins reports, however, that "the considered judgment of some

1909), 545–546; obituaries in the New York *Times,* the New York *World,* and other newspapers on 20 May 1909; Rogers's own brief but revealing account in *Who's Who in America;* a more dispassionate account in the *Dictionary of American Biography;* Clemens's reminiscences in *MTA,* his family correspondence in *MTP,* and statements by Albert Bigelow Paine in *MTB.*

later Standard leaders was that the organization would have been better off had he never entered it" (*Study in Power*, I, 274, 272).

For Rogers stood out even among his associate overlords. Of bold and regal bearing, his head held high, he was attractive, magnetic, and a natural leader, whose friends, says Nevins, "found him an unmatchable raconteur and a prince of entertainers. But his competitors in business—and some associates—knew him as exacting, cold, relentless, and tyrannical" (*Study in Power*, I, 272). His first contribution to Standard Oil Company operations was in the supervision of production; he knew this part of the business from first-hand experience in the oil fields, where he had invented and, in 1870, patented a method for extracting naphtha from crude oil. But he soon moved confidently into other areas of activity. He reached beyond production to distribution by becoming president of the National Transit Company, which would put down a system of pipelines to carry oil, he hoped, to every state in the union. In 1884 he and William Rockefeller were instrumental in forming the Consolidated Gas Company, which fought for control of plants in all major cities and which brought them into head-on conflict with J. Edward Addicks of Boston in legal battles which stretched over many years. Those battles led the Consolidated Gas Company into business practices which a disgruntled former colleague, Thomas W. Lawson, zealously exposed in *Frenzied Finance* (1905). Rogers caught the public eye as a debonair evader of questions asked by government commissions investigating the methods by which he and his associates established their monopolies. An "irascible and contemptuous witness," the New York *World* called him in an editorial the day after his death, who mocked "the efforts of a sovereign State to investigate his business methods." Rogers was called a butcher, a pirate, "Hell Hound Rogers." No punishable offense, observed the New York *Times*, was ever "formally proved against him," but his "share in the unfair and abhorrent methods of Standard Oil was so considerable that he ought therefore to have suffered from increasing torments of remorse; and undoubtedly he did not so suffer."

When the Standard Oil Company was reorganized in 1890,

Rogers became a vice-president and director. From his office, which looked out over the Statue of Liberty from the eleventh floor of the company's building at 26 Broadway, he virtually controlled its burgeoning activities. Ida M. Tarbell was impressed by the many ways there were to enter his office, circuitous ways which guaranteed that she would not be seen by anyone from whom Rogers wished to conceal her visits (*All in the Day's Work*, p. 216). Clemens found the office sultanic:

> a kind of fortress with outworks, these outworks being several communicating rooms into which no one could get access without first passing through an outwork where several young colored men stood guard and carried in the cards and requests and brought back the regrets. Three of the communicating rooms were for consultations, and they were seldom unoccupied. Men sat in them waiting—men who were there by appointment—appointments not loosely specified, but specified by the minute hand of the clock (*MTA*, I, 253).

He enjoyed lounging in Rogers's fortress, "stretched out on a sofa behind his chair, observing his processes," admiring the efficiency of the chieftain's attendant-page, his capable private secretary, Katharine I. Harrison, who had a desk within the fortress also. He admired Rogers's stamina and resiliency in "reasonings with the captains of industry":

> Every day these consultations supplied a plenty of vexations and exasperations for Mr. Rogers—I know this quite well—but if ever they found revealment in his face or manner it could have been for only a moment or two, for the signs were gone when he re-entered his private office and he was always his brisk and cheerful self again and ready to be chaffed and joked, and reply in kind. His spirit was often heavily burdened, necessarily, but it cast no shadow, and those about him sat always in the sunshine (*MTA*, I, 253–254).

Rogers's interests became increasingly diversified, his influence increasingly large, and the outcry against him in the press and legislative chambers increasingly loud. Criticism was heaped on him for his share in the formation of Amalgamated Copper, a giant trust built on the corpses of competitors from Boston to Montana, with an initial capital investment of $75,000,000, more than half of which was said to have been in watered stock. He had become the transportation magnate of Staten Island, controlling its traction lines, railroads, and ferries. He joined with Edward H. Harriman as a power behind the Union Pacific Railroad, and he then became a director of that and other lines. Rogers, like Harriman, made extensive investments in insurance and imperturbably survived the governmental investigations of 1905 which looked into their practices. He invested widely, but wisely, in whatever promised profit.[2] "As fine a pirate," said Ida M. Tarbell, "as ever flew his flag in Wall Street" (*All in the Day's Work*, p. 10). To be known also as a friend and protector of so popular a public figure as Mark Twain must have been helpful to Rogers—to be seen with his friend at sporting events, to maintain him as a kind of private jester for cruises on his yacht. For Rogers also "may be regarded," said Ida M. Tarbell, "as the first public relations counsel of the Standard Oil Company" (*All in the Day's Work*, p. 214).

But in another sense, Clemens was the king and Rogers his powerful vizier. The friendship between them was public and often playful, but it was real. There was a doubleness in Rogers not unlike the doubleness in the Clemens who was also Mark Twain and who was never comfortable with money nor satisfied without it. If in business Rogers could seem unfeelingly rapacious, in personal relations, in drawing room or club, he could be the most charming of gentlemen, gracious and kindly. His eyes could be flint-hard at

---

[2] The New York *World* on 20 May 1909 listed some of his corporate positions: Besides being vice-president of the Standard Oil Company, he was president and director of the Amalgamated Copper Company, the National Transit Company, the National Fuel Company, the New York Transit Company, and the Richmond Light and Railroad Company; vice-president and trustee of the Anaconda Copper Mining Company; vice-president and director of the Brooklyn Union Gas Company and the United Metals Selling Company; trustee of the Mutual Life Insurance Company of New York. And he was director of the United States Steel Corporation; the Atchison, Topeka, and Santa Fe Railroad Company; the Chicago, Milwaukee, and St. Paul Railroad Company; the Union Pacific Railroad Company; the New Jersey and Staten Island Railroad Company; the Staten Island Ferry Company; the Atlas Tack Company; the Farmers' Loan and Trust Company; the Guaranty Trust Company; the National Bank of Fairhaven; the Tennessee Copper Company; the Staten Island Midland Railway Company; and the Atlantic Coast Electric Company.

one moment and a friendly, sparkling blue the next. As open-handed to friends as he was ruthless to competitors, he donated generously to the village where he had spent his boyhood; he gave two schools, a library, a town hall, a public park, a Masonic hall, a church with parish house and parsonage, and improvements for all its streets. He built a palatial summer residence in the outskirts of the village; and in order that Fairhaven might have a first-class hotel, he built the Tabitha Inn, named in honor of his grandmother. His largesse to Booker T. Washington and Helen Keller was known only to closest associates, for he preferred quietness in personal affairs. When relaxed, he was a raconteur capable of vying with Clemens. He liked poker and billiards and swearing and the exchange of gruff insults with his friends. "I always play poker," he is reported to have said, "when the market is closed . . . Saturday afternoons I almost always make up a poker party" (*All in the Day's Work,* p. 218).

Rogers was many things that Clemens was not: consistent, careful, conscientious; his tact seemed to Clemens as great as his generosity: "His character is full of fine graces, but the finest is this: that he can load you down with crushing obligations, and then so conduct himself that you never feel their weight. . . . He was born serene, patient, all-enduring, where a friend is concerned . . . He is not only the best friend I have ever had, but is the best man I have known" (Appendix G). Joseph Twichell of Hartford was a great friend of long standing; William Dean Howells was a literary friend, closer to him than any other; but Rogers, Clemens said, was "the only man I would give a *damn* for" (SLC to OLC, 15 February 1894). He could calm the troubled waters of Clemens's spirit; he could laugh, and he could afford expensive play. The more he helped Clemens, the more Clemens admired him; each played to the other's need.

Stories about their friendship continue to circulate, like the one told by Finley Peter Dunne about a literary luncheon club that was being planned ("Mr. Dooley's Friends," *Atlantic Monthly,* CCXII [September 1963], 95). After Dunne and Clemens had agreed to invite Robert Collier and Howells, Clemens said:

"How about H. H. Rogers?"

"I thought you said this was to be a literary lunch."

"So it is."

"Then why ask Rogers?"

"Why ask Rogers?" Mark cried. "Why ask Rogers? To pay for the lunch, you idiot."

Harper's Weekly, ten days after Rogers's death observed that: "He was one of the 'big men' of the country. . . . His audacity and courage—the sporting blood in him—caught and held the attention of that sporting element which takes so large a share in affairs. Besides all that, he was personally interesting; a man of humor; a good comrade and an affectionate friend." During the last few years of his life, he had some setbacks, for the temper of the times was changing; the muckrakers were at large, and reforms were setting in. His worst public defeat came as a result of an ouster suit brought by the State of Missouri in 1905, when, with reporters present, he had to admit that the Standard Oil Company did have secret investments in subsidiary companies. But soon afterwards Rogers had a final personal triumph.[3] In 1909 he completed—and all with capital of his own or that he had raised by himself—the Virginian Railway, which stretched for almost five hundred miles from the mining fields at Deepwater, West Virginia, to tidewater Virginia at Sewall Point near Norfolk. When the road was ceremoniously opened, Rogers was ill and Clemens was ill, but they journeyed to Norfolk, where Clemens made a speech in which he revealed something of his admiration for the achievement and the bounty of his friend.

When Rogers died suddenly of a stroke less than two months

---

[3] But at large cost to his private fortune, for when unexpectedly high production costs forced him to borrow money, rival financiers, "generally believed to have been captained by J. Pierpont Morgan, who had been camping on his trail for years, gave him no mercy in the spring of 1907. Dozens of times Mr. Rogers had done the same things to others," said the New York *World* on 20 May 1909, "grinding up the poor and rich in his money-making machines, but it was a crushing blow when he was caught himself." When he tried to sell securities, prices were beaten down; when he tried to borrow, interest rates were raised: his fortune which a few years before had been estimated at $100,000,000 had shrunk to an estimated $50,000,000 by the time of his death.

later, newspapers filled columns with stories about him—the "Dual
Personality of Henry H. Rogers," his gifts of "Millions to His
Home Town," John D. Rockefeller's warning to him that he had
been working too hard, how "Norfolk Mourns His Death," and
about "Flags Half Masted at Copper Mines." Clemens could not
have agreed with the judgment expressed by the New York *Times,*
that "Mr. Rogers was one of that class . . . who, with opportunities
and with the ability to make a great fortune, made that fortune
colossal by not giving the other fellow a fair chance." To him, his
friend represented the epitome of modern chivalry; he was exactly
what a gentleman should be. Of all his great qualities, said
Clemens:

> the one which I most admired, and which was to me a constant
> reproach because I lacked it, was his unselfishness where a friend or
> a cause that was near his heart was concerned, and his native
> readiness to come forward and take vigorous hold of the difficulty
> involved and abolish it. I was born to indolence, idleness, procrasti-
> nation, indifference—the qualities that constitute a shirk; and so he
> was always a wonder to me, and a delight—he who never shirked
> anything, but kept his master brain and his master hands going all day
> long, and every day, and was happiest when he was busiest, and ap-
> parently lightest of heart when his burden of labor and duty was
> heaviest.
>   He could take trouble; . . . to see him take trouble, no end of
> trouble, days and days of trouble, and take it so patiently, so placidly,
> so interestedly—and so affectionately, too, if it was for somebody else
> —was to me a strange and marvelous thing, and beautiful (*MTA,* I,
> 264).

Perhaps the most telling tribute appeared in *Harper's Weekly.* It
may have been written by George Harvey, with whom six years
earlier Rogers had drawn up a contract for the publication of books
by Mark Twain which would free Clemens and his heirs from
financial worries:

> He did a great many things, including a number that he ought not to
> have done. A huge fortune is like a tall, strong, obstreperous horse,
> only useful to a man who is able to catch and ride him. Mr. Rogers

caught and rode his horse—rode him over, or through, some pretty tall fences and across some wide ditches; and at times observers held their breaths, and at times they scolded, but he did ride the horse. There was nothing bogus about him. He was delightfully free from hypocrisy, and did not know how to be a snob. What was best in his life—his kindness, his companionableness, his benefactions—is largely matter of private knowledge. He did not advertise that side of himself. If he had to choose whether to advertise his good deeds or his misdeeds, the misdeeds would have had the notice. That was the manner of faulty man he was.

The correspondence between Clemens and Rogers does not reveal all details of the financial life of either man, but it does set forth some of the moods and crotchets of two aging men who found frequent comfort in being together. The letters reveal within Clemens, as his secretary Isabel V. Lyon once wrote, some of the "deep disturbed moods which rose to the surface like foam, and vanished as they found escape in these letters of affection, to the man who understood him better than could any other."

I

"Fussing with Business"

(DECEMBER 1893–FEBRUARY 1895)

> "I am so tuckered out with 5 months of daily and nightly
> fussing with business, that I shall not feel any interest
> in literature or anything else until I have had a half-year
> of rest and idleness to compensate that account."
>
> SLC to Arthur S. Hardy,
> 3 February 1894, Bancroft Library

W HEN Samuel Clemens arrived in New York from Europe on 7 September 1893, he was miserable with a cold and apprehensive about his financial future. To cure the cold, he "went to bed before dark and drank almost a whole bottle of whisky, and got up perfectly well" the next morning (SLC to Clara Clemens, 10 September 1893, TS in MTP). But the apprehension was not so easily done away with. The country was gripped by the Panic of 1893, and the development of the Paige typesetting machine, in which Clemens had invested many thousands of dollars during the past twelve years, had come to a standstill. Charles L. Webster & Company, Clemens's publishing firm, was in serious trouble also.

10

Bankruptcy had barely been averted a few months earlier; now the debts had to be paid at once, but "Money can not be had, at any rate of interest whatever," Clemens wrote his wife on 13 September, "or upon any sort of security, or by *anybody*."

Clemens went to Hartford, hoping for help there, but was disappointed; he "raced around Wall street . . . assailing banks and brokers—couldn't get anything" (SLC to OLC, 17 September 1893). When prospects seemed darkest, Dr. Clarence C. Rice, at whose home at 123 East 19th Street Clemens stayed during his first weeks in New York, "told me he had ventured to speak to a rich friend of his who was an admirer of mine about our straits. I was very glad. Mr. Hall was to be at this gentleman's office away down Broadway at 4 yesterday afternoon, with his statements; and in six minutes we had the check and our worries were over till the 28th" (SLC to OLC, 17 September 1893).

The rich friend was Henry Huttleston Rogers who, like so many others, had been reminded of his own boyhood by the writings of Mark Twain. Clemens was later fond of recalling that they first met in this autumn of 1893: a chance encounter in the lobby of the Murray Hill Hotel, an introduction by Dr. Rice, an instant friendship, with Rogers in perpetual gales of laughter at Clemens's stories. At the time, however, he wrote his daughter that he had first met "the best new acquaintance I've ever seen" two years before, on a yacht (SLC to Clara Clemens, 15 September 1893, TS in MTP). Rogers now began his sixteen years of involvement in Clemens's affairs. Rogers arranged for his son-in-law, William Evarts Benjamin, to buy the *Library of American Literature* from Charles L. Webster & Company for $50,000. "This," said Hall, "will insure our safety for several months to come" (Fred J. Hall to SLC, 18 October 1893). Clemens reported to his wife: "I have got the best and wisest man of the whole Standard Oil group—a multi-millionaire—a good deal interested in looking into the type-setter" (*MTB*, pp. 970–971).

The affairs of the typesetting machine designed by James W. Paige needed looking into. The complete and complicated story of Clemens's participation in its fortunes and misfortunes since 1881, when he first invested in the Farnham Type Setting Company in Hartford, can perhaps never be recovered, but the outlines are clear. By 1887, he was contributing over $3,000 a month toward salaries and expenses for Paige and such expert mechanic-assistants as Charles E. Davis who were working to perfect the machine. In 1885, and again in 1890, he and William Hamersley, of the Farnham Company, tried to form a new joint-stock company that would buy out Paige, but with no success. In June 1891, having exchanged his stock in the machine for royalties on future sales, Clemens retreated with his family to Europe, where expenses would be less than in their big house in Hartford, and where he might be removed from the temptations which his fascination with the machine and its possibilities provided.

Paige found a new backer in Towner K. Webster of the Webster Manufacturing Company in Chicago, who moved Paige and his still unfinished typesetter to that city. A capital investment of $3,000,000 was promised by Chicago investors (H. C. Robinson to SLC, 26 August 1892), which seemed sufficient to guarantee that at least one machine would be completed in time to be exhibited at the 1893 Chicago World's Fair. In the spring of 1893 Clemens hurried back to the United States to inspect the progress on the machine, for he considered his potential royalties on sales or rentals of the typesetter to be among his most valuable assets. What he heard then in New York and saw in Chicago allowed him to return to Europe convinced that the machine was in good hands: "By the end of this year the Co will be making 1 machine per day—next year 2—the year after, 5" (Notebook 27, TS p. 7).

Actually, there were too many hands, and none had access to the capital necessary to insure success. A group of New York brokers, which included H. S. Ward, George Frink, and the three Knevals brothers (Caleb B., Lambert, and S. W.), had bought interests in the Webster Manufacturing Company. They called themselves the Connecticut Company and apparently planned to manage sales of the machine and of stock from their New York offices. None of them seems to have had special knowledge of typesetting or machine-shop operations, nor even—Clemens sometimes seems to have thought—of ordinary business practices. He found it amusingly portentous that the Knevals brothers were also agents for the Woodlawn Cemetery—which he consistently called the "graveyard"—in New York.

The Chicago group, composed of T. K. Webster, his attorney George N. Stone, and Charles E. Davis, who had followed the machine from Hartford, could not supply Paige with the funds which he had been promised. Associated with them were investors from Hartford, like Hamersley and some Pratt & Whitney Manufacturing Company people, in whose shops Paige had formerly tinkered over the machine, and, of course, investors like Clemens and Charles R. North, who had invented the typesetter's automatic line-adjuster. Each of them had given time and money in confident expectation of success; all were now confused and apprehensive. Nevertheless, most were still hopeful that Paige with his inventiveness and Davis with his mechanical skills could lead them, despite persistent aggravating delays, toward the anticipated riches. There was, however, no effective leader among them until Rogers went to Chicago in December 1893 to inspect the operation. He then supplied money for immediate working capital and began the task of uniting the disparate interests into a solidly organized, but short-lived, Paige Compositor Manufacturing Company. Negotiations toward this end stretched out over many months. During this time it became increasingly evident—as the letters indicate—that Rogers and Clemens formed a team, oddly matched but effective, to which the others must finally submit.

Clemens moved on 29 September 1893 to the Players Club at 16 Gramercy Park in New York. He visited often at the Standard Oil Building at 26 Broadway, where he enjoyed watching Rogers at work and wished that he himself could be more in the midst of the contest. His notebook jottings and his letters to Mrs. Clemens reveal excitement and pride, but they only hint at what went on: "Mr. Rogers wants to see me Thursday. I shall be there, you may be sure" (SLC to OLC, 14 November 1893); "Await message from

Rogers till 7" (Notebook 27, TS p. 38); "Make appointment with
Lambert Knevals to have Frink or his brother or Ward for Mr. R.
at the graveyard Tuesday 4.30" (*ibid.*, p. 43).

Sometimes details of negotiations are briefly sketched, as when,
after a meeting on 3 December, Clemens noted that it had been
agreed by Rogers, Webster, and Davis that "my option shall be to
demand and receive any time during 3 years, $240,000 cash, or
$500,000 stock, or keep my royalties, as I shall elect" (*ibid.*, p. 41).
The next day he wrote Mrs. Clemens:

> Mr. Rogers mapped out a reformed contract and Webster will have it
> drawn by a lawyer here and submitted to Mr. Rogers for approval.
> Then he will take it to Chicago and see if he can get Paige to sign. If
> it shall seem best, Mr. Rogers and I will go out there. . . . A
> singularly clear-headed man is Mr. Rogers—this appears at every
> meeting. And no grass grows under his feet. He takes his steps
> swiftly, yet no step is bungled or has to be taken over again.

Sometimes it seemed great sport as Rogers and Clemens, partners
united against "the other braves," schemed privately about "how
much stock to stand out for, in exchange for my royalties. And also
as to how many royalties to refuse to give up" (SLC to OLC, 8
December 1893, TS in MTP). Clemens told his wife how Rogers
had advised him to let the new company buy options on other
people's royalties:

> "but don't you give them any option on yours. When they have
> secured those options & you know the terms, then you can say you
> are ready to listen to a proposition, but that it must be at considerably
> higher rates than those others get, & that on the whole you think you
> will leave your wife's royalties undisturbed" (SLC to OLC, 9 De-
> cember 1893; *LLMT*, p. 283).

They chuckled together over the $150,000 which Clemens had
"persuaded" Rogers to promise to advance the new company—a
maneuver that gained Clemens a bonus of shares for bringing in
desperately needed capital. But the miscellaneous jottings which
Clemens made in his notebooks do not reveal the precise financial
structure of the new company, and his letters to Mrs. Clemens are

characteristically more acute in recording his reactions to people than as a source for exact financial accounts.

After weeks of conference, word finally came from Chicago that Paige would agree to new terms, if he could get "$2,000 down, from Conn. Co., $5,000 down from Webster Mf. Co., $600 a month till a certain dividend is reached," and if the new company —the Paige Compositor Manufacturing Company—would assume debts of $8,000 and $70,000 owed, respectively, to the Pratt & Whitney Company and to Newton Case of Hartford (Notebook 27, TS p. 43). Paige was willing to exchange his 1,271 royalties and his $210,000 in stock of the old company for 20 per cent of the $5,000,000-aggregate stock in the new, consolidated company. This, Clemens calculated, would make his own 470 royalties worth about $330,000 of the new stock (*ibid.*, p. 37). However, he planned "to stand out for $500,000 stock, or retention of royalties in the same proportion" (*ibid.*, p. 42).

That potential profit pleased him, although he confidently expected the machine to bring him much more. Meanwhile, he was happy to act as Rogers's lieutenant, traveling with him to Chicago in a special car, conferring with him in private, or going alone to the office of the Connecticut Company "to warn them against intimating in any letter or telegram that Mr. Rogers & I will yield any inch or half an inch of our requirements" to the demands of any opposition. "It heavily taxes their nerve & staying power," he said, "but they have to stand it." Clemens reveled in the excitement of the negotiations, even the disagreeable business interviews with other royalty holders, "a function which I have insisted on performing myself with no others present—& they have yielded the privilege to me with a good deal of alacrity" (SLC to OLC, 29 December 1893; *LLMT*, p. 287). His purpose, in accordance with Rogers's wishes, was to persuade them to exchange their royalties for stock, so that his own royalties would become more valuable.

But he seems seldom to have felt completely confident when acting alone. Following an interview with a lawyer from New Haven named Newton, who represented the interests of the royalty-holder Charles R. North, Clemens reported:

The moment Mr. Newton was out of sight around the corner I ran to Fourth avenue and boarded the first car and reached Mr. Rogers's house in 57th Street at 6 o'clock, to report in detail my interview with Newton and my earlier interview with the Vice President of the Conn Co., (the one wherein I was obliged to make him squirm a little). Advising Newton to go to Mr. Rogers within 24 hours and see if I had made any statements that were defective, rendered it necessary for me to get in ahead and warn him that Newton was coming and prepare him to back me up at all points with an unyielding front (SLC to OLC, 30 December 1893).

His balloon of anticipation was deflated when he found Mr. and Mrs. Rogers were just going out to dinner as he rushed up to their door—so Clemens had to settle for supper with the Rogers children. Yet when Rogers arrived at the Players Club just as Clemens was finishing his coffee the next morning and they compared strategies, Clemens preened (or pretended to) because Rogers remarked that "great commercial intellects" like theirs "were pretty sure to break out in kindred inspirations." "It is interesting," Clemens continued, "to play games with a partner who knows how to play and what to play and when to play it" (SLC to OLC, 30 December 1893). Despite the seriousness of their business-game, Clemens and Rogers often found reason for laughter:

> Sometimes when I reflect that our great scheme may still at any moment go to ruin before our eyes and consign me and mine to irretrievable poverty and want, my three months' work are but acts of a tragedy; but all the rest of the time it is a comedy—and certainly the killingest one, the darlingest one and the most fascinating one that ever was. I don't laugh easily, I believe, but there are two men who make me laugh without any difficulty—to-wit, Mr. Rogers when he comments on the C[onnecticut] C[ompany], and Frank Jenkins (of this Club) when he comments on his opponent's shots in a game of billiards (SLC to OLC, 27–30 January 1894).

The negotiations were often like a game: watching telegrams arriving from Chicago which begged them to "accept Paige's terms —*don't* let him get away from us—he is bound to lose patience presently"; answering that "Mr. Paige must accept *our* terms." Late in December, they were warned, " 'If you don't hurry, Paige will get tired waiting.' " Members of the Connecticut Company became anxious: " 'What shall we answer, Mr. Rogers?' Mr. R. said pleasantly but gravely: 'Say, at this end we are *already* tired waiting.' " What a master stroke, thought Clemens: "That card was well played. It shed a new light on the situation."

To watch Rogers in action, knocking heads together, "is better than a circus. . . . It was beautiful," said Clemens,

> to see Mr. Rogers apply his probe & his bung-starter & remorselessly let out the wind & the water from the so-called "assets" of these companies. And he did it so sweetly & courteously—but he stripped away all the rubbish & laid bare the fact that their whole gaudy property consisted of just $276,000 & no more! Then he said, "Now we know where we stand, gentlemen. I am prepared to listen to a proposition from you to furnish capital." There was a deep, long silence. Then their [the Connecticut Company's] spokesman proposed a basis of 50 cents on the dollar. Mr. Rogers said, "We will all think, to-night, & come together in the morning—early. Shall we say 9?" That was agreed to, & he & I went away (SLC to OLC, 9 December 1893; *LLMT*, p. 282).

Rogers seemed even something of an artful bamboozler, like Tom Sawyer, and Clemens reported him as speaking in words and rhythms much like those which Tom might have used:

> Along the street he said, "They ask 50, & would be glad to get 12. But we will not take advantage of their necessities. I know exactly what it is worth, to a farthing. I will offer them that in the morning; they will accept, & try not to look as glad as they feel. When that business is settled you will go at once to the President of the Connecticut Co & claim the block of stock which you, conspiring against me, two months ago, required & were to get in case you succeeded in beguiling me into taking hold of this swindle; & you want to magnify the trouble you've had with it, & how hard you've had to work to keep me from squeezing them down to 12 cents" (*LLMT,* p. 282).

When they met the next morning, "everything came out as Mr. Rogers said it would. He pays 20 when they only hoped for 12 or at

the very most 15—therefore there is rejoicing in their camp, now."
After the meeting, they rode together "away down in the Elevated" because Rogers "wanted to talk & laugh." He told Clemens:

> Once when you were out of the room I said "Please hurry this
> matter, gentlemen; you understand I am not going into this thing for
> any rational reason, but because I don't see any other way of getting
> rid of Clemens. I feel sure I ought not to pay 20, but when a person is
> harried as I am he loses a good share of his judgment."

Clemens accompanied him "clear down to Rector Street & then he
said I had better go right back & catch Ward & nail him in writing
to give me the block of stock I was to get in case I bunco-steered Mr.
Rogers into the scheme" (*LLMT*, p. 283).

For all his scurrying about on business matters, Clemens's social
and public lives were not neglected. The Lotos Club gave a dinner
in his honor. He went to the theater with Howells to see Sir Henry
Irving and later dined with Irving at Delmonico's. He spent a
weekend with Frank Fuller at his model farm in Madison, New
Jersey. He dined often with the Rices or the Rogerses or the
Laurence Huttons, at whose home he gave an occasional informal
reading to a group of friends; he refereed a debate on kindergartens
between Kate Douglas Wiggin and Mrs. Bisland Wetmore, and he
joined James Whitcomb Riley in two public lectures (*MTLC*, p.
235). He attended boxing matches with Rice and Rogers, and
Stanford White introduced him to World Champion James J.
Corbett in his dressing room at Madison Square Garden. He spoke
in Boston at an "Author's Reading and Music for the poor" and
dined at Mrs. James T. Fields's house with Oliver Wendell Holmes
and Sarah Orne Jewett. Clemens spoke at the dedication of the
town hall which Mrs. Rogers had donated to the Rogers's childhood
home in Fairhaven; he met Helen Keller at the Laurence Huttons's; he talked with Chauncey Depew about raising money for
the unemployed of New York. Ellen Terry, Richard Harding Davis
—anyone who came to New York—was eager to meet Mark Twain
(Notebook 27, *passim*).

He wrote Mrs. Clemens that Dr. Rice said, "that my welcome to

New York has been phenomenal, and that the manifest affection of the people for me was the sort of fame that was worth having." And he was especially proud of Mr. Rogers's comment that "other people's successes in this world were made over broken hearts or at the cost of other people's feelings or food, but that my fame had cost no one a pang or a penny." These things were comforting, especially at this time: "I can stand considerable petting," Clemens admitted to his wife (SLC to OLC, 4 January 1894).

Nor was his literary activity allowed to lapse. He had come to New York with a scheme for a magazine of reprints, to be called *The Back Number,* which he thought his nephew Samuel Moffett might help to edit (Notebook 27, TS p. 39a), and in which he tried to interest John Brisben Walker of *Cosmopolitan.* A little more than a month after his arrival in New York, he wrote Mrs. Clemens:

> with all the interruptions, I am making good progress with "Tom Sawyer's Mystery," for I have written 10,000 words, which is one-seventh of a book like Huck Finn or Prince & Pauper. The last two days I have written very slowly & cautiously, & made my steps sure. It is delightful work & a delightful subject. The story tells itself (SLC to OLC, 10 November 1893; *LLMT,* p. 277).

At William Rideing's request he contributed an essay on "How to Tell a Story" to the *Youth's Companion* (Rideing to SLC, 23 January, 27 April, 1894). He discussed with William Dean Howells possibilities for making a play out of *Don Quixote.* After sitting through an evening of amateur theatricals in Hartford, he rode back to New York in a smoking compartment with Rudyard Kipling and found him not so shy as he had seemed when they first had met (SLC to OLC, 12 January 1894, TS in MTP).

But mostly it was business and worry and excitement. By 4 January 1894, it seemed clear to Clemens that he and Rogers were about to force Paige to concede to their wishes. This was to be "the last of the games in the long tournament. Mr. Rogers and I have not lost a single one, thus far, and we think we are equal to this occasion. If we can hang this last remaining scalp at our belt the victory will be complete." Rogers was obdurate and had the upper hand: " 'In all negociations of this kind,' " he told Clemens, " 'there presently comes a time when one must drive his stake down and stand by it. I have driven mine and it is final' " (SLC to OLC, 13 January 1894). When on 15 January 1894 a telegram from Chicago announced that Paige had finally been brought to terms, Clemens was jubilant. "This is a great date in my history," he wrote. "Yesterday we were paupers, with but 3 months' rations of cash left and $160,000 in debt, my wife and I, but this telegram makes us wealthy" (Notebook 27, TS pp. 47–48). He wrote at once to Mrs. Clemens:

> I came up to my room and began to undress, and then, suddenly and without warning the realization burst upon me and overwhelmed me: I and mine, who were paupers an hour ago, are rich now and our troubles are over!
>
> I walked the floor for half an hour in a storm of excitement. Once or twice I wanted to sit down and cry. You see, the intense strain of three months and a half of daily and nightly work and thought and hope and fear had been suddenly taken away, and the sense of release and delivery and joy knew no way to express itself (SLC to OLC, 15 January 1894).

The details of an agreement with Paige remained to be worked out, however, and Clemens could not return at once to his family in Paris. He explained metaphorically to Mrs. Clemens why he had to stay in New York. And, he promised:

> When the anchor is down, then I shall say:
> "Farewell—a long farewell—to *business!* I will *never* touch it again!"
> I will live in literature, I will wallow in it, revel in it, I will swim in ink! Joan of Arc——but all this is premature; the anchor is not down yet (SLC to OLC, 27–30 January 1894).

It wasn't until the first of February 1894 that Clemens could cable his wife: "A ship visible on the horizon coming down under a cloud of canvas." That night he sent another cable to inform her of the consummation of "the great Paige Compositor Scheme," timing the message so that it would reach Paris on the morning of their twenty-fourth wedding anniversary: "Wedding news: *Our ship is safe in port.* I sail the moment Rogers can spare me" (Notebook 27, TS p. 51).

He had been glad to let Mrs. Clemens know that others involved in the Paige affairs also thought highly of Rogers, for she had sometimes worried that her husband and his new financial adviser were too high-handed:

Yesterday evening on my way out, in the hoss kar, to play billiards and take dinner with Mr. Rogers, Mr. Knevals, Second Vice President of the C.C., got into the hoss kar and his great fat face was radiant with joy. He said:

"Well, I guess everything's all right at last. Satisfactory news from the Farnham Co. The last nail will be driven home inside of 48 hours—don't you think so? And doesn't Mr. Rogers?"

"Yes, we both think so."

"I'm glad. Well, Mr. Clemens, we've had pretty savage feelings against Mr. Rogers from the start all through—he has certainly been the most exacting, and pains-taking, and particular, and cool-headed, and im—*movable* human being I ever saw in my life. But now that it's all finished, *we* see, as plain as anybody, that every single step he took was an advantage to every individual concerned and for the benefit of every individual concerned, both here and in Chicago. And what contracts we've got this time!—*ain't* they! Why, Mr. Clemens, talk about masterly negociation—bless my soul, I've never seen anything to *begin* with it. There's that mangy Paige who was always bragging about *his* gifts in that way (and he *was* too smart for *us,* I'll admit it)—where is he *now?* Mr. Rogers has tucked strand after strand around his wings and his body and his legs till he is just merely a *cocoon*—and he'll never stir again, and you'll never hear him buzz any more in *this* life! Grateful for that? I'm the gratefulest man alive. Mr. Clemens, we of the C.C. all think Mr. Rogers is the most extraordinary man in America to-day" (SLC to OLC, 27–30 January 1894).

Clemens also thought Rogers extraordinary. On behalf of Charles L. Webster & Company, Clemens refused to publish a book arraigning "the Standard Oil fiends." He told his wife that he had wanted to make his refusal a demonstration of personal loyalty:

> I *wanted* to say—
> "The only man I care for in the world; the only man I would give a *damn* for; the only man who is lavishing his sweat and blood to save me and mine from starvation and shame, is a Standard Oil fiend. If you know me, you know whether I want the book or not" (SLC to OLC, 15 February 1894).

During the months when the typesetter required principal attention, the ailments of Charles L. Webster & Company had been almost forgotten. Hall wished that Clemens would sell some of his royalties in the Paige machine, to provide a backlog of cash, just in case the bank "should happen to get cranky" or Benjamin should have trouble keeping up his payments on the purchase of the *Library of American Literature* (Fred J. Hall to SLC, 3 January 1894). "One thing at a time," said Clemens. He explained to his wife on 15 February:

> I never laid Websterco's disastrous condition before Mr. Rogers until to-night after billiards. I did hate to burden his good heart and over-worked head with it, but he took hold with avidity and said it was no burden to work for his friends, but a pleasure. We discussed it from various standpoints, and found it a sufficiently difficult problem to solve; but he thinks that after he has slept upon it and thought it over he will know what to suggest.

Decisions had to be made at once about an offer from the Century Company to buy rights to books by Mark Twain which were owned by Charles L. Webster & Company. Clemens hoped that they would take over all the other books published by Webster, too, even the ones which did not sell:

> [Rogers] will tell me exactly what to say to the Century people and how to say it, and then I will go back to him and report what progress I have made—if any. They want *my* books badly; so he believes I can crowd them into giving me something for the rest. He wants me to be absolutely clear of business and *stay* clear (SLC to OLC, 23 February 1894).

Early in March, Clemens could say: "We rather expect to get a trade out of them which will emancipate me from business. There will be heavy loss, but that is no matter if it will only get me free of debt to the banks and the manufacturers" (SLC to OLC, 2 March 1894). On 7 March 1894, having made over a power of attorney to Rogers the day before, Clemens left New York to rejoin his family after more than seven months of separation. But the visit could not be long; after three weeks in Paris, Clemens sailed again for New York on 7 April, arriving in seven days to find his old room at the Players "swept and garnished and ready" (SLC to OLC, 14 April 1894). Two days later he wrote confidently to Mrs. Clemens:

> Mr. Rogers feels so much encouraged about Websterco's probable ability to pull through alive, that he suggested, without my saying anything, that we hold on and try to work out, paying a hundred cents on the dollar and finally closing the concern out without any stain upon its name. Mr. Rogers has been at Websterco's several times and kept close watch upon its affairs, and has kept it out of financial trouble by the strength of his name—and with his money, too, the other day where two or three thousand dollars were immediately necessary (SLC to OLC, 16 April 1894).

On 18 April 1894, however, fortunes were reversed. The bank called in its loans, and Charles L. Webster & Company declared itself bankrupt. "Mark Twain Loses All," reported the New York *World* the next day:

> The assignment of Samuel L. Clemens, known over the entire world as "Mark Twain," and his partner, Frederick J. Hall, who compose the firm of Charles L. Webster & Co., book publishers, at No. 67 Fifth avenue, was filed in the County Clerk's office yesterday, just at the close of business. The assignee is Bainbridge Colby, of No. 40 Wall street, with Stern & Rushmore, attorneys.

Clemens wrote at once to reassure his wife:

> All my friends say I was wisely advised, & did right. I think your desires made Mr. Rogers think, for a while, that he wanted the assignment prevented—but I haven't a doubt that that was merely a momentary weakness on his part; the moment he saw the rigorous

attitude of the Mt. Morris Bank his sanity returned to him & we precipitated the assignment (SLC to OLC, 20 April 1894; *LLMT*, p. 299).

He hoped that Mrs. Clemens had met Rogers's daughters, "Mrs. Duff and Miss May," who were then in France: "There aren't any better girls than *they* are; *that* I know. I am eating their meals for them while they are away" (SLC to OLC, 20 April 1894).

About the future of the publishing company he was again briefly optimistic: "We all think," he told her, "the creditors are going to allow us to resume business; and if they do we shall pull through and pay the debts" (SLC to OLC, 22 April 1894). When that proved to be clearly impossible, Rogers took firm control of the meetings with creditors, who were "bent," he told Albert Bigelow Paine many years later, "on devouring every pound of flesh in sight and picking the bones afterward." Rogers shrewdly insisted that Mrs. Clemens, to whom the company owed more than $60,000, was a preferred creditor, and that as such she had first claim on the copyrights to Mark Twain's books. He further protected Clemens by helping to arrange a settlement which provided that Clemens should pay fifty cents on each dollar owed (*MTB*, pp. 984–985). Clemens, confident that the Paige machine would ultimately pull them through, insisted that he would eventually pay every debt in full. Then on 9 May he left again for Europe, "to be absent indefinitely," said the New York *Times* on the day following. "He has a number of important engagements abroad, but will return at once should there be any need here for his presence."

But on 14 July he was back in New York. When Rogers spent a short time in Washington, Clemens stayed with the Rogers family at Manhattan Beach on Long Island, where there were evenings of games and readings and glorious fireworks: "I didn't know they could do such flaming and gorgeous miracles outside of perdition." They planned to go to Fairhaven also, "where I was to make a cruise with Harry in his boat." But that, like everything else, had to wait on Rogers (SLC to OLC, 20 July 1894).

Mrs. Clemens thought Rogers was perhaps too forceful in his

control of business affairs. She worried about the Webster creditors:

> We want to treat them all not only honestly but we want to help them in every possible way. It is money honestly owed and I cannot quite understand the tone which both you and Mr Rogers seem to take—in fact I cannot understand it at all. You say Mr Rogers has said some caustic and telling things to the creditors. . . . I should think it was the creditors place to say caustic things to us (OLC to SLC, 31 July 1894, TS in MTP).

Clemens's chief errand in New York, however, was not connected with the affairs of Charles L. Webster & Company. He had originally come to New York, he reminded Mrs. Clemens, in order "to ransack the country and sell [stocks or royalties] to make myself safe in the pool" which Rogers had formed to finance completion of the typesetting machine (see letter 10). But, Clemens explained, he found that the Chicago *Herald's* test of the typesetter, scheduled for the fall, made it more practical for him to hold on to his stock in the machine:

> Mr. Rogers dropped a remark which made me think he was not holding me to the limit of time required of the others—for he said, "If I were you I wouldn't spoil my market by trying to sell now; it could give the impression that you were anxious to unload; whereas if you wait till the Herald test it is fair to believe that people will come to *you* for the stock instead of your having to go to *them*. If I were you I would be patient and wise, and wait" (SLC to OLC, 3 August 1894).

So Clemens returned to Europe, to wait there for word of the success of the typesetter in its sixty-day competition with other machines. When news that it had failed reached him in December 1894, he was numbed with disappointment. The dream of sudden riches was finally shattered. Even Rogers's corporative skill could not put the Paige Compositor Manufacturing Company back together again. The two machines which had been completed became museum pieces—exemplars of mechanical ingenuity, too complicated for day-to-day use. "Certainly it was a marvelous invention," remembered Rogers many years later. "It was the nearest approach to a human being in the wonderful things it could do of any machine I have ever known. But that was just the trouble; it was too much of a human being and not enough of a machine. It had all the complications of the human mechanism, all the ability of getting out of repair, and it could not be replaced with the ease and immediateness of the human being" (*MTB*, p. 991). The royalties which Clemens held were valueless; the stock which he and Mrs. Clemens owned was exchanged, ten shares for one, for that of a Regius Manufacturing Company, hastily organized, with Rogers's future son-in-law, Urban H. Broughton, as its president. In December 1895 some of the assets of that company were sold, and a dividend of $14 a share was distributed to stockholders (Regius Manufacturing Company to Orion Clemens, 10 December 1895). This may have been the time when the machine was taken over by the Mergenthaler Linotype Company (John S. Thompson, *History of Composing Machines* [Chicago, 1904], pp. 24–25), but the Regius Manufacturing Company continued to exist, at least on paper, for some time (see stock certificate for 44 shares at $100 a share to OLC, 19 April 1897, CWB).

Its records and those of the Mergenthaler Linotype Company for that period are not available, and what Clemens occasionally recorded in his notebook or scratched in calculation on the backs of envelopes suggests that he himself was often uncertain about what was happening. It was clear that the marvelous machine was a financial failure. That debts existed which should be, perhaps even could be, paid—this was also clear. What small confidence Clemens took with him on his recuperative world tour was that, if any man could, Henry Rogers would steer him back toward solvency.

1. CLEMENS TO ROGERS

New York
13 December 1893 [1]

Dear Doctor Rogers:

I can't feel sorry you had to postpone Chicago, for I think a little delay will be good medicine for Paige. Next week will be better for me, too, because I brought home a cold two sizes too large for me from New Jersey; and as you were not handy I had to call in Rice—and you can imagine the rest. His jealousy on account of our growing practice is such that—well, it's only human nature.

Don't go any further with that untruth. Make another appointment with Dr. Mayo,[2] and give me a chance to whet-up in the meantime. In cases where I have no personal feeling, but where merely a cold pure Work of Art is required, I have my merits.

I have engaged to talk, to-morrow night,[3] but there is not going to be any voice to do it with.

Sincerely Yours

SL Clemens

---

[1] Even preceding this first surviving letter to Rogers there is a letter from Clemens (10 December 1893) to the secretary of the Millicent Library. Rogers had given the Library to Fairhaven as a memorial to his daughter, who died at the age of seventeen. Although not mentioned in the correspondence, the letter does provide early evidence of his appreciation for Rogers's generosity in involving himself in Clemens's tangled business affairs: "I have allowed myself the privilege of sending two or three of my books to the Library. They are not instructive, but I feel sure you will like the bindings." In the next few months Clemens sent the library several inscribed copies of his books, including *Huckleberry Finn* and *The Prince and the Pauper*. He inscribed the latter volume "To the young contingent among those who enjoy the privileges of the Millicent Library, from one who would like to trade years and reputations with them and start over again. Mark Twain" (2 February 1894, Fairhaven).

[2] Probably Frank Mayo, the actor who was later to dramatize *Pudd'nhead*

Wilson; Mayo was a member of the Players and, it can be presumed, had recently been victorious at billiards, or perhaps poker.

³ On 15 December 1893 Clemens wrote Livy: "I promised, the other day, to talk to a Workingmen's Society last night. But I told Clarence Buel at the time, that I had a cold, and would not talk unless I got rid of it in the meantime. Well, I could have gone, last night, if it had been reasonable weather, but it wasn't; it was fearful weather, snowing and blowing and bitter cold. So I sent and had the thing postponed till the weather improves."

2. ROGERS TO CLEMENS

New York
19 December 1893

Dear Mr Clemens

I send herewith the powders for your cold. If you will observe faithfully the rules laid down I am sure you will soon be a better man.¹

Wayne MacVeagh came in after you left but he no longer looked like the Coffee-Cooler; having taken on a fine Italian bake, at the hands of the President, and looked like a scorched gunny-bag. How gracefully he sits. He must have practiced in a harem. I believe he once was

"A malignant and turbaned Turk" ²

I digress. Don't let Rice know we are taking the shingles off his house, but take the powders "in spirit and in truth."

I hit the P. R. R for passes ³ and will know the result to-morrow when I will advise you.

Don't forget those heavier shoes. You'll need them in Chicago. It is always unpleasant overhead and twice as often underfoot.

Yours truly

Rogers M. D.

¹ "Mr. Rogers has been buying homeopathic powders and feeding them to me," Clemens wrote his wife (30 December 1893). But these, along with "whiskey" and "starvation," were only part of his assault on a chronic cold and cough. While staving off Livy's worry (denying a "newspaper report that I am sick. It is

a lie"), he admitted to others that he was "still in bed, and waiting for Dr. Rice" (15 December 1893, SLC to OLC; and 14 December 1893, SLC to Clarence Buel, TS in MTP). The cough had already caused him a rupture two months earlier (SLC to Clara, 23 September 1893), so he finally resorted to a Madison Avenue physician for a "mind cure": "[I] don't know if *he* is the reason, but I haven't coughed since" (Notebook 27, TS pp. 43–44).

[2] Wayne MacVeagh was Ambassador to Italy (1893–1897) for President Cleveland. Rogers compares his appearance to that of the Negro pugilist Frank Craig, the "Coffee-Cooler," as well as to that of Othello.

[3] Clemens and Rogers were bound for Chicago on the 21st, intent on inspecting Paige Typesetter affairs. In response to the request for passes, Frank Thompson, president of the Pennsylvania Railroad, is reported to have said: "No, I won't give Mark Twain a pass over our road. I've been reading his 'Traveling with a Reformer,' in which he abuses our road. I wouldn't let him ride over it again if I could help it. The only way I'll agree to let him go over it at all is in my private car. I have stocked it with everything he can possibly want, and have given orders that if there is anything else he wants the train is to be stopped until they can get it" (*MTB*, p. 982).

3. ROGERS TO CLEMENS

New York
28 December 1893

Dear Mr. Clemens:

The enclosed dispatches have been received from Mr. Stone [1] to which I have made answer as follows:

"Dispatches received. I will consult with some of the Connecticut people this afternoon but my present judgment is to refuse a proposition and wait a little."

Please make appointment with the Knevals at 23rd St., at 4 o'clock this afternoon and be present yourself at that time. [2]

Yours truly,

H. H. Rogers

[per] K. I. H. [3]

[1] George N. Stone, an attorney in the firm of Rich & Stone of Chicago, was conveying the various proposals and counterproposals between Paige, Rogers, and the other investors.

² Clemens sent this letter on to Livy in Paris, with the following notations:
3.30 p.m
I hain't got no time to write you to-day, dear old Sweetheart. Busy trying to get our ship into port.

SLC

6 p.m. We held the talk and then telegraphed that Paige must come to our terms—we would yield nothing.

1.30 a.m. Dinner party at Dr. Rice's; Mr. and Mrs. Rogers and ten other nice people, including me. At 10 p.m. sixty people came, and were seated in camp chairs in the library, and I stood by the fire-place and read The Californian's Tale and then talked an hour, and had a roaring good time. Now I tell you it *was* a good time, and everybody said so, in the most outspoken way. I don't know *when* I have so enjoyed hearing myself talk.

2 in the morning, now, and I better go to bed. I love you my darling and think you are the dearest woman in this world.

Saml

³ This letter, like most from Rogers, is typed on stationery on which is printed in the upper left: "H. H. ROGERS, 26 BROADWAY"; and on the upper right: "DICTATED." In this case Rogers's signature was added by his private secretary, Katharine I. Harrison.

4. CLEMENS TO ROGERS

New York

29 December 1893

Friday, 2 p.m.

Dear Mr. Rogers:

Mr. C. B. Knevals asked me to read this Chicago letter, then send it to you and ask you in your turn to pass it on to the other Knevals at 32 Nassau.

I have just left Mr. Frink feeling rather depressed on account of that $75,000 commission.¹

Newton ² will probably arrive from New Haven an hour from now.

The Farnham Co. of Hartford have apparently agreed to do whatever Hamersley ³ advises.

Sincerely Yours

SL Clemens

[1] Clemens was to receive $75,000 in stock as commission for "inducing" Rogers to invest $150,000 in the Chicago company. Rogers, however, invested only $78,062.69, so Clemens's commission was reduced (Urban H. Broughton to KIH, 13 May 1901, CWB).

[2] Newton was attorney for Charles R. North, who had invented a method for automatic line justification for the Paige machine.

[3] But Hamersley apparently did not advise in a manner which suited Clemens. The Farnham Company was unwilling to trade its 150 royalties on the Paige machine for stock:

Does the ship seem so *very* near in? No. The Farnham Co. in Hartford are hanging back. That inveterate blatherskite Bill Hamersley conspired with the C. C. [Connecticut Company] to gather the Farnham Co's 150 royalties in for $75,000 of paid-up stock provided his 50 royalties could remain on the machine. He has now resigned his Presidency of that Co. without waiting to get their acceptance in writing. The new President proposes to ignore the agreement and stand out for more stock. . . . Oh, if the C. C. would only send me up there to address the Farnham Co (of which I am a member) with that bilk, Bill Hamersley in front of me as part of my audience! (SLC to OLC, 27–30 January 1894).

The Farnham Company eventually settled for 1,000 shares of stock.

5. CLEMENS TO ROGERS

New York
30 December 1893

Dec. 30—1 p.m.

Dear Mr. Rogers:

If Newton accepts,[1] won't it be kind of judicious to make him put it in writing?

(⟨It⟩ This is only a suggestion—just a mere humble and very diffident suggestion, from one accustomed to teach his grandmother how to suck eggs.) [2]

With my homage to the ladies, I am

Sincerely Yours

S. L. Clemens

[1] Paige had promised Newton's client, Charles R. North $200 a month and $400 to $500 royalty on each machine until North had received a total of

$2,000,000 (Notebook 27, TS p. 8). Attempts were now being made to exchange these royalties for stock in the new company.

[2] On this same day he wrote Livy about this letter:

P. S. I had an idea. So I wrote a note [to] Mr. Rogers and sent it at once to his house by a messenger—to wit:

"Dear Mr. Rogers:

"If Newton accepts, won't it be kind of judicious to make him put it in writing?

"This is only a suggestion—just a meek little humble and diffident suggestion, from a person accustomed to teach his grandmother how to suck eggs" (30 December 1893).

6. CLEMENS TO ROGERS

New York
1 January 1894

Dear Mr. Rogers:

This is the rough draft of the letter which has gone to Brer Newton.[1]

Yours Sincerely

SL Clemens

P. S.   Jan 1, 6 p.m./94.

Dear Mr. Rogers:

I *did* want to stand out and say "$50,000 of stock and retain 50 royalties, and that is our *last* and final offer, Mr. Newton"—but I am so troubled about Susy Clemens[2] and so anxious to send the family some inspiring good news that I am losing my strenuosity and coming to accept the better wisdom of your suggestion that he be allowed his 125 royalties if you see that he can't be silenced for less.

We should still capture the $25,000 of stock, and that is the main thing, since I didn't know enough to claim all the royalties saved out of the 125. I do suppose I shall land in heaven just about the time that I have learned how to conduct business on earth. We will go partners there if there should happen to be anything in our line.

Sincerely Yours

SL Clemens

[1] This letter is written at the bottom of the penciled "rough draft" which Clemens mentions. In the letter to Newton he advises that "if you would like to see Mr. Rogers I will make the appointment for you, or you can communicate directly with him. He will be able to explain his position and his reasons for it much better than I can do. . . . You will not be able to reach a clear understanding of the whole matter and its relation to your own and your client's interests without a talk with Mr. Rogers. I know this to be true. Therefore I recommend it."

[2] Mrs. Clemens had written that their oldest daughter was ill.

7. Clemens to Rogers

New York

3 January 1894

Dear Mr. Rogers:

Caleb and Ward and Frink were still here at the Graveyard [1] when I returned, a few minutes ago. They thought $50,000 of stock would be due me when your $100,000 cash came in; and that the rest would be due when or *if* the other $50,000 cash was needed and furnished. Also, it was the business of the Paige Company to pay these commissions; that a resolution of that Board would authorize the payment; that the 3 here present would vote aye; and finally you would be a member of the Board yourself. They feel sure that no objection would arise from Stone, Webster and the other Chicago members.

I can't get the privilege of giving up 200 royalties, but only 150.[2] There ain't stock enough left in the Tank to spare me any more than $150,000.

I was hoping to have the privilege of raising a third of the

$150,000 cash capital and clearing $50,000 cash for myself. But these boys are purposing to divide that privilege up among us all and raise it by sales of stock at *par*.

Sincerely Yours

SL Clemens [3]

---

[1] This letter is written on letterhead stationery of the "Office of Woodlawn Cemetery / 20 East 23d Street," with which the Knevals brothers were associated.

[2] Clemens owned 470 royalties on the Paige typesetter. He was finally able to trade only 150 royalties for stock, receiving 1,500 shares valued at $100 each for a total of $150,000. This did not include his commission of 750 more shares for "inducing" Rogers to invest in the new company.

[3] Clemens apparently used this letter for notes during the discussion. In pencil at the bottom of the page he had written:

825/150	500	100,000	500
			75

750/75

$825 000

8. ROGERS TO CLEMENS (telegram)

New York

5 January 1894

Unless you hear from me to the contrary please meet me at rices at about five oclock = H H Rogers

9. CLEMENS TO ROGERS

New York

27 January 1894

Dear Mr. Rogers:

I'll be there at 6.30, (un)loaded for bear—in case you are going to have any for dinner. Otherwise, ham will do.

I am very sorry Mr. Benjamin [1] is still ill, but you are right in what you said to him. There will be no difficulty about settling the Hall matter.

Yrs Sincerely

SL Clemens

[1] William Evarts Benjamin, husband of Rogers's oldest daughter (Anne Engle Rogers). He was proposing to buy the *Library of American Literature* from Charles L. Webster & Company.

10. ROGERS TO CLEMENS

New York

3 March 1894

My dear Sir:

To avoid all misunderstanding in regard to the "initial memorandum" between us regarding two pools relating to the business of the Paige Compositor Co. I conclude to write you a letter,[1] acceptance of which by you shall serve as a contract between us. The pools as understood, are based on a certain contract [which] I have with the Paige Co. agreeing to advance from time to time, as occasion requires, the sum of $150,000. Copy of which Contract I herewith attach.

Pool # 1 is to be shared in the responsibility and advantages equally between us, subject to an option given, Messrs. Geo. N. Stone, S. W. Knevals, Geo. A. Frink, C. B. Knevals, T. K. Webster, H. S. Ward and T. F. Rowland,[2] copy of which is herewith attached. The pool as made up will stand as follows:—

For payment by us of $100,000 we receive $450,000. of the stock.[3]

25,000	125,000
25,000	166,667.
$150,000.	$741,667.

Pool # 2 is to be shared equally between us in all respects the same as # 1, and is made up as follows:

For payment by us of $100,000 we receive $450,000 of the stock.

25,000	125,000
25,000.	166,667.
Commissions.	75,000.
$150,000.	$816,667.

Of course the option given Knevals and others, applies to both pools alike. Interest on my advances, according to the contract, will be charged you at the rate of 6%. I am to reserve the right to exercise my judgment in regard to the sale of the stock from either pool for joint account.

Yours truly,

H H Rogers

[1] This agreement indicates what might have been. In 1904 Clemens wrote on the envelope in which his copy of a similar agreement of 20 January 1894 is contained: "The machine failed to stand the test and the fortune went up in air."

[2] The contract gave these men, collectively, the option of taking "one-quarter interest in my contract with Paige Manufacturing Company, at any time before or at the completion of the first Paige Compositor referred to in my contract with said Company, on condition that you pay each to me one-quarter of the amount I have paid out with interest, and the assumption on your part of one-quarter of the then unexpired obligations of the contract" (HHR to Geo. N. Stone, S. W. Knevals, G. A. Frink, C. B. Knevals, T. K. Webster, H. S. Ward, T. F. Rowland, 3 March 1894, CWB).

[3] An undated list in CWB indicates the proposed division of stock:

NAME	NUMBER OF SHARES	AMOUNT	REMARKS.
J. W. Paige	10,000	1,000,000.	Issued March 5th.
Connecticut Company	6,000	600,000.	
Webster Mfg. Co.	4,000	400,000.	
H. H. Rogers	7,417	741,700	Number of Shares contingent upon money advanced. 500 Shares issued March 9th.
S. L. Clemens	1,500	150,000.	To be held on order of Mr. Clemens or Mr. Rogers. 750 Shares issued to Mr. H. H. Rogers, March 9th.
Farnham Type Setter Co.	1,000	100,000.	Not to be issued at present.
C. R. North	500	50,000.	Not to be issued at present.
S. Coit	300	30,000.	Issued March 6th.
S. L. Clemens (additional)	750	75,000.	Contingent upon Mr. Rogers' advances.
Stone Trustee			
for Davis	250	25,000.	
for Grohman.	75	7,500.	
for Bates	50	5,000.	
for S. Knevals	200	20,000.	
for Slattery	20	2,000.	
for Rich & Stone.	355	35,500.	
	32,417	3,241,700.	
In Treasury	17,583	1,758,300.	
TOTALS.	50,000	5,000,000.	

When the machine failed in December 1894, Rogers had invested only $78,062.69 out of the proposed $150,000 advance, so he never received all of his 7,417 shares (Urban H. Broughton to KIH, 13 May 1901, CWB). Similarly, Clemens finally received only part of his 2,250 shares since 750 were contingent on Rogers's advances.

11. CLEMENS TO ROGERS

New York
4 March 1894
Sunday night

Dear Mr. Rogers:

The enclosed note [1] arrived six or seven days ago, and gave me a pleasant surprise; for although I secretly hoped Mrs. Clemens would write to you I did not expect she would be able to get her courage up to it, for she is a shrinking person and cautious about intruding. I think it was your photograph that gave her confidence; I sent it to her.

She says I may withhold her note if I think she has done wrong; but I shall not withhold it, for it contains words ⟨of Livy's⟩ of mine which I would many a time have liked to say to you, but I should have been awkward about it and would have embarrassed two people. Even with a pen, and behind your back, and knowing my letter will not reach you till I am away, I am not able to put into words ⟨the⟩ how grateful I am to you. In truth there are no words that could do that. You have saved me and my family from ruin and humiliation. You have been to me the best friend that ever a man had, and yet you have never by any word made me feel the weight of this deep obligation. And Lord, how welcome is the sight of your face to me!

S.L.C.

[1] See letter 12.

12. OLIVIA CLEMENS TO ROGERS

Paris
14 February 1894

My dear Mr Rogers:

I am going to venture to send you a little note in order that I may quote to you a paragraph in one of Mr Clemens' last letters.

I have had the good fortune to be Mr Clemens wife for a goodly number of years, therefore I know him pretty thoroughly.

One of his peculiarities is that he does not say a thing when he thinks it and ought to say it. Or if he does voice his thought he does so to the wrong person and therefore it never reaches the one that it ought to reach.

Now I intend that some of the things that he says about you get to your ears. I quote,

"Yes at two p.m. yesterday we were paupers and five minutes later we were rich people. It is a miracle and a quite dramatic one. And who achieved it for us? Who has saved us from separations, unendurable toil on the platform, and public bankruptcy? *Henry Rogers.*

And he was the only man in America who both could and cheerfully *would.* His name is music in my ear.

Assemble the family now and drink long life and happiness to Henry Rogers."

I assure you, Mr Rogers, that was most earnestly and heartily done. For six months Mr Clemens letters have been full of affectionate admiration of you, and I have given you a little sample of what his letters have contained.

Hoping the day is not far distant when I shall be able to know you personally

believe me

very sincerely yours

Olivia L. Clemens [1]

[1] "Your letter to Mr. Rogers is just right, sweetheart," Clemens wrote to Livy on 27 February 1894. "I'm going to write him a letter, and enclose yours in it, and leave it to be handed to him after I have sailed. That will spare him embarrassment."

13. CLEMENS TO ROGERS

New York
4 March 1894

Please deliver to Bram Stoker, Esq.,[1] 20 shares of Paige Compositor stock on my account. The stock is to be paid for in 10% instalments, and delivered when $1000 has been paid.

SL Clemens [2]

[1] Bram Stoker, British author and agent for Sir Henry Irving, with whom Clemens had recently been pleased to dine; both men invested in the Paige machine. A memorandum dated 9 March 1894 (CWB) explains that "Mr. Stoker is to send to me from time to time money on payment, and we are to send to him our receipts for the same until he has paid for 20 shares of stock at which time we are to forward to him the stock [to the] Lyceum Theatre, London." A penciled notation in CWB reveals that Stoker made one payment of $50 on 5 March, a second on 5 May, 1894.
[2] Written diagonally across the face of the letter: "Accepted H H Rogers 26 Broadway New York." At the bottom of an office copy in CWB appears: "RECEIVED of Henry Irving, Esq., S. L. Clemens order for 10 shares Paige Compositor Co. stock which I agree to forward to Lyceum Theatre, London, as soon as received from Chicago. (Signed) H. H. Rogers."

14. CLEMENS TO ROGERS

At Sea
8 March 1894

S. S. New York [1]

Dear Mr. Rogers:
How would this scheme do?
Benjamin, Bliss [2] and Clemens to join teams on the Uniform

Edition on the basis of a third of the profits to each; Benjamin to furnish the capital and Bliss to do the work.

The first outlay would be on a "dummy"-book for the canvassers to use—three or four hundred dollars.

When 1,000 subscriptions have been secured, set the type and make the plates—cost about $3,600.

Then the printing and binding would proceed merely at a pace necessary to keep up with the orders, and not any faster, thus avoiding all risk of loss.

By this scheme Mr. Benjamin would be free of the labors of publication, unless he chose to take the General Agency for New York.

I sat up until 2 in the morning waiting for Mr. Colby,[3] but he did not arrive. It was very kind of Mrs. Duff and Harry the Energetic to come down with me and take the cheerlessness out of my exodus, but it was a pity Mr. Colby made them wait so long. I was a good deal troubled about it, but they said it wasn't any worse than being in a house full of doctors without the privileges of the floor and the vote.

Mr. and Mrs. Benjamin are on board, so I am provided with pleasant company.[4]

By this time Mrs. Rogers is in her chair again,[5] I am perfectly sure, and I am very glad of it, too.

> Sincerely Yours
>
> SL Clemens

I wish you would cable me that you and Mr. Benjamin approve of my scheme and that by the authority in you vested you have consummated it.

The spirit of self-sacrifice is blossoming in Harry. He had a chance to play a joke on me and didn't do it.

---

[1] Clemens embarked at New York on 7 March: "I talked all my various matters over with Mr. Rogers and we decided that it would be safe for me to leave here . . . I should reach Southampton March 14, and Paris the 15th" (SLC to OLC, 15 February 1894).

    [2] Frank Bliss, president since the death in 1880 of his father, Elisha Bliss, of the American Publishing Company, which owned the copyright on Clemens's early volumes.
    [3] Bainbridge Colby, a lawyer with the New York firm of Stern & Rushmore, handled legal matters for Rogers and Clemens before he was appointed assignee for Charles L. Webster & Company on 18 April 1894.
    [4] Evidently not the William Evarts Benjamin family, although perhaps related to them.
    [5] Mrs. Rogers had been a semi-invalid for several years. Clemens described her to Livy (4 January 1894) as:
    a cheerful person [who] goes to dinner parties and theatres—Mr. Rogers carries her up the steps in his arms—and she violates the doctor's commands pretty regularly. Still, she gets along very well until she tries to climb three or four stairsteps—then the throes of pain come and for a few hours they think she is not going to pull through. In her own house they watch her and make her use the elevator always, but away from home she sometimes tries to climb the steps of a stoop, and then disaster ensues.

15. ROGERS TO CLEMENS

New York
8 March 1894

My dear Mr. Clemens:

Mr. Colby came in this morning and said there was a misunderstanding in regard to his making an appointment to see you at the steamer. All the papers were prepared so no embarrassment was occasioned by your going away.[1] Mr. Hall has been in to-day and I have gone over his papers and concluded to advise him to accept an offer which he had for the first story and basement of his building[2] at $2500 per year. This reduces the C. L. Webster obligations to $900 a year, plus certain expenses for heating, but Mr. Hall will try and get from the new tenant the responsibility of heating the new building by making reasonable allowance. Mr. Hall reports somewhat favorably in regard to business. He expects to hear from the Mt. Morris Bank people in regard to renewals to-morrow. The U. S. Bank have renewed for three months.

I have a letter from Mr. Whitmore[3] of Hartford, copy of which I enclose herewith. I appreciate that nothing will suffer if I wait until you give me instructions as to what I shall say to him in reply.

Mr. Colby will write you concerning the transfer of royalties to Mrs. Clemens, and send papers forward to you for execution. I understand from Mr. Colby that he has communicated with Mr. Broughton at Chicago, and that I may expect to receive the stock either to-morrow or next day.

I have heard nothing from Mr. Hall since writing yesterday and so I assume that everything is going smoothly with him as regards Russell and the Mt. Morris Bank.[4]

Bram Stoker came in to-day with the breeziness of a typhoon. Presented Mr. Irving's letter and gave me yours. I settled the matter with him by agreeing to send the stock to Mr. Irving as soon as I could get it from Chicago. Regarding his stock, I told him I would see that it was issued when he had paid me the $1000.[5] As fast as he sent me money, I would receipt for the same. All this was satisfactory, and he went away in good humor.

Yours truly,

H H Rogers

P. S. Since dictating the above, Colby has been in and I have executed the paper to Mrs. Clemens by virtue of my Power of Attorney. Colby will forward you a similar paper and instruct you to execute it at Paris. In the event of anything transpiring between this time and your execution of the paper, Mrs. Clemens is fully protected by reason of my action to-day.

---

[1] On 6 March 1894 Rogers had received a power of attorney from Clemens. On 9 March, using that power, Rogers assigned all of Clemens's property to Mrs. Clemens, including rights in the Paige machine and copyright on his books (CWB). On 8 March 1894 Urban H. Broughton had written Clemens (CWB): "I am in receipt of your esteemed favor of 6th inst, enclosing two copies of agreement between yourself and the Paige Compositor Mfg. Co. I will execute and return the same to Mr. Rogers." Details of the agreement, other than those set forth in letter 10, have not been discovered.

[2] Headquarters of Charles L. Webster & Company at 67 Fifth Avenue.

[3] Franklin G. Whitmore, a real-estate and insurance man in Hartford, supervised many of Clemens's minor business matters, particularly in that city, while the Clemens family was absent.

[4] Thomas Russell, owner of a printing and bookbinding firm, was a major

creditor of Charles L. Webster & Company. Apparently he and the Mount Morris Bank were pressing for payment of money owed them. In July 1895 Russell would sue Clemens for settlement of the debt.

[5] Shares of the Paige Compositor Manufacturing Company (face value, $100 each) were being marketed for $50 a share because of their speculative nature. Stoker had arranged to pay his $1,000 in twenty installments. (See the undated office memorandum in CWB.)

16. ROGERS TO CLEMENS

New York
13 March 1894

My dear Clemens:

I have nothing of special interest to report. Mr. Hall called this morning and reports progress in affairs, but as he will write you in detail, I will not undertake to say anything more.

I enclose copy of a letter from Mr. Davis [1] which I would ask you to read and send me such comments as you have to make. My judgment is to let him have about 3% or 4% of our holdings in pool #1 and no more, because Stone as Trustee, is carrying for him $25,000 of the stock. They have now on their payrolls 55 men the average of whose wages are $2.58 per day.

I have a very interesting letter from Mr. Broughton [2] concerning the affairs of the Company. He expresses himself very positively at last in regard to the machine. He says he has given it careful study, and can see nothing to prevent it from being a mechanical success, and thinks so well of it, that he would like to avail himself of our offer and allow him to take a share. This I consider one of the best endorsements we have had, because he is a pains-taking fellow, and is going to invest his own money, without being carried in any way by me.

We are having just a little friction with Webster in regard to the rental of the shop, as Messrs. Broughton and Moffett [3] think $1000 a month pretty steep.

I have been to Fairhaven for a day or two trying to adjust my fire losses. The trouble was with water and not fire,[4] and I am reminded

of the experience of a town in one of your stories where they
dreaded the fire engine more than the fire itself.[5] It seems about
concluded that the old house is unfit to be repaired, and as Mrs.
Rogers and the girls are getting to a point of commanding me, I
suppose it means a new house.

Yours truly,

H H Rogers

P.S. I neglected to say to you that the transfer of the stock is
going along satisfactorily.[6] Now from what I have said in regard to
Broughton's judgment of the machine, do not allow yourself to get
too enthusiastic. Still if faithful and persistent endeavor will accomplish anything, I am sure the Paige Compositor will have an opportunity of speaking for itself at a later time. If it speaks correctly,
that is all we desire.

R

[1] Davis's letter suggests that Rogers was attempting to divide the Chicago camp
by making "confidential" offers to its members. Davis indicated ("in relation to
the option which you and Mr. Clemens offered to me") that he would like as
much as 5 or 6 percent of the whole stock issuance in pool #1. He added, in the
emerging spirit of conspiracy, that "in accordance with your request, I have said
nothing to any one regarding any terms of this option. Something you said to
Messrs. Dewey and Stone led them to ask a question which I answered by saying
I might have a chance at some of the stock sold. No one will join me in this
matter in any way. It will be my own venture and in no sense in a speculative
way but on the lines you suggested in regard to your own" (Charles E. Davis to
HHR, 6 March 1894, OC in MTP).
[2] Broughton's letter has not survived. Rogers relied heavily on this civil
engineer in his assessment of the workability of the typesetter. Broughton, who
became Rogers's son-in-law by marrying Mrs. Duff in 1895, would soon be
elected president of the newly formed Paige Compositor Manufacturing Company
(see letter 42, note 2).
[3] James A. Moffett (1851–1913), a leading executive of Standard Oil, was
stationed in Chicago. Moffett would soon be elected, along with Broughton, to
the board of directors of the Paige Compositor Manufacturing Company.
[4] Rogers's summer home had burned on 18 February 1894. According to the
Fairhaven *Star*, the local volunteer firemen "succeeded in extinguishing the
flames on the first floor," only to discover "that the second floor was ablaze." By
the time they finished, "every thing was soaked with water which was several
inches deep upon the floor." The occasion (the *Star* observed with mingled pride

and chagrin) was "the first time that the water works service has been used and it is rather a remarkable coincidence that the water should be turned upon the residence of Mr. Rogers who was one of the prime movers in the affair." Final tallies showed that "18,000 gallons of water were used for the fire, lowering it over 2 feet in the standpipe" (Fairhaven *Star,* 24 February 1894).

Rogers soon decided to raze the water-soaked remains and began construction almost immediately on the new house.

[5] In chapter 11 of *Pudd'nhead Wilson* (*Century Magazine,* February 1894) Clemens had described the costly efforts of the volunteer fire department of Dawson's Landing: "Then the fire-boys mounted to the hall and flooded it with water enough to annihilate forty times as much fire as there was there; for a village fire-company does not often get a chance to show off, and so when it does get a chance it makes the most of it. Such citizens of that village as were of a thoughtful and judicious temperament did not insure against fire; they insured against the fire-company" (p. 557).

[6] Rogers was presiding over the formation of the Paige Compositor Manufacturing Company, which was capitalized partly by the transfer of stock from the Farnham Company, the Webster Manufacturing Company, and the Connecticut Company.

17. Clemens to Rogers

Paris
19 March 1894

Dear Mr. Rogers:

I am always forgetting! I meant to say you must not trouble to answer that letter of mine, but I forgot it. I am glad, now, that I did forget it, for by consequence I have words from you which give me the deepest and sincerest pleasure. But you must not bother yourself to write Mrs. Clemens, indeed you mustn't; your hands are abundantly full, without that. You have sufficiently answered her in what you have said to me.

Mr. Whitmore has paid my Hartford bills for me for the past 8 or 10 years, and is familiar with my small affairs there. He must not pester you with those trifles. I guess the simplest solution of the matter will be to transfer the money in the U. S. Bank, Hartford, to Whitmore, and let him pay my bills from it with his own check. (There is never more than $2,000 there.)

Also, he might receive the Am. Pub. Co. royalties and receipt for them as usual—due Jan., April, July, etc.

If you approve of this plan, will you send the enclosed orders to Whitmore, countersigning them or making new ones in their place, if necessary?

I am glad to have Mr. Hall advised to take the $2500 rental—he was only wasting money waiting for a better offer.

I have your kind order on Messrs. Bedford [1] to allow me to draw on you for $1,000, and I thank you very much; but Mrs. Clemens is better off than I supposed, and we shall not need to draw.

If we can get Clara and Jean satisfactorily housed here, Mrs. Clemens and Susy and I will sail for home together in the New York, April 7. I shall come then, *any*way.

I beg to be remembered kindly and gratefully to all that bear the name of Rogers; and I remain

Sincerely Yours

S. L. Clemens

[1] Probably Bedford et Compagnie; see letter 21, note 1.

18. ROGERS TO CLEMENS

New York
20 March 1894

My dear Mr. Clemens:

I have to-day succeeded in making reply to Mrs. Clemens's note but I was obliged to fall back upon my common weapon, the typewriter. I have so accustomed myself to dictation that Miss Harrison is mightier than the sword—or I mean something like this, which perhaps you will put in suitable quotation marks.

Everything seems to be going smoothly at Chicago. Hall was down yesterday about some financial disturbance and I am to call and see him on my way home to see if it is possible to bridge matters for a time longer. I am sure that we settled upon the wise and proper course. It is going to take such a load from your mind that I am sure your days will be lengthened. Do not worry, but believe it to be for the best.

I received your cable and am waiting for your letter to arrive before Mr. Benjamin has his talk with Mr. Bliss. I know you are having a delightful time with your family and I dislike saying anything about your coming back. Yet I feel that it will be wise for you to come at about the time I suggested.

Henry Irving's stock has been delivered and I have Bram Stoker's acknowledgment for the same.

It is barely possible that Mrs. Duff will go out on the "New York" a week from to-morrow, with May, who the Doctor urges to go abroad for a time. If they sail, I will cable you because they will want to see you if possible. May came near being asphyxiated at school a short time since and is in an enfeebled condition in consequence. One of the Sisters went into her room after May had retired to remove a screen, and in doing so turned the cock on the gas fixture and as a consequence May inhaled the gas, but fortunately was discovered in time to save her life. Her blood is in wretched condition and her heart is somewhat out of order all of which the Doctor thinks will be improved by a change.

Yours sincerely,

H H Rogers

19. CLEMENS TO ROGERS

Paris

22 March 1894

Hotel Brighton

Dear Mr. Rogers:

I've had a tough time persuading Mrs. Clemens to stay here and allow me to go back. She consents to let me go; but it is on condition that I remain in America only 3 weeks and take ship for

France again May 7. She wants to go home with me, but the physician will not hear of it—says she would lose all she has gained—and she is gaining pretty satisfactorily. Susy is a deal better, and has acquired a valuable appetite.

I have begged off from ⟨one⟩ two New York World interviewers, and from interviewers connected with two London and two Paris papers; so, if you see any interviews from me they'll be spurious ones, that is to say, unauthorized. I've got some things to say, but not in interviews.

I bought this elevated railway ticket for you, and then came off and forgot to give it to you.

Sincerely Yours

S. L. Clemens

20. CLEMENS TO ROGERS

Paris
26 March 1894

Hotel Brighton
Easter Monday/'94.

Dear Mr. Rogers:

In answer to yours of March 13. Yes, 4% of Pool #1—or even ⟨2%⟩ 3%—will answer for Davis I should think.

Evidently the work on the machine is booming along. That and Mr. Broughton's enlarged confidence makes me feel pretty comfortable. I am impatient to get over there and stir Shoemaker [1] up. It was time he was booming, too.

I received the document from Stern & Rushmore Saturday, but too late to go to the Consulate with it. I have been there this morning, but it's no use—the whole town is shut up, on account of Easter Monday—we are right in the centre of a bunch of holy holidays, when everything is sinful except going to horse-races. Heaven is going to be full of Frenchmen, I reckon—so I shall try to fetch up at the other place.

As regards the Fairhaven house, my advice—if you feel that you need any—is, that you succumb. *One* against a family is not a good working majority. I would make a show of resistance—for that is policy, and will have a good effect—but I would build the house.

Sincerely Yours

S. L. Clemens

Easter Monday.

P. S. I forgot to mention my scheme. If Shoemaker fails to "get there," I want to try England when I come back presently. So I have written and stirred up two old-time friendships there of many years' standing—Henry M. Stanley and Sir Francis de Winton, Governor of the Duke of York's household. They know everybody in England. I am not intending to say anything about the matter when I dine with them on the 6th, the night before I sail, but I'll throw out some feelers, in a general way, as a preparation for a possible future campaign.

Sincerely Yours

S. L. Clemens

---

[1] J. M. Shoemaker, a representative of the Standard Oil Company for the Elmira district, had been commissioned by Rogers to sell a block of Mrs. Clemens's Paige stock. Because Shoemaker was not immediately successful, Clemens later blamed him for the assignment of Charles L. Webster & Company:

Charley [Langdon] looked in yesterday morning, and I told him Shoemaker's fooling around so long had caused my assignment; and I would like him to go to Shoemaker and ask him to step down and out, and return to me the letters which Mr. Rogers gave him. . . . If he fails to sell your stock in 30 days I mean to have Mr. Rogers cancel his privilege. Then I will come back to America and sell it myself. *I* can do it in 30 days, and if I had undertaken it the job would have been finished before this. But I am glad I didn't, and glad he fooled around. If we had sold the stock, we wouldn't have been assigned— and that would have been a big blunder. By fool luck and accident, everything has happened just right for me (SLC to OLC, 22 April 1894).

21. CLEMENS TO ROGERS

Paris
30 March 1894
Hotel Brighton

Dear Mr. Rogers:

We have been hoping to get the cablegram, but as it has not come I judge that Mrs. Duff and Miss May are still with you. It makes one shudder to think what a narrow escape Miss May had. I hope she is over the ill effects of the gas by this time and that that is the reason a sea voyage has been considered unnecessary. We have had a little accident here this morning; a kettle of boiling water was upset and Jean is nursing her leg, now, in consequence. It has no skin on it from the knee down.

I've got my ticket for the "New York" sailing April 7.

I shall read here next Thursday afternoon at the British Embassy, and try to put some money into the empty purse of a first-rate charity—⟨the English⟩ a school for destitute English and American children. Then leave next day for Southampton *via* London.

I have seen Mr. Southard, a delightful man; also Mr. McGowan.[1] If the social duties will give me a chance I mean to go there again.

Mrs. Clemens received your welcome letter and was mightily pleased. She wants to go home for the summer but the doctor forbids. She is improving decidedly now under the electrical treatment.

I'm sent for. Good-bye and good luck!

Sincerely Yours

SL Clemens

---

[1] George Franklin Southard was a partner and James G. Macgowan a manager in "Bedford et Compagnie, a partnership registered in France on July 15, 1893,

legally separate from Standard Oil," but acting on its behalf by setting up a modern refinery at Rouen. (See Ralph W. and Muriel E. Hidy, *Pioneering in Big Business: 1882–1911* [New York, 1955], pp. 241; 491–492.)

22. CLEMENS TO ROGERS

New York
8 May 1894

26 Broadway
Noon

Dear Mr. Rogers:

Enjoy your trip; be perfectly tranquil concerning this office.[1] Miss Harrison and I are running its affairs in the most admirable way. I am going up, presently, to eat your luncheon for you, for you need to keep well nourished when on a long trip, and I don't think much of that West Virginian cuisine.

I invited myself out to dinner last night, and I've got the brooch and a letter for Mrs. Duff.[2] I invited Rice to come out and play billiards, and no doubt he would have come if he hadn't said he would. However, I took it out of Harry and we didn't need the doctor.

Mrs. Clemens writes:

"What a tremendous debt of gratitude we owe Mr. Rogers, and it can never be paid" (all of which is exactly true). We can't ever pay even a tenth of it.

They have given me those same palatial quarters in the ship again, and I move aboard with my crown and sceptre and gripsack this evening.

Mrs. Clemens says I can't have any more furloughs, but she *must* let me come and be on hand when the public test begins in the Chicago Herald office. I expect to take her to Aix-les-Bains immediately—for a 6-weeks course; then deposit her for a sea-bath course somewhere within easy reach of Paris; then ⟨I can⟩ it will be past the beginning of July and I can start at any time for America.

But if at any time it should seem well for me to come earlier, I hope you will notify me.

⟨It was⟩

I had a notion to see you aboard your train and warn the conductor to take the right sort of care of you, but as I was hankering to go on that trip myself it seemed best to keep out of the way of temptation.

Sincerely Yours

SL Clemens

[1] This letter was written from Rogers's office while Rogers was on a business trip to West Virginia.

[2] Mrs. Rogers had asked Clemens to deliver a brooch to her daughter Mai and a letter to her elder daughter while they were touring in England.

23. CLEMENS TO ROGERS

At Sea

16 May 1894

Wednesday.

Dear Mr. Rogers:

It was ever so good and kind of you to tell me to draw on you if I got short, and I did not half thank you for it; but I *do* thank you, ⟨all⟩ nevertheless, in my heart. I shan't need to draw—I feel quite sure of that—and of course I wouldn't till I *did* need to.

You are just about arriving home, now, from your ten-day scout with the coffee-cooler's bottle-holder. It was a pity that I lost that spree; I want to go on the next one.[1]

I have been at work on a magazine article all through this trip, but I didn't get it finished. That is because it will make three articles. The first is nearly done and the notes are made for the other two and the articles themselves blocked out in my head.

It is a review of an old-time novel. I think I will review (and blackguard) all the novelists the last two generations of English-men and Americans admired. I ought to make a vicious and entertaining book.[2]

I told Bliss to keep in touch with Mr. Benjamin. ⟨I said I was⟩ I told him, ⟨I was⟩ Mrs. Clemens would be willing that he should publish Puddnhead Wilson[3] by subscription on a basis of half of the profits above cost of manufacture—same contract, as to all details, that I made with his father on "A Tramp Abroad"—and that if you approved, he could get at it whenever you considered the time ripe.

I also told him that if he could arrange with you and Mr. Benjamin about a Uniform Edition the terms of it would be satisfactory to Mrs. Clemens.

I've got the lumbago.

I have not lost the brooch nor the letter which Mrs. Rogers gave me, and I am expecting to arrive in time to deliver them to Mrs. Duff this evening.

Sincerely Yours
SL Clemens

[1] John D. Archbold had accompanied Rogers on a trip to West Virginia; it seems likely that he is "the coffee-cooler's bottle-holder"; see letter 2.

[2] Probably "Fenimore Cooper's Literary Offenses," which Clemens conceived as one in a series to be called "Studies in Literary Criticism." (See Bernard DeVoto's introduction to "Fenimore Cooper's Further Literary Offenses," *New England Quarterly*, XIX [September 1946], 291–292.) Clemens's "A Cure for the Blues," a piece deriving from the same impulse, had been collected in *The £1,000,000 Bank-Note and Other New Stories* in 1893.

[3] *Pudd'nhead Wilson* had been appearing serially in *Century Magazine* since December 1893. As the date of its last installment in June 1894 approached, Clemens became increasingly eager that it appear soon as a book, and on his terms (see letters 27 and 33). It was published, almost simultaneously, late in November 1894 by Chatto & Windus in London as a trade book, and by the American Publishing Company as a subscription book.

24. Clemens to Rogers

Paris
22 May 1894

Hotel Brighton

Dear Mr. Rogers:

Mrs. Duff and Miss May had escaped into Switzerland before I arrived. The Brown's Hotel people in London were expecting them there, and said they had some letters and telegrams for them; so I left with them the letter sent by Mrs. Rogers, but kept the brooch, fully expecting that the wanderers were still in Paris; but Mrs. Clemens said they were making a trip into Switzerland. I am on their track this morning, and have traced them to the Hotel Victoria, London. I am telegraphing them that Mrs. Rogers's letter is at Brown's, and am inquiring when they intend to sail. I suspect that they sail to-morrow; in which case Miss May will still be minus her brooch, for I shall be afraid to send it to her with so little time to spare. Their society was a thorough charm to Mrs. Clemens and our girls, and I and they wish they could have had more of it. Their native sincerity, simplicity and genuineness are a refreshment to the spirit in this stuffy artificial atmosphere of Paris.

I was two days in London. Mary Anderson's [1] agent offered me £2,000 to lecture 10 nights there, but I declined because the London season would be over in three weeks, therefore there was not sufficient time to advertise. I promised to consider a fall or winter engagement, to be extended to 2-night stands in the other chief cities. Bram Stoker said I must require a part of the proceeds besides the specific sum.

Mrs. Clemens goes to Aix-les-Bains 5 weeks hence—which gives me a handsome big writing-interval. Then she comes to Étretat, on the coast near Havre for August, Sept., and part of October. We examined a cottage there day before yesterday and secured it. I shall be indispensable there, because the cottage stands by itself in a big garden and the family would be afraid without somebody to chew up burglars and other intruders. So I think the madam will have to leave for Aix as early as the 20th June, so that I can go ⟨then⟩ to America as soon as she is settled there and get back to Aix in time to take her to Étretat in the first week of August. There is a cottage adjoining the hotel, but the madam would not have it because it was too expensive. It would have required no policing, and I would have *made* her take it, but the doctor said no, she must not be close to the water.

[The remainder of this letter is missing.]

¹ Mary Anderson was an American actress who had settled in England.

25. CLEMENS TO ROGERS

Paris
25 May 1894

Dear Mr. Rogers:

Those children of yours have certainly got lost or mislaid somewhere. They are not at the Victoria, London. I get no answer from them—so they are not there. I think I will go to the Chief of Police and see if he knows anything about them. I do wonder if they have gone home.

I shall conduct this family to Aix-les-Bains about the end of June or *toward* the end of June, and then return and sail from Southampton.

If by chance the machine should be finished before then, do be good and send me a cable saying—

Clemens
Care Drexel, Paris
Finished.

I would very very much like to hear that news.

Wouldn't it be a good scheme to pay Paige a year's salary in advance? He is not half improvident enough these days. Consound him I am afraid he is trying to reform.

With my very kindest regards to you and the household, including Harry the Storage Battery,

Yours sincerely

SL Clemens

26. CLEMENS TO ROGERS

Paris

31 May 1894

10 p.m.

Dear Mr. Rogers:

Miss Harrison's letter came twenty minutes ago. I have walked the floor, shut up in my study, and tried to realize it, but I cannot. It seems impossible that she is gone,[1] and that I shall never see her face again. I cannot bear to think of it. I knew that my affection for her was strong and deep, but I did not realize how strong and deep it was until now. She had such a gift for making one feel welcome. It was in her eyes, and in her face and her hand-clasp—she did not need to speak a word. In the very beginning, and always afterward, her welcomes touched me so that it was hard for me to keep the moisture from showing in my eyes. I would have gone miles at any time to get one of them; but now—now I would go around the globe. She always had that glass of milk put at my place, and never forgot it; and it always gave me a new pleasure to think that she could keep me in her mind like that, and would take that trouble for me. And now she will never know but that I took that attention as a matter of course, but I never did. The spirit that was back of it made it a dear and beautiful grace to me. It seemed a little thing to her, no doubt, but it was never so to ⟨her⟩ me, and I shall keep the memory of it, for it was one of her unspoken welcomes.

I cannot realize that she is gone, and that there will be a void in the house when I come again. She was so young; and in all ways so lovely. She was not even entering age yet. It seems impossible; and yet for all my grief I must believe it. When I think of yours, words fail; they cannot measure your loss. And they have no power to lessen your sense of it, or bring you any comfort. I can offer sympathy, out of the bottom of my heart, and I do; but I know no healing words, and indeed there are none. If there were, I would find them. I will let myself hope, and dream, that you will come abroad with me and find some help in rest and change. It may be that you cannot see your way to it, but I will hope.

I am glad I have her picture, and that it is by her own consent that I have it.

We all feared it—and more than once—and now that it has come, it is as if we had never dreamed of it. It is incredible.

In sincere and affectionate sympathy,

S. L. Clemens

---

[1] Abbie Palmer Gifford Rogers died on 21 May 1894. After returning to New York, Clemens wrote Livy (17 July 1894):

Mr. Rogers tried to tell me about the last days of Mrs. Rogers this morning, but it was finally too hard for him and his voice broke and he could not go on. She was suffering intolerable pain (from the unsuspected tumour, which was as big as a man's fist) and was glad to undertake the surgical operation. It was to take ¾ of an hour, but it took an hour and three-quarters. Before it she made various arrangements: wrote a cablegram to be sent to Mrs. Duff saying the operation had been successfully performed and all was well. She called for some bills and her check-book and signed checks for them. Mrs. Benjamin suggested that she sign some more in blank, but she said no, there would be no occasion for that. She told Mr. Rogers and the doctors that soon she would have the advantage of them—she could eat grapes without fear, and they couldn't. Then the surgery began; after its completion she began to sink and never rallied. Mrs. Duff says all the family were dependent on her and rested in her, and that in losing her they have lost more than can be described. Mr. Rogers says his hardest time is when he gets up every morning—for, coming out of sleep he is expecting to see her, and then comes the daily shock and the new realization.

Let us be spared this, my darling. May we die together.

27. ROGERS TO CLEMENS

New York
1 June 1894

My dear Mr. Clemens:

It was very considerate in you to send me the cablegram, and I appreciate it fully, because I know that it comes in all sincerity. Miss Harrison tells me that she wrote you quite fully of our great sorrow and so I will not refer to it in detail. Of course, the whole experience is like a dream and as yet I have not reached a full realization of what it means to me. Our attempts at concealment from Mrs. Duff proved fruitless, and she poor girl, read of her mother's death in a foreign paper the day before she sailed, and my heart has been aching for her ever since. She is due to-morrow morning and I am going down the Bay to meet her. If I can find her in good health, I will feel relieved of the great anxiety I have for her, because of her great troubles.[1] Mrs. Benjamin is well, and with her family are at present at our house. Poor Harry is quite heart broken, but he seems to feel that I am the one on whom the blow has fallen and so with his sister, they make every effort to appear brave, and in many ways they study to comfort me. I feel that you will be interested to know that he said the other evening, "Come Papa, let us go down for billiards. I wish 'Uncle Sammy' was here to cheer you up," and perhaps you will not think me speaking for effect when I say that I could have said Amen! to his expression. I am trying to get absorbed in business as much as possible, and so without further reference to my personal affairs, I will undertake to reply to your letter, and tell you of the C. L. Webster & Co. matters.

I note that you are at work on some magazine articles. I think if you are to carry out the suggestion of reviewing all the novelists, that you will very thoroughly advertise yourself to say the least. Mr. Colby was obliged to follow me to Fairhaven in order to make proper transfers of the copy-rights to Mrs. Clemens, it being necessary to go into detail and specify each of the books. Colby is arranging for a meeting of the creditors within a day or two. I will attend. As yet the proposition for Mrs. Clemens to assign the copy= right and waive royalties on your books for a year, on condition that you be released has not been accepted. I think Colby now inclines to the opinion that if the creditors receive a proposition from you to agree to pay a certain percentage on liabilities and give to the assignee the power to sell off the stock and conduct business for a year with privilege of copy-right and the waiving of royalties, that it will be accepted, and on the whole the best way out of the matter. However, that need not disturb you for the present. I will attend the meeting and try and catch the temper. Business is so terribly depressed that it seems almost impossible to do anything in the way of selling books. Mr. Benjamin complains very much about his business and tells me that the entire trade is prostrated. I note the willingness of Mrs. Clemens and yourself to allow Mr. Bliss to publish "Pudd'nhead Wilson" by subscription but I hesitate in giving my approval at present, because I am afraid it will not prove satisfactory in the end. However, I am talking with Mr. Benjamin about it and discussing the whole scheme from the many standpoints and hope to reach an intelligent decision.

Mr. Archbold and I were away for ten days and had a rough but pleasant time. I feel sure you would have enjoyed the trip and that you would have seen a phase of life perhaps somewhat new to you, although in a degree like your early experiences in the West.

I will write you after the meeting of the creditors. I have not heard from Chicago for fully two weeks. Mr. Broughton, I hear, was thrown from his horse last week and is now nursing a broken arm. I am quite sure that everything is going satisfactorily, but in my next letter I hope to be able to give you some positive information.

Please remember me most kindly to Mrs. Clemens as also to

Susie, Clara and Jean, whom I feel that I know.

With warmest regards to your good self, I am,

Yours sincerely,

H H Rogers

[1] Mrs. Duff's husband, Bradford F. Duff, had died on 6 September 1893. The young New York stockbroker had contracted pneumonia soon after their marriage on 17 November 1890, and his death at the age of twenty-four followed subsequent "lung trouble" (Fairhaven *Star,* 9 September 1893).

28. KATHARINE HARRISON TO CLEMENS

New York
1 June 1894

Dear Mr. Clemens:

I received your letter to-day in regard to the extension of time to Mr. Brusnahan.[1] He has been to see me two or three times, and although he is working hard to sell the stock, he finds it pretty hard work, as the majority of those printers are such poor fellows, and in some cases they are not to be depended upon. He asked me if he might make an arrangement with Mr. Chas. B. Knevals to help him sell the stock, and give him part of his commission. I thought over the matter for three or four days, then came to the conclusion, that what you wanted was to sell the stock, that it didn't matter much who bought it as long as you got the money, so I thought as I could ask nobody about it, the best thing to do was to let Mr. Brusnahan and Mr. Knevals sell all they could. I hope this will meet your approval. As yet, they have reported no sales, although Mr. Brusnahan did not expect to get many in before the 10th of July. This Mr. Knevals is a broker, so I hope he will be able to sell a great deal of it for you. He seems anxious enough to do so at any rate. I will also suggest to Mr. Brusnahan the next time he comes about selecting some Union foremen in two or three other cities, and getting them to sell some stock.

Mr. Rogers has written you a long letter to-day. Whenever I learn anything about the machine, I will certainly write you.

I spoke to Mr. Rogers about sending the 5 shares of stock to your brother, and it is to be attended to the first of next week. Mr. Rogers's absence from the office has delayed this matter, although I wrote to your brother and told him, so he would know the cause.

Do not think you are giving me trouble. It is a pleasure I assure you, and I only hope you will sell all of Mrs. Clemens stock that you want sold. With kindest regards, I remain,

Yours sincerely,

Katharine I. Harrison

P. S. Since dictating the foregoing I have had a call from Messrs. Colby and Rushmore.[2] They have modified their opinions and are now hopeful that if we give the creditors the use of the copyright and waive royalties for a year, that it will be accepted. I am waiting in my office, subject to call from them this afternoon they having hoped to get a meeting with Payne, Barrow and Whitford.[3] If anything important transpires, I will add a few lines before closing.

Mr. Rogers wishes me to add that the meeting was not held after all.

K. I. H.

[1] John Brusnahan, a printing foreman for the New York *Herald,* had agreed to dispose of Olivia Clemens's stock in the Paige company. A surviving draft of the arrangement, in Clemens's hand, outlines the terms under which Brusnahan undertook the task:

May 7,/94.

Agreement entered into with John Brusnahan. He to sell $100,000 or less, of Mrs. C.'s stock at 50, and pay into Miss Harrison's hands 45, taking the remaining 5 as commission. Payments to be in instalments—⟨15⟩ 10 per cent down, and 10 per cent a month till the whole is paid—the stock to be then delivered. He to have also, as further commission, one share of paid-up stock for every 10 shares ⟨ten⟩ sold through him and *paid for.* This agreement to terminate June 15, 1894 (Enoch Pratt Free Library).

² Charles E. Rushmore, of Stern & Rushmore, attorneys.

³ William H. Payne, president of the Mount Morris Bank; George Barrow, who represented the Barrow family, to which Charles L. Webster & Company owed $15,416.90; Daniel Whitford, who had been retained by Clemens in 1885 and 1890 (*MTLP*, p. 266), who now, as attorney for the Mount Morris Bank, was suspected of taking advantage of his previous knowledge of Charles L. Webster & Company affairs in the present negotiation.

29. ROGERS TO CLEMENS

New York
2 June 1894

My dear Mr. Clemens:

Since writing you yesterday, I have information from Mr. Broughton saying, "everything is going on satisfactorily at the Paige Factory and I have got Mr. Paige to sign the Patent Specifications and they have gone on to Washington." When Mr. Broughton was here about ten days ago, he informed me that Mr. Paige was holding back his signature to the applications for Letters Patent on the plea that he was negotiating sales for his foreign rights, and he felt as he was not quite prepared to take out his foreign patents, he would prefer to wait. After careful consideration of the matter, it was decided that Mr. Broughton should see Mr. Paige immediately on his return and politely but firmly tell him to immediately sign the patents[1] or the factory would close, and to say as coming from me, that I trusted that our relations, which had been so pleasantly inaugurated, were not to be marred by any prejudicial conduct on his part. That they are now all in perfect harmony and that we could only continue it by co-operation on the part of all to make the Paige Compositor a perfect success. I confess that I had some misgivings as to how he would act in the matter when Mr. Broughton interviewed him, but I am rejoiced to learn that he has signed the papers. There does not seem to be any further cause for anxiety in our matters with Paige. Of course, he is likely to step over the traces at any time, but Broughton is diplomatic and I think can manage him successfully.

The "Paris" arrived at Sandy Hook last evening at 9:20 and I stole down on the tug that went for the mails and met Mrs. Duff, who looked very well, but I learn has had a very trying time. Everybody on the ship was extremely kind to her so that the passage was made bearable. She left May at school on the other side, and on the whole perhaps it was the best thing that could have happened. She learned the news of her mother's death the day before sailing and was in doubt as to what to do with May. She finally decided that if I wanted May to return we could easily send for her, so she gave May the sad news and received a message in reply full of courage and concern for her sister. Mrs. Duff arranged with Miss Delaney to stay abroad for a time in order to be near May until May felt she had made some friends in school. This fact makes me feel comparatively easy. I will ask Mrs. Duff to write you in a day or two and she can then give you instructions regarding the brooch. I received four pages of your letter written on the 22nd ult. and note the contemplated movements of your family. If you ever are startled by housebreakers in your cottage, I am sure your appearance, as I have once or twice seen you in the night, would be quite enough to drive them away, if they did not drop dead on the spot. I might suggest that you put your spectacles on the tip of your nose to add to the effect.

I note what you say in regard to your lecturing in London and I have no doubt of its entire success when you choose to go on the platform.

Yours sincerely

H H Rogers

---

[1] It is not clear whether this crisis involved any of the three patents on the Paige machine registered in the *Official Gazette of the United States Patent Office,* LXXIII (15 October 1895), 324–341: Machine for Setting, Distributing, and Justifying Type, No. 547,859, filed 5 December 1882; Machine for Distributing, Setting, and Justifying Type, No. 547,860, filed 19 August 1887; Automatic Type-Justifying Machine, No. 547,861, filed 14 February 1893, by James W. Paige and Charles R. North.

30. CLEMENS TO ROGERS

Paris
16 June 1894

Dear Mr. Rogers:

The dismal work of trunk-packing has begun; we leave here next Friday, 21st for La Bourboule, down in the centre of France, 12 hours from Paris. ⟨It⟩ This is ordered on Susy's account, and cuts Mrs. Clemens out from going to Aix-les-Bains. The family will go from Bourboule to Étretat on the coast near Havre the first week in August and stay until early in October, living in a cottage a little ⟨be⟩ back from the seashore. I sail in the New York June 30, and shall expect to arrive at The Players at noon July 6th. If Harry has any billiard-opportunities open in those days, he will find his Uncle Sammy mighty glad to take a chance; and mighty glad, too, to have him umpire the game, if he won't go further and set up the balls.

I have arranged for the brooch so that it will be safe. If I do not hear from Mrs. Duff before I leave, I am going to hand it to Mr. McGowan, who will hold himself responsible for it. Anybody else would have thought of him and of Mr. Southard the first thing, but I didn't. In trying to find Mrs. Duff I went to banks, and tele-graphed hotels—in vain, of course—and never thought of those men once. But I went there a day or two ago to return a call, and found that Mr. McGowan was Miss May's banker and had her address. There are a good many different kinds of fools in the world, but I seem to be a new kind. You will see by the enclosed card that my mind is giving way. The Bodleys and I got all mixed up on a dinner engagement some days ago, and I never got there at all. This time I got my acceptance in, for a breakfast, all right and on time, making merely the mistake of beginning my note "Dear Mr. Clemens," instead of Dear Mr. Bodley. However, I got the breakfast.

I have spent a considerable portion of two days in buying a family ticket—second class and return—to Bourboule. The red-tape and discussion connected with it was something formidable. It was like the old days of negociating the Compositor-scheme in the Graveyard. Of course there will be a flaw in it somewhere. We never shall see Bourboule.

I am glad Paige has signed. I wish it was his death-warrant. Well, maybe it is. His European patents ought to furnish him money enough to spree himself into Perdition on, if he makes a trade.

I am very sorry to hear of Mr. Broughton's accident, and very glad it was no worse—it could have been fatal.

Mrs. Clemens and the children were very glad to get your message, and they wish to be most kindly remembered to you and to Mrs. Duff—and I wish to be included.

> Yrs Sincerely
>
> SL Clemens

31. CLEMENS TO ROGERS

> La Bourboule-les-Bains
> 25 June 1894

Dear Mr. Rogers:

As the cablegram hasn't come, I suppose the scheme for continuing the business a year did not meet with the bank's approval—con-sound that stupid concern! You have got a good reserve-stock of patience—I hope those people will not exhaust it. I cannot understand their attitude. To go on a year would not injure their chance to "go for" me in accordance with that profound Whitford's desire, and might profit them somewhat during the year—so I don't see why they hold back.

I judge by Mr. Broughton's guess that the machine will be done by the time I arrive—the which will make me glad.

We are up here in the bottom of a cup in the hills, but the cup is not empty; it is full of sunshine and heat; but there are shady places, and they are cool. The nights are very cool, the air is fresh and fine, the table-fare is good, the rooms are unspeakably small, and the family are doing their best to believe they can survive the month. I am sorry to have to leave them before they get wonted, but I must. One can't come *down* in the lift without sending a servant to the main floor and securing a special order from the landlord.[1] Exquisitely European!

The news of the assassination of the President of the Republic [2] has come. We live in strange times. While the French and the Italians were celebrating the anniversary of Solferino and weeping lovingly on each others' necks by telegraph, the bottom Italian of the period stabs the top Frenchman of the period to death.

Sincerely Yours

SL Clemens

[1] The "Grand Hôtel des Iles Britanniques" evidently regarded its elevator with proprietary awe. The hotel facade, as depicted on its letterhead, boasted three signs in bold letters: "J. DONNEAUD" (the owner) at the first floor; "HOTEL DES ILES BRITANNIQUES" on the second; finally and most grandly on the third, "ASCENSEUR."

[2] Marie François Sadi-Carnot, fourth President of France, was assassinated by an Italian anarchist at Lyons on 24 June 1894.

32. CLEMENS TO ROGERS (cablegram)

La Bourboule-les-Bains
29 June 1894

Unavoidably detained

33. CLEMENS TO ROGERS

La Bourboule-les-Bains
29–30 June 1894

Dear Mr. Rogers:

This family is out of luck. We were sent to this place for Susy's sake, and now she is sick abed—yesterday afternoon and to-day. She had fever day before yesterday, and it continues; she does not get rid of it. It was much aggravated, no doubt, by the events of night before last. When we were about to go to bed we heard a good deal of noise about a hundred yards away—shoutings of a great crowd. These continued—burst after burst of shouts—louder and louder—and at last the shouts became furious howlings. We have Italian waiters in the house, and I became uneasy, but I tried to make the family believe it was only a mob of drunken merry-makers. However, that assertion soon lost force. The noise approached, and took the form of the Marseillaise. Then stones began to fly. They rattled against our windows and considerably frightened the family. We put out the lights, and no more stones struck our windows, but a lady in another room went too near her open window and got knocked down by a stone. Then the rioters gathered in front of the hotel and demanded the Italians, proposing to hammer them; but the landlord refused to give them up, and sent them to the upper story for safety. There ⟨are⟩ were but two policemen. These argued with the mob, but were not listened to. Toward midnight the mob came around under our windows again and began to smash windows on the floor below and there was also the crash of smashing woodwork. It looked serious, then. I was afraid they would fire the house. But they didn't. They kept everybody up to the small hours with their threats and howlings and cries of "À bas les Italiens!"—then at last they went away saying the Italians must leave next day or the hotel must take the consequences. I was to leave at 10.30 in the morning to catch the steamer, but I of course decided to remain. I didn't wake until 9, and then I had no time to consider much. Jean came in and said some soldiers and eleven policemen had arrived from Montluçon and there wouldn't be any more trouble. So at 10.30 I started in the diligence for Laqueille, the RR station; but on the way I had time to think. It goes without saying that I turned back. The President's funeral is not until Sunday. There can be no assurance of quiet in France until some days after that. Susy is too sick to travel. We must stay here for the present.

The soldiers and the eleven policemen stayed in the hotel last night and there was no demonstration. But all the soldiers are gone, now, and some of the policemen. A while ago I was over at the hotel de Ville and saw the ringleaders of the mob (well-dressed, good looking fellows, with their well dressed peasant-families about them to say good-bye), marched out of town by three cavalrymen. They are to walk 32 miles and remain that distance from here until pardoned. It is a sort of banishment, you see. Groups of peasantry stood talking together here and there about the square and looking gloomy. It is thought that the banishment has made the people very bitter against our landlord, who did the prosecuting, and that there is further trouble in store.

I telegraphed ⟨Paris⟩ the American Line yesterday and asked them to postpone me to the Paris.[1] By that time I hope Susy will be well enough either to travel hence or to let me go.

Don't you think Puddn'head can be put into the hands of some publisher, without waiting longer on the creditors? It will take pretty brisk work to get it ready for the fall trade, if it is published by "the trade." If Bliss or some other subscription house should publish it there would not be so much press of time, because such a house could begin taking subscriptions as late as the 1st of October and issue all right by Dec. 1.

There's an excitement out in the square—I must go and see what it is.

June 30. It wasn't anything. The people get excited over next to nothing, these days.

News has come that the New York had a collision at sea and will need some repairs; it is reported that she will not be able to sail to-day.

Susy still has that fever this morning—and here we are, a thousand miles from a doctor. For a bath-village doctor is necessarily a doctor who can't make his living anywhere else and would starve anywhere else. This one here said Susy had no fever. I went and got a thermometer and took her temperature—102°. Then I went to him and he ciphered with his pencil and showed me that 102° Fahrenheit was only 28¾ centigrade—[as] if that affected the matter in any way. Mrs. Clemens administers medicines of her own, now, and I throw the doctor's out of the window. *His* are for constipation; he gives nothing for the fever, contending that there *isn't* any.

No more mobbing, up to now. But there is still rioting all over France—and will continue to be until a week after to-morrow's funeral, no doubt.

I am glad Mrs. Duff got home safe. We all wish to be kindly remembered to you all.

Yours sincerely

SL Clemens

[1] The SS *Paris* was scheduled to depart for New York from Southampton on 7 July 1894.

34. CLEMENS TO ROGERS

Étretat
25 August 1894

Étretat, (Normandie)
(Chalet des Abris.)

Dear Mr. Rogers:

I find the Madam ever so much better in health and strength;

but disappointed, for she hoped you and Mrs. Duff would come and let her take care of you as she proposed; but I told her I didn't get the letter, which was true. But I don't see how she would take care of anybody in this little Chalet des Abris, which is such an incredibly small coop that the family can't find room to sleep without hanging their legs out of the windows.

But the air is superb and soothing and wholesome, and the chalet is remote from noise and people, and just the place to write in. I shall begin work this afternoon.

Won't you assign to yourself the privileges and powers of proxy for Mrs. Clemens by virtue of your power of attorney? I suggest this because if she must perfect the proxy before a U. S. consul to make it good she will have to make the fatiguing journey to Havre to find one—in fact as tough a journey as from here to Paris. She will make the trip if necessary, of course, but I am hoping that the other way will answer.

She is in great spirits on account of the benefit which she has received from the electrical treatment in Paris and is bound to take it up again and continue it all the winter, and of course I am perfectly willing. She requires me to drop the lecture platform out of my mind and go straight ahead with Joan until the book is finished. If I should have to go home for even a week she means to go with me—won't consent to be separated again—but she hopes I won't need to go. I tell her "all right," I won't go ⟨until⟩ unless you send, and then I *must*.

She keeps the accounts; and as she ciphers it we can't get crowded for money for eight months yet. I didn't know that. But I don't know much anyway.

I am hoping to hear from Colby the result of the dicker with Bliss; in fact I was hoping to hear the morning I sailed.[1]

The passage of the bill sent a lot of people over in our ship to buy goods and start the business-boom.[2]

I should like to know and shall hope to learn that Mrs. Duff's health is now wholly restored. Mrs. Clemens and the children wish to be remembered to her, with their kindest regards. And I the same to you and all the household, including Harry the Storage Battery.

Sincerely Yours

SL Clemens

---

[1] Clemens was not yet aware that a contract had been signed on 24 August with Frank Bliss for the publication of *Pudd'nhead Wilson* by the American Publishing Company.

[2] The tariff bill of 13 August reduced tariffs on imported goods and added more items to the free list.

35. CLEMENS TO ROGERS

Étretat

2–3 September 1894

(In bed—noon)

Dear Mr. Rogers:

The facts are distorted in that "Sun" squib.[1] (When you see it in the Sun it ain't so.)

Here it's more than 2 weeks and Colby hasn't told me yet how he came out with Bliss. I shall cable him to-morrow evening. B'gosh he builds a fire under me and then says "Don't worry." I've *got* to worry. There isn't a moment to be lost (on Puddnhead), but *weeks* are being lost.

You write on the 22d, which shows that you have signed no contracts with Bliss, I judge, or you would mention it.

Puddnhead had some value; but if no contract is signed for it before Sept 15 it won't be worth as much as a last year's almanac.

However, I'll banish these uneasinesses until I hear by cable to-morrow.

I arrived here on the 28th,[2] Thursday; and worked ⟨Frid⟩ Saturday and Sunday on a magazine story ⟨which⟩. I failed to finish it to suit me. It must be re-written on a different plan and from a different stand-point some day by-and by.

Monday morning,[3] Joan. I hadn't any trouble there. That is a book which writes itself, a tale which tells itself; I merely have to hold the pen. At 7 yesterday evening my aggregate on that book for the 6 days was 10,000 or 11,000 words—plenty good enough, considering how much time was daily lost in freshening-up on history, and in thinking. I think the mill is fairly started for a long grind; I hope so, anyway. I would like to finish Book II before we leave for Paris a month hence; but I can't tell. The artist [4] has been here to discuss illustrations. His views and sympathies are right.

The thing that delights me is that Mrs. Clemens's health is so ⟨im⟩ very very *much* improved. She is even going to venture on house-keeping in Paris, for economy's sake.

With my warmest regards to Mrs. Duff and the Sand-Blast,

Sincerely Yours

SL Clemens

---

[1] A search of the New York *Sun* in late August 1894 failed to identify this "squib."

[2] Clemens apparently wrote "28," which was not a Thursday, for "23," which was. Letter 34 places him in Étretat by 25 August 1894.

[3] Clemens evidently returned to the letter which he had begun on Sunday, 2 September.

[4] Frank Vincent Du Mond did the illustrations for *Joan of Arc.*

36. CLEMENS TO ROGERS

Étretat
9 September 1894

Dear Mr. Rogers:

I drove the quill too hard, and I broke down—in my head. It has now been three days since I laid up. When I wrote you a week ago I had added 10,000 words or thereabout to Joan. Next day I added 1,500, which was a proper enough day's work though not a full one; but during Tuesday and Wednesday I stacked up an aggregate of 6,000 words—and that was a very large mistake. My head hasn't been worth a cent since.

However, there's compensation; for in those two days I reached and passed—successfully—a point which I was solicitous about before I ever began the book: viz., *the battle of Patay*. Because that would naturally be the next to the last chapter of a work consisting of either two books or one. In the one case one goes right along from that point (as I shall now do); in the other he would add a wind-up chapter and make the book consist of Joan's childhood and military career alone.

I shall resume work to-day; and hereafter I will not go at such an intemperate rate. My head is pretty cob-webby yet.

The madam has made up her mind to take a flat in Paris and keep house all winter. I am not sorry. It will be economy, and we shall have a home. She expects to ⟨derive⟩ get vast benefit from the electrical treatment this time; and I am sure she will.

I am hoping that along about this time I shall hear that the machine is beginning its test in the Herald office. I shall be very glad indeed to know the result of it. I wish I could be there.

I got so uneasy about Puddnhead that I cabled Colby. I'm satisfied, now. Let's see how Bliss will succeed.

The Harpers wrote me (Aug. 24) that they had sent me a type-written copy of Joan, express paid—and by gracious it's 16 days out and not here yet!

Cuss these French, their postal system is mighty poor.

Sincerely Yours

S. L. Clemens

37. Clemens to Rogers

Étretat

14 September 1894

Dear Mr. Rogers:

I am very glad to know that the matter you were so busy about when I left is progressing to suit you. That's the Brooklyn one, I reckon. I am strongly interested to know how it comes out.[1]

Barrow's offer of $9,000 was not very gaudy, still it proved something—proved that Mr. Hall's poor old literary ash-pile is worth *something*, anyway—a thing not easily believable.[2]

Mr. Broughton calls 1500 shares the total of Mrs. Clemens's stock—but that is an error which would deprive you and Mrs. Clemens, ⟨of 7,500⟩ between you, of 750 shares—"commission," you remember. I wish they would issue that 750 without any further delay and put it into your hands so that ⟨could⟩ can vote its weight Oct. 3. It ought to be done, I am sure.

Necessarily you are right about postponing Scott's "Supplement" [3] till the end of the test. But I am hoping that the test will go through to your satisfaction, so that Scott can whack out his supplement then and with a full head of steam. We have always kept the machine out of print before, but that was because it wasn't ready for business, and therefore no use to waste a ⟨stink⟩ ⟨stench⟩ fragrance that could come good another time.

⟨Yes⟩ Thanks for the duplicate of Mr. Wright's letter. I will hang it around my neck the minute there is a vacancy; places all occupied now, with reminders to do this and this and this and this—and also a lot of *thats*. I am trusting in God for a result.

Yesterday I found a letter which I wrote you and mislaid, I don't know when—all ready for the mail. To-day I find some more letters —2—⟨which⟩ for people on the other side—I don't know when I wrote them. I wish I had a nurse—*any* kind, wet or dry. Understand, I am not alarmed; I have not lost my mind, but only my sense. And I don't really care for that; it was never around when I wanted it.

I am shoving my work along—not swiftly, but persistently, steadily, surely; and not losing a day that can be saved. I have now written 224 pages, which is say, 25,000 words.

Sincerely Yours

SL Clemens

¹ Rogers was making a vigorous attempt to prevent J. Edward Addicks of the Bay State Gas Company of Delaware from providing service to Brooklyn, a Standard Oil territory. The battle was engaged, however, not in Brooklyn but in Brookline, Massachusetts. Addicks already controlled through his company the major gas companies of Boston. However, Rogers "got control of the Brookline Gas Light Company, extended its mains to Boston and cut the price of gas in that city from $1.25 to $1 a thousand cubic feet," thus forcing Addicks to withdraw from his attempted invasion of Brooklyn. "When the war came to an end in 1896 Mr. Rogers and certain of his associates were made trustees of the Bay State Gas Company of Delaware, to manage the Boston, South Boston, Roxbury and Bay State (of Massachusetts) gas companies" (New York *Tribune,* 20 May 1909). Litigation in the matter dragged on until 1907, and Rogers's frequent testimony in the Boston gas suit is mentioned often in this correspondence.

² Barrow apparently offered to purchase some part of the assets of Charles L. Webster & Company.

³ James Wilmot Scott, of the Chicago *Herald,* planned to issue a supplement to that paper printed by the Paige machine.

38. CLEMENS TO ROGERS

Étretat
16 September 1894

Dear Mr. Rogers:

Oh, that's all right—don't you worry; I'll find a way to get an invitation.¹ I selected my quarters when I was there—mattrass on the billiard table.

I am sending Colby the order for $500. I had already done that in a letter to him, thinking the Bliss money would be in his hands. I don't know whose name the money is in; I have signed the order with my own name. But if that won't do Colby must let me know and Mrs. Clemens will repeat the order.

Yes, that was just like Frink. But God made him. (I shall get hit with lightning some day for throwing that kind of slanders around.) I wish *I* had a subpoena-server and an elevator, for I never take exercise, and I know I need it. Which reminds me that I feel pretty dull and heavy these last few days: wrote only 500 words yesterday—100 to be torn up; and failed to turn out a full crop the day before, I believe—that is, I had to tear up 800 words of it. But these things are of no consequence—just so the book is done right, it is small matter how long it takes. And it is pretty sure to be done at my level best; for the madam and Susy are prompt and frank about squelching inferiorities. They would not hesitate to tell you you are right in "expecting great things" from the work I am now doing. They make me proud of it myself.

I am thundering glad to hear that the Brooklyn campaign went your way. Being right around on the outskirts of the camp myself while the pourparlers were exchanging and the assault preparing, I naturally felt a kind of warm unsalaried non-assessable *personal* interest in it.

Sincerely Yours

SL Clemens

P.S. We'll be settled in Paris and housekeeping by the middle of October. Now surely between that and no long time later you and Mrs. Duff and Harry can run over, can't you? Just the mere change will be a great and valuable rest for you; and a little general looseness and dissipation with me will do us both good and start Harry right. Do take a vote of three on this and do as the majority shall decree.

[1] Probably to Rogers's new house at Fairhaven.

39. CLEMENS TO ROGERS

Étretat
24 September 1894

Monday
Midnight.

Dear Mr. Rogers:

There isn't anything to write, but to-morrow is mail-day, and I have been to bed and can't get sleepy because I am all nerves and over-wrought and spiritually raw to the touch. And when it is mail-day and there isn't anything to write, one would best get up and have a smoke and write it. It is thundering and lightning and raining, and it irritates me; and when it stops, *that* irritates me; and there is a clock down stairs which splits one's ears when it strikes, and it takes four minutes to strike twelve, and then it rumbles its bowels and starts in and strikes it all over again—the most maddening devil of a clock that was ever devised. I would God I could afford it, I would build a fire in it. I have damaged my intellect trying to imagine why a man should want to invent a repeating clock, and how another man could be found to lust after it and buy it. The man who can guess these riddles is far on the way to guess why the human race was invented—which is another riddle which tires me.

I suppose we shall have to break up and strike for Paris before long, and I am sorry. This place is a kind of paradise; it is beautiful, and still, and infinitely restful.

In the 27 days that I have been ⟨here⟩ at work on the book [1] here I have lost nine or ten through head-fatigue and consequent incapacity; but of the 35,000 words written only 300 have been condemned by Mrs. Clemens and short of 3,000 destroyed by myself. It is not a large output, considering the time expended, but is large enough considering the fact that it has to be done with unusual carefulness. I am drawing toward the end of Book II. Book III will be difficult, and will require a good while, much study and thinking, and very great pains-taking in the writing.

I would like to have my warm regards conveyed to Mrs. Duff and the tar, Harry and the like to you. And now I will go to bed. I don't mind the clock so much when its industry is obstructed by the small hours.

> Sincerely Yours
>
> S. L. Clemens
>
> c/o Drexel Harjes, Paris

Hope to hear from you by to-morrow's mail.

[1] *Joan of Arc.*

40. Clemens to Rogers

Étretat
30 September 1894

Dear Mr. Rogers:

As your letter hasn't come, I judge that there wasn't any news in the locker. There isn't any at this end, either. Four days ago I got to the point I was struggling for and anxious about, and now *that* bridge is behind me and all right. It foots up 40,000 words since I arrived. Since then ⟨I⟩ we have had visitors—relatives. I got through exactly in time for them. In front of me now is a long course of study and not much production—on the book. But I'm safe. To-day Mrs. Clemens is packing trunks for Paris, and I am translating a French article which I wish to abuse in a magazine paper.[1] This keeps me out of the way of the packing—otherwise I would be obstructing it with my assistance and advice.

We leave for Paris to-morrow ⟨I think⟩ if Susy is well enough to travel. She has been in quite good health until yesterday, and may be all right again to-morrow. No, I believe it is Monday that we go. Anyway it is along there some where.

Sincerely Yours

SL Clemens

---

[1] Paul Bourget's "Outre Mer," which appeared in Sunday editions of the New York *Herald* from 23 September 1894 through 17 February 1895 and in *Le Figaro* from 26 September 1894 through 6 February 1895. Clemens's "What Paul Bourget Thinks of Us" was published in the *North American Review,* January 1895.

41. Clemens to Rogers

Rouen
5 October 1894

Fridayoctobersomething.

Dear Mr. Rogers:

We are stalled here, tight and fast. We left Étretat last Monday. Susy was not well; so we came four hours and stopped over here to let her have a rest. It turned out to be congestion of the right lung. Temperature during three days, 104, 103, then 101. Necessarily we were a good deal alarmed, but she is ever so much better now. We shall be captives here indefinitely, of course.

All my Joan of Arc bibliography went through to Paris in the trunks, but it is no matter; I do not need it. I know what there is here—and it isn't much. There is no scrap or stone in Rouen that she ever saw. Even the spot where she was burned is not as definitely located as ⟨it⟩ one would expect it to be. But there is a new statue of her—and the worthiest one that has been made yet.

To put in my odd time I am writing some articles about Paul Bourget and his Outre-Mer—laughing at them and at some of our oracular owls who find them "important." What the hell makes them important, I should like to know!

I don't know that Mrs. Clemens will allow me to print them, but I hope to manage to work them into a shape that she will approve. I discarded the first one, myself; but I think better of the one which I began yesterday noon and finished at 2.10 this morning. It is noon again and I will begin another now.

Yours Sincerely

SL Clemens

42. Clemens to Rogers

Rouen
7 October 1894

Dear Mr. Rogers:

Yours of the 24th Sept has arrived, filled with pleasantness and peace. I would God I were in my room in the new house in Fairhaven, so'st I could have one good solid night's sleep. I might have had one last night if I hadn't lost my temper, for I was loaded up high with fatigue; but at 2 this morning I had a W.C. call and jumped up, in the dark, and ran in my night-shirt and without a candle—for I believed I knew my way. This hotel d'Angleterre must be a congeries of old dwellings—if it isn't, it is built up in a series of water-tight compartments, like the American liners, that go clear to the top. You can't get out of your own compartment. There is only your one hall; it has 4 rooms on each side of it and a staircase in the midst[1]: Would you think a person could get lost in such a place? I assure [you] it is possible; for a person of talent. We are on the second floor from the ground. There's a W.C. on the floor *above* us and one on the floor *below* us. Halls pitch dark. I groped my way and found the upper W. [C.] Starting to return, I went *up* stairs instead of down, and went to what I supposed was my room, but I could not make out the number in the dark and was afraid to enter it. Then I remembered that I—no, my mind lost confidence and began to wander. I was no longer sure as to what floor I was on, and the minute I realized *that,* the rest of my mind went. One cannot stand still in a dark hall at 2 in the morning, lost, and be content. One must move, and go on moving, even at the risk of getting worse lost. I groped up and down a couple of those flights, over and over again, cursing to myself. And every time I thought I heard some body coming, I shrank together like one of those toy balloons when it collapses. You see, I was between two fires; I could not grope to the top floor and start fresh and count down to my own, for it was all occupied by young ladies, and a dangerous place to get caught in, clothed as I was clothed, and not in my right mind. I could not grope down to the ground floor and count ⟨from⟩ *up*, for there was a ball down there. A ball, and young ladies likely to be starting up to bed about this time. X X X. And so they did. I saw the glow of their distant candle, I ⟨heard⟩ felt the chill of their distant cackle. I did not know whether I was on a W.C. floor or not, but I had to take a risk. I groped to the door that ought to be it—right where you turn down the stairs; and it *was* it. I entered it grateful, and stood in its dark shelter with a beating heart and thought how happy I should be to live there always, in that humble cot, and go out no more among life's troubles and dangers. Several of the young ladies applied for admission, but I was not receiving. Thursdays being my day. I meant to freeze-out the ball, if it took a week. And I did. When the drone and burr of its music had ceased for twenty minutes and the house was solidly dead and dark, I groped down to the ground floor, then turned and counted my way up home all right.

Then straightway my temper went up to 180 in the shade and I began to put it into form. Presently ⟨a disapproving voice said, at a temperature of about 8° below:⟩ an admiring voice said—

"When you are through with your prayers, I would like to ask where you have been, all night."

It was Mrs. Clemens; waiting in the dark; waiting for a reposeful atmosphere and tranquillizing speech; for Susy's tossings and semi-deliriums had fagged her out, in her watch-weary state, and she had come to my room to rest her nerves a bit.

I told about my adventures, and ⟨got not a single compliment. I fired⟩ that took her out of her troubles for the present. Then I fired up on my lamp and read until 6 this morning; thus adding one more to the string of wakeful nights which I have passed in this town.

Your letter is a great pleasure to me, all through. The next time you get a Herald with some machine-matter in it, I'd like to have it, to see how it looks along-side the hand-set matter. [The preceding sentence has vertical lines drawn through it in the MS.] I do hope the election went right; evidently it was going to do that anyway, whether the molasses agreed with Paige or not.² And by *George!* it delights me to know that the matter of raising the capital is assuming a more favorable look to you. That big lion was standing right in the road when I came away—and he had an aspect!

Some day the Mergenthaler people will come and want to hitch teams with us. And we'll do it if they've got a long-life patent left then, on an essential feature. They seem to have a capital of $10,000,000 which they are not going to need after we get started. With their machine suppressed, we should have no competition but hand-composition—5 and 6 cents against 45 and 50.

The Herald has just arrived, and that column is healing for sore eyes. It affects me like Columbus sighting land.³

Attendez! as we French people say. As soon as we get that flat on approval, I am going to take the measure of your feet. There's got to be plenty of room for you, even if we have to take the Place de la Concord.

Susy is coughing all the time, to-day, and is a sick child; but we have a doctor of great reputation, and he seems cheerful about her, and confident. In Mrs. Clemens she has a mighty competent nurse and a mighty willing one; with a mother's faculty of outlasting thirty men when the fight is for a child. The case is doing as well as could be expected. And we are lucky to be here—in one way. We know nobody. Nobody calls but the Consul and the Vice Consul; whereas in Paris, with the kindest intentions in the world, the friends would add to our burdens.

With very kindest regards from us to you all,

Yours Sincerely

SL Clemens

I hope to be at the house-warming. I shall need a vacation by that time.

---

¹ Clemens sketched in the margin a rough cross-section of the hotel, with the staircase zigzagging up the middle.

² The election of the board of directors for the Paige Compositor Manufacturing Company took place on 3 October 1894 (see letter 37). The board included Caleb B. Knevals, H. S. Ward, and George A. Frink, representing the Connecticut Company; Urban H. Broughton, Charles E. Davis and James A. Moffett, representing Clemens and Rogers; D. H. Fletcher and one "Walker," representing Paige; and George N. Stone, T. K. Webster, and D. B. Dewey, representing the Webster Manufacturing Company.

A memorandum in Rogers's hand lists the board, naming Broughton as president and placing Dewey and Fletcher on the executive committee with him. Clemens penciled the following analysis of the board beneath Rogers's notation:

The Board. Selected by Mr. Rogers. Each individual or Company owning $300,000 of paid-up stock is allowed a representative on it. Broughton and Moffett represent *us*, but we regard Davis as our representative too, for we know he will vote with ⟨us.⟩ our men. So will the C. C. men; so also will the Webster Mf men.

Consequently 9 of the 11 Directors are ours, and 2 out of the 3 members of the powerful and all-important Executive Committee. Paige's representatives are excellent men—which shows that *he* didn't select them, you see.

³ If certain columns in the Chicago *Herald* of this period are machine-set, and by the Paige machine, they are not identifiable to an eye less keen than Clemens's.

43. CLEMENS TO ROGERS

Rouen
11 October 1894

Dear Mr. Rogers:

I have your note and Miss Harrison's, both of Sept. 28th, and am kind of glad you made Colby sweat a little for his second $250. Serves him right, and evens us up: the Bliss matter was probably decided within 24 hours after I sailed, yet anxious as I necessarily was to get my mind away from that and onto my work I had to finally cable Colby to know.¹ Serves him just right!

Mrs. Clemens has had a wearing hard week of anxiety and day-and-night nursing. Susy is pretty thoroughly exhausted, but the fever is gone. It left day before yesterday. Some of the congestion remains. That lung will have to have further doctoring, further repairing. The physician says we shall be detained here 2 weeks yet, and maybe 3. But we are pretty comfortably housed, and I believe Susy is better off, here, than she would be in the hotel in Paris.

I wrote ⟨2 or⟩ 3 malicious ⟨articles⟩ chapters about M. Paul Bourget and his idiotic "Outre Mer" which satisfied Mrs. Clemens but they did not quite suit me; so I have begun over again and started on a new basis—and a better one, I think. I expect to work portions of the rejected MS in, but if I don't succeed I shan't burn it; I'll send it to you, for there are things in it that you will enjoy—that I can *swear* to.

Yrs sincerely

SL Clemens

[1] The money probably was part of Colby's fee for supervising the drawing up of a contract with the American Publishing Company for the publication of *Pudd'nhead Wilson*. Clemens was annoyed because he had not heard until 28 September that the contract had been signed on 24 August 1894.

44. CLEMENS TO ROGERS

Rouen
13 October 1894

Dear Mr. Rogers:

Yours of the 2d, with enclosures, has just arrived, and I can hardly keep from sending a Hurrah by cable. I would certainly do it if I warn't so superstitious. The Germans say that every time you hurrah you attract the attention of the Devil. That ain't *my* trouble. I don't want to attract the attention of Providence. I always get along best when I am left alone. There are other wise people. Shelley, you know, down there at the Oriental,[1] a naturally pious man, had to stop praying because he found that he couldn't pray ⟨without giving himself away.⟩ without exposing his hand.

All the words are charming—from Scott, Webster, Davis—and it is astonishing, the way Paige took his molasses. I think he will march to your diplomatic music right along. The Heralds have come, and certainly the machine's work is as neat as neat can be.

I think I can't bring myself to use the articles which I have written about Bourget—he is too small game to go after elaborately.

But I can't quite give him up—I can't ever give *any*thing up right off—so last night I tried him on a new lay; this time not with a newspaper in mind, but the North American Review. I worked from mid-afternoon till night, and from 2 a. m. till 9.30; then breakfasted and walked the town over trying to freshen up, but I don't seem to have managed it. But I shall be ready to begin again when I wake up in the night, I think. I am contrasting America's contributions to modern civilization with France's, and naming all the great things our patent office has turned out since 1794 when our first patent law was passed; and I dreadfully want to name our machine but I suppose it is not quite time yet to speak of it—and a mighty pity it is.[2]

'George it was lucky I was here. Mrs. Clemens would have died of fright if I had been in America. But Susy is progressing well, now. A week or two more and we can leave for Paris.

Sincerely Yours

SL Clemens

[1] Clemens had stayed with the Rogers family at the Oriental Hotel at Manhattan Beach in July 1894.
[2] "Have We Appropriated France's Civilization?", a MS of 43 pages is in MTP (DV 317).

45. CLEMENS TO ROGERS

Rouen
19 October 1894

Dear Mr. Rogers:

Gill makes a proposition to Mrs. Clemens: he wants to become publisher of the Twain books that Webster & Co had; and pay half-profits or a royalty.[1]

It seems a good chance to squelch that old Gill-contract which ties up "Old Times on the Mississippi;" so I have written some suggestions to Colby and sent Gill's letter to him, and have just written to Gill to say that whatever arrangement you and Sterne & Rushmore approve of will be satisfactory to Mrs. Clemens. I ⟨also⟩ consider Gill a rusher in his line—that is, I think Hall thought him so; and he is prompt pay. He might take those books for 3 or ⟨4⟩ 5 years on condition that Mrs. C. can use them in a Uniform Edition and that Gill remove the Embargo from "Old Times."

The Chicago Herald interests me gaily. I haven't ever seen such nice work as the Compositor does. And it shows up handsomest when put alongside of Mergenthaler. I shall soon know, now, how the annual meeting went off, and how the suggestion to pool and lock up the stock and strengthen its grip and keep its bowels open, was received by the boys. Getting corraled here delays our mail,—that is, the part which still goes to Étretat first and then by way of Paris. Without question ours is the only mail matter that goes to Étretat now, and when it quits, that postoffice will be out of business.

I wish I had Harry here. There is absolutely nothing to do, and I have so little skill in doing it.

I have ⟨finished⟩ written the second article of my new series, and I hope I can finish with one more—can't tell; the subject is bulky.

I am taking it for granted that Mrs. Duff is well, to whom I send best regards and homage.

Mrs. Clemens was taken ill last night in consequence of over-fatigue from watching; but I said if we had any more of these experiments I would desert the family. And so she is all right again to-day.

Susy is about well, but is required to keep her room till about the end of the month. Still we rather hope to get away for Paris a little sooner than that.

Sincerely Yours

S. L. Clemens

---

[1] Watson Gill had previously purchased remaindered copies of *Life on the Mississippi* (see MTLP, pp. 216, 252, 264–265, 268; see also letter 56).

46. Clemens to Rogers

Dear Mr. Rogers:

It seems to me that things couldn't well be going better at Chicago than they are. There's no other machine that can set type 8 hours with only 17 minutes' stoppage through cussedness. The others do rather more stopping than working. By and by our machines will be perfect; then they won't stop at all.

I am very glad you miss me—more glad than I can tell. I know it is melancholy in the 57th street house now. I should be sad there, too; for I should be reminded at every turn of that gracious presence which is gone and which filled all the place with the spirit of welcome and friendliness. It is good that you have the relief of the home-interest in Fairhaven and the interest which watching the new house develop furnishes. This has been a hard month on our household here, and I shall be very glad of a change. Neither Susy nor her mother are strong yet, but they are strong enough for the 2-hour trip to Paris, and we go to-morrow.

I congratulate the Dude. And I am glad of his change for interested reasons; I can help him wear his clothes, now. And his other change is good, too—the school; a school where he will be taught *how* to learn. It is the whole secret. They lacked that in the schools of my day, and so I have never had a rational *method* by which to acquire what I wanted to learn.

Now that I know more about the house at Fairhaven, I think I will change my room and go higher where I can have the view—up where you are going to shake the flag at me.

You *are* a special partner in that book, and there are inspirations in it that flowed from you, too; and you are a special partner in a way which no one else is.

We shall be very glad if Colby can pay something to the creditors; I hope he can; it would be a comfort all around.

I would like to have my regards conveyed to the Benjamins and to Mrs. Duff and Harry. To-day I mailed some chaff to Laffan— about 6 columns of the Sun,[1] I should think—chaffing Bourget.

Sincerely Yours

SL Clemens

[1] In May 1891 William Mackay Laffan, of the New York *Sun,* had "proposed to join with McClure in paying Mark Twain a thousand dollars each for a series of six European letters" (*MTB*, p. 919).

47. CLEMENS TO ROGERS

Paris

2 November 1894

Dear Mr. Rogers:

The doctor delayed us 2 days at Rouen after we were packed and ready. We could not make out what amount of risk there was; so at the end of 2 days we concluded to take it *without* knowing; so I secured a compartment by paying 2 extra fares, and we bundled Susy up and came through all right. It happened to be the mildest and sunniest day of the whole season, and it did Susy good instead of harm. We have our old rooms in the hotel [1] and are very comfortable. Mrs. Clemens started out at once to look at flats which had been hunted up by friends and agents; overdid herself and has to lie up a day or two in consequence.

The report of the machine's first 16 days' work in the Herald office arrived night before last just as we arrived ourselves. It seems a pity they didn't put the *old* machine in, instead of the new one, for *it* was in good and sound condition, I think.

When the machine is in proper working order, it *cannot make a mistake*. When the operator is a good operator, *he* will not make any mistakes worth speaking of—say 2 in 1000 ems, 16 in an hour.

These 16 should be corrected in 4 minutes. Half an hour is enough to devote to correcting an entire 8-hour output.

A *good* hand-compositor will correct his whole day's work in half an hour; and when it comes to doing clean work he stands no chance against the machine.

When we come to turning out perfect machines, the newspapers will not *have* an operator whose hour's proof cannot be corrected in 4 minutes. I mean, a plodding slow 8,000-an-hour (solid) man. But *I* don't believe they will keep a man who can't turn out 10,000 (solid) per hour and correct it in 5 minutes.

Their choice men will turn out 12,000 solid per hour, and their AA1 stallions 15,000.

We have to put a tariff on the machine based on Wood and Slattery's capacity [2]—we can't help that; but *they* don't represent what is going to be the average in printing offices any more than the Coffee-Cooler represents what is going to be the average of saint-ship in heaven.

A big daily employs the very fastest men it can find; and those are the men who will go from the case to the machine,—not the second-rates. In each great office there are a couple of men who are one-third faster at the case than the best of the others. Those men set 1,500 ems an hour. I have seen them do it. On the machine they will multiply that by ten—just as Slattery multiplies the good fair high-class compositor by ten.

I wish we had a man *between* Slattery and the lightning expert —for the reason that *that* is the man who is going to be hunted out for machine-work by and by and will create and establish the standard of wages. But b'gosh we haven't got him, and so I'm not going to worry about it.

Good-bye, I'm going out flatting, now.

Yours Sincerely

SL Clemens

[1] The Hotel Brighton, 218 rue de Rivoli.
[2] Charles H. Wood and William J. Slattery were Hartford printers.

48. CLEMENS TO ROGERS

Paris
6 November 1894

169 rue de l'Université

Dear Mr. Rogers:

It isn't a flat, but a whole house.[1] We get it, furnished, for $250 a month. It belongs to a friend who has to go south for 6 months. He pays $300. It has 4 bedrooms. When you come we'll sleep two of the girls together, and that will vacate a room for you. Take a vacation and come; it will rest you up, and you will be glad you took a holiday. We are growing old, and must not put off the holidays.

We are still in the hotel, but shall move a week hence. Mrs. Clemens is digging for servants now. She has dug up a cook, and is close after a manservant and a chambermaid. Jean will have to go about 5 miles to school, and change horse-cars twice.

Susy is just about well again.

We expect to save $200 a month, housekeeping, *but*——we'll wait and see.

I am pretty impatient to get to work again.

Sincerely Yours

SL Clemens

Very glad Mrs. Rice is coming.

[1] See *MTB,* pp. 989–990, for a full description.

49. Clemens to Rogers

Paris
7 November 1894
169 rue de l'Université

Dear Mr. Rogers:

Just as long as you "confess to being pretty well pleased" with the machine, I myself shall confess to being quite content, and quite willing that Scott [1] or de Young [2] or anybody else may do ⟨their⟩ his little best to knock out the un-knock-outable. When a bastard cripple like the Mergenthaler can fight its way up through ridicule and hostility during seven years to prosperity and a goodly share of respect, there's no occasion for the Paige Compositor to have any doubts about the future. When the N.Y. Tribune had about 25 Merg's, and Stillson Hutchings [3] had 10 in his Washington "Post" office, the Merg had then been publicly at work a year or two, yet nobody was allowed to sit down in the Tribune office and watch it and time it. After all that time it couldn't bear inspection. And here are Scott and De Young ⟨passing judgment⟩ delivering their expert verdicts upon a machine which stands a good test in the first month of its public existence!

Hutchings got a little uneasy about our machine, and he sent me word by Col. John Hay that I might come and freely inspect it there in Washington. I sent to Hartford for Paige and Davis, and we sat down by the Mergenthaler. The smartest of the operators set 5,000 ems in 2 hours, and the proof showed 108 errors—errors made by the MACHINE almost exclusively. ⟨Re-setting—⟩ The 5,000 ems would comprise ⟨at 25 ems per line⟩ about 200 lines. Re-setting the lines containing errors reduced the operator's output to twelve or 1,300 ems per hour *corrected matter*. Yet with a *concealed* machine, which couldn't bear daylight, and by gaudy advertising and large but poor-quality lying, those people have splendidly marketed their bastard.

I wish I were in Chicago for a few minutes—just to inquire *why we wish to know how long it takes to correct* OUR PROOF? Do we wish to know how long it takes to correct the proof of a typewriting machine? No. It can make no errors. We buy the machine and put the operator to work; if he makes a bad proof we discharge him.

In our machine there are 108 characters. In half a minute anybody can touch the 108 keys and see if the types and spaces accurately respond. If they do, that is the last that we care to know about good-proof and bad-proof. An expert pianist will play ⟨a piece⟩ *by the hour* and not strike a wrong key. When we have competent operators they will not strike wrong keys. Their proof will be as clean as a pianist's. Or they will be discharged.

The Merg people always claim in their advertisements that the output is so-much an hour. But they should add "corrected matter" —for their *machine* makes errors—it makes in effect all the errors that *are* made. But with us, when matter needs correcting, it means that the *operator* needs correcting.

⟨"5,066 ems corrected matter," for Oct. 17.⟩

Afternoon. I'm staying in, all day, because I scoured my head this morning and I seem to have caught cold in my skull. I keep hearing it crack.

Mrs. Clemens was in here a moment ago and asks to have her love and the children's sent to Mrs. Duff; and I would like to add mine, and extend it to all of you. I suppose you will have to remain in New York for the winter, but I see how lonesome it is and must continue to be. I am glad to be in your minds there, and I wish I could be there in person. The Prince of Activity is going to be useful, now, in that billiard room, until his game goes so far ahead of yours as to take the fun out of the contest. It won't take long, I am afraid, because the rascal is so young—and youth is so exasperatingly capable. I will turn out, now, and go and see the people the new servants refer to.

Sincerely Yours

SL Clemens

[1] James Wilmot Scott of the Chicago *Herald*.
[2] Michel Harry de Young, of the San Francisco *Chronicle*.
[3] Stilson Hutchins, former owner of the Washington *Post*, who was a founder of the Mergenthaler Linotype Company.

50. CLEMENS TO ROGERS

Paris
11 November 1894

Dear Mr. Rogers:

I wonder if you are in Chicago? You are right about thinking you are competent to take care of the pooling matter, but I wish I were there to help sit on the rear platform of Mr. Thompson's[1] car and help do the traveling.

I am writing this line only to say that we expect to move to our house at noon to-morrow. I am in bed with grippe—a slight attack but the doctor made me go to bed. And so I have lain here several days, and have been not the slightest use to Mrs. Clemens, who is raiding around everywhere after servants and having two or three times as much work to do as her strength is gaged for.

I haven't smoked for three days; that is because of the bronchial cough; but I am to re-begin to-morrow morning, and I will see what can be accomplished between that and night.

I reckon even Cheeseborough's[2] poetry failed to kill him, for it appears that anything and everything that was Republican was safe for a ride into camp on the avalanche. To my mind, Republican government is mighty bad government, but there seems to be plenty of evidence that democratic government is worse. I am not sorry for the change.[3] It will bring the sort of relief I had last night; my back and breast had been painted 4 times with iodine; it was doubtful if either could stand another application, but we chanced it and painted my breast. There was an uncertainty for about 3 minutes, then there was no uncertainty any more. Well, sir, ⟨you⟩ I had to turn over and have a fire built on my back ⟨as a counter-⟩

or I should have died. It was the kind of counter-irritant the Republican party is getting ready to furnish me, I reckon.

I've received the Chicago Heralds, and I see that the machine is doing neat work; and I hope it has learned to set a clean proof. However, I guess it's the operator, not the machine. I don't care how bad a proof *he* sets, for he can be discharged when his efforts become discomfortable and a scandal.

With the warmest regards to all of you,

Sincerely Yours

S. L. Clemens

Thanks in advance for the Riley poems [4]—I shall watch the mails; I want them very much.

[1] Frank Thompson, president of the Pennsylvania Railroad (see letter 2).

[2] Robert Augustus Chesebrough was an inventor and a poet, and latterly a politician. He had been a manufacturer of petroleum products since 1858, and in 1870 he patented Vaseline. Contrary to Clemens's supposition, Chesebrough was defeated as Republican candidate for Congress from his New York district. Such lines as the following from his *A Reverie and Other Poems* (New York, 1889), must have delighted Clemens and Rogers:

Enough! Enough! I will not look
Too long upon the past,
A gleam of hope at last remains,
The present cannot last. (p. 47.)

[3] The 6 November 1894 election of Levi P. Morton as Governor of New York State and of William L. Strong as Mayor of New York City was an overwhelming Republican victory.

[4] Probably James Whitcomb Riley's *Poems Here at Home* (1893).

51. CLEMENS TO ROGERS

Paris
15 November 1894

Dear Mr. Rogers:

I have been in bed ever since. Just as I was going to move over to 169 rue de l'Université, I got knocked flat on my back with gout. It

was in my starboard ankle-bone. It took very little while to disable
me. I supposed it was some new kind of super-devilish rheumatism,
and imagined it would stop hurting presently. But it didn't. It made
me so tired that I went to sleep at midnight slept till 3. Then
followed 5 or 6 hours wherein the gout was the only presence
present, Mrs. Clemens and I counting for nothing at all. This is
one of the oldest pains known to medical science, and is perhaps the
most competent. When we got the doctor at last, he said it was only
the gout, and an attack of no importance. He seemed to regard it as
a pleasure trip. He gave me a hypodermic and appeared to think
the business was done—which it wasn't. At the end of ten minutes
another. It didn't phaze that pain a bit. So he began to respect it
himself, I think. After half an hour he gave me another, and that
made me very comfortable.

The servants are in the house and everything ready. I couldn't go
yesterday, but I can go to-day, I think. I can bear my foot on the
floor this morning. However, I am not kept back by the gout; the
gout is no consequence; the doctor says so himself; neither is hell, to
a person who doesn't live there; but my cough *was* of consequence;
in the doctor's opinion; but the bronchial end of it passed away
yesterday, and only the laryngeal end remains; and so he will say,
this morning, that we can leave this hotel to-day, I think; and I shall
be glad.

Yours Sincerely

SL Clemens

P.S. No, he says to-morrow, Nov. 16. Meantime the letters are
come; you are gone West, and Miss Harrison has sent me Mr.
Broughton's detailed account of the machine's misconduct. Great
guns, what *is* the matter with it!

52. Clemens to Rogers

Paris
21 November 1894

169 rue de l'Université

Dear Mr. Rodgers [1]

It seems an age since I wrote you. It must be ten days or two weeks. I have had the gout a couple of weeks; it struck me hard and without warning, and kept us all at the hotel a day or two longer than necessary. But I was finally bundled into a close carriage, and brought to this house and this room, and this bed, whence I have not stirred since. Yesterday I was comfortable at last, and supposed I was going to be soon well; but last night I was hit hard in the other ankle by the gout, and now I am disabled in both legs. I heard from you last on the second of this month; you were then just starting for Chicago. In two or three days now the test will be over, and I am putting in these dull hours of pain and cussedness with interesting anxieties and wonderments regarding the result of it.

I do hope it will be satisfactory to you and that things will go on comfortably and prosperously from that time.

The family are charmed with this house, and I think I shall be if I ever get a chance to see it. It is infinitely more comfortable and homelike than the hotel, but we are getting afraid that it will not be much cheaper living.

I find dictating awkward and difficult and will take a rest now and give Clara a rest. With a great deal of love to all of you.

Sincerely Yours

S. L. Clemens

[1] As the last paragraph indicates, this letter was dictated to Clara Clemens; it was evidently she who could not spell Rogers's name.

53. Clemens to Rogers

Paris
28 November 1894

169 rue de l'Université

Dear Mr. Rogers:

I am out of bed at last, and seem to have got the best of the gout. I don't know how long I have been in bed, but it seems several ⟨weeks⟩ years; the fog is thick, the daylight is black, and I feel defeated and in a state of surrender to fate.

And now that I observe that by the last report received the machine seemed to be getting into shape at last, I reproach myself for not saying, "Let's tell Mr. Scott we won't begin the test on a particular date, but only when we can put a perfect machine on exhibition"—but that would have been *fore*sight, whereas hindsight is my specialty. I ought to have remembered that they used to test a mere sewing-machine a couple of months before they allowed it to go to a customer, and therefore we couldn't hope to get off cheaper with a machine like the Paige. I believe a watch is not allowed to go out until it has undergone an extended and searching test. I guess Davis ought to have "driven a stake," for he knew something about untried new machines. Land, I wish now that the machine had spent those two months in the shop! Then we would give an exhibition just for speed; and in the proof, mark none but errors made *by the machine*. The showing would leave the Mergenthaler not a leg to stand on.

It hurts me all through, that after you have put so much money, and brains, and good hard work into that machine there was nobody to save you from this disappointment. I am to blame. I should have said "Put none but a thoroughly perfected machine on exhibition to please Mr. Scott or any one else." I ought to have clearly seen that if Davis was putting in a long string of hours over the

machine every day it meant that it was not nearly in condition for
business yet.

If I could be of any use to you I wish I were there. But
Providence has arranged these last two months, and not to my
satisfaction. Susy tied me in Rouen a month. We hardly got away
from there before I fell into the doctor's hands and am there yet. I
might be able to go to work by day after to-morrow, possibly, but it
will be best for the work that I wait till I get your next letter, for I
shall not be sleeping well meantime.

By the time this reaches you I ought to be in my usual health;
and then if I can be of any service, cable me and I will take the
next steamer.

This house is very comfortable, and the expense really promises
to be noticeably lighter than the hotel, notwithstanding we could
buy some things cheaper than the manservant if the custom would
allow us the privilege of trying.

⟨I was 5⟩ Mrs. Clemens was 49 yesterday, I shall be 59 tomorrow.
You will feel older something less than two months hence than you
do now. Many happy returns!

With cordial salutations to you all, including the lad in the adult
clothes,

SL Clemens

54. CLEMENS TO ROGERS

Paris
29–30 November 1894

169 rue de l'Université
Thanksgiving Day

Dear Mr. Rogers:

Your letter, written after your return from Chicago came at 8 this
morning, and I had a bit of a shiver and says to myself, "Clemens,
stand by for a cyclone! for if Mr. Rogers finds it wise and best to

remove his supports from under that machine, your fine ten-year-
old dream will blow away like a mist and you will land in the
poor-house sure."

Then, just before the Thanksgiving dinner this evening arrived a
letter from home announcing that Mrs. Clemens's only brother is
in an alarming state of health.

It seems to me, take it all around, that the President hasn't
chosen a Thanksgiving date with much judgment this time.

Birthday, Nov. 30/94.

Mrs. Clemens and I made a lot of plans between the departure of
our one Thanksgiving guest and midnight. We decided one thing
without the least trouble in the world: that whatever course you
have made up your mind to take, *that* will be the wisest one. Next,
we decided that if you have drawn out, Mr. Brusnahan of the N.Y.
Herald must have his money returned to him; ⟨for he is⟩ also, that
Bram Stoker must be stopped from paying any more instalments.

Next, that we will all come to America when the lease of this
house expires (May 1st) and live on top of the hill at Elmira on
what is called "the farm," very cheap. By that time Mrs. C.'s
electric treatment here will have carried its health-restoring work a
long way toward completion. Her doctor is very proud of the
progress he has made. And there I will prepare my books for a
uniform edition to follow immediately after "Joan" a year hence.

Also we decided that I shall take advantage of the doctor's
command that I remain shut up in the house a week or two yet, to
extend that time to two months and pull Joan through to a finish.

We considered some other ways to add to our bread and butter
which can be further considered and decided later. Then we slept
the sleep of the damned—which is always sound—and woke up
refreshed this morning. The mother and the three children spent
two francs on birthday presents for me, and we have begun life on a
new and not altogether unpromising basis.

Also we decided that it was best that I was here and not there;
for if I were there I might try to persuade you to go against your
better judgment, whereas after all that you have done for us that

would be ungrateful, and ingratitude is a crime—and the meanest
one there is.

I have got my feet out of the pillows, and am able to get about
the house in cotton paddings and slippers. I am expecting to be
strong enough in a day or two to get to work. I shall bury myself in
it—*deep*.

Laffan sold that Bourget article to the North American Review.[1]
I have a letter from the Review asking me to write a sympathetic
article about Joan of Arc. I'll plead press of business and decline.
Perhaps; I am not perfectly sure.

A year ago Mrs. Rogers was looking so well. I had a fleeting
glimpse of her in a dream last night. I hope Mrs. Duff and the
Benjamins are well; best wishes of the season to them. And congratulations to Harry—his birthday is in this month, I think. I hope to
have a sail with him next summer.

Sincerely Yours

S. L. Clemens

[1] "What Paul Bourget Thinks of Us" appeared in the *North American Review*, January 1895.

55. CLEMENS TO ROGERS

Paris

7 December 1894

169 rue de l'Université

Dear Mr. Rogers:

I haven't any news to write, except that the days are wasting
away and leaving me behind. Behind and hard aground. Not with
gout, for that seems to be gone; but there isn't any life in me
because I am not allowed to go out and get air and exercise except
in heavenly weather, and that is a slim show for me, for they
import all their weather from the other place, ⟨past⟩ to avoid the

duties. I do not wish to put any of my present spirit into my book, therefore I leave the book strictly alone. I try to write other stuff— magazine stuff—but it won't go. I but little minded the month lost in Rouen—I could stand one month—but this past one! I couldn't spare it. I need to be at work now especially, to keep my mind absorbed while I wait for the verdict concerning the machine. I'll be glad to get that. You'll cable it, won't you?

You never say anything about Miss May, nor her program. Does she like it where she is? Is it a French school? *Does she like the French?*

Sincerely Yours

SL Clemens

56. Clemens to Rogers

Paris

9 December 1894

169 rue de l'Université

Dear Mr. Rogers:

Yours of Nov. 30 has just arrived. I shall welcome the Kipling poem. There were good things in Riley's book, but you have noticed, of course, that there's considerable padding in it, too. Also in his other books, as per the indexes advertised in this one. A little padding can be allowed to pass, no doubt, but Riley must certainly damage himself if he keeps his ratio up. He is unwise—in fact one may say reckless. But Kipling *can't* pad. He's always got a line or two at least that saves each piece that he writes. Remember the "lousy ulster" line in the poem we read in the "L"? All by itself it made a good poem out of an indifferent one.[1]

I think I made the Gill matter plain—*perfectly* plain—in a letter to Colby a couple of months ago. If he will refer to it he will know how to talk to Gill.

Gill wrote to Mrs. Clemens some such letter as the one you enclose.[2] I answered, asking him—as well as I can remember—to talk with Colby and that you would then ratify any arrangement arrived at. Then I immediately wrote Colby that here was probably a tip-top chance to get control of the "Mississippi" book for the Uniform Edition by some clever trade with Gill. I indicated the particulars of the trade, and tried to impress upon Colby the importance of the thing.

And now here after all this delay comes Gill to *us* again (and meantime to you) and the blamed thing is standing stock still.

I think I will tell Gill *again* to go to Colby. No—I haven't his address. I'll enclose it and ask you to send it to him.

Gill is an excellent man to handle books, and is prompt pay; but Mrs. C. doesn't want the books put into his hands in any way that could hamper or defeat the "Uniform"—and she wouldn't want any trade closed with him which Bliss would consider a detriment to the Uniform. But she *does* want to capture that "Mississippi" from him. Seven hundred dollars ought to *buy* it of him if we can't trade any other way.

I am feeling ⟨very⟩ in better shape yesterday and to-day. Last night we had a dinner party and I sat up till midnight without observable fatigue. If this family were in a hotel, now, or in a flat, I would take the next ship for New York, for I see you believe that that would be well. But here we are, in this little private house, with two stories, eight staircases, no end of cells and passages, and *little or no room*. It was built by an idiot, I think. There is but one bedroom (ours) on our floor. All other bedrooms are far away, and one couldn't make anybody hear if one were in trouble. We have French servants whom we know little or nothing about. The man-servant is sometimes impudent—in *manner,* not words—and I guess he'll have to go, before long, though he is alert and capable, and *another* stranger ⟨brought⟩ admitted. I can't seem to invent any scheme of proper protection in my absence. (I must continue to think and contrive.)

You must cable me to come, when things require it, and then we will manage somehow.

———

I note that you are not strongly expecting a favorable opinion from the Herald. I am catching around for straws to swim ashore on, in case of disaster, and something like this has been passing through my mind:

1. In case you decide to withdraw, wouldn't it be a good idea to put it off a while for consideration, and in the meantime put the money which is to come to us and to Broughton, Davis, etc., from the wreckage into Mergenthaler stock at as low a figure as possible before your decision is made public?

For this reason. Paige will be crowded for bread, and will be obliged to sell his patents to the Merg for a song—(a *salary*, that is what he will get.) That will boom the Merg. stock, for their machine will then be cock of the walk, and *permanently*, without possibility of rivalry.

I might be of use in privately purchasing that stock ⟨through Dean Sage [3] as go-between—&⟩.

2. If you decide to go on, couldn't you make it a condition that Paige give up about half of his stock and turn it either into your pocket or into the treasury?

He can't start another Co to save his life. He must either go on upon your terms, or sell to the Merg for a song.

———

Sho! *you* don't know how to manage the "Kid." I wish we could borrow him for a while. I think you are entirely out of practice. And that cynic, Harry, has never been *in* practice.

With love and kisses for you, and lots of thanks for yours,

Yours Sincerely,

SL Clemens

P.S. I see that a Boston house is advertising a new edition of "Innocents Abroad." I have written Bliss about it. I wonder if that copyright is imperfect. [4]

¹ Kipling's poem "Back to the Army Again," first published in the *Pall Mall Magazine*, III (August 1894), 589–594, opened with the lines, "I'm 'ere in a lousy ulster an' a broken billycock 'at,/A-layin' on to the Sergeant I don't know a gun from a bat." When the poem was collected in *The Seven Seas* (1896), the language was altered to "ticky ulster."

² Rogers had sent Clemens a copy of an undated letter (Salm) from Gill, which asked:

> On what terms could I get from Mrs. S. L. Clemens the right to publish the books of her husband formerly made by the late firm of C. L. Webster and Company. I have just made a purchase of a large amount of this stock of the assignee and of the parties the assignee sold to, and Mr. Clemens writes me that you and Mr. Colby have full power in the premises. At Mr. Clemens suggestion I was in New York to see you the past week not being able to meet you I write for terms. I think with all modesty my experience will enable me to work for Mrs. Clemens interests as anyone she'd get on these books.

At the bottom of that letter Clemens drafted a reply, dated 9 December:

> Watson Gill Esq.
> Dear Sir: Mr. Colby has all the details, in a letter written by me some time ago. Will you please confer with him?
>
> Very Truly Yours
> O. L. Clemens
> per S L Clemens

³ Dean Sage, a New York businessman who was a classmate and close friend of the Reverend Joseph Twichell of Hartford, had been Clemens's friend also since the 1870's (*MTHL*, pp. 138–141). The friendship between Clemens and Twichell had begun in 1868.

⁴ Clemens noted just below the postscript: "(*As per Xmas 'Scribner.'*)" The Joseph Knight Company was advertising a "New Edition. Fully illustrated with thirty photogravure illustrations." The two-volume edition had been advertised as early as 29 September in *Publishers' Weekly*.

57. CLEMENS TO ROGERS

Paris
16–17 December 1894

169 rue de l'Université
Sunday night,
Think it is the 17th.

Dear Mr. Rogers:

I started the mill again 6 days ago and have ground out a good average:

```
    1300
    2600            It is 6 consecutive days,
    2100            ending this Sabbath evening,
    2000            of uninterrupted work.
    1800
    2000
   ─────
11,800 words.
```

Uninterrupted because I am not allowed to go out save on dry days, and we haven't had any. I have been out of the house only twice since we moved in. That was two or three days before I began work.

I already perceive that Book III will be as long as Book I, and twice as long as Book II, which I wrote in Étretat. It can't go into the magazine. It will be too long. Joan, therefore, will make two full volumes of the proposed Uniform edition.

The gout seems to be entirely gone, and I am as well and strong as I ever was. The profound weakness disappeared all of a sudden a week ago. I could return some visits, now, and lose some time; but fortunately I haven't any clothes. But they will be on hand in a week and then the interruptions will begin. But they will not be serious. I'm not going to make any serious plunge into social life until away yonder when the book is done.

When the afternoon tea people come in at 4 and 5 I only say howdy and go back to work. They excuse the laborer.

Next Morning. Yours containing Cole's [1] and Paige's letters to Brusnahan came to my bed just before I got up. By George, that wolf does seem to be approaching my door again! I wish he would apply somewhere where he hasn't worn out his welcome.

My hindsight is getting to be very sharp. *Now* if we were back at the starting-place, we could have a safer thing. We wouldn't start up the works at all—wouldn't spend any money on a machine. No, I guess we would test the *old* exhaustively and under Broughton's eye for two months and then we would know whether to try it in the Herald or not.

Has the notion of putting the *old* machine in the Herald ⟨at this⟩ in place of the new one, ⟨at the⟩ now, been canvassed?

I wish Paige and the rest would give you full control of the patents, so that they could be traded to the Mergenthaler Co for stock. However, I reckon Paige ⟨can⟩ is in a position to make that scoop for his sole advantage if our Co winds up.

If you wind up don't you think there is some way to delay it a while and get into the Merg Co on easy terms? You see that stock is an absolutely sure investment, with the Paige patents suppressed.

If I have to cross the sea I am in good shape for it now, because it would not interrupt my work entirely, at all. I am on my course, now; it is clearly charted, I know my road. I could go on with my work—on shipboard; in your office; in my lodgings; in fact anywhere. While it would be of course very hard on Mrs. Clemens to spare me, she would manage to do it, if necessary.

The more I think of it the more it gravels me to think that perhaps we've been making all this struggle and doing all this work just to secure that dam Paige a fortune. It's looking horribly like it now, *isn't* it?

But I must go right to work and bury myself deep down in it and among the phantoms flitting vaguely through the mists of the Middle Ages, or there will be a sudden inquest and a verdict "died of the blues."

Merry Christmas to all of you from all of us!

Always gratefully yours

The Clemenses.

Poor Brusnahan! Well, if we wind up, the assets will pay him back half and enough of the money now in your hands can be put aside and reserved to pay the other half. It was his whole fortune; he cannot afford to lose any of it.[2]

---

[1] Charles J. Cole was a lawyer from Hartford.
[2] Clemens's concern for Brusnahan's dilemma was implemented by Livy's decision to pay Brusnahan $850; see letter 60, note 1.

58. CLEMENS TO ROGERS (cablegram)

Paris
21 December 1894

Can you delay final action one month

Clemens

59. CLEMENS TO ROGERS

Paris
22 December 1894

169 rue de l'Université

Dear Mr. Rogers:

I *seemed* to be entirely expecting your letter,[1] and ⟨sup⟩ also prepared and resigned; but Lord, it shows how little we know ourselves and how easily we can deceive ourselves. It hit me like a thunderclap.[2] It knocked every rag of sense out of my head, and I went flying here and there and yonder, not knowing what I was doing, and only one clearly-defined thought standing up visible and substantial out of the crazy storm-drift—that my dream ⟨was⟩ of ten years was in desperate peril, and out of the 60,000 or 70,000 projects ⟨that⟩ for its rescue that came flocking through my skull, not one would hold still long enough for me to examine it and size it up. Have you ever been like that? Not so much so, I reckon.

There was another clearly-defined idea—I must be there and see it die. That is, if it must die; and maybe if I were there we might hatch up some next-to-impossible way to make it take up its bed and take a walk.

So, at the end of four hours I started, still whirling, and walked over to the rue Scribe—4 p.m—and asked ⟨if⟩ a question or two and was told I should be running a big risk if I took the 9 pm. train for London and Southampton; "better come right along at 6.52 per Havre special and step aboard the New York all easy and comfortable." Very! and I about two miles from home, no packing done, and with just barely head enough left on my shoulders to protect ⟨myself⟩ me from being used as a convenience by the dogs.

Then it occurred to me that none of these salvation-notions that were whirlwinding through my head could be examined or made available unless at least a month's time could be secured. So I cabled you, and said to myself that I would take the French steamer to-morrow (which will be Sunday).

By bedtime Mrs. Clemens had reasoned me into a fairly rational and contented state of mind; but of course it didn't last long. So I went on thinking—mixing it with a smoke in the dressing room once an hour—until dawn this morning. Result—a sane resolution: no matter what your answer to my cable might be, I would hold still and not sail until I should get an answer to this present letter which I am now writing or a cable-answer from you saying "Come" or "Remain."

I have slept 6 hours, my pond has clarified, and I find the sediment of my 70,000 projects to be of this character:

———

Our machine (modified) *is* valuable, and maybe we ought not to take it out of the Merg's way gratis, but see if we can't make it worth their while to pay us for that service. To-wit:

Make a new deal with Paige and continue the Co. 6 or 12 months with Paige and Davis under reduced wages, and no others. That would trouble the Mergs, who are expecting our immediate dissolution of course.

If anybody wants information, let him freely have it—to-wit:

1. It was shown in the Herald office that the stereotyping process weakened the type—hence the breakage. Therefore we are going to make *brass* type, and stop all that.

(One can't *cast* brass type; nor aluminum type, either, perhaps; ⟨nor bronze?⟩ but Paige (and I think Davis) made some experiments once with die-stamped cold brass and said the thing could be done and cheaply. If you or Mr. Broughton would ask a fine-brass worker, and aluminum-expert also Davis and ALSO THOMAS A. EDISON, the truth could be come at.)

2. The Herald test also showed that we must put on the *circular* (and slow) type-driver, because we need to make 200 or 250 revolutions a minute in order to get up to Slattery's capacity, which must be 9 or 10,000 an hour if we could speed-up the machine sufficiently without making that long type-driver rip and carry-on so. (The plans and drawings of the circular type-driver are all made and ready long ago.)

3. Also the machine is more heavily loaded with work and iron than necessary, and we are considering how much the cost of manufacture might be reduced and sureness of action enhanced by discarding the

I. leading mechanism; and

II. About half of the keyboard.

I think we have 108 or 9 characters in the keyboard, now. They include *small-caps*—not necessary; also, diphthongs, fractions, &s, and other rubbish which heavily load ⟨the⟩ us up with machinery and yet are used but very *very* seldom. We could reduce to these:

$$\begin{array}{r} \text{Capitals} \ldots .26 \\ \text{Lower-case} \ldots .26 \\ \$/£/,/;/:/—/-/ \ldots . \ \underline{7} \\ \text{Total keyboard} \ldots .\overline{59} \end{array}$$

Set a false type (equivalent in thickness) for the semi-occasional diphthongs, fractions, etc., and correct them in the proof.

Let them set market reports by hand or have one machine in each big office with a special key-board.

With 60 letter-channels in place of 106 or 8; and 60 key mechanisms in place of 108, ⟨the machine⟩ and the unnecessary (though somewhat valuable but mainly ornamental?) leading-device removed, it ought to lighten up the machine's load a good deal and its cost also. [written in left margin:] Wouldn't this reduce the cost to Pratt & Whitney's original estimate—$2,000 to $2500?

I think that in a few months we could get up a showing that would put us in good shape to do either of two things—sell out or go on.

But don't suggest *any* of these ⟨things⟩ *details* where they can get to Paige if it can be avoided. He would go [to] the Mergs and say "wait till this contract runs out—then I'll trade with you on easy terms."

But *to-day* P. couldn't trade with them, I guess. They would point to his helpless condition and the Herald test, and laugh at him.

———

Don't say I'm wild. For really I'm sane again this morning.

———

I am going right along with Joan, now, and wait untroubled till I hear from you. If you think I can be of the least use, cable me "Come." I can write Joan on board ship and lose no time. Also I could discuss my plan with the publisher for a *de luxe* Joan, time being an object, for some of the pictures could be made over here cheaply and quickly, but would cost much time and money in America.

———

If the meeting SHOULD decide to quit business Jan. 4, I'd like to have Stoker ⟨and the Keokuk man⟩ stopped from paying in any more money, if Miss Harrison don't mind that disagreeable job. And I'll have to write them, too, of course.

Meantime I want Harry to save some of the next soup for his Uncle Sammy, who would do as much for him.

With love and kisses,

SL Clemens

<hr/>

¹ Evidently it explained that the Paige machine had failed the Chicago *Herald* test.

² The number of parenthetical phrases, phrases written in margins, parentheses within parentheses, and shifts in direction, as well as the pleading tone of much of this letter, all testify to Clemens's extreme agitation while writing it.

60. Clemens to Rogers

Paris
27 December 1894

169 rue de l'Université

Dear Mr. Rogers:

Notwithstanding your heart is "old and hard," you make a body choke up. I *know* you "mean every word you say," and I do take it "in the same spirit in which you tender it." I shall keep your regard while we two live—that I know; for I shall always remember what you have done for me, and that will insure me against ever doing anything that could forfeit it or impair it. I am 59 years old; yet I never had a friend before who put out a hand and tried to pull me ashore when he found me in deep waters.

It is six days or seven days ago that I lived through that despairing day, and then through a night without sleep; then settled down next day into my right mind (or thereabouts,) and wrote you. I put in the rest of that day till 7 p.m., plenty comfortably enough writing a long chapter of my book; then went to a masked ball blacked up as Uncle Remus, taking Clara along; and we had a good time. I have lost no day since and suffered no discomfort to speak of, but drove my troubles out of my mind and had good success in keeping them out—through watchfulness. I have done a good week's work and put the book a good way ahead in the Great Trial, which is the difficult part; the part which requires the most thought and carefulness. I cannot see the end of the Trial yet, but I am on the road, I am creeping surely toward it.

"Why not leave them all to me." My business bothers? I take you by the hand! I jump at the chance! I ought to be ashamed, and I am trying my best to *be* ashamed—and yet I do jump at the chance in spite of it. I *don't* want to write Irving, and I *don't* want to write Stoker. It doesn't seem as if I *could*. But I can⟨t⟩ suggest something for *you* to write them; and then if you see that I am unwise, you can write them something quite different. Now this is my idea:

1. To return Stoker's $100 to him and keep his stock.

2. And tell Irving that when luck turns with me I will make good to him what the salvage from the dead Co fails to pay him of his $500.[1] *P.S.* Madam says *no*, I must face the music. So I enclose my effort[2]—to be used if you approve, but not otherwise.

There! Now if you will alter it to suit your judgment and bang away, I shall be eternally obliged.

I'll attend to the dab of Keokuk stock[3] as soon as I know that the Co has formally dissolved itself.

As to Rice[4]—well, I will arrange that when I come, in June or July, with the family. (I believe Mrs. Clemens doesn't want any one to know that we are coming.) You see I can't arrange with Rice till I come, for there must be something outstanding between you and me and him on medical consultations there in his office. He has never settled up on those, I think. Then there were those men whom he was treating for something that he called gastritis and charging them burglar rates. I never said a word, though those people were merely drunk, that was all. I could have given that thing away, but I didn't. He must owe us something ⟨for⟩ on that.

I am not letting Brusnahan weigh heavily upon me, because I am not going to die till I have got him squared entirely up. If I can't do any better, I will square him up with a public reading.

I am very glad you are going to Lakewood for a rest—but why *didn't* you two come here? It would have been twice as restful. If you will come I will take to my Scotch whisky again and we will be disorderly and have a grand time.

I thank your mother ever so much for remembering me, and I wish to send my homage and best regards to her. I note, in connection with Fairhaven, that the stable looks almost good enough to live in,[5] and I take that as a feeler—but it won't do. Now that I am in adversity I am prouder than ever. I intend to occupy Harry's room. Pretty soon the house will be Kodakable—and when you Kodak it, I would like to have one.

We shall try to find a tenant for our Hartford house; not an easy matter, for it costs heavily to live in. We can never live in it again; though it would break the family's hearts if they could believe it.

⟨Land! n⟩ Nothing daunts Mrs. Clemens or makes the world look black to her—which is the reason I haven't drowned myself.

I got the Xmas journals which you sent, and I thank you for that Xmas remembrance.

We all send our deepest and warmest greetings to you and all of yours and a Happy New Years!

SL Clemens

P.S. I am almost robustly well again. Laffan is going to put in the improved "McMillan." [6]

P.S. Don't you think I would be just the man to advertise to the world the unrivaled value of the Mergenthaler if I had a handsome interest in it? I would so *much* like to write about the Paige.

[1] This decision was endorsed by Mrs. Clemens when she wrote Rogers on 28 March 1895: "Please pay Mr John Brusnahan $850: Mr Bram Stoker $100: and Mr Henry Irving $250. out of any moneys in your hands belonging to me and charge the same to my account" (Salm).

[2] Clemens did enclose a note for Stoker which said:

I am not dating this, because it is not to be mailed at present.

When it reaches you it will mean that there is a hitch in my machine enterprise—a hitch so serious as to make it take to itself the aspect of a dissolved dream. This letter, then, will contain cheque for the $100 which you have paid. And will you tell Irving for me—I can't get up courage enough to talk about this misfortune myself, except to you, whom by good luck I haven't damaged yet—that when the wreckage presently floats ashore he will get a good deal of his $500 back; and a dab at a time I will make up to him the rest (*MTB*, p. 994).

[3] Clemens's brother Orion, then living in Keokuk, Iowa, had been sent five shares of stock; see letter 28.

[4] Rogers's office records (CWB) indicate that Dr. Rice also invested at least $2,000 in the Paige enterprise; for this amount he had received 40 shares of Clemens's stock (although the shares had a face value of $100).

[5] The construction at Fairhaven had begun with an elaborate barn and stable (118 by 150 feet, 41 feet to the ridge, with 19 stalls for horses and 6 for cows). The building was constructed by August and was judged to "surpass anything of its kind ever built in this section" (Fairhaven *Star*, 24 March, 7 July, and 18 August 1894).

[6] The McMillan typesetter had been, with the Mergenthaler, a competitor of the Paige machine; apparently Laffan planned to use it for the New York *Sun*.

61. Clemens to Rogers

Paris
2 January 1895

Dear Mr. Rogers:

Yours of Dec. 21 has arrived, containing the circular to stock-holders and I guess the Co will really quit—there doesn't seem to be any other wise course.

There's one thing which makes it difficult for me to soberly realize that my ten-year dream is actually dissolved; and that is, that it reverses my horoscope. The proverb says, "Born lucky, *always* lucky," and I am very superstitious. As a small boy I was notoriously lucky. It was usual for one or two of our lads ⟨to⟩ (per annum) to get drowned in the Mississippi or in Bear Creek, but I was pulled out in a ⅔ drowned condition 9 times before I learned to swim, and was considered to be a cat in disguise. When the "Pennsylvania" blew up and the telegraph reported my brother as fatally injured (with 60 others) but made no mention of me, my uncle said to my mother "it means that Sam was somewhere else, after being on that boat a year and a half—he was born lucky." [1] Yes, I *was* somewhere else. I ⟨was⟩ am so superstitious that I have always been afraid to have business-dealings with certain relatives and friends of mine because they were unlucky people. All my life I have stumbled upon ⟨sing⟩ lucky chances of large size, and whenever they were wasted it was because of my own stupidity and carelessness. And so I have felt entirely certain that that machine would turn up trumps eventually. It disappointed me lots of times, but I couldn't shake off the confidence of a life time in my luck.

Well, whatever I get out of the wreckage will be due to good luck,—the good luck of getting you into the scheme—for, but for that, there wouldn't *be* any wreckage; it would be total loss.

I wish you had been in at the beginning. Then we should have had the good luck to step promptly ashore.

Miss Harrison has had a dream which promises me a large bank account, and I want her to go ahead and dream it twice more, so as to make the prediction sure to be fulfilled.

I've got a first-rate ⟨schem⟩ subject for a book. It kept me awake all night, and I began it and completed it in my mind.[2] The minute I finish Joan I will take it up.

Love and Happy New Year to you all.

Sincerely Yours,

SL Clemens

[1] See *MTA*, chapter 20.
[2] Probably *Tom Sawyer, Detective*.

62. Clemens to Rogers

Paris
3 January 1895

169 rue de l'Université

Dear Mr. Rogers:

All night I have been thinking out the details of my Uniform Edition, and this afternoon and evening I have completed it and set it down on paper.

I want the canvass to begin just a year from now. If I don't kill my reputation meanwhile, I think it will set me up financially and enable the family to live in their house again. When I come, I shall want to show it to you and talk it over with you.

I have lost time. I ought to have knocked CL Webster & Co in the head 3 years ago when it owed only ⟨$25,000⟩ $16,000, and gone into the Uniform edition-business with Bliss. And that would have been a good time to shove the machine out of my dreams, too.

I hoped Colby would get up a trade with Watson Gill which would release "Old Times on the Mississippi" so that I could add it

to the Uniform—but I don't hear from him and don't know
whether he succeeded or not.

Sincerely Yours

SL Clemens

I have not been sleeping, these many nights past, but the Uniform has brought light and cheer and I shall sleep, now.

P.S. I sent for my London publisher and he gave me help and information on the Uniform.

63. CLEMENS TO ROGERS

Paris
8 January 1895

169 rue de l'Université

Dear Mr. Rogers:

As usual, Whitmore says not a word until his exchequer has run
dry. And he never sends me an account of any kind; therefore I can't
foresee what is going to happen.

I have just written him that he must make the Am. Pub. Co.
check (now due) on my old books last him several months. Will
you turn it over to him?

I have told him to send me an itemised account every month. He
will send me just *one*—and when the second one fails to arrive, I
will put another man in his place.

We have offered to rent our house to a friend. I guess he will not
take it, for he won't like the expense of living in it. But we shall try
again. Apparently it costs $200 a month to support it untenanted,
even without counting the taxes. Part of the money spent by
Whitmore in the reported 9 months went to my brother—$50 a
month; $40 a month to Whitmore; $70 a month to the gardener
and his wife. Insurance $300 a year, I think.

I have proposed to Whitmore to reduce himself to $20 a month. If we can rent, or sell, or burn the house, it will rid us of the other wages and the taxes.

Whitmore's letter and 10-line account (covering 9 months) came this morning from Mr. Colby and has made me lose my day—the first day's work I have lost since I got over the gout, I think.

If I had not lost this day I believe I would have arrived in sight of the end of the second division of Joan. I have written about ⟨40,000⟩ 35,000 words on it since I began in Paris, which was about Thanksgiving, I think.

I expect to finish the whole book by the middle of Feb., and complete the revision by March 1st. Can't tell, but that is my calculation.

However, if I add a large Appendix I shan't get through so early. As soon as it is ready for the printers I will carry it over and make arrangements.

Happy New Year again, to all of you!

Yrs sincerely

SL Clemens

64. CLEMENS TO ROGERS

Paris
21 January 1895
169 rue de l'Université

Dear Mr. Rogers:

Yours of the 8th is received.

That is the very thing. If you will write that ⟨to Stoker⟩ sort of a letter to Stoker, I'll be very glad, and will keep diligently aloof myself.

Meantime the thing for me to do is to begin to teach myself to endure a way of life which I was familiar with during the first half of my life but whose sordidness and hatefulness and humiliation long ago faded out of my memory and feeling. With the help of my wife this will not be very difficult, I think. I think, indeed, that she and I could adjust ourselves to the new conditions quite easily if we were alone,—in fact I know it—but the reflection that they are going to be hard on the children (and incomprehensible by them) will string out the probation of course. The first step has been taken: we have written to Hartford and offered our house for rent. With that idle and expensive institution off our hands we think we can pull along somehow—not in America, perhaps, but in Paris or Vienna.

Of the rags left of Mrs. Clemens's Elmira interests she may count upon $3,000 a year for herself and $1,000 for the children. Then there is about $1,500 a year from the Hartford books and $2,000 from the London publisher—total, $7,500. To that I must add $5,000 a year by work, and that will keep the tribe alive.

This last item would be quite easy if I might venture to raise it by magazine articles, but that is dangerous and to be avoided if possible. A man who is on the down grade must not print too often —he must keep out of the public view as much as he can; and when he prints be sure he is not printing anything that is not up to his very best. I shall be cautious about that—and have already begun. That New York syndicate [1] offered me $1,000 a week ago for a short story to contain not less than 5,000 words. I took a day's holiday from Joan and began the story in the afternoon and finished it at 11.10 p.m—6,200 words. Formerly I would have mailed it; this time I pigeon-holed it. Perhaps it was within the central ring, but Mrs. C. and I decided that it was not in the bull's-eye.

We were hoping we might live in New York; but so far as we can learn, the best terms obtainable there for a flat large enough to contain us, is $3,000 a year unfurnished. Moreover Mrs. Clemens is not strong enough to walk the distances that lie between the horse-car lines. Therefore we have been obliged to give up the New York idea, and we don't want to live elsewhere in America—certainly not in Hartford, in the circumstances.

We shall all go over to America—in May is our plan—and while ⟨the family⟩ we spend the summer in Elmira I can edit and prepare the uniform edition for issue next ⟨Decem⟩ January, preceding it with Joan in the previous month.

Tell me—what does Broughton say Paige talks like? What is he going to do with his new machine? What are his plans? [2]

PRIVATE——PRIVATE.

As a rule I have not damaged my ribs laughing, of late, but when I was lying awake in bed this morning a project came into my head which broke me all up—and made Mrs. Clemens mad because I wouldn't tell what I was laughing about and give her a share in the fun.

This is my project—a conspiracy against the gullibility of the world. And you are to consent to be a fellow-conspirator. You are to insert this $1,000 ad. a single time in the Sun or Herald or some other big Sunday edition,—*and gather in the newspaper comments* from all over the country and save them. Laffan could have the exchanges watched and saved. (But perhaps he ought not to be let into the secret.)

Also, save up the guesses sent to "XXX." From the two sources one might get some pleasant reading.

Now if you could get a hint to the police that there is a swindle in the wind, and then send Rice to the newspaper office to collect the mail addressed to "X X X" and get him arrested, that would be jolly. Or go and get *yourself* arrested—jollier still.

Being required to explain, you will say you were asked to do this for me; that you examined the ad., and as it did not ask the guessers to send stamps or money, you saw no possibility of a swindle in it, therefore you did as I requested. Being asked what the missing word is, you will say *you don't know*—which will be perfectly true, and a sufficient answer. Being asked if you are always muggins enough to do any fool errand any idiot asks you to, you will look embarrassed and say you don't know any better. Sometime I will ⟨send⟩ tell you the missing word—but no one else.

$1,000. The forthcoming new magazine *The Wayside* offers this great prize to the first furnisher of the missing word in this sentence:

Man is like a ⎯⎯⎯⎯ : welcomed and courted when he is young and rich; courteously but earnestly avoided when he is old and stale. Address XXX, Herald office (before) until Feb. 28.

⎯⎯⎯⎯

There, now, go ahead and get Rice arrested—or yourself—and save up the answers and the newspaper comments.

With love to all of you

SLC

[1] The Bacheller & Johnson Syndicate of New York had made this offer in a letter of 8 January 1895 (Salm). Arthur Waugh also wrote, from London, on 21 January 1895 (Salm) urging that Clemens "give Mr. Bacheller a provisional promise of a story within, say, six or nine months."

[2] Paige continued as an inventor: on 17 August 1895 he applied for a patent on a pneumatic tire (*Official Gazette of the United States Patent Office*, LXXV [23 June 1896], 1950).

65. CLEMENS TO ROGERS

Paris

23 January 1895

169 rue de l'Université

Dear Mr. Rogers:

After I wrote you, two or three days ago I thought I would make a holiday of the rest of the day—the second *deliberate* holiday since I had the gout. On the first holiday I wrote a tale of about 6,000 words, which was 3 days' work in one; and this time I did 8,000 before midnight. I got nothing out of that first holiday but the recreation of it, for I condemned the work after careful reading and some revision; but this time I fared better—I finished the Huck Finn tale that lies in your safe,[1] and am satisfied with it.

The Bacheller syndicate (117 Tribune building) want a story of 5,000 words (lowest limit of their London agent) for $1,000 and offer to plank the check on delivery, and it was partly to meet that demand that I took that other holiday. So as I have no short story that suits me (and can't and shan't make promises,) the best I can do is to offer the longer one which I finished on my second holiday —"*Tom Sawyer, Detective*."

It makes 27 or 28,000 words, and is really written for grown folk, though I expect young folk to read it, too. It transfers to the banks of the Mississippi the incidents of a strange murder which was committed in Sweden in old times.

I'll have it all type-written here and corrected ready for the press; then I will ship it to you and ask Miss Harrison to hive it in the safe, till I hear from Bacheller (and also from Walker[2] of the Cosmopolitan.)

I've written both of them to-day and asked them to make me an offer "conditioned on your (their) approval of the story after examination and my approval of the offers *before* it."

Now if both men are financially good, I'll know what to do. If neither offers enough, then I will try the Century and the Harper, but not earlier—I know *their* terms. That is, I know what they *have* paid me.

As Howells is running a story in the Cosmopolitan[3] I suppose Walker must be still able to meet his engagements, but of course I don't know; neither do I know anything about Bacheller's syndicate. I notice that the latter is offering a $2,000 prize (which I don't wish to compete for) for a short detective story, and that he appends the fac-simile signatures of 7 or 8 newspaper proprietors as a guaranty—as if he thought his own credit might be doubtful.

I'll refer applicants for a sight of "T.S., D." to you or Miss Harrison. I *must* find something for you to do in these dull times.

Yrs sincerely

S. L. Clemens

Do you think Harry would read the story when it comes and pledge himself to a favorable verdict? Usual terms for billiard-marking.

I hope our Chicago machine shop will prosper. It won't take

much of a dividend from it to piece out this family's income sufficiently to disappoint the wolf.

<hr>

[1] Apparently an earlier version of *Tom Sawyer, Detective*, now completed.

[2] John Brisben Walker was editor of *Cosmopolitan*. On the margin of the letter of 8 January 1895 (Salm) from the Bacheller & Johnson Syndicate Clemens penciled: "P.S. Jan. 23. I don't think *he'll* offer enough. I'd rather be in the Cosmop at a lower rate than he is going to offer, anyway." The "he" referred to may have been Irving Bacheller, or it may have been Arthur Stedman who in the summer of 1894 had first approached Clemens for the syndicate.

[3] *A Parting and a Meeting* ran serially in *Cosmopolitan* from December 1894 to February 1895.

66. CLEMENS TO ROGERS

Paris

29 January 1895

169 rue de l'Université

Dear Mr. Rogers:

Your felicitous and delightful letter of the 15th arrived three days ago and brought great pleasure into the house. I note what you say about helping me with your heart and head and pocket in the matter of the uniform edition; and I shall surely call on the first two gratefully; and if I find I can't pull through without invading the third, why then I'll attack *that* if the edition promises to justify such conduct.

My scheme is modester than it was. It contemplates a cloth set of 12 volumes (90 to 100,000 words each; small octavo; 300 pages each, small pica:) for $12. *No pictures.* Single volumes $1.50. And suppress all the old editions.

The sets to be sold by subscription: $4 down, and two instalments of $4 each. Cash down in full for high-priced-binding sets.

Cost of plates......$2,500.00

"   " cloth volume....⟨2⟩20 [1]

There are a lot of other details, but that is the general idea. My

London publisher came over and figured it out with me; and left with me two models for the volumes.

No, don't put Harry on the roof. There's no need of that. He can sleep under my bed.

I have a hope that the Hospital trouble will end in making Rice President.[2] I suppose that what is needed in a President is not morals, but business faculty. I should think that those people, with all their fussiness and obstructiveness, would see that. They have no eligible man but Rice, no man who can fill the whole bill. They will not let you retire, unless they lose the rest of their minds, and so I consider Rice's elevation pretty certain.

There is one thing that weighs heavily on Mrs. Clemens and me. That is Brusnahan's money. If he is satisfied to have it invested in our Chicago enterprise, well and good; if not, we would like to have the money paid back to him. I will give him as many months to decide in as he pleases,—let him name 6 or 10 or 12—and we will let the money stay where it is in your hands till the time is up. Will Miss Harrison tell him so?—I mean if you approve. I would like him to have a good investment, but would meantime prefer to protect him against loss.

At 6 minutes past 7, yesterday evening, Joan of Arc was burned at the stake.

With the long strain gone, I am in a sort of physical collapse to-day, but it will be gone to-morrow. I judged that this end of the book would be hard work, and it turned out so. I have never done any work before that cost so much thinking and weighing and measuring and planning and cramming, or so much cautious and painstaking execution. For I wanted the *whole* Rouen trial in, if it could be got in in such a way that the reader's interest would not flag—in fact I wanted the reader's interest to *increase;* and so I stuck to it with that determination in view—with the result that I have left nothing out but unimportant *repetitions*. Although it is mere history—history pure and simple—history stripped naked of flowers, embroideries, colorings, exaggerations, inventions—the family agree that I have succeeded. It was a ⟨dan⟩ perilous thing to try in a tale, but I never believed it a doubtful one—provided I stuck strictly to business, and didn't weaken and give up; or didn't get lazy and skimp the work. The first two-thirds of the book were easy; for I only needed to keep my historical road straight; therefore I used for reference only one French history and one English one— and shoveled in as much fancy-work and invention on both sides of the historical road as I pleased. But on this last third I have constantly used five French sources and five English ones, and I think no telling historical nugget in any of them has escaped me.

Possibly the book may not sell, but that is nothing—it was written for love.

I believe I cannot let the Harpers have the Martyrdom. It is not a wig, and separable—it is the heart; it is a part of the living body, and not detachable without assassination. I suspected that this might be the case, in the beginning; but could not be sure of it.

I think I will add a few finishing-up chapters this week; then put in a week or ten days' revising; then the book will be done.

The family are arranging to go over in May or June and spend the summer with the relatives in Elmira—then (this is private) spend the winter in our house in Hartford if we can afford it. Mrs. C. has made acres of figures, and has decided that without horses and coachman we can live there the winter on Paris rates—$1,000 a month. Her calculations have always come out right, I believe, and so she is right about this, I guess.

A friend wants our house from March 1 till Sept. 1—and that comes very handy. I am quite willing somebody else shall pay our taxes for us a while.

There—I'm called to see company. The family seldom require this of me, but they know I am not working to-day.

Yrs Sincerely

SL Clemens

---

[1] The relationship of this figure to production costs is obscure.
[2] Dr. Rice was a founder and, with Rogers, a trustee of the New York Post-Graduate Medical School and Hospital.

67. Clemens to Rogers

Paris
3 February 1895

169 rue de l'Université

Dear Mr. Rogers:

Yesterday was our silver wedding. I gave Mrs. Clemens a bran new 5-franc piece, and she will frame it. Nobody else put up anything, all the family but me being poor.

I suppose we have rented our Hartford home to some particular friends (John C Day and family) for 5 or 9 months. I hope they will keep it indefinitely.

I expect to sail in the New York the 23d of this present month. To consult with you first and then arrange a contract to issue Joan next December and follow it with the Uniform Edition.

Also to consult with you about another project, which is—(take a breath and stand by for a surge)—to go around the world on a lecture trip.

This is not for money, but to get Mrs. Clemens and myself away from the phantoms and out of the heavy nervous strain for a few months. By the urgent help of the doctor I have got her more than half persuaded—provided Susy or Clara will go with us. Also, it will be a rest for you and Mrs. Duff and Harry. You all need just such a trip. (It would do the Benjamins good, too, and I hope to persuade them to join the procession.) I suppose I can hire myself out to Mrs. Clemens as a platform-reader and thus escape trouble from (the) my creditors. I must ask Colby about that. For my scheme is, to start west in September, read twice in Kansas City, four times in Chicago, four times in San Francisco, two or three times around about there, and sail for Australia about Oct. 1. Read 60 times in Australia, New Zealand and Tasmania; once in Colombo, Ceylon; 4 times in Bombay; maybe read also in Calcutta or around there somewhere; then go on to the gold and diamond mines of South Africa and put in 20 or 25 readings there; then to Great Britain and read in London, Dublin, Edinburgh, and so on, 20 or 30 times; then home and read a few times in Boston, New York, Phila, Baltimore, Washington and Richmond.

I have discussed the matter with Stanley [1] and got all the items. Also I have to-day written his lecture-agent in Melbourne ⟨and told him⟩ and asked him to make me a proposition and send duplicate (signed) contracts for consideration, together with his guess as to ⟨whether I⟩ how much my profits might exceed my expenses. Of course I should come out ahead if I went alone; but going alone would be to worsen Mrs. Clemens, not improve her. I estimate my land expenses in Melbourne and Cape Town (120 days) at $4,000; and the steamer fares from ⟨San Francisco to London⟩ beginning to the end at $6,000. If I get half the gross proceeds (Stanley's terms) it ought not to take the whole hundred lectures to pay that. Stanley estimates my clear winnings in Australia and the Cape at $15,000; but *I* don't. I would sell them for $5,000. But I *should* expect the trip to help sell my uniform edition, and I should also expect to make a trifle reading in England and on the Atlantic seaboard later. I should be a novelty in one way down there in Australia and the Cape of Good Hope—the only Yank that ever appeared there or in India on the platform.

Now all of you get ready, and while I am instructing the ⟨native⟩ Zulus around about the Cape, you can speculate in gold and diamond stocks.

My land! if I undertake this, it will take me all summer to train myself for the platform. I know what it is to be out of training; I found that out when I made those unspeakable botches at Madison Square Garden with Riley.[2] I was a fool to go on that platform— but I had to have money.

Whitmore reports a balance of $67.40 in bank at Hartford. He never gives a body sufficient notice ahead. I must try and replace him with another idiot when I come.

If I go on that trip I may possibly get a book of travel out of it; and books of travel are good sellers in the subscription trade.

If we go, it is our project to get the Elmira relatives to ⟨keep⟩ board two of our girls for us while we are away. That is, half of the time; and Twichell in Hartford the other half. He has offered, more than once, heretofore. With that kind of change of scene I think the girls would have a very good time and not miss us severely. Miss their mother, I mean. Girls don't miss their fathers as much as they ought to.

Get ready now; and tell the others to get ready.

Sincerely Yours

S. L. Clemens

Maybe a better way would be to read in England Ireland and Scotland all October; then to South Africa; then *straight across* to Australia; then China and Japan; then to San Francisco—turning the whole trip around, you see, and bringing home a foreign reputation.

---

[1] Sir Henry M. Stanley, whom Clemens had known since 1867 and had met again in England in 1872; and then most recently during one of Stanley's several lecture tours in the United States.
[2] Clemens had lectured with James Whitcomb Riley in Madison Square Garden on 26 and 27 February 1894 at $250 a night; he had not been well received (see *MTLC*, p. 235).

68. CLEMENS TO ROGERS

Paris
8–9 February 1895

Dear Mr. Rogers:

Yours of Jan. 17 has just arrived, in which you mention $200 check received from American Pub. Co. It puzzled me for a moment, because Bliss wrote me ten days earlier (Jan. [7]) [1] that he would presently send check to New York of something more than $1,000 on the old copyrights. I think this $200 must be a part of the $1,500 which he was to pay for "Those Extraordinary Twins."

The thing has happened which was bound to happen. Bliss got hold of Pudd'nhead so late that he lost the holiday trade; consequently achieved no sale.

News has just come that the interest on Mrs. Clemens's Buffalo mortgage has defaulted. So that is $1,500 withdrawn from her bread and butter. Da-a-m—*nation!* Isn't there *ever* going to come a turn!

Mr. Macgowan shipped that Tom Sawyer to you yesterday for me, and got it registered. I enclose the P. O. receipt.

Yesterday I engaged passages in the New York—from here Feb. 23; and return from New York March 27.

I also engaged passage for the whole 5 of us in the same ship for May 18.

I have had a talk with Mr. Macgowan's friend Mr. Libbey,[2] and he found the sail between San Francisco and England, via Australia delightful—also much cheaper than I had supposed;—$600 for one first-class the whole trip.

Apparently I've *got* to mount the platform next fall or starve; therefore I am examining into this thing seriously. You and Mrs. Duff and Harry, Mrs. Clemens, Clara and me—that is the way we are planning that long voyage. You are 55 and need the rest; Mrs. Duff needs the voyage for her health, and Harry needs it for exercise. Don't disappoint us. This is our last chance to go around the world. If we don't do it now we never shall.

I'm afraid it's a bad case for the hospital if you four resign.

With warmest regards to all,

Sincerely Yours

SL Clemens

Feb. 9/95.

P.S.[3] I didn't know it, but Mrs. Clemens doesn't want anybody to know she is thinking of dumping two of our girls upon her sister on top of the hill near Elmira for the summer. She wants to find out privately first, whether they would be an inconvenience to Mrs.

Crane or not, and that she can't manage till she gets to America. So if you should innocently go and mention it to Rice, you see, the cat might get out of the bag; for Mrs. Crane runs down every little while and buys Rice's professional help, and he might happen to mention the matter to her. She and Rice are great friends. Rice breeds some kind of an animal in her nose—an octopus, I think—and then charges her for letting on to take it out. He *is* the most ingenious cuss!

I finished revising and completing Joan yesterday evening, and shall take the MS along when I sail the 23d. Will you warn Harry that his uncle Sammy is coming over to see about that wall paper?

Sincerely Yours

SL Clemens

---

¹ Clemens mistakenly wrote "17" instead of "7."
² Allan Nevins, in *Study in Power: John D. Rockefeller* (New York, 1953), II, 350, calls William H. Libby "the Standard's diplomatic agent abroad."
³ The postscript to this letter is taken from a typescript in MTP.

69. CLEMENS TO ROGERS

Paris
12 February 1895

169 rue de l'Université

Dear Mr. Rogers:

More Mental Telegraphy. About the end of January I wrote and asked Stanley for the name and address of his Australian lecture-agent, and he told me R. S. Smythe, Melbourne. So I wrote Smythe nine days ago—*and got a letter from him from Melbourne last night answering my questions!* There—how's that! It is true that his letter left Melbourne Dec. 17 and went to America and then back to Paris—still it was odd that he should take a notion to write me just about the time that I was going to write him. I hadn't thought of Australia away back there in December; so I conclude that his mind telegraphed the idea into ⟨mind⟩ mine across the ocean.

I sail in the New York 11 days hence; and so I shall soon see you all.

[The remainder of this letter is missing.]

II

"As Long as the Promise Must Be Made"

(MARCH 1895–AUGUST 1896)

> "Well, as long as the promise must be made, it was necessarily well to make it *public;* and so I have made it public."
>
> SLC to HHR, 17 August 1895

O N 23 February 1895 Clemens left Southampton on the SS *New York,* bound again for the United States. His errand was twofold: to arrange for publication of *Personal Recollections of Joan of Arc,* and to consider a plan for a uniform edition of his works. *Joan of Arc* was not difficult to sell, although Mark Twain insisted it be published anonymously for fear that association with his name would prevent readers from taking the work seriously. It was taken up at once as a serial for *Harper's Magazine.* A penalty, in the form of an increase in the author's royalties, was to be invoked if Mark Twain's name was mentioned in connection with the serial, and Harper & Brothers also promised to bring it out soon thereafter as a dignified volume. Arrangements for a uniform edition of Mark Twain's works, however, were to stretch out over several years. The Harper brothers, Frank Bliss, F. N. Doubleday, Watson Gill, and Frederick A. Stokes were prominent among those who bid for the opportunity to become Mark Twain's publishers.

Not until 23 May 1895 was an even partially satisfactory solution arrived at. By an agreement of that date, the following books, formerly published by Charles L. Webster & Company, were turned over to Harper & Brothers: *Adventures of Huckleberry Finn, A Connecticut Yankee in King Arthur's Court, Tom Sawyer Abroad, The Prince and the Pauper, Life on the Mississippi, The Stolen White Elephant, The American Claimant, The £1,000,000 Bank Note,* and *Mark Twain's Library of Humor.* The American Publishing Company, which controlled *The Innocents Abroad, Roughing It, The Gilded Age, The Adventures of Tom Sawyer, A Tramp Abroad,* and *Pudd'nhead Wilson,* was "at the earliest practical date" to turn those books over to Harper & Brothers for inclusion in the uniform edition. But, as Rogers's letters to Clemens explain, complications of all kinds arose, chief among which was Frank Bliss's claim that the American Publishing Company owned renewals of the copyrights of its books by Mark Twain for forty-two years and refused therefore to allow Harper & Brothers to include those books in its uniform edition.

True, or not, his claim led to the drawing up of a new agreement on 31 December 1896, giving the American Publishing Company the right to publish a uniform edition which would include those works by Mark Twain controlled by Harper & Brothers. Most of these negotiations were carried on while Clemens was abroad, by Rogers, who firmly and finally drew Clemens away from the American Publishing Company, after it had published a number of sets of his collected works, toward Harper & Brothers, which eventually became his sole publisher.

Meanwhile, on 27 March 1895 Clemens had left New York again on the SS *Paris,* on which Mrs. Rice and her children and Andrew Carnegie also sailed. Welcomed in London on 4 April at a dinner given in his honor by Sir Henry Stanley, Clemens proceeded then to Paris to join his family. The next month the Clemenses started home, embarking at Southampton on 11 May 1895 and arriving in New York seven days later. They went immediately to Elmira, where Clemens was afflicted with carbuncles and troubled by creditors of Charles L. Webster & Company, by suspicions about former associates in the Paige Compositor Manufacturing Company, and by worries about his ability to whip lectures into shape. It was almost with relief that he and Mrs. Clemens and Clara set off on 14 July for their journey around the world. A week before he left Vancouver for Australia, Clemens made public his promise to pay the creditors of Charles L. Webster & Company in full. The New York *Times* of 17 August 1895 reported him as concluding that "if I live I can pay off the last debt within four years, after which, at the age of sixty-four, I can make a fresh and unincumbered start in life."

70. OLIVIA CLEMENS TO ROGERS

Paris
28 March 1895

Mr H. H. Rogers:
My dear Sir:
Will you kindly honor any drafts made on you by my agent Mr Whitmore, for my Hartford expenses and greatly oblige

yours truly

Olivia L. Clemens [1]

[1] Clemens was on board the *Paris* at this time. In a letter to Whitmore on 27 March 1895 he had indicated the necessity for Mrs. Clemens's supervision of the family's financial matters: "At first I thought I would drop a note to Mr. Day and tell him to pay the rent to you; but next it occurred to me that I am warned every day to venture no orders concerning Mrs. Clemens's properties and affairs" (Mark Twain Memorial, Hartford). For further evidence of Livy's formal control, see letter 60, note 1.

71. CLEMENS TO ROGERS

At Sea
3 April 1895

11 a.m.

Dear Mr. Rogers:

Mrs. Rice and the children have been sick part of the time, but on the whole they have had a pleasant voyage; and as the channel is smooth to-day and the weather fine I think they will have a comfortable trip to Havre to-night. If we get in in time to catch the boat—and the experts say we shall.

The usual "concert" last night. Carnegie in the chair. Something prompted me to risk telling my dream about my trip to heaven and hell with Rev. Sam Jones and the Archbishop of Canterbury—and I did it. It was good fun—but just scandalous. When Mrs. Clemens finds it out there will be a scalp lacking in the Clemens family.[1]

It was mighty good and kind of you three to make that long journey down to the ship with me, and I thank you for it with my very best thanks. I lost a final glimpse of Mrs. Duff and Miss Hammond through being caught and introduced to a number of people; so that by the time I got to the ship's side they were gone and I was very sorry. I have never half thanked Mrs. Duff for coming down and fetching me when I arrived in New York; but I thank her to myself every time I think of it.

It was lucky that I named the 4th of April for the dinner in London instead of the 3d, for we are not going to get into South-ampton till along in the night.

Tell Harry to be good and he will be happy. I have not tried it, but I know it's so.

Sincerely Yours

SL Clemens

The purser asked me for a ticket, but I told him you had it but forgot to give it to me.

---

[1] In the winter of 1891–1892 Clemens had written "A Singular Episode" (DV 329, MTP), an account of a dream in which Mark Twain leaves the world by celestial railroad and surreptitiously exchanges his ticket to Sheol for the sleeping archbishop's ticket to Heaven. Clemens wrote at the top of the manuscript: "Not published—forbidden by Mrs. Clemens."

72. CLEMENS TO ROGERS

At Sea
3 April 1895

Steamer *Paris*

Dear Mr. Rogers:

We are approaching Southampton, and have not had a suggestion of weather yet. The weather has been summer weather, and the sea has been smooth all the way. But I have done no work. Every attempt has failed—a struggle every day, and retreat and defeat at nightfall. *Now* you see you ought to have come! It would have been a health-giving voyage for Mrs. Duff, I think. I beg to send my regards to her, and hope she is entirely well by this time.

[The remainder of this letter is missing.]

73. CLEMENS TO ROGERS

Paris
7 April 1895

169 rue de l'Université
Sunday.

Dear Mr. Rogers:

Now I *am* in a sweat—or close upon the verge of it!—concerning the Mayo contract. Our original basis of agreement was, one-fifth of the profits to me and four-fifths to him. My understanding of that was, that it was the same sort of partnership that I had with Raymond, except in the matter of proportions. We shared half and half in the profits. If Raymond cleared $5,000 in a week (which happened now and then), I got half of it.[1]

But I remember, now, that in your office Mayo said he had had trouble to place his piece because managers objected to giving me a fifth of the *"profits of the* PIECE," but that he had stuck to his point and had had to lose many months in consequence. I vaguely wondered *why* they objected; I wondered how it could affect *them*.

But look here! Suppose Mayo should play at "half gross" to a $1200 house. Does he carry off $600 and leave me to get my fifth out of the remnant left of the other 600 after paying the ⟨company⟩ advertising, rent, etc.? I should be lucky if I got $60.

And suppose he should play on a salary of $500 a night and the management cleared but $100; is $20 my share? And suppose the management clears *nothing?*—is the fifth of nothing my share?

Shucks, I *must* be wrong—and yet I'm scared. I have ⟨not⟩ never thought of making a contract with managers for a fifth of *their* profits; I have had no idea of dealings of *any* kind with *them*. My only idea was that whenever Mayo cleared $5, one dollar of it came to *me,* no matter whether the theatre made money or didn't.

Do please tell me how you understand the contract—and tell me quick! My fifth seemed plenty small enough when our agreement was first made—it seems to have nearly *disappeared,* now. I shall be horribly angry with myself if I find that I have once more gone and ⟨signed⟩ ratified a contract without understanding it.

If you have a copy of Mayo's contract[2] with his manager I reckon it will throw all the light required on this matter.

Mrs. Rice is here at the hotel Brighton and she and Mrs. Clemens are busy contriving her arrangements. Clara and I thought we had discovered exactly the flat she needs, last night, but we couldn't get it. It was already taken; the people who were moving out a month ahead of their sailing-day were not doing it voluntarily. Mrs. Howland[3] has arrived, and she will be a good planner and helper.

The reason I am not enclosing Helen's [4] letter is because I didn't write a line of any kind on board ship. First time I've failed.

Stanley is magnificently housed in London, in a grand mansion in the midst of the official world right off Downing street and Whitehall. He had an extraordinary assemblage of brains and fame there to meet me—thirty or forty (both sexes) at dinner, and more than a hundred came in after dinner. Kept it up till after midnight. There were cabinet ministers, ambassadors, admirals, generals, canons, Oxford professors, novelists, playwrights, poets, and a number of people equipped with rank *and* brains. I told some yarns and made some speeches. I promised to call on all those people next time I come to London, and show them the wife and the daughters. If I were younger and very strong I would dearly love to spend a season in London—provided I had no work on hand; or no work more exacting than lecturing. I think I will lecture there a month or two when I return from Australia.

There were many delightful ladies in that company. One was the wife of His Excellency Admiral Bridge,[5] Commander-in-Chief of the Australian Station, and she said her husband was able to throw wide all doors to me in that part of the world and would be glad to do it; and would yacht me and my party around, and excursion us in his flag-ship and make us have a great time; and she said she would write him we were coming, and we would find him ready. I have a letter from her this morning enclosing a letter of introduction to the Admiral. I already know the Admiral commanding in the China seas and have promised to look in on him out there. He sleeps with my books under his pillow. P'raps it is the only way he *can* sleep. You and Mrs. Duff and Harry *must* go with us. It will rest you up and restore your youth.

According to Mrs. Clemens's present plans—subject to modification, of course—we sail in May; stay one day, or two days in New York; spend June, July and August in Elmira and prepare my lectures; then lecture in San Francisco and thereabouts during September and sail for Australia before the middle of October and open the show there about the middle of November. We don't take the girls along; it would be too expensive, and they are quite willing to remain behind anyway.

Mrs. C. is feeling so well that she is not going to try the New York doctor till we have gone around the world and robbed it and made the finances a little easier.

Mr. Macgowan is well and happy, and so is Mr. Southard. I saw them yesterday.[6]

With a power of love to you all,

SL Clemens

[1] Clemens may have been mistaken: John T. Raymond in 1884 had suggested the possibility of playing "Colonel Sellers as a Scientist" in one-night stands. Raymond questioned the proposed division of income, since receipts might be "three or four hundred dollars—and to pay a royalty of one hundred dollars would leave me on the wrong side of the track" (*MTBus*, pp. 253–254); it is suggested in *MTLP*, p. 176, that Raymond "made an alternate offer the details of which are unknown. . . . Raymond decided the play would not be successful and withdrew his offer."

[2] Clemens later realized that he need not have worried: the agreement of 29 September 1894 (CWB) which gave Mayo sole right to produce *Pudd'nhead Wilson* in the United States, Great Britain, and Canada guaranteed Clemens 20 per cent of the net profits.

[3] Probably Mrs. Henry E. Howland, wife of Judge Howland of New York. In 1901 Clemens would wish to invite the Judge for a cruise on Rogers's yacht, the *Kanawha;* see letters 275 and 277.

[4] Helen Keller had written Rogers on 25 March 1895 to thank him "for leaving your carriage to take Teacher and me home yesterday" and asking him to "give my love to dear Mr. Clemens if he is still your guest. I can not tell you how glad I was to see him." Rogers had apparently loaned the letter to Clemens before his departure, and when Clemens finally did return it, Rogers sent it to the Millicent Library in Fairhaven. "I consider it a most valuable paper" he wrote on 22 May 1895, "and ask you to take the best care of it for the Millicent Library" (Fairhaven).

[5] Sir Cyprian Bridge.

[6] See letter 21, note 1.

74. CLEMENS TO ROGERS

Paris
9 April 1895

Dear Mr. Rogers:

I invented the form which appears on the other page,[1] but Mrs. Clemens thinks she could have phrased it better herself.

Yrs sincerely

SLC.

[1] On "the other page" was written in Clemens's hand, but signed by Mrs. Clemens:

H. H. Rogers, Esq—Please pay to yourself $270.00, borrowed by my husband and charge to my account.

Olivia L. Clemens

75. CLEMENS TO ROGERS

Paris
14 April 1895

169 rue de l'Université

Dear Mr. Rogers:

Yours of the 2d has come, and it is a very genuine pleasure to me to know that I am missed. I had such a good homelike time there that I missed the house and everybody in it and found it lonesome in the ship and hard to reconcile myself to the change.

Tell me—aren't you and Mrs. Duff going around the world with us in case we go? I do hope so. A couple of days ago Clara concluded that she would go, because her mother was refusing to take a maid, but I think we will leave her behind and take a maid;

for the experts seem to have decided that she is a musical genius, ⟨and is going to be a composer;⟩ therefore I don't want her to lose any time from her studies if I can make money enough to keep her at them. We are not dead sure, yet, that we are going, but we imagine we are. I think we shan't hear from the Australia man before we leave for home.

We expect to sail in the New York May 11, rest-up the family Saturday and Sunday 18th and 19th in New York and leave for Elmira at 9 Monday morning.

⟨This will give us time to⟩

We were to have stopped at the Waldorf a few days as Charley Langdon's guests, but Mrs. Clemens's head is too level for that. People would think we were splurging there on our own footing and it wouldn't look modest for bankrupts. Charley may take the children there if he will see to it that their names do not get into print, but the head of the family and I will stop at the Everett.

Bliss is an ass. It would be a mistake to publish with him on any terms. He did his best to prove to me that the books were not valuable, and now he seems to be chiefly engaged in eating his own words. I hope Mr. Benjamin's plans about the books will go through.

I wonder if it would interfere with Stokes's editions if we should let the Harpers issue the same books in a high priced and uniform form? I wonder if Stokes would object? If not, Bliss would presently want to copy the Harper form, and then a uniform edition would come to pass at last.

I am tired to death all the time, and my head is tired and clogged, too, and the mill refuses to go. It comes of depression of spirits, I think, caused by the impending horror of the platform.

I've got a photograph for Mr. Broughton and will send it or bring it.

We all send our warmest regards to you all. Mrs. Rice is pleasantly housed.

Yours Sincerely

SL Clemens

76. Clemens to Rogers

Paris
28 April 1895

Dear Mr. Rogers:

Within the last few days I have completed my arrangements for Australia, India and South Africa and signed the papers [1] and sent the cablegram. So that much is settled and put out of my head and out of my way. If I can talk a little on the Pacific coast before sailing, without being bothered by Webster & Co's creditors, I will do it; if not, I will sail without it. I am going to prepare more than one reading, and I am going to have insufficient time to do it in; for if I talk on the Pacific coast I must start out there ⟨early⟩ about the first of July, for I sail from Vancouver August 16. I can get ready I think, but it will be a close fit and take hard work.

I hope we can arrange with Harpers or Stokes or Gill for issuing the books, and that the arrangement can be made and completed as soon as I arrive; if it should take three days, maybe I could reduce Book III of Joan for the magazine in that time, and so have both of those things out of the way. Then I could begin preparing my readings as soon as I reached Elmira. I am already making a few selections now while I've got a new touch of the gout.

We have been hard at work many days, now, trunk-packing and breaking up housekeeping—I say *we;* but in fact Mrs. Clemens has done all the work herself; for I am no account. It is the most heart-breaking, soul-damning business the world can furnish. I would rather see the stuff all burned, next time. I don't think the madam will get over this exhaustion soon.

To-morrow we go to the hotel, and we expect to sail from Southampton May 11. And then I'll see all of you soon!

Sincerely Yours

SL Clemens

[1] On 23 April 1895 Clemens had written J. H. Harper: "To-day I shall sign a contract [with R. S. Smythe] which has just arrived from Melbourne, for a six to nine months' reading tour next fall and winter in the Sandwich Islands, New Zealand, Australia, Ceylon, Madras, Calcutta, Bombay and other Indian cities, then South Africa and the Mauritius. After the which I shall probably read in England a spell, then talk across America to Pacific coast and then back again through the Southern States.

"And then die, I reckon" (TS in MTP).

77. Clemens to Rogers

Paris
29 April 1895

169 rue de l'Université

Dear Mr. Rogers:

I have been hidden an hour or two, reading proof of Joan, and now I think I am a lost child. I can't find anybody on the place. The baggage has all disappeared, including the family. I reckon that in the hurry and bustle of moving to the hotel they forgot me.[1] But it is no matter. It is peacefuller now than I have known it for days and days and days.

Your this-morning's letter suits. *Now* you're shouting! You and Mrs. Duff and the Judge, Mrs. Clemens, Clara and I—it will be a perfectly darling pleasure-trip! There will be enough of us to afford a private car, and we can stop and do a lecture whenever we get tired. (*Mrs. Duff, begin, now, and work all your persuasions—the quicker you get it settled and clinched, the better.*)

In these Joan proofs which I have been reading for the September Harper I find a couple of tip-top platform readings—and I mean to read them on our trip. If the authorship is known by then; and if it isn't, I will reveal it.[2] The fact is, there is more good platform-stuff in Joan than in any previous book of mine, by a long sight.

By Jackson the Mayo contract *is* all right, after all. Glad of that.

And I am very very glad the play pleases and promises to succeed. I don't value the commendations of critics at as high a rate as

I value the commendations of personal friends—for these latter are naturally in a state of solicitude and anxiety, and this makes them ever so much harder to please or move than the indifferent and disinterested stranger. So your letter brought me the first *real* confidence I've had in the play yet.

Most of my gout is gone, and I have been on my feet all day without discomfort. Electricity did it.

We see Mrs. Rice often. She is well and comfortably situated and equipped now.

Yes, every danged member of the tribe has gone to the hotel and left me lost. I wonder how they can be so careless with property. I have got to try to get there by myself, now.

All the trunks are going over as luggage; then I've got to find somebody on the dock who will agree to ship 6 of them to the Hartford Customhouse. If it is difficult I will dump them into the river. It is very careless of Mrs. Clemens to trust trunks and things to me.

Sincerely Yours

SL Clemens

I'll have to get you to pay the postage—they've carried off the stamps.

---

[1] Clemens seems persistently to have believed that he had once been so abandoned as a child. See *SCH*, p. 53; *MTB*, pp. 24, 30.

[2] Clemens vacillated on the question of anonymity for the *Personal Recollections of Joan of Arc* which had begun to appear serially in *Harper's Magazine* in April 1895. On 17 August 1895 he would write J. Henry Harper:

> I hope you will put my name to the "Joan of Arc" now, for all that I wanted to accomplish by withholding it has been accomplished. Before making this request I have weighed the matter thoughtfully and am convinced that a longer delay may be a disadvantage. I wish to be appearing in print periodically during my trip around the world; for I shall return and make a wide lecture tour in America next year, and all the advertising I can get will help that enterprise. I can't expect to pay off all the Webster debts in a single lecturing-bout, but I think I can come pretty near it if my name is kept alive while I am away on this long journey. (J. Henry Harper, *The House of Harper* [New York, 1912], pp. 575–576.)

Mrs. Clemens, however, countermanded this decision, and Clemens wrote Harper again to ask him to continue to publish it anonymously.

78. Clemens to Rogers

Paris
1 May 1895

Dear Mr. Rogers:

This is very good and strong from Mary Mapes Dodge.[1] I was going to send it to Mayo, but I wanted you to see it. Will you send it to him? She's another personal friend, you see, and her testimony is therefore valuable.

I have been offered a press-banquet and Australian "send-off" in London for May 10, but I am still ⟨down⟩ in a whirl of preparation —that is, superintending and obstructing while Mrs. C. does the work—so I felt obliged to decline; and did. And besides, it was too soon. The powder would all be wasted and the public interested in some newer thing long before we got started from the Pacific coast. It's an immense pity it couldn't happen a couple of months later.

Sincerely Yours

SL Clemens

[1] Clemens recorded in his notebook that a gentleman just back from India "told Mary Mapes Dodge those people claim to know all about America till you corner and sift them with questions; then it turns out that they know just 3 things about it and no more: 'George Washington, Mark Twain, and the Chicago Fair.' What's the gratefullest compliment ever paid me? Why the above" (Notebook 28, TS p. 12).

79. OLIVIA CLEMENS TO ROGERS

At Sea
15 May 1895

H. H. Rogers, Esq.,

Dear Sir: Please honor Mr. Clemens's drafts upon such funds of mine as are in your hands, and greatly oblige

Yours Very Truly

Olivia L. Clemens [1]

[1] All of this letter except the signature is in Clemens's hand.

80. CLEMENS TO ROGERS

Elmira
26 May 1895

Dear Mr. Rogers:

It seems plain that I am not going to have time enough to do the work in front of me with thoroughness before starting west. We leave for the hill-top to-morrow, and then I shall begin at once and work ten or twelve hours a day—half the time on Joan, Book III, and the other half on my three readings: thus shifting the burden back and forth and resting both shoulders. I have already arranged to begin about a week from now and practice the 3 readings privately once and perhaps twice on the convicts at the Reformatory —twice, is my intention; next I am to go to Ithaca and practice them on the Cornell students. This provides for 9 nights (if Joan can spare them to me), and will put me in fairly good shape for the platform.

I have not written Ward or Knevals, yet, for I conceive that it will not be wise to accuse them until I am sure they are guilty. The number of Paige Co shares in your hands for Mrs. Clemens (1,940,) exactly accounts (apparently) for the 1500 shares sold to me for 150 royalties, and for four hundred and odd shares (promised) due as commission on the money which you put into the venture.[1]

When Broughton comes he will know if this surmise of mine is correct or not. If he says those people backed down from their agreement as to the commission I shall write them no letter, but proceed in a quite different and more effective fashion.

Also, when Broughton comes he will know if the new Co have actually made up their minds to try to shove onto Mrs. Clemens a lot of worthless royalties and gobble the 1500 shares of Paige stock the Paige Co bought the royalties with. Please hang on tight to every share of Mrs. Clemens's Paige stock, and let's lay for that new Co. They sent Mrs. Clemens the same printed invitation which went to the other Paige Co stock holders, to exchange old stock for new at the rate of ten for one. I hope you will tender to them the whole of her Paige stock on those terms, and let me know if they offer the slightest shade of a shadow of an objection, so that I can have Colby ready to take immediate measures. Perhaps I ought to have spoken to him before leaving New York; I would have done it, but when I saw that Mrs. Clemens's stock was still in your possession and that you were not troubled as to the outcome, my anxiety passed away. Of course I have no reasonable occasion to be troubled now, but I have had so much ill luck in the past eleven years that it takes very little to scare me and certainly the attitude of the new Co is not altogether tranquilizing. When I reflect soberly I know I am perfectly safe, for you are quite competent to beat the new Co's game and (if) I am competent to take care of the Cemetery gang in 23d street—at least I have that superstition.[2]

Mrs. Clemens does not suspect that her rights have been threatened by the new Co, for it couldn't do any good to disturb her with it, and there is no way for them to consummate the threat anyway.

Pond is making out the route,[3] and expects to have it done in a week. I am hoping it will so shape itself as to let us start west from Boston and give us a week in Fairhaven. In which case I should very much like a chance to practice my 3 readings on that village in the new Town Hall—either free or with a trifling admission, the money to go to the Library or to some local charity. After that, I ought to be able to go on the road without a book in my hand. Think it could be managed?

All of us join in hearty acknowledgments and kindest regards to you and Mrs. Duff. (They are not present—those others—but I am reporting their feeling as I have heard them express it.) And I wish to strongly commend ourselves to the Admiral, and inquire how he feels about letting me have his room when we come.

Sincerely Yours

SL Clemens

Harpers will send you $200 (when they get ready) for a small article entitled "Mental Telegraphy Again." [4]

---

[1] Rogers paid only about $78,000 of the funds he had contracted to advance before the machine failed.

[2] Clemens seems never to have been completely clear about details of the financial transactions when the Regius Manufacturing Company took over the affairs of the Paige Compositor Manufacturing Company. During the spring of 1895 he recorded in his notebook:

> Mr. R. put in $80,000 cash, which entitled him to $400,000 in the old Co.
> Then they gave him $48,000 old Co for the release of some royalties. (Does he return those royalties?)
> For this mass he gets $50,000 new Co. stock—one-fourth of the whole capital.
> He gave me the $75,000 old (commission stock) and I had $150,000 old stock, traded for royalties.
> Thus I had just half as much old stock as he, and am entitled to $25,000 stock of the new Co.

"But," he continued, "there's an error here":

> He *couldn't* give me $75,000 (commission) stock, but only *half* as much, for the 75 was based on his putting in $150,000 *cash,* whereas he put in but half of it.
> And yet I think an order was passed giving O.L.C. at the rate of $75,000 (commission) stock (Notebook 28, TS p. 7).

Livy's stock in the Paige Compositor Manufacturing Company was exchanged, ten shares for one, for stock in the Regius Manufacturing Company (see certificate of 19 April 1897, CWB). Except for an occasional outburst of interest, such as is evidenced in this letter, Clemens apparently put the typesetter and everything connected with it out of his mind, depending on Rogers to salvage for him whatever he could.

[3] James B. Pond was to have a commission of 25 per cent for arranging lectures for Clemens between New York and San Francisco, and 20 per cent for the lectures originally planned for San Francisco; he and his wife accompanied Clemens, Mrs. Clemens, and Clara as far as Vancouver (see SLC to Pond, 24 May 1895, Berg; and J. B. Pond, *Eccentricities of Genius* [London, 1901], pp. 200, 224–225).

[4] It appeared in *Harper's Magazine*, September 1895.

81. CLEMENS TO ROGERS

Elmira
4 June 1895

Quarry Farm

Dear Mr. Rogers:

Well, I *am* a pretty versatile fool, when it comes to contracts, and business and such things. I've signed a lot of contracts in my time; and at signing-time I probably knew what the contracts meant— but 6 months later everything had grown dim and I could be *certain* of only ⟨three⟩ two things, to-wit: 1. I didn't *sign* any contract; 2. The contract means the opposite of what it *says*.

I perceive, now, that ⟨in⟩ I didn't *sell* any royalties, but only *deposited* them temporarily and took stock as security, the royalties to be returned to me at a certain time if certain conditions failed of effect. I haven't a doubt that I understood the thing at the time; and I probably continued to understand it for nearly a week. But after that, the trade took the form of a *sale* in my mind; and this impression was so solidified that I wouldn't have hesitated to sell my stock out and out; and if I had done that, and spent the result, what a fix I would be in now! Everybody would regard me as a deliberate swindler.

It's a valuable lesson—for to-day. To-morrow it will be gone from me and I'll have to learn it over again. But *to-day* is all right. I shall withhold my signature from the Contract proposed to me by the Century Co for the 12 articles.[1] They have put in one or two new conditions which are better avoided, I guess.

That "boil" turned out to be a carbuncle. I could have done without it, for I do not care for jewelry. It has furnished me a week of admirable pain. We lanced it yesterday, and seemed to get no result; but it began to flow a little last night, and to-day it is attending to business pretty satisfactorily. I have discovered and squelched three others in their infancy and am discouraging still another. I've got one on the back of my right hand which has crippled it for a week, but it came to a head yesterday.

Meantime, I have lost all this time. I cannot expect to get out of bed for 3 or 4 days yet. Therefore, my project of preparing and familiarizing myself with *three* readings, is knocked in the head. To do that with *one* reading is the most that I can do. Also—therefore, I must not think of lecturing all the way across to the Pacific; I must go at one bound, to the Pacific, read in 6 northern towns there, stay clear away from Frisco, and sail from Vancouver Aug. 16.

Everything is at a standstill. Pond is sick abed, I am sick abed, we are determining nothing, accomplishing nothing, and the devil is on deck and having everything his own way.

Land, don't go to Chicago this weather! Go to Manhattan Beach—go to Fairhaven—those are rational places.

Thank you ever so much for your thinking of me and my affairs, and your generosities toward me. I hope we can get to Fairhaven, but I suppose the devil will bar *that,* too.

Mrs. Clemens and Susy send their love to Mrs. Duff (and so do I), and their cordial greetings to you.

Yrs sincerely

SL Clemens

[1] See letter 84; Clemens also refused an offer from Walker of the *Cosmopolitan* of $10,000 for twelve articles on Australia.

82. CLEMENS TO ROGERS

Elmira
11 June 1895

Dear Mr. Rogers:

Bliss is plucking up quite a spirit. He offers a guaranty of $10,000 on a round-the-world book. It makes me hesitate. I can write the *very book* for the subscription trade, and do it without difficulty; but those 12 articles for the Century at $12,000 would be *horribly* difficult. It may be that the Harpers will object; but if they don't, I can⟨t⟩ write a book that Bliss can sell 60,000 copies of in 6 months and pay me $30,000—or, as he suggests, a possible $40,000.

I'm going to write the *book,* anyway; then if I want to sell some of it to a magazine, very well; but I am not going to make any previous contract, with any magazine.

Have the Harpers sent that contract to you, yet, for signature?

I am progressing. There is more Clemens than carbuncle, now. This is a considerable improvement. It puts the balance of importance where it properly belongs. I shall be up and around in a week or ten days, I reckon.

Will you tell Mrs. Duff, with my love, that the coat came—and many thanks to her.

I'm *away* behindhand, of course. I've got to work like a slave if I leave here for Cleveland or Duluth July 7—and that seems to be the program.

Yours sincerely

S.L. Clemens

P.S. First piece on my program is *"My First Theft."* [1] Can you send me the Fairhaven speech?

¹ Clemens had told his "Stolen Watermelon" story at the dedication of the
Fairhaven town hall on 22 February 1894. The story was one of Rogers's
favorites, and Clemens eventually presented a copy of his speech to the Millicent
Library in Fairhaven.

83. Clemens to Rogers

Elmira
15 June 1895
Saturday

Dear Mr. Rogers:

Since writing a P.S. to Miss Harrison a minute ago, your note
has come and I am very glad you are back. Also, this mail has just
brought a notification from Pond that he has got my first reading
postponed a week; therefore we shan't have to leave for Cleveland
till Monday July 15. This ought to give me a chance to run down
and see you and the Harpers a moment, about the 10th or 12th, or
along there. I do hope so, anyway.

I have a good reason for inclining to Bliss this time: I can write a
subscription book of travels without any effort, but to write travels
for *serial* publication is hideous hard work. I am not committed to
any magazine yet—and I believe it will be wisest to remain unfettered.

The Century people actually proposed that I *sign a contract to be
funny* in those 12 articles. That was pure insanity. Why, it makes
me shudder every time I think of those articles. I don't think I
could ever write one of them without being under the solemnising
blight of that disgusting recollection.

The mail is leaving. Good-bye.

Yrs Sincerely
SL Clemens

P.S. Mrs. C. says I *am* committed for the 12 articles. Upon
examining the documents, she seems to be right. Dam——nation!

P.S.—*4.30 p.m.* Miss Harrison's telegram with Dr. Rice's message just received per telephone. Good! If they don't send for me again, you'll come up here, *won't* you?—and you'll telegraph, so you can be met at the station.

The wagon is waiting for this. *So-*long!—(which means Au revoir) if you don't know.

84. CLEMENS TO ROGERS

Elmira
19 June 1895

Dear Mr. Rogers:

Will you please keep this copy [1] for me—otherwise I shall say, some day, that I never wrote and don't remember anything about it. My memory is pretty useless.

I never *could* write those mag. articles to my satisfaction, for I would always be trying to write them according to Mr. Scott's requirement—whereas I have never written with chains on, in my life, and wouldn't know how to manage it. Madame and I are fully expecting to have a Sunday at Fairhaven.

Love to all of you,

SLC.

In a hurry—mail waiting.

[1] This note is written on a copy of a letter Clemens sent to Frank Hall Scott, president of the Century Publishing Company, on 18 June 1895. It says in part:

To be virile and fresh, the articles would have to be written as three-fourths of the Innocents Abroad was written—*intransitu.* To do that, and at the same time run the lecture-business and the social business, would make a botch of all three. For an old man to write a young book under exhausting pressure of other work and in trying climates—well, it could not be done.

And so, to save the making a bad mistake for both of us, let us stop now (before) in time and give it all up. In the beginning I was charmed with the unhampered, uncharted $10,000 offer which was made me last March, but if the sum were doubled it could not tempt me, now that I have done my belated thinking.

85. Clemens to Rogers

Elmira
22 June 1895

Dear Mr. Rogers:

I have made some notes, which I enclose. I wish I could come down and talk with you and Colby and the Harpers, but I can't. I shan't be able to put my clothes on till—I don't know when. Carbuncles are extravagantly slow.

My main objection is the absence of a time-limit. At least that is the mainest. I don't mind it half nor a tenth as much in this case as in Bliss's, and yet I do mind it. I think Harper's contracts are usually for 5 years. I think the Boston houses make it less.

I hope Colby can get the contract sufficiently amended without my presence, and that he will try to do it, for time is flying.[1]

No, we don't want the *money*. We only wanted to know the amount in your hands, so that in case we left an insufficiency in Elmira for Jean and Susy's needs we could supply them from your end of the line if there was anything there to be levied on.

We dined lately in Paris with the greatest of the French ⟨opti⟩ oculists. He had been an enemy to eye-cutting, but is whacking away at people's eyes now, with confidence and enthusiasm.[2] I guess you are all right. I believe so, "solid."

Mr. Lawson called?[3] I do not call him to mind.

I've got my photograph for Mr. Broughton, and I'm going to get it to him yet; but I procrastinate right along, while I am in bed.

The carbuncle is gone, and there is a raw hole in my leg where it was. It will heal by and by, I reckon.

I would like Miss May to reconsider that. If you tell her ⟨the⟩ you and the rest of the family are going, she will change her mind.

With the best regards of all of us to all of you,

Sincerely yours

SL Clemens

[1] Colby had been negotiating with Harper & Brothers for many weeks. On 20 May 1895 he had written Rogers (CWB): "I have been expecting to hear from you regarding the purchase of the plates of Mr. Clemens' books. I understand that we had agreed upon the price, and that you were only waiting for a word from Mr. Clemens approving the purchase." On 23 May Harper & Brothers replied (CWB) to Clemens's proposal that he give Harper & Brothers rights to exclusive publication in this country of all of his books then under his control or which would thereafter come under his control. Harper & Brothers suggested that they publish "a new, uniform library edition of those books, from new plates" and pay Clemens a royalty of 15 per cent on the retail price of the first 5,000 copies sold and 20 per cent on the retail price of all copies sold beyond that number, if Harper & Brothers supplied the plates. They offered to pay 20 per cent and 25 per cent if Clemens supplied the plates (presumably those owned by the American Publishing Company). Carbuncles and other distractions, however, seem to have prompted Clemens to leave these details in Rogers's hands. When the contract of 23 May 1895 (see Appendix A) was delivered on 26 July 1895, it bore his signature, as attorney for Clemens.

[2] Rogers was to have an eye operation; see letter 89.

[3] Thomas W. Lawson was a Boston broker who promoted stock for the Standard Oil Company, but who later attacked that company in *Frenzied Finance* (1905).

86. CLEMENS TO ROGERS

Elmira

[? 22] June 1895

Dear Mr. Rogers:

Mr. Colby thinks that if you *could* have the interview this afternoon it would be a very great help.

And he wanted me to suggest to you my notion as to royalty and profits.

I think a royalty better and surer and simpler than for Mrs. Clemens to take the profits and pay the publishers a royalty.

I think that a royalty to Mrs. Clemens of 20 per cent would be a liberal one—and 15 per cent a good one. (The customary royalty in the trade—to authors of mere ordinary reputation—is 10 per cent.)

20 per cent has been paid to authors of wide reputation, but I have heard of no instance of a higher one being paid.

Sincerely Yours

SLC.

87. CLEMENS TO ROGERS

Elmira
25–26 June 1895

Dear Mr. Rogers:

Good—I hope Mayo can give me a ⟨flying⟩ call.

I am having a good enough time, all things considered. No pain, but the doctor still comes daily and the bandaging goes on. It will be all of a week yet, before I can put my clothes on.

I do hope I can get to New York within ten days, and that I can manage to finish up the Harper contract suitably, and have a day or two at Fairhaven; and take Mrs. Clemens along.

[half a page torn off]

⟨it when we went to the Murray Hill.⟩

By gracious, it looks as if I've got to go on the platform only half prepared!

I am in a good deal of a fidget to see the new house. I know it is lovely; it was already that, when it was only half done.[1]

We-all join in warmest regards to you-all and I abide

Yours Sincerely

SL Clemens

P.S.

Elmira, June 25.[2]

Dear Mr. Rogers:

A Buffalo mortgage belonging to Mrs. Clemens may possibly be paid off in July—*pretty doubtful*—but if this money should come in (it is about $26,000), maybe you could point out a good investment for it. And so—by your leave—I will tell her brother Charles J. Langdon to call on you one of these days and see if you can advise him, if it won't inconvenience you. This is an estate matter, and he has charge of the estate matters.

I believe I have got *one* reading about ready for the platform. I've got to leave the others till I get aboard ship.

> Yrs sincerely
>
> SLC

> June 26/95.

P.S. This paper has just been served on me. Is it necessary that I obey it and appear in court in New York July 5? [3]

The doctor has just gone from here; he says I'll be able to travel by that date.

> SLC

[1] The Rogers house was begun in March 1894, and Clemens had visited the unfinished building late in July of that year. The house at Fairhaven became, for Rogers and for Clemens, a favorite retreat from business and care. Its eighty-five rooms and extensive grounds (near old Fort Phoenix on the shore of Buzzards Bay) provided an ample summer playground for all the Broughtons, Coes, Benjamins, and Rogerses. The house was bequeathed to Harry when Rogers died in 1909.

[2] The postscripts were added on separate sheets and in pencil.

[3] Clemens had been subpoenaed by Thomas Russell & Son, printers and bookbinders, a creditor of Charles L. Webster & Company. Another subpoena (now in CWB) ordered Mrs. Clemens to appear on 19 July 1895 before the Honorable M. L. Stover, one of the justices on the Supreme Court of New York. Clemens's eagerness to settle the matter resulted in an arrangement which was worked out before the case was taken to court.

88. CLEMENS TO ROGERS

> Elmira
> 26 June 1895

Dear Mr. Rogers:

How exasperating it is! The Devil and Colby would necessarily choose this time for junketing when I am tied by the hind leg and can't go and 'tend to my matters myself. Why good Lord, I *must* make a book-contract with somebody before I leave this country;

can't have the books standing still any longer. Dang it, I'm getting desperate. This carbuncle is not going to allow me to stand on my feet for two or three weeks yet. It is slower than chilled molasses. I'll go to Cleveland on a stretcher, sure.

Don't you think *you* can arrange a meeting with J. Henry Harper and amend and sign the contract? And *won't* you, please?

It should not be difficult. In the present draft he has left himself a limit—he can terminate the contract in 10 years. All right, let me have the *same* limit; let both sides have the privilege of quitting in 10 years from date.

Isn't that reasonable? and aren't our other suggested modifications (heretofore sent you), fair and reasonable?

Doctor has come. Don't you think you can do that for

Yours sincerely

SL Clemens

89. Olivia Clemens to Rogers

Elmira

27 June 1895

Dear Mr Rogers:

I have been greatly distressed today by the paper that was served on Mr Clemens, and I feel that in some way these Webster & Co. matters must be arranged.

You have so stood our friend in all these troubles that I naturally turn to you.

Mr Clemens does not know of this writing although I shall tell him before I send it.

I have, as I think Mr Clemens wrote you the other day, about thirty thousand dollars that will fall in to be invested in July. By using that money to pay the Webster & Co. debts could we not get a settlement with them?

I know that Mr Clemens and my brother will feel that it ought not to be used in that way—but if it could make us at ease on the Webster matters, during our trip, I should feel that it could not be better employed.

My brother would not approve of this plan I know because he has felt very sorry to have my income so cramped as it has been by the machine and Webster & Co. But I believe that it would repay us because of the greater peace of mind that it would give us.

Would it trouble you to send me just a line telling me whether you think it would be a good plan? I am not going to consult my brother until I hear from you.

Mr Clemens is steadily gaining but he is still far from well, and sometimes he looks so white that I feel troubled about him. I doubt very much whether he will be able to get to New York on the 5th but he may be. The doctor said this morning that he might possibly be well enough to go in ten days, but the 5th is only eight days.

I was very glad to learn by your letter that the operation on your eye was proving satisfactory.

Please give my love to Mrs Duff and believe me

Sincerely yours

Olivia L. Clemens

90. CLEMENS TO ROGERS

Elmira
29 June 1895

Dear Mr. Rogers:

No, indeedy, it won't answer. It would [be] a bad advertisement for my lecture-trip to have all the papers here and in Australia saying I have dodged the courts and fled the country. I mustn't do it. If Colby had told me of this danger I wouldn't have remained in this State.

Now my project is this. Send down my doctor's certificate to-night and get the court-proceedings postponed till the 8th of July.

Then go to New York the 4th and meet the creditors the 5th or 6th and propose a composition in the form of an addition of 10 per cent to what the Webster assets produces.

I hope you will approve this, and that Colby to issue an immediate call for that assembly of the creditors (if he ever *can* be got to stir his stumps.)

⟨Good by⟩

You are just as dear and good as you can be, and the madam and I are building high and getting to Fairhaven.

Charley Langdon is waiting to carry this down the hill.

Sincerely Yours

SL Clemens

91. Clemens to Rogers

Elmira
30 June 1895

Sunday

Dear Mr. Rogers:

In case Mr. Langdon should be prevented from going down, Mrs. Clemens and I desire this, to-wit: That Mr. Colby call a meeting of the creditors for just as early a day as possible; but *before the 8th;*

2. That he then talk with Russell and ask him if he will agree to the compromise suggested (10 per cent additional to Webster assets);

3. If he refuses, ask him on what terms *he* individually will release me. Get his terms and ask a few days to consider them in; then compromise with the other creditors if possible, meantime. And finally silence Russell, even if we have to pay his *entire* bill.

After which I will try to get out of the reach of anybody else's supplementary proceedings.

The fact is, the assignee *can't* assume the above suggested job, I imagine, but maybe there is somebody else that can.

Mrs. C. is dead set against having me keel-hauled and fire-assayed in that court for the benefit of the newspapers; though I myself do not much dread it—hardly at all, in fact.

I find I mixed the dates up pretty well yesterday. Mrs. Clemens's project was, that we should leave New York for Fairhaven next Friday and be back there for the proposed judicial dissection the following Monday, but I think I mixed that, and got it wrong.

However, the way this carbuncle is acting, I suppose I really *couldn't* travel as early as 4 or 5 days hence.

Yrs sincerely

SL Clemens

P.S. Look here, don't you think you'd better let somebody else run the Standard Oil a week or two till you've finished up these matters of mine? Why *I* can keep you busy, you don't need any outside industries.

92. OLIVIA CLEMENS TO ROGERS

Elmira
1 July 1895

My dear Mr Rogers:

I feel as if you would get tired of the Elmira post mark.

I come however with an other proposition—in case Mr Clemens is not able to go to Fairhaven the last of this week could not you and Mrs Duff and Dr Rice come here? [1]

My brother and his wife will be most happy to have you and Mrs Duff their guests for the time that you could remain here. My sister wants Dr Rice to be her guest and will write him. She would ask you all only their little hill top house is so small that we fill it full. My brother will send you and Mrs Duff up here every morning to spend the day with us and you will be taken back to spend the night with them.

We should all be so happy to see you and Mr Clemens feels so anxious to have a talk with you before he goes that I hope you can come.

By Wednesday the doctor will be able to say whether Mr Clemens can travel and we will send you a telegram on that day giving you his decision—If we cannot go to you I hope you can come to us.

Believe me

Very Sincerely yours

Olivia L. Clemens

[1] Mrs. Clemens wrote the following note to Rogers's daughter (Salm):
My dear Mrs Duff:
    If Mr Clemens does not get well enough to go to you the latter part of this week, we want you to come here with your father and Dr Rice. Will you? I am sure we could make you happy for a time here and it would make us so happy to see you.
    We want very much to see you and to see you in your Fairhaven home but I fear it must be put off until our return. So do urge your father and Dr Rice to bring you here.
    We have no excitements, we live most quietly and have nothing to offer you but our own society but we will all be as agreeable as we know how to be.
    Did you receive your mother's photograph in good order?
    Hoping to see you the latter part of this week believe me

affectionately yours
Olivia L. Clemens

93. CLEMENS TO ROGERS

Elmira
5 July 1895

Dear Mr. Rogers:

Mrs. Clemens was inclined to think, last night, when we went to bed, that we could have been on our way to Fairhaven if we had done my leg up in good compact shape and made a vigorous effort. Yes, very well; but if Fairhaven was *jail*, instead of a nest of friends and comfort and peace, she would have had a different opinion about it. However, it was rather the swan-song over a frustrated hope and desire than a serious conviction that it would be good for me to make an all-night journey to Albany; then to Boston; then to Cape Cod, and then not know *which* way to go to get to New Bedford. It is a dam shame and a sign of poor progress that at this late day the railroads *still* follow the old mouldy methods, instead of hanging a brass tag on a person and checking him through, same as they would any other trunk.

I've been on my back 40 days, now, and—sho! I could make the trip if the doctor believed in it, but he doesn't. Yet I ⟨will⟩ *would* make it if you couldn't come up here—that's dead sure.

I had come to a dead stand-still, and lost all interest in life and work and lecturing and everything else; but ⟨yesterday⟩ my brother-in-law's account of his visit with you, and Colby's subsequent letter confirming all he said, made things look plenty well enough, and so I will either get at my lectures again this morning or write an article which the Century wants in a desperate hurry.

It is mighty good and lovely of you to be doing all this work and taking all this trouble for me, but I can tell you *one* thing—God shall reward you for it. I am going to look after that detail *personally*.

Now you are to come up here as soon as you find you can, you know. I could explain to you which railroad to take and just how to come, but you would not have any confidence in it.

With love to all of you,

SLC

94. Clemens to Rogers

Elmira
6 July 1895

Dear Mr. Rogers:

It is of course under bad and uncomfortable conditions that I shall travel Monday, and I'm pretty sure the doctor will not much like it; but our time is so short that I couldn't possibly manage a *further* adjournment; therefore Mrs. C. and I are going down on the D L & W.[1] Monday, leaving here at noon and arriving at Everett House 7.30; then return here ⟨per night train the next night⟩ next day at 1 p.m. This will give me 3 or 4 days to rest-up in, before leaving for Cleveland—*and I shall need* as many. I will read, here, to the Reformatory convicts Wed and Thurs. nights.

Yrs sincerely

SLC [2]

[1] The Delaware, Lackawanna, and Western Railroad.
[2] This letter is written on the back of a note to Rogers, which was written by Clemens and signed by Mrs. Clemens:

H. H. Rogers, Esq

Dear Sir: If you can buy from the Charles L. Webster & Co estate the plates of the Mark Twain books for $100, please do so and charge to my account.

Olivia L. Clemens

95. CLEMENS TO ROGERS

Elmira
8 July 1895

Quarry Farm

Dear Mr. Rogers:

A telephone message from town has stopped me just as I was about to put on my clothes for the first time in 44 days. Dr. Wales [1] had just gone, not pleased about the New York journey, and outspokenly discontented because a professional nurse (mighty capable man), was going with me instead of Mrs. Clemens. After all the trouble the tribe of us had been at, to persuade her to remain here! She is not well, and I could *not* endure the idea of her making that big journey—no good preparation for the long trip Pacific-ward. My uneasiness about her would have made the journey all the harder for me.

Of course I shall obey all orders from New York; but I was all keyed up and ready for the examination; and now in a day or two

I'll have to do all that keying-up *over* again, I judge. All right, I'll manage it.

But I am sure I could have gone, very well. I had a stateroom engaged. I would have undressed and lain down at once. I would have gone to bed the moment I reached the Everett. I would have saved myself in every possible way, and I should have fetched up here again all right. I swear I think I am as able to go to-day as I shall be 5 days hence. Two or three weeks ago the raw sore was the size of your watch-crystal; a ⟨quarter of a⟩ trade dollar would just cover it now. It does not reduce its dimensions *fast,* but its work is steady.

I shan't be able to stand on a platform before we start west. I shan't get a single chance to practice my reading; but will have to appear in Cleveland without that essential preparation. Nothing in this world can save it from being a shabby poor disgusting performance.

I've got to *stand;* I can't *sit* and talk to a house—and how in the nation am I going to do it? Land of Goshen, it's *this night week!* Pray for me.

Doctor Rogers—*look* you! I can't *stand* it to have that N. Y. examination postponed beyond Friday!

Sincerely Yours

SL Clemens

[1] Theron Augustus Wales, M.D., practiced in Elmira until his death in 1914.

96. CLEMENS TO ROGERS

Elmira
14 July 1895

Dear Mr. Rogers:

You will feel a good deal like blowing me up, I suspect,—*I've thrown up the Russell sponge.*

I found Mrs. Clemens in the deeps of despair and misery when I arrived, because my name had gotten into the papers in connection with the examination,[1] and because I was not able to say Wilder[2] would not try to attach the gate-money in Cleveland—which would start another newspaper-item afloat, whether he succeeded or failed. She was ill, over the situation, and I at once administered the only medicine that could stop her from getting worse. I said we would immediately compromise with Russell or pay him in full. Maybe *I* might be able to endure further annoyance, but she has reached her limit and is entitled to a release. So I have formally instructed Sterne & Rushmore to settle or pay in full, and draw on Mr. Langdon for the money. There is probably not enough in your hands for the purpose; so I beg you to invest what you can of it when you get a chance, ⟨leav⟩—all but about $1500, which will be needed by ⟨the⟩ Susy and Jean, for board, etc.

I saw Rushmore on the train yesterday afternoon and told him I didn't want any annoyance at Cleveland; ⟨that⟩ (it would be difficult enough for me to pull an untried lecture through in *any* case, without any added clogs and distractions;) but he said I could rest easy; said ⟨I⟩ he was sure Wilder was now satisfied that I had no concealed property and would leave me alone in Cleveland.

And yet, after all, he was not *certain*. However, that is neither here nor there. Wilder *can* play that card, and I will take no risks with *that* man. Mr. Rushmore thinks he knows Wilder. It is a superstition. Cleveland is a good card, and Wilder is not a sentimentalist. I wish I had listened to Stanchfield[3] here when he wanted to vacate the order of the Court. It would have taken some of the value out of the Cleveland card and put us in a better position to negotiate with Wilder. Stanchfield says my right to vacate the order was absolutely clear; that they hadn't the shadow of authority to summon me to New York. He says the statute is crystal-clear.

As the matter stands now, settlement with Wilder means payment in full, I judge. He *did* offer, before I went to New York, to settle for 75 per cent (which meant 50, I guess) but that's gone by.

If he will take less, it will not be through negociations conducted by Colby or the firm, *that's* sure. He and they are bitter enemies. I hope they will select somebody else, with you to do the selecting or help them do it. But you mustn't touch it if you would rather not, for it troubles me to put ⟨so much⟩ so many loads on your generous shoulders; and it troubles Mrs. Clemens, too. She thinks I ride you too hard, when you are so patient and uncomplaining. She is full of gratitude to you, and most certainly I am, also.

Oh, but wasn't it a comical defeat—Randall's Island! [4] Delivering a grown-folks' lecture to a sucking-bottle nursery! No, only *trying*—I didn't do it—and couldn't. No man could have done it.

However, I am very glad I went, for the plan of the lecture was bad—yes, and trivial; silly, in fact, and I've thrown it overboard, and invented a totally different plan, and I think a pretty good one. I am going to try it on the Reformatory convicts to-night. I shall feel freer—in fact unhampered—because I shan't memorize what I call the *lecture* part, but deliver it extempore. I know the *substance* of what I wish to say, and will ⟨put⟩ choose the wording for it as I go along. After Cleveland I will write and tell you how I'm getting along. But I shall be half way to the Pacific before the thing takes final shape. There's *one* good thing—the old plan would fit only one lecture—the new one will fit any number—if it succeeds.

Mrs. Clemens and ⟨S⟩ the children send their warmest regards to you and their best love to Mrs. Duff. I send my love to all three.

Yours sincerely

SL Clemens

[1] Clemens had gone to New York where on 11 and 12 July the grievance of Thomas Russell & Son was brought before the court. On 12 July 1895 the New York *Times* reported:

The examination of Mark Twain yesterday was upon a judgment against him and Frederick J. Hall . . . that Thomas Russell & Sons, printers, of 34 New Chambers Street, obtained in the sum of $5046.83. Upon the return of the execution unsatisfied, Justice Patterson issued an order for the examination of Messrs. Clemens and Hall. . . .

Henry H. Rogers, a Director in the Standard Oil Company, the other member of the firm, was present yesterday, waiting to be examined after the judgment creditors finished with Mr. Clemens. . . .

Mr. Colby said that Mr. Clemens has done all in his power to aid him in paying the firm's creditors, and to dispose of the assets, which consisted of books that accumulated in the nine years that the firm was in business.

The assignee has paid dividends amounting to 20 per cent. of the claims proved against the firm.

With the exception of Russell & Sons, the creditors of the firm have taken no action against Mr. Clemens, but have been satisfied with Mr. Colby's efforts to realize and pay them as much as possible, knowing that Mr. Clemens will do what he can to pay them in full.

At the time of the failure, Mr. Clemens became ill through worrying over his business affairs, and has not yet fully regained his health. He was attended yesterday by a nurse, who came from Elmira to care for him until he is ready to return. . . .

[2] William Wilder was attorney for Russell & Son.

[3] John Stanchfield, an Elmira lawyer and an old friend.

[4] On 12 July 1895 Clemens tried out his new lecture on 700 boys in the Randall's Island House of Refuge. Although the New York *Sun* applauded the program, Clemens felt that it had been over the boys' heads (*MTLC*, p. 244).

96a.[1] ROGERS TO CLEMENS

New York
16 July 1895

My dear Clemens:

I telegraphed Mrs. Clemens yesterday as follows:—"I shall do everything to carry out your wishes even though it conflicts with my judgment. In order to make progress, I have talked with your brother on the telephone to-day and he is coming here on Wednesday to help us in the matter. Everybody is friendly. I will send newspaper clippings with letter to Sault Ste. Marie. Kindest wishes all around." I now beg to confirm the same.

When I received your letter yesterday morning I arranged for an interview with Colby and discussed the matter of treating with Russell. It seems to me your judgment in regard to bringing Wilder and Rushmore and Colby together is right, and I told Colby as much. On reflection I concluded that Mr. Langdon was the very best person to treat with Russell and we called him up on the telephone. After explaining the matter to him he consented to come here and I expect to see him to-morrow morning at 10:30. As soon as anything definite is reached, I will telegraph you as I have before me your route to the Pacific Coast. Don't worry about troubling me. You are in such a state of mind that you seem to worry about everything. It was not a comical defeat at Randall's Island. It may have been a mistake to go up there to talk to a lot of hoodlums, nine-tenths of whom perhaps have never seen the inside of a book, but Miss Harrison says, that anybody of sense would have appreciated and enjoyed it. Let us kick over the whole of this miserable Russell business and we will attend to that here. In the meantime, let me say that everybody is in sympathy with you and feels most kindly. Why, Payne of the bank, even criticises Russell's conduct as absolutely outrageous and poor old Whitford melted to tears over your troubles. They may have been of the crocodile kind, but in my judgment, came from a kindly feeling. The newspapers are agreeable and I send you two or three little clippings. Your examination is like one of New York's nine days' wonders, and will be forgotten within the prescribed time. Benjamin tells me that Russell bragged of having made out of the C. L. Webster & Co. all the money he had in the world. That he made $35,000 in one year out of the concern, and Benjamin thinks if we were to make the strongest kind of a fight we could cut Russell's bill in two, in view of the fact that he charged in it a lot of leather for bindings which was never used.

I wonder if I could make you laugh. I guess I will try it, by sending you a letter of Joe Howard's to the Boston Globe.[2] I don't often get a newspaper notice and do not consider this as an honest tribute to my many virtues and qualifications, because old Joe is sure to come around later. In fact I may say that he has blown his whistle to let me know that he is moving toward me. I know to a degree, what it is to be as sensitive as you are and I am heartily sorry for Mrs. Clemens, but I hope that distance will remove all this unpleasantness.

Mrs. Duff joins me in most kindly messages to Mrs. Clemens, Miss Clara and your good self.

Yours sincerely,

HH Rogers

P.S. Just as a little comforting P.S. let me say I received a letter from Harper yesterday, enclosing a check for $6,982.[3] which I have safely stowed away, and added to the amount I have in my hands $3,728.22 ($10,710.22) makes quite a comfortable nest egg.

P.S. Excuse this disjointed letter. Since dictating the above I have appealed to Benjamin as to the best person to treat with Russell. He recommends a man by the name of Williams who was formerly with Webster & Co. but now with Benjamin. I have requested Williams to come here to-morrow morning to meet with Mr. Langdon, Mr. Colby and myself.

[1] This letter and letters 99a, 100a, and 151a became available for this collection only after the volume was partly set in type, and so they have been placed in the sequence without renumbering subsequent letters.

[2] Joseph Howard, Jr., (1833–1908) was a newspaper editor, correspondent, and writer for numerous American papers. Over the signature "Howard" he contributed a weekly column to the Boston *Sunday Globe,* and on 14 July he offered a meandering report of meeting celebrities at Manhattan Beach, Long Island. "One of the most interesting, one of the most instructive personalities there was Henry H. Rogers of the Standard oil association. He is a product of New England, with a face and head classic in their severe, yet simple, beauty, with a record for industry intelligently directed, with a reputation for veracity which makes his word as good as his bond, with a character childlike in its ingenuousness, a business capacity recognized in the selectest circles of financial endeavor, with a fortune placed far, far along the line of millions, beyond the possibility of the conception of a majority of us, with a charming home, with a New England clientele ever regarding him with affectionate pride . . ."

[3] On 12 July 1895 Harper & Brothers had sent this check as the balance due Clemens on the sum which *Harper's Magazine* had contracted to pay for the serial rights to "Tom Sawyer, Detective" and "Joan of Arc." The Harpers paid a total of $9,382 for "Joan" and $2,600 for "Tom Sawyer, Detective" (H. M. Alden to HHR, CWB).

97. CLEMENS TO ROGERS

Cleveland
16 July 1895
(Forenoon.)

Dear Mr. Rogers:

We both thank you ever so much for your telegram, received yesterday afternoon, and its contents. So far, we have not been molested by the enemy. Pond collected the money in advance from the parties to whom he had sold the show for $300. I didn't allow him to give any of it to Mrs. Clemens. I don't want her in it any more. I gave him a receipt for $200 myself—yesterday morning approaching Cleveland.

Had a roaring success at the Elmira reformatory Sunday night. But here, last night, I suffered another Randall's Island defeat— and by George, for the same cause—children. There were a couple of hundred little boys behind me on the stage, on a lofty tier of benches which made them the most conspicuous object in the house. And there was nobody to watch them or keep them quiet. Why, with their scufflings and horse-play and noise, it was just a menagerie. Besides, a concert of amateurs had been smuggled into the program (to *precede* me,) and their families and friends (say ten per cent of the audience) kept encoring them and they always responded. So it was 20 minutes to 9 before I got ⟨into⟩ on the platform in front of those 2,600 people who had paid a dollar apiece for a chance to go to hell in this fashion.

I got *started* magnificently, but inside of half an hour the scuffling boys had the audience's maddened attention and I saw it was a gone case; so I skipped a third of my program and quit. The newspapers are kind, but between you and me it was a defeat. There ain't going to be any more concerts at *my* lectures. I care nothing for this defeat, because it was not my fault. My first half hour showed that I had the house, and I could have *kept* it if I hadn't been so handicapped.

Yours sincerely

SL Clemens

P.S. I find that there were *five* hundred boys behind me, two-thirds as many as Randall's Island, and that they flowed past my back in clattering shoals, some leaving the house, others returning for some more skylarking!

98. Clemens to Rogers

Mackinac, Michigan
20–22 July 1895

Dear Mr. Rogers:

Your telegram saying the suit had been silenced was a great and solid relief to us, and at once gave us peace of mind and enabled me to turn my whole attention to my infamous readings. And your letter completed our comfort. At Sault Ste. Marie and here I ⟨gave⟩ satisfied the Ponds and Mrs. Clemens and Clara, and they say I satisfied my houses. As to satisfying myself, that is quite another matter. It will be some time before I reach that point—but I shall reach it. I have already reached it in "The Watermelon," "A Midnight Adventure," "Tom Sawyer's Crusade" and "Grandfather's Old Ram." I have *not* reached it in "The Jumping Frog" and "The Bluejays." I foresee that I am going to discard these last two. Then the thing will go.

It was lovely in you to take hold of that Russell settlement and push it through. It is incredible, the worry and anger that that Russell business has cost me since the day my idiot lawyers allowed me to be dragged to New York by a court which had no more authority over me than the Mikado of Japan. There was no "technicality" in the matter, and no "quibble." My personal liberty was invaded without due process of law—wholly without right or reason—and those lawyers did not know it.

Now that I've been through the fire once, I'm not willingly going through any more. I am going to ⟨wait in the old world till⟩ hope that presently the creditors will agree upon ⟨the⟩ terms which they are willing to allow me. If the terms are not unreasonable, I will accept them and work them out; but I'm not ⟨going⟩ anxious to face the chances again under an uncertainty. I can make a lecture-season in the U. S. pay me $25,000 or $30,000; and I am willing to give one-third of the profit of such a season to the creditors if they will let me off with that; yes, I would give a *larger* share than that. Don't you think I am right? I can support myself in the old world and be at peace, while waiting for a decision.

We all greet you-all warmly and gratefully.

Sincerely Yours

SL Clemens

Monday.[1]

P.S. Had a satisfactory time at Petoskey. Crammed the house and turned away a crowd. We had $548 in the house, which was $300 more than it had ever had in it before. I believe I don't care to have a talk go off better than that one did.

Shall get to Duluth just in time to go on the platform. I shall dress before leaving the boat, then go straight to the train after the lecture.

---

[1] The remainder of the letter, written on 22 July, is on stationery with the letterhead "NORTHERN STEAMSHIP CO./ GREAT NORTHERN RY LINE./ S. S. NORTH WEST." It is in the Salm Collection.

99. CLEMENS TO ROGERS

Minneapolis
24 July 1895

Dear Mr. Rogers:

I have Mr. Colby's letter in which he suggests that a settlement with the creditors be arranged as soon as possible—and I heartily agree with that idea, (Privately, he thinks my lack of fighting-stuff makes this course necessary). I like the serenity and complacency of this idiot and his associate-idiot Rushmore. What cheap, cheap material one can make a New York lawyer of. This jack-rabbit has made blunder after blunder, and one worthless prophecy after another, until he got me into a scrape which his youth and obscurity disenable him to appreciate; then he blandly intimates that ⟨I⟩ settlement is the correct course for a client who lacks nerve. I wish I could say to him, "When I find myself marching to battle under the leadership of a corporal who doesn't know anything except how to ⟨be⟩ get licked by the enemy three times a day, and who pipes up complacently after every flogging and says 'DON'T WORRY—*we'll take care of you!*' I have but one desire, one longing, one lust: and that is, to get out of that fight just as soon as possible."

I've told him how he can get the $15,000 he thinks he can settle for. He will tell you.

I am getting into good platform condition at last. It went well, went to *suit* me, here last night.

Yrs sincerely

SLC

P.S. Pond swears he sent the Cleveland papers to you. He promises to cut out the things hereafter and enclose them in envelops. If he fails of his promise, I'll do it myself.

P.S. No, I'll enclose the letter; and if you approve, you can send it to Colby.

99a. Rogers to Clemens

New York

25 July 1895

My dear Mr. Clemens:

Five minutes ago I was saying to Miss Harrison that I thought it time for me to hear from Clemens. Immediately the boy entered and brought me your letter from Mackinac. You may be sure that I was delighted to think, from the reading of your communication, that you were getting yourself into shape and consequently doing creditable work.

I note what you say about the invasion of your personal liberty and I know you are right, and think I knew it all along. At least, I tried to impress on those lawyers that you could easily be spared the annoyance to which you were subjected. However, it is a question of the past and we must let it bury itself and look only to the future.

I have had some pleasant correspondence with Gen. Langdon in reference to the compromise of the creditors and perhaps that will be brought about in the near future. I am interested in all your movements and particularly interested in your lectures. I have heard the "Watermelon" story. Miss Harrison has heard the "Midnight Adventure." "Tom Sawyer's Crusade" also, but "Grandfather's Old Ram" I always hankered for. I suppose I have read it—I don't know, but surely more times than you have, and I am rejoiced that your audiences appreciate it. The "Jumping Frog" and the "Blue Jays" always amused me, but I like to read them in perfect quiet and simply chuckle over them.

I haven't much of interest to communicate. Mrs. Duff and I went to Fairhaven last Saturday and took along Miss Shelley, Clinton Gilbert and a young fellow named Harry Santana who was a cousin of Mrs. Duff's husband. He has been raised in South America and is slower than cold molasses. I never saw a man who could at all compare with him in moderation. We had a delightful time however, and returned to New York on Monday. Mrs. Benjamin and Will arrived at Southampton yesterday evening on the "St. Louis."

We are having beastly weather. Rain, fog, heat and humidity. I want this to reach you at Crookston and so will hurry it off by the afternoon mail.

Not a word from the Webster business and so I imagine things are very quiet. I have had to pay the lawyers $700 which we spoke about before you left.

Remember me most cordially to Mrs. Clemens and Clara, and with kindest messages for yourself, believe me,

Yours Sincerely,

HH Rogers

P.S. I overlooked your question in regard to giving a share of your platform proceeds to the creditors. I think we can compass it in a more direct manner and advise you to wait patiently for a time and see what General Langdon and I will accomplish.

100. CLEMENS TO ROGERS

Crookston, Minnesota
29 July 1895

Dear Mr. Rogers:

We got your good letter here, last night and it was very very welcome. I judged we'd have to pay that $700—whereas a brass farthing would have overpaid those people. They ought to have collected that money from Russell; by their ignorance and idiocy they played into his hands from the very day, months and months ago that he brought suit, plumb down to the hour that he got his money. They never made a prophecy that came through—and they are fuller of prophecies than old Isaiah; they never made a move that wasn't silly; they were mere children in Wilder's hands; he played with them; told them lie after lie, and made them believe every *one* of them. That pitiful Rushmore had no more dignity than to repeatedly insult Wilder—acted like a child. And as for B. D. W. W. T. C. O. Y. Colby—(Bainbridge Don't-worry-we'll-take-care-of-you Colby), he is a mere nine-days' miscarriage, just a pulpy foetus. I reckon he wants that $700 to buy a sugar-teat with. He told me that after that order of the court went to Elmira, Wilder's partner offered to compromise for 75 per cent (meaning 50, no doubt, for he knew the court's order was worthless, whereas my jackasses didn't), and then my jackasses allowed me to come to New York, which made a compromise at less than par wholly unnecessary, for it threw the game into Wilder's hands past hope. Lord! and see what a whaling compliment Stern & Rushmore have paid Wilder—made him promise he wouldn't champion any more of the Webster creditors! If I were Wilder I would paste that on my hat-front to show the world that there's *one* lawyer that

Stern & Rushmore are horribly afraid of. I wish to write Colby a letter when the right time comes.

If I had tried to fight under the instructions of such idiots as S. and R., Wilder would have dropped on me at sailing-hour Aug. 16 and got his money, sure, or I'd lose my ship and all my Australian swag; but when I return to America no creditor will have that chance to destroy me. They can obstruct me, perhaps, at every town on my route, but they can't destroy my tour. And I'll have a lawyer who knows something, then—not S. and R. or Alphabet Colby.

I have written Colby to compromise with the creditors at $15,000, but if he is in the way, bundle him *out* of the way; for whatever he touches he will botch. I stand ready to pay the creditors in full *when I can*—but I can't say when it will be.

I'm stealing a moment to scribble this line. I have to *steal* my odd moments, for I am at work *all* the time on my lectures, on board the trains and everywhere. I've got No. 1 where I am no longer afraid of it or in doubt about it; and now for the past few days I am at work on No. 2. I tried it in Winnipeg Saturday night and found it was 35 minutes too long; and so at the end of an hour and a half I offered to let the audience go; but they said "go on,"—so I did. To-day I have knocked out one long piece and put in a shorter one; and I hope the audience to-night will allow me to add the new piece to No. 1's program so that I can try it. But I won't without their consent, for a special train-load of them are coming 180 miles and I must not tire them. Thus far I have had more people in three opera houses than they've ever had in them before, winter or summer; and they swelter there with admirable patience; they all stay and see me through.

You *must* hire a private car some day and take a swing through this splendid country.

Love to you all. Mrs. Clemens has said to me in confidence several times that you are the dearest man in the world, and I keep her secret as well as I can.

Sincerely Yours

SL Clemens

I cannot tell you how much your telling us to disabuse our minds of the idea that you were being fatigued with our matters solaced us. The truth is, Mrs. Clemens was a good deal troubled, and I wasn't a great way behind her.

100a. ROGERS TO OLIVIA CLEMENS

New York
2 August 1895

My dear Mrs. Clemens:

Messrs. Harper and Brothers after having signed the contract sent me a letter which reads as follows:

"Our counsel Mr. George L. Rives, suggests that the words 'each of' might be inserted between the words 'each copy of' and 'such' in line 6 section 2 of the contract with Mrs. Olivia L. Clemens, making the clause to read as follows—'on their respective trade-list (retail) prices for each copy of each of such books by them sold etc.' Upon reflection we did not deem it necessary to make any change in the contract which had already been signed by you. It seemed to us and to Mr. Bainbridge Colby that the clause as it stands conveys our meaning as well as if expressed by the suggested change of words.

We would be obliged if you would kindly favor us with a line to the effect that your understanding of the clause is the same as ours."

My reply was that inasmuch as the original contract had your approval I did not feel warranted in permitting any insertions without consent from you. Therefore I ask your advice in the matter.[1] The following is the extract from the clause referred to in Messrs. Harper Brothers' letter.

"Harper and Brothers agree that they will publish a uniform edition of said works at their own expense, at such time and in such style as they deem best suited to their sale; and will pay to said Mrs. Olivia L. Clemens, or her representatives or assigns, fifteen (15) per cent. on their respective trade-list (retail) prices for each copy of each of such books by them sold up to five thousand (5000) copies and twenty (20) per cent on their trade-list (retail) prices for each copy of such books sold by them over and above five thousand (5000) copies. The trade-list (retail) price on which percentage shall be paid, shall be that of the cloth binding. And Harper and Brothers shall render always on application therefor, semi-annual statements of account, in the months of January and July and make settlements in cash four months after date of each statement. But for copies sold to canvassers or otherwise, for the purpose of introducing said books, at a discount greater than customarily allowed by them to the largest buyers in the regular trade in the United States, Harper & Brothers shall pay the fifteen or twenty per cent. only on the actual price received for each copy. Said Harper and Brothers hereby agree that work upon said series is to begin within a month after the date of the signing of this agreement.

With warmest regards, believe me,

Yours sincerely,

HH Rogers

[1] For Mrs. Clemens's answer see letter 104, note 1. Despite her willingness the changes were not made. For the full contract, see Appendix A.

101. CLEMENS TO ROGERS (telegram)

Spokane
7 August 1895

Certainly no objection would like a type written copy[1] of it mailed to Melbourne all well and send love to you all

SL Clemens

[1] At the second annual reunion of The High School Association, held in Fairhaven on 8 August 1895, Rogers stepped to the front of the stage and asked

the audience if it would like to "hear a new story by Mark Twain. . . . Mr.
Rogers said that he had in his possession the manuscript of a beautiful little story
written by the noted humorist which has never been published and which is a
little out of the humorist's line. 'I telegraphed to Mr. Clemens, who is in
Spokane, yesterday,' continued Mr. Rogers, 'and asked him if he had any
objection to having his story, "The Californian's Tale" read in Fairhaven, at the
High School reunion. I received the following answer this morning: Certainly;
not the slightest objection and give my love to them all'" (Fairhaven *Star,* 10
August 1895).

102. CLEMENS TO ROGERS (telegram)

Vancouver
15 August 1895

Steamer does not sail until the twentieth.[1]

SL Clemens

[1] Clemens had expected to embark for Australia on 16 August; when his ship,
the *Warrimoo,* ran aground on entering the harbor, he was delayed a week
(*MTLC,* p. 251).

103. CLEMENS TO ROGERS

Vancouver
17 August 1895

Dear Mr. Rogers:

I *wish* you'd get acquainted with J. Henry Harper and make sure
that he is going to be perfectly willing that I shall publish my
volume of travel through Bliss or a Chicago subscription house for
the first three or four years before adding it to the Harper books.

There are 3 or 4 reasons why I want it published by one of those
houses.

1. ⟨The⟩ One main one is, that it is going to be a book peculiarly
suited to the subscription market—for it will take the attitude that

the reader is wholly ignorant of the countries I am writing about—
and one mustn't take *that* attitude toward Harper's clientele.

2. I want that $10,000 cash in advance from Bliss or the other
man.

3. I want a clean and clear $40,000 out of that book in the first 6
months; and that is achievable by the subscription method only, I
judge.

I have been making a calculation to-day. I believe that between
Australia and London I shall have about 3 months' sea-voyaging.
Therefore I expect to reach London next March or April with
almost the entire book ready for artist and printer.

Colby wrote me that in order to arrive at the proposed settlement
by putting up $15,000 cash, it would be necessary for him to
promise the creditors that I would go ahead and work till I had paid
them 100 cents on the dollar,—a promise which I could have made
a year ago just as well and with more advantage.

Well, as long as the promise must be made, it was necessarily
well to make it *public;* and so I have made it public.[1]

"Dr. Clemens" and family were very glad to get your telegram. I
judge by the date that it crossed ours to you postponing our sailing
to the 20th. I've been hoarse for several days, and here the other
night and in Whatcom I had very great difficulty in pumping out
any voice *at all.* I was booked to talk in Victoria to-night, but we got
it postponed to next Tuesday. Been in bed ever since, and am now
getting back some voice. I knew the Vancouver audience would be
English, and therefore no trouble to talk to; otherwise ⟨I⟩ it would
have been insane for me to try to succeed with such a dilapidated
voice. I went through all right—by whispering, mainly.

Lots of love to you all. Good-night; I'll say good-bye in a day or
two.

SLC

[1] Clemens had the day before given an interview to a correspondent of the
New York *Times*, which on 17 August 1895 reported:
VANCOUVER, B. C., Aug. 16.—Samuel L. Clemens, (Mark Twain,) who is

about leaving for Australia, made a signed statement to-day concerning the purposes of his long trip and his business troubles, in part, as follows:

"It has been reported that I sacrificed, for the benefit of the creditors, the property of the publishing firm whose financial backer I was, and that I am now lecturing for my own benefit. This is an error. I intend the lectures, as well as the property, for the creditors. The law recognizes no mortgage on a man's brain, and a merchant who has given up all he has may take advantage of the rules of insolvency and start free again for himself; but I am not a business man, and honor is a harder master than the law. It cannot compromise for less than a hundred cents on the dollar, and its debts never outlaw.

"I had a two-thirds interest in the publishing firm, whose capital I furnished. If the firm had prospered, I should have expected to collect two-thirds of the profits. As it is, I expect to pay all the debts. My partner has no resources, and I do not look for assistance from him. By far the largest single creditor of this firm is my wife, whose contributions in cash, from her private means, have nearly equaled the claims of all the others combined. In satisfaction of this great and just claim, she has taken nothing, except to avail herself of the opportunity of retaining control of the copyrights of my books, which, for many easily understood reasons, of which financial ones are the least, we do not desire to see in the hands of strangers. On the contrary, she has helped and intends to help me to satisfy the obligations due to the rest.

"The present situation is that the wreckage of the firm, together with what money I can scrape together with my wife's aid, will enable me to pay the other creditors about 50 per cent. of their claims. It is my intention to ask them to accept that as a legal discharge, and trust to my honor to pay the other 50 per cent. as fast as I can earn it. From my reception thus far on my lecturing tour, I am confident that, if I live I can pay off the last debt within four years, after which, at the age of sixty-four, I can make a fresh and unincumbered start in life.

"I do not enjoy the hard travel and broken rest inseparable from lecturing, and, if it had not been for the imperious moral necessity of paying these debts, which I never contracted but which were accumulated on the faith of my name by those who had a presumptive right to use it, I should never have taken to the road at my time of life. I could have supported myself comfortably by writing, but writing is too slow for the demands that I have to meet. Therefore I have begun to lecture my way around the world. I am going to Australia, India, and South Africa, and next year I hope to make a tour of the great cities of the United States. In my preliminary run through the smaller cities on the northern route, I have found a reception the cordiality of which has touched my heart and made me feel how small a thing money is in comparison with friendship.

"I meant, when I began, to give my creditors all the benefit of this, but I begin to feel that I am gaining something from it, too, and that my dividends, if not available for banking purposes, may be even more satisfactory than theirs."

104. CLEMENS AND MRS. CLEMENS TO ROGERS

Vancouver
17 August 1895

Dear Mr Rogers:

Days ago my letter ought to have gone to you regarding the Harpers' contract,[1] but with this constant traveling I have found it almost impossible to write letters.

We were very glad to receive your telegram on reaching here the other day and thank you most heartily for it.

I am very glad that our steamer did not sail on Friday because Mr Clemens has taken a hard cold and I think it would have been unsafe for him to travel. Tuesday and Wednesday and Thursday evening he found it difficult to make himself heard.

I was very anxious about him fearing an attack of bronchitis or lung fever. We have kept him in bed now for two days and he seems better. When he found that the steamer did not sail on Friday he made an engagement to go to Victoria for Saturday night.

Naturally he thought he must fulfill that engagement, but I was sure if he did that he would not get off on the steamer for Australia. I sent for the Doctor and he said it would be very perilous for Mr Clemens to read that night, he was in a condition that could easily develop pneumonia or lung fever. So the reading was postponed until Tuesday evening. We go to Victoria Tuesday and take ship for Australia from there on Wednesday.

I want to thank you once more for all your kindness to us and to mention particularly your kind letter in which you assure us that our unbusiness-like methods did not disgust you and make you tired of the entire thing.

Please give my love to Mrs Duff. I am very desirous to see the result of her work in the Fairhaven house. Mr Clemens and I look forward with great anticipation to accepting your extended invitation when we get back.

With our affectionate greeting to you all
believe me

very sincerely yours
Olivia L. Clemens

P.S.

It seems as if there should be some date specified [2] between now and which the Harper Brothers should begin their publication of Mr Clemens' books.

I wondered if now when these changes in the contract are to be made would not be a good time to suggest that addition.

O.L.C.

It seems to me that that is only reasonable. It runs in my head that the contract is silent in that regard.

SLC

[1] On 17 August 1895 (CWB) Mrs. Clemens did send a formal letter "regarding the Harpers' contract":

H. H. Rogers Esq.

Dear Sir:

I very readily agree to the changes which Messrs Harper & Brothers desire made in their contract with me, as per your letter of recent date

very truly yours
Olivia L. Clemens

The contract had been signed by Rogers (for Livy) on 23 May, and had been delivered on 26 July 1895 (see letter 100a).

[2] Clemens added the word "specified" and the last two sentences of the letter.

105. Clemens to Rogers

Vancouver
19 August 1895

Dear Mr. Rogers:

It was always my strong impression that the Paige Mf. Co. had no shadow of right to throw my royalties back on my hands and seize my stock whether I liked it or not.

I have been carefully reading clause Third of the paper signed by me Jan. 27, 1894 (a copy of which you sent me some time ago) and I now seem to see that I was right.

In clause Third the party of the second part covenants and agrees (that is, solemnly promises) to return me my royalties IF I surrender my stock and make the demand.

There is no compulsion upon me. The word *shall* does not occur. I am left wholly free. I can surrender my stock or keep it, just as I please. There is nothing in the paper which can force me to make the exchange.

If I surrender my stock I can compel the other party to keep their covenant and restore to me my royalties. They can compel *me* to nothing; power to compel is vested in me, *alone*.

Now I have never surrendered my stock, and have never *offered* to.

⟨Won't you take hold of this matter for me⟩

I will bring suit when I get back and can have a talk with you and secure the proper lawyer. Why not try John Stanchfield, of Elmira? I believe I will. I like him. Charley Langdon doesn't, but that is merely a superstition, I think. Charley would agree that Stanchfield is an able man, that is sure. Stanchfield must talk with you, if you will let him.

There is blood in my eye, do you perceive? I was utterly amazed when that gang returned my royalties and coolly proposed to gobble my stock. It seemed to me that I must have signed a paper without comprehending its meaning. But it ⟨is⟩ seems plain, now, that I did understand its meaning, and that that gang's action in shutting the door in my face was a clean cold attempt to rob me. Land, if I can only make them disgorge it will be a proud day for me. I think you had your doubts, too, or you would not have been surprised at the gang's action. Read clause Third, examine it closely, and I think it will mean to you just what it means to me. ⟨If you haven't a copy—but anyway I will send my copy to Stanchfield and he can show it to you.⟩

If you approve—and land, I do hope you will!—won't you mail the enclosed letter to

John Stanchfield, Elmira.

And don't you think the suit can be begun right away? It will have to proceed in my wife's name, anyway, and you are fully empowered to represent her. If I can only capture that $15,000, I'll be out of the Webster chains a year earlier than otherwise. I wish we could sell this claim to the creditors for its face.

———

We (Mrs. C. and Clara) are busy packing. The trunks will go on board the ship in the morning. The vessel has been on a reef and is now about to come out of the repairers' hands. She was not greatly damaged. The smoke is so dense all over this upper coast[1] that you can't see a cathedral at 800 yards. It makes navigation risky even in daytime—and at night very difficult and dangerous.

It's a long good-bye, now; and we all accompany it with love and gratitude to you and all of you. Don't forget us, and don't forget our underworld address.

Sincerely Yours

SL Clemens

Balwyn,
  Melbourne
—till the end of this year.

[1] Forest fires burned just outside the city.

106. CLEMENS TO ROGERS

At Sea

13–15 September 1895

Dear Mr. Rogers:

I think it has been a charming voyage—two days hence we shall reach Sydney. A very pleasant 3 weeks thus far—no rough weather, no rain, a rich abundance of sunshine and moonlight. Everybody wore white linen from the day before we reached the Sandwich Islands (Aug. 30) till day before yesterday—from 25° north of the equator to 25° south of it. So the white-linen region covers just 50 degrees of latitude at sea.

I had a big audience at Honolulu, but the cholera was bad, there, and we couldn't go ashore. Had to send the freight ashore in lighters, and it took 30 hours, because we could have no navvies from shore to help.

We had half a day in Fiji a few days ago—a lovely island and splendid stalwart natives, a fine race, both sexes.

We dropped Monday out of the calendar there, skipping from Sunday over to Tuesday, although we had not yet reached the 180th meridian.

Mrs. Clemens and Clara have enjoyed the voyage; and perhaps Clara would not object if we had to take it over again. Amusements —reading, shuffleboard and cards.

Found a letter at Fiji from my agent notifying me that I was advertised to lecture in Sydney Sept. 8—five days ago. I can't do it.

Sept. 14. Shuffleboarding is rather violent exercise for me. At first a single game of 100 points lamed me and took the life all out of me for the rest of the day; but to-day I played 10 games, winning 7 of them, and came through without fatigue. On the voyage we have played two tournaments. I beat all the winners in one of them and a Mr. Thomas beat the winners in the other. Two champions. To-day he and I played best 2 in 3 to see who should be sole "Champion of the South Seas." I won.

Sept. 15. Atlantic seas on to-day—the first we have had. And yet not *really* rough. Satchels keep their places and do not go browsing around. We shipped one sea—the only one so far. Clara "fetched away" from the piano stool while playing the hymns at divine service.

We left America in the summer, reached Fiji in mid-winter, and shall reach Australia to-night in the spring. Variety enough for *one* three weeks.

Pond is superannuated; [1] hasn't any sand or any intelligence or judgment. I must make no contract with him to platform me through America next year if I can do better. Who *can* I get?

With warmest greetings from all of us to you-all—

SLC

---

[1] "Superannuated" Pond was three years younger than Clemens.

107. CLEMENS TO ROGERS

Sydney
25 September 1895

Dear Mr. Rogers:

I perceive that you had a very good time at the Highschool reünion; [1] I would have liked to be in it myself.

I am in bed with what seems to be a new carbuncle; not in bed on *that* account, but in order that the poultice may have a chance to stay on. This one is half way between my left knee and ancle, right astride a big tendon. Also I am in bed (at this late hour, 11 a.m.) to rest. Mrs. C. and the maid are packing the trunks; we leave for Melbourne this evening. We have had a darling time here for a week—and really I am almost in love with the platform again.

⟨I⟩ Mrs. Clemens has sent you the newspapers; so I've nothing to write about. Well, that isn't so; I've got lots to write about, but I've never had a moment's time that was honestly and positively *mine* since I arrived. I don't know what would become of me but for

Mrs. Clemens and Clara; they slave away ⟨writi⟩ answering letters for me half the day and night and paying not only their own calls but as many of mine as can be brought within their jurisdiction. I work at my lectures ⟨a great⟩ all I can, trying to get them to a point that will suit me.

I will turn out now, and pay my final visits. We leave for the station at 4.30.

> Love to ye's all.
>
> SL. Clemens

Oh look here—do give our love to those Rices; we were glad to hear they were having a good time in France.

[1] In addition to a reading of "The Californian's Tale" (see letter 101) Rogers had enjoyed a clambake, a band concert, and a farce—"Professor Baxter's Great Invention" (Fairhaven *Star*, 10 August 1895). In fact, Rogers's strong interest in his high school is in evidence throughout the period of this correspondence. In 1905 the *World's Work* noted that "Mr. Rogers has never lost interest in the Fairhaven High School. He attends all the reunions and takes an active part in the business discussions" ("Henry H. Rogers—Monopolist," X [May 1905], 6130). (See also letter 293.)

As early as 1883 he had contributed a grammar school and would eventually add a new high school to the Fairhaven school system. "He was fond of telling his friends of later years how the seats in the schoolhouse in that village used to cramp his legs when, as a pupil, he was compelled to sit at the poorly constructed benches. 'If I ever get rich,' he told the teacher one day when he was more uncomfortable than usual, 'I'm going to build a schoolhouse in which the boys can be comfortable.' This promise he fulfilled; for his first gift to his native home was a handsome brick school-building that cost approximately $75,000" ("Henry H. Rogers: Captain of Industry," *Harper's Weekly*, LIII [29 May 1909], 9).

108. CLEMENS TO ROGERS

> At Sea
> 1 January 1896
> New Year's /96.

Dear Mr. Rogers:

There is nothing to write, but we want to send New Year greetings to the Rogerses and the Benjamins and the Broughtons.[1]

We came back from New Zealand and lectured a couple of times in Sydney and a couple in Melbourne while waiting for this splendid P. & O. ship. We have touched at Adelaide and are now just leaving for Ceylon. We shan't hear any more war-talk [2] for ⟨ten⟩ 14 days to come.

Love to you all—and peace!

S. L. C.

We sent you about two hundred pounds a few days ago in Sydney; and by this present mail Mrs. Clemens expects to send about £850 more.[3]

[1] Urban H. Broughton, a young Englishman whom Rogers had recently brought to Fairhaven to supervise installation of the town's drainage system, had married Rogers's second daughter, Cara Leland (Duff), on 12 November 1895.

[2] On 1 January 1896 President Cleveland appointed a commission to explore the Venezuelan boundary dispute which threatened to bring the United States and Great Britain into conflict.

[3] During the tour Clemens sent Rogers money for safekeeping. On 3 October 1895, he recorded in his notebook that he had sent him £437.13.6 (Notebook 28a, TS p. 56). Late in the year, he noted: "Shipped about £200 to Mr. Rogers. . . . Shipped £437 to same . . . 2 or 3 months ago. Will ship £850 from Adelaide" (Notebook 28b, TS p. 11).

109. CLEMENS TO ROGERS

At Sea, nearing Ceylon
12 January 1896
S. S. "Oceana"

Dear Mr. Rogers:

I am shut up in my cabin with another ⟨hellf⟩ allfired cold on my chest. I shall have to read in Colombo if there is time; and we are trying to doctor-up my voice. But *I* don't care if it *never* gets audible again. I have been persecuted with carbuncles and colds until I am tired and disgusted and angry.

I've been writing a note to J. Henry Harper to ask him to renew the copyright of "Innocents Abroad" for Mrs. Clemens's benefit. She and I have told him you will furnish any writings or authorities in her name if any shall be needed.

There is one Webster debt which the creditor, (the U.S. Grant estate), ought to be ashamed to collect. It is about $700. In 1885 early—when the family were still poor—I lent Jesse Grant $500; and neither that nor any interest has ever been paid.

I saved the family $200,000 by keeping [them] from signing a contract with the Century for a 10 per cent (!) royalty on his book. I paid the General more than double that.

It is roasting hot here within fifty yards of the equator. Mrs. Clemens doesn't allow me to leave this room to-night. Still, I think I will dress and go on deck.

Do give my love to all of you.

Mark L. C.[1]

I think that when I get through in South Africa I will settle down there or in England for half a year or more and write two books before I take up lecturing again.

Please remember me to Miss Harrison.

SLC

[1] Clemens seemed to delight in his double identity; see also letter 134.

110. CLEMENS TO ROGERS

Bombay
5 February 1896

Dear Mr. Rogers:

I was delighted to see by enclosure from Langdon a few days ago, that you had decided to take the creditors individually and get releases from them at 50 cents on the dollar. And I was glad to see that the first to respond was that Boston firm. They were always nice men to deal with; their only fault was that they were too easy with Hall—they ought to have made him pay up occasionally.

Yes, it *would* be a good thing if a trade could be made with Bliss which would release my old books early. ⟨May be if⟩ I wasn't thinking of that, but I *was* thinking of requiring him to pay down an advance of $10,000 cash (as he proposed);—contract to run 3 or 5 years—and instead of *half profits* ⟨after⟩ above cost of manufacture, I was thinking of asking ⟨a trifle⟩ ⟨a *royalty of*⟩ either 55 per cent of the profits—or a royalty of 16 or 17 per cent on retail price of book (which would be about the same thing.) Then you could *come down* to half profits or 15 p. c. royalty as a condition that he release my old books early.

I mean to write my book (or books) before I decide on an American lecture season. I don't see how I can stand Pond, he is such an idiot. Yet I know no other American lecture agent.

I have been barking around on the platform (troublesome cough), in Bombay, Poona, Baroda, etc., for a week or so, but now at last I've got my health and voice back in time for Calcutta—we leave for there to-morrow. From Calcutta we loaf and talk back toward Bombay again, visiting Delhi, Agra, Lahore, etc.

You've got an excellent man in Bombay—Major Comfort.[1]

They're calling me—I never get a moment's time to myself.

Love to all of you,

Clemens

---

[1] Major Samuel Comfort was the manager of Standard Oil's business in western India and had his headquarters in Bombay. He was also the American vice-consul and would soon become the American consul to Bombay.

111. CLEMENS TO ROGERS

Calcutta

8 February 1896

Dear Mr. Rogers:

Yours of Dec. 7 met us here yesterday, and I perceive that a letter of yours of an earlier date has failed to reach us. The first paragraph —about the finding of the Referee—plainly refers to something we know nothing of—also the paragraph at the top of the 3d page. You speak as if May has been in trouble of some sort. Is it so? We hope not. But at any rate, whatever it was she is evidently out of it again and we are very glad of that.

We are very glad to know that Webster & Co can pay 38. That is probably better than the average of failures that occurred at that time.[1]

It will be an everlasting shame if it turns out that Bliss is really entitled to my copyrights for 42 years.[2] Bliss's father robbed me of $25,000 on a single contract—("Roughing It.")

Certainly, let's let the Century put in an offer for the book if they want to, but *only* to be published by *subscription*, and comprehending an advance-payment of $10,000 or $12,000 cash—Bliss offers the first figure. But it will be much better that Bliss have the book if it shall turn out that he can legally hold the old copyrights till their second death. I wrote you ⟨basis of⟩ the other day what I thought ought to be the terms with Bliss—raise them higher if you and Mr. Benjamin think best.

We are very glad indeed to learn that you have made one or two thousand dollars for Mrs. Clemens. We are very much obliged to you for thinking of it and putting it through.

I've had a kind of a time of it, as to roughness. Seven days in bed in Melbourne,—carbuncle; Couldn't go on platform the second night in Napier, New Zealand; ⟨carbuncle;⟩ ⟨seven day⟩ couldn't lecture in Colombo, Ceylon—cold and cough;
in bed 3 days at sea—   "   "   "
ditto 7 day in Bombay   "   "   "
Respite for a week or so—and now my first 2 days in Calcutta I am spending in bed with a cold, and hoping [I] shan't develop a cough for the platform here next week. However, yesterday I dropped back onto my long-neglected remedy for cold in the head—starving; and now, after 24 hours of starving the cold is entirely gone. I am well enough to go out with the family and dine with the Lieutenant Governor this evening [3]—and that will be my first outing here, whereas the family have been gadding around and dissipating socially just the same as ever since they left home. It is wonderful

the way they keep up, considering the tax that is put upon their strength. We came through by rail from Bombay to Calcutta, only breaking the trip at Allahabad and Benares; and at the latter place they were up at 6 in the morning and off sight-seeing the whole day —and I also. We have struck it fine here, for the Indian Army is turning itself loose on a series of magnificent military tournaments —regular mimic war. I shall see some of it next Monday and Tuesday.[4]

Love to all of you and lots of it,

SLC

The Century people haven't a very large "moral right" over me, for they wanted a contract in writing, and that broke the matter down. They drew a writing which ⟨was ful⟩ had things in it which hadn't been mentioned before and which I couldn't possibly agree to.

[1] Rogers apparently relayed one of Colby's more optimistic estimates of the Webster assets. The assigned estate finally paid only 27.7 per cent from its assets. See letter 176, note 2, for further details.

[2] This claim of the American Publishing Company was accepted by Harper & Brothers, the contract of 23 May 1895 was put aside, and negotiations started for a new contract which would allow Bliss to publish books on the Harper list. Clemens was later to decide that Bliss's claim was false, but by that time the damage had been done.

[3] Clemens recorded in his notebook: "To-day and yesterday I lay abed and starved a cold. This evening went to Belvedere and dined with Lt. Governor of Bengal (Sir Alexander Mackenzie) and a dozen—private dinner party" (Notebook 28b, TS p. 40).

[4] Clemens had been invited by Col. F. W. Chatterton of the tournament committee.

112. CLEMENS TO ROGERS

Calcutta
17 February 1896

Dear Mr. Rogers:

Yours of Jan. 9 has just arrived, and we now see what poor May has been through,[1] though who that blatherskite is, or how she came to know him isn't clear. However, she is out of it, and that is the important thing.

There's a lot of good news in your letter. All that about the Webster creditors accepting the 50¢ basis and Frank Mayo's increasing success[2] is very comforting. If the arrangement with the Harpers falls through by reason of Bliss's possible ownership of the full life of the copyrights I shall have to put all the books in Bliss's hands for a term of years, but he can bring them out one at a time in uniform style and wide apart and make them go successfully, I think.

We are just in from a long trip—2 p.m., now—and I am going to bed and rest up a little, for I leave for the west at 9 to-night and travel till noon to-morrow. After I finished my Calcutta series of lectures we went by rail 24 hours to Darjeeling so as to have a big view of the Himalayas; stayed over Sunday (I lectured there Saturday night from 9.30 to 11)—then we came down the mountain (40 miles) at a dizzy toboggan gait on a six-seated hand-car and never enjoyed ourselves so much in all our lives.[3] We started in rugs and furs and stripped as we came down, as the weather gradually changed from eternal snow to perpetual hellfire.

Our love to all of you.

SLC

The government railway treated us well. Private car and elegant food etc., the way Frank Thompson served us when we went to Chicago.

---

[1] On 28 July 1893, Mai Rogers had eloped with and married Joseph Cooper Mott at Sheepshead Bay on Long Island. They never lived together, and an annulment was secured in December 1895.

[2] Mayo had begun touring in the title role of his own dramatization of *Pudd'nhead Wilson*.

[3] Clemens's notebook records: "From the breakfast station we started in a small low 6-chaired car—canvas—and by and by came to the foot of the rise. Ascended the mountain—all curves—at apparently 100 m. an hour, but really it takes 7 or 8 h to climb the 40 m. to Darjeeling. What a world of variegated vegetation!— and ribbony roads squirming and snaking, cream-yellow over the rounded hills below" (Notebook 28b, TS p. 48).

113. CLEMENS TO ROGERS

Jeypoor
6 March 1896

Dear Mr. Rogers:

Whether Harper gets my books or not, I do hope the copyright of Innocents Abroad will be renewed and not suffered to run out. If Bliss turns out to be owner of the old copyrights all through their life and their renewal (a thing apparently *impossible* unless the renewal is expressed in the contract,) I suppose it will be best to put all my Webster & Co copyrights into his hands too—on a ½-profit basis, say; (or better still, a 15 per cent royalty) on *all* my books in his hands. In that case he could use the Webster plates if it seemed advisable.

I am in the doctor's hands again. He made me cancel a week's engagements and shut myself in my room and rest. Said he would not be responsible for the consequences if I didn't. We leave here to-morrow night and go lecturing along up to Lahore and so-on; and we fetch up in Madras near the end of this month and take ship there for Ceylon and the S. Africa.

Enclosed please find a "Duplicate" or "Second" for £101. If you will strike out the words in parenthesis I think you can collect it, for they will not notice and will think it a "First." [1] You could get Dr. Rice to work it.

I have to go to S. Africa, but I suppose that that will end my lecturing in this world. Mrs. Clemens is not willing that I shall continue the risk any further.

Love to all of you, including yourself.

SLC.

---

[1] The enclosure was a check for £101 / 12d dated 19 February 1896 from the National Bank of India; the "words in parenthesis" were "(First of the same tenor and date being unpaid)" (Salm). Mrs. Clemens had apparently sent Rogers the original of which this check was a duplicate; see letter 116.

114. ROGERS TO CLEMENS

New York [1]
6 March 1896

My dear Clemens:

Since writing you I have had a letter from Frank Mayo, in which he advises me that at last "Pudd'nhead Wilson" is on his feet, and in evidence of which he sent me a check for $511.61, being Mrs. Clemens' interest in the royalty.

Walter Bliss [2] came down yesterday, and said that his brother Frank was still ill, and unable to come to New York. I think I have about as much patience as the average man in dealing with people, but there is a point where my patience stops and my positiveness asserts itself. Yesterday was one of my bad days, and Walter Bliss and I had a very plain talk. I need not go into the general details, but I think I forced him to the position of saying that he would be willing to surrender all of the old books to Harper & Bros. for the uniform edition, if such edition is sold in sets only, and he (Bliss) be privileged to continue the sale of books singly, as he has been doing in the past. If he could have the books C. L. Webster & Co. publish under the same terms, I think that would help the trade through. I told him of the new book, and that it was in great demand, and, in fact, we were offered a great deal more than he offered for the privilege of publishing it for a short period of years. He, of course, will demand, if he surrenders the old books to Harper & Bros. on the terms suggested, a certain amount of royalty received on such books.

Looking at it from your standpoint it strikes me that it would be a reasonably fair trade, viz; for Bliss to surrender the books and receive a portion of the royalty on same from Harper Bros. The American Publishing Co. to continue the sale of your books singly and adding those that Webster & Co. published. Of course, Bliss to pay Mrs. Clemens a royalty on such books as are sold by them.

In regard to the new books, viz; "Joan of Arc" and what you may write hereafter, will, of course, be subject to a trade with anybody, for a period of years, but ultimately to go to Harper Bros. for the uniform edition. I have written Harper & Bros. to learn if they would favor such a trade, but as yet have received no reply. Of course, I will do nothing in the matter without consulting you, and will be glad of any suggestion you may make.

May I ask you to decide only after careful deliberation. To review, please consider first, that the scheme provides for Mrs. Clemens's receiving a royalty from Harper & Bros. on the uniform edition entire. She will also receive a royalty on all of the books sold by the American Publishing Co. singly as at present, including those originally published by Webster & Co. She will surrender a portion of the royalty from Harper & Bros. on "Innocents Abroad," "Roughing It," "Tramp Abroad," etc. now controlled by the American Publishing Co. This may be perfectly visionary on my part, and impossible to carry out, because of an objection that Harper & Bros. may make to it, but I believe that the American Publishing Co. can be whipped into line, particularly if they can secure the privileges on your new book for a short term of years.

Colby has dropped into a state of lethargy for the moment, and we are dropping carpet tacks in his way to stimulate his ambition. He is a rather spasmodic sort of a cuss.

The Rices, Rogerses and the Benjamins are all well. The Broughtons, I suppose, are in Paris, and they sail for home on the 21st inst.

With kindest regards to Mrs. Clemens and Miss Clara, believe me,

> Yours truly,
>
> (Signed) H. H. Rogers.

---

[1] This and eight subsequent letters from Rogers to Clemens (now in CWB) are typewritten office copies apparently kept for Rogers's records. Clemens was of course traveling throughout 1896, and Rogers probably had copies made to insure against the uncertain mails. With the exception of letter 131, they are not carbon copies and bear no autograph additions or signatures. See Calendar of Letters, p. 718.

² Walter Bliss was secretary of the American Publishing Company, of which his brother Frank (Francis E.) Bliss was president.

115. CLEMENS TO ROGERS

Jeypoor
15 March 1896

Dear Mr. Rogers:

Your cable has just arrived through Major Comfort. Thank you ever so much for your generous offers, but things are going along pretty well with us considering that we are not acclimated. We have been here two weeks, and each of us (including the manager) has been in the doctor's hands in turn. I have not been seriously ill —nor any of the others. I was going to start last night for Lahore but wasn't yet in condition; but we all start to-night and lie over a day for rest in Delhi. A couple of weeks now will complete my lecturing in India, (for this fortnight's loss) and we sail from Bombay for Ceylon and South Africa about April 1st.

By Jackson! the idea of Bliss claiming the *new* life of the old copyrights when there is not a word in the contracts to compel me to *take out* the new life, beats me. There is no shadow of sense in it. ⟨If⟩

Well, I am commanded to get ready for the train, now. Good-bye and love to you all.

SLC

116. ROGERS TO CLEMENS

New York
20 March 1896

My dear Clemens:

I have nothing from you since my letter of March 20th. I have from Mrs. Clemens enclosing draft on London for 101/12. Since

my last of the 5th inst. I have a letter from Harper & Bros. in which
they express themselves in a general way as not unfavorable to the
scheme proposed. They have asked me some questions which I am
not able to answer until I can see the Blisses, which I hope to do on
Monday next, when they are coming down to the city. Gen'l.
Langdon [1] was here a day or two since, and he approved of the
Harper scheme, taken as a whole, without, however, going into the
details, which we have not yet come to. Gen'l. Langdon had a talk
with that miserable man, Payne of the bank,[2] and I think they had
quite an animated time, at any rate the Gen'l. left Mr. Payne in a
very pleasant sort of way, so that no harm was done.

   The question of a Manager I have not forgotten, but you are
indebted to Gen'l. Langdon for a suggestion, which I think will
meet the case very thoroughly. He has had a talk with Henry E.
Abbey, to see if it were possible to get hold of anybody as a
Manager, in preference to Pond. Yesterday he had the talk with
Mr. Abbey and his partner, John Schoeffel, and in the conversation
it developed that their manager, John Warner, who next year will
be somewhat relieved, could, perhaps, give time to you. They spoke
of him in the highest terms, saying that he had been in their
employ for years at a large salary, and was thoroughly competent,
etc., and if Mr. Clemens would make a proposition which would
seem fair, they would give him the benefit of their name, Abbey,
Schoeffel & Grau,[3] as Managers, putting the business in Mr.
Warner's hands. Mr. Abbey would be very glad to hear from you as
to what your idea of compensation would be. The trouble in the
matter seems to be that you are not likely to be here for next
season's business, and it is possible that Mr. Warner could not be
secured for any other time, still, I do not know your plans entirely,
and it is possible that Mr. Warner may be disengaged all next year.
I think it would be well for you to write me concerning compensa-
tions and such other details as pertain to the subject, and either
through Gen'l. Langdon or directly I will undertake to communicate with Mr. Abbey. I think it would be a very good card to have
the name of Abbey & Co. as your Managers. It would give the
enterprise a very good standing, as they are very particular as to the

business, and only undertake to manage for the very best artists. This, I admit, is entirely superfluous, but at the same time, I throw it in and leave you to swear about it, if you want to.

We have been quite disturbed in regard to the newspaper reports concerning your illness, and I cabled Major Comfort at Bombay on Saturday last as to your condition, and he replied on Monday that you had been ill, but that you had gone on, in improved health. I am sorry to hear so unfavorably of your trip; notably, in reference to your health. Do try and take care of yourself. Mrs. Clemens wrote me a very pleasant letter, saying that she was having a delightful time, but for the draw-backs, incident to your physical condition. I hope, ere this, you have fully recovered, and that the balance of your journey will prove delightful in every sense. I have nothing later from Frank Mayo, and in fact do not know just where he is playing at the present time. I will forward the letter which you enclosed for him, as soon as I can learn his whereabouts.

Mrs. Broughton sails from Southampton to-morrow.[4] I had a letter yesterday stating that she and Mr. Broughton were well. The rest of my family are in fine healthy condition. I have bought Harry a small sloop yacht,[5] and he is looking forward with much pleasure to its use.

With kindest regards to Mrs. Clemens and Miss Clara, believe me as ever,

Yours truly,

(Signed) H. H. Rogers.

---

[1] Livy's brother Charles had in 1880 been appointed Commissary General by Governor Alonzo B. Cornell of New York, hence his title. He was also a major in the 110th Battalion of the New York militia and a member of the Elmira volunteer fire department.

[2] William H. Payne, president of the Mount Morris Bank.

[3] The agency of Abbey, Schoeffel, & Grau had managed American tours for Sarah Bernhardt, Edwin Booth, and Henry Irving.

[4] The Broughtons were returning from their honeymoon in Europe.

[5] The "cutter Lotowana" had been built in South Boston in 1889. She was "51 feet long on deck, 39 feet 10 inches on waterline" and was commanded by Rogers's personal pilot, Daniel Egan of Fairhaven (*Fairhaven Star*, 28 March 1896).

117. CLEMENS TO ROGERS

At Sea
2 April 1896

Dear Mr. Rogers:

I didn't *quite* finish in India, because I got laid up in Jeypore, Rajputana, with diarrhea, but I came very near doing it. Perhaps I might not have had to cancel any engagements at all if this ship had stuck to her advertised sailing-day instead of suddenly shortening up her date. We had to jump for the train and travel two nights and a day to catch her.

We reach Colombo, Ceylon, to-morrow; and my talks there will end this part of the campaign. We then go on in this vessel to the Mauritius; then change for South Africa.

I've been sick a good deal; the rest not so much; but we have had a good time in India—we couldn't ask a better. They are lovely people there, both in the civil and the military service, and they made us feel at home.

I am dropping this line to say howdy to you and the Benjamins and the Broughtons and Harry; and I would like to be remembered with best respects and good wishes to your mother, too.

SLC.

118. ROGERS TO CLEMENS

New York
10 April 1896

My dear Clemens:

I have nothing from you since my letter of March 20th. I have been working away as best I could with the Bliss people, and got a half way proposition from them. I gave it to Colby to take up with the Harper people, and he has been so busy as to wear out my patience, and I am now in communication with Harper Bros. direct, and am to have an appointment with Mr. Henry Harper on Monday next, when I believe we are going to make substantial progress. I have the following memorandum initialed by Walter Bliss and myself. Of course you must not pass hasty judgment on the matter for the reason that everything I do is subject to your approval later on, but I wanted to get something down in writing. They can talk longer and cover a wider range than anybody I know. The only mistake those fellows made was in going into the Publishing business instead of the preaching business. I am sure their prayers, if they were allowed to run loosely would go out over the Pacific Road, ramble over the Pacific Ocean into Australia, then to India through Europe and down through the slums of London and back to New York, and up to New Haven, and the Lord knows where they would stop if they ever got to praying. However what we put on paper was very brief, and what we said you will find it just along here next door.

New York, Mar. 24th, 1896.

"H. H. R.
W. B.

The American Publishing Co. to permit Harper Bros. to publish 'Innocents Abroad,' 'Roughing It,' 'Tramp Abroad,' 'Gilded Age,' 'Tom Sawyer,' 'Sketches' and 'Pudd'nhead Wilson' in a uniform edition to be sold by them in full sets only, on condition that Mrs. Clemens pays to said Company per centum of her royalty received on such books from Harper Bros.

The American Pub. Co. to have the exclusive sale of all the single volumes of the above named books and the books published by the late firm of C. L. Webster & Co. during the life of their copy-rights and any renewals thereof.

The American Pub. Co. to have the rights of publication of the new book contemplated by S. L. Clemens (embracing his journey around the world) if written, for which the said Company will pay one half profits and advance $10,000. and guarantee the one-half profits shall amount to not less than that sum within five years, and further agree to cancel all existing contracts with Mrs. Clemens for the publication of the old books so called and 'Pudd'nhead Wilson' and take a new contract which shall give Mrs. Clemens one-half profits on all the 'Mark Twain' books sold by them.

If Harper Bros. want the said new book 'Pudd'nhead Wilson' for the uniform edition at the end of three years after date of its first publication, then the American Pub. Co. is to have the exclusive continuous legal right to sell the book singly."

Of course you understand the first article of the above. About the second article let me explain. The American Publishing Co. want to publish your books singly, and keep up their continuous sale. You will notice that it is contemplated to give them your books published by the late firm of C. L. Webster & Co. That means that the American Publishing Co., if the trade goes through, are to buy the plates of the C. L. Webster & Co. books, and pay Mrs. Clemens at least what she paid for them when she purchased of Colby, the Assignee. From little talks that Colby has had with the Harper Bros. and from letters that I have received from them I think they are rather agreeable to the arrangement, provided the books are not put out at such low prices, as would interfere with their sale of the sets. That is one of the questions that Mr. Harper and I have to discuss on Monday. In regard to the third article: It reads very clearly concerning the new book which you contemplate writing. Instead of giving $10,000. bonus, they make another suggestion, but, of course, you will not consider that final until we are through trading. The next important question in the same article is the matter of cancelling all existing contracts. I thought at first that that was a mighty fine thing, and I was prepared to jockey with the Blisses. When I saw them on the 23rd of March in a very diplomatic sort of way I broached the subject, so as to gradually get them committed to the scheme, but to my amazement, as soon as I raised the question they yielded so readily that I concluded there must be something behind it, which I did not understand. I took it, however, as being one of the things *they offered,* and now it comes home to me, that it is barely possible, that the higher royalties paid on "Tramp Abroad," "Tom Sawyer" and some of the others perhaps was a little burden-some, and that the lesser royalties on "Innocents Abroad" and "Roughing It" did not equalize for what they paid on the first named books, so we have got to make a little mathematical calculation and see where we would land if we traded with them on their offer to cancel existing contracts. I am not sure that I make it clear to you, so I am going to take the liberty of illustrating just a little. Take the case of the "Tramp Abroad," where the royalty is, I think, 15% on a $3.50 book; you are entitled to receive 52-½¢ per volume. If they are to put out a new edition at $1.50 or reduce the price of the old one to the same figure, 15% of $1.50 would be 22-½¢. If it were on the one half profit basis, the question would be if you would get as much as 22-½¢, however, if the method is satisfactory to you, and it is desirable to change existing contracts, why we will make the calculations for you, so that there will be no mistake so far as the figures go.

"Joan of Arc" was concluded in the April "Harpers," and in the publication advertisement they announce the early appearance of the book. They pay a great compliment to the writer, whose name they do not give. Referring to the matter of authorship, I am presumptuous I suppose in saying that I believe "Mark Twain's" name on the title page would give great commercial value to the book. Of course you are the Doctor concerning that.

I think I have given you the full particulars now in regard to Harper Bros., and the American Publishing Co. to date. I will write you next week after my interview with Mr. Henry Harper. I suppose you think that I have been very negligent in these matters: I confess to it all, but I have had some very slow people to deal with. I trust you will therefore, excuse me for all the delays. I have heard nothing from Mr. Frank Mayo, excepting in the way of newspaper criticisms, which he has sent me from time to time. I was in hopes that I would be able to announce to you the receipt of further remittances from him. General Langdon was down some time ago and saw that old idiot at the bank, but nothing seemingly has come of the interview, as Colby tells me that he has not heard from Payne since the meeting. I used to swell up a little bit with pride because I could declare that one of my great, great, etc. grandfathers was a great, great etc. grandfather of General Grant, but since I have got to learn what a puny little weasily, good-for-nothing, ungrateful kind of a man Fred Grant is, I have about concluded to abandon the thought which I have had for some time, namely; of restoring the grave and nickel plating the grave stone of Lieut. Jonathan Delano, who was the ancestor of General Grant and myself. Grant is suing Colby as Assignee for the royalties on the books that Colby sold in liquidation of the business. I see no reason why we should change the policy which we have pursued concerning these creditors. I am pressing Colby to close up the affairs of the concern, and hope to succeed with him as soon as Grant's case is out of the way.

We have had a great deal of trouble down at Fairhaven in the past three or four years in regard to the money which has been spent on the streets and high-ways. The Superintendent, which they have had, succeeded in spending the money there with great punctuality, but with little apparent effect. In fact all the town officers were in bad odor, and last fall I made a little campaign, and told certain people that they would have to stand as officers of the town at the election, because I intended to kick out everybody then in office. I had plenty of good help, and my friend, Winsor, whom you surely remember, consented to serve on the Board of Select-men,[1] on condition, however, that I would in some way direct the matters concerning the high-ways and streets. He was elected to office by a unanimous vote. He then said "Now my friend, I want you to carry out your part of the promise." I said "All right, I will make application for the position of Superintendent of Streets." The Board heard me and promptly after election appointed me, and I took the oath of office. Some of my friends in New Bedford took it up as a pretty good joke, and gave it to the United Press Association, and it was telegraphed all over the States, and published, of course, as a matter of news, although I was entirely unknown to about 110 per centum of its population. Then some friendly idiot wrote an article and published it with my picture in the Boston Sunday Globe. Some of the Chicago papers, thinking it was a funny thing for a man who is said to be well-to-do in life to take the position of Superintendent of Streets, took the matter up and also published pictures etc. The result is that I have been inundated with letters from people who wanted to borrow much money, and from people who wanted to borrow little. Other communications from marriageable women, who have noticed in the article that I was unmarried. While it has been annoying it has had its bright side, as some of the letters were really amusing. I regret now that I did not keep all that I received, but I have destroyed a great many which I am sure careful reading of them would have found much that was amusing if not interesting. One in particular has so appealed to my sense of the humorous, and I may add to my feelings of sympathy, that I have had a copy of it made and enclose it herewith.[2] I hope it will entertain you as it has me. The sweet simplicity of this poor old woman as shown in the whole letter, and the pathetic story of her husband, who has to take a hot stone to bed with him even in July, and the description of her home, and the desire to take one or two children to board with her for the summer, makes the letter one which I hope will strike you pleasantly.

The Broughtons have returned from England and are now in Chicago. The Benjamins are well. Mai and Harry are in good health, and the "electric spark" has grown about three inches since you saw him, and has almost reached that important point of being able to "lick his daddy." We have a good many rough and tumbles just because we both like it, and I can see that each time he develops a little more strength, and that I must be very guarded in my language toward him within six months.

We are in doubt as to your movements. We hope, however, each and all of us, that the next news we have will be of a favorable kind concerning your health. I think of you about all the time, and have tried to put myself in your place, with all your discouragements and sicknesses, because of my genuine sympathy.

Kindest regard to family, and I am,

always yours truly,

(Signed) H. H. Rogers.

---

[1] The Fairhaven *Star* reported on 8 February 1896 that "Walter P. Winsor had consented to be a candidate for selectman." Winsor was president of the First National Bank and active in Fairhaven's affairs. The Boston *Herald* described him as "probably more intimate with Mr. Rogers in both business and social connections than any one else in New Bedford or Fairhaven" (20 May 1909).

[2] Mrs. Abbie G. Bates of West Sumner, Maine, had written Rogers of her poor health and had requested financial aid—two dollars (CWB).

119. ROGERS TO CLEMENS

New York
13 April 1896

My dear Clemens:

I am in receipt this morning of your letter of the 15th of March, and note that you are still far from well. I am going to address this letter just the same as previous letters until further advised.

I have been up to talk with Mr. Henry Harper this afternoon, and I can positively say if the American Publishing Co. are as reasonable as the Harpers seem to be, that we can make a good trade all around. Harper likes the idea very much of getting the earlier books immediately. They are going to write me a letter in three or four days saying exactly what they are willing to do,[1] and on receipt of it I will submit it to the Blisses, and hope for the very best outcome. Of course, I am not going to make any trade except on your approval, but I hope to be able to lay the matter before you in such an attractive way as will command your hearty endorsement. In regard to the copy-rights for the old books, I am of opinion that the American Publishing Co. took out the copy-rights for

"Innocents Abroad" and "Roughing It," and that your contract was simply for the book. However, we won't worry about that at the moment; let us wait and see if we cannot make amends for the past.

I don't know but what you have heard of the Rev. Mr. Twichell. He has been writing a sketch of you, which the Harpers are to bring out in their "May" Magazine. Mr. Harper showed it to me while there, and I only glanced at it. I will say, however, that the picture is an excellent one, and Mr. Harper says the sketch is fine; and further I may add, that it is the first article in the Magazine.[2]

Yours truly,

(Signed) H. H. Rogers.

[1] Harper & Brothers did write on 16 April 1896 (CWB) to confirm "our conversation of the 13th inst.," and to set forth their terms. They authorized Rogers to proceed "to make a mutually satisfactory arrangement with the American Publishing Company" whereby the Harpers could secure the right to publish Clemens's five early books. The "general outlines of the proposed arrangement" specified that a "reciprocal interchange" of books between the two companies would allow books controlled by the American Publishing Company to appear in the uniform edition of the works of Mark Twain, which Harper & Brothers had already announced, while books controlled and printed by the Harpers could be sold by the American Publishing Company through the "recognized channels of the subscription book-trade" for "not less than three dollars ($3) per volume."

The Harpers's letter also noted that Rogers had authorized them "to proceed with the manufacture of the new edition of 'Life on the Mississippi' and that you agree for Mrs. Clemens to protect us from loss or injury through any obstacles, legal or otherwise, which Mr. Watson Gill" might interpose. The Harpers had "instructed the printers to resume the composition and electrotyping of the work, which was suspended last autumn."

[2] Twichell's sketch did appear as "Mark Twain," the lead article in the May 1896 *Harper's Magazine*.

120. CLEMENS TO ROGERS

Curepipe, Mauritius
24 April 1896

Dear Mr. Rogers:

We have been here about ten days, and shall be here 3 or 4 more before our ship will be ready to receive us on board. This holiday

comes very handy for me; I am very glad to have a resting spell; I
was getting fagged with platform work. We had a perfectly delightful voyage of nineteen or twenty days from Calcutta by Madras and
Ceylon to Mauritius. That was a holiday, but not enough of it.
There *are* no sea-holidays any more; the voyages are all too short,
unless you take a sailing-vessel.

This village of Curepipe is up-country, 2 hours (16 miles) by rail
from the Port. It is on high ground, and is cool, and rains all the
time, and is very damp and pleasant. Cigars are mushy and clammy,
and a match that will light on *any*thing is a curiosity. It is believed
to be the wettest place in the world except the ocean. But it is in a
beautiful country, surrounded by sugar plantations and the green-
est and brightest and richest of tropical vegetation, and we like it.
The island is a British possession, and has an English governor; but
there are few English people and many French; so the French have
everything their own way—and the French way is seldom a good
way in this world. The population of the island is guessed at
360,000. French 20,000; English 8,000; the rest is made up of East
Indians, creoles, niggers, and mongrels—but the bulk are East
Indians. These latter are temperate, industrious and valuable. The
French and other mongrels are well enough, but the East Indians
are the boys for value. The manufactures consist of sugar, molasses
and mongrels. Formerly there was a bounty paid for mongrels; but
this was found unnecessary; indeed of late years the market has
suffered from over-production; for several successive seasons all who
sold short got left. It is believed that nothing can save the business
but to form a Trust; but that cannot be done because the whole
thing is in the hands of the French and they wouldn't have it
because it would limit individual effort.

There are some Protestant missionaries here, but there is nothing
doing in their line. The Catholics control the market. There are 18
daily newspapers in the island, but there wouldn't be any money in
it if there were a million. Nobody knows what they live on.

Clara has a large carbuncle, and suffers a great deal with it; but
her mother's health keeps in pretty good shape.

If I think of any more facts about Mauritius that will be valuable in Wall street I will write again. Meantime I send love to you all, and if you think Harry would like a mongrel I will get him one.

Sincerely Yours

SLC

121. ROGERS TO CLEMENS

New York

29 April 1896

My dear Clemens:

Since my last letter of April 12th, I have heard nothing from you. I have been faithfully at work with Harper Bros. and the Blisses, with a view of coming to some understanding in regard to the publication of the books, but I don't know whether we are making progress or not. Harper Bros. last suggestion to the Blisses, was for the Blisses to take the uniform edition and publish it and let Harper publish all the single books.[1] The Blisses have gone home to consider their proposition. I have written Messrs. Harper Bros. if they desired to see me in reference, I could keep any appointment for this week. On Sunday I am going away for a couple of weeks [2] to the Oil Fields of Kansas, Tennessee, Kentucky and Virginia. This is one of the trips you have always wanted to go on, but I suppose your going will have to be put off for this year.

We have a letter from Frank Mayo this morning enclosing check for $1457.87 being royalty to and including April 11th. I also enclose copy of his letter.[3]

At last the Grant case is settled and Colby is going on now to close up the affairs of the C. L. Webster & Co. Payne and Barrow are the stubborn ones and we are unable to make settlement with them. The only thing to do is to let the matter rest for a time and hope for something favorable to turn up in the future.

With kindest regards to all, believe me as ever,

Yours sincerely,

(Signed) H. H. Rogers.

P.S. I have just had a letter from Mr. Harry Harper in which he wants to see me and I will see him to-morrow or next day.

---

[1] The Blisses had apparently rejected the proposal which the Harpers and Rogers had discussed on 13 April 1896. The Harpers's "last suggestion to the Blisses" completely reversed the scheme of that proposal.

[2] Three days later on 2 May 1896, Katharine Harrison would write the Harpers to notify them that "Mr. Rogers has been called out of town, and will probably be absent about two weeks" (Fairhaven).

[3] Mayo had been playing *Pudd'nhead Wilson* from Pittsburgh to Kansas City to San Francisco: "the play is an assured success," he wrote. "I was so glad to read that Sam had made such a success in his travels, and that he had been fully restored to his health. Kindly remember me to him always in your writings and to his dear family" (CWB).

122. CLEMENS TO ROGERS

Durban, Natal
8 May 1896

Dear Mr. Rogers:

We reached here day before yesterday, 41 days out from Calcutta—breaking the journey a couple of days in Ceylon and near a fortnight in Mauritius. We have been in the pitiless and uninterrupted blaze of summer from the time I saw you last until we reached this place—more than ten straight months of it. We had the American summer all across America and the Pacific; then struck Australia the middle of September, just as *their* summer was (about) getting ready to open; we left Australasia 3 months later in Midsummer—Xmas and New Years—and reached Bombay in what *would* have been winter if there had been anything to make it out of; but there wasn't. It was always summer in India; at least we found it so—particularly in the winter. Of course we never saw any of the *real* summer; they do say that when that comes Satan himself has to knock off and go home and cool off.

But here in Durban it is cool. Their (summer) autumn is closing; before this Month of May is ended their winter will have set in. The days are warm, but not too warm; coolness begins with sunset; an hour later you must put on an overcoat; and your bed must have several blankets on it.

We shall be in South Africa 3 months—address Cape Town—
then sail for England end of July or early in August—most likely
August.

No letter here from you, but maybe there's one at the Cape. We
have sent for it.

A power of love to you all.

SLC.

123. ROGERS TO CLEMENS

New York
22 May 1896

My dear Clemens:

Since writing you on April 29th, I have been out of town for
nearly three weeks with Mr. Archbold. We were making our
annual pilgrimage through the oil regions of the South and West.
We were at Jamestown, Tennessee, where there is much excitement, but as yet no oil has been found in paying quantities. To the
South they have some good wells and I am of opinion that oil will
be found all through that country. The quality is somewhat inferior, but I think the quantity is there.

I had about given up accomplishing anything with Bliss and
Harper Bros. but Bliss was here yesterday, after an interview with
Harper Bros. He had a memorandum from Harper Bros. which I
think *he* ought to be willing, at least, to accept. Of course, it is all
conditional on its being agreeable to you. In substance, it was, that
Harper Bros. were to go on with the publication of the books of C.
L. Webster & Co. and "Joan of Arc"; selling the same to the trade,
or retailing them as is customary with their publication. Bliss to
issue new editions of the old books, such editions to be of the same
size and style of books published by Harper Bros. Bliss to have the
uniform edition business entirely and to purchase from Harper
Bros. at some agreed price the books required to make up the sets.
The uniform edition to be sold by subscription only. I asked Bliss if

it was not acceptable and he said he would have to take it home and confer with his people as to selling the uniform edition by subscription only. The point I think Harper Bros. are trying to make, is that Bliss shall be confined to the sale of his old books for single editions, just as he is now printing them, and that the new editions that he prints are to go into the uniform edition only. I don't know if they will succeed, and I don't know if a trade of that kind can be made satisfactory, but all things considered, I should favor closing up the trade in some way, so that the public can get "Mark Twain's" books. It is fair for me to say now that everybody says that "Mark Twain" is on the boom. It is high water mark with him for a lot of reasons, and his books should be before the public. I enclose copy of a letter addressed to you by Harper Bros. As it was unsealed, I have taken the liberty of copying it, because I fear the loss of the original, if entrusted to the mails.

Nothing further has been done in the affairs of C. L. Webster & Co. Payne and Barrow are acting the "dog in the manger" and I suppose we will have to let the matter go on. I would not allow it to worry me, because it will surely work itself out in the end.

I am sorry to hear that you have not been in good health, but I trust my next letter will bring me more encouraging news. We are all very well at 57th Street, and in response to your kindly messages, they desire me to extend to you their cordial good wishes.

Harry's yacht is being fitted out and he is about the biggest nuisance there is in the vicinity of 57th Street. He puts on too many airs, and it will require the services of a man to take him down. I wish when you come home you would avoid making any appointments until you have engaged with me to give him a blamed good thrashing. You haven't any idea, Clemens, really how sassy he is. He has grown so big that he can tire me out because my wind is poor, and I shall want somebody to ease me up when we have the battle. I would send for the "Harlem Coffee Cooler" but I understand he is under a permanent engagement in London.

With warmest regards to you all, I am, as ever,

Yours sincerely,

(Signed) H. H. Rogers.

124. Clemens to Rogers

Pretoria, S. A. R.
26 May 1896

Dear Mr. Rogers:

It is intensely interesting here—the political pot is boiling vigorously. I have seen the prisoners, and made them a nonsensical speech.[1] They are trying to be cheerful, but I suppose that by and by their captivity will begin to tell heavily upon them. It is believed that the sentences of the 4 leaders will be reduced to 5 years, but no man can tell. However, I am sending you the newspapers; if the situation interests you you will find matter in them on the subject.

We have been having in South Africa a repetition of the charming times we had in India and the other places. In truth I am sorry to remember that the lecture trip is drawing to a close. I would like to bum around these interesting countries another year and talk. I suppose that within 2 months I shall retire from the platform at the Cape and be ready to go to England and sit down and write my book. My London address will be Brown Shipley & Co, bankers.

My health is in good shape at last. Mrs. Clemens and Clara are well. They will join me 3 or 4 weeks hence at Port Elizabeth from Durban by sea, and then go with me to Kimberly and around, and then down to the Cape.

I haven't heard from you for a couple of months, but you are in my mind all the same, and I send love to you and all the house.

SLC

[1] Among the prisoners was John Hays Hammond, an American mining engineer associated with Cecil Rhodes in developing South African resources and a leader of the Transvaal reform movement. He was taken prisoner and sentenced to death; but his sentence was commuted, and he was released on paying a fine of $125,000. Clemens described his visit to the prison in his notebook:
Pretoria, May 23. . . . Visited the prison with the Chapins, Mrs. Hammond and Smythe. . . . Found I had met Hammond many years ago when he was a Yale Senior—visitor at Gen Franklin's. An English prisoner heard me lecture in London 23 years ago. Guard barred me off from crossing a line—called the death-line. Made a talk—or speech—sitting. Explained to the prisoners why they were better off in the jail than they wd be anywhere else; that they would

eventually have gotten into jail anyhow, ⟨by the look of their countenances⟩ for one thing or another, no doubt; that if they got out they wd get in again; that it wd be better all around if they remained quietly where they ⟨are⟩ were and made the best of it; that after a few months they wd prefer the jail and its luxurious indolence to the sordid struggle for bread outside; and that I wd ⟨go and see Pres. Kruger and⟩ do everything I could, short of bribery, to get ⟨him⟩ the government to double their jail-terms (Notebook 30, TS pp. 11–12).

125. CLEMENS TO ROGERS

Queenstown, Cape Colony
6 June 1896

Dear Mr. Rogers:

I find myself well scared. The May Harper (London edition) is here. Evidently Joan has finished appearing in the magazine, but I hear nothing of its being published in book form.[1] Is it *possible* that there is a hitch there, and that it hasn't *been* issued in book form? If so, I don't think it is of any use for me to struggle against my ill luck any longer. If I had the family in a comfortable poor-house I would kill myself.

We are poking along from town to town, from village to village. Shall be in East London to-morrow evening, and maybe have a glimpse of Mrs. C. and Clara as they pass by on board ship for Port Elizabeth. ⟨We⟩ They join me at Pt. Elizabeth and go to Kimberly, and presently to the Cape (middle of July.)

I have enjoyed being in Pretoria and Johannesburg in the thick of this political storm. A week ago if I had had $100,000 I would have dumped it into stocks. They were down at the bottom, and I knew that the body of minor prisoners were going to be released. The best stock in the lot jumped up 33 points when the news came.

Love to you all.

SLC

[1] The announcement of the forthcoming publication of *Personal Recollections of Joan of Arc* as a volume had appeared in the April issue of *Harper's Magazine;* it had run serially from April 1895 through April 1896, attributed to the Sieur Louis de Conte and "freely translated out of the ancient French" by Jean François Alden.

126. CLEMENS TO ROGERS

Port Elizabeth, S. A. R.
18 June 1896

Dear Mr. Rogers:

Your ⟨long⟩ *very* long delayed letters of the end of February have just arrived—via India. Honest, if I had had the selecting to do for you, I would have chosen Mrs. Hart every time;[1] and so it has cost me not a pang to praise you up, to her, a blame sight higher than you probably deserve; for I want her to be satisfied with you. I wanted to make her feel restful and easy about her bargain; and at the same time I was determined to earn the million you owe me if it cost the last rag of conscience I had in stock.

You say "May or June." Well, she will be at 26 East 57th by the time ⟨this⟩ to-day's letter reaches New York; or she will be in the new house at Fairhaven; so I will direct to 26 Broadway in your care. No—I will enclose it in *this*. That's the rational way. I hope my cable-congratulations will arrive in time or close to it.

I am sending a few wedding presents per first vessel—to wit:

Pair of elephants;
Pair of rhinosceroses;
Pair of giraffes;
Pair of zebras;
30 yards of anacondas;
Flock of ostriches;
Herd of niggers.

The wedding-present business is expensive when you work it from Africa.

I wish joy and prosperity to both of you, out of my heart.

Sincerely Yours

S. L. Clemens

---

[1] Rogers was married on 3 June 1896 to Emilie Augusta Randel Hart, the former wife of Lucius R. Hart.

127. Rogers to Clemens

New York
18 June 1896

My dear Clemens:

Since my letter to you of May 22nd. I am in receipt of your favors of April 2nd written at Sea, April 24th written at Mauritius and May 8th written at Durban, and am pleased to note that you are [in] better health and spirits. I have not the time to reply in detail to your several letters because I am meandering through my honey-moon, and as you must know, everything else must be put to one side until that important season is over. However, I must write you on your business affairs, and so shall undertake the task although I have very grave doubts as to my being able to make myself thoroughly intelligible. Before I go farther, I may say that I was married on the third of June and to the present time have no special reason for regret. Some of the newspapers gave me considerable of a roasting and others treated me with fair indifference. The most insulting thing was, that I was worth $65,000,000. and 66 years old, but that my youthful spirits and buoyancy of manner enabled me to pass for a man of 25 years younger. I used to think I was not at all sensitive on the age question. I believe I am getting to be a little that way now, but as for the wealth,—Holy Moses! if I only had the wealth I get credit for, I shudder when I think of the load it would be. But jesting aside—let us go to business.

I am going to send you a copy of my letter of May 22nd so that when you read this you will have something to refer to if the original has not reached you ere this arrives. I received Mrs. Clemens cable from East London in regard to the dramatization of "Joan of Arc" and have opened negotiations with Harper & Bros. and am expecting to have their reply in a few days. The affairs of C. L. Webster & Co. are now gradually drawing to a close. The accounts have been handed to the Courts and we expect to get the whole business cleaned up within 20 or 25 days. Nothing further was done with Payne or Barrow but we do not despair of getting them later on through a new lead we have found.

Those Hartford fellows are enough to perplex a saint. No doubt, I may say in dealing with them they *are perplexing one,* but the godly qualities I possess I think are quite sufficient for the job, and I can exercise as much patience to the square inch as they can. They get a proposition and then sit back in the traces waiting to tire me out, or hoping for a better trade. On Wednesday last I sent a letter to Bliss of which the following is a copy:—

"I have news from Mrs. Clemens and it is very important that you decide as to an agreement with the Harpers, and unless I hear from you to the contrary, I shall assume that you do not care to negotiate further and shall act as I deem best in the interest of Mrs. Clemens on all matters in which she and Mr. Clemens are concerned."

This morning I have a reply as follows:

"Will you kindly telegraph as soon as you receive this, to the Grand Union Hotel, (42nd St.) at what hour to-morrow I can confer with you about the Clemens business? If the evening would suit you better than during business hours, thus allowing a little more time, then fix it for evening; any portion of the day, however would suit me."

Consequently I have telegraphed him that I would see him this afternoon at 3 o'clock. I have coaxed, plead, bullied and blustered to mighty little purpose with those people but I am not going to give up until we get the job finished. I will add a P. S. to this letter after my interview with Bliss.

Poor Frank Mayo. I suppose before this reaches you you will have learned of his sad fate. If you have not heard however, the story is that he had finished his engagements for the season at Denver, Col. and was on his way to Philadelphia where his wife was lying dangerously ill, when the life quietly slipped out of his body, as he sat sleeping in the smoking end of a sleeping car, just West of Omaha.[1] Some of his company were on the train with him and it being a warm night, he concluded that he would sit up and get his sleep in the smoking room rather than to crawl into a stuffy berth. Somewhere about midnight, one of the Company went into the smoking room, and fearing that Mayo would take cold or that he might want to go to bed, tried to arouse him, but to no purpose. His spirit had flown. I believe the Doctors said he died from paralysis of the heart and attributed it to the high altitude. I had a letter from him only a short time ago, and I think I sent you a copy of it. He had made a great character of "Pudd'nhead Wilson." The papers spoke most highly of him after he had gone. I have decided to wait a reasonable time and then communicate with his son, whom I think was a member of his Company and undoubtedly knows of his affairs. It seems such a sad story all around, and looking at it in your interest, I am at a loss to know who can play the character of "Pudd'nhead Wilson." I can say no more at present, but hope to be able to communicate something in a subsequent letter. I enclose the last newspaper notice we received from Mr. Mayo.

4 o'clock, P. M.

Mr. Frank Bliss has just been in in response to my telegram. He had a better story to tell than I expected. It seems that he and Harper Bros. have come practically to terms with the exception of the figures at which the Harper books should be sold to Bliss. Harper Bros. want 80 cents for the printed sheets of "Huckleberry Finn" a $1.75 book—Harper & Bros. to pay you the royalty. This seems a very high price, and I have sent Bliss to Harper Bros. to try and get the price reduced; failing in which I will undertake to influence Harper & Bros. to make a reduction. I suppose I ought to qualify my remarks in this letter about the Blisses, because Frank Bliss to-day showed more willingness to be reasonable than ever before. We have got so close to a trade that it seems too bad for the Harpers to hold out for something that is unreasonable. I hope, however, within a fortnight to submit a memorandum of agreement between Harper & Bros. and the Blisses, together with my recommendations in the matter. You understand of course that if Bliss makes the arrangement with Harper & Bros. it seems that Bliss is to be the publisher of your new book if you write one, on the terms expressed in an earlier letter which undoubtedly is before you. When the memorandum goes forward for Mrs. Clemens' approval, I will embody the whole.

With warmest regards to you all, I am, as ever,

Yours sincerely,

(Signed) H. H. Rogers.

¹ On 8 June 1896.

128. CLEMENS TO ROGERS

Port Elizabeth, S. A. R.
19 June 1896

Dear Mr. Rogers:

Mrs. Clemens wrote me the other day and copied a paragraph from Harper's letter to you about division of dramatic profits on Joan; and I cabled you:

"Harpers share dramatic profits too high. Offer one-fifth or fourth.

Olivia Clemens"

and followed it with this cable:

"Private. But conclude dramatic contract anyway.

Olivia Clemens."

You see, we want the book dramatized and produced, even if we have to let Harper take a third of the spoil. Privately—to you—I don't know how there comes to be anything about dramatic business in the Joan contract. But that can rest till I come. There's a memorandum in your safe on a little piece of paper (unless my memory is astray) containing the basis for the Joan contract; and by and by when I come we will look at that and see what it says. I'm sure it would have taken my breath away if Harper had proposed to ⟨div⟩ share dramatic swag with me on a book of mine. ⟨Of course he never did⟩

—————

Yes, I think with you, that a trade might be made with Bliss on the basis you name: he to let Harper use the old books on a small royalty (Bliss pays *me* only a small one and therefore is reconciled to small ones) and he (Bliss) get Harper's permission to use the Webster books etc. Won't Bliss make a distinct proposition? If he will do that, we and Harper can soon arrive at an arrangement with him no **doubt.**

We expect to sail from Cape Town July 15 and reach London 1st or 2d August. ⟨There⟩ ⟨(Address Brown Shipley & Co)⟩ ⟨Address Chatto & Windus, 214 Piccadilly.⟩ Then hunt up village quarters in the country and have the book done by Nov. 1 and ready for a contract. If things have not by that time been settled between Bliss and Harper, I'll want Bliss to run over to England and contract for the new book independent of Harper. I don't see why Harper doesn't begin the publication of my books. He has no *valid* excuse. I have no contract with Bliss allowing him the use of *renewed* copyrights. I think it but fair to me that Harper should begin on the books at once or relinquish the contract.

—————

It is good news from Mayo. He got out of debt just at the time I estimated he would.

I am very glad the big creditors have all come in except bank and Barrow.

Now how much do we owe the bank and Barrow at present?

And how much do we owe the *rest* at present?

And how much money have we in your hands now?

I think it's a good idea to pay a 5% dividend to those who have come in on the 50% basis.

Also Mrs. Clemens and I think it would be well to pay off the *little* creditors in full, now? Don't you?—unless it will take more money than can be spared.

The Grants needn't come in; I'm never going to pay *them* a cent *any*how.

—————

I think the Harpers would object to being required to sell my 7 old books in *sets* only, but we will see.

Hang it, they ought to go ahead and publish my books without *regard* to Bliss. After the original copyrights expire what can *he* do?

[The remainder of this letter is missing.]

129. CLEMENS TO ROGERS

Port Elizabeth, S. A. R.
22 June 1896

Dear Mr. Rogers:

I don't know *yet* if the marriage has taken place, but I heartily hope it has; for both of you are lovable people and you could not fail to make each other happy. I was minded to cable my congratulations, but that is a dangerous thing to do when the distance is so great and the tidings that suggest the cablegram are so time-worn; so I tore up the message and did not send it. I mean it is dangerous because such a cablegram could reach you in the midst of mourning for some bereavement—for Providence generally makes the most out of a chance like that.

That reminds me of the time I cabled ⟨my⟩ the words "*Hearty Congratulations*" from New York to ⟨Berlin⟩ a bride in Berlin— timing the cablegram to hit the wedding-hour but it came within only an hour or two of congratulating her on her father's sudden death. And all this reminds me to wonder if you ever got the cablegram that went through Major Comfort when I was sick in Jeypore. However, of course you did, if *he* got it. But the one I sent ⟨from⟩ to Gen. Langdon never left Jeypore, I guess. A receipt for it came back from the Jeypore post office all right, but they hogged the money and destroyed the cablegram I guess. They say the native officials do not waste opportunities.

About the time this reaches you we shall be cabling Susy and Jean to come over to England; and so I hope you will let Miss Harrison engage passage for them in an American liner when they or Langdon let you know the date they wish to sail on. Please pay the fares and charge to ac/ of Mrs. Clemens.

I wish to *gosh* you had cabled the marriage—do *you* like suspense? Love to both of you and all the others.

SLC

130. ROGERS TO CLEMENS

New York
22 June 1896

My dear Clemens:

I have just received a line from Harper & Bros., copy of which I herewith enclose.

"Dear Sir:—We thank you for your very kind and courteous letter of the 18th inst. Mr. Daly was desirous of an immediate answer to his proposition as to the dramatization of 'Joan of Arc,' and we are not at all sure, in view of the lapse of time, that he would be disposed to take up the matter now. If he should still look favorably upon the idea, we have no doubt, but that we could, in accordance with our agreement, make an arrangement that would be mutually satisfactory to Mrs. Clemens and ourselves. In further explanation, we would say that if Mr. or Mrs. Clemens had been in this country to give the matter their personal attention and to decide the many important and annoying details sure to arise, we should have been entirely content to accept one fourth of the profits, as suggested. Assuming that we would be called upon to bear all the responsibility, we do not think the division of profits suggested in our proposition an unreasonable one."

I assume that Harper & Bros. will take the matter up with Mr. Daly, and that I shall hear further from them again.

Yours truly,

(Signed) H. H. Rogers.

131. ROGERS TO CLEMENS

New York
9 July 1896

My dear Clemens:

Mr. Bliss is here this afternoon and brings to me a paper addressed to him by Harper & Bros.[1] in which they have consented to allow the American Publishing Co. the use of the plates of their books published by C. L. Webster & Co. as well as the plates of "Joan of Arc" for their use in preparing the uniform edition; the understanding being that the American Publishing Co. are to set up anew the old books in the same style as those published by Harper & Bros.; Harper & Bros. to continue the sale of the C. L. Webster & Co. books in their trade as arranged in the contract. I have asked Mr. Bliss to write me a letter which I can forward to you covering the general details of the business, and what is contemplated by the American Publishing Co. if they accept the proposal of Harper & Bros. This he will do but not in time for to-morrow's mail.

As I view it the conditions of affairs will be in substance: if the trade is made between Harper & Bros. and the American Publishing Co. as follows, the American Publishing Co. will get out the uniform edition and continue the sale of books already in their possession, both old and new editions and sell the Harper books only in complete sets. Harper & Bros. will confine themselves to the sale of the C. L. Webster & Co. books, "Joan of Arc" and perhaps "Tom Sawyer, Detective." The American Publishing Co. to publish the new book you are going to write of your trip around the World, and to make an advance payment of ten thousand ($10,000.00) dollars as a guarantee on the profits of the new book for a stated time. The American Publishing Co. proposes to make a new contract (destroying the old one) with Mrs. Clemens for their publications, giving her half the profits on all the books or perhaps 15% as Mrs. Clemens may elect.

I think I have given you briefly just what is contemplated, and of course I should be glad to hear from you as soon as possible in approval, but before you decide fully in the matter I want to lay before Mrs. Clemens a full text of the contemplated arrangements between Harper & Bros. and the American Publishing Co.'s offer to me in regard to the whole trade.

Yours truly,

HH Rogers

[1] The letter from Harper & Brothers to Bliss, 25 June 1896 (copy in CWB), said:

Dear Sir:

Your letter of yesterday has had our careful consideration.

Under the circumstances, we would be disposed to an arrangement such as the following for "The Adventures of Huckleberry Finn":

I. We to sell you a duplicate set of electrotype plates of our edition for two hundred and seventy-five ($275.) dollars cash, and you to pay us a royalty, upon all copies sold of your edition, of four (4%) per cent upon the retail price of our edition. *Or,*

II. We to loan you our plates, and you to pay us a royalty, upon all copies sold by you, of eight (8%) per cent, also based upon the retail price of our edition.

III. The copies printed by you from our plates, as above, to bear your imprint and the proper copyright-notice; and a note to the effect that your edition is printed from our plates.

IV. The above quotation does not include the photogravure portrait of Mr. Clemens, included in this book.

V. An arrangement of similar character, *so far as the principle is concerned,* to be applied to the other books by Mark Twain published by us.

VI. You to sell the copies of Mark Twain's books, printed from our plates, as above, only in complete sets along with a complete uniform edition of his books published by you.

VII. The price put by you upon such volumes as you may secure from us for this complete and uniform edition to be fixed so that it will be impossible for us to be undersold in this market.

This proposal is tentative and is subject to the approval of Mr. Henry H. Rogers, Mrs. Clemens's legal representative, who, with you and ourselves, should sign the agreement when it is drawn up in complete form.

Very truly yours,
(Signed) Harper & Brothers
per J. I. R.

F. E. Bliss, Esq.

The second option was chosen when agreement was finally reached on 31 December 1896. See Appendix C.

132. Clemens to Rogers

At Sea
[22] July 1896

SS. *Norman*
On the Equator
July something 1896.

Dear Mr. Rogers:

I think we have been out about a week from Cape Town [1]—speed, an average of 410 miles a day. Very fine ship.

You have been having a tough job of it with the Blisses *et al*. I don't see how even your trained and wonderful patience has held out. I am ashamed of being the cause of putting so much work on you; but I am grateful to you for *doing* it, anyway. We are looking forward with a heap of interest to the Memorandum of Agreement.[2] We shall find it when we reach England no doubt. I do most heartily hope it will settle my publication matters once and for all. The tentative steps already achieved amongst you promise exceedingly well, I think.

I should think it would be better to have the *sets* sold by subscription and the single volumes by Harper, but that may be merely a superstition. The *main* thing is to get the books *going* again, after their long and calamitous rest.

I got horribly tired of the platform toward the last—tired of the slavery of it; tired of having to rest-up for it; diet myself for it; take everlasting care of my body and my mind for it; deny myself in a thousand ways in its interest. Why, there *isn't* any slavery that is so exacting and so infernal. I hope I have trodden it for the last time; that bread-and-butter stress will never crowd me onto it again.

This is a perfectly lovely voyage; all three of us are enjoying it to the full. I wish you and all your gang and its ramifications were here and that we were a thousand days from port. If Harry wants to take me out on a year's holiday in his yacht, I am his man.

We are hoping to find comfortable quarters in some village a couple of hours from London and go into hiding there a few months till the book is finished.

With love to the old members of the family and also the new,

Yours sincerely

SLC

¹ They had left Cape Town on 15 July.
² The Memorandum of Agreement drawn up on 3 August 1896 was in substance the same as that of 31 December 1896. See letter 135, note 2.

133. CLEMENS TO ROGERS

Southampton ¹
31 July 1896

P.S.

Dear Mr. Rogers:

We are just arrived, 16 days out from the Cape, and now I will telegraph London to send down the letters.² Love to you all.

SLC

¹ This postscript is written on stationery of the South Western Hotel, Southampton; Clemens may have intended it as a continuation of the preceding letter to Rogers, despite the interval of more than a week.
² On that same day Clemens telegraphed Chatto & Windus to forward all of his mail to his hotel in Southampton (Berg).

134. CLEMENS TO ROGERS

Guildford
12 August 1896

c/o Chatto & Windus
214 Piccadilly. W.

Dear Mr. Rogers:

Land, but the Harpers must be acquainted with the road to wealth! Just imagine: Bliss to pay them 8 per cent on the retail

price of my books for the *use of the plates!* Suppose Bliss sells
25,000 of one of my books at $1.50—*cost of plates, say $450* (at
the outside $500)—is he to pay Harpers $3,000? They could give
Bliss a duplicate set of plates at cost of $100. Why, this is murder in
the first degree, isn't it?

And Bliss was ⟨actually⟩ willing ⟨!⟩ ? All right, let him go ahead,
it's his funeral. And it's about time somebody was squeezing that
gang—they've robbed me for a quarter of a century; and wherever I
catch Bliss's old thief of a father, be it in hell or heaven, over the
balusters he goes.

Apparently there was no hitch but the guaranty of 12% to me.
No wonder he strains at that gnat after having gorged that camel.
How *is* he going to be sure of any profits if Harper takes them all?

⟨The Harpers pay 5 per cent themselves for the use of plates—
⟨it is what they pay ⟨Howells.⟩ a certain author and it is what
Houghton used to pay one of his authors.⟩⟩

A 10 per cent guaranty is sufficient for me—I'll be satisfied with
that; but I think that Bliss for his own sake and mine ought to do
his level best to crowd Harpers down to ⟨the ⟨Howells⟩ "certain
author" basis.⟩ a 4 or 5% basis.

The figures:

Bliss claims to pay a commission of 60% on retail price to his
general agents. ⟨My⟩ Consider the book's price ⟨will⟩ to be ⟨—presumably—$3.50:⟩ $1.50.

Genl. Agt. Commission.............................	$ 90
Harper's 8%.......................................	12
Cost *(to make the book)*..........................	30
	1.32
Remainder	18 cents

9 cents apiece to Bliss and me.

Whereas 10% guaranteed to me would be 15 cents, and Bliss
would have 3 cents left to pay office-rent with.

However, if he will guarantee me 10%, I'll be very well satisfied.

Moreover, if in addition to half profits on my new book he wants
to pay *me* 8% for the use of the plates, I'd like it. Said plates not to

cost above $2,000. He to make them and illustrate them in his own way, but not bring a bill against me for more than $2,000. I would leave him $2,000 of the advance-money to make them with. I mean, if it is to be not less than a three-dollar book.

I think you must enjoy tough work and plenty of it or you would have thrown this troublesome book-matter overboard early, and Bliss out of the window. I am ever so much obliged to you. Bliss has not written me. If he should write me I will send you a copy; and I will send my answer through you. If he comes over to see me I hope he will bring a contract or something approved by you.

I think it *must* be about time to re-copyright the Innocents— Colby will know. If it *is* time, won't you send the enclosed application to Washington, with 50 cents (for registration fee) and charge to me.

We are in a house in Guildford for a month, and Mrs. Clemens is scouring around after one for a longer period. We've invited Miss Harrison to pay us a visit.

With lots of love to all of you.

SL. C. M. T.

III

"Our Unspeakable Disaster"
(AUGUST 1896-JULY 1897)

> "Our original plans are all swept away by our un-
> speakable disaster"
>
> SLC to HHR, 10 September 1896

S USY CLEMENS'S death from meningitis on 18 August 1896 put an end to immediate plans for further lecturing. The Clemenses hid themselves for a year in London, seeing few people. Clara had her piano, Jean her horseback riding, and Mrs. Clemens her modest household duties; Clemens himself was determinedly at work finishing his account of the world tour. He continued to worry about the settlement of the Webster business affairs and about publication of the uniform edition of his writings. He was often physically ill, but he was ill in spirit also, discouraged and dejected. Though he wrote in detail concerning his affairs in the United States, more than ever before he was satisfied now to leave decisions, even about his publishing contracts, in Rogers's hands.

135. CLEMENS TO ROGERS

Guildford
14 August 1896

Dear Mr. Rogers:

We have been expecting disastrous news from America, and it has come this morning; in the form of—silence. I suppose it means that Susy is still ill; therefore if no better news comes this afternoon in answer to my cable of this morning, we shall sail for home in the Paris to-morrow.[1]

Your letter arrived yesterday evening containing the news of the agreement with Harpers and Bliss, and carried me off my feet with delight.[2] You have had a long and tedious fight of it, and we are deeply grateful to you for sticking to it and fighting it out to this handsome conclusion. I couldn't want the thing in better shape, and I never could have accomplished it myself.

My letter of day before yesterday was a pretty ignorant one. I see, now, why Harpers charged 8%, and why they were right about it and why Bliss apparently made no objection.

It is most fortunate that I have made no engagement to lecture in Great Britain. Still, I wasn't very likely to do it, I was so impatient to get at my book.

This letter will sail to-morrow, whether we do or not. I think we must take a cheap flat in New York and furnish it from our Hartford house.

We cabled to have Susy removed from Hartford, but I see by the papers that no sick person can travel in such heat.

Always Yours

SLC

⟨Please sign the Harper-Bliss contracts for me⟩ [3]

[1] Clemens finally decided not to accompany Livy and Clara, who left Southampton on 15 August. Three days later, Susy died in Hartford. The New York *Times* (23 August 1896) reported:

Among the passengers who arrived yesterday on the American Line Steamship Paris were the wife and daughter of Samuel L. Clemens (Mark Twain), whose eldest daughter, Olivia Susan Clemens, died on Tuesday night last, at the home in Hartford, Conn.

Mr. Clemens, who was expected also, had started, with his wife and Miss Clara, the second daughter, when news of their eldest daughter's illness reached them, but was detained on business at the last moment in Southampton. He, therefore, was advised of the death by cable while Mrs. Clemens and the sister were on the ocean.

They were notified by Dr. Rice, a friend of the family, who boarded the Paris at Quarantine. The mother was prostrated and swooned when the news was conveyed to her.

A carriage awaited the party at the pier, and they went directly to the Grand Central Station.

Mr. Clemens sailed from Southampton yesterday for New York.

In fact Clemens remained in England, since he could not have reached Elmira in time for the funeral.

[2] On 3 August 1896 Frank Bliss had written Rogers (CWB):

As we seem to have arrived at a satisfactory arrangement with the Harpers Brothers, relative to the proposed "Uniform Edition" of Mr. Clemens' works, —a copy of Harper's proposition to us being enclosed herein,—we now have to submit the following suggestions or propositions for a new contract between Mrs. Clemens and ourselves regarding Mr. Clemens' writings.

First: All old contracts now in existence between Mrs. Clemens and the American Publishing Company to be destroyed and a new contract to be made to cover all of Mr. Clemens' writings, as well as for what he may write in regard to his present "Journey Around the World"; the said contract to be on a basis of one-half profits, similar to that of "Tramp Abroad" and "Pudd'nhead Wilson," which call for one-half of the gross profits to be paid Mrs. Clemens. Said profits to consist of the difference between the actual receipts from the sales of the books and the cost of the plates, use of plates, and repairs thereof, paper, printing, binding, wrapping, boxing and all expenses incident to manufacturing the books, and getting them ready for shipment, insurance on plates and on book stock; the advertising and expenses of doing business, etc., being borne by the A. P. Company, out of their portion of said profits. The contract to cover any renewals of copyrights of said books.

Second: The American Publishing Company to issue a "Uniform Edition" of Mark Twain's entire works,—except such writings as may be deemed advisable to omit,—from new plates of the old books and Harper Brothers' plates of their books, as per arrangement with Harper. The A. P. Company to have the exclusive sale of said "Uniform Edition."

Third: The American Publishing Company, to pay Mrs. Clemens $10,000. in cash as an advance on the one-half profits to arise from the sales of the book, on the acceptance by them of a satisfactory manuscript of original matter written by S. L. Clemens sufficient to make an octavo volume of at least 550 pages, of an account of his late journey around the world. The said Company to have exclusive use of said manuscript and the right to publish the same, and the said Clemens not to write or furnish any portion of the same subject matter that will come in competition with the proposed new book, nor do anything that will interfere with the sale of said volume. The American Publishing Company to publish the book as soon as practicable and advisable after receipt of manuscript of the same, and to use all their best efforts to make a large and satisfactory sale of the same; and they are to further agree and guarantee that the profits to Mrs. Clemens arising from the sale of said book, shall amount to at least the $10,000. which is to be paid her in advance, within five years after publication.

Fourth: The American Publishing Company to guarantee that the one-half profits above referred to shall in no case fall below 12 1/2% of the retail price of each book respectively, except those of the cheap editions of "Tom Sawyer," "Sketches," "Pudd'nhead Wilson," and any other that may hereafter be mutually agreed upon.

³ The canceled line was replaced by the two following notes, written on the verso of manuscript page 2. The first, except for the signature, is in Clemens's hand.

Guildford, Aug. 14/96.

Dear Mr. Rogers:
I beg to thank you for the good work you have done in my behalf. Please sign the Harper-Bliss contracts for me.

Sincerely Yours
Olivia L. Clemens.

The second is all in Livy's hand:

Dear Mr Rogers
Yes I suppose that says what I wanted to say but I had in my mind something much longer. However our news of this morning has greatly upset us.

Sincerely yours
Olivia L. Clemens

136. CLEMENS TO ROGERS

Guildford
10 September 1896

Dear Mr. Rogers:
I have just read the sheaf of letters brought from you by my wife, and it makes my bones ache to think of the work and thought and persistency and patience they represent. I do not see how you ever held out to finish such a lagging and discouraging and troublesome job. If I had done it I should have considered it a heroic achievement. Which it is, anyway, although I didn't do it. And you got the victory at last—as you always do. You have brought about a consolidation of my interests which is far more advantageous to me than I could have expected or could have counted upon. It secures to my

wife and children one sure source for their bread and butter, and I am deeply grateful to you. Chatto said that a better arrangement could not have been invented.

It was most kind of you to place my wife and daughters so comfortably in the St. Louis. Mrs. Clemens says that the communicating nest of cabins was airy and spacious and homelike—and in every way so wholesome and health-protecting that she was spared all necessity of going outside her door the whole voyage to encounter the eyes of either the curious or the compassionate. They arrived early yesterday morning, and came up at once with me to this house. Our original plans are all swept away by our unspeakable disaster; therefore we go to London to-morrow, and shall get a house there and shut ourselves up in it and bar the doors and pull down the blinds and take up the burden of life again, with one helper the fewer ⟨in⟩ to put heart into my work as it goes along. I shall write the book of the voyage—I shall bury myself in it. But if I only had time and money and no bread-and-butter pressure upon me I would write a certain other book and make this one wait.

It kills me to think of the books that Susy would have written, and that I shall never read now. This family has lost its prodigy. Others think they know what we have lost ⟨, but⟩—intimates of hers —but only we of the family know the full value of that unminted gold; for only we have seen the flash and play of that imperial intellect at its best.

Fortunate Frank Mayo, to die in prosperity, not in adversity. I wonder his son does not attempt to take his place in the piece. Charley Langdon thinks Evans claims commanding rights in it. If he possesses them it must be by some contract with Frank Mayo which you and I know nothing about.[1]

I hope you are all well and happy, and that you still have as much of Mrs. Rogers's approval as you deserve. And more—more.

SLC

Future address:
Care Chatto & Windus
214 Piccadilly
London W

¹ After Mayo died, his partner Charles E. Evans hoped to continue producing *Pudd'nhead Wilson,* but he could not make satisfactory arrangements with the Mayo family. When he tried to sell the assets of the partnership, Mayo's son, Edwin, prevented the sale. Edwin later took over the play himself, but with little success (Contract of 18 August 1896 dissolving the Mayo-Evans partnership, enclosed with a letter from C. H. Butler, attorney, to HHR, 19 August 1896, CWB).

137. CLEMENS TO ROGERS

London
20 September 1896

Dear Mr. Rogers:

I gathered the idea from Frank Mayo that Evans was a capital manager; so I think, with you, that a quarrel in that camp is bad for all concerned, and ought to be patched up if possible. I guess it would be to young Mayo's advantage to let Evans select a new Puddn'head and go on and do the managing.

And yet, where's the use? Straightway something else would happen. Luck has turned her back on me for good, I reckon. Sometimes it looks like it. It is *good* luck that you have managed to bring order out of chaos in the Harper-Bliss matter, but until the contracts are actually signed I shall always be expecting Satan to mix in and spoil everything.

I cannot find it in my heart to be sorry that the Bank and Barrows still stand out against the 50 per cent. I shall be glad if they never consent. It was the Bank's criminal stupidity that caused my destruction, and I never greatly liked Barrows. I don't want to pay those two anything until all the others have been paid in full—if that day ever comes. My chances to pay are far poorer than they were. Our unspeakable bereavement has put my proposed 2-years platform-campaign entirely (and I think permanently) out of my list of intentions. It was my purpose to pay those debts in that way, and reserve all proceeds of my pen for my family.

I want to pay off the *small* debts as soon as that useless Colby closes the estate and lets us find out what they aggregate. I mean such of them as are owing to people of slender means—Mrs. Custer ¹ and a few others. But not including small debts owing to people who are well off. If Colby were only dead it would be an advantage; for then we could galvanize the corpse and put some energy into it; and what is more, some intelligence.

We are still house-hunting. Our difficulty is to find a furnished house for 5 guineas a week. We could get one for 6, no doubt, but we cannot afford that. Some years ago this was not the case.

We heartily wish well to young Broughton who lacks a name [2] —first of the No Name Series, but not the last, let us hope—and the same to the mother and father. And all the rest of you, big and little. We hope to see you here by and by, and shall rely on Mrs. Rogers to bring you.

I do not come up out of my misery and desolation in the least degree yet; but presently I shall submerge myself and my troubles in work.

SLC

[1] Elizabeth Bacon Custer's claim for outstanding royalty payments on *Tenting on the Plains; or, General Custer in Kansas and Texas,* which Charles L. Webster & Company had published in 1887, amounted to $1,825.46. (For some details of previous dealings with Mrs. Custer, see *MTLP,* pp. 252–253.)

[2] Urban Huttleston Rogers Broughton was born 31 August 1896 to Rogers's daughter Cara.

138. CLEMENS TO ROGERS

London
27 September 1896

c/o Chatto & Windus
111 St. Martin's Lane, W.C.

Dear Mr. Rogers:

I was glad to get the letter of last November which Miss Harrison remailed to me, for it flooded with light an episode about which I was in doubt and darkness before. It all stands explained, now, and I see that you did the right thing, followed the only right and manly course. I would have done just so, myself—even to the hiring of Hummell.[1] That was clean, straight wisdom. I wish I had Wilder [2] instead of Colby for my lawyer—that paltering ass. I suppose he will *never* collect the two or three thousand dollars owing to me by Frohman.³ I want to put that matter into Wilder's hands when Colby gets through with the Webster affairs.

We have searched London high and low for a house,⁴ and at last we have found one, for ⟨fifteen⟩ $1,350 a year; ⟨what⟩ which is a little more than we wanted to pay. We shall move into it in about a week; but possibly we may not like it well enough to stay in it; so we shall continue to use Chatto and Windus, 111 St. Martin's Lane, W.C. as our letter-address. My *cable* address is care BOOK-STORE, London—if Miss Harrison will make a note of it.

With love to you all

SLC

P.S. Was nothing said in the New York or other papers about Susy's death? If ⟨so,⟩ there was, nothing has come to me.

---

¹ Probably Abraham Henry Hummel, an attorney frequently accused of sharp practices, who, in addition to his criminal cases, also specialized in lawsuits involving theatrical people.

² William Wilder had impressed Clemens the year before when he had acted as attorney for Thomas Russell & Son in their suit against Charles L. Webster & Company.

³ Daniel Frohman was manager of the Lyceum Theatre in New York City. When *The Prince and the Pauper* was playing there in 1890, Clemens and Frohman were sued by Edward H. House, who claimed that the adaptation by Abby Sage Richardson, which Frohman was producing, had been plagiarized from a version which House had written for Clemens years before. To prevent House from having the play legally closed, Frohman paid him from Clemens's royalties. In 1894 Clemens sued Frohman for this money, which amounted, he said at that time, to five or six thousand dollars (SLC to OLC, 7 February 1894). While the suit was in progress, Frohman remembered, "Mr. Clemens and I played our nightly games of pool at The Players with unruffled amity" (*Memoirs of a Manager* [London, 1911], p. 52).

⁴ Clemens described the hazards of house-hunting and housekeeping (Notebook 31, TS p. 7):

> Chelsea, Oct. '96. In London it takes 5 weeks to find a house (furnished) that will suit both your convenience and your means; five more to find a cook—not many are advertised, even in the Morning Post where, it is said, they mainly go to be thought high-class; and it takes the former occupant 9 weeks to persuade the postmaster to respect his new address. We already had maids or maybe it would take 11 weeks to get them. Got a good man the first day to do the odd jobs—carry up coal, black boots, scour knives, etc. He is the authorized messenger of the block and has to show a good character before the police authorities will appoint.

139. CLEMENS TO ROGERS

London
6 October 1896 [1]

Dear Mr. Rogers:

The proposed Bliss-contract has arrived,[2] and is so entirely satisfactory that I shall be very glad and quite at rest in my mind the day that it is signed and goes into effect. Thank you ever so much for pushing it to this hopeful condition.

I am grown superstitious in these dreadful days, and was resolved not to write until I should hear good accounts from Mrs. Broughton and the little fellow that got crippled. I take it, now, from what you say, that you are no longer uneasy about either of them; and for that happy outcome I am very thankful.

I am glad you are keeping track of the Puddnhead play in Mrs. Clemens's interest. I shall be curious to see how the play will pan out, with poor Mayo's part in other hands. I had begun to think it possible that Mayo would succeed in making the play a permanency, like Rip Van Winkle; and I imagine that he had a like hope.

We are at last settled in a house, after scouring London several weeks. It only just exactly holds us—not an inch of spare room. However, we'll put up a bed in the drawing-room for you and Mrs. Rogers when you come.

I have concealed the address, in order to keep it out of the newspapers. But I shall reveal it to you and to Harry Harper and Miss Harrison, for you are trustworthy fellows. This is it:

23 Tedworth Square
Chelsea, S.W.

With the love of

SLC

[1] Clemens headed this letter: *"See address on page 3."* where it appeared at the end of the letter.

[2] Although a "Bliss-contract" dated November 1896 survives, it would appear that the agreement did not become final until 31 December 1896, when an identical contract went into effect (see Appendix C and letter 152).

140. CLEMENS TO ROGERS

London
13 October 1896

Care Chatto's new address:
111 St. Martin's Lane W C
(Or our dwelling house if
you prefer)

Dear Mr. Rogers:

I enclose answer to Mr. Harper's question.[1] You can retain it if you prefer, and convey the decision to him by your own hand.

Well, you *do* have a time of it trying to make Bliss and Harper trot in harness together! First one and then the other breaks over the traces when you are least expecting it. Bliss's turn next—I wonder what *he* will do, this time.

However, this is all noble good tuition for you. When you get done you can advertise as an expert who knows how to handle publishers. There's millions in it—perhaps.

Yours Ever

SLC

[1] Harper & Brothers had written Clemens on 12 May 1896 (CWB) to ask whether certain of his essays might be gathered into a volume in the series of "Harper's Contemporary Essayists." Not having received an answer, they wrote again on 12 October to repeat the request. Clemens noted on the envelope of their second letter: "I said Yes . . . provided the matter was used again in my own books."

141. CLEMENS TO ROGERS

London
20 October 1896

Dear Mr. Rogers:

Yours of Oct. 8 arrived last night. By George I am glad your patience is holding out. I should have been buried before this if I had had to conduct the negociations with the Harpers. You tell me not to give up. All right, I won't; at least I won't until you think the time has come for it. You'll be in a position to know.

Also I'll try not to worry over the Webster matters, though I perceive that there *is* formidable load of debt on me. It is bigger than I thought. When I left America I thought $40,000 would set me clear of debt; and it was my purpose to put in 200 nights on the platform in America and pay it off. But my trip has taught me that I am too old a wreck for such a job. I should break down almost at the start.

I find, now,—or seem to find, per the statement sent me by Miss Harrison—that my debt was nearer $70,000 than $40,000. In which case, I need not dream of paying it. I never could manage it.

My impression was that the debt was between $80,000, and $90,000, and that the Webster wreckage would pay ⟨half of it⟩ 43 per cent of it.[1] I don't know where I got that idea, but I had it. Whereas in truth that wreckage pays but 35 per cent, I suppose. I make this guess because Mrs. Custer's claim was $1800, and I see we have paid her $547—to piece out the Webster dividend and make up 50 per cent of the claim, as I judge.

I find we have paid Mrs. Grant $882.95. That surprises me, for Fred Grant told me in Colby's presence that the whole Grant claim was only $700—and I was lately sorry that I didn't remember, at the time, that Jesse Grant owes me $500 (borrowed money) and eleven years' interest and ask the family to let *that* square their claim. I suppose Colby has allowed them to enlarge their claim.

I am glad the Mt. Morris bank and Barrow declined to let me off at 50 per cent. I find it a relief now. If ever I get the others paid I will then tackle the Barrows debt, and pay that if I can. But I expect to be dead before I get a chance to begin on the Bank; and First-Assistant Archangel before I begin on the Grants. However, long before that I shall pay Fred Grant off in full in my Autobiography. I saved that family considerably over $200,000, and in return Fred Grant robbed the firm of many thousands by going back on an oral agreement, wherein that ass Webster had trusted him.

Colby will never collect the money that is owing to me by that

Lyceum Theatre Jew. It has been lying in the Court's hands for years. Just as soon as we are through with Colby I would like Wilder to go for that money. Hubbell [2] is that Jew's lawyer. The two will make a fine fight. If Colby's senior, Russell, were dead, Colby would be the head idiot of this century; and I wish Russell would die and give him a chance.

Mrs. Cara must not hurry about a name for the baby. And don't *you* hurry. You will be sure to make a mistake unless you wait till you find out what its sex is. I know you don't know, or you would have told me long ago. A mistake was made in my case, at first—or maybe it was afterward.

If they elect Bryan and a silver Congress, send me our balance and I will wait and buy silver and settle some of those debts on an economical basis. Are you wanting this political fight to go against *me?*

With love to all of you

SLC [3]

---

[1] The total debt was actually $79,704.80, and the assigned estate had paid 27.7 per cent of it.

[2] Clemens may have meant Abraham Henry Hummel. See letter 138, note 1.

[3] Clemens appended a note to Katharine Harrison (Salm):

Dear Miss Harrison:

Ever so many thanks for the Statement. It is a very good showing for us.

How many of the creditors agreed to the 50 per cent deal? Am I right—was Mrs. Custer's claim $1800? And did the Webster & Co assets pay 35 per cent?

I was very sorry I missed seeing you when you were here.

Yours Sincerely
SL Clemens

Katharine Harrison replied 10 November:

Dear Mr. Clemens:

I enclose a letter from Mr. Colby which I thought might be of interest. I have been trying to find out about Mrs. Custer's claim, but cannot succeed in getting hold of Mr. Colby. I will follow it along and as soon as I get anything, send it along.

With kindest regards believe me, as ever

Yours sincerely,
Katharine I. Harrison

Colby's letter to Miss Harrison of 2 November 1896 explained: "Practically all the creditors whose claims are admitted have accepted Mr. Clemens' settlement, except Mr. Barrow and the Mount Morris Bank." He added: "I cannot tell definitely whether the assigned estate will pay thirty-five per cent.; I doubt if it pays quite that. . . . I think that when everything is cleaned up, the estate will pay, at the very least, thirty or thirty-one per cent. and it may reach thirty-two or thirty-three per cent."

142. CLEMENS TO ROGERS

London
1 November 1896

Dear Mr. Rogers:

My goodness, have I gone and weakened your hands! I didn't know you were holding back a card in Tom Sawyer, Detective; and so when the Harpers wrote the other day to ask about how to fill out that book—what to use as padding, that is—I answered and told them to fill it out with anything they pleased (for in fact I was getting pretty impatient with the delay).[1] Dear me, a year ago I was taking comfort in the fact that at last I was in the hands of the Harpers, but in truth I am feeling less restful about it now.

If you are holding back any more cards I will try my best not to spoil the hand, as soon as I know what they are.

Possibly the Harpers are disgruntled because I was purposing to give the new book to Bliss. But I wanted it published by subscription, for it is not suitable stuff for the "trade."

If ever you get the Harpers to agree upon anything reasonable again, do make them *sign*—and you sign too—don't wait to hear from Mrs. Clemens—I am bail that she will be satisfied. Since my daughter's death my interest has centered itself upon the books: they will be the only support of my family in case of my death; yes, and their only support while I remain alive, for I am done with the platform. For a year or more, at any rate. I wish to make the list of books as large as I can. And so, after I finish the present subscription book, I shall go straight on and clear out my skull. There are several books in there, and I mean to dig them out, one after the other without stopping. The first one will be a "trade" book—about the others I don't know. One of them—my Autobiography—should be sold by subscription, I judge.

Since I am cut off from the platform I am thinking much more about creating an income for my family than I am about paying creditors. That is not Mrs. Clemens's attitude, but it is mine.

Give my love to the electric spark and the others, and let me know young Broughton's name as soon as you remember what it is—for your latest report is not definite enough.

Sincerely Yours

SLC

When the contracts are signed won't you please cable me:

Clemens care Bookseller [2]

London

Signed

———

As soon as I get the news I will start Bliss to renewing the Innocents copyright.

SLC

[1] "Tom Sawyer, Detective" was included in *Tom Sawyer Abroad* when Harper & Brothers published the volume, 17 November 1896.

[2] He meant "Bookstore," which was Chatto & Windus's cable address; see letter 160.

143. CLEMENS TO ROGERS

London
6 November 1896

Dear Mr. Rogers:

I am very glad indeed that the contract is accomplished at last, both for your patient indomitable sake and for my sake—I can work the better now. And I am glad of what you say of Harry Harper. He always seemed to me to be a frank and straightforward man and a man of a good heart and an obliging disposition.

Poor little Benjamin! [1] I am sorry for him. It doesn't seem fair to expose to him what this world is, so early. He ought to have been allowed to live in a pleasant misunderstanding of it for a long time yet.

I perceive that Brer McKinley has arrived. I supposed he would. Now then, let us have a quiet spell for a while, if we can.[2]

With love to you all

SLC

[1] A penciled notation on the manuscript reveals that Henry Rogers Benjamin, four-year-old son of Rogers's eldest daughter, had broken his arm.

[2] William McKinley had defeated William Jennings Bryan on 4 November after a particularly stormy campaign for the presidency, which centered on the issue of free silver. See letter 146 for Rogers's views on the contest.

144. ROGERS TO OLIVIA CLEMENS

New York
10 November 1896

My dear Mrs. Clemens:

You will recall that I some time since complained that Harper & Bros. had put into the contracts certain stipulations, which I did not feel were warranted, all things considered. At my suggestion the contracts were rewritten and the objectionable clause left out. I did however, promise Harper & Bros. that I would submit the matter to you without prejudice, and leave you to decide as to whether you were willing to put such a clause in the contract. About the 21st of October Messrs. Harper & Bros. sent me the enclosed letter[1] which I took the liberty of holding until I could have a conversation with Mr. Harry Harper, which took place, and concerning which I wrote you last week. There are some features in the contract which Mr. Harper desires inserted, which it will be impossible for you to do, because of your arrangement with the American Publishing Company. However this feature of the contract stands by itself, and it is for you to determine.

If I may be permitted I would like to give a little expression of my feelings as to Messrs. Harper & Bros. and their relations with you. It is true that they undertook the publication of some of Mr. Clemens' books, in the belief that they would ultimately get the publication of his entire works, old and new. They are therefore much disappointed because of the contracts with the American Publishing Company, which prevent the carrying out of the original plan with them. My belief is that Harper & Bros. are quite as friendly to Mr. Clemens as any publishing house, and I am quite free to say and I desire to emphasize the fact that I believe Messrs. Harper & Bros. will prove in the long run to be the most satisfactory people that Mr. Clemens has dealt with. If my advice can in any way influence you I would ask you to consider very fully and carefully the matter of making terms with Harper & Bros. for all time, and I most cheerfully urge upon you such permanent arrangement.

Yours truly,

HH Rogers

[1] In the letter of 21 October 1896 from Harper & Brothers to Mrs. Clemens it was requested that the following clause be inserted into the new contract:

WHEREAS, the contract dated May 23, 1895, and executed July 26, 1895, between the said parties of the first and third parts [Harper & Brothers and OLC], for the publication of a Uniform Library Edition of Samuel L. Clemens's works was based upon the understanding that the said party of the first part shall eventually include in the Uniform Edition all of the books thus far published by said Samuel L. Clemens; and WHEREAS, it was subsequently found impracticable to put such stipulation into effect; it is now hereby understood and agreed that the said party of the first part shall be at liberty, five years after first publication, to include in their edition any future books by the said Samuel L. Clemens hereafter published, upon the same terms and conditions as are stipulated in the aforesaid contract between the said parties of the first and third parts.

The letter continued: "Mr. Bliss having strongly objected to this provision, and Mr. Rogers not being prepared to decide the question, we have followed his advice in bringing the subject directly to you for consideration." On a page containing the clause which Harper & Brothers wished included, Clemens had written:

and that said future books so added, to the Harper list may also (be adde) be used by Bliss in his uniform edition upon the same terms and conditions specified in the contract (proposed) between Harper and Bliss as regards those books of mine which are already in Harper's hands. (Otherwise Bliss's uniform edition would not be uniform, but incomplete.)

The agreement of 31 December 1896 (Appendix B) does not contain this clause. But Rogers was trying as late as 24 December 1896 to get Bliss to "contract to put [Clemens's future books] in the uniform edition, after a period of five (5) years. I think this would be a protection to both you and Mr. Clemens" (HHR to Bliss,

24 December 1896, Yale). Bliss agreed, but thought the "fairest way to arrange this item" was for Clemens to handle each new book (or publisher) individually, reserving "the right to have us publish it in the uniform set after a proper period." He noted that this procedure "would relieve us from having to pay Harper or any one else the 8% royalty for the privilege, which takes about all the profit out of the publication of a book" (Bliss to HHR, 26 December 1896, CWB).

145. Rogers to Olivia Clemens

New York
10 November 1896

My dear Mrs. Clemens:

Will you read the enclosed contracts and if they meet your approval please sign them as indicated and return to me by an early mail, that I may complete the execution of the same. That you may have with you a full knowledge of what you have signed I send also a blank contract for you to keep while you are on the other side. I hope that the contracts will be satisfactory to you in every respect. I do not believe that it is in my power to do anything better, but will, however, if not satisfactory to you, undertake to make such changes in the contracts as you desire, but I am rather afraid of accomplishing anything; I may be anticipating trouble, and it may be that the contracts are all that are required.

Yours truly,

HH Rogers

146. Rogers to Clemens

New York
10 November 1896

My dear Clemens:

I sent to-day to Mrs. Clemens copies of the contracts for her to sign. Of course you will see all the papers and the letters, etc. I believe that I have done the very best that I could under the circumstances. Should you feel differently, and feel that I should make another exertion in any particular line you have but to command me and I am your obedient servant. I have thought this whole business was to turn out as a bad job a great many times, but fortune has favored us and things have come round after a while to pretty nearly what we have been asking for.

Archbold and I are going on Thursday morning on one of our visits to the Oil fields of Ohio and Indiana. You know you wanted to make the West Virginia trip a number of times; I only wish you were here to go with us.

We are getting along very smoothly at #26 East 57th Street. Mrs. Broughton and her baby are still with us, while Mr. Broughton has gone to Chicago to settle the house and arrange for the coming of his family.

We have just had an election, and we have just saved ourselves from going to the eternal bow-wows. I believe, however, that the Lord was on our side, and that he only gave us a good big scare, so that we might take heed and attend a little more closely to National business. The truth is that the politicians have been running the country for a good many years, and it is quite time that some business sense should be exercised, and I have the feeling that we are on the right track.[1]

With best wishes, I am,

Yours truly,

HH Rogers

[1] According to Thomas Lawson, Rogers was responsible for raising a fund of $5,000,000 to ensure McKinley's victory over Bryan (*Frenzied Finance*, p. 177).

147. CLEMENS TO ROGERS

London
[? 20] November 1896

Dear Mr. Rogers:

The contracts clear my head.

I had the impression that the Harpers could use all of my Bliss books; and that my 'Round the World would fall into their list, too, after a reasonable time. I had the notion that all the books would be sold by both parties, but that Bliss would sell them in uniform *sets* only.

However, I see it isn't so. I don't know why. I suppose Bliss was the objector.

And he objects to the additional clause proposed by Harper. I don't know why. He ought not to object, I should think.

Bliss does not engage to sell the new book and the sets *by subscription*. He allows himself to sell in any way he pleases. I haven't any use for ⟨Bliss in these two cases⟩ Bliss, in case of a *new* book and *sets* of old ones, *except* by subscription. Necessarily he means to sell by subscription, for he would lose money by any other plan; but he might as well have said so, I should think.

You do not believe it is in your power to "do anything better," and *I* don't see how anything better can be done. I am clearly of opinion—after thinking over the situation 3 hours—that it would be dangerous to try to alter these contracts. It is my opinion that they should be signed and sent.

If I knew of anything to hold over Bliss's head to make him consent to ⟨let Harper have the new book after a y⟩ the clause proposed by Harper, I would furnish it. How would this do: release Bliss from half or the *whole* $10,000 advance on the new book, on condition that he accept the additional clause proposed by Harper. I would do that.

That advance has no value to me as a *shover* of Bliss, (since he is not required to make the book earn it in 3 months but in 5 years), whereas it would be a happy thing for him to be relieved of the necessity of raising the money in a lump.

———

I think that my reason for wanting my travel-book in Bliss's hands is sound. Harper publishes very high-class books and they go to people who are accustomed to read. That class are surfeited with travel-books. But there is a vast class that isn't—the factory hands and the farmers. *They* never go to a bookstore; they have to be hunted down by the canvasser. When a subscription book of mine sells 60,000, I always think I know whither 50,000 of them went. They went to people who don't visit bookstores.

I planned this book, from the beginning, for the *subscription* market. I am writing it according to that plan. If it doesn't pay me $30,000 in the first six months, it will be because the new Blisses lack their old father's push and efficiency.

I have half a dozen books in my head, half of them suited to subscription, the other half to Harpers. But I shall not need to publish again with Bliss unless he will turn books over to the Harper list after reasonable delay.

[The remainder of this letter is missing.]

148. CLEMENS TO ROGERS

London
24 November 1896

Dear Mr. Rogers:

In ⟨one⟩ two of your letters of Nov. 10 you favor the execution of the contracts, but in your other of the same date you "urge us to consider carefully the matter of making terms with Harper for all time." I take this latter to mean, drop Bliss entirely and publish my new book and future books with Harper alone.

Or, it may be that the first mentioned two letters were written last, and mean, "These contracts seem the best that can be done, ⟨but⟩ and I am doubtful about being able to improve them, but if you wish to try, suggest the amendments and let us see what can be done."

PROJECT No. 1.

I wish I could talk with you. Are you coming over? Or would Bliss come over.

We have discussed the contracts two days. With this result: that before signing, they would better be amended thus:

1. Bliss to accept the clause proposed by Harper—with this addition: that my future books so added to Harper's list 5 years after publication remain *also* in Bliss's list. Otherwise his uniform edition would not be complete.

2. That clause II of our proposed contract with Bliss shall re-

quire him to canvass and publish my forthcoming new book *by subscription* and that it be not sold in any other way (that is, the "trade" way) until *after the day that the delivery to subscribers has begun.*

3. That clause III of said contract shall be so altered as to require Bliss to canvass and sell the uniform sets by *subscription* at first.

(This not to be insisted upon if he can satisfy you that he can do better with the sets by some other plan.)

4. Said clause III be further amended by striking out the indefinite as-soon-as-practicable business, and inserting a distinct *when* —on what *date* in the future the complete set shall be ready and deliverable.

I should say, one year after the delivery to Bliss of the MS of the new book ("Another Innocent Abroad")—or if that is too early, then *a year and a half* after such delivery.

(Bliss was horribly afraid of the uniform edition when I flung it at his head; said it would cost a world of money to sell it by subscription; the result couldn't be collected without great loss, etc. Why isn't he afraid of the uniform now? I think it is because the proposed contract leaves him at liberty to get it out at his leisure and sell it in any way he pleases.)

PROJECT 2

Another scheme—which you may have already considered—I don't know:

Could the thing be *turned around?*—end for end—the *Harpers* to issue the *uniform,* not selling the Bliss books singly, but only in the set⟨.⟩

⟨Could that in any possible way hurt Bliss?⟩

—"Another Innocent Abroad" and any other book or books of mine published by Bliss to be conceded to Harper a year or two years after issue, for use and sale *in the set only.*

Could that hurt Bliss in any possible way?

1. To accomplish this; 2, and reduce the ancient Bliss contracts to the ⟨newly prop.⟩ new 12½ or half-profit basis; and 3, to make him issue the new book by subscription and *within 6 or 7 months*

*after the MS goes into his hands, I would release him from the
necessity of paying me $10,000 advance* or ANY advance.

The truth is, the 12½ royalty requirement is a much stronger
incentive to energy on Bliss's part than is the $10,000 requirement,
since he proposes to take 5 years to earn ⟨it⟩ the latter in if he likes.

You will think me foolish about the subscription business, but it
isn't so. I have tried it, and I have tried the trade too—and really
there is no comparison between them. The sub. plan can outsell the
"trade" five to one with any book of mine whose subject is *foreign
travel.* Bliss will sell 60,000 copies of my new book in 6 months
⟨; the trade couldn't do it in six years.⟩.

PROJECT No. 3.

By gracious, I'm appalled! Here I am trying to load you up with
work again, after you have been dray-horsing over the same tiresome ground for a year. It is too bad; and I am ashamed of it.

Tell you what—if you approve, let's do this. Won't you put on a
separate paper, in legal phrase, the things which I have suggested
in PROJECT No. 1 and No. 2, and ship the paper to me and tell
Bliss (not his brother) to come over here. Then I will discuss with
him, and if there is a result I will submit it to Chatto and his lawyer
before letting Mrs. Clemens sign the papers.

How does that strike you? It is not fair to let you waste any more
time on Bliss.

Mrs. Clemens's leanings are *all* toward the Harpers—she doesn't
believe in Bliss. I add this in fairness to her. But I keep insisting
that if I fail to compromise with Bliss this time I can never get my
books together and never get the income from the old books aug-
mented.

Sincerely Yours

SLC

P.S. Is Colby, as assignee, on a *salary?* If so, let us not get in a
hurry—it wouldn't be any use. I'd like to have our Broughton baby
educated to succeed him when he dies in the harness of old age.

This letter bears date to-day, but it took me four days to study out the situation. Mrs. Clemens and I thought it best to take time and go into the matter carefully.

149. Clemens to Emilie Rogers

London
26 November 1896

For and in behalf
of Helen Kellar [1]
Stone blind and deaf, and
formerly dumb.

Dear Mrs. Rogers:

Experience has convinced me that when one wishes to set a hard-worked man at something which he mightn't prefer to be bothered with, it is best to move upon him behind his wife. If she can't convince him it isn't worth while for other people to try.

Mr. Rogers will remember our visit with that astonishing girl at Laurence Hutton's house when she was fourteen years old. [2] Last July, in Boston, when she was 16 she underwent the Harvard examination for admission to Radcliffe College. She passed without a single condition. She was allowed only the same amount of time that is granted to other applicants, and this was shortened in her case by the fact that the question-papers had to be *read* to her. Yet she scored an average of 90 as against an average of 78 on the part of the other applicants.

It won't *do* for America to allow this marvelous child to retire from her studies because of poverty. If she can go on with them she will make a fame that will endure in history for centuries. Along her special lines she is the most extraordinary product of all the ages.

There is danger that she must retire from the struggle for a College degree for lack of support for herself and for Miss Sullivan, (the teacher who has been with her from the start—Mr. Rogers will remember her.) Mrs. Hutton writes to ask me to interest rich Englishmen in her case, and I would gladly try, but my secluded life will not permit it. I see *nobody*. Nobody knows my address. Nothing but the strictest hiding can enable me to write my long book in time.

So I thought of this scheme: Beg you to lay siege to your husband and get him to interest himself and Messrs. John D. and William Rockefeller and the other Standard Oil chiefs in Helen's case; get them to subscribe an annual aggregate of six or seven hundred or a thousand dollars—and agree to continue this three or four years, until she has completed her college course. I'm not trying to *limit* their generosity—indeed no, they may pile that Standard Oil Helen Kellar College Fund as high as they please, they have *my* consent.

Mrs. Hutton's idea is to raise a permanent fund the interest upon which shall support Helen and her teacher and put them out of fear of want. I shan't say a word against it, but she will find it a difficult and disheartening job, and meanwhile what is to become of that miraculous girl?

No, for immediate and sound effectiveness, the thing is for you to plead with Mr. Rogers for this hampered wonder of your sex, and send him clothed with plenary powers to plead with the other chiefs—they have spent mountains of money upon the worthiest benevolences, and I think that the same spirit which moved them to put their hands down through their hearts into their pockets in those cases will answer "Here!" when its name is called in this one.

There—I don't need to apologise to you or to H.H. for this appeal that I am making; I know you too well for that.

Good-bye with love to all of you—

SL Clemens

Laurence Hutton is on the staff of Harper's Monthly—close by and handy when wanted.

---

[1] Clemens was consistent in misspelling Helen Keller's name.
[2] Helen Keller describes this occasion and her subsequent visits with Rogers in *Midstream: My Later Life* (New York, 1929), pp. 288–289.

150. Clemens to Rogers and Emilie Rogers

London
18 December 1896

Dear Mr. and Mrs. Rogers:

This is a line to wish you Merry Christmas.

I do not wish this family one, for the wish would achieve nothing in that line. We are bearing Susy's wholly unnecessary death as well as we can. The hard part to bear is the knowledge that if she had been with wise and thoughtful friends those last six months instead of with ⟨fools⟩ the other sort, she would be as well to-day as she was when we left her. If she had had only *one* wise and courageous friend among the crowd of friends in Hartford, we should not have lost her.

I myself can keep cheerful—much more so than the others—for I have my work. I work seven days in every week, and seldom go out of the house. I don't rush, and I don't get tired, but I work every day and sleep well every night. I got to work on the book at the earliest possible moment—⟨Nov.⟩ October 26—and I have not missed a day since, I believe. The book requires about 250,000 words. I have written 65,000. My idea is to always turn out 30,000 a month. And certainly that is not difficult.

With love to you all

SLC.

151. Clemens to Emilie Rogers

London
22 December 1896

Dear Mrs. Rogers:

It is superb! And I am beyond measure grateful to you both. I knew you would be interested in that wonderful girl, and that Mr.

Rogers was already interested in her and touched by her; and I was sure that if nobody else helped her you two *would;* but you have gone far and away beyond the sum I expected—may your lines fall in pleasant places here and Hereafter for it! [1]

The Huttons are as glad and grateful as they can be, and I am glad for their sakes as well as for Helen's.

I want to thank Mr. Rogers for crucifying himself again on the same old cross between Bliss and Harper; and goodness knows I hope he will come to enjoy it above all other dissipations yet, seeing that it has about it the elements of stability and permanency. However, at any time that he says *sign,* we're going to do it.

> Ever Sincerely Yours
>
> SL Clemens

[1] Rogers supported Helen Keller at Radcliffe.

151a. ROGERS TO CLEMENS

> New York
> 24 December 1896

My dear Clemens:

I have been out of town and ill and had other things to annoy me, hence my neglect in writing you. At last I have a letter from Bliss, copy of which I enclose [1] which I think meets the questions you raised in your letter of the 24th of Nov. or at least, as near to the same as I can get. Bliss in closing up his letter says, these are all the points I raised with him, (which is not quite true,) but as much as I was able to get him to yield.

In regard to the acceptance by Bliss of the clause proposed by Harper Bros., I think on reflection you will see that it will work out naturally, without committing Bliss to the matter in any way. Bliss will be very glad to add the Harper books to the uniform edition, and I have no doubt that in a personal interview I can get him to consent to it if you think wise. Please read Bliss's letter, and if the same is acceptable, sign the contracts and I will attach Bliss's letter to your copy of the contract and it will therefore become part of it.

I haven't anything of personal interest to write about, excepting to say to you, which Mrs. Rogers may have already done, that the Helen Keller matter has been adjusted satisfactorily with Mrs. Hutton for the time being, at any rate. If I had time I could tell you of a singular coincidence in connection with that matter, and as I have started on it, I guess I will take the time.

I went to a Lotus Club dinner given to Ian McClaren (Rev. Dr. Watson) and met Mr. Lawrence Hutton there. I referred to the pleasant afternoon that I spent at his house when you and I went there to see Helen Keller, and in asking him about her, learned that Mr. Spaulding,[2] her benefactor had died without making any provision for her. I suggested to Mr. Hutton that I would be willing to contribute a little in that direction and he thanked me very heartily. Monday morning at the breakfast table I received a letter from Mrs. Hutton and Mrs. Rogers received a letter from you; they were both on the same subject, viz: Helen Keller. Mrs. Rogers went that day to call on Mrs. Hutton and had a very pleasant talk, and the arrangement that I before referred to was consummated. I do not know whether you would bring that coincidence into your mental telegraphy business or not, at any rate, I thought I would tell you about it, and knew it would please you to say the least.[3]

We are all very well at home. Mrs. Broughton is settled at Chicago and Harry is to start on his maiden voyage to that City on Saturday morning entirely alone. Frank Thompson didn't send him a private car but he did give him free transportation and a fine stateroom on the Limited.

Colby has been in and tried to explain to me about his affairs, and I judge in due process of time, if the world exists long enough, that we will get the Webster matter settled so far as Colby can do so.

I don't imagine that you will have a very Merry Christmas, but certainly all our wishes are that you may. Remember me with much kindness to Mrs. Clemens and your daughters, and believe me, as ever,

Yours sincerely,

HH Rogers

¹ F. E. Bliss to Rogers, 15 December 1896 agreed that his firm would:
. . . assent to Mr. Clemens' requests as follows:

First, that the proposed new book shall not be sold by us in any other way than as a subscription book until after the day of delivery to subscribers has begun; which is entirely within our proposed plan of selling.

Second; That the proposed "uniform edition" shall also be sold by subscription at first; and as to the time that the complete "uniform edition" shall be ready for delivery, we are willing to name a date, although it is a matter of guess-work largely, as not merely the actual time necessary to the mechanical part of it has to be considered, but the circumstances under which it may be sold, the condition of the times, etc. You have suggested one year, and I doubt not that we should have it ready and be delivering it within that period, yet it would please us better to have eighteen (18) months as the date, thus giving us a little extra time to cover unforseen and unanticipated difficulties which may come up. There will be a number of new pictures to be made for the various volumes, and the engravings of the same, and it will take time to do all these things, and we feel that one year *might* be pretty close work for us, so ask that eighteen (18) months be taken as the time (office copy in MTP).
At the bottom of the page Clemens has written: "This letter is added to the contracts of Dec. 31/96, and completes them. SLC" For the contracts of 31 December 1896, see Appendixes B and C.

² John Spaulding, "the 'Sugar King' of Boston . . . was a generous and unselfish friend" of Helen Keller and Miss Sullivan, "furnishing them lavishly with money when they stood in need of it" (Nella Braddy, *Anne Sullivan Macy: The Story Behind Helen Keller* [Garden City, 1933], p. 164).

³ Clemens described another case of "telegraphy" involving Helen Keller in an Autobiographical Dictation of 30 March 1906 (*MTA*, II, 298). The incident occurred at the Hutton home during the first meeting between Helen and Clemens. Miss Keller, who was then fourteen, astonished the company by unconsciously repeating the same words that Clemens had just spoken across the room.

152. CLEMENS TO ROGERS

London
4 January 1897

Dear Mr. Rogers:

Yours of Dec. 24, enclosing copy of Bliss's of Dec. 15 of which the original is to be attached to the signed contracts and become part of them, arrived duly.

We have signed the contracts, ⟨this morning⟩ I using visible American ink and Mrs. Clemens using partly visible English ink. In one case her result was so doubtful that I thought it best to witness her signature, just to show that there *was* a signature.

In turning the word November into December I preserved part of the original word—the last 5 letters of it, and turned the first 3 into *Dec* with the pen—neatly, too, I think.[1]

I have cabled you this morning, "Contracts signed." ⟨So as to⟩ So that Bliss can get straight to work.

I have started the package of contracts to you, not by mail, but by an Express-Co. Their New York office is close to you—J.W. Hampton & Co 41 Broadway. If they do not arrive promptly, please ask Miss Harrison to step over there with her tomahawk.

Well, I am mighty glad that that business is finished up at last, and so tight and shipshape. Accept my deep gratitude. But for you I never should have arrived *anywhere* in it.

I am sure the Harper clause can be arranged by and by. If they are in no hurry, let us drop it for the present.

I think that the Helen Kellar "coincidence" case is exceedingly interesting. And I think that it is more easily explained as an instance of telegraphy than in any other way. I've got another one which I think is of the same nature—a New Zealand experience— and I mean to get a page or so out of the two.[2]

You guessed rightly as to Xmas. It was a desolate time. It was the first, since our marriage, that the day came and went without mention. No presents were exchanged, and we studiously pretended to be unaware of the day.

I am grinding steadily along with the book—7 days in the week, 31 in the month. I shall get 31 into February. It will crowd me, but I shall do it.

I've got a new book in my head—3 or 4 of them, for that matter —but I mean one that occurred to me a day or two ago. I shall write *All* of them—a whole dam library.

And I've struck an elegant new idea this morning for a lecture next winter in New York—a lecture that I can *enjoy;* and it has been 20 years since I actually enjoyed standing on a platform.

I wouldn't let Harry go out there and boss the Broughtons around. He will break up that family. But I send him my love, anyhow.

We all wish you and Mrs. Rogers and all of you a happy New

Year. We had none ourselves, because of thinkings; and because one was absent.

SLC

---

[1] Evidence in MTP suggests that Clemens made this change in a copy of the agreement reproduced here as Appendix C.

[2] The "New Zealand experience" is related in *Following the Equator* (Hartford: American Publishing Company, 1897), pp. 316–317.

153. CLEMENS TO ROGERS

London
15 January 1897

Dear Mr. Rogers:

We liked the contract, and were glad to sign it. Give yourself no trouble about that. As for Harper and Bliss, neither of them has done best for himself. Bliss could have had *all* the books, a year or two ago, but showed no strong desire; *now* he is so anxious that he takes the lacking ones on hard terms. Harper fulfils *part* of his contract with me, by publishing only those which there is no shadow of dispute about, and elects to avoid fulfilling the rest of it on the plea that I can't deliver the goods—i.e. Innocents Abroad, (to begin with.) He could have tested that, in a court, with a "dummy" Innocents—and he would have won, *I* believe.

I beg that you will offer my best wishes and homage to your mother. I am coming to dine with her again some day.

I suppose Harry struck 16 in October; and probably tried to vote in November.[1] Yes, we will transfer the "electric spark" to Colby, now that Harry is developing into a volcano. Dear me, that Colby! Why, when he took the Frohman matter out of Whitford's hands he was loud in criticism of Whitford's slowness—*he* would collect that money right away—it was a perfectly simple matter, and all that; whereas the chances are that in his hands Frohman will escape by the statute of limitations. I am glad of what you and Charley said to him about the Bank. It was that bank's free way of lending money to Hall while I was abroad that made the bulk of the trouble.

I'll keep the Helen Kellar subscription private.[2] I don't want you to be flooded with begging letters. The magazine came, and I am much obliged.[3] Helen's name will be familiar to the world five centuries from now. In her line she is the most extraordinary product of all the ages.

The reason I have been tardy about writing you is, that I wanted to wait till I could announce that the back of the book was broken —that is, that it was half done. So I have stuck steadily to it day after day and given my attention to nothing else. ⟨All right⟩ The first half of a book is a tough job; a body thinks he never can hold his grip and pull through to the middle, the summit; but the summit once passed, he doesn't mind the down-hill spin. Well, I've crossed the ridge, and I'm homeward bound. I shall move faster, now.

You've got a "Roughing It" at home. Please take a full page of it, uninterrupted by blanks, dialogue or pictures, and *tell me how many words it contains,* by actual count. I am proposing to make this book the same size as that; that is, 550 8vo pages.

With love to all of you,

SLC

P.S. *Jan. 15.* I forgot to say this—that I think I won't at present write the Harpers about future books, but leave that to arrange itself later. I am curious to know whether they can make sales of my books or not—in fact I haven't large faith in any but the subscription method of selling *my* books.

But no doubt I shall soon know how they made out with Joan. You will be receiving their ½-yearly statement about this time. Tell me the result.

SLC

[1] Actually Harry was seventeen on 28 December 1896.
[2] Clemens did not speak publicly of Rogers's generosity to Helen Keller until

he made a speech at Norfolk, Virginia, on 3 April 1909, at the opening
ceremonies for the Virginian Railway.

[3] Possibly the January 1897 issue of the *Century* magazine, which contained
an open letter by Arthur Gilman on "Helen Keller at Cambridge," and an article
on speech-reading for the deaf which cited Helen Keller's miraculous case (pp.
473–475, 342–343).

154. CLEMENS TO ROGERS

London
19 January 1897

Dear Mr. Rogers:

As soon as I hear that Bliss and Harper have executed their end
of the contracts [1] I'll write Bliss and send through him an application for renewal of Innocents Abroad.[2] I have already written the
letter.

By letting *on* powerfully, Bliss may have convinced Harper that
he (Bliss) would own all renewals, but in his heart he didn't
believe it. Doesn't he confess it in the lines which I have under-
scored on the second page of his letter? [3]

But I think it happens all the better for me. Harper's 8 per cent
royalty cuts the profit out of the books he allows Bliss to use.

I am a good deal further along than I thought I was. I could
finish my book by the first of March if I chose. But I shan't. I will
write a deal more than necessary—then I can cut out as much as I
choose.

Maybe Bliss's letter possesses importance; so I think it had better
go into Miss Harrison's keeping.

I have lost yesterday and to-day. Tired. Also, stupid. But it won't
last.

Yours Sincerely

SLC

[1] Harper & Brothers delayed signing until 26 February, and Bliss until 4 March
1897. See Appendix B.

[2] Bliss had written Clemens two months earlier on 16 November 1896 (Salm) that *The Innocents Abroad* would "not be legally ripe for renewal before Jan. 29th 1897, and any time within six months after that date will do for making the application." Clemens did write Bliss (19 January 1897), enclosing an application for copyright renewal and asking him to submit it "at what shall seem to you to be the proper time." But Bliss seemed inclined to take his time, and Clemens repeated his request on 30 January, 19 March and 31 May.

[3] Bliss professed ignorance of the fact that "the *copyrights* themselves had been assigned" to Mrs. Clemens, and yet evidently conceded that Clemens (or his wife) retained "ownership of the book." Clemens underlined relevant passages on both pages of Bliss's letter: "The former copyright was taken out in OUR name; this time *it will have to be done in* YOUR *name* . . ." (page 1). And ". . . I see no harm in the new copyright on "The Innocents" remaining in your name just as it will be issued, as *it seems as if your late transfer to Mrs. Clemens would continue to hold on the renewal as on the other copyrights still standing in your name*" (page 2). Bliss was as shrewd as he apparently was naïve, however, and Clemens probably valued this concession too highly (Bliss to SLC, 16 November 1896, Salm).

155. CLEMENS TO ROGERS

London
2 February 1897

Dear Mr. Rogers:

The moment the Bliss and Harper contracts are signed, over there, I want to make a suggestion to Bliss—a proposition. You see, this book is stringing out. I finished it yesterday, but I have covered only about half of the trip. 180,000 words does not allow me room enough. So I think of going on and making it a 2-volume book of 140,000 words each—say 450 pages each, and sell the volumes ⟨independently⟩ separately at $3 or $3.50 each, and the set at $5 or 6.

The first volume would contain the Pacific Ocean, Fiji, Honolulu, Australasia and a day in Ceylon.

The second volume would contain India, the Mauritius, South Africa and ⟨the Bermudas⟩—no, not the Bermudas—those other islands, I can't recal the name at the moment.

Oh—*Madeira*.

What do you think of it? I could have the first volume ready for

Bliss at nearly any time, and the other one by the end of May I should think.

All well.

Yours ever

SLC

My brother writes that Puddnhead had a crowded house in Keokuk and was splendidly played to an enthusiastic house, with several curtain-calls after each act.

156. CLEMENS TO ROGERS

London
8 February 1897

Dear Mr. Rogers:

Well, I've had my feathers cut. I was feeling too cocky. The minute I concluded to go on and make 2 volumes of this book I broke down. I haven't touched a pen since. I am all right again, and shall go to work again to-morrow—but not to make 2 volumes. No, I've dropped that idea. I mean to write a third more matter for the one volume than necessary, then weed out and leave one compact and satisfactory volume.

I am much obliged to you for counting those words for me. Your count confirms my estimate.

I wonder what Harry shoved his age ahead a year for. He will want to shove it back again by and by. *I* know his age—but it is safe with me. I won't give it away.

I was very glad to get Mrs. Rogers's letter, and am going to write her again presently. I am very glad everything has come out so well for Helen Kellar. If she doesn't go into the publishing business she'll be all right, now.

I am going to write with all my might on this book, and follow it up with others as fast as I can, in the hope that within three years I can clear out the stuff that is in me waiting to be written, and that I shall then die in the promptest kind of way and no fooling around. But I want you and the rest of you to live as long as you would like to, and enjoy it all the time.

With love to you all

SLC

Curse that Colby, why *does* he fool along so!

157. CLEMENS TO ROGERS

London
26 February 1897

Dear Mr. Rogers:

I am grown so nervous about the contracts that such sleep as I get doesn't do much good, and so my work drags badly and lacks life. I should think that if Bliss meant to sign at all he would get at it; for he knows that if the book were in his hands at this moment his time would be crowded, and that every day that is lost now is a sure money-loss. I am not strenuous now. If he wants concessions, let's grant them. It will be good business if it saves the book from being delayed too long. I want to strike Chatto for a new and better arrangement, for I have a good bid from another London publisher; but I don't wish to move in the matter until I know that Bliss is secure.

I should think the creditors would be entirely out of patience with Colby. I am. Is there a Judge whom I could appeal to to force him to close up the concern? Or, would you advise me to drop a hot paragraph about his laziness and incompetence into the American papers? The nights that Bliss lets me sleep, *Colby* interferes.

I believe I will follow my old superstition and cable you Monday or Tuesday to know if the contracts are signed—in the hope that a cablegram coming from you will cross it under the ocean.

By George, if Bliss shouldn't sign! Well, that *would* be a disaster!

For I have written this as a subscription book, and it is not suited to the "trade."

I am ashamed to seem so nervous and scared, but by gracious it's just the way I feel. Part of it is this long unbroken strain of work, but the other is the main part, I am sure.

I sent you a part of this billiard-game between Roberts and the "all-around" champion—spot-barred game, Roberts giving Peall 12,000 in 24,000.[1] But I begin to believe it is a "fake." At first everybody supposed it was an honest game. Roberts can win it easily if he wants to. But with the spot-shot allowed, Peall can beat Roberts easily.

Sincerely Yours

SL Clemens

[1] John Roberts was the 1893 English billiard champion; apparently a London newspaper had printed a description of a game between Roberts and W. J. Peall.

158. CLEMENS TO ROGERS

London
5 March 1897
5.30 p.m.

Dear Mr. Rogers:

The cable "Signed" has just arrived, and I can't tell you how glad I am. It is like a new start in life. It takes a great deal to stir me up now, but this has done it. I am ever, *ever* so much obliged to you. You are the best friend a man ever had, and the surest.

I'll start Bliss to getting a renewal of the Innocents copyright, now. And also I will presently have a business-talk with Chatto.

If I had time I believe I would make a 2-volume book of it, for the canvasser would rather have that than a 1-vol, and a good canvasser will take hold of a 2-vol when he wouldn't the other. But I believe there is not time. Not time because I am going to destroy a good deal of this book and I couldn't rewrite it in time for Bliss to get his canvassing-book ready by the *1st of September*—which he *must* do, or he can't get in a long enough canvass before the right and proper publishing Day—which is *Dec. 15* or thereabouts.

Ever so many thanks, with love to you all. Now I will go and tell the Madam.

SLC

159. CLEMENS TO ROGERS

London
19 March 1897

Dear Mr. Rogers:

I have just written Bliss, and told him I should finish the book about June 1, and that ⟨before⟩ now pretty soon I shall send over the first part of it to select canvassing-matter from.

I didn't say to whom I should send it. I shall send it to you, of course. If I sent it to him it might not be wise.

I finished the book three weeks ago, then began the process of gutting. I gutted out one-third. I am revising and re-revising the remaining two-thirds, and am getting them into very satisfactory shape.[1] Am very much pleased.

I think I shall be through by June 1. I am trying my very best to make a good book of it.

Poor old Puddn'head! Why didn't the useless *son* die, instead of the useful father? That is the way this universe is carried on. I wish we could get its affairs into the hands of the Standard Oil.

Love to all of you

SLC

Yes, we think, with you, that Bliss ought to have at least 12 months from now before the publication of the uniform edition; in fact he could just as well have till October 1898—a year and a half from now—for he will not issue in the summer time, of course.

I shall consider Mr. Warner pretty shabby if he doesn't ⟨retire⟩
cease from any further claim upon the Gilded Age.

[1] On 19 March Clemens wrote Frank Bliss asking him again to renew the
copyright on *The Innocents Abroad* and telling him of the new book:
> I finished the book (in the rough) March 1st, then spent a week gutting it.
> I gutted a third of it out, and then began a careful revising and editing of the
> remaining two-thirds. I shall complete this revision in two or three days. I set
> the type-writer to work on the first 10,000 words a couple of days ago.
>   When she finishes the first 100,000 words I will carefully revise that and it
> will then be ready for you.
>   I must do all this extraordinary revising because this book has to come into
> comparison with the Innocents, and so I must do my level best to bring it
> chock up to the mark.

As an old hand in the subscription book business, he had marked, he said,
"passages which I think will be useful in the canvassing-dummy." And he had
suggestions about illustrations also: "There are several places—3 or 4—where you
will need an artist with a poetical imagination and a fine touch, if you illustrate
them at all; illustration not really necessary, but if done let it be *well* done." And
he continued:

> I suppose A B Frost is an expensive artist; but if he is not *too* expensive it
> might be well to get him to make 3 *or* 4 *full-page humorous pictures.* He is the
> best humorous artist that I know of, and he might not be difficult to deal with
> for the reason that he told me 3 years ago that he had long had an ambition to
> make some illustrations for me.

(When *Following the Equator* appeared, Frost was one of its eleven illustrators.)
Clemens told Bliss, "I fully expect to write the remaining third and complete the
book by June 1 and then ship it straight to America . . . If I get the book to suit
me thoroughly, I shall know the title to give it" (TS in MTP).

160. Clemens to Rogers

London
26 March 1897

Dear Mr. Rogers:

Dammmm*nation!* That cable address is Book*store.* I had an idea,
at the time, that I was getting it wrong.

So Colby has pulled through at last—thank goodness for that.

I wrote a line to Harper yesterday, and forgot *again* to ask him
for a statement. I wonder if they never send one till it is asked for.

I sent the renewal-application to Bliss about a week ago, and told
him that if [he] would ask you what course to take concerning it,
you would tell him.

Give my love to the electric spark and tell him to be a credit to us.

It is long since I have added a chapter to my book, but Mrs. Clemens and I have done a world of revising and editing. The book improves every day. And I don't mind saying, now, that I am getting to be most offensively proud of it and satisfied with it.

I have in mind two names, and shall settle on one or the other of them, I think:

Imitating the Equator.

Or this:

Another Innocent Abroad.

The book-agent would be asked, as to the first one: "What does it *mean?*" And he would answer, "The equator goes around the world."

Which one do *you* vote for? And what does Harry say?

With love to you all
SLC

I want Bliss's judgment, too, as a publisher.

P.S. I have asked Robert Chapin, a friend of mine (late U.S. Consul at Johannesburg) to step in and tell you I am well. He is a very nice man indeed, but desperately quiet.

161. CLEMENS TO ROGERS

London
8 April 1897

April 8, I think, 1897 I know.

Dear Mr. Rogers:

I signed the big photograph and mailed it. But I was afraid to put "patiently"—it seemed kind of crusty, and I didn't feel that way.

I could finish the book in a week, now, but I shan't. I'm going carefully. My type-writer is fearfully slow. By the time you and

Mrs. Rogers get back from junketing, though, I'll have part of the book in your hands, I hope.

Wayne MacVeagh is going to call on you (he sails Saturday) and will be able to tell you that I am healthy. He told me to bust up Mrs. Clemens's desire to pay some of the small debts in full. I said that that was your view, too, and he said it was sound. I shall try to do the busting.

I've done my day's work, my conscience is clear, and dinner is ready.

With love to you all

SLC

162. CLEMENS TO ROGERS

London
14 April 1897

23 Tedworth Square
Chelsea, S.W.

Dear Mr. Rogers:

I finished the book yesterday. The workmanship is of course better than that of the Innocents, and in my opinion—however, maybe my opinion isn't valuable. I have put this in the front of it:

THIS BOOK

is affectionately inscribed to

my young friend

HARRY ROGERS

with recognition

of what he is, and apprehension of what he may become unless he form himself a little more closely upon the model of

THE AUTHOR

But if you think he wouldn't like it, just suppress it when the manuscript reaches you.

Four days ago came Bliss's quarterly statement. On a 3-months' sale of 7 books (2 of them on ½-profit) he enriches ⟨her⟩ Mrs. Clemens to the extent of *260 dollars!*

It is ghastly. Mr. Doubleday came in, to-day when I had just finished the first page of this. He wants to make a deal with Bliss or me or somebody, for my new book and the uniform edition. I told him I thought Bliss would be willing. I think Laffan knows D. At any rate he knows his partner, McClure of McClure's Magazine and the syndicates. I have given D. a note of introduction to you.[1]

I have not received a line from Bliss, either about the renewal of the Innocents copyright or anything else. I judge he wishes he hadn't signed the contract. Moreover I don't think he can raise the $10,000. If he can't, will that release me and all my books and set me free?

The first thing I know, he will fail to renew the Innocents copyright, dang him.

I mean to ship you some of my MS in a few days, and follow it as fast as my typewriter will let me. I will have all of it in your hands as quickly as possible, so that if Bliss fails to connect, we can arrange with Doubleday or somebody before midsummer.

You say it is spring weather and the buds are starting. Then you say *you* are ⟨going to⟩ starting—to Fairhaven, etc. Why *you* are no bud. Come, this is scandalous complacency. Love to you all.

SLC

P.S. The Harpers have done first-rate with the old books. Joan didn't take with the public.

---

[1] The note read:

London
14 April 1897

Dear Mr. Rogers:

This is to introduce Mr. Doubleday. He wants to talk some publishing business with you. He has been talking with Bliss and knows how matters stand.

Sincerely yours
S. L. Clemens

In presenting the note to Rogers, Doubleday attached a printed card:

141 East 25th Street
New York, March 3d, 1897
Mr. F. N. Doubleday begs to announce that he has severed his connection with Charles Scribner's Sons, and has become Vice-President of the S. S. McClure Co. In the autumn of 1897 a new book-publishing company will be formed to be called the Doubleday & McClure Co. The close relations between the two interests, the magazine and the books, will be of the greatest mutual benefit (Coe).

163. CLEMENS TO ROGERS

London
16 April 1897

P.S.[1]

Dear Mr. Rogers:

I wrote Frank Bliss 5 or 6 weeks ago, I should say, and sent him an application like the enclosed, and asked him to consult you as to measures to be taken to keep the Webster creditors from capturing the renewal; and I asked him to do the necessary ⟨two⟩ public advertising of the consummation of the renewal—and charge all to me. But I have received no line from him; and since you have offered to bother yourself with this renewal-matter, I flock to you with it now, for the time is very short and I am a little uneasy. You will know by this time whether Bliss has attended to it or not.

Mrs. Clemens is charitable to me, and restricted herself to saying, "Mr. Rogers urged you to deal solely with the Harpers, and I urged you; and so you have no one to blame but yourself that you are in the hands of a sleepy and timorous publisher whom you call 'the late Frank Bliss.'"

It's true, every word. The only answer I can make is, "The Harpers went back on the contract which they first made with me because their lawyer made them believe Bliss owned the renewals (a thing which Bliss has naively confessed that *he* doesn't believe, himself), and then, in order to get my books together in a set, I *had* to get up an arrangement with Bliss—but if it was to do over again I wouldn't do it."

At the same time I do know one thing—that even Frank Bliss,

asleep and with one hand tied behind him, can sell ⟨three⟩ twice as many copies of a ⟨real⟩ travel-book by subscription as any house can sell by trade methods. This new book of mine is distinctly a *sub-scription* book; and if Doubleday or some other live young person had it you would see it thrive.

Doubleday thinks our terms are so hard upon Bliss that he can't make a cent out of the new book. I thought maybe he was right. But now that I reflect upon it I remember that this ½-profit basis is exactly the one that *old* Bliss worked under, on the Tramp Abroad, and under which the Am. Pub. Co. scored a profit in the first 3 months, of $32,000 and I the same. The sale was 64,000.

Which reminds me that those people probably made me pay half of *all* expenses—otherwise their profit would have been smaller than mine. Maybe so. They used to rob me in every way they could think of.

If Bliss fails on the $10,000, lucky for me. But he belongs to Twichell's church and God won't let him. God takes care of all of Jo Twichell's riff-raff; it was a commercial mistake when I sold out my pew there. People of other affiliations have to work and *pay* to get into Heaven, but Twichell can glide his in on a pass. You ought to know Twichell.

SLC

[1] This may indicate that Clemens intended letter 163 as a supplement to letter 162 and that he mailed the two letters together. Distinct datelines and salutations, as well as the length of letter 163, however, warrant their separate presentation here.

164. CLEMENS TO ROGERS

London
26–28 April 1897

Dear Mr. Rogers:

Yours enclosing Bliss's of April 14th, has arrived.

I have been trying to get at Bliss's desires a good while, but have had no luck.

It is 52 days since the contract was signed, and in all that time I have not had a ⟨word⟩ line from him. I fully expected a letter 40 days ago—that, or some other sign of interest.

I wrote him about 40 days ago, but have had no answer.

I have written him about several things and asked him questions. No answer.

At one time I believed I could make a 2-volume book. I knew that in the subscription business a 2-volume is a better property than a 1-volume book; and I thought he would jump at the proposition and that I should get a cable to "go ahead."

When it failed to come I naturally lost interest in the scheme, and went on to finish the 1 volume.

Later, I was very glad I got no cable; for I foresaw that it would be necessary to make South Africa take up a great deal of room, in order to fill out—a country which was absolutely barren of interest when I was there, except the *political* interest—a matter which is as dead as Adam to-day, and will never be resurrected by me, during this life. It is just as I told the Archbishop of Canterbury this very morning: "I wouldn't write a chapter on South Africa to save Your Reverence from being damned."

South African politics had interest until the other day, when the Parliamentary Committee investigated the Raid, punctured the flabby poor thing and let out the wind. It was a shabby and trivial episode and all the heroics have vanished out of it. It is dead, and its interest will never be revived again.

I went on, as I say, and finished the book on the 1-volume plan.

Am I to take hold again at this late date and ⟨go⟩ end it up with a dozen chapters that will put the reader to sleep? ⟨I am not dreaming of it⟩

A successful book is not made of what is *in* it, but of what is left *out* of it. I have left out South Africa—and saved ⟨its life⟩ the book's life.

The public are "expecting"—the public will be "disappointed," etc. The public are in a position to expect only one thing, and one only, that is binding upon me; and that is, that I will make the *best* book I can; and if they know me they know that I will use my own judgment as to ⟨the bes⟩ how to do that, and will consider it sounder than ⟨any one else's.⟩ their own.

Walter Bliss suspects that I am keeping back the best stuff, to sell to another publisher. His father was a thief, and he has inherited the fancy that nobody is honorable.

Those people are scared. They have no pluck, no energy, no brains. They are going to fail on their $10,000,[1] and I shall be rid of them, and not sorry. I mean to begin to rush the MS over to you soon. To be any good to any publisher for the fall trade, it is necessary that said publisher have the MS in his hands by the end of May. I mean to have it all in your hands by then. Then if Bliss's money isn't ready, straight off, we can cancel the contract and give the book to Harper, or Doubleday, I think ⟨either will do.⟩ a *subscription* house is best for a book like this.

I came near adopting "An Old Innocence Abroad"—then I perceived that the Electric Spark was laying a trap for me, and trying to bring my gray hairs down in irony to the public. And so I am awake. I will call it "Another Innocent Abroad," and still pass for young and gay.

I have shoved in 20 pages of brisking-up matter to-day, where a chapter seemed to need it—and now the book is finished.

My best love to you, one and all.

SLC

P.S. Oh, you are just starting to the Hot Springs. Well, I hope you both will have a restful good time. And you will, if you leave the Spark at home.

I note that you feel as Bliss does—that South Africa ought to be in. By George, then I am sorry. To do it I should be obliged to dig 300 pages of MS out of the present book to make room—and it is not any easier to take a completed book apart than it is to take an Indian rug apart. Each figure would be spoiled—obliterated. One would have to write the book all over again—5 months' work, as a sacrifice to Bliss's long silence and destitution of interest.

The publishers are speaking up vigorously here—my latest offer is 25 per cent royalty.

Latest P.S. Apl. 28. Mrs. Clemens urged that you and Bliss were right. She said—but that ain't any matter. The only thing is, that *I have started in on South Africa,* and have done two chapters on it and am moving along.[2]

That makes this long letter unnecessary—but it has to go. I'm not going to write long letters just to waste-basket them. You've got to read them.

I have done 7,000 words in these two days, and I'll have Africa in and the book finished once more in two or three weeks.

[1] If Bliss failed to pay $10,000 advance against royalties, he would forfeit the right to publish the book.

[2] Clemens added chapters about South Africa; he wrote Frank Bliss on 3 May 1897:

I got Mr. Rogers's letter a week ago in which he said that you and he thought that the book ought to cover the whole trip. I went to work at once, and have carried it to Mauritius, then to Delagoa Bay, then to Durban, then to Pietermoritzburg, and to-day shall either take up the gold mines of Johannisburg or begin the chapters in which I wish to make fun of the Jameson Raid and the "statesman" Cecil Rhodes.

He did wish Bliss had come over to confer with him: "if you had come here in March, it might have been worth while to reserve Australasia (and possibly even South Africa) to work by subscription. A house in Sydney wanted to try it. It may be that Chatto will yield those regions to you yet if you have a talk with him." And he added: "Yes, I will sign the de luxe. Here they make a plain de luxe with not a picture in it—1,035 signed copies—I speak of the Meredith and Louis Stevenson. If you make a costly one you (might) could charge like smoke for it in America, I should think, and perhaps make *it* 1,035 copies. But we will talk about it when you come" (Berg, TS in MTP).

165. Clemens to Rogers

London
18 May 1897

23 Tedworth Square

Dear Mr. Rogers:

I am unspeakably glad to be able to say that I have just this minute finished this book *again.* I have added 30,000 words. Part of it has been most enjoyable work to me—chaffing Rhodes and making fun of his Jameson Raid.

Yes, I remember urging you to release Bliss from his $10,000 obligation if we could push him ahead any in that way, but as you did not write anything about it I didn't know it had been done. It is all the better, since he is to publish the book—it lightens his load.

I was offered 20% royalty here by one good house and 25 by another; but as Chatto ⟨has⟩ is anxious to pay the latter rate I think I shall end by staying with him.

The $10,000 being no longer in the way, I suppose I would better send the book straight to Bliss now—but I must think about that, first, there being a custom house in the way.

It has taken me 7 months to write this book—and all of a sudden I feel tired. Love to you all.

SLC

166. CLEMENS TO ROGERS

London
3 June 1897

Dear Mr. Rogers:

Your order to secure from Bliss the de luxe privilege was mighty definite, and I resolved to carry it out ⟨if⟩ or bankrupt my ingenuities trying.

You know Bliss, therefore you know that I would have an entertaining time; for he is the most *indefinite* man that ever was. He is intangible. He is a gas, and nothing but a pressure of 250,000 atmospher⟨ic⟩es ⟨pressure can con⟩ can solidify him.

If he had come equipped with full powers to act, I think I could have solidified him—I feel quite sure I could. But he could sign nothing without discussing it with his people. However, I think I am safe in forecasting that after a discussion with his people and ⟨an hours⟩ a small talk with you, he will sign.

For when all arguments had left him still hankering after the de luxe, I came out plainly and said in substance this:

"Frank, you have exposed the fact that you and your brother know nothing whatever about the de luxe business; it is a brand= new business to you; you would be apprentices to it. I have paid for several apprenticeships and will never pay for another one. I wholly refuse my consent to ⟨you⟩ allow your Company to touch the de luxe. Without my consent it would not do for you to proceed. My published opposition would badly damage the thing and possibly destroy it. I have drawn up, here, a perfectly fair proposition, and you would better accept it and sign it, relinquishing to me the de luxe unfettered."

That put a new aspect upon the matter, and if he had had power to sign ⟨he⟩ I am quite sure he would have done it. He began to take a warm interest in the Japanese book, then, and said he would see his people as soon as he reached home ⟨⟨the⟩ ⟨about 22d June⟩ and would cable me the result.

I enclose my proposition,[1] and will explain it.

But first I will begin at the beginning—then you will understand better:

1. I wanted a de luxe privilege *unlimited as to number*—since it might be easier to sell 1000 at $100 than 500 at $200.

2. I wanted to make the book *myself*, through De Vinne[2] ("Century" printer), the most capable man in the world.

3. I had to have something to offer Bliss in *place* of the deluxe.

About ten days ago arrived from Japan a little book dedicated to me, which was full of beautiful Jap. illustrations. (I will mail it to you; don't let Doubleday see it—or anybody outside of the family.) (Bliss is to mention it to none but his Co.) It is about 40 pages, and cost about 10 cents a book to manufacture it, I judge, (for it is sold, retail, in Japan, at 48 cents a copy.)

I had already (a week ago) resolved to have one of my old books done in Japan by that artist—he to illustrate it in *his* way, not mine. Tom Sawyer for instance, or the Yankee at King Arthur's Court. It would be infernally comical, and at the same time beautiful. It would be nearly as big as an atlas, and something more than half as thick as a brick—a splendid centre-table ⟨novelty,⟩ ornament and an *absolute novelty* to 99 people in 100. It could be made in Japan and delivered in New York, customs paid, for less than $1.50 a copy, I think. Even Bliss could sell 20 or 30,000 copies at $12 or $13 a copy; for every prosperous mechanic and head-clerk would be powerfully attracted by it. I told Bliss that *he* must sell it at the price just suggested, for then it would be in his line; but that if he backed out of it I should give it to Doubleday and *he* would sell it to swells, but would charge $25 a copy—and *get* it.

However, you must understand that all the above was *later* conversation. I never said a word to Bliss until I had gotten from him every detail of his de luxe scheme.

Then I asked him, first, if you had released him from his advance-payment of $10,000. He said no. (So I shall send the last half of the new book to *you*, instead of letting Bliss carry it away. Also, if all other arguments should fail (which is not likely) we can get the de luxe by releasing the $10,000 advance or part of it.

Next I began to ask questions about his de luxe scheme (and I set down the answers.) When he got through, I was able to say:

"You people have made no estimates. You have no definite idea ⟨bu⟩ about your project. You have come here freighted with mere foggy *guesses*. And here is the result—drawn from your own answers:

1. It will be 15 volumes, anyhow.

2. It *may* be 20.

3. You will use in it the Harper plates and ⟨add⟩ make plates like them of your own books to go with them.

4. Each volume will contain about 6 photogravures—new and special pictures.

5. Price of the set, from $100 to $180,—but you *think* $100.

6. Cost of paper, printing and binding for each volume, $1.

7. You had thought of venturing an edition of 300 sets, but had concluded that 250 was the utmost that you could sell.

8. "Wally" thinks general agents will undertake the selling at a commission of 55%.

9. The plates made by you will cost $5,000.

10. The artist's fee for drawing the pictures will probably be $3,000.

"Frank, have you ciphered these figures out?"

"No."

"Let us cipher, then—on a 15-volume set at $100 per set."

Artist (pictures)	$ 3,000
Plates	5,000
Making the books	3,700
Packing, insurance, prospectus, advertising, telegraph, soap, candles, chewing-gum, house-rent and clerk hire for a year	1,000
Commissions	13,000
Total—$25,700	
250 sets at $100 each	25,000
Profit	700

"How much of this profit do I get?"

"Half."

"That is $350. Do you believe it would pay me to put in 15 weeks reading proof of 15 volumes for $350? I can make more sawing wood, Frank. Now then, let us knock out the commissions, and imagine that you are going to sell the 250 sets clean and clear *without* commissions:

"$13,000 subtracted, leaves $6,350.

"Half of it is yours—about $3,000. I will never consent to let you people handle the de luxe upon any conditions whatever—and that is final, Frank.

"Turn the de luxe rights over to me without reserves or limitations, and you may have the Japanese book and *keep* the first $3,000 that would accrue to Mrs. Clemens from its sale. Take it or leave it, Frank—business tires me; I should die if I should try to chase you up a year on a stretch, as Mr. Rogers has done. If you elect to *leave* it, you get nothing at all—no de luxe nor anything else."

He said he would go home and see if he could manage to back

out of such arrangements as he has already made with people concerning the de luxe, and hoped he would be able to do it. I said—

"You will have no difficulty; tell them you forgot to consult an important partner, and that the partner refuses to allow you to go on. You say 20 or 25 people have applied for sets regardless of what the price may be. There will be no trouble about those people. We will supply them."

Now *I* was proposing to make 1000 sets at $100 a set and do the whole canvassing *myself*. I would go to Washington and stay there 2 months and make the 700 Senators and Congressmen each give me the name of a man at home who, to please his representative and keep on the good side of him, would take a set—heelers, barkeepers and other persons near and dear to Congressmen. I would load up every important jail and saloon in America with a de luxe edition of my books.

But Mrs. Clemens and the children object to this. I do not know why.

In England the de luxe edition is always 1000 sets. It has not a single picture. It is bound in coarse dull-colored cloth and has no gilding. It costs half a dollar a volume to make the book. No advertising is done. Only circulars are sent to people. The money comes to the author himself, or to a bank named by him. If the book is not delivered the bank will return the money. Out of 1000 sets an author has cleared upwards of $70,000. My arrangement with Chatto here on the de luxe will leave me a liberal margin.

My family vote that Doubleday shall handle the de luxe. On subscriptions sent in by me, here, Chatto will not charge me a commission. Couldn't I have that chance in America? I know a good many men there whom the average canvasser couldn't easily get at.

Well, anyway, after you and Doubleday have talked, won't he come over and discuss with me about the get-up of the book, the printer of it, and the number of sets? ⟨And Chatto⟩

———

I find that there was a report in New York yesterday, that I was dead. Don't you believe anything of the kind.[3]

———

If Bliss attempts the de luxe, I certainly will come out in print and repudiate it and urge the public not to buy it. Those people are timorous, and will never face that.

We leave London July 2, but remain in *England* till middle of July, then go to Vienna for fall and winter.

With love

SLC

[1] Clemens wanted Bliss to accept the following agreement (Salm):
    For and in consideration of certain conditions hereinafter set forth, the American Publishing Co. of Hartford, Conn., hereby agrees that S. L. Clemens shall have the sole right to issue an edition de luxe of his complete works, said American Publishing Co. to receive no part of the profit ⟨, if⟩ therefrom.
    The conditions above referred to are these: Mrs. ⟨S.⟩ Olivia L. Clemens agrees that the American Publishing Co. shall have the sole right to make ⟨and sell⟩ one of said Clemens's present books in Japan according to a plan already devised by said Clemens and sell the same in America, said Mrs. O. L. Clemens to receive the same share of the accruing profits as she now receives under h⟨is⟩er ⟨latest⟩ present contract with said American Publishing Co., except that the first $3,000 which shall accrue to ⟨him⟩ her on said Japanese book shall go to the American Publishing Co. instead.
[2] Theodore Low De Vinne, who in 1906 would print the private edition of Clemens's *What Is Man?*
[3] Clemens explains this in his notebook (Notebook 32a, TS pp. 27–28):
June 2, '97
    Came Mr. White, representing N. Y. Journal, with 2 cablegrams from his paper:
    (1.) "If Mark Twain dying in poverty, in London, send 500 words."
    (2.) "Later. If Mark Twain has died in poverty, send 1000 words."
    I explained how the mistake occurred, and gave him a cable in substance this: "James Ross Clemens, a cousin, was seriously ill here two or three weeks ago, but is well now. The report of my illness grew out of his illness; the report of my death was an exaggeration. I have not been ill. 'Mark Twain.' "

167. ROGERS TO CLEMENS (cablegram)

New York
16 June 1897

All friends think Herald movement [1] mistake withdraw graciously Langdon approves this

Rogers [2]

[1] On 1 June 1897, responding to rumors that Clemens was seriously ill, the New York *Herald* announced that it would sponsor a subscription fund for his relief. James Gordon Bennett, of the *Herald,* and Andrew Carnegie initiated the fund with contributions of $1,000 each; the newspaper regularly printed lists of donors and their contributions.

[2] Three days later Frank Bliss would send a similar message: "Herald Fund hurting you will you cable us disapproval."

168. CLEMENS TO ROGERS

London
16 June 1897

Dear Mr. Rogers:

Your cablegram came to-day, but I can't retire gracefully from the matter because three months ago when I was down in the depths and everything was looking black and hopeless a friend of mine approached me upon this thing and over-persuaded me and I finally gave him my word that if it was ever put before the public I would stand by it and not repudiate it. I had had time to forget all about it, since, but if I should try to back out now, he would bring me to book and I could make no answer. But even to-day it is not objectionable to me.[1] The project may end in a humiliating failure, and show me that I am not very popular, after all; but no matter, I am used to humiliations these years, and they do not come so hard now as once they did. $250,000 were raised by private subscription for Gen. Grant after the G. & W. failure,[2] and I myself helped to raise $20,000 for Dr. John Brown [3]—at least was starting in to do it in America on a promise when I was stopped by a message from Edinburgh that the full amount was already raised and I needn't proceed. The only difference that I know of between a public subscription and a private one is, that the public one leaves a man free to give or not, as he pleases, but the private one collars him personally and makes him contribute or explain.

If I had ever laid this matter before my wife she would have forbidden me to touch it—and for that reason I didn't mention it to

her 3 months ago. She is troubled about it now, but is good and
kind, since I have told her I can't alter the matter now.

You see, the lightning refuses to strike me—that is where the
defect is. We have to do our own striking, as Barney Bernato did.[4]
But nobody ever gets the courage till he goes crazy.

I have given Bliss half of the MS to-day, and shall send the other
half to you as soon as the type-writer finishes.

⟨If⟩ He didn't say anything more about the de luxe. If he is hard
to persuade, no doubt a release from half of his $10,000 advance-
payment will fetch him. But I wonder if the Harpers won't object?

Good bye—and don't ever get as low-spirited as I am. It isn't
healthy. Love to you all.

SLC

[1] In a draft of what was probably meant to be a letter either to Bennett or to
the *Herald*, Clemens had expressed an acceptance born of desperation:
> This way out ⟨of debt⟩ would not have occurred to me, and a year or two ago
> my self-love would have rebelled; but I have grown so tired of being in debt
> that often I think I could part with my skin and my teeth to get out. I know
> that the custom is to wait till a man is dead and then gather up money for a
> monument for him, when he can't enjoy it; but if friends want to ⟨collect⟩
> advance money for the monument now, my creditors will think that the ⟨wiser⟩
> more rational course, and so shall I. If I can get on my feet again I will be the
> monument myself, and shan't ever need another one.

[2] No evidence has been found of a fund for Grant at the time of the failure of
the Grant & Ward brokerage firm; earlier, after Grant had lost the nomination for
a third term as President, George Jones of the New York *Times* had set in motion
a campaign to raise $250,000 for him; and later, at the time of Grant's final
illness, other efforts were made to assist him financially.

[3] While Clemens and his family were in Edinburgh in 1873, Dr. John Brown,
author of *Rab and His Friends,* was ill and had to abandon his medical practice.
A private subscription for Dr. Brown was so successful that Clemens later
recalled: "No public appeal was made. The matter was never mentioned in print"
(*MTA,* II, 45).

[4] Barnett I. Barnato, who had made a spectacular fortune in the South African
diamond mines, had committed suicide by leaping from a ship in mid-Atlantic the
day before. Reuter's dispatch in the London *Times* (16 June 1897) said that
Barnato had been suffering from "an overtaxed brain" and was being kept "under
close observation." He had distracted his companion, "wrenched his arm away
and jumped clean overboard."

169. ROGERS TO CLEMENS (cablegram)

New York
21 June 1897

Twenty two hundred looked upon as Herald fake [1]

Rogers

[1] Rogers's cable message may have been garbled by the operator. A clipping in MTP suggests that nearly two weeks later the *Herald* fund "take" still amounted to only $2,938.

170. CLEMENS TO ROGERS

London
23 June 1897 [1]

Dear Mr. Rogers:

I wrote the enclosed interview to-day, intending to have it cabled to the N. Y. Journal, but Mrs. Clemens will not allow it. She says *I* must not advertise the fact that the Herald scheme was a failure. She made me write to Bennett in Paris last Saturday and ask him to stop the scheme and return the money.[2] I didn't *want* to; for, failure or no failure, I wanted to see how the scheme would fare. To my mind there was nothing discreditable to me about it, whether it failed or succeeded. Bennett is probably off yachting somewhere, and I hope he is; for it is late in the day, now, to enter Mrs. Clemens's protest—the scheme will die before this week is out, of pure inanition.

All the newspapers in America have jumped on it, no doubt.

If I were younger I should be in an awful state of mind, now, but I am old and played-out and pretty nearly callous; and distresses do not distress me as much as they ought. I am willing to do almost any dreadful thing to wipe off the debts and satisfy my wife who has made so many sacrifices for me; but ⟨personally⟩ if I had consulted her she would have throttled this one promptly.

This is a strange time for my market-value to go up; but it has. To-day there is a cablegram from a magazine offering me a third more per page than it has ever offered me before.

I wish you would collect $40,000 privately for me from yourself, then pay it back to yourself, and have somebody tell the press it was collected but that by Mrs. Clemens's desire ⟨⟨and mine⟩⟩ I asked that it be returned to the givers and that it was done. ⟨Come⟩ Now if your conscience will let you do that, it will reverse things and give me a handsome boom, and nobody will ever be the wiser. I like the idea; I don't see any harm in it. You see you could do it just as soon as the Herald scheme ceases and Bennett returns those subscriptions; then it will be ship-shape and consistent.

Mrs. Clemens is to have an operation performed next Friday. We shall start for Switzerland a week later, and leave there for Vienna early in September.

The Jubilee has worn everybody out. It will end to-night, and I shall be glad, for it has cost me considerable labor and fatigue.[3]

With love to you all,

SLC

[Enclosure, in pencil]

Certainly I am willing to talk about the ⟨H.⟩ Herald subscription fund. I was glad Mr. Bennett started it. If it had succeeded it would have been a ⟨prize⟩ compliment to me and I should have been proud of it. Cablegrams tell me it has not succeeded. Therefore I have thanked Mr. Bennett and asked him to close the subscription and return the money to the contributors. When my ⟨wife⟩ family learned of the ⟨proj⟩ Herald undertaking they were strongly opposed to it, but I was not, if I had friends enough to make it succeed. Do I regret that the Herald made the attempt? Not in the least. No enemy was expected to subscribe, ⟨and⟩ ⟨nor⟩ and no friend who did not wish me well. There was no compulsion upon anybody; the result proves it. Does it distress me to find ⟨I have so few friends?⟩ that my friends did not come forward? No, for I think they were like my family and disapproved. Otherwise they would have stood by me and saved me harmless. ⟨The Herald could not save me by itself⟩ Did the report that I was living in luxury influence their action? No, for they knew it was not so. They had better reasons than that, I do not know what they were. But they were good ones or they would have prevented the scheme from failing. The Herald could not save me by itself. It could do only what it did—offer the scheme and let it take its chance. Months ago personal friends offered me a benefit lecture in New York ⟨and two⟩ and five other cities, with tickets at fancy prices, and said they would make it pay off my debts in ⟨three⟩ six nights. ⟨I was under⟩ I had to write my book and could not go.[4] I am still revising and finishing. Their proposition convinced me that I had friends; the failure of the present scheme does not prove that they have ceased to exist, but only that they do not approve this method. I am not distressed about this failure. I have many personal friends, and only crimes could alienate them, not blunders. I commit twenty-four blunders a day, and they always expect that. I have not kept up my average for a while back, but that was because I was busy. I can make it up, now.

[1] Clemens mistakenly dated this letter "June 23/95."
[2] Clemens had written to Bennett in Paris:

I concealed this matter from my family, and hoped that when they found it out I could persuade them to be reconciled to it, but I have been disappointed in that, and have failed, after three days of strenuous effort. I hoped and believed, and I still believe, that a sufficient fund could be raised to lighten my debt ⟨considerably⟩ very greatly and possibly even discharge it, but my family are not willing, and convinced me that I have no right to take your money and other men's to smooth my road with, and so I have to come to you and ask you to cable the enclosed letter to the Herald to the end that I may once more stand well with the household (19 June 1897).

[3] The public ceremonies honoring Queen Victoria's sixtieth year as British sovereign included a lengthy procession of troops from all the colonies. Clemens witnessed the spectacle and wrote a dispatch on it for the American newspapers (*MTB*, p. 1043).

[4] This scheme which Clemens found tempting as a means for early release from debt is described in a letter he had written to Frank Fuller on 27 May 1897:

Intimations have reached me a while back that friends of mine in New York and also in San Francisco would like to know if I would like to be invited to come next fall or winter and be treated to a "special benefit" lecture, at big prices for tickets and an auction of a dozen first-choice seats at Jenny Lind prices. I was not greatly taken with the idea and so I put it off and said I couldn't have time to weigh it in my mind until my book should be off my hands. . . . Lately the matter has come to me again. This time, with this suggestion: that a dozen men, each with influence over a millionaire, go each privately to his millionaire and get him to put up $1,000 and sign his name to an invitation to me to come and do a "benefit" lecture in the lecture-hall of the Waldorf hotel, and sell one seat privately at auction to the highest bidder—the highest bidder to agree beforehand as to the bid he would be willing to make—and that the rest of the tickets be put at $5 or $10 or $100 (privately sold) and if the boom failed to sell them, resort to papering the house. . . . And that this private scheme be also worked by trusty men in Chicago and San Francisco—in which latter place it was believed that my old pal, Adolf Sutro would head the paper with $5,000.

Could such a scheme be practicable? he asked. "Would it 'go'? and pull me suddenly out of debt? If it would the income from my wife's inheritance would enable us to go home and live in a modest way in our own house." He had hoped that another lecture tour would clear him from debt, but "I am not strong enough for the work and am too old" (TS in MTP).

171. CLEMENS TO ROGERS

London
25 June 1897

Dear Mr. Rogers:

Mrs. Clemens was strong in her disapprobation as soon as she heard of the Herald fund, so I wrote Bennett her feeling about it on the 19th and asked him to cable over and stop the subscriptions and return the contributions.

I wrote ⟨young⟩ Mr. Mitchell, ⟨too⟩ yesterday,[1] and learn to-day by telegram that my letter had not been received by Bennett, but B. would be glad to do anything he could. So I wrote Bennett the following,[2] to-day and asked him to cable it to the Herald:

I suppose that that will appear in the Herald in New York day after to-morrow June 27 and close the incident.[3] But I send you this copy so that you may know just what I did write, in case any cable mistakes occur.

Mrs. Clemens had an operation performed on her eye to-day and is ill in consequence. But it had to be done, and we hope she will get benefit from it. I am too solicitous about her to be able to worry much about this other distress.

Good night—I will go out and post this at once.

SLC

[1] Clemens sent the letter for publication to Percy Mitchell of the *Herald* bureau in Paris, asking him to cable it to New York immediately: "*This* I know I would like to have in print in the N. Y. Herald." Clemens's letter to the *Herald* appeared on 27 June:

> I made no revelation to my family of your generous undertaking in my behalf and for my relief from debt, and in that I was wrong.
>
> Now that they know all about the matter they contend I have no right to allow my friends to help me while my health is good and my ability to work remains, that it is not fair to my friends and not justifiable, and that it will be time enough to accept help when it shall be proven that I am no longer able to work.
>
> I am persuaded that they are right. While they are grateful for what you have done and for the kindly instinct which prompted you, it is urgent that the contributions be returned to the givers with their thanks and mine. I yield to their desire and forward their request and my indorsement of it to you.
>
> I was glad when you initiated that movement, for I was tired of the fact and worry of debt, but I recognize that it is not permissible for a man whose case is not hopeless to shift his burdens to other men's shoulders.

[2] The second letter to Bennett read:

> When my family learned that a subscription had been started by the Herald they urgently insisted that I had no right to shift my burdens to other men's shoulders, and begged me to write and ask you to close the subscription list and return the money to the contributors, with their thanks and mine for the kindness which they had tried to do me. I did so, five days ago, but you were absent and I failed to reach you, then and since. I am trying again, in the hope that you will have returned by this time. For your attempt to reduce my indebtedness and for your large contribution to that end you have my and my family's sincere thanks (Middlebury College).

[3] But the *Herald* letter did not close the incident. On 15 July 1897 *The Chap-Book* editorialized:

> For years there has been more or less sniveling in the press about Mark Twain's poverty and his debts. We have never believed that this lachrymose sentimentality was at all pleasing to Mr. Clemens. To be sure, his misfortunes were to be regretted, but we have understood that they were legitimate business losses, due largely to the fact that Mr. Clemens could not force himself to be content with one trade only—that of author. It has been very pleasant to feel that the real sufferer faced his troubles bravely and cheerily; that he was working diligently in the hope of making good the past. . . . [But] in what appears to us a most unseemly way [he revealed in the *Herald* letter] what a nasty time family pride had, in private, conquering his own lack of scruples. We have tried in vain to look upon Mr. Clemens's communication as a humorous composition, little suited as humor seemed to the occasion. The only refuge seems to be in the belief that his health is really broken, that he has lost his grip on himself, and that the present false position is due to an act for which he is as little accountable as a sick child which escapes its nurse. We should like to believe still that the real man in health and happiness is somewhat more sturdy than the pathetically flaccid and groveling figure we are trying not to see to-day.

172. CLEMENS TO ROGERS

London
7 July 1897

Dear Mr. Rogers:

Chatto was about to mail you the last of the book yesterday.[1] My, what a long terrible job the writing and double-revising of that book has been!

We are just leaving for the continent. Chatto will forward my letters to me. I shan't know what our address is going to be for a month or six weeks yet.

Pond is here trying to get me to lecture in America all the fall and winter, and I desperately want to do it, but Mrs. Clemens is not in favor of it—still I sort of hope to bring her around.

The people here seem determined to get up a fund for me, without regard to whether I need it or not, and they think they can convince Mrs. Clemens to-night—but that is because they don't know her.

If you should run across Jesse Grant, I wish you would hand him the enclosed[2] and see what he says. I wish I had thought of it a year or two ago. I expect they are a poor lot, those Grants. Through Webster's treachery to me, they got more than $20,000 that belonged to me. He gave them two-thirds of the New York General Agency commissions. We ran that agency ourselves and they were not entitled to a penny of it. Webster was a particularly low-down dog.

Do you think the Harpers will let their share of my books go into the de luxe?

Good-bye and love to you all.

SLC

---

[1] Clemens had written Chatto & Windus, 15 June 1897 (CWB):
Please send for some more MS.—say 10 or 11 Monday.
I shall want you to send the *type-written* lot to
H. H. Rogers, 26 Broadway, New York
—either as cheap mail matter or any way you think best.
Chatto & Windus wrote Rogers, 30 June 1897 (Salm):

As requested by Mr Sam L. Clemens we are sending you by book post registered, type written portion of his book *"The Latest Innocent Abroad"* pages 406 to 562. Mr Clemens informs us that he has written you concerning the placing this portion in the hands of Mr Bliss, as well as other matters concerning the publication of the volume.

[2] "The enclosed" might have been a note reminding Jesse Grant of the $500 loan made to the Grants about 1885. (See letter 141.)

173. CLEMENS TO ROGERS

London
12 July 1897

Dear Mr. Rogers:

We broke up housekeeping yesterday,[1] and we leave to-morrow morning early for Lucerne. Yesterday Clara was flung out of a hansom and struck the dashboard and carried it with her—the horse had suddenly slipped and fallen—she disappeared from her mother's view. Clara landed on the horse's hind legs and hung on to them while he struggled; then he sprang up and spilt her on the ground in front of the wheels and she scrambled out from under the shafts. Neither she nor her mother was much hurt, only rudely shaken up. It was a very narrow escape.

Pond has been offering me $50,000 and expenses to come over in October and lecture 125 nights; but he is so unbusiness-like that I was afraid to consent—and Mrs. Clemens was dead opposed to having him for agent. It seemed to me impossible that he could secure halls and theatres this late in the season.

During the fall and winter I mean to prepare a lecture or two; then if I can arrange satisfactory terms with Hathaway[2] or some other sane person I will make a final and farewell lecture-campaign in the fall and winter of '98–99.

Goodbye, and love to you all.

SLC

[1] Clemens was staying at the Hans Crescent Hotel.
[2] George Henry Hathaway had become proprietor of the Redpath Lecture Bureau.

IV

"You and I Are a Team"
(JULY 1897-MAY 1899)

"You and I are a team: you are the most useful man
I know, and I am the most ornamental."
SLC to HHR, 21 December 1897

AFTER THE better part of a summer in the village of
Weggis on Lake Lucerne, the Clemens family went by way of
Salzburg to Vienna in September 1897. There they spent the
winter at the Hotel Metropole, still attempting to economize in
every way they could. The gloom which had settled over them after
Susy's death was slowly lifting, the debts of Charles L. Webster &
Company were soon to be paid in full, and Rogers was patiently
working out a satisfactory contract between Harper & Brothers and
the American Publishing Company. But there was still, Clemens
wrote to Laurence Hutton, "a blight upon us all." Mrs. Clemens
found "some trifle of relief from sorrow in taking care of the rest of
us." Clara worked at her music "hard and faithfully under Lesche-
titzky; and between her work and her society-intercourse she gets
some sleep now and then, but not much." Jean studied language:
"She could be learning Russian, which has a large literature and is

292

a beautiful language besides, but it is her caprice to learn Polish." It was a busy and, quietly, a social season: "We all like Vienna. Among our numerous acquaintances we count several friends— friends whom we love and profoundly value. It is friends that make life" (20 February 1898, Princeton, TS in MTP).

Clemens kept himself busy with scheming and dreaming of new ways to wealth through writing, salesmanship, inventions, or brave speculation; for debts still oppressed him, and the burden of being poor blighted his pride. He buried himself in literary work of one kind or another—translating plays, working up new novels or ideas for novels, producing miscellaneous articles and sketches and stories. He later recorded in his notebook the titles of twenty-two separate short pieces, most of which he had written and offered for publication during this period. He set his own price for such works: for sketches "$140 per 1,000 words, up to 4,000; each additional 1000, $60"; for stories "The same, up to 4,000; beyond that, special terms" (Notebook 32, TS pp. 60–61).

Clemens must have been gratified when in March 1898 newspapers in London and New York announced that "Mark Twain has paid all the debts that led to the bankruptcy of the publishing firm with which he was connected." It seemed "a fine example of the very chivalry of probity" deserving "to rank with the historic case of Sir Walter Scott." Rather than content himself with paying only what the law required him to pay, Clemens "preferred to make good the entire loss, and to this end he had to make a fresh start in life at the age of sixty." But he did it, and with profits from his lecture tour and his latest book "has carried out his high-minded and generous purpose" (from the London *Daily News*, quoted in *Saturday Review of Books and Art*, New York *Times*, 12 March 1898).

But mainly and finally and most consistently, he depended on Rogers to market his sketches and stories, to deal with publishers, to invest what money was left when the debts were paid. He found him, he said, the most useful man he knew, and Miss Harrison, his secretary, was useful also. As publication of the uniform edition finally drew near, Clemens wrote to Frank Bliss on 31 March 1899:

I want *set No 1* of the *de luxe* edition to go to Mr. Rogers, and to be charged to me (minus agent's commission).

And I want the first set of the ordinary Uniform edition to go to Miss Harrison and be charged to me (minus agent's commission) (TS in MTP).

174. CLEMENS TO ROGERS (fragment)

Lake Lucerne
23 July 1897

Dear Mr. Rogers: [1]

In case all other means should fail with Bliss, I hope you will show him the enclosed notice to the Public.[2] And if he persists in going on, I hope you will insert it as an advertisement prominently in Harper's Monthly. . . .

How far are you along with the Testament? You are getting pretty old—don't you think you would better glance through my book first? You wouldn't like to appear before Satan . . . familiar with a work which he does not allow on the premises, and ignorant of the book of his nearest friend. . . .

---

[1] The first paragraph of this letter, whose original has not been found, is quoted in Feldman's *Literary Manuscripts Catalogue* (New York, May 1956), item 268. The second paragraph appears in the *Byron Price Library Catalogue* of the City Book Auction, Inc. (New York, December 1954), item 118. The letter was laid in a first edition of *Life on the Mississippi*. The City Book Auction catalog describes the letter as four pages, Octavo, "on numerous topics, 74 lines, plus six-lines crossed out by the author."

[2] The enclosure is reprinted in the City Book Auction catalog:

To The Public

In regard to this de luxe edition of my books which the American Publishing Co. of Hartford are proposing to issue, I desire to put possible subscribers on their guard against investing in it. The scheme has been undertaken without my authority and the goods will not be delivered.

Mark Twain.
Dated . . .

175. KATHARINE HARRISON TO CLEMENS

New York
30 July 1897

Dear Mr. Clemens:

Mr. Rogers wanted me to write you a line and let you know that we have the ten thousand ($10,000.00) dollars from Mr. Bliss. I received it from him this morning, when I gave him the balance of the manuscript.

Yours truly,

K. I. Harrison [1]

[1] Clemens passed this note on to Chatto & Windus, writing at the bottom of the page:

Weggis, Tuesday.

Dear C. & W: You can send perfected revises to Bliss, now, to the end of the book.

I forgot to say you don't need to send me my MS. Thus far I have not needed it; and I shan't need it at all, if the printers will exactly follow it. ⟨No writing⟩

⟨If you could get a line in the papers to say I am not going to lecture this year in either England or America it might save me some letter-writing; and I should value that.⟩

SLC

176. CLEMENS TO ROGERS

Lucerne
6 August 1897

Dear Mr. Rogers:

Yours of July 23d is to hand.

I am glad you are standing out for the 1-year limit on the uniform edition; for, with that and the relinquishment of the $10,000-advance to work with, Bliss will probably let go of the *de luxe.* He knows I am not going to let *him* publish it, for I told him that if he made the attempt I would fight it in print, tooth and nail, and do what I could to damage its chances.

A couple of days ago McClure sent me, from London, ⟨a let⟩ a copy of a letter written to you by Doubleday, May 26, in which Doubleday laid before you his scheme for the de luxe. It is a far bolder one than Bliss's, yet is still not quite bold enough, I think.

I would make the de luxe 1,000 sets at $100—not 250 at $200; and I would not set the printer to work until 250 sets had been subscribed for and the venture made safe. I would find a market through Chatto for a number of sets. Eventually there would be $70,000 profit in it, or in the neighborhood of it.

I would not want to ask those authors to contribute articles to it. I would rather ask a man for money, straight out, than for handiwork of his trade which might represent a larger sum than he could afford to give away. I'm in a sweat to publish the de luxe with Miss Harrison—still, I am going to keep quiet and kind of rational, and wait and see how the eventualities eventuate.

Your splendid news that the Bliss money and what is in your hands foots up $27,000 and that you are doing a little gambling for Mrs. Clemens has set us both up in spirits, and we are feeling pretty fine. Mrs. Clemens went to ciphering at once and found that by adding to the $27,000 sums lying in the London bank, Langdon's hands and Whitmore's she could swell the gross amount to $49,000, and pay off the Webster debt at once. She wanted me to ask you to pay $39,000 straightway, leaving us $10,000 to live on till we get ahead again. But I have advised her to wait, and keep still, say nothing, ⟨—otherwise she might damage Bliss's chances; his canvassers will want to use my load of debt as a persuader, and make people buy the book to get me out. By George it's a shabby business, but I suppose Bliss would be in a state of consternation if we should suddenly step up to the captain's office and settle. I judge he would consider himself cruelly betrayed.⟩ and you will let us know when the right time has come. (*I didn't edit that* out.) [1]

Moreover-besides, the Mount Morris claim is for $29,381.67—whereas $9,000 of that represents pure vacancy—false notes—

money which Webster & Co never had. Whitford and Hall know this. At least neither of them has ever told me that the $9,000 of false notes was ever handed back to Hall. They still stood against the firm the 12th of March '93, and in that month the bank lent Hall $30,000 more—and so it doesn't seem reasonable that the bank would hand back those venerable notes at *that* time.

We owe the Mt. Morris only $20,000. I am willing to pay that, but I will not pay the stolen $9,000. Shan't I write Mr. Payne and place this case before him and ask him to prove to me by Hall and Whitford's oaths—aided by better evidence—that the $9,000 of false notes were returned to Hall and do not form a part of the Bank's claim against Webster & Co.?

We have the 2 lists of creditors of date Jan. 30 eighteen months ago.

The Grant estate appears in neither of them. Is it possible that those people have withdrawn their claim?

Among the "Settled" I find Thos Russell & Son. We paid that debt in full, 2 years ago, didn't we? Then does the heading "Settled" mean that the ⟨cred⟩ claims set down under it have all been paid in full? ($25,546.31.)

However, that cannot be. Then does "Settled" mean that these have agreed to the 50% arrangement? But that won't quite explain it, for Russell & Son have been paid in full.

Under the "Unsettled" appears the Mount Morris with its old original claim of $29,381.67 unreduced; but a note in the margin says that a 20% dividend has been paid to these Unsettled people [2] —"Except those proved after the div. was declared." But I suppose the Mt. Morris ⟨was⟩ claim had been proved and allowed before that.

Apparently the original indebtedness was ⟨about⟩ $74 or 75,000.

The full payment of Russell & Son reduces it to about $70,000.

Apparently the Webster estate is going to pay ⟨about⟩ in the neighborhood of a third of that—say $23,000.

Leaving about $47,000 for me to pay.

Subtracting $9,000 from the Mount Morris claim

Leaves me in debt less than $40,000.

Is it so?

If it is, we will square up and go out of debt the minute ⟨Bliss no longer needs the indebtedness as an advertisement to sell his book, and the de luxe has been marketed, or at least safely started.⟩ you advise it.

Meantime I will write a book—maybe a couple; and a year from now I will prepare for the platform—a farewell shout—and then retire on what's left, and stop worrying. I have stopped now, for a spell.

It will be a pity if the Mount Morris has to go into the hands of a receiver. I will try to cry. Can't you get Colby appointed? Because I want a long cry.

If you can get the de luxe by relinquishing the $10,000-advance (Harper agreeing not to stand in our way) I think it a good trade. We shan't need the $10,000 before it comes in from Bliss's book.

You have given me a great shock about Mrs. Rogers. I do hope she is fully recovered, and that this sordid business-talk of mine will not find you still troubled concerning her. It is one of the horrors of wide distances—one never knows when he is choosing the wrong time to write a letter, and the wrong topic. Out of our hearts we all say, Fortune speed you both!

SLC

P.S. Alas! Mrs. C.'s addition was defective—the accumulation is $39,000, not $49,000.

---

[1] The parenthetical remark follows immediately after the canceled passage and clearly refers to it. The last 12 words of the sentence directly preceding the parenthetical remark, "and you will let us know when the right time has come," were inserted above the canceled matter, but are here printed in the order of composition (according to the practice described in the "Editor's Preface").

[2] Technically, Colby paid two dividends to the Webster creditors from the assigned estate: one of 20 per cent in May 1895, and a second of 7.696 per cent two years later. With certain important exceptions, including the Mt. Morris Bank, the creditors were settled with "on a basis of 50% of their claims." But only 20 per cent was paid them from the assigned estate, the remaining 30 per cent being made up in cash earned elsewhere. When the decision to pay 50 per

cent was announced, the creditors assigned their remaining claims to "Genl Langdon, who thus became entitled to such further dividends as the estate yielded—which amounted to 7.696%" (Colby to HHR, 1 September 1897; Colby to KIH, 9 November 1897, CWB).

177. CLEMENS TO ROGERS

Lucerne
[?13] August 1897

Lucerne, Augustthesomething-orother, 1897.

Dear Mr. Rogers:

Miss Harrison's note has come with the news that Bliss has paid the $10,000.

Good. Maybe now he will like to save himself the trouble of publishing the de luxe if he can get as much out of it as he was expecting to get *without* that trouble—by turning it over to us for $1800. That was all he expected to make. He ciphered it out in my study, and I've still got his figures, somewhere.

I am writing a novel,[1] and am getting along very well with it.

I believe that this place (Weggis, half an hour from Lucerne), is the loveliest in the world, and the most satisfactory. We have a small house on the hillside all to ourselves, and our meals are served in it from the inn below on the lake shore. Six francs a day per head, house and food included. The scenery is beyond comparison beautiful. We have a rowboat and some bicycles, and good roads, and no visitors. Nobody knows we are here. And Sunday in heaven is noisy compared to this quietness.

Miss Harrison said nothing about Mrs. Rogers's illness, and so we take that for a good omen. I wish you would bring her here.

Sincerely Yours

SLC

[1] On 4 August 1897 Clemens recorded: "Began ⟨Hellfire⟩ Hotchkiss" (Notebook 32b, TS p. 24). See also *MTSatan,* p. 31; *S&B,* pp. 172 ff.

178. Clemens to Rogers

Weggis
13 September 1897

Dear Mr. Rogers:

Your letter has given us a grand uplift. Dear me, our wealth piles up faster under your handling of it than it ⟨does⟩ did under my labors on the platform. It might be good business-partnership for you to have all the money I can make on the platform and ⟨you t⟩ give me the profits you make it yield, over and above its own personality. Mrs. Clemens asks me to say to you that she is "perfectly delighted, and very grateful." So am I.

As to the disposition of the money—now won't you just keep it and do what you like with it a spell longer, until we know there's enough to sweep off our debts at one wipe? I want to pay everybody in full except the Mount Morris. I shall be very glad if they can be persuaded to come to the 50% basis. Then when I paid the rest of the creditors in full, I would pay that bank in full on the basis of an indebtedness of $9,000 less than the claim as allowed by the assignee; and stop there until they explain to my satisfaction what they did with the $9,000 of fraudulent notes.

When Miss Harrison's letter arrives, we will cipher; and if there is enough money to pay everybody off in full except the bank, I think that that is what we shall want to do. And if there isn't enough, wait a while.

However, if there's enough to pay ¾ of the debt, I guess it would be best to do *that* ⟨, and publish the fact.⟩. If we paid it all at once it might make us seem to scrape money together too easily. ⟨It could stop the tear of sympathy from flowing.⟩

Pond has renewed his offer of $50,000 for 125 nights; but I don't intend to go on the platform any more if I can pay the debts without it; and I am feeling pretty sure I can, now.

From your letter I can see that you are having very good times at

Fairhaven; and I am glad to know that Mrs. Rogers is able to be in them. Say—when is Harry going to work? I mean on shore. Of course on the sea the yacht supports him.

I would like to be remembered to all the vast household—may it increase 300 per cent a year right along and be correspondingly happy.

SLC

179. CLEMENS TO ROGERS

Weggis
18 September 1897

Dear Mr. Rogers:

The Swiss vacation is ended and I am packing the trunks for Vienna. That is, I am superintending. We have had more sunshine and more rain here in these 10 weeks than ever got mixed together before in that space of time. Still, it has been perfectly satisfactory to me, and (I would as soon spend my life in Weggis as anywhere in the geography.) I leave all places with regret; and if there is ever to be an exception, this is not the one. We shall reach Salzburg next Wednesday 22d—no, a day or two later—and remain a week. We reach Vienna about Oct 1. Our address there for a few days will be c/o Thos. Cook & Son, while we hunt up a house to live in.

Hang it, I wish Rice had come here. I wonder if he came to Switzerland at all, and if his family were with him. We should have been very glad of a sight of them. I could not have offered any billiards, but German 9-pins are to be had. There is good exercise in it, but that is all. You can't hit anything but the game-keeper. We have played, all these weeks.

Very reposeful here. I have seen a newspaper only 3 times in 10 weeks. I do not know what has been happening in the world, and do not seem any the worse for it. I believe it has been a distinct gain, in fact; and so I intend to continue the deprivation for a year and see what the result will be.

By Langdon's monthly statement I perceive that Colby has been charging me $800 for something or other. This is the third or fourth similar robbery he has committed upon me—and he hasn't collected the money due from Frohman *yet*. Colby is a bilk.

With love to you all.

SLC

180. CLEMENS TO ROGERS

Vienna

8 October 1897

Hotel Metropole

Dear Mr. Rogers:

We have been here nine days and I have spent seven of them in bed—with gout. I am up and around, ⟨the⟩ yesterday and to-day, but the rainy and snowy weather keeps all of us except Mrs. Clemens in the house—colds, coughs and gout-possibilities the reason.

We can't get on the track of a furnished flat, and an unfurnished one would be expensive; so we rather expect to remain in this hotel. They have given us here all the room we could use in a flat, and have reduced the rent of these rooms 40 per cent; ⟨so⟩ we shouldn't be able to live cheaper except in a furnished flat.

The mail is made up of letters that are written in the difficult German script. This blocks off all possible idleness and keeps all of us busy; for it takes us as long to spell out a German letter as it does to answer it. All the gouty people in Austria and Germany write me and tell me what is good for gout, and some of the remedies are good. I mean to try the whole ⟨?darned⟩ lot the next time I get the disease. They can't all fail.

So far, I've seen nothing of Vienna except what is visible from the hotel windows.

With love to you all.

SLC

181. Clemens to Rogers

Vienna
10–11 November 1897
Hotel Metropole

Dear Mr. Rogers:

I throw up the sponge. I pull down the flag. Let us begin on those debts. I cannot bear the weight any longer. It totally unfits me for work. I have lost three entire months, now. In that time I have begun twenty magazine articles and books—and flung every one of them aside in turn. The debts interfered every time, and took the spirit out of the work. And yet I have worked like a bond slave, and wasted no time and spared no effort. A man can't possibly write the kind of stuff that is required of me unless he have an unharassed mind. My stuff is worth more in the market to-day than it ever was before—and yet in 3 months I have not succeeded in turning out fifty acceptable pages.

Peace of mind is easily attainable—and let's go for it. If Miss Harrison sent those figures, they got lost; but any way they are not necessary to my present scheme. Which is this: (and let Bliss like it or not as he pleases—I am tired of having my mendicancy flaunted in the world's face as an advertisement):

Please pay (pro rata) the Webster creditors (pro-rata $10,000) (*except the Bank and the Grants*), $10,000 on December 1st; also $10,000 on January 1st; and finish paying them in full on February 1st.

This is Mrs. Clemens's desire as well as mine. If the Grants want to (credit in all) assume Jesse Grant's indebtedness to me of $500 and twelve and a half years' interest, all right, I will pay the rest of their claim—otherwise I will pay them only what is due them over and above the Jesse Grant swindle, and let them skirmish for the rest.

Leaving out the Bank and the Grants, $30,000 will pay off all the others, according to my reckoning.

The Bank debt will never trouble me. Its claim is a false one—that is, half or more than half of it is. When it is ready to knock off half, I am ready to compromise on that basis.

———

Nov. 11. After 24 hours, the above scheme looks as sound and rational to me as ever; and I feel good over it. But I wish I had thought of it twenty days ago, for it has been raining and snowing and storming politics here, and I ought to have been taking advantage of that harvest, instead of growling around cursing life and ⟨the intolerable way [remainder irrecoverable]⟩ its humiliations.

Your letter has come, and by George you seem as young at 58 as *I* was at that early day. Wait till you are 62! You will not be the frivolous young thing you are now. The comedy of life will have played its gay curtain down, by then; ⟨and four⟩—you wait and see.

However—not necessarily. Some people are *born* young, and stay so. Like my mother, who was still young and full of the zest of life at 88; and like yours, who at 86 is her counterpart. I beg you to give her my affectionate homage, with the wish that she may never grow old.

Yes, and I will send you and Mrs. Rogers that same message.

SLC

182. Mrs. Clemens and Clemens to Rogers

Vienna
17 November 1897

P.S.

Dear Mr. Rogers:

Please divide pro rata among the creditors of Charles L. Webster & Co whose claims have been allowed by the Assignee ⟨with the exception of the Mount Morris Bank and the U. S. Grant estate⟩

$10,000 on Dec. 1, 1897; $10,000 on Jan. 1, 1898; and $10,000 on Feb. 1, 1898, from money of mine in your hands.

> Very Truly Yours
>
> Olivia L. Clemens

It just occurred to me last night that as between my unsupported say-so and Mrs. Clemens's formal endorsement of it you would prefer the latter if you were going to pay out money of hers;—this explains the foregoing paragraph.

If the paying of this money at this time is going to be a fatal mistake, of course we must abide by your judgment and not do it. But I hope you will not regard it so. If I can heave the main debt off my shoulders I shall feel free again and shall not mind the Bank-debt.

I am beginning a new book this morning. (Of all the work which I have begun since last August I have finished *not one single thing*.) [1] Shall I throw *this* aside next week?

> Sincerely Yrs
>
> SLC

---

[1] The variety of surviving uncompleted manuscripts which Clemens began in Austria amply supports this statement but prevents identification of the "new book."

183. ROGERS TO CLEMENS

> New York
> 10 December 1897

My dear Clemens:—

I know your heart will be made glad by the accompanying sheets [1] which express the appreciation shown by the creditors of the firm of Charles L. Webster & Company, of your kindly act. These acknowledgements are the only ones we have at present, but as they come in later, we will send you copies. We will keep the originals and put them among your effects, so they may stand as permanent recognitions of appreciation.

Harry received in due time your book, and will duly acknowledge its receipt.[2] I have monopolized it to the present time, and I cannot express to you how much pleasure I have had in the reading. I like it particularly well. It is a good book.—My word!

I am just head and heels in business winding up a very important gas deal in Boston, which you will remember I went into some five years since. I am glad to say it is finally closed, and of course we get a profit.[3]

Sincerely yours,

H H Rogers

[1] Typescript copies of letters of thanks from a number of creditors written in early December 1897, most of them addressed to Mr. K. I. Harrison, or K. I. Harrison, Esq., are in MTP (the original letters are in CWB). "I appreciate Mr. Clemens' manliness no less than his incomparable humor," said one; another could not "refrain from a word of appreciation in praise of the high honor and strict business spirit evinced by Mr. Clemens in his endeavor to settle in full the claims against his publishing firm." One creditor wrote: "We have read of examples of such sterling integrity but this is the first time where a similar thing has occurred to us in our business experience"; another enclosed a personal letter to Clemens in which he refused to accept any further payments of the Webster debts.

It must have been at about this time that Miss Harrison also forwarded a three-page document listing 101 creditors of Charles L. Webster & Company to whom $79,704.80 had been owed, indicating amounts they had been paid, first by Colby, then by Miss Harrison for Rogers, until only $7,990.82 was outstanding. These figures did not include, she explained, the $33,862.72 (see letters 188 and 193) owed to the Mount Morris Bank, Mrs. J. D. Grant, and the Barrows.

[2] *Following the Equator*, with the dedication to "my young friend Harry Rogers," was in print by November 1897. Clemens had sent a copy of the London Chatto & Windus edition called *More Tramps Abroad*.

[3] Rogers refers to his battle with J. Edward Addicks (see letter 37, note 1). At about this time "Mr. Rogers sold his interest in the Brookline and Dorchester gas companies to the New England Gas and Coke Company, and delivered to that company the management and control of the four Boston gas companies." Rogers's "profit" from this sale proved to be the main issue of litigation which continued into 1907, when the United States Circuit Court ordered him to return half of $3,000,000 which he had received "in excess of any value which was visible to the court" (New York *Tribune*, 20 May 1909).

184. CLEMENS TO ROGERS

Vienna
16 December 1897

Hotel Metropole

Dear Mr. Rogers:

We are delighted with your plan. Go on with it, on the lines you propose. Only, don't leave the *Barrows* out. Apparently that claim has been inherited by some women—daughters, no doubt. We don't want to see them lose anything. Barrow is an ass, and disgruntled; but I don't care for that. I am responsible for the money, and must do the best I can to pay it.

Leaving out Grant and the Mt. Morris, how much will it take to clear us entirely of debt?

I wish I could have seen that game.[1] Ives ought to go to England and punch the stuffing out of Roberts. He did it in New York once. You know that at the *full* English game (whatever that is) Roberts can give any man in Great Britain 50 per cent and beat him—and *does* it—does it every time.

How is the 18-inch balk marked off? Draw me a diagram of the table. ⟨Then⟩ Is it thus:

Charley Langdon says you turned over to him a dividend of $171 on the Gas stock you bought for us. By George you mustn't pay out *that* fertile hen [2] to the Webster creditors till the very *last!* Let her lay as long as she can.

Clara and I had started into society, and were dining and lunching and going to operas, and were getting at times cheerful once more; ⟨?and indeed almost gay;⟩ but we are all once more under a cloud, through the death of my brother,³ and have resumed our former seclusion.

I am glad Rice is to have a new house, and glad he is to be near you. He will be handy when I drop in on you by and by when the debts are cleared off.

I am writing hard—writing for the creditors.

Has Miss Harrison received my new book? I think I wrote Bliss to send one to Harry and one to Miss Harrison and go down [to] sell one to you. I know I wrote about Harry, and I believe I wrote about Miss Harrison. If I am mistaken I wish to rectify it *quick*.

Blame it, why didn't Laffan tell me about that Monotype Machine!⁴ I could have helped to get up that Company in London, and now I should be out of debt.

The cable said a Czech hit me over the head in the Reichsrath,⁵ but it suppressed what I did to the Czech. There are orphans in that family now.

Sincerely Yours

SLC

¹ Clemens refers to the World's Championship Billiard Tournament in Madison Square Garden, in which Frank C. Ives, "the Napoleon of billiards," had made a record run of 140 (New York *Times*, 3 December 1897). In 1893, Ives, then described as "the smooth-faced billiard champion from the backwoods of Michigan," had played the English champion, John Roberts, in New York. The English rules seriously inhibited Ives's play, and, although he did break all records in winning one game, he lost the match to Roberts (New York *Times*, 2–8 October 1893). The new eighteen-inch balk line game about which Clemens inquires here was a matter of some dispute. It had been introduced in order to prevent just such large runs as Ives's 1897 record run, but, while failing to restrict players of Ives's caliber, the new regulation made the game more difficult and less satisfying for men of inferior skill.
² Recurring allusions to the hen which hatches profit for Clemens represent Clemens's earliest approach to the familiarity of using Rogers's first name.
³ Orion Clemens died 11 December 1897.
⁴ Clemens may even have been serious about wishing that he had invested in the Lanston Monotype Machine Company, of which William Mackay Laffan, of the New York *Sun,* was vice-president.
⁵ In a letter of 10 December 1897 to the Rev. Joseph Twichell (Yale), Clemens described the incident:
    Pond sends me a Cleveland paper with a cablegram from here in it which says that when the police invaded the parliament and expelled the 11 members

I waved my handkerchief ⟨with the rest of⟩ and shouted Hoch die Deutschen! and got hustled out. Oh dear, what a pity it is that one's adventures never happen! When the Ordner (sergeant-at-arms) came up to our gallery and was hurrying the people out, a friend tried to get leave for me to stay, by saying "But this gentleman is a foreigner—you don't need to turn him out—he won't do ⟨him⟩ any harm."

"Oh, I know him very well—I recognize him by his pictures; and I should be very glad to let him stay, but I haven't any choice, because of the strictness of the orders."

And so we all went out, and no one was hustled. Below, I ran across the London Times correspondent, and he showed me the way into the first gallery and I lost none of the show. The first gallery had not misbehaved, and was not disturbed.

185. Clemens to Rogers

Vienna
21 December 1897

Dear Mr. Rogers:

Yes, you are right. The replies of the creditors have indeed "made my heart glad." And the fact that I am soon to be wholly clear of all of the hateful burden of Webster and Hall's debts that I care a rap about makes that same heart as light as Colby's brain or the soul of the Mount Morris.

I am very glad you like the book. The London papers and the Vienna papers like it, and so do my personal friends in England and here. I believe this testimony to be square. And I can add to it my own—I like the book myself. All this shows—what? That the common notion that a book infallibly reveals the man and his condition, is a mistake. This book has not ⟨revealed⟩ exposed me. It pretends to an interest in its subject—which was mostly not the case. It pretends that it was freely spouted out of a contented heart —not the forced work of a rebellious prisoner fretting in chains. Well, Gott sei Dank it is over and done with; I would rather be hanged, drawn and quartered than write it again. All the heart I had was in Susy's grave and the Webster debts. And so, behold a miracle!—a book which does not give its writer away.

Oh, you are winding up the Boston gas-deal, are you? Acting as

Coroner, I reckon. Luck to you! Coroner to the Webster corpse, too.
And that is luck for *me*. You and I are a team: you are the most
useful man I know, and I am the most ornamental.

Good-bye—I am feeling gay. I had nearly forgotten how it felt.

Yours ever sincerely

SLC

186. CLEMENS TO ROGERS

Vienna

29 December 1897

Hotel Metropole

Dear Mr. Rogers:

Yours of the 17th arrived this morning and is immensely gratifying in various ways. Land, we are glad to see those debts diminish-
ing! For the first time in my life I am getting more pleasure out of
paying money out than pulling it in. When I get everybody paid
but the Bank and the Grants I shall be as full of spirit as a
distillery. Then my plan will be to pay the Bank a small sum yearly
—$1,000 or $2,000—until I have paid $10,000, then quit. I think
it quite likely that I owe the Bank that much. That I owe it more I
shall not believe until I find out what went with the $9,000 of false
notes.

I think the Bank and the Grants are going to come good when I
get to that part of my Autobiography.[1] Also James W. Paige. Also
Thomas Russell & Son. I hope it won't turn out that the Assignee
paid Russell & Son the figure that appears in the Statement—or
any other sum. Unless it was a dividend which was paid before
Charley Langdon cleared off the debt.

I think the Harpers are doing mighty well with the old books,
but I wish they would advertise them a little more—just to give
them an important look. Still, I think they know their own business
⟨better than a⟩ pretty well.

I am very very glad that you like the book, and that others do. The notice in the Sun delighted me all over. I think John Wagner must have written it.[2]

I guess the World article [3] will help Bliss, rather than hurt the business. I was getting a little tired of being traded on as the only real living, unrivaled, genuwyne marketable pauper.

We seem to have lots of money in your hands. Very glad of it, too. Pay it out to creditors. But save the gas stock.

This is a most cussed expensive town. When I get out of debt I will burn it and build a cheaper one.

I have had a troublesome time trying to get hold of a satisfactory subject to write a book about, but I think I am all right, now. I have gotten along up to 30,000 words without running against a snag—a good sign that I am on the right track. As a rule I find it out earlier when

[The remainder of this letter is missing.]

---

[1] Among the many literary projects undertaken by Clemens in 1897 were sporadic returns to his autobiography. None of the material in *MTA* identified with this period deals with the Grants or Clemens's bankruptcy.

[2] The review of *Following the Equator* in the New York *Sun* on 11 December 1897 was unsigned. Clemens had met John H. Wagner in Melbourne, Australia, in 1895; on 28 October 1895 Clemens had written a letter of introduction for him to J. Henry Harper.

[3] The New York *World* on 13 December 1897 had described Clemens, his debts paid, as the most popular figure in Vienna.

187. ROGERS TO CLEMENS

New York
6 January 1898

My dear Clemens:—

I have your interesting letters of the 16th and 21st of December. I note what you say in regard to the Barrow claim, and will try and get in communication with him. I did not quite understand the case but I know I do now, and it shall be treated just as you wish.

The $171.00 you refer to is a 3% dividend on 57 shares of Brooklyn Union Gas Company's stock, which we bought for Mrs. Clemens; General Langdon placing $5,000.00 in our hands for the purpose. We bought the stock, I think, at something less than $90. and it is now selling at $120., so that will not go to the Webster creditors.

We have now in our hands $29,982.95 in cash. After we pay the last 25% dividend, namely $6,648.33 (leaving out Barrow, Grant and the Mt. Morris Bank) we will have remaining $23,334.62.

The balance due the Mount Morris Bank	$21,244.13
The balance due Mrs. J. D. Grant	1,471.55
The balance due Barrow	11,147.04
	$33,862.72

I can appreciate under what trials you wrote your book, and I think it a remarkable production when we consider the fact. The book is spoken of most pleasantly by every body. The people in New York, of course, do not get hold of your book promptly by reason of the fact that it is sold only by subscription. I very frequently hear it spoken of and always in the kindest terms. I enclose a criticism from Harpers' Magazine, which you will probably see before this reaches you. Of course it is by Laurence Hutton.[1]

Poor Helen Kellar has gotten into trouble over in Boston. Mr. Gilman the tutor and Miss Sullivan seem to have a variegated difference, and there is the "old Harry to pay." Mrs. Hutton is an active participant and is much distressed because of the trouble, still I guess it will work out in some way. Helen has been getting along very smoothly in her studies for the past year and has shown remarkable aptness and ability.

Dr. Rice is getting on slowly but surely with his new house. I think the cellar is dug and the foundation walls in. One of the little girls, Margerie has been ill and Mrs. Rice has taken her to Lakewood for a short stay, otherwise the family are all well. Rice was in one night last week and we played billiards. I used your cue and beat him easily. We never get together in that old room but we are reminded of and talk of you most incessantly. I judge your ears burn on such occasions, but as it is occasionally late in the night with you I suppose you sleep right through without noticing it. Harry received his copy of "Following The Equator" from Bliss as also the one you sent him from London. That reminds me, I wonder if I ever thanked you for the picture that Chatto & Windus sent me. Miss Harrison interrupts me to say that I did acknowledge receipt of the picture; at any rate I haven't told you that Mrs. Rogers had it framed in pure gold, and it is hung in the library. You know her father was in the diamond business for a great many years. He retired a year or so ago, and he has a barrel or two of diamonds, rubies, emeralds, etc. under the bed. Mrs. Rogers expects in the near future to be able to steal some of the precious stones and have them inserted in the frame, then I shall want your autograph on the picture and the thing will be complete for posterity and eternity.

We are all very well at 57th Street. Mrs. Benjamin's children have been spending two weeks with us, while she and Will have been to Chicago on a visit to Mr. and Mrs. Broughton. They are expected home on Saturday. They did not have to travel in private cars as you and I do when we go to Chicago. There are no restrictions against them on the Pennsylvania Limited.

We have been moving from the office to the eleventh story of the new building. From the windows we have a fine view of the river, and it seems very hard to work when there are so many attractions out of doors. We have fine quarters and I have some spare rooms, one of which we will be very glad to offer you when you are in town and desire to re-establish yourself in business.

I will ask Miss Harrison to answer in reference to your remarks concerning Mrs. Grant.

> Love to you all
>
> Yours truly
>
> H H Rogers [2]

P.S. We received shortly after New Years a letter from Edwin F. Mayo, copy of which we enclose herewith. The statement of the Mayo account shows a loss under the new management for

1896 and 1897 of	$4,045.33
from December 18th	266.73
making a total loss of	$4,312.06

so it would appear that this last named sum would have to be made up this year before we can expect to receive further dividends. I think the death of Frank Mayo meant a serious loss to you, because the Play is very attractive, and as played by Mayo was getting into great favor. Mr. Mayo wants to know your address. We don't propose to gratify him unless you approve.

This is the 18 inch balk line.

---

[1] Hutton in his "Literary Notes" in *Harper's Magazine,* January 1898 found *Following the Equator* "not so 'funny' as are the Innocents and the Tramp Abroad," but, he wrote, the "cause is not far to seek": it was "undertaken to raise the burden of a business debt which he considers a personal obligation, and concluded in the midst of an almost overwhelming domestic sorrow," however something of "the old-time, Mark Twainy flavor" survives.

[2] All of the letter was typed (and dictated) except the last six words and the signature, which were added in Rogers's hand.

188. Katharine Harrison to Clemens

New York
7 January 1898

Dear Mr. Clemens:

I have your favors of the 18th and 21st ult. I have sent the Calcutta letter to John Brusnahan and as soon as I hear from him will communicate with you again.

Now, about the statement I sent you. I was afraid at the time I was not making it clear, but my excuse must be that I was hurried. Mrs. Grant was paid her 50%. There is only owing her $1471.55

which amt. I think you will find at the end of my statement. As I made over the statement three times owing to different information I received from Colby, I may have neglected to add it on. Mr. Rogers has written you today and as I made up the figures, I won't repeat them again. I think everything will be clear.

About Russell—Without knowing anything about him I did send him a check, but he returned it and for further information referred me to his lawyer. Then I found from Colby that he had been settled with so he does not get a penny. If I can learn the detail, I will send you word later. I would like to get all the creditors settled, but Mr. Rogers says it would be unwise just now.

You ask if Bliss sent me your book—No, but I received the English edition and have enjoyed it immensely. I thought I acknowledged its receipt but in the hurry I may have overlooked it, if so I trust you will pardon me.

I have just been turned out of one room, as there are six men at work painting. Such a week as we have had moving. I shall be thankful when it is in order again. We have fine offices—quite an improvement on the 4th floor.

Please tell Mrs. Clemens I don't want any pay for the little I have done. I am only too glad to be able to do it for you both, and I shall not stop until it is all settled. We have it well under way now.

With kindest regards, and best wishes for the New Year, I am

Yours truly,

Katharine I. Harrison

189. Clemens to Rogers

Vienna
20 January 1898

Met Hotel

Dear Mr. Rogers:

Yours of the 5th is to hand. It is very very good news: that when you have paid Barrow up, and the last 25% div. to the other creditors (except Grant and the Bank), we shall still have about $1[2],000 [1] left in cash. This is exceedingly bully; the best music we have heard lately.

Since we began to pay off the debts I have abundant peace of mind again—no sense of burden. Work is become a pleasure again —it is not labor, any longer. I am into it up to my ears, these last 3 or 4 weeks—and all *dramatic*. (I always believed I couldn't write a play that would *play*, but this one will that I am putting the finishing touches to.)

And there's another one—a joint production. An Austrian playwright is plotting it out, and we are going to write it together.[2]

Thirdly, I've ⟨been⟩ acquired the American and English rights in a new and powerful and successful Austrian drama, and have nearly finished translating it. The author and I share the American and English profits half and half.[3]

They are going to stage the Prince and Pauper in England [4] again—they have started on a preliminary tour through the country. If it should be successful I may want to have a *real* lawyer—not an imitation—get it a chance in America by forcing a compromise with Dan. Frohman, who owns the American right and owes me a lot of money, which is lying all these years in Court waiting for some ignorant loafer like Colby or Whitford to come and collect it.

I'm grateful that you didn't give young Mayo my address.

I think I see, by Harry's letter, what he is up to. (In fact it is almost a confession.) When the swag is all in, on the book, he is going to garnishee it, on the ground that it is the dedication that sold the book. And the customers. Will you and Mrs. Rogers block that game? I never saw a boy act so.

Yes, I shall want seven rooms in the eleventh story of the new building next year, to conduct my dramatic business in. Please have them frescoed. Put in a billiard table. I will send you further details as they occur to me.

Mrs. Clemens wishes me to ask you to do her a large favor, as she does not feel quite courageous enough to ask it herself. She encloses Chatto & Windus's check (new book returns) for a thousand pounds-odd, and begs that you will invest it for her when you get a

chance. Of course she isn't expecting another oil-well like the gas
stock, but you'll jam it in somewhere, won't you?

With love to all of you

SLC

[1] This figure is irrecoverable from the manuscript. A tear in the paper has
obliterated the second digit. The figure has been reconstructed on the basis of
Rogers's statement in letter 187 that, without paying Barrow (to whom $11,147.04
was owed), the Mount Morris Bank, and Mrs. Grant, "we will have remaining
$23,334.62."
[2] It must have been at this time, not in 1899 (*MTB*, p. 1075), that Clemens
began his short-lived collaboration with Sigmund Schlesinger. A contract in
Clemens's hand, governing the management of a comedy entitled "Der Gegen-
candidat, or Woman in Politics," was signed a month later in Vienna on 24
February 1898 (State University of New York at Buffalo).
[3] Letter 198 indicates that this play was probably *Bartel Turaser*, by Philipp
Langmann.
[4] Bram Stoker was to be agent for Clemens's plays (see letter 195). No production of *The Prince and the Pauper* is on record as being staged at this time.

190. CLEMENS TO ROGERS

Vienna

5–6 February 1898

Hotel Metropole

Dear Mr. Rogers:

Yours of Jan. 21 was just full of charm. It will be a nobby thing
if you do get that letter out of the Mount Morris. I am afraid to
think about it, and almost to write about it, I am so superstitious.
But if you *should* land those fellows! (I'll shut up and wait.)

I had a letter from Bliss ⟨two or three⟩ several weeks ago from
which I seemed to gather that the most he could say was that he
had issued 20,000 books up to the end of the year. I haven't
answered, because I didn't quite know what to say.[1] All things
considered, it is not quite a third as good as he ought to have done.
And it is less than a fourth as good as his old fox of a father would

have done. I don't want to hurt his feelings, for he has done the best that was in him to do—so I don't quite know how to write him. Ever since he came over to England with a scheme to issue 250 copies Edition de luxe and make *1800 dollars* for me out of it, I have believed it might improve him if he could lose the rest of his mind. *He* mustn't touch an edition de luxe! I will have his scalp if he tries.

When his letter came I was well along with what I know will make a rattling good subscription book—and of course I had his firm in my mind.[2] I put that manuscript away—suddenly! and haven't touched it since. I resolved to stop book-writing and go at something else. Just then an Austrian professional dramatist came along and proposed to write an American comedy with me (woman in politics) on half-profit basis; and that comedy is about finished, now—it won't take many more days. Meantime I have translated a new and strong Austrian melancholy drama and secured the English and American rights on a half-profit basis. And between-times I have written a comedy by myself, entitled "Is He Dead?"—and I put on the finishing touches to-day and read it to Mrs. Clemens, and she things it is very bully. I think, myself, that for an ignorant first attempt it lacks a good deal of being bad. I am learning the trade pretty fast—I shall get the hang of it yet, I believe. I shall stick to the business right along until I either turn out something real good or find out I can't.

Meantime, also, I've made my last final permanent appearance on the platform—I hope. It was for a Viennese charity, and we had a staving good time. Many of the seats were $4 each. Packed house, and lots of "standees." Six members of the Imperial family present and four princes of lesser degree, and I taught the whole of them how to steal watermelons. Now all this sounds like brag, but[3]

We like Vienna immensely—and by and by if we can persuade Mrs. Clemens to go out a little and mingle with people once more, we shall like it better still. But that is well along in the future.

With a great deal of love to you all.

                                                                       SLC

Feb. 6. Your letter has arrived! And you've crucified the Bank, sure enough! I shake you by the hand! and am your obligedest and humblest servant. *Now* it's plain sailing. I still owe the Bank (after this $6,612.46 is paid) fairly and squarely about $6,000, more, and that I will pay, a little at a time, at my leisure. When they prove to me that they never collected the $9,000 false notes, I will pay that, too. But the burden of proof is upon them—they must do the proving, themselves. And I don't quite know how they will do it: for Hall and his book-keeper cooked a false statement of the Webster assets and liabilities once and played it off on me; and another time Hall deceived me ⟨to the⟩ and got my name on $15,000 of new Mt. Morris notes, allowing [me] to believe I was endorsing the old ones—therefore the testimony of those two has no value for me.

Now as to the Barrow claim. I want to pay that in full—no *interest*, of course, but the full sum allowed by the assignee. And so we don't need to make *him* agree to any compromise, do we? We only want a receipt out of him acknowledging that we owe him nothing more—isn't that it? Evidently there are women concerned —his sisters, no doubt—and we are afraid ⟨it⟩ they may be in sharp need of the money.

I thought I was going to finish this letter, this time, but no— there's some company—ladies—and I must put on my shirt and go and see them. (This is Mrs. Clemens's idea; she is particular about clothes.)

No—I won't wait—I'll mail it now.

SLC

[1] Clemens would write to Frank Bliss, 11 February 1898: "Considering all the circumstances a 20000 sale is certainly a little disappointing for it is a most attractive looking book, however may be the times will improve. They have been bad about long enough" (TS in MTP).

[2] None of Clemens's books was published by subscription after *Following the Equator* in 1897, and none of his published or unpublished works after this time appears to have been suitable for this kind of exploitation.

[3] Clemens added at the bottom of the page: "that's what it *is.*" On 1 February 1898 he had spoken in Vienna and read the watermelon story (Notebook 32, TS p. 8). See letter 82, note 1.

191. CLEMENS TO ROGERS

Vienna
7 February 1898

Dear Sir:

Please accept for me the compromise-offer made by the Mount
Morris Bank through its President, Mr. Wm. H. Payne in his
letters to you of Jan. 22 and 26, 1898,[1] concerning the C. L.
Webster & Co debt; and please pay the $6,612.46 required.
And greatly oblige (and charge to)

Yours Very Truly

S. L. Clemens

This is a postscript, to a letter which I was writing yesterday, and
which will be finished and forwarded to you within a day or two.

SLC

I send this without waiting, for this is financial business, ⟨and⟩
whereas the other is literary business. There is little or no connection between literature and finance, except when Grant writes the
book and Webster handles the money.

⟨I'm *going* to write Bliss some time or other. Meantime I'd like
the enclosed card sent to him, please.⟩

SLC

[1] On 22 January 1898 (Salm) William H. Payne of the Mount Morris Bank
sent Rogers a statement of the bank's claim against Clemens:

Notes made by *C. L. Webster & Company,*
endorsed *S. L. Clemens,*

Due June 1st. 1894	$ 2500
" " 22nd. "	$ 4500
" May 25th. "	$ 5000
" April 18th. "	$ 5000
" " 21st. "	$ 5000
" July 5th. "	$ 3000
" Aug. 20th. "	$ 1000
Note made by S. L. Clemens endorsed by C. L. Webster & Co.	$ 3500
	$ 29500
Interest to date	6495
Charges for protest	7
	$ 36002
Received from Assignee	
$ 5876.33	
$ 2261.21	$ 8137.54
Amount due..........	$ 27864.46

"The account does not include," Payne explained, "Alexander & Green charges or costs and expense of procuring judgement on some of the notes." He continued:

In accordance with your suggestion at our interview, I offer to compromise and release this claim for $6750, which with the amount paid us by the assignee will be about 50% of the principal of the original notes.

On 26 January Payne acknowledged Rogers's amendment, "making the balance of 50% on the original notes $6612.46," to be an amount that "is correct and will be satisfactory to us."

192. ROGERS TO CLEMENS

New York
9 February 1898

ORIGINAL CLAIM [1]
$2,613.33

RECEIVED of S. L. Clemens $653.34 which added to $1,959.99 previously received makes the full amount of my claim against the late firm of C. L. Webster & Company at the time of its failure. This receipt is given in full of all demands.

H H Rogers

[1] The receipt is typewritten, and signed in Rogers's hand.

193. Katharine Harrison to Clemens

New York
11 February 1898

My dear Mr. Clemens:

Your last 25% is paid to all the creditors excepting Bank, Barrow and Grant. I wish I could shout it across the water to you, so that you would get it ten days ahead of this letter, but I'm afraid my lungs are not strong enough. As soon as we hear from you we are to take up the remaining three, and hope soon they will be settled.

The amount to your credit today is $19,444.47.

Amt. due Mt. Morris Bk.	21,244.13	
" " Mrs. J D Grant	1,471.55	
" " Barrows	11,147.04	
Total	$33,862.72	

The total amt. of Mt. Morris Bank was $29,381.67. They were paid 27% or $8,137.54.

2/29,381.67

14 690.84	or	50% of claim
8 137.54		27% pd. by Colby
$ 6,553.30		Amt. now to be paid them.

Mr. Rogers is going away for three or four days to get a little rest. He wishes to be remembered.

With kindest regards, I am

Yours truly,

Katharine I. Harrison

194. KATHARINE HARRISON TO CLEMENS

New York
25 February 1898

Dear Mr. Clemens:—

Enclosed please find copies of the various expressions of the creditors received to date. You will note on the very first page the settlement of the Mount Morris Bank.[1]

I want to thank you for your kindness in sending me "Following the Equator" which arrived a few days since.

Yours truly,

K. I. Harrison

---

[1] See letter 183. Copies of further letters from creditors, dated 4 March to 16 April 1898, were later forwarded to Clemens. According to Clemens's notations on envelopes in which they were received, other collections of "Thanks from Webster creditors" were mailed from New York on 7 January and 26 April 1898; they and a copy of the settlement by the Mount Morris Bank for $6,612.46 are in MTP.

195. CLEMENS TO ROGERS

Vienna
7 March 1898

Dear Mr. Rogers:

The copies of the letters from creditors arrived to-day—first in the list the Mount Morris release, and I was very glad to see that. Mr. Dodd clothed it in boiler-iron! All right, I shall be very glad to "let you raise questions" with the⟨m⟩ Mt. Morris when it comes to further payments. I believe you will find that there are some quite legitimate questions to raise.

Bram Stoker is willing to be my dramatic agent in England and maybe in America;[1] and I asked him because I was ashamed to ask you to potter with it. He has not said he would act for America, and

I hope he will decline; for if *you* don't mind, I would rather have you for dramatic agent than any other expert in the business, I don't care where he hails from.

On a first reading he doesn't much believe in my play, but says he is going to examine it more closely. I was very near getting hold of a rattling good German play the other day, but Augustin Daly heard of it first and got in ahead of me. I must wake up. There will be other chances.

Why, you are all in the doctors' hands! I do wish Mrs. Broughton would have that operation performed; not now, but as soon as she gets well. As I understand it, the operation is not dangerous when one is in good health. I am anxious to know the state of her health now.

Why do you go to Virginia? Come here—cut the telegraph wires, shut off the mails, and take a real holiday. Suggest this idea to Mrs. Rogers. The Ministry was changed again night before last, and there is going to be some more political fun, probably. That is what you need. And bring Harry—I'll prepare him for Yale.

I wonder when I *am* going to get into my new quarters in the Standard Building. There is no immediate prospect. Jean is deadly homesick, but Clara has to stay here a year yet, to study music, and the rest of us must stay, too, for Mrs. Clemens will not hear of the family ever being divided again. But I suppose we couldn't go home anyway, for we are not able to live in our house. And I don't suppose we could afford a flat in New York.

I had a letter from young Barrow 3 or 4 days ago. I told him that if he called on you he would find that we had not forgotten his case. I told him I did not answer his father's appealing letter last summer because I could not reveal our plans of payment; that we wanted to secure a 50 per cent release from some of the creditors first; not from his father, but I couldn't tell his father that—it would be revealing too much. I said you were a business man and no doubt wanted that release, also, but that now the need of it was gone by.

Mrs. Clemens has always been particularly anxious to have the Barrow claim paid in full; and indeed so have I—for although he was not very agreeable about it it was a perfectly straight indebtedness.

Mrs. Clemens has been reading the creditors' letters over and over again, and thanks you deeply for sending them, and says this is the only really happy day she has had since Susy died.

With love to you all,

SLC.

---

[1] Clemens had recorded on 12 February 1898: "From letter to Bram Stoker: If he is willing, his commission for acting as agent for my plays, to 15% of the profits accruing to me, all over the world, and *he* to pay the commissions of all of his sub-agents out of his 15%" (Notebook 32, TS p. 12).

196. CLEMENS TO ROGERS

Vienna
15 March 1898

Dear Mr. Rogers:

Indeed I do rejoice with you in the rehabilitation of the health of Mrs. Benjamin and Mrs. Broughton. I was well able to sympathise with you in your anxieties—this family has been undergoing a sharp education in troubles of the heart this past two years.

I am glad you liked the Austrian article.[1] I noticed with gratification that one of the London dailies made extracts from it more than once and also said it was the most interesting article in the magazines of the month—a good compliment for an article on an unfresh subject.

Darn it I wish I had not written to Barrow. But I thought you were ready to pay him but didn't know how to find him. I didn't imagine that he was standing out for *interest*. If I had known that, it would have hardened this Pharaoh again that child of Israel. I don't feel in the least degree merciful toward him, now. It was a little difficult to feel merciful toward him at any time, for without a doubt he was on the inside when Mr. Hall laid before me the false statement (4 or 5 months before the failure) which fooled me into trying to save the concern by emptying into its stomach the last money ($24,000) ⟨which I had in the world. He must have known that Hall was playing that fraud upon me. I think that both he and Hall belonged in jail. As to Hall I am quite certain. My sympathy with Barrow is dead. I would squeeze him if I had a chance.⟩[2]

Bram Stoker has sent you my so-called play. Thinks it is good ⟨enough⟩ for America, possibly—not for England. I think that if it were put into the hands of a professional playwright it might perhaps be made a playing piece. An American one, I mean. Frohman, of the Lyceum Theatre, used to have such a man. There are others, but I don't know them.

Meantime I have arranged to translate a couple of plays—a melancholy one ("Bartel Turaser") and a funny one ("In Purgatory.")[3] I have the stage-rights for England and America. Of the money-results I get half. ⟨If⟩ Agency and other expenses in England and America (up to 10 per cent of the "take") are to be subtracted before the division; expenses in excess of that figure are to be paid out of my half of the profits. Contract holds for 6 years.

Within a fortnight I shall ship Bartel to you, and hope you can find an agent to take care of it in America—and maybe he could place it in England, too, for I'm tired of Stoker; he promises with energy, but is too slow and uncertain and unsatisfactory.

This dismal but interesting piece first saw the light the 9th of last November; and it made such a hit that within 2 months it was being played with great and fine success in the cities of Germany, Spain, Italy and around generally—but Bram didn't ask to look at it —says dismal plays won't go, in England.

It costs nothing to "stage" Bartel; $100 will buy the scenery,— and as for costumes, any old clothes of Harry's will do. It's the quaintest thing—doesn't much resemble a play—but it crowds the houses every time it is billed.

I want to send the "Purgatory" to you, too, when I have finished it—say a month or six weeks from now.

Be patient, don't get uneasy—I am hunting up all the work for you that I can think of.

Please tell us how little Margery [4] is getting along, we are troubled about that news.

With love

SLC

---

[1] Clemens's "Stirring Times in Austria" appeared in *Harper's Magazine* for March 1898.

[2] This deletion was made by Mrs. Clemens, who added her initials in the margin in a playful pretense of censorship. The canceled sentences are marked out so lightly that she patently intended them to be read.

[3] *Bartel Turaser* was written in 1897 by the German dramatist Philipp Langmann; *In Purgatory* was by Ernst Gettke and Georg Engel. None of the plays which Clemens mentions in this and other letters of this period was published in his translation or adaptation, and none survives among the unpublished dramatic writings by Clemens in MTP.

[4] Rice's daughter Marjory had been ill.

197. CLEMENS TO ROGERS

Vienna

17–20 March 1898

Dear Mr. Rogers:

I've landed a big fish to-day. He is a costly one, but he is worth the money—worth it because America has *got* to buy him whether she wants to or not. It isn't a type-setter, which people may take or leave, as they choose.

(I haven't had such a good time since we (meaning *you*) used to fry those people in the cemetery in the type-setter days. You ought to have been here; you would have enjoyed it.)

Night before last I heard by mere accident that the American patents on the ingenious and capable Designing-Machine [1] had not yet left the hands of the young inventor [2] and his backer (Mr. Kleinberg, banker.) I lost no time, but sent and asked them to come and talk with me—and appointed 9 last night. Then I went statistics-hunting all day yesterday. It was poor pickings at our Consulate General. The youngest book in the whole place was 18 years old;

still it answered well enough. It gave me the number of factories and the capital employed in America, and that was a fifth part of the information desired by me. The other four-fifths ⟨wouldn't be in a book⟩ ⟨that is, number of designers employed on Jacquard looms in America and their wages⟩ wouldn't be in a book.

Then I made out a list of questions ⟨which I will enclose in another envelop⟩ [3] and went through them with the banker and the inventor in the evening. The questioning lasted 3 hours. ⟨Mighty n⟩ Nice men, both of them. The banker is ⟨just⟩ a love of a man—a thorough-bred gentleman; educated; and used to be a jurist. You would like him. I was ashamed to question him as if he were on trial in a court, but it had to be done, ⟨and I had to imitate you, the Master of the art,⟩ and he said he didn't mind it. Said I could get my living as a financier if authorship should fail me—a very nice compliment and quite true, too, though you probably don't believe it.

I couldn't beat him down any from his price—$1,500,000; he is well in cash, now, and knows the value of the invention nearly as well as I do. He said he would dearly like the fame of being associated in business with me, but that *I* knew he was not asking a high price. ⟨I intimated that he *was*, but I thought I knew better.⟩

Had a very good time indeed. I said I would think the thing over and he could come ⟨again⟩ and get my answer at 4 ⟨to-morrow⟩ Friday afternoon. ⟨My answer was already ready, but I thought I wouldn't say so.⟩ ⟨I had been figuring—by mere guess-work, of course—on 2 designers to a factory—$2,000 salary—1,000 factories—$4,000,000; the machine to reduce that to a tenth; but when I found that a factory employs 20 to 30 designers and that the machine could weave colored cheap calicoes, I judged I better land the fish.⟩

This morning I sent for him again and said I had overlooked the fact that I must write New York to-day if I would catch the Saturday steamer; that I had reflected, was satisfied, and he could go and draw up the Option and add to it a private letter to me extending the time if I found it necessary.

A few months from now an additional machine will be completed and patented, whose office is to ⟨poke the threads⟩ automatically ⟨through⟩ punch the holes in the Jacquard cards. I cannot get a price on that at this time, but I take a writing which gives it to me ten per cent cheaper than anybody else's offer—in case I want it and demand it. I probably shan't want it. It is no great thing, ⟨and it⟩ (as far as I can see at present,) and can't be used without the help of this machine, and I've already *got* this one.

Mr. Kleinberg says that the business of making textiles requiring patterns (and therefore the Jacquard device) has very greatly increased in America of late years, and is growing.

In Austria 800 out of the 1500 textile factories have the Jacquard.

In America in '80 we had 3,237 textile factories (also 1005 cotton). By the Austrian ratio 1500 or 1600 of these 3,237 factories should have been employing the Jacquard.

Maybe there are 2,000 by this time, if the business has been greatly increasing.

With 10 designers to a factory, that is 20,000. With an average wage of $1,000 the expense is $20,000,000.

This invention will do that work for $2,000,000.

We employ $5 or $600,000,000 in textile manufacturing.

Ruling cotton out, ($220,000,000) and halving the rest, one may guess that $200,000,000 of capital use the Jacquard.

If they clear 6 per cent at present, ($12,000,000 ⟨is⟩ ain't it?) we can hog $3,000,000 of the $18,000,000 saved, and let them have the $15,000,000 to enable them to compete with the machine in Europe.

If they try to do without the machine they will have to put up with a 4 per cent dividend, and the value of their stock will suffer a slump which will give them the belly-ache.

The machine will make the output very much greater than it is now—never mind that, I haven't time to explain the reasons.

⟨You will run over here⟩

You are now to do as follows—and don't be trying to shirk:

You will run up to the Cheney Silk mills at South Manchester, 8 miles from Hartford; or, you visit mills nearer New York; and you will also post yourself in other ways; and when you've got accurate statistics in place of my faulty ones, you will then run over here a fortnight after you receive this, and examine the machine and its work. And then you will run back home and get up a Company of about $5,000,000 or $10,000,000, and take my fish off my hands, and give me one-tenth of that Company's stock, fully paid up, for my share. I can get along without cash, but I can't live without that stock.

Then the whole Jacquard industry in America will be in the hands of that Company. And people will call it a Trust. And in fact that is what it will amount to. But you must not be troubled by that; such things cannot be helped.

———

PLANT. It is inexpensive. When you receive the descriptive pamphlet which I will mail to you to-morrow, you will see that this is necessarily true. One small plant to start with—others as required.

———

APPLICATION of the invention. The thing can get to work in a very little while. The Co. will not have to wait, and wait, and wait, and chew its bowels, and moan about hope deferred, and all that. (Because it isn't a type-setter.)

I think you better make a $2,000,000 Company, and pay the money all in, in 3 or 4 instalments. That will buy the patents and furnish a deal more capital than is necessary, besides.

And *I* think the Standard Oil should take the *whole* of it.

You can make it pay 200 per cent a year on that capital and still leave the industry entirely competent to compete with the patent in Europe.

Within a year or two the $2,000,000 of stock would be worth—a good deal; I am ashamed to say how much. But I would not sell my tenth for a song, (Even with Patti to sing it.)

Now you and Mrs. Rogers come along over here. I will board you for nothing while you stay.

If this were an oil tract away down yonder in Kentucky, you and Archbold would go down there and live hard and travel hard for a month, and examine it. *This* is several oil tracts, the travel is easy and elegant, and your board free, except wine.

If you can't come, send Archbold; if he can't come, send Broughton; if he can't come, send me a financial giant who is out of a job and would like to get up the Company. If that isn't possible, cable me thus:

Mark Twain, Vienna.
LONDON.

Then I will go to London and do the best I can with my fish.

If you can come (or Archbold or Broughton or some one else,) cable me thus:

Mark Twain, Vienna
ROGERS

(or in place of your name put the name of the man who is coming). Even if the name be Smith or Jones or Brown I shall understand.

Of course it would occur to you—(still I better mention it, because you are so poetical and absent-minded) that so I get my one-tenth of paid-up stock gratis, *I* don't care if you make the Company *ten* millions and require it to give *you* as many paid-up tenths as you please. (I am trying to take care of you, lest you forget to do it yourself.)

Yours with love

S. L. Clemens

[The page is torn off.]

Sunday, 20th.

P.S. But really you should come yourself—for some good sense and good diplomacy are necessary, on account of the promised auxiliary invention. You might find it worth while to want to include it in the present Option, and you are the very man to know how to make them do it.

If there's war here, go to Germany. You can see the machine in practical operation there, and you will not need to visit Austria (or what's left of it) at all.

Parliament meets to-morrow afternoon—and there'll be music. I've got a front seat for the season (which will be short, perhaps.)

I will send you my Option in another envelop, registered. I keep a stamped copy of it.

P.P.S. Mr. Kleinberg would like to have a third of the American stock in place of $500,000 cash, but I told him that could be talked when my principal arrives from New York—I couldn't say, myself.

SLC

[1] Clemens's Notebook 32 is filled with evidences of his excitement about the textile-designing machine, which employed a photographic process:

March 18, 1898. On the 15th I heard by accident (through a chance remark of Miss Levetus to my wife) that the American patents on Szczepanik's designing-machine were not yet sold. I sent a note at once to Miss Levetus and asked her to arrange an interview for next night—16th for 9—here in the Hotel Metropole in our rooms. I spent the 16th in gathering American statistics at our Consulate-General (the youngest were *18 years old!*) and British ones through Mr. Wm. Lavino, Correspondent of the London Times: he got others for me by telephoning the British Consulate.

I ciphered on the data, and wrote 11 pages of questions; and when the inventor and his capitalist (Mr. Ludwig Kleinberg) arrived at 9 with Miss Levetus and Dr. Winternitz, I was ready for business, and rich with my new learning. My extraordinary familiarity with the subject paralyzed the banker for a while, for he was merely expecting to find a humorist, not a commercial cyclopedia—but he recovered presently.

We talked till midnight and then parted: I to think over the data and the price ($1,500,000) and we to meet again at 4 p.m. to-day. (18th) By breakfast time the 17th I had thought it over sufficiently; so I sent word and Mr. Kleinberg came and we entered into an agreement:

1. I to have an Option for 2 months at $1,500,000.
2. This to be payable in several instalments.
3. The term of the Option to be extended if I should need it and ask for it.
4. I to have No. 2 (an auxiliary device now approaching completion—it is to ⟨poke the threads through⟩ punch the Jacquard cards automatically by electricity) ⟨at⟩ ten per cent cheaper than the best offer made by any one else, if I want it and elect to take it.
5. I to have the *first* opportunity to take No. 3 for America when it is patented, if I want it. (No. 3 is a secret; it does away with the Jacquard loom entirely, and performs all its functions in another way and automatically.)
6. Mr. Kleinberg to pay me 12 per cent. commission if I effect the sale; as each instalment of the $1,500,000 reaches him he is to pay me 12 per cent of it immediately. (TS, pp. 13–14).

[2] Clemens liked Jan Szczepanik and wrote about him in "The Austrian Edison Keeping School Again," *Century Magazine,* August 1898. The inventor was "an interesting young creature," he wrote Richard Watson Gilder on 2 April 1898:

He comes and drinks beer with me every now and then, and talks till midnight. Is well born, educated, dresses nicely, and is an echte gentleman. He was a village school teacher in the provinces a few years ago, with a salary in proportion; but he is comfortable, now, and has a laboratory 3 or 4 stories high, in the centre of Vienna, and has inventions enough in his head to fill it to the roof.

Clemens hoped, he said, that "Rogers and his elbow-mates of the Standard Oil will furnish the whole capital and take hold of this large thing" (Notebook 32, TS p. 15).

[3] Clemens did enclose ten additional sheets on which he had first written his

barrage of questions (in pencil), then added Kleinberg's answers (in ink). He wrote out extensive inquiries into the variety of fabrics for which the machine could be used, the estimated operating costs, wages, and the probable profits—everything except the probable demand for its services in American factories. Rogers no doubt found his frantic notes less than enlightening as documents, but it seems likely that Clemens sent them chiefly to assure him that the cross-examination had been thorough.

198. CLEMENS TO ROGERS

Vienna
22 March 1898

Dear Mr. Rogers:

To-day I am sending you by very slow express the play entitled "Bartel Turaser," for you to exploit in America through your sub=theatrical agent.

Terms of my contract:

1. I alone am authorized to make contracts for staging the piece in America and collect the money.

2. After subtracting from the money 10% for American agent and other necessary expenses over there, the remaining profit is to be divided—half to me and the other half to ⟨Ernst Gettke and Alexander Engel.⟩ Heinrich Hirsch (the Author's agent.)

3. My American agent must send a monthly statement of the business to Hirsch (address: "I Nibelungengasse 7, Vienna,") together with the Author's half of the profit.

4. Title in bills and programs must read, "Bartel Turaser, by Philip Landmann,[1] ⟨translated⟩ adapted by Mark Twain." (I make no claim for a share when the piece is played in the *German* tongue.)

5. Contract holds 6 years, *provided* the piece gets on the stage within 18 months from the present time—failing which it perishes.

6. Violation of the contract, 300 florins (600 francs) fine—to be proven in a Viennese Court. (A formality and valueless, but the law requires it.)

I have a great curiosity to see how Bartel will go, in America. With the right actor for the chief part, it is bound to go, I suppose.

It is still filling the houses here on the continent. If it goes in America I will then try it in England.

I've contracted to translate a Comedy—"In Purgatory"—and try *that* in England and America.—Terms and conditions exactly the same as in Bartel, except that at this end the author's half doesn't go to Hirsch but to the *authors* of the Comedy (Gettke and Engel.)

———

I was going to translate a good drama ("The New Ghetto") on the above terms, but shall not contract to do it, yet awhile. My project to put the Jacquard looms of America into the hands of the Standard Oil will furnish me entertainment enough for a spell.

You must come over here. You will find it worth your while. This is not a small scheme, but a large one. It is going to need some diplomacy, unless I succeed in working the diplomacy myself to=morrow night. I will try.

But really if I succeed, ⟨that⟩ then *all the more* will a visit from you be necessary. (You remember the negro's prayer, time of the Charleston earthquake? "Come down, Lord, come *quick!* Come down yo' own self, *don't send yo' Son*—dis ain't no time for chillun!")

I beg Mrs. Rogers (as a personal favor) to pack up and come over. I judge you'll come, then.

Sincerely Yrs

SLC

———

¹ Clemens meant Philipp Langmann, who wrote *Bartel Turaser*.

199. CLEMENS TO ROGERS

Vienna
23 March 1898

Dear Mr. Rogers:

I was present at the opening of Parliament, but it was peaceable and dull; so I have not been there since. I had mislaid my present-session ticket, but I got in on my *last-year's* ticket. I am a vain person, and I was proud of that handsome treatment, for admissions were at a premium.

There is a very pleasant American named Wood [1] nibbling at my option. Of course he does not know the length of the option nor the price, and he does not expect to get hold of those details at present; all he wants now is a promise that if my New York friends decline to buy my option, the American carpet man whom he represents shall have the next chance to make me a bid. I am to think about it till day after to-morrow and then let him know. I suppose I shall then tell him that I don't think such a promise worth while, for the reason that if my New Yorkers, after close scrutiny, find the option ⟨very⟩ valuable, they will take it; ⟨if they don't,⟩ otherwise they won't; and if *they* don't want it *his* man won't want it.

He seems a good fellow, and nice, but he is either not extraordinarily smart or is concealing his brains from me. He arrived a week ago—just the day that I got my option arranged, but three days before it was signed and sealed; and as he had evidently come with orders to secure an option for his principal, he gave me 3 days of mute discomfort—during which I chewed my bowels. He went straight to Mr. Kleinberg as soon as he arrived; but K would give him no information; said he was too late; said America was in my hands for the present, and I was the only person with authority to furnish information—and he must not mention my name to anybody, for I did not want it to get into the papers until my undertaking should *succeed*—if it failed, then not at all.

So he came at once to me. Was there a machine which he could see? I said I didn't know. What—hadn't *I* seen it? No, I hadn't. Was I actually taking an option on a thing which I had never seen? Yes, that was what I was doing. Would I mind explaining why I was acting in this way? Yes; because *my* evidence wouldn't be worth anything; my men were business men; they would value none but evidence furnished by experts—experts of their own selection. He thought it strange. Surely I must tell my men *something* to proceed upon; would I mind saying what it was? I said I was quite willing—I was merely proceeding upon *circumstantial* evidence.

Why that?

Because circumstantial evidence is among the most valuable of all testimonies. I would give him the details:

1. The machine professes to make a notable reduction in the expenses of a business which employs $200,000,000 of capital in America; hence it is worth inquiring into for that mere reason.

2. When so important an official as the Director of the Weaving School at Aachen testifies over his official signature that after *careful study and practical test* of the invention he finds that its claims are justified, *that* is evidence No. 2 that the thing is worth looking into.

Evidence No. 3. The English patent has been sold. This gives the invention a *distinct* value.

Ev. No. 4. The German patent has been sold. This evidence increases the value 5-fold. It may be a fool that buys the first patent, but the second sale diminishes the fool-likelihoods.

Ev. No. 5. It is a German *banking* house that is exploiting the invention in Germany. Bankers are not generally fools.

Your man has sent you here to get an American option. In a sort of a way, that is circumstantial evidence itself.

A detail worth noting. In the present case it is not ⟨an idiot⟩ ⟨a hum⟩ a *humorist* that is backing the inventor, it is a *banker*. In the present case it is not the inventor that owns the backer—the backer owns the inventor.

This morning I said to Mr. Wood: A week ago you seemed to be kind of indifferent: no time to fool away; if there's anything to show, *show* it—got to leave here in 24 hours. *But you are here yet.* This is Wednesday. You have telegraphed your man that the invention will be seeable Friday or Saturday—shall you stay? ⟨They an⟩ He answers stay—although *your business in the South is very urgent.* You are going to stay, even till Sunday, if necessary. And without knowing the terms of my option, you are asking me to name the *cash* profit at which I will sell, so you can cable it to your man, who wants it *all*, instead of letting me have part cash and part in stock. Don't you notice that you are furnishing me some circumstantial evidence yourself? And don't you begin to believe that as between sworn testimony and circumstantial evidence the advantage is quite likely to be with the latter?

I hadn't the least curiosity to see the invention myself, but under your influence I have acquired some. I will make an appointment for you for Friday, and I will go *with* you.

(Parting flattery from Wood: "You don't seem to be as much of a fool as you look.")

Thine

SLC

---

¹ Clemens recorded (Notebook 32, TS p. 14):
To-day (18th) Mr. William M. Wood, representing American carpet interests, arrived. He is a very charming man, but he is exactly one day too late—which seems to show that I am a more charming man than he is. We talked a couple of hours very pleasantly. He wanted me to furnish him a price at which I would sell my Option. I declined, and got away from the subject. I was afraid he would offer me half a million dollars for it. I should have ⟨felt⟩ been obliged to take it. But I was born with the speculative instinct and I did not want that temptation put in my way.

200. CLEMENS TO ROGERS

Vienna

24 March 1898

Dear Mr. Rogers:

(I feel like Col. Sellers.)

Mr. Kleinberg came according to appointment, at 8.30 last night, and brought his English-speaking Secretary. I asked questions about the auxiliary invention (which I call "No. 2") and got as good an idea of it as I could. It is a *machine*. It automatically punches the holes in the Jacquard cards, and does it with mathematical accuracy. It will do for $1 what now costs $3. So it has value, but "No. 1" is the great thing—(the designing-invention). It saves $9 out of $10, and the Jacquard looms *must* have it.

Then I arrived at my *new* project, and said in substance, this:

You are on the point of selling the No. 1 patents to Belgium, Italy, etc. I suggest that you stop those negociations and ⟨write⟩ put those people off two or three months. They are anxious now, they will not be *less* anxious then—just the reverse; people always want a thing which is denied them.

So far as I know, no great world-patent has ever yet been placed in the grip of a single corporation. This is a good time to begin.

We have to do a good deal of guesswork here, because we cannot get hold of just the statistics we want. Still, we have *some* good statistics—and I will use those for a text.

You say that of the 1500 Austrian textile factories, 800 use the Jacquard. Then we will guess that of the 4,000 American factories, 2,000 use the Jacquard and must have our "No. 1."

You say that a middle-sized Austrian factory employs from 20 to 30 designers and pay[s] them from 800 to 3,000-odd florins a year —(a florin is 2 francs.) Let us call the average wage 1500 florins ($600.)

Let us apply these figures (the low wages, too) to the 2,000 American factories—with this difference, to guard against over-guessing: that instead of allowing for 20 to 30 designers to a middle-sized factory, we allow only an average of 10 to each of the 2,000 factories—a total of 20,000 designers. Wages at $600, a total of $12,000,000. Let us consider that No. 1 will reduce this expense to $2,000,000 a year. The saving is $5,000,000 per each of the $200,000,000 of capital employed in the Jacquard business over there.

Let us consider that in the countries covered by this patent, an aggregate of $1,500,000,000 of capital is employed in factories requiring No 1.

The saving (as above) is $75,000,000 a year. The Company holding in its grip all these patents would collar $50,000,000 of that, as its share. Possibly more.

Competition would be at an end in the Jacquard business, on this planet. Price-cutting would end. Fluctuations in values would cease. The business would be the safest and surest in the world; commercial panics could not seriously affect it; its stock would be as choice an investment as Government bonds. When the patents died the Company would be so powerful that it could still keep the whole business in its hands and strangle competition. Would you like to grant me the privilege of placing the whole Jacquard business of the world in the grip of a single Company? And don't you think that the business would *grow*—grow like a weed?

"Ach, America—it is the country of the big! Let me get my breath—then we will talk."

So then we talked—talked till pretty late. Would Germany and England join the combination? I said the Company would know how to persuade them.

Then I asked for a *Supplementary* Option, to cover the world, and we parted.

You and Mrs. Rogers need not hurry. If you reach here by the 1st of May it will do. The country will be lovely, then.

I am taking all precautions to keep my name out of print in connection with this matter. And ⟨I⟩ we will now keep the invention itself out of print as well as we can. Descriptions of it have been granted to the "Dry Goods Economist" (New York) and to a syndicate of American papers. I have asked Mr. Kleinberg to suppress these, and he feels pretty sure he can do it.[1]

With love

SLC

[1] While business engaged him, Clemens gave only perfunctory attention to other matters. On 25 March 1898 he wrote laconically to Bliss: "Oh, as to the books that are to go into the Uniform Edition? *Begin* with Innocents Abroad, and put in all the books that have been published by you and by Webster and by Harper" (TS in MTP).

201. CLEMENS TO ROGERS

Vienna
12 April 1898

Dear Mr. Rogers:

A week or two ago I received the enclosed letter from Barrow; it is in reply to my letter (the one which you think may not have reached him.)

This first page of Barrow's letter is exasperating. I find I cannot answer it and keep my temper.[1] He ignores Benjamin's interview with him (middle paragraph.)

In the bottom paragraph he seems to think *you* are going to turn out and hunt him up, or inaugurate a correspondence with him. He is probably in error.

In my letter to him I told him to go to you. On his second page, now, he wants to deal directly with me, or go to you armed with an ultimatum.

Is he an ass? Is he an idiot? Is he a child? *What* is he? He does not seem to be aware that it is *he* that is walking the floor—thinks it is us.

How would it do to let him go on walking? Till he gets tired, and goes to you of his own accord. I have lost interest in him and his claims.

I have tried to write a letter to him but I can't seem to stomach it. The best I could do was to grind out the enclosed one. If you approve it will you send it to him? Or—if preferable—return it to me and I will send it to him. The idea of it is to let him know that I have dropped back to a cold business basis with him and am not having any more sentimental bellyaches on his account.

I am at work on translations (plays) these days, and on magazine articles. *Was.* There is a lull at present, for Charley and Jervis Langdon arrived yesterday, and while their visit lasts I shall take holiday.

Also I am waiting for Mr. Kleinberg to hunt up some *exact* statistics concerning the design-industry. I have fairly-healthy statistics for Germany. They take the value of the invention down several pegs. They make it well worth what the patent sold for in Germany, and worth a fourth of what he asks for it in America. This upon the argument that the invention ought to pay back its purchase-price in a single year; though perhaps he would hold that it ought to be allowed 3 years to do it in.

You have not cabled me, and so I think you are taking testimony and will presently know whether America and the world are a large field for the invention or a small one. Mr. Wood writes from

Paris and would like to know what would be a fair price for the French patents in case Mr. Kleinberg will let him have an option. I can't seem to make him understand that if he can find out what France pays her designers annually, he will then know, himself.

No doubt you knew, *yesterday,* whether it is war with Spain or not.[2] In this slow country we shan't know till tonight.

Sincerely ever

SLC

[1] When Clemens learned that Barrow demanded interest on his debt, he wrote him two letters on 12 April 1898, the first of which, he noted, was "(Disapproved by Mrs. C. and not sent)":

To Mr. Barrows:

In answer to your cablegram I am able to say that I did get your letter.

I remember writing you some months ago in substance this: that *my wife and I* had earned and placed in Mr. Rogers's hands the amount of money necessary to pay in full yourself and other (claims against) creditors of Webster & Co. (accredited and allowed by the assignee.) It presently turned out that you wanted greater favor extended to you than to any other creditor—for some reason not divinable by me, (for) unless you imagined that an (offensive) uncourteous attitude from the beginning had entitled you to peculiar consideration.

Meantime you have said (to the gentleman who reported it to me), that it is not my wife and I who are paying my debts, but that Mr. Rogers is paying them out of his own pocket.

Since it is you that have said it, it must be true.

Your word is better than mine; you have better means of knowing my private affairs than I have; and so I withdraw my assertion that my wife and I (are) were paying the debts. You will now go to the *real* debt-payer. I declined to pay you interest on your claim; I declined to favor you above the other creditors. Perhaps he will do better by you. In any case you and your claim are henceforth matters of indifference to me.

The second was more moderate, but was also noted as "Not sent."

Dear Sir:

Your letter conveys to me the impression that you expect interest as well as principal. I have therefore withdrawn all suggestions previously made to Mr. Rogers, and the matter has now reverted to the condition in which it was in the beginning, before any arrangement was made with the creditors. He possessed full powers at that time; he possesses them yet. When you call upon him he will talk with you; and quite uninfluenced by me.

[2] The Spanish-American War began on 24 April 1898.

202. Clemens to Rogers

Vienna
21 April 1898

Dear Mr. Rogers:

You have furnished me facts which are intelligible—and worth a good deal more than foggy guesses gotten out of a census-report 18 years old.

I think that your investigations [1] are likely to establish one very important thing: to-wit, that the designer has no existence in America, and that the introduction of a new pattern there is not common, but unusual. I find that many of the Austrian factories use the same old designs, year in and year out.

Germany pays no such figure for designing as was supposed. She pays about $750,000 a year. The invention makes a stir there and is much discussed and praised. The patent sold for $200,000 there, and is worth two or three times that. It is probably well worth its English price, too—$250,000. It is owned there by a syndicate of manufacturers. When I hear from you next I shall know its American value—if it have one. Meantime—as the men here concede—it is best left alone in these war times.

Charley Langdon has been here—he left yesterday. He did not feel any interest in the design-business; so I said nothing to him about my later project. I couldn't have said anything definite anyhow, as I was thoroughly ignorant concerning it myself. But Mr. Kleinberg and his partner told me about it last night. It was all in the air before, but I have something of an idea of it now. It is another patent—the invention of a Dutchman. It has been patented everywhere, and the patents are in the hands of Mr. Kleinberg and his partner. They built a small mill over the border in Hungary a year ago when the patents were a year old, and have now proved the value of the invention, they think. It makes blankets and other cloth out of peat—peat-fibre mixed with cotton—or with wool if you want better goods. Nearly half cotton or wool—40 to 50 per cent.,—the rest peat. They claim to make stuff enough for a suit of clothes for 36 cents—soft, good, and durable. Peat is plenty in most countries, and is a sure crop and not subject to defeat by capricious weather. In the case of this invention they say they can furnish exact and exhaustive statistics. They say they can make certain low-grade stuffs at a cost of a cent or two a yard.

I am afraid you will not care for this. Would you? I want a holiday, and am going to England with a project to market this thing there—shall start ten or twelve days hence, with cloth samples and statistics of cost, etc. By that time maybe the war will be out of the way and you will take a holiday and come to London and examine it and put it on its feet. In that case you will cable me care of "Bookstore, London," won't you? (It is Chatto's cable address.)

I know you are doubtful about patents, and it is natural. Still the whole vast modern civilization is built up, course by course, upon patents, and without that protection none of the innumerable devices of the inventors could have secured capital for their development.

I wish Doubleday were over here.[2]

Doubleday writes that you advise against the publication of that note about the *de luxe*. All right—your judgment is right, I think. I will leave you to beat Bliss. I think you can.

I am prepared to pay $1,000 more to the Mt. Morris bank on condition that they satisfy ⟨me ⟨and you⟩⟩ you that the account is correct. How does the proposition strike you?

Charles Frohman (Savoy Hotel, London) wants to see my play. I have written him that he'd better apply to you, as you have the only copy that anybody can read. I told him you wrote that you were going to submit it to the Frohmans.

But *I* don't care what Barrow thinks as to who pays my debts for me—as long as it makes him unhappy.

I will write him if you require it, but otherwise I'll let him sweat and fume and cuss.

(If I write him, what's the good? Mrs. Clemens won't allow me to send it.)

Love to you!

SLC

---

[1] Rogers had investigated possibilities in the United States for the textile-designing machine, and sent Clemens a report by William Whitman of the Arlington Mills in Boston (Whitman to James Phillips, Jr., 5 April 1898, Salm):

It would require quite an investigation to give an accurate report to you of the value of the invention described in the pamphlet left with me this morning, entitled "Photography in Weaving," and I do not understand that you wish me to give much time to the consideration of the subject. I do not feel that it would be of any value to us in our mills, and the number of Jacquard looms in use in America is so limited that I am of the opinion that there is no field for the exploration of a company to develop the invention here. It would appear from the reading of the pamphlet as if it would be more useful in carpet and upholstery work than in any other. A cursory examination of the pamphlet leads me to place no very high value upon the invention, from a practical standpoint.

At the top of Whitman's letter the Arlington Mills was identified as "4000 people employed Worsted and woollen dress goods."

[2] Clemens wrote page 4 of this letter on an inverted piece of Hotel Metropole stationery. He found himself interrupted by the letterhead, and began again on manuscript page 5.

203. CLEMENS TO ROGERS

Vienna
29 April 1898

Dear Mr. Rogers:

We are securing a nice house, satisfactorily furnished, at a little health-resort an hour from Vienna—beautiful wooded hills all about. The family will go there the first [of] June, and if they like it will remain till October. Mrs. Clemens and Jean will take the baths. For company there will be a number of old Vienna friends. If a Revolution should happen here we shall pull out and go to Cuba. Or to Spain, or some other health-resort.

But it must happen before the first week of June or I shall probably be in England on this peat-wool scheme. By that time I

⟨shall⟩ expect to have samples of the cloth, and of the peat-wool ⟨as prepared for the weaver⟩ and also be equipped with all necessary statistics.

The idea is, to get up a company in England to *manufacture* the peat-wool ⟨and sell it to the weavers, *not* weave it.⟩ Mr. Kleinberg estimates that by the time the peat-wool has been delivered to the weaver it will have cost a cent and a half a pound. It must be a mistake. It surely cannot cost any more than half a cent—if worked on a fairly large scale. However, statistics will be worth more than guesses; and I will wait for those. I mean to go to Mr. Kleinberg's little mill ⟨on my way to England⟩ where the peat-wool is made, and see the process and look at the machinery. I find it is at Düsseldorf, in Germany.

I am still translating. ("Im Fegefeuer"—In Purgatory.) Translating is dull and stupid work, and I'll do no more of it. For the present, anyway.

I am expecting that your investigations of the design-industry will prove that it has no importance in America. That is already foreshadowed. Your verdict will be valuable, and not doubtful and I wish you were here to pass one upon this peat-wool—and, in case it promises well, squeeze the water out of it and conduct the negociations. You found the Paige-industry with $2,000,000 of property on hand, and reduced it to $78,000 in one sitting.

[The remainder of this letter is missing.]

204. Clemens to Rogers

Vienna
13 May 1898

Dear Mr. Rogers:

They find it slow and difficult work to get the necessary statistics from here and there in Europe to prove the value of the design-invention and *how much* value it possesses in each country. They apply to consuls for the information. It will take a very long time, I think—judging by the progress already made; and will be loose and unsatisfactory anyway. It defers my trip to London—some years, perhaps. I can't go unprepared.

The peat-wool seems good, but in its case also the statistics are not worked down fine enough. Still, they are worked down fine enough to prove that it cannot be made at a less cost than 2 cents a pound. The chemicals and the treatment are expensive.

I have seen the cloth—12 or 15 varieties and qualities of it, and it looks ⟨like⟩ and feels like any goods in a tailor's shop. In some cases it was mixed with cotton, in others with wool. Per centage of peat, from 30 up to 90. But all of it looked and felt like woolen goods.

Unbleached, the peat-wool is brown; (sample enclosed) bleached, it is white. It dyes in all colors.

Bliss's letter about the de luxe and the Uniform (sent to me by Miss Harrison) reads fine.[1] Is it sound?—or a fairy tale?

Shall I come over and help argue the case with the Harpers? ⟨Or will they⟩ It is most likely that you can get along better without me than with me—still, if by chance I can be of use—what do you think?

Bliss's project looks very grand, and I am waiting with large curiosity to hear what you think of it.

A week hence we move to the country for the summer. We have taken a furnished villa at the end of a water-cure village, and Mrs. Clemens and Jean will try the treatment. It is ½ to ¾ of an hour from Vienna by train. The villa is most pleasantly situated, with a dense pine wood bordering immediately on its back-garden, and with wooded hills all about. And so our address is now—

Kaltenleutgeben
(Near) *Vienna*
Villa "Paulhof."   Health and long life!

                                                     SLC

---

[1] In writing Rogers on 20 April 1898, Bliss had been detailed and optimistic: 28,500 copies of *Following the Equator* had been "shipped"; 10,000 more were being printed; and, he continued:

We are just now discussing with Harper & Brothers the advisability of changing the contract between us, allowing new plates to be made for the Uniform set of "Mark Twain" books of those volumes which the Harpers control. We hope in due time to have this matter satisfactorily adjusted and with that done, it seems to us that the prospects for the Uniform set will be very bright indeed, far exceeding the anticipations of anyone. We have spent much time and effort in working up an interest in the set and we now begin to get a glimmer of what is coming in the future; I would not undertake to estimate the amount of business that is likely to be done. As an instance, however, of what is in hand I will say that we have now a memoranda contract from one agency alone to take of the "Mark Twain" works, as follows:

"Author's Signed Edition" from 300 to 500 sets.

DeLuxe Edition, not less than	1000 "
Popular Edition " " "	8500 "
Total not less than	10000 sets of various editions.

On a copy of this letter Clemens later penciled marginal notations estimating that the author's signed edition of "10,000 vols at $10. per vol." would bring in $100,000; the de luxe edition of "20,000 vols at $4. per vol." would net $80,000; and the popular edition, with "170,000 vols at $2.50 per vol." would produce $425,000, for a total amount of "about $600,000." Bliss continued:

This means of itself 200,000 volumes, as we expect, each set will make 20 volumes. Now there are quite a number of different agencies to be supplied and while this instance, perhaps, is likely to be the largest, yet, if we assume for all the others the very moderate figures of doubling the above amount, but which we think is small, we should have the pleasant result of 400,000 volumes.

The plan is to start in with the highest priced edition first, in order to market it before following with the lower priced ones, and in that way work off as many as possible of the expensive editions. The probability is that the "Author's Signed Edition" will sell for about $200. a set, the "DeLuxe" about $80.00 a set, and the Popular Edition about $50.00 a set. It looks to us as if we are going to do an overwhelming business with the set, and I want the hearty co-operation of everyone interested in it to help it along, and I wish you or Mr. Clemens would write a line to Harper signifying your approbation of the change we want made in the contract with them.

When I was over in London Mr. Clemens had an idea that he would like to publish the fine edition himself, and try to sell it himself, and thus get all the money there is in it for himself. Of course I could not say anything definite at that time for I did not know just how the conditions would be. Now, however, it is quite plain to be seen that it would be a very grave mistake for him to undertake to do anything of the sort. In the first place I do not believe that he would succeed in selling very many sets from personal efforts. He might easily place a few, but I imagine that he would find it very distasteful when he had to settle down to asking people to buy the books. He would not like to do it.

Second: It has been a long and stupendous fight to bring the public mind to the fact that this Company was to publish the Uniform set. The Harpers so advertised their books that it was almost impossible to eradicate the idea that their books were not the complete works. We think, now, however, that we have established our point. Now, if Mr. Clemens should undertake to set up a different publication there would be a greater confusion in the minds of the people than has ever existed, and we think the injury to the whole cause would be far greater than any advantages which he might secure.

Third: Our agencies are all equipped for selling, and we have through them

almost every *good* DeLuxe edition canvasser in the U. S. tied up and engaged
to sell the fine editions; they will not listen to any proposition which does not
give them a chance to sell all the different editions. We have talked over the
matter with them, and almost without exception, they will throw the whole
thing over and have nothing to do with the enterprise unless they can have all
the benefits; the contract referred to above is conditional on having *all the*
editions. To use a homely phrase, they do not want their milk skimmed, they
want whatever cream naturally belongs to it.

For these reasons neither Mr. Clemens or ourselves can afford to entertain
the idea of his attempting to market the fine edition himself. Since my visit to
London Mr. Clemens has never referred to the subject nor has anything passed
between us concerning it, and we have gone ahead and made our arrangements
to manufacture and market all the various editions, as has been frequently
announced in the papers during the past year, and expecting Mr. Clemens to
sign the "Author's Edition," as he wrote us last May that he would do.

205. CLEMENS TO ROGERS

Kaltenleutgeben
31 May 1898

Dear Mr. Rogers:

I am very glad indeed to hear that that standing peril to Mrs.
Broughton's health and life no longer exists, and that her thorough
recovery is assured. It is a standing peril to *every*body's life, from
the cradle onward. The human being is a stupidly-constructed
machine. He may have been a sufficiently creditable invention in
the early and ignorant times, but to-day there is not a country in
Christendom that would grant a patent on him.

No, I am not in London. I made my arrangements to go there
and be the guest of a rich South African, but the testimony collected by you and by Mr. Wood [1] troubled me, and I thought it best
not to hurry—I mean, best to cool down and *stop* hurrying. Those
testimonies astonished me. I asked Mr. Kleinberg how he explained
it. He said all the experts here talked in the same way until they
made a practical examination of the thing—then they were convinced. I think I will wait till a practical examination is get-atable
in Vienna. Col. Frank W. Cheney's South Manchester (Conn.)
Silk ⟨Mill⟩ Factory has an office in New York. Do you know those

people? I am afraid to write to Cheney although he is an old friend of mine—I don't want to get into print in this connection.

I have mulled a couple of hours over Barrow this morning; but I *can't* write him. So far as I know he is the only similarly-situated creditor in all history since Shylock's time who has demanded blood in addition to flesh. I cannot write him a polite letter, and neither you nor Mrs. Clemens would permit the other kind.

And besides, he has now reached the acute walking stage. He *cabled* me three days ago to know if I had received his letter. I did not reply. If I let him alone he will give in and call upon you presently. I think he will call within the next 30 days. I think it would not be judicious at present for me to interrupt his walk.

Hello, we are waiting at both ends of the line!—for I was waiting for ⟨you⟩ you to say what *you* thought of Bliss's Uniform and De Luxe scheme. It looked so stunning and splendid on paper that I thought it more than likely you would write me to come over and help him argue with Harper—he seemed to think I might have a little influence. While there is a prospect that I may be needed ⟨over⟩ in America on this matter I shall not tie myself up with London speculations. But if you think well of Bliss's scheme, and it can go into effect without my presence, don't wait for me, but authorize him to go ahead with it.

This is not a hasty notion of mine. Whenever a Uniform and a De Luxe can be marketed, *that's* the time to do it; a delay of a year can be fatal, for a literary reputation is a most frail thing—any trifling accident can kill it; and its market along with it. We are settled, and have a cook. I hope we shall stay in this house 5 or 6 months.

With love to you

SLC

---

[1] Clemens must have meant Mr. Whitman (see letter 202, note 1).

206. CLEMENS TO ROGERS

Kaltenleutgeben
10 June 1898

Dear Mr. Rogers:

I will enclose with this a full authority from Mrs. Clemens to act for her with Bliss in regard to the books.[1]

I would like Bliss to engage to furnish and ship to Chatto a de luxe edition at about cost.

As I have to pay, not Chatto (he is merely my agent) I want Bliss to take his order from *Chatto,* as only Chatto and ⟨I⟩ not I, will know how many sets he will want and *when.* I don't want Chatto to order any more than he has a sure market for. (He is merely under contract to be my agent and take a 10 p.c. royalty for his services.)

I have lost Bliss's letter, but I remember that his scheme was so gorgeous that it took my interest out of peat wool. I wonder what has wakened him up! In any case now is the time to work the market—for by and by there won't be any market. I want him to pull his Klondyke in and materialize it, for I want to be able to come and die at home. Funerals are too expensive here for my means.

I'm not cabling you. No, I don't wish to interrupt the trade.

You are all in the big house at Fairhaven now, and I wish I could be there a spell. Not to play billiards, but to look on; you are out of my reach on that game.

By to-day's news I judge that if Harry doesn't clear for Cuba soon with his yacht he will be too late. Then he will have to wait till the question of what to do with the Phillipines sets the world on fire.

Mrs. Clemens is grateful for what you are doing for us, and so indeed am I, as you know; and she is sorry we burden you with so much work, but I think it keeps you healthy; in fact I know it. You don't have time to run around now and get yourself out of order through idleness.

It just occurs to me: this place is a cold-water-cure, and has an immense reputation. Come over, bring Mrs. Rogers, and try it. You can't do a better thing. It will set you up, sound as a drum, for ten years.

More health and long life!

SLC

[1] The enclosure, dated 10 June 1898, read:
H.H. Rogers Esq.
Dear Sir:
   I hereby formally vest in you full authority to arrange on my account and in accordance with your best judgement terms and conditions with the American Publishing Co. for the proposed issue of my husbands work in collected forms and I also hereby invest in you full authority to sign the resulting contracts for me and in my behalf. I hereby confirm in advance your acts in these matters.
Sincerely yours
Olivia L. Clemens

207. CLEMENS TO ROGERS

Kaltenleutgeben
10 July 1898

Dear Mr. Rogers:

   At a first glance it seemed easy to run over to America—but upon second thought it turns out otherwise. This furnished house is on our hands and paid for in advance till ⟨October⟩ November. The family will not allow me to leave them. We cannot divide the family again after our disastrous experience.[1] If we all go it would end Clara's music in the middle and the past twelvemonth would be wasted. But this last is the thing we shall do if you decide that my presence is necessary. Then we shall come back to Europe no more. We'll stand ready to come when you say the word.

   I think the Harpers ought to yield that point. They owe me a grace for retiring from the understanding which we arranged, since their retiring was due to the mistake of their own lawyer, who was afraid that the renewals of the Innocents and the rest of the Bliss books would belong to Bliss and couldn't be turned over to Harper; whereas there was no word about renewals in my contracts with Bliss. Bliss never dreamed of making a claim for the renewals; he never made one and had no thought of it. But for their lawyer's blunder my book affairs would be in smooth shape, now, and eventually all of my books would be where I wanted to put them— in the hands of the Harpers. Of course I don't want them to suffer damage in order to do me this favor—but will they? Is it a serious matter do you think? If you will have a talk with Harry Harper he will grant me that grace, I believe.[2] And if he doesn't do it he will make clear to your business head why it is that he cannot.

I am not happy about this water-cure. I expected it to do great things for Mrs. Clemens, but I think she is not as strong as she was when she began. It may be that the benefit comes *after* the course. I hope so.

                                                        With love

                                                        SLC

Later.

The madam says that now that we have endured this Austrian exile a year for Clara's sake, she must complete the job, not leave it half finished; and thinks I'd better let the book wait till we go home next spring if the Harpers won't yield meantime. Well, I robbed the family to feed my speculations, and so I am willing to accommodate myself to their preferences. The loss of the Bourgogne[3] has not helped to persuade them to let me go.

---

[1] Clemens attributed Susy's death to neglect as a result of being separated from the family.

[2] Rogers made an appointment to see Harper on 29 July 1898 (Harper & Brothers to KIH, 27 July 1898, Salm). Meanwhile Clemens wrote Bliss on 20 July:

Yes, it *was* best to talk direct with the Harpers; also, if you needed me to help I was there to do it, from the very beginning, *in the person of Mr. Rogers.* . . . he is always there representing me and armed with full authority to transact business for me and for Mrs. Clemens. He is still ready to do anything wise and needful—so I do not need to cable. There is nothing I could do by cabling which he can't do himself if he approves (TS in MTP).

³ 560 persons were killed when the French passenger steamship *La Bourgogne* sank in a collision on 4 July 1898.

208. CLEMENS TO ROGERS

Kaltenleutgeben
26 July 1898

Dear Mr. Rogers:

A couple of months ago I translated a farce-comedy ("In Purgatory") which was having a fine run in Vienna and still is, and as Charles Frohman wanted a look at it I sent it to him in London. But he says it's no good in England—(and that includes America, no doubt.) He says it's all jabber and no play. ⟨Still⟩ Curious, too, for it tears these Austrians to pieces with laughter. When I read it, now, it seems entirely silly; but when I see it on the stage it is exceedingly funny. I mean to send it to you; and you can return me word that it is not marketable in America—then I'll drop it out of my mind and off my conscience.

At odd intervals I am translating another play; by and by I'll finish it, and then I'll translate no more.

I have written 3 mag. articles:

1. "About Play-Acting." (Forum).
2. "The Great Republic's Peanut Stand."
3. "Concerning the Jews." [1]

I intend No. 1 for the Forum, for it is exceedingly serious.

I think I will send 2 and 3 to Harper and ask him to ⟨take⟩ select one and send the other to you. I should like you to send it to the "Century."

I sent an article to the Century lately ("From the London Times of 1904"). They paid me $140 per magazine page for it. [2] I think I charged them too much, but I can tell better when I see the article in print. I prefer the Century to other mag.s in one way—they *advertise* an article so liberally.

I never expect the Harpers to pay more than $100 per mag. page, even for the shortest article—whereas they ought to pay 50 per cent more per page for a 4-page than for a 10-page article.

They haven't advertised my books in the magazine for about a year, now. If the Bliss-Harper deal were completed—however, that's another story.

"The G Rs Peanut Stand" is an article on copyright. I wrote it because the matter is being stirred in a Parliament-Committee. There is no hurry about it. It will keep.

The Jew article is my gem of the ocean. I have taken a world of pleasure in writing it and doctoring it and polishing it and fussing at it. Neither Jew nor Christian will approve of it, but people who are neither Jews *nor* Christians will, for they are in a condition to know truth when they see it. I really believe that I am the only man in the world who is equipped to write upon the subject without prejudice. For I *am* without prejudice. It is my hope that both the Christians *and* the Jews will be damned; and to that end I am working all my influence. Help me pray. You and Rice.

If I have any leaning it is toward the Jew, not the Christian. ⟨There is one thing I'd like to say, but I dasn't: Christianity has deluged the world with blood and tears—Judaism has caused neither for religion's sake.⟩ I've had hard luck with *them*.

I *must* remember to ask Bliss to send Mrs. Clemens's July ½ year money to you. Whitmore has $2,500 in Hartford—a great deal too much. It tempts him to spend. Aloha—aloha-nui! I want W. to send $1500 to you—I'll write him.[3]

                                                SLC

[1] "About Play-Acting" appeared in the *Forum*, October 1898. "The Great Republic's Peanut Stand" was not sent to Rogers (see letter 209). It is "a dialogue between Statesman and ⟨Ordinary Ass⟩ Wisdom Seeker"; the MS (Box 4, MTP) is marked in Clemens's hand, "Never published SLC." "Concerning the Jews" appeared in *Harper's Magazine*, September 1899; Clemens received $500 for it (Henry Mills Alden to KIH, 5 October 1898, Salm).

[2] It appeared in the November 1898 issue.

[3] He had already written him, on 20 July 1898: "please subtract $1500 from the $2500 in your hands and send it to Mr. Rogers in New York" (Mark Twain Memorial, Hartford).

209. CLEMENS TO ROGERS

Kaltenleutgeben
3 August 1898

Dear Mr. Rogers:

I must stop work a minute and congratulate you upon to-day's telegraphic peace-prospects.[1] I imagine you are feeling comfortable now.

Here the matter would be immensely discussed and written about—*would* have been, a week ago—but now it is cut down to a dozen lines, for now the whole reading-matter space in the papers is crowded with Bismarck's life and death.[2] It has been so for several days and will continue to be so for many days to come.

To-day is a warm day—only about the fifth one this summer. But in the house it is cool. It is a fortunate summer-country—Europe. Its foliage and grass remain dense and green and fresh all summer —no parched and browned places. And no flies nor bugs or other insects; and no mosquitoes nor gnats. This house is not afflicted with any of these things; yet its garden is full of trees and thick shrubbery—a good place for them.

We shall return to Vienna by the middle of October; and meantime we must be looking out for hotel quarters if we mean to change from the Metropole, for the Jubilee[3] is going to crowd the town when winter begins. They want us at the new hotel—the Krantz—which is a kind of Splendid Waldorf, but I think they knock off only a third of their regular rates, whereas the Metropole knocks off half. At the Metropole we have 2 parlors, a study and 4 bedrooms for $6.20 a day, and the food and other things bring the total up to ⟨$407 a month⟩ $460 a month. At the Krantz the same would be $704—but it's a palace! and the food is much better. If they'll come down $125 lower, I think we'll take them up; if not, we'll have to go back to the Met—to my immense dissatisfaction; not that the rooms aren't good enough and the ⟨rooms⟩ food good

enough, but I *do* like lovely furniture. We wrote yesterday and
declined their first offer; and are waiting with some anxiety for
their second. It's a bran-span new hotel, just opened. Mrs. Clemens
happened in there and found on the lobby wall the finest portrait of
me she has seen. We don't know who made it nor when, but we
recognize that it is a hotel that has taste.

I've been trying to think of something for Miss Harrison to put
in her idle time with when she gets back from her vacation, and I
have struck only one—I will think up some others presently. ⟨I'd
like it if she would collect and tear out and keep my magazine
articles as they appear; I seldom see them. At present I recal
these.⟩ [4]

"In Memoriam, Olivia Susan Clemens"
Harper's Monthly last November.

"Lively Times in Austrian Parliament"
Harper's Monthly last spring.

"From the London Times of 1904"
Century—about to be published.

"The Appetite-Cure"
The Cosmopolitan—about to be pub. [5]

"About Play-Acting"
Forum—mailed to New York to-day.

Not yet mailed:
"The Great Republic's Peanut Stand;"
"Concerning the Jews."
"My Platonic Sweetheart."

I got $2,075 for the first four; am to get $200 for the fifth.

I think I shall keep the article on copyright ("Peanut Stand") for
the present.

I've a notion to send the "Sweetheart" story to you, and then write Edward Bok of the Ladies' Home Journal that if he wants to pay $1000 for it he can write you and get it. I half promised him a $500-article a year ago. If he declines, I'll send you the "Jew" article, and let Harper's take choice between it and the "Sweetheart" [6] (at their own price) and let the Century have the unchosen one (at its own price.) They are thundering good—I don't know which one I like the best.

Yours sincerely

SLC

[1] Terms of peace outlined by the United States to Spain were accepted on 12 August 1898.

[2] Bismarck had died on 30 July 1898.

[3] The jubilee of the coronation of Emperor Francis Joseph of Austria was to be celebrated in Vienna on 2 December 1898.

[4] Written in the margin on either side of the deletion are these words: "CONDEMNED / by the CENSOR."

[5] "At the Appetite-Cure" had been mailed to the *Cosmopolitan* on 30 May 1898 (Notebook 32, TS p. 21); it appeared in the August 1898 issue.

[6] "Concerning the Jews" would be published in *Harper's Magazine,* September 1899; "My Platonic Sweetheart" would not appear in *Harper's Magazine* until December 1912.

210. CLEMENS TO ROGERS

Ischl
19 August 1898

Dear Mr. Rogers:

We are in a state of great thankfulness to you for finishing up the Barrows business for us. It is a relief—more of a relief than I can put into words. I was so cussed tired of the name of Barrow! Now he can go hang himself as soon as he wants to; I have no further use for him.

The news came just as we were packing to start on this pleasure trip; and thus far it was a better pleasure trip all by itself than this one has been. We left a cool and comfortable house, and after a long and hot railway trip we have been sweltering two days in this hot town in a hot hotel which has no lights but candles, and puts *them* out in every hall and corridor all over the house at 11 p.m. It is all so primitive and depressing. We have dropped back into the dark ages. There isn't a bath room in the house.

Moreover, Mrs. Clemens has had a cinder in her eye for two days and a half, now, and it can't be found nor seen—has bedded itself out of sight, and she must submit to a surgical operation. She came away to get a rest from house-keeping; but I am afraid it isn't going to pay her. However, I am not meaning to intimate that this isn't a good pleasure trip; for really it is. It is above average; for a cinder in your eye can improve *any* pleasure trip. They are always mournful orgies, and any little thing helps.

I suppose you are all having luxurious times in Fairhaven now. Try to deserve them. But enjoy them, anyway.

You've got peace at last, and I congratulate you. We have it here, still, but the Austrian political sky remains cloudy, and in some degree threatening: I hope we are going to pull through in a quiet way, and that we can get home alive in the spring.

Oh, hot and dark!

Good-bye, and be good to yourself.

SLC

211. CLEMENS TO ROGERS

Kaltenleutgeben [1]
28 August 1898

Dear Mr. Rogers:

A dozen days ago we went traveling [2] for heat (I suppose.) At any rate that is what we got. We reached home and coolness again last night, and find yours of Aug. 12.

Put "Is He Dead" in the fire. God will bless you. I too. I started in to convince myself that I could write a play or couldn't. [3] I'm convinced. Nothing can disturb that conviction.

Harry Harper is right: Mrs. Clemens would indeed be glad to have his house as her exclusive publishers.

Is Mr. Rives [4] the Harper lawyer; and is it he that is going to examine the 3 contracts and your correspondence with Bliss and determine when the forfeiture-clause works as against Bliss? If so, I'm on the anxious bench! I think it was he that examined my contracts with the Am. Pub. Co. and made the Harpers withdraw from their agreement with me—whereby I tumbled back into Bliss's hands after having almost escaped. He decided that the *renewals* of my copyrights would belong to Bliss and that I couldn't convey them to the Harper's! Colby—even Colby—could have read the contracts better than that. Colby drunk—Colby insane—Colby dead, would have a more competent brain than Rives. ⟨If Rives had consulted just one single clause of the copyright law he would have seen (as Bliss did)⟩ Renewals were not once *mentioned* in my Bliss contracts; and Bliss and his 3 lawyers never had a doubt that I would own the renewals and could do as I pleased with them. Bliss talked no otherwise in London to me.

If you yourself have examined what Rives is going to examine, your judgment is valuable—his isn't worth any fraction of any *kind* of a damn.

I hope you *can* get Bliss into ⟨a corner which will enable you to take⟩ the arrangement you have mapped out. I believe I will enclose Bliss's letter in this, so that you can be posted from all directions. I have this moment answered him—and I took occasion to mention that he got $1000 from McClure's Magazine for some advance-extracts from "Following the Equator," and that I did not find it mentioned in the statement of book-sales for the last half-year, although he had promised some time ago (according to my memory) to deliver up that spoil next pay-day.[5] I told him he could send the money to you. I hope you will receive that money right away. I shall lose my temper, otherwise. He did an impudent thing when he made that publication without my knowledge or consent—and then shoved the money into his own pocket.

We engaged our winter quarters when we passed through Vienna yesterday afternoon, and we shall leave here ⟨one or⟩ two months from now and occupy them. We lived at the Metropole last winter, having a parlor, a music room, a study and 4 bedrooms, for a trifle under 2200 francs a month, which included food, fire, light and attendance ⟨—but not⟩ and baths. The bathroom on that floor was 50 yards distant, and ⟨the⟩ as I was often tired and they didn't allow bicycles in the halls, I didn't take any baths that year. I was never so healthy and warm in my life.

There is a new hotel, now, just finished—the "Krantz"—and they offered to give us all of the above necessaries of life at 3,500 francs a month, and we said we couldn't afford it. They said they must have us, and would knock off 500 francs. We said we ⟨that is, Mrs. Clemens⟩ would talk further when we returned from our excursion for heat in the Salz-Kammergut regions.

Then we sent the Metropole word that we were dickering for other quarters, and would like to know his terms for 7 rooms etc. on a lower floor than we occupied before. The manager came out here and said he would do it for 200 francs a month more than last year. This was putting *room*-rent at half price—(for in Vienna the room-rent is always placarded on the wall of the room where you can't overlook it.)

Yesterday we called at the Krantz to get *their* finality. They dropped another 200 francs (thus making a total reduction from the original 3,500 to 2,800 a month) and said our being in the house would be the best advertisement they could have, and indicated that they were ready to come lower still; but really ⟨th⟩ it was already robbery, and we surrendered and said 2800 would answer.

The Metropole is a *long* way short of being as fine a house as the Murray Hill, but the Krantz is a fine building and is completely and richly furnished like the Waldorf—there is nothing approaching it in France, Germany or Austria. We have a dining room, a parlor, a music-parlor, a study, and 4 bedrooms—and there are bathrooms attached to 3 of the bedrooms. And the whole cost to feed and house the family is but sixty dollars a month higher than the Metropole terms. I used to be a little ashamed when Ambassadors and dukes and such called on us in that rusty and rather shabby Metropole, but they'll mistake us for millionaires next fall and will probably lend us money. Send your friends there—they'll thank you for it.

Love to you

SLC.

P.S. I hope you will have a lovely Californian trip with your questionable gang.[6]

P.S.

If you *can* only "make an arrangement with the Harpers to publish the whole of my books for the trade and with Bliss to publish them by subscription" that will be very jolly.

There is no way for Bliss to get anything out of the books *except* by a Uniform edition sold in sets—his semi-annual statement amply proves that.

———

Copying is pretty slow here, but the copyist promises to have those mag. articles ready for me *very* soon—means several days, I guess.

P.S. *Next Day.*

Yours of the 19th has arrived, enclosing letter of Mr. Harper and opinion of Mr. Rives.

Good, I am glad a settlement is close at hand, though I wish Rives wouldn't always keep on interfering with people's arrangements.

I believe Bliss would gladly name a *date,* this time, for the Uniform edition, as a *condition* upon which the Harpers yield to his desires about new plates: a condition giving him still another year yet,—or more.

Evidently "a reasonable time" (with him) is too indefinite.

I reckon you are off for California now. Good times to you!

SLC

[1] Clemens's impatience with this long place-name is indicated by his slurring all the letters from *K* to *g* so that they are almost illegible.

² The Clemenses had been vacationing in Hallstatt, as well as Ischl.

³ Clemens had begun to write this comedy in mid-January 1898 (Notebook 32b, TS p. 53); it survives among the unpublished manuscripts in MTP.

⁴ George Lockhart Rives was attorney for Harper & Brothers; he had been examining relationships between that firm and the American Publishing Company, as outlined in the agreement between them of 31 December 1896 (see Appendix B), laying the groundwork for the supplement to that agreement of November 1898 (see Appendix D). Details of negotiations are set forth in G. L. Rives to Harper & Brothers, 12 August 1898 (Salm); Harper & Brothers to Rogers, 16 August 1898 (Salm); Walter Bliss to Harper & Brothers, 23 and 31 August 1898 (Salm); Harper & Brothers to American Publishing Company, 16 September 1898 (copies of all are in MTP).

⁵ Clemens wrote Frank Bliss on 28 August 1898 (Yale): "I have yours of Aug. 16 with Statement for past half-year—for which, thanks. But you said you were going to add the $1000 paid by McClure for the 'previous publication' extracts. You have not done it, but it will be all right if you send it to Mr. Rogers."

⁶ Rogers's trip to California probably was made in connection with his interest in the Union Pacific Railroad; his "questionable gang" might well have included William Rockefeller and Henry M. Flagler, both of whom were also interested in E. H. Harriman's enterprises.

212. Clemens to Rogers

Kaltenleutgeben
14 September 1898

Dear Mr. Rogers—

Are you home again? I guess you'll be there by the time this reaches you, since you are due there the 25th.

Fortunes continue to be offered me, but I haven't collected on any of them yet. One offer yesterday from Ohio—but it is too agricultural; and the other day came the enclosed.

The collection is genuine, of course, and the pictures named are doubtless worth a great sum, though not as much as *he* wants, I reckon. I wasn't going to answer the letter—and shan't, at present —but ⟨then I thought Mr. Rockefeller⟩ will wait, and will keep the page bearing the writer's signature and address. Meantime Mr. Rockefeller might want to add this Museum to his University if it can be had at a bargain after verification of values by experts.¹ Will you ask him?

This man hasn't mentioned a picture that the government would allow to leave Italy—except in the usual way: by the underground railroad; yet he thinks (*seems* to think) he can deliver the goods. Possibly he can; plenty Old Masters have been shoved over the border, but not by the shipload, I reckon.

I sent a little cheap two-hundred dollar article to the "Forum" a while back—"About Play-Actors." [2] I haven't heard of it since, so I suppose it got lost. If you see it mentioned, I should like to know.

We closed the bargain with the new hotel in Vienna—the "Krantz"—and I am glad of that. It will be much better winter quarters than we had before.

The Austrian Empire is hung in black. [3] The lamentings (particularly in Hungary) are deep and universal. I have not seen anything like it since General Grant died. The French mourning for President Carnot was a mild thing compared with it.

The Bliss-Harper documents have not come yet, but I am very glad you succeeded in appeasing that conflict and arranging a bargain. I hope Bliss is in earnest, and I am persuaded that he *is*. He gets nothing out of the old books; so I think he believes he can mend his fortunes with the Uniform.

An artist here has painted a perfectly superb portrait of Clara, and has given it to us. And so I am going to sit to him myself. Not that I expect him to give me the result, for he couldn't afford it; and not that I expect to buy it, for *I* can't afford it; but because I want to see *one* stunning portrait of myself before I get homely. [4]

Gratefully Your

SLC

[1] John D. Rockefeller was continuing his benefactions to the University of Chicago, which he had supported since three years before its formal establishment in 1892.

[2] "About Play-Acting" would appear in the *Forum*, October 1898.

[3] Elizabeth, Empress of Austria and Queen of Hungary, had been assassinated in Geneva on 10 September; Clemens described this episode as "the largest of all large events" in "The Memorable Assassination," *What Is Man?* (New York: Harper & Brothers, 1917), pp. 167–181.

[4] Of his own oil portrait by Ignace Spiridon, Clemens would write Frank Bliss on 17 November 1898 that it was "a long way the best I have ever had, and much better than any photogaph from life can ever be." The portrait would be

used as a frontispiece to Volume XX of the Edition de Luxe (1899) of *The Writings of Mark Twain.*

213. CLEMENS TO ROGERS

Kaltenleutgeben
21 September 1898

Dear Mr. ⟨Bok:⟩ Rogers:

I am finishing an article about the assassination of the Empress. I will forward it presently. Meantime if Bok of the Woman's Home Journal, Phila., has returned the "Platonic Sweetheart" unaccepted, I would very much like Miss Harrison to offer him this—for it will be cheaper, and that is what he likes.[1]

This promises to be a quiet winter in Vienna; there will be no public balls nor court balls nor any other public carryings-on, but only private things; and even the private things will not begin till the season of full mourning is over. I am sorry for the cause, but this is all an advantage to me.

I suppose you have come back restored, refreshed, and in fighting trim. I hope so, anyway, and that you all had a good time.

Love to you.

SLC

P.S.
Finished.

Price, to Bok,—for the first 4,000 words, $140 per 1000; each additional 1000 words, $60. It seems to be about 5,000 words, or 6,000. But I doubt if it goes over 5,500 ($650).

P.S. If by any chance Bok should *keep* the "Platonic," I would like to have this "Assassination" article sent to another magazine—Harper or Century (the one that hasn't at present an article of mine—and I don't know of any except the Jew article).

SLC

¹ On 6 September 1898 Clemens had recorded in his notebook (Notebook 32, TS p. 32):

Am sending to Bok "My Platonic Sweetheart" (about 9,000 words—price $1000). Am writing him if he doesn't (or *does*) want it, *inform Mr. Rogers.*

Am sending "Concerning the Jews" to Mr. Rogers. If Bok keeps the above send *this* one to Harper. But if Bok declines, send *both* to Harper, let him have his choice, then send the remaining one to Century.

On 26 September he noted (TS p. 46):

Wrote Bok he could have Assassination in place of Platonic S if he liked, at $600.

Wrote Miss H. the same and that I was no[w] mailing to her said sketch.

"The Memorable Assassination" apparently never was published in any magazine (see letter 212, note 3).

214. CLEMENS TO ROGERS

Kaltenleutgeben
26 September 1898

Dear Mr. Rogers:

In something short of 3 weeks we shall take up fall and winter quarters at the Hotel Krantz in Vienna. They have given us handsome terms; I don't remember what they are, but Mrs. Clemens does. It is getting pretty cold here, but we can stand it awhile yet; we are used to cold, anyway—we have had plenty of it here the whole summer. It has been a good place for me; I have written a raft of stuff—for publication when I'm dead, mainly.

Spiridon has given us that admirable portrait of Clara. He wanted to paint one of me, and said he would make short work of it and not tucker me out; so I sat, and he made the best portrait that ever was—and did it in *eight hours*. I never saw such a man to handle oils and skirmish with a brush. He is terribly accurate. From charcoal sketch to finish he never rubbed out a stroke; once made, it stayed. If he should offer to give the portrait to me I wouldn't let him, but I should *want* to, all the same. I have never been anxiouser than other people to own a portrait before, but it is different this time; with a little pains this one could be taught to speak—not German, of course, but the other tongues.

The papers are telling about the vast steel trust, and they add that you are in it.[1] I hope you have remembered to insert me into it too on the ground floor. Mrs. Clemens has $10,000 banked in London, and I reckon we can live on that about a year and make steel with the rest. Meantime I reckon Bliss will make us a fortune with the Uniform.

With my prayers and love—

SLC

P.S. Spiridon has been here and has given me that portrait. If I had purchased (which I refrained from doing,) it would have cost me $1,000 and Clara's $2,000.

---

[1] The New York *Times* of 25 August 1898 announced that the merger of the Illinois Steel Company and the Minnesota Iron Company with several smaller concerns "finally has been accomplished." On 10 September 1898 the *Times* reported the official incorporation of the Federal Steel Company with a "capital of $200,000,000, half preferred, half common stock." Rumors of the merger had moved the *Times* to speculate as early as 12 August that "should the consolidation . . . be effected, a formidable rival to the immense Carnegie interests will have entered the lists in the iron and steel field of the world."

215. CLEMENS TO ROGERS

Kaltenleutgeben
1 October 1898

Future address for 7 months:
Hotel *KRANTZ*
Neuer Markt, Vienna.

Dear Mr. ⟨Harper:⟩ Rogers:

(I am a little undecided, but if I am going to make any more mistakes it'll be safer to make them to *you*—so I believe I won't write Mr. Harper just now.)[1]

When yours of 25th August told me terms had been arranged and Bliss started home saying he was happy, I at once did a foolish thing—jumped to the conclusion that nothing I could now say could kick up a new complication; so I wrote Mr. Harper that I was sorry it hadn't turned out so that he could handle all my books in the trade and Bliss handle them by subscription. (You see I was thinking of the fact that each book in Harper's hands is now paying me just three times as much per year as each book in Bliss's hands pays me; ⟨by⟩ but I was quite *overlooking* a much more important fact: that that arrangement would put *two* cheap uniform editions into the field, and the *Harper* set would kill the *Bliss* (cheap) set, because its price would be a deal cheaper.)

I wish you would stay close enough by, so that you could kick ⟨upon⟩ me upon occasions of this kind. [This sentence is circled.]

Well, I expect that that letter of mine arrived in New York just in time to produce the closing sentence of Mr. Harper's letter to Bliss of Sept. 16 (herewith enclosed) [2] and institute a new complication.

If you think the two sets issued by rival firms would be a mistake, I wish you would talk Mr. Harper out of the notion and close up the contract solid, so that I can't interfere again—and I'll swear in advance, NOW, that I won't ever do another stupid thing again as long as I live.

Meantime, I did *another* ill-considered thing. Remembering that the book "How to Tell a Story" was too small, I sent Bliss a list of recent magazine articles with the idea that they should be added to that book to make it large enough. But later I wrote him not to do that, for these articles were becoming numerous enough to constitute a book by themselves.

I have written several since; and there is now *plenty* of matter for a new book. (70,000 or 80,000 words.) It is better to issue it as a new book, get six months' board out of it and *then* add it to the Uniform.

Now then, I want to put this book into *your* hands, you to give it to Bliss or to Harper, whichever you please; if Harper takes it, Harper to let Bliss add it to the Uniform within (say) 6 months or such a matter, after its issue by Harper. But I think Harper ought to pay more than 12½ per cent royalty on it. I didn't know Harper was paying me less than 15, but I find that on one book he is. By my new contract Chatto pays me 24.

To-day I mean to get to work on an article for Harper's about the Shipwreck of the Hornet—he has sent me the magazine I wanted for a text.[3]

Bliss seems so desperately in earnest that I think he fully means to accomplish something with his Uniform and his de luxe.

The Hornet article will be needed to fill out the new book.

I am pretty well along with a new story,[4] but I am not expecting to get *that* into that volume. It won't be long enough for a book by itself, perhaps, yet too long to crowd into that one.

You will be home Oct. 15—the day we set up shop in Vienna again. Receive my blessing!

SLC

[1] Clemens evidently thought he had been indiscreet in having written J. H. Harper (30 August 1898; Indiana):

O dear, dear, I'm in despair! I was hoping for that new arrangement whereby you would handle all my books in the trade and Bliss the uniform sets —and it didn't materialize. I was getting pretty full of the conviction that Bliss would agree to that. He would have considered his letter urging that he ought to have 18 months on his uniform edition as a binding thing, for he is a conscientious man, although his father wasn't. He was square about the renewals of my old books, and claimed no ownership in them. I could have transferred them to you, as originally agreed, without objection from him. Knowing him so well as I did, I ought to have had wit enough to ask him about it when Mr. Rives doubted my ability to carry out my contract.

If it is not too late to get a *date* fixed for the Uniform, I think Mr. Rogers will manage that; I have written Mr. Rogers and suggested it.

[2] The closing sentence of Harper's letter read: "But, frankly, in view of the circumstances and considering Mr. Clemens's wishes, don't you think it due to us that some reciprocal arrangement should be made whereby we could publish a trade edition of his books now on your list—an edition that would be uniform with the volumes we have?" (office copy in Salm).

[3] He had written to Harper on 30 August 1898:

I want to write a magazine article of a reminiscent sort. The first magazine article I ever published appeared in Harper's Monthly 31 years ago under the name of (by typographical error) MacSwain. Can you send it to me? I think it appeared in the first half of 1867. It is the diary of a passenger who was shipwrecked in the "Hornet," a clipper ship which was burned on the Line.

On 19 November 1898 Clemens "Mailed Hornet article to Harper" (Notebook 32, TS p. 51). Clemens later wrote of it to Richard Watson Gilder, 25 February 1899 (Yale):

I have abandoned my Autobiography, and am not going to finish it; but I took a reminiscent chapter out of it and had it type-written, thinking it would make a readable magazine article; and sent it to my friend *H. H. Rogers, 26 Broadway.* If you would like to look at it, send there and get it. It is about the burning of the clipper "Hornet" on the Equator thirty-three years ago. The survivors made 4,000 miles in an open boat on 10 days' provisions, and I was in Honolulu when those scarecrows arrived.
The article eventually was published in the *Century,* November 1899, as "My Début as a Literary Person."
[4] "The Man That Corrupted Hadleyburg."

216. CLEMENS TO ROGERS

Vienna
18 October 1898

Dear Mr. Rogers:

I am undergoing crucifixion (deserved!) on account of my blunder that I made in exposing to the Harpers the fact that I should have been glad if Bliss ⟨had been⟩ could have been crowded into giving the Harpers *all* the books for the trade, leaving Bliss only the sets by subscription. ⟨Apparently the⟩ I only ventured to write that because the contract had already been *settled*—whereas I guess nothing is really settled with the Harpers until they have *signed.*

Reflection has taught me what you had already perceived, no doubt: that if Harper had the trade-use of all the books it would kill Bliss's edition or badly cripple it; and so I wish I had kept my foolish tongue still.

I have written Bliss that talking with Harper and then running back to Hartford before the papers are signed will never accomplish anything. His only chance is to have your help and *stay* in New York till the thing is finished.[1]

Consound it, every time I start a piece of work along comes a complaining letter from Bliss and knocks the brains out of it for a day or two. I began a good thing (I think) yesterday—and straight off comes Bliss's letter this morning.

Blame it, I wish I hadn't sent that "Memorable Assassination," and I hope Bok won't want it; for I don't want it printed at all. Nor the "Platonic Sweetheart" either. I shall have other and better matter, and I don't want to be in print too frequently—it can hurt my market.

Meantime Bok has sent me a copy of his magazine—I had never seen one before. Why, bless my soul, it is a mere literary night-cart. I would rather steal nickels for a living than earn it writing for such a rag as that. It is full of Wanamaker and his Sunday schools and other hypocricies.[2] It ought to be medicated, and restricted [to] the Bleeding Piles Hospital.

I'm longing to see the handwriting of your type-machine again.

With love,

SLC.

P.S. A year ago Bliss allowed McClure's Magazine to insert some stuff from my unpublished book [3] for $1000. Instead of sending the money to me, he *didn't*. I wrote him about it and he put off sending till a later day.—About a month ago I wrote him again—this time I get silence.

I am writing Whitmore to go to him and collect that $1000 and 6 per cent interest; ⟨and⟩ or get Bliss's note for it made out in your name. But it occurs to me that you will probably see Bliss soon, and if *you* go at him he will take water very suddenly. He musn't *argue* the point—a man mustn't argue about a theft; it is adding insult to injury.

Cuss him, his not answering my recent letter with a check has made it necessary for Mrs. Clemens to break into her interest-bearing London deposit, and it makes me mad.

Gott behüte Dich!

SLC

[1] Clemens had written Frank Bliss that same day (18 October 1898):
Come! Haven't you found out, yet, that you mustn't agree on the details for a contract and then go back to Hartford before it is signed? Now do go down there, and get Mr. Rogers's help, and *stay* there until the thing is completed beyond recall. You have had experience enough to know that no other way will ever succeed (TS in MTP).

The contract was not signed until 11 November 1898 (see Appendix D).

[2] Clemens had sued John Wanamaker, the department store owner and benefactor of the YMCA, in August 1886 for allegedly having sold surreptitiously obtained copies of Grant's *Memoirs* in Philadelphia; the motion of Charles L. Webster & Company to restrain Wanamaker's sale of the books was denied.

[3] *Following the Equator.*

217. CLEMENS TO ROGERS

Vienna
2 November 1898

Dear Mr. Rogers—

That is immense news. For 24 hours I have been trying to calm down and cool off and get sane over it, but I don't succeed very well. I would rather have that stock than be free from sin.[1] The news came in the right time to do me a couple of good services. It lifted from me the fatigue of the Bliss-Harper suspense—I am not going to walk the floor any longer about that. I think the unfairnesses proceed from Harper, not Bliss, and I hope Bliss will win; necessarily it is the *canvassers* that want the Bliss-form of book— Bliss wouldn't want to make new plates just for the amusement of it; he is a placid person and doesn't care for excitements; and Bliss's new plates would cost Harper neither expense nor inconvenience.

Another thing. The New York World had just asked for a story for Xmas. I needed a stiffened spine, for I didn't want to write for the World. You have furnished it. I have replied, to-day that my price is $200 per 1000 words.[2] That will put the World's feverish desires on ice—those highly-enterprising concerns have their economies, like other people.

In declining the "Platonic Sweetheart," Alden (Editor Harper's Monthly) did me a kindness. Upon a re-reading of it it seems to me to be neither fish, flesh nor fo⟨u⟩wl. I would have cabled you to withdraw it from the Century, but I didn't, for I was sure I could depend upon Gilder's declining it. If he hasn't done it, please take it away from him and charge him with being drunk and misattending to his duties. This will come with more force and effect from you than it would from me. But if you feel too fastidious about it, let Rice do it; though the more I think of it the more I am satisfied that it will come best from you.

I wanted the Memorable Assassination to remain in your hands, in a state of suppression. I believed you knew me; and would know that my silence meant "Mr. Rogers knows he has performed his whole duty of courtesy in cabling—the absence of an answer won't disturb his sleep;" and besides, the answer was already half way to America in a letter.

My backbone is stiffened in several ways. For instance, I mean to write as much as ever, but only *stories*—and not print very often. And I will trust the Century and the Cosmopolitan to name prices for me, but not Alden. He calls the Jew article "timely" (in the sense of fresh and new *and* of immediate and large interest because of the Dreyfus matter), pays half price for it and finds a precedent for that in the fact that he paid me the same price for "Mental Telegraphy" 8 years ago—an article a shade longer. He forgets that the reason he ⟨paid⟩ gave for paying half price 8 years ago was, that the subject of Mental Telegraph *wasn't* new.

He closes thus: "I was sorry to see the announcement by the Century of a short story of yours. The next time you have a short story I wish you would let us have it."

That was meant to fool me into imagining he wasn't ashamed of himself. It didn't do it. Eight years ago he was ashamed, and he wasn't any luckier in concealing it then than he was this time. You see, he has to pay Harry Harper's estimate and let on that it is his own.

I will be politic, and write him an unantagonising letter; and I'll send him a story, too; but I'll put it at $140 per magazine page and then when he declines I will sell it to the Century or the Cosmopolitan and let them put their own price on it. By instinct I *preferred* to put the Jew in Harper (I don't know why), and I kind of expected to be gouged a *little* in the matter of pay, but derned if I'm going to trust those fellows again!

My stuff for a new volume of sketches now foots up 100,000 words. I can leave out the Empress Assassination and the Platonic and still have matter enough. But whether to give it to Bliss (in case he should *want* it) or to Harper—can you advise?

Well, I *am* glad that I am not sweating any more over the Bliss-Harper deadlock. Will you look at the stock-report and see what the latest rates are for a Tinker's Damn? I don't care *one* for that muddle, and if the rate is low enough I don't care *two*.

LATER. There, b'gosh, I've answered Alden [3]—and softly and sweetly and diplomatically, too; and sent my love to Franklin Square; and told him I've got a story and am ready for a bid (*per magazine page*), subject to his approval of the MS when he comes to examine it.

Many many thousands of thanks to you—and may you live forever! (Partly here, and partly in the other place.) Which place are you going to? And Rice? Let's make up a party, and go together. I can work you in at either place; I've got a pull.

Sincerely Yours

SL. Clemens

[1] Rogers had purchased stock for Clemens in Federal Steel: "201[7] Preferred shares at 69, and 249[3] Common, at 28, for $17,139.87. Glad of that. Represents $50,000 par of stock" (Notebook 32, TS p. 49).

[2] Clemens recorded on 2 November 1898 (Notebook 32, TS p. 48) that he had answered James M. Tuohy of the New York *World*, "offering Hadleyburg, 20,000 words, for $4,000, or Wapping, 'more than 8 and less than 9,000,' at $1,600. His order was for '7 to 10,000 words for 250 guineas.'" Tuohy took neither: "The Man That Corrupted Hadleyburg" appeared in *Harper's Magazine*, December 1899; "Wapping Alice" remains in manuscript in MTP.

[3] Henry Mills Alden had written Clemens on 5 October 1898 that in his opinion "My Platonic Sweetheart" was "neither a downright story nor a downright essay"; he returned the manuscript and offered $500 for "Concerning the Jews." On 2 November 1898 Clemens wrote Alden (Yale):

> I hold myself your obliged servant and friend for rejecting the "Platonic Sweetheart." I thought it was good; I think differently, now; I have been examining it again—by aid of your eyes this time—and have written to ask Mr. Rogers to put it away and suppress it if it is still in his reach.

Rogers meanwhile had submitted it to the *Century Magazine*, and Clemens wrote Richard Watson Gilder on 6 November 1898:

> I have been looking over the MS. of the "Platonic Sweetheart," and if you haven't already rejected it, reject it *now*. I wouldn't have it printed for $3,000. I liked it when I sent it, but that was because it was *recent* and I hadn't had a chance to give it a cold examination. I am generally more careful; but this time I felt cock-sure—and it was a mistake.

218. Clemens to Rogers

Vienna
6–7 November 1898

Hotel Krantz

Dear Mr. Rogers:

The other day I was going to cable and ask you to buy me $25,000 worth of Steel stock; and my idea was to have Mr. Whitmore mortgage our Hartford house for the money; and I would take up my uncompleted Autobiography and finish it, and let Bliss and Chatto each make $15,000 out of it for me next fall (as they did with the Equator-book) and pay off the mortgage; and also go on the platform in New York and a dozen other cities next November at $500 a night and make up the deficit—if any. I was strongly minded to write Pond and agree to do 20 or 30 nights, in place of the 100 he wants; and I got out my uncompleted lecture of a year ago and was going to put in the finishing touches. ⟨About⟩

I was full of the scheme; and it looked good. There were arguments in favor of it. At present Mrs. Clemens's income is about $4,000; the books, in England and America together, furnish ⟨another⟩ $⟨4⟩6,000; and I scrabble for the rest of the year's necessities with magazine-work. The steel stock will pay 5 per cent by and by; and if I had the second block of it it would complete the necessary income, and I could be a person of importance and not have to damage my reputation by too-frequent appearances in magazines.

But at this point I found that a man who has been in debt once is afraid to venture it again. So I didn't cable. I think I am a fool. I think I ought to have braced up and cabled. I should never have written the Equator book if I could have gotten out of it; I shall never write the Autobiography till I'm in a hole. It is best for me to *be* in a hole sometimes, I reckon.

Now it is a plain case to me that in not cabling I have choused myself out of that book; that is to say, I have robbed my own pocket of $30,000; and what is worse, I have robbed it of the extra block of steel stock. Give me your opinion. Was I wise, or have I acted foolishly and like a coward?

———

Later. Here's a chance for Rice! It has just come. The "Neighbor-Chain." It is a New York scheme, and the idea of it is to link the human race together, all round the globe in an unbroken hand-clasp, a rope of spiritual sausage, each individual a Link, and the whole to constitute and make perfect and beautiful the Universal Brotherhood of Man. Rice is the Missing Link. Insert him.

Nov. 7. It just occurs to me: am I a Vice President, or a Director in the Steel Company, or only a General Manager? And what do I get? What is the wages? And will I get anything for advice? Would you advise me to charge high, or go cautious, along at first? Will you collect, or had I better send in a bill? Do you think I had better go on with literature for a while, or begin to run the Company *now?* You know more than I do about these things. Tell me.

Hochachtungsvoll

SLC

219. CLEMENS TO ROGERS

Vienna
12 November 1898

Dear Mr. Rogers:

Your welcome cable came just as I was getting out of bed at 9 this morning, and at 10 my answer "Sign thanks splendid" left here.[1] If I had only been thoughtful enough to address it to your home it could have fetched you and Mrs. Rogers out of bed at 4 this morning and you could have had a good long day and got in a lot of work. I think I was born careless. Forgive me.

I am immensely grateful to you for pulling that thing through; I don't think any one else could have done it; and I don't think any one else would have had the patience to stick to it. I hope to goodness I shan't get you into any more jobs such as the Typesetter and Webster business and the Bliss-Harper campaigns have been. Oh, they were sickeners!

I am feeling pretty independent, now, and ready to do any rash thing that offers. I have already sent off one telegram to London putting prices on a couple of ⟨miscellaneous articles⟩ short stories ("Wapping Alice" and "The Man that Corrupted Hadleyburg") which will so modify the applicant's desire to possess them that I expect them to go from him to you by next mail. I told him to send them to you.[2] I don't know what I shall do with them yet a while. There is no hurry.

I will go at that Introduction, now, and with all the more satisfaction now that you have made Bliss disgorge that $1000, consound his skin. It must have been the sage Walter that invented the idea of confiscating that swag; it wasn't like Frank.

I supposed the Introduction [3] would occupy me half a day, but it ⟨already begins to string out in my head pretty formidably.

I have resumed my Autobiography, and I suppose I shall have Vol. 1 done by spring time. ⟨I hope so⟩ I expect so. I want Bliss to have plenty of time on it before next autumn.⟩ will probably absorb several. ["Edited *out*" is written in the right-hand margin.]

                                             Most gratefully Yours

                                             SLC.

I could run the Plagiarism Department of the Steel Works satisfactory if you could get me the place. I have had more experience than any body and can get recommendations.

---

[1] Rogers had cabled: "Harper Bliss myself agreed on contract papers drawn shall I sign cable answer introduction wanted thousand dollars all right Rogers" (Notebook 32, TS p. 50). For the contract, see Appendix D.

[2] Clemens had followed his telegram to Tuohy with a letter, dated 2 November 1898:

One of these stories ("The Man that Corrupted Hadleyburg") is longer than you want: 20,000 words—price $4,000; the other ("Wapping Alice") is more than 8,000 words and less (I think) than 9,000—price $200 per

1,000—To be within certainties I will call it sixteen hundred dollars, which goes $300 beyond the $1,300 offered by you for the minimum of 7,000 words. On 10 November he wrote again:

I made a bad miscount. If I am committed to the price named—$1,600—all right, I stand to it; but if I'm not committed, I'd rather raise it to $2,000, if my present count is correct (10,220 words.)

But—committed or not committed—if you find you don't want the tale I shall take it as a great favor if you will mail it to

H. H. *Rogers, 26 Broadway, New York.*

(Both letters are in the Doheny Collection, St. John's Seminary, PH in MTP).

[3] Clemens was having trouble with the introduction which Frank Bliss wanted him to write for the uniform edition. On 28 August 1898 he had written to Bliss: "I haven't any idea what to put into an Introduction. Have you? Can you suggest something? An Introduction *may* have value—I don't know—I've never seen one that had." He suggested that "Mr. Howells or Brander Matthews would write the Biographical sketch—You might ask them. Very little material is needed. The facts and dates are in some of the cyclopedias" (Yale). Meanwhile, he kept an eye on the production of the edition. "Your sample page," he wrote Bliss on 18 October 1898 (TS in MTP) "is very attractive. Please keep a sharp eye on the proofs." As for the introduction—"When the contract has been actually signed, cable me so, and under that inspiration I will drop everything and write an introduction. There's no inspiration now—for the contract seems as far off as ever" (Clemens did not know that it had been signed just six days before). Bliss did ask Howells to write the introduction, but, as Howells wrote Clemens: "he had not the courage to pay what I asked for it,—fifteen hundred dollars,—and he wanted something less in quantity than I was willing to do; so the thing is off" (W. D. Howells to Clemens, 23 October 1898, *MTHL*, pp. 679–680). An introductory essay, "Biographical Criticism," was ultimately written by Brander Matthews.

220. CLEMENS TO ROGERS

Vienna

17 November 1898

Dear Mr. Rogers—

Oh, dear me, you don't have to excuse yourself for neglecting me, you are entitled to the highest praise for being so limitlessly patient and good in bothering with my confused affairs, and pulling me out of a hole every little while.

I finished the Introduction yesterday, but I shall let it lie a day or two to make sure that it is worded to my satisfaction before I forward it. I have never had the habit of hurrying MSS off while they were still hot; and when I did this latter thing a couple of times lately you know the result.[1]

A MS (about "Hadleyburg") went to you a day or two ago from London.[2] It is more than 20,000 words. I haven't any purpose in view about it as yet. The "World" took a look at it. I think it just possible that it didn't like my price—$200 per 1000 words. (I didn't expect it to!)

It makes me lazy, the way that Steel stock is rising. If I were lazier—like Rice—nothing could keep me from retiring. But I work right along, like a poor person. I shall figure up the rise, as the figures come in, and push up my literary prices accordingly, till I get my literature up to where nobody can afford it but the family. (N.B. Look here, are you charging storage? I am not going to stand that, you know.) Meantime I note those encouraging illogical words of yours about my not worrying, because I am to be rich when I am 68; why didn't you have Cheiro [3] make it 90, so that I could have *plenty* of room?

It would be jolly good if some one should succeed in making a play out of "Is He Dead?" [4] From what I gather from dramatists, he will have his hands something more than full—but let him struggle, let him struggle.

Is there some way, honest or otherwise, by which you can get a copy of Mayo's play, Pudd'nhead Wilson, for me? There is a capable young Austrian here who saw it in New York and wants to translate it and see if he can stage it here. *I* don't think these people here would understand it or take to it, but he thinks it will pay us to try.

A couple of London dramatists want to bargain with me for the right to make a high comedy out of the "Million-Pound Note." Barkis is willing.

I reckon the Broughtons are coming to New York; [5] I hope so, anyway, and doubtless you do, too. You are getting to have a nice large family-plant, now, and you ought to consolidate it in a Trust and have it under your own eye where you can look after it personally. I could be a Director, if I could get in on the ground floor. I believe the prospects are good; and then the Electric Spark is going to be along pretty soon, now, and I foresee a boom. If I can't get Preferred, I'll take Common.

I haven't a doubt that it was Pond who emptied that sewage down the back of the Chambermaid's Home Journal.[6] It's in his taste. Some of it has dribbled into these Vienna papers.

Young Dr. Freeland who is going to run over in December thinks he can find us a flat in the Washington Square region which will not bust us when we go home next October, but I am doubting it. From what I hear New York is growing more and more expensive every day.

By Jackson! I forgot, in my last to ask you to send us Bliss's $1000. But maybe Bliss hasn't turned it in, yet. In that case we will draw from London again.

I am touting for this hotel. Send your friends here. It is the best one in Vienna.

⟨With my bes⟩ With this family's best regards to you all,

Sincerely Yours

SLC

[1] Clemens composed a draft of letter 220 on the reverse of page 5 of his MS notes for the "Schoolhouse Hill" version of "The Mysterious Stranger" (DV 327C, MTP):

Nov. 17/98

Dear Mr. Rogers:
I put in 5 days on an Introduction. I had pretty good hopes of it—also some suspicions. After the finish the hopes retired and the suspicions had a walk-over. I was totally unsatisfied, and tore up the MS.
But the one which I enclose suits me. I can't improve on that, for steering clear of the immodesties.
By George, if Bliss could get an Introduction from Howells, *that* would be a thing worth *reading!*
On the same day, he wrote to Frank Bliss:
I put in 5 days on 50 pages of Introduction, and then put it in the fire. A thousand dollars' worth of work for nothing. An author cannot successfully write about his own books nor a mother about her own children—nothing but a poorly-concealed parade of silly vanities results. No one can do the job creditably but an outsider. No one can do it best for me but Howells or Brander Matthews.
The 3 pages of Introduction which I enclose are satisfactory to me. They do not exhibit me turning handsprings in my shirt-tail.
A three-paragraph preface by Clemens, dated Vienna, January 1899, appears in

Volume I of the Edition De Luxe, issued by the American Publishing Company
in 1899.

    [2] Clemens recorded (Notebook 32, TS p. 51):
        Monday, Nov. 21/98. Cabled:
        "Harper Publisher New York
        Rogers has Hadleyburg. Clemens
        7 words—about $2.45

Puzzled by the cablegram, Alden wrote Rogers on 21 November 1898 (Salm):
"In answer to our request for some stories he has written, Mr. Samuel Clemens
sends us the following cablegram: 'Rogers has hadleyburg.' We do not know
exactly what this means, but we shall be glad to consider anything of his that you
may have."

    [3] Pseudonym of Louis Hamon, palmist, who in 1895 in New York and again
two years later in London prophesied that Clemens would become very wealthy
in his sixty-eighth year (Notebook 35, TS p. 10).

    [4] Clemens had tried, but apparently felt that he had failed; see letter 211.

    [5] They had been residing in Chicago.

    [6] "The Anecdotal Side of Mark Twain—Told in Stories and Anecdotes
Contributed to the Journal by the Closest Friends of the Great Humorist, and
Now Published for the First Time" appeared in the *Ladies' Home Journal*,
October 1898; many of the anecdotes were of Clemens on the lecture circuit.

221. CLEMENS TO ROGERS

                                                    Vienna
                                                    8–13 December 1898

Dear Mr. Rogers:

    It is 12 days since I handled a pen. It seemed to be an attack of
fatigue, and I tried to *rest* it off, but that was a failure; so I think it
is a touch of malaria or piety or something like that and will go off
of itself if let alone. I am letting it alone by lying around in my
study reading and smoking all day—couldn't even write an ordinary letter—couldn't make it say what I wanted it to say. If I could
afford it I would be like this all the time; merely lie around and
manage the Steel Company and never do any work.

    December 11.

    I worked yesterday and day before, and am in trim this morning
to continue.

    I have had two letters from Bliss since you signed the contract,
but they contain not a whimper of dissatisfaction with the bargain
—seems only delighted to be footloose and free to get to work on

the Uniform. I couldn't *give* the books to him 3 years ago; now he is glad to get them on any hard terms. It's the same old human nature; Adam was the original Bliss; if God had told him to help himself, the crop would have rotted on the trees; but as soon as He loaded the apples up with extra-territorial royalties and other wanton exactions and obstructions, Adam was bound to sample the orchard if it cost him his shirt-tail. Bliss is happy, now, and I am, too.

Bliss is satisfied with the brief Introduction I sent—and that is better luck than I expected.

He *isn't* so well satisfied with that $1000 McClure-article matter, but I have written him the kind of soft letter which turns away sorrow and leaves a check the same size it was before.[1]

Cablegram from Harpers yesterday offering $2500 for Hadleyburg and an account of the Wreck of the Hornet. Those people are not going to fetch up in the poorhouse through lack of literary economy. I didn't chance their judgment *this* time; I asked them to name a price. They have done it. I will answer them with ⟨?a price which will⟩ a perfectly fair price, but it will probably land those articles in your hands ⟨with⟩.

Later I will get you to send them to other magazines—there is no hurry. The same with "Wapping Alice." The "World" offered something over my magazine rates—in fact about double—but I put on a price which I judged would discourage them, and it did. It was really a syndicate in disguise. One never knows where those buccaneers are ambushed.

There is a letter this moment from Miss Harrison in which she says Cheiro is coming to New York by and by. I wish you would see him personally when he comes, and get him to reduce the time-limit on that fortune of mine. If he can pull it down to next year I am willing to take 15 per cent and leave the rest to you and him.

December 12.

December 13. Mrs. Clemens wouldn't *let* me charge the Harpers a fair price, so I cabled them that their offer "lacks $500."[2] I would have made it double that. And she says the cablegram was from you, not the Harpers. Women are full of superstitions, and don't know anything.

Did the Harpers pay you the $500 they "allowed" me for the Jew article? They didn't send it here.

I think—but am not quite sure—that Dr.

[The remainder of this letter is missing.]

[1] On 10 December 1898, Clemens had written Bliss again about the McClure money:

I must give you my side of the McClure matter. You were dead opposed to having any part of the book get into print before publication-day. I was of your mind—it could do no possible good, and *would* do very serious harm (to a subscription book) *without the slightest doubt in the world.* Your McClure publication cost you and me ten times the McClure check.

That is one item. Another: You bound me not to sell an advance sheet. We were partners: therefore you bound yourself, as well. Another: You should have consulted me—I was entitled to a voice. I always sent people to you when they applied to me—of course expecting you to say no, and say it promptly. And finally: You sold to McClure at half price. That would not have happened if you had told me you had changed your mind and wanted to make an advance-publication (Syracuse University).

[2] Alden was somewhat puzzled when having offered $2,500 for "The Man That Corrupted Hadleyburg" and "My Debut as a Literary Person" (Alden to HHR, 9 December 1898, Salm), Harper & Brothers received another cable from Clemens saying "Lacks five hundred" (Harper & Brothers to HHR, 13 December 1898, Salm). Ultimately Clemens received $2,000 for "The Man That Corrupted Hadleyburg" (Alden to HHR, 30 December 1898, Salm).

222. CLEMENS TO ROGERS

Vienna

27 December 1898

Hotel Krantz

Dear Mr. Rogers:

Yours of the 16th is a very enchanting Christmas letter and introduces a striking and in all ways commendable novelty. Christmas has always been an expense before; this is the first time it has gone the other way. That $17,000 has been a very industrious and fertile old hen, and I am very glad you have set her again. She is doing a dazzling business on the new nest.[1] And there is Puddn'head—I was not expecting to hear any promising thing from Puddnhead again. I think Cheiro is beginning to realize that his reputation is at stake and that he had better begin to hump himself. I hurt a zealous believer in him last night by telling her he was an unreliable man in financial prophecy. I will go and apologise.

I am cabling you to-day "Accept $2000"—for Hadleyburg.[2] Now *that's* a decent price, and I am glad we have crowded them into a reasonable degree of commercial propriety at last. All magazine people are like all other people—insane in one detail or another—but the Harper detail is the funniest I know of. Plainly their editorial gospel is this:

New subjects are valuable.

Old subjects are not.

And then at Christmas they forget all that, and ⟨put o⟩ empty a whole magazine-full of mouldy old moth-eaten ⟨sentimental ⟨holy slush⟩ slush onto the nation,⟩ poetical tin haloes onto the nation, that they scour and polish ⟨and burn⟩ and patch up fresh every year —and even the *rhymes* are hardly changed.

Until I revealed it there was not a double handful of men left alive on the planet who knew that the Hornet matter had ever been in print. I could have played it for a brand new discovery on the Harpers themselves.

I have the impression that in the Hornet article I permit the reader to fool himself (with my help) with the impression that the *diary* part has not been in print before. I will look at my copy, and if that isn't so I'll *make* it so, and the next magazine-puddnhead it goes to shall examine it from *that* point of view and see how it affects him. It is now 33 years since I copied and published that diary free gratis for nothing, and before I get through somebody has got to pay for that job. I am ⟨a reasonably⟩ not a patient creditor. When I do a piece of work I ⟨mu⟩ want the money—and pretty reasonably quick, too, or I will sue the whole ⟨dam⟩ nation.

We of the Krantz greet all you of 57th street with best wishes and the holiday salutations, Broughton baby and all.

SLC

¹ On receipt of Rogers's letter, Clemens had recorded (Notebook 32, TS p. 52): "Mr. Rogers invested $17,140 for me in October in Federated Steel stock. Has sold it for 22,789.78 and bought in 712 shares of the Common stock at 32 and it has already gone up to 38½—a profit of $4,628 in 2 weeks."

² The cablegram which reads "Accept two thousand" survives in the Salm Collection.

223. CLEMENS TO ROGERS

Vienna
3 January 1899

Dear Mr. Rogers—

Yours of Dec. 23 arrived yesterday afternoon. Federated Steel does certainly brisken up these holidays with handsome surprises! ¹ By grace of you, we have had a Christmas and a New Year this time which knocked the gloom out of a season which we have grown accustomed to anticipate with dread. There has been no dismalness —we have been gay. We went out to several late-hour suppers and private theatricals, and furnished return-festivities and dissipations ourselves. We are resembling the long-vanished Clemenses of 10 years ago. God knows what we should be resembling if it had not been for you.

I was a good deal puzzled as to what kind of a cable to send. If I said "Yes, $10,000," and you cabled back and said you were sorry to disappoint my fine dreams but the stock had dropped below that in the meantime, I should recognize that I ought to have been smart enough to hedge a little on that remark. So then I *did* hedge, and placed you where you would do the thing which you deemed wisest, and leave the results to me. I knew that whether it was hold or sell, you would know better which to do than I could tell you. It's a grand hen,—⟨the Feder⟩ keep her setting till she wears the seat out of her pants!

Those magazine articles—well, I think I will let them alone a while. Perhaps I have been in print enough for the present. "Hadleyburg" will fill the gap for a while. I wondered—rather—that the Harpers took it; it had a sort of profane touch in the tail of it.

I have written a blamed sight profaner one, about Monaco and Monte Carlo [2]—if Mrs. Clemens allows it to pass her frontier I think I can beguile the Cosmopolitan into printing it.

I hope you did gather the whole family together, and that you all had the good time you deserve. Certainly you have made us have a good one, and we all greet you all heartily and wish you many happy returns.

S.L.C.

P.S. Do you believe Cheiro can come on me for commission?

Speaking of gaieties, the children and I are going to a fancy dress ball at a private house to-morrow night—the children in splendid costumes, with much jewelry; one of them as "Night," the other as a Hindoo ⟨girl.⟩ princess. These things are very expensive. Mrs. Clemens designed these costumes herself, and the maid constructed them, and they are striking and beautiful. Altogether they cost, including jewelry, seven dollars. It is the jewelry that comes so high.

[1] Clemens recorded (Notebook 32, TS p. 53):
Letter dated Dec. 23 from Mr. Rogers says the 712 shares show a profit of $10,000 altogether, since he bought them the week before. Shall he sell at that? I have just cabled him: "Follow your judgment whatever it is, I take the risk. Clemens."
[2] This survives as a TMS, "The New War Scare" (MTP, Paine 46).

224. CLEMENS TO ROGERS

Vienna
24 January 1899

Dear Mr. Rogers:

I am gradually getting over the disorganizing effects of sudden wealth, steadying down and resuming normality. It was a gaudy trip that that $17,000 made when it went lecturing for half a semester under your able management.[1] I wish to retain your services, sir; and it is my intention to raise your salary. Let us get back on the financial platform, now, and do another tour. It is much better than literature. Literature is well enough, as a time-passer, and for the improvement and general elevation and purification of mankind, but it has no practical value.

I have been doing some of it of late, but haven't finished any of it except a short article ("Diplomatic Pay and Clothes") which I sent to the "Forum" five or six days ago and told them to send it to you if they didn't want it.[2] I didn't put any price on it. If they don't want it (but they will, I think), I reckon McClure would like to have it if he is privileged to name the price himself.

This is like any other city—a bad place to work in, in the season. It makes late hours; then I have to sleep till noon to make up; two or three hours of disjointed, unconcentrated work, and the social mill goes to grinding again. Summer is the time!—I wish there were more of it; I wonder how Howells manages to work in New York. Before the year is ended I may be trying to answer that conundrum out of my own experience. Maybe a body could work better in Washington. Or Richmond. I think either place might be less expensive than New York, though less satisfactory in other ways.

I'm not asking questions—I'm only thinking aloud. You are not to waste your moments on letters to me. A long letter from you gives me pleasure, but it also gives me a pang, because I know the cost of it to a man driven as you are. Just shout me a line, and leave me to imagine the rest. I'm competent.

Aufwiedersehen! with the best thanks and regards of us-all to you-all!

SLC

[1] Clemens recorded (Notebook 32, TS p. 53):
Cable from Mr. Rogers: "Profit $16,000." Cabled back: "Splendid bird, set her again." (11 words—about $4.)
[2] The piece appeared in the *Forum*, March 1899.

225. Clemens to Rogers

Vienna
2 February 1899

Dear Mr. Rogers:

Now that I am prospering at such a rate, thanks to you, I am feeling pretty young and very comfortable.[1] I wish I were there, to sit in the office and see you bet, and then watch the hen perform; it would give life a new zest. Maybe that can happen, by and by; I hope it may. The other day I wrote Bliss to send his January money here, but we shan't need it for a long time yet, so I have now written him to send it to you. It is $5,500, and will swell that hen-fruit up to $48,000 and will make a jolly nice stake to bet with or put into securities, according to the way your judgment shall suggest. I hope you will see a safe chance to bet and will bet the whole pile; but if you buy securities, won't you please *keep them in your own hands,* so that you can sell them whenever you see a good chance to gamble? Charley Langdon already has Mrs. Clemens's securities in his hands ($75,000) which pay $4,000 a year, and I would rather have mine where you can exploit it. You see, the more things you have to attend to, the robuster you will be and the more advantageous it will be, because health is a great thing and it is my duty to keep yours up to the mark.

For a whole week, now, Mrs. Clemens has been having a rough time with rheumatism in the hip, and has had but little sleep. She is up and around all day, and movement seems to modify the pain somewhat; but the nights are too wearing, so we have notified the doctor to furnish some sleep for to-night, and he has sent a soporific.

I am glad the Broughtons are nearer you, but sorry they didn't settle in New York. We shall settle there for a while, I hope, and it is my plan to join the poker game, with Mrs. Rogers for a pal, and live on Rice.

This is our wedding-day; 29 years married!
Live long and prosper!

Yrs Sincerely

SL Clemens

I have written Bliss that the volume of Sketches will be in your control, to place it in any hands you please, and this will enable him to trade it to Harpers for some Uniform concessions he desires, merely seeing to it that if they take it they pay me 15% royalty as usual.[2]

---

[1] On 31 December 1898 Rogers had written that he was now holding $43,000 for Clemens (Notebook 32, TS p. 53).

[2] Clemens wrote Frank Bliss on 2 February 1899:

There's as much as 100,000 words for the volume of Sketches—say half as much more as Huck Finn or Tom Sawyer contain. Half of it has not yet been in print and half of *that half* is especially good, and ought to be put into a magazine but I don't much care, one way or the other, as to that, provided *you* publish the book. *New* is important to you but not to the Harpers. I am too far away to conduct the scheme with the Harpers, but you and Mr. Rogers can manage it, I guess. In this way: Let us consider that Mr. Rogers has full control of the book, to give it to you or to Harpers just as he pleases—if Harper gets it, Harper to pay me 15% royalty, as usual. But I wouldn't promise *new* matter to *them*, unless you can make a leverage out of it. Then Mr. Rogers can empower you to turn the book over to the Harpers, and you can go ahead and with Matthews' help no doubt you can get from the Harpers the concessions which you have indicated in pages 2 and 3 of your letter. You see you can consider the book your *own* and that puts you in shape to dicker. But try to avoid talking about *new* matter if handy, for I might want to print a couple of these articles in a magazine—a couple which I am now engaged in finishing. I hope Brander Matthews *will* do the rearranging, for in that case, it will be done well, whereas I could not promise that if I did it myself. . . .

If I am not speaking too late, send that $5,500, to Mr. Rogers: I have no use for it here, I find (TS in MTP).

In 1900 two volumes were published: *The Man That Corrupted Hadleyburg and Other Stories and Essays*, by Harper & Brothers; and *How to Tell a Story and Other Essays*, which became Volume XXII of the various uniform editions by the American Publishing Company.

226. Clemens to Rogers

Vienna
19 February 1899

Dear Mr. Rogers:

Why, it is just splendid! I have nothing to do but sit around and watch you set the hen and hatch out those big broods and make my living for me. Don't you wish you had somebody to do the same for you?—a magician who can turn steel and copper and Brooklyn gas into gold. I mean to raise your wages again—⟨blamed if you don't deserve it.⟩ I begin to feel that I can afford it. I think the hen ought to have a name; she must be called *Unberufen*. That is a German word which is equivalent to "'*sh! hush!* don't let the spirits hear you!" The superstition is, that if you happen to let fall any grateful jubilation over good luck that you've had or are hoping to have, you must shut square off and say "Unberufen!" and *knock wood*—⟨other⟩ the word drives the evil spirits away: otherwise they would divine your joy or your hopes and go to work and spoil your game. Set her again—do!

If at any time you should think it best that the Brooklyn Gas be sold and the harvest raked in, won't you tell Langdon to do it? Otherwise I want him to leave it undisturbed. And of course he will; he will easily divine that as long as you don't advise the sale, a sale is not the judicious thing to exploit.

Oh, look here! you are just like everybody; merely because I am literary, you think I'm a commercial somnambulist, and am not watching you with all that money in your hands. Bless you⟨r soul⟩ I've got a description of you and a photograph in every police office in Christendom, with the remark appended: "Look out for a handsome tall slender young man with a gray moustache, and courtly manners, and an address well calculated to deceive, calling himself by the name of Smith." Don't you try to get away—it won't work.

The "Forum" will print that little article.[1] I've just finished a very short one (2,000 words) for the swell new London political periodical ("Lords and Commons.")[2] They pay $500 for it, which is double "Century" rates, and twice-and-a-half Harper's best.

I think maybe we could live cheaper in Washington than in New York, but of course we would rather live in New York—not on account of the "quiet and retirement," for I don't take any stock in that superstition of yours—but because I want to be near you so that you can have my character as a model to shape-up your own by, and because I am practising poker, now, and shall want to be where I can make my living out of Rice. Laffan must be prospering greatly, now, and will need a large house, and will want to rent his present one to a capitalist of high character; and so I am going to write him and let him know that I am approachable. It is right on the horse-car line to your desirable billiard-room and cigar box, and in easy reach of Rice's house and portmonnaie.

That umbrella never looked better than it does now. Through prosperity it is fatter than ever. I have offered it to the Emperor, and he was very much pleased, but thinks it is too showy for a person of his age. This is a pretext; he has some other reason, I believe, which he does not want to disclose; I wish I could find out what it is.

With the gratefulest and kindest regards to all of you

Yours sincerely

SLC

---

[1] "Diplomatic Pay and Clothes."
[2] Clemens's essay appeared in the 25 February 1899 issue of *Lords and Commons* as "The 'Austrian Parliamentary System'? Government by Article 14." It summarized the fourteenth article of the Austrian constitution as "a Constitution all by itself . . . It means anything you please, but it does not mean the same thing to any two people . . . the Government can commit political adultery with it every day, and while everybody may know it, nobody can prove it."

227. Clemens to Rogers

Vienna [1]
14 March 1899

Dear Mr. Rogers:

Unberufen—keep her a-squatting! Miss Harrison's report makes me a capitalist of a very swell sort.[2] Pretty soon, at this rate, it will become Rice to speak of me as *Mr.* Clemens—yes, and even *Colonel*. I don't like to suggest it to him myself, but you might remind him. He is [a] man who has a passion for titles—when they are conferred upon him. He used to hint around that it would be becoming in me to call him the Wood Violet. Now you know, that was a little *too*-too. Rice *is* a modest man—as New York modest men go—but he is not *that* much of an exaggeration.

Yes, Hutton offered me a chance in his Trinity, and it seemed a [good] [3] idea, with a lot of econom[ies] in the way of house-expenses and such; and I have written and asked him what board and three bedrooms might cost us in that inn.[4] Three only, because I think Clara will want to get quarters with some lady friend and live in New York where there's things going on, and music. We *all* want to live in New York, but I judge we couldn't afford the expense—particularly if ⟨he⟩ Rice is getting so well up in poker that he goes home now with Mrs. Rogers's money in his pocket. I was expecting to get a part of my living out of him, but this last development is discouraging.

They are scaring us about the [. . .] [5] *any* of their accumulation of odds and ends cost. I wrote Hutton that I was a patriot, with no heart to cheat the government, but I couldn't afford the duties and should come ashore in my shirt-tail, and you ⟨get⟩ must make the Collector let the family come in with some of their clothes on. My baggage has never been examined before, but I reckon those halcyon days are gone by for the Clemenses.

Dr. Freeland, who met Rice, kept his promise and looked for a flat for us in New York, but he has come back and reports that the best he can do is $3,000 unfurnished. He says rents and all things have gone up high. Mr. Tatlock, of the New York Life Co is to see what *he* can do. But there is plenty of time, as we shall not arrive before the end of September. Maybe [Tatlo]ck will find the right thing for us; [then] I can sit around and see you set the hen. I don't expect her to hatch out $3586 every time she goes on the nest, but it would be a pleasure to be in the hennery and see her exercise herself, anyway.

Don't try to paint the house, you haven't had experience enough. Put it off a year, then I will superintend, and it will be done right, and I shan't mind the labor.

We are all going down to Budapest the forenoon of the 25th to do a reading,[6] to begin with the Stolen Watermelon. That always goes.

I hope Miss Mai will come back well—and the Electric Spark, too; but if you will make him pay his own way he will get well sooner.[5]

----

[1] A penciled headnote, dated 3 April 1899, indicates that part of this letter was sent to Rudyard Kipling.

[2] *"March 14.* Received letter from Mr. Rogers. Last sale brought $3586. Total in his hands, $51,995. Brooklyn Gas is up to 155—cost us 75. . . . *Miss Harrison*—date, Apl. 28/99: To our credit, $51,995.29, cash. Invested in American Smelting Co., $5,000—now worth $6,300. 50 pfd and 35 com—selling at 90 and 52" (Notebook 32, TS p. 55).

[3] A corner of the manuscript has been destroyed; conjectures for the missing pieces appear in square brackets.

[4] Laurence Hutton, who lived in Princeton, New Jersey, tried to persuade the Clemenses to settle there, at the Princeton Inn. (See SLC to Hutton, 12 March 1899, Princeton.)

[5] The bottom of the page has been cut off, probably to send to Kipling (see note 1). At least six lines of manuscript are missing here, and the complimentary close and signature (on the verso) are also missing.

[6] Clemens lectured on 26 March 1899 at the jubilee celebration of the emancipation of the Hungarian press. (See *MTS* [1923], p. 176.)

228. CLEMENS TO ROGERS

Vienna
18 April 1899

Dear Mr. Rogers:

All right, I am glad you are keeping that capital at work and making it earn its living; there isn't any *other* member of this family that is so diligent and so capable. As for myself, I have talent but not efficiency. I wish Rice would re-dramatise "Is He Dead." It would keep him out of mischief, and shorten his gambling-hours, and postpone the gallows; [1] and *I* know, quite well, that that play will never play until it is reconstructed. Meanwhile I've a notion that Puddnhead will resume dividends one of these days; a letter received yesterday from the Mississippi valley speaks warmly of it and of its big houses.

The landlord of the inn in Princeton offers us very good terms indeed; but naturally we can't decide anything until we are on the ground and can look around.

I should like to try the inn a spell, but I think we shall end by keeping house. Mrs. Clemens prefers it, and I am not by any means averse from it. There is one little trouble about that inn, but not one which I should much mind: Hutton says it is in the rainy end of the town, and he thinks we should be healthier in the sunny end. It seems strange to me that they do not distribute the rain there according to some kind of system; for that is the usual way: sometimes it is arranged to fall upon the just and the unjust alike, for spite, and indeed this is the common custom, although stupid, and I think that this new idea of trying to discriminate between Mr. Cleveland and Mr. Hutton is a mistake and will cause remark. But as for me I shall not care for the rain, for I am always dry anyway. I wish the Fairhaven house were in Fifth avenue; I would rent it. I hope we shall get back in time to have a glimpse of it, anyway, before you close it. Don't be in too big a hurry closing it.

Do not go to any expense about my smoking in the barn; I am not particular, and can get along in the parlor.

The enclosed has wandered to me from America.[2] I suppose you knew the Whitfields. It is a pleasant story. I suppose I have met the old Captain myself if he is the one who was a teetotaler 3 years and became profane when he got back home and learned he hadn't been elected to the Society.[3]

Prosperity and best regards to you all; and I am taking warning from that poetry about the ex-Millionaire—and carefully arranging to *be* one.

Sincerely Yours

SLC

[1] Clemens recalled, in a note of introduction to Laurence Hutton, that Dr. Rice "wrote a play once, and when advised to burn it, did it. That is the kind of people we want" (Princeton, undated fragment). On 27 February 1899 Alf Hayman, manager for Charles Frohman's Travelling Companies, had written to Dr. Rice that he was unsuccessful in finding producers for Clemens's three plays, *Bartel Turaser, In Purgatory,* and *Is He Dead* (CWB). Hayman quoted a letter (Klaw & Erlanger to Alf Hayman, 2 February 1899, CWB) which suggested that if *Is He Dead* "were revised by some clever and practical dramatist, particularly in the last act . . . there is a favorable opportunity for it."

[2] The enclosure has not survived, but Clemens probably refers to an account about Manjiro Nakahama, a young Japanese fisherman who had been rescued at sea and taken to Fairhaven in 1841 by Captain William H. Whitfield, a whaling master. Nakahama had learned the English language and Yankee ship building before returning to Japan, where he played an important role as translator in Perry's negotiations with the Japanese in 1853. The Fairhaven *Star* reported on 5 November 1898 that M. P. Whitfield had "received a very interesting letter" from Manjiro's son, hoping to make contact with his father's benefactor.

[3] Apparently in November 1894 Rogers had told Clemens the story of the whaling captain who had spent three painful years at sea living up to his "pledge," only to find on his return that he had long since been blackballed from the Temperance Society. On 18 December 1905 at a benefit in New York City, where Clemens shared the stage with Sarah Bernhardt, he claimed to have met the old Captain "some years ago with a friend of mine" while attending "the dedication of a great town hall" in Fairhaven. His friend, Clemens said, had given him the Captain's story (*MTS* [1923], pp. 265–268). The next year, a profile of Rogers in *Human Life* (April 1906) cited the anecdote as "one of Rogers' stories" about "real" persons from Fairhaven; on his copy Clemens wrote at the bottom of the page: "That *was* a good story when I told it to Sara Bernhardt and her audience on the stage of the theatre, but this person doesn't know how to tell a story. He has no art."

It seems likely that some "old Captain" from Fairhaven was the original for

Jimmy Starkweather, the whaling captain in Clemens's "The Great Dark," who curses his pledge to a temperance society throughout a long, dry cruise in the Bering Strait, then returns to find that "he'd been black-balled three years before —*hadn't ever been a member!*" (*WWD*, pp. 115–117). But Clemens could never actually have met Whitfield, who died on 14 February 1886.

229. CLEMENS TO ROGERS

Vienna
10 May 1899

Dear Mr. Rogers:

Three removes are as bad as a fire—and we were projecting them: 1. To Reichenau, in the mountains, 50 miles from Vienna, June 1 to July 1; 2. Then to London; 3. then to the Channel Islands or somewhere till we sail for home. But, two removes are only two-thirds as bad as a fire, of course; and I have persuaded the family to abolish No. 1 and go to London *now*. That is to say, a fortnight from now; it takes us a fortnight to pack up. This is because I only superintend, and do not do the packing myself.

And so our address, from now on, is Care Chatto & Windus, 110 St. Martin's Lane.

Miss Harrison says we have about $52,000 on hand; and $5,000 under the hen, who is hatching upwards of 20 per cent out of it. That is good news, and shows that Cheiro can work his prophecy-mill very well when you stand behind him and turn the crank.

For a week, now, the Vienna papers have been excited over the great Copper combine, and sometimes they say you are president of it, other times they call you vice-president, but *all* the time I seem to gather from them that you are the Company and the Board of Directors.[1] I feel perfectly sure that you are arranging to put that $52,000 under that hen as soon as the allotment of stock begins, and I am very glad of that, for you know how to make a copper hen lay a golden egg. Oh yes, Hochwohlgeboren, you have got that art and mystery down fine. Put it in! you don't want all that money stacked up in your daily view; it is only a temptation to you. ⟨I⟩ Am I going to be in the Board?

It is a pity we can't go home now. We are all pretty home-sick. But we should have to go to some summer resort, and it would be crowded and uncomfortable and I couldn't work; and besides, if it were ⟨at⟩ a satisfactory place it would be too costly for us. Why, even here I can't afford Scotch whisky enough to keep my morals from stinking, for these highwaymen charge a dollar and ten cents a bottle for it; and as for cigars, they are 3½ cents apiece, and there is no way for a really conscientious economist to do but steal them. It shames me to do this, and it makes a good deal of talk; but I feel as Rice does about such matters: that it is better to be economical than honest, as a general thing. I have learned many useful things from Rice.

> Gott behüte dich!
>
> Ihr ergebenst—
>
> SLC.

---

[1] Marcus Daly was president, Rogers vice-president, and William Rockefeller secretary and treasurer of the Amalgamated Copper Company. Organized in New Jersey with a capital of $75,000,000, the company purchased interests in the Anaconda, the Butte and Boston, the Boston and Montana, the Isle Royale, the Parrott, the Boston and Colorado, and the Washoe companies.

Abbie Palmer Gifford Rogers

Olivia L. Clemens, September 1895

Emilie Augusta Randel Rogers

Harry Rogers, about 1898

Harry Rogers, about 1889

From *Life,* January 1905

From *Life,* October 1905

The *Kanawha*

On board the *Kanawha,* March 1902: Colonel A. G. Paine, Rogers, Thomas B. Reed, Clemens, Laurence Hutton, Wallace T. Foote, and Dr. Clarence C. Rice. (See letter 297.)

Mai Huttleston Rogers (Mrs. William R. Coe)

Cara Leland Rogers (Mrs. Urban H. Broughton)

Anne Engle Rogers (Mrs. William E. Benjamin)

Jean Clemens

Clara Clemens

Susy Clemens

63 points above
what it cost us?

NEW YORK. Dec. 26, 1901.

Monday Tuesday
or Thursday

Samuel L. Clemens, Esq.,

      Riverdale, N. Y.

My dear Clemens:

      I send you a clipping from the "World" relating to the much advertised history of the Standard Oil Company now being prepared for Mc Clure's Magazine by Ida M. Tarbell. It would naturally be supposed that any person desiring to write a veritable history, would seek for information as near original sources as possible. Miss Tarbell has not applied to the Standard Oil Company, nor to anyone connected with it, for information on any subject. On the contrary, I have reason to believe, she is seeking all her information from those not disinterested enemies of the "Standard" who have for years invented and published falsehoods concerning it. She may in this way make her work more striking and spectacular, but a reputable magazine should have some assurance that what purports to be history is truthful as well as interesting. I do not know whether you can be of any service in the matter, but it would be a kindness to Mr. Mc Clure as well as myself if you could suggest to him that some care should be taken to verify statements which may be made through his magazine, whether affecting corporations or individuals.

                    Yours truly,

                    H H Rogers

I got a stocking full of water. I hope you found better. Have got his filled with oil.

Rogers to Clemens, letter 290

Mark Twain drawn by Harry Rogers, 1901 (Log of the *Kanawha,* Salm Collection)

Clemens in London, 1897

Rogers and Clemens, Bermuda 1908

Another picture of Rogers and Clemens in Bermuda, 1908

Isabel V. Lyon, 1906

The Paige Typesetter

MR. H. H. ROGERS, THE STANDARD OIL MAGNATE AT HIS DESK IN HIS PRIVATE
OFFICE, NO. 26 BROADWAY, N. Y. CITY. FOUR MONTHS AGO, MR. ROGERS HAD
AN ATTACK OF APOPLEXY IN THIS OFFICE, AND WAS QUICKLY REMOVED TO HIS
HOME AT FAIR HAVEN, MASS., WHERE HE HAS BEEN CONFINED EVER SINCE.
From a stereograph copyright by Underwood & Underwood, New York.

From the *Overland Monthly*, January 1908

From the New York
World, 20 May 1909

Clemens at Rogers's funeral, 21 May 1909

V

"This Everlasting Exile"

(JUNE 1899-AUGUST 1900)

"I am tired to death of this everlasting exile"
SLC to HHR, 8 January 1900

AN ATTEMPT to find a cure for Jean's illness, which had been diagnosed as epilepsy, was responsible for keeping the Clemens family abroad longer than any of them wished. They spent more than a year in Sanna, Sweden, and in London, while Jean received osteopathic treatment, which Clemens was sure could also cure the illnesses of the entire family. But they all grew increasingly homesick. "Why, hang it, we haven't seen a home-face for generations," Clemens wrote Laurence Hutton. "I suppose Mr. Rogers is old and fat and wearing a wig, now, and dyeing his moustache, but I hope not. Go and see him, and tell me privately of the ravages of time and piety" (18 September 1899, Princeton).

230. CLEMENS TO ROGERS

Broadstairs [1]
6 June 1899

Dear Mr. Rogers:

I am very glad to know I am in Amalgamated Copper, for considerable copper will be needed to pay this week's bills. We had been only 2 days in our nice rooms in the Prince of Wales Hotel, Kensington, London (£30 a week, including everything,) when the doctor ordered Clara down here for a week, and of course we all came. We kept our rooms at the P. of W. (£19 a week for the interval), and rushed immediately down here, where it costs a shilling to look at a cup of coffee, and two to drink it. Send Rice over.

We expect to return to London next Friday the 9th and remain at the P. of Wales till the end of July. We shall then go to ⟨the⟩ Jersey or Guernsey for 2 months, I think. We shall still be at the P. of Wales when the Electric Spark arrives the 28th of this month, and shall be very glad to see him. If he would care to put up there and take his dinners with us in our parlor, it goes without saying that he will be very welcome. We take our breakfast while we are dressing, and ⟨the fam⟩ our luncheon in the public dining-room. (*Our* luncheon means the others—I don't feed in the middle of the day.) If Miss May comes over while we are still in London she must come to the P. of W.—she must not go elsewhere. Without a doubt we can be of some use to her; and we want to try, anyway. I am so sorry her health is affected, and very very sorry she has to go so far as Switzerland. She would find it much more agreeable to take her dinners and lunches with us than with strangers.

I showed Chatto Bliss's canvassing book of the de luxe a day or two ago, and he was vastly taken with it, and wants to put 1000 on the English market for me at 10% commission.[2] I have asked Bliss what he will charge me for the volumes—suggesting *cost*, or thereabouts.

Behüte dich Gott!

SLC

---

[1] The Clemenses were staying at the Grand Hotel in Broadstairs on the Dover coast.

[2] Clemens had written Chatto & Windus from Vienna on 25 April 1899:

Bliss seems to be having an easy thing with his handsome signed and numbered edition (of 512 copies.) President McKinley and other big guns have subscribed, and Bliss is feeling very well.

Do you think you could work off a similar edition in England? I suppose there is abundance of time to feel the pulse there; for I don't suppose Bliss has as yet manufactured any but the first of the 20 or 22 volumes. I think the American price for the set is $200.

The books are made by the Riverside Press—and of course that means the best of taste and much expense.

In an interview in the London *Daily Chronicle,* 3 June 1899, Clemens is reported to have said that he was in London to arrange for the publication there of a twenty-two-volume de luxe edition of his writings.

231. CLEMENS TO ROGERS

London
25 June 1899

Prince of Wales Hell of a Hotel
Sunday

Dear Mr. Rogers:

I judge the Electric Spark will be arriving to-morrow, and I hope he will come here and educate himself in the knowledge of what an English private hotel is. There isn't a convenience known to civilization which it doesn't lack; there isn't a detail pertaining to its business which it isn't ignorant of; there is no attainable incompetence in the art of running a hotel which it hasn't acquired. It is always kept by a woman; there is no supervision, it takes care of itself and goes as you please. Its religion is, to skin whom it can catch.

We have hunted around and found a satisfactory *public* hotel where the cost is a third less, and we shall go there when we return to London a few months hence.

It was our purpose to remain in London till the end of July; but I want to turn the family loose on the Swedish Movement Cure for a change; so ⟨our⟩ passage is booked in a ship which leaves London for Gottenburg, Sweden, about 2 weeks hence (July 7.) The sanitarium is all alone by itself on a lake 4 hours from there. We expect to be there three or four months, then return to London, and finally leave for America in the winter or toward spring. It is a radical change of all the plans, you see, and cuts us out of our visit to Fairhaven, where you were going to foot all the bills, if I remember rightly. ⟨I am only doing this to save your pocket [very lightly canceled].⟩ ⟨No—on second thoughts I suppose I couldn't work that statement off on you at par.⟩

Kipling remained in town part of a day, and called, but I was out; then he went to his home. Doubleday came yesterday morning with a cable from Harper wanting to issue Tom Sawyer at 75 cents. I referred him to you. I had no objections, and did not think there was anything in the Bliss or Harper contracts that would be in the way, but I said you would be able to ⟨sett⟩ determine that point.

We are having a very good time here, but there is most too much of it for old second-hand people. We cannot leave before the 7th, on account of social engagements that can't well be canceled; but we have none after the 7th which cannot be dissolved.

Miss May ought to join us in Sweden and try that cure. I am sure of it. It fetched Poultney Bigelow [1] up out of the grave—his was an absolutely desperate case. He is a sound man, now, and blooming with health. *You* come and try it, too! Love to you all.

SLC

---

[1] Poultney Bigelow (1855–1954), American journalist and author, had been a correspondent for the London *Times* in the Spanish-American War in 1898.

232. CLEMENS TO ROGERS

London
3 July 1899

Dear Mr. Rogers:

I have been getting up my muscle all these past five days, and when I get hold of that young Eleck T. Rickspark I mean to make him think Sandow has arrived. He left your letter of introduction at Chatto's, but not his address; Miss May called yesterday and named her own hotel and also the one he is stopping at, but Mrs. Clemens entrusted the matter to her memory and that hotel has slipped out of it. I am hoping he will turn up to-morrow, for Miss May said he would. If he doesn't, I will start the police on his track. Why, his conduct is just scandalous—this comes of associating with Rice, you see.

Miss May was looking well—thoroughly well, and beautiful; and she was admirably bright and charming. She told us about you all, and said you thought of building a yacht to travel in between New York and Fairhaven. Don't discard that idea—and put in a berth for me. Miss May was to leave London this morning.

We shall leave for Sweden on the 7th, and be gone about three months. Meantime our address will be Chatto & Windus.

Doubleday said Harper wanted to issue Tom Sawyer at 75 cents. I liked the idea, but told him you would know whether there was anything in the various contracts to bar it; so he said he would refer the matter to you.

I have been rather rushing it for four weeks, but am brisk yet and healthy. To-morrow night is my last speech—4th of July.[1] That emancipates me from speech-making and then I shall be a free and independent citizen.

Sincerely Yours Ever

SLC

¹ Clemens's Notebook 32, TS pp. 56–57, shows he was busy in London. He dined at the Whitefriars, at the National Club, the Savage Club, with the New Vagabonds at King's Hall, and at the Sesame Club, to which he was given honorary membership. He lunched with the U.S. ambassador to Britain, Joseph Choate, and with Canon Basil Wilberforce; and he called on Sir Henry Irving. On 4 July he spoke before the American Society of London (see *MTS* [1923], p. 187).

233. CLEMENS TO ROGERS

Sanna
3 August 1899

Address, Chatto, etc London

Dear Mr. Rogers:

Yours of July 6 is just to hand. I wondered where it could have been spending its vacation; but I find by the N. Y. postmark that you didn't mail it until it was 14 days old. After it started it came a good gait, making the trip via London [to this vil]lage ¹ (Sanna, Sweden), in 14 [days to] the hour. ⟨No, I am wrong.⟩ [It we]nt to London in ⟨12⟩ 11 days, reaching [there Ju]ly 31, then to this place in 3 more. [I gue]ss I see what the trouble [was:] you were waiting to enclose [Harpe]r's letter about the cheap Tom [Saw]yer edition —and then you gave it up! For you didn't enclose it. You've been mixing your drinks again—how often I have implored you not to do that!

I had an impression (but wasn't sure) that Bliss's consent would be necessary before the Harpers could proceed with that project. I am quite content that Bliss should refuse it if he thinks it good judgment to do it.

I don't get over missing Harry. He had the news of years stored up in him, and I got not a bit of it. He didn't put his address on his card, either at our hotel or a[t Cha]tto's. I guess he thought I was misbehav[ing and that] his hotel people would get [suspicious] of him if doubtful charac[ters] called on him. But he wa[s wrong,] for

I was running mainly [with] clergy and making a reputa[tion that]
he would have envied and tried to [?spoil.] Miss Mai said he would
be in L[ondon] a fortnight; so I expected to catc[h him] without
any trouble; but by the time [I] had hunted him down with the
telephone he was gone.

Private.

Bok was mistaken. I think we were packing up for Sweden when
he called with Doubleday. I am unspeakably sorry to lose the steam
yachting[2] and the Fairhaven visit, and I wasn't *expecting* to lose
the whole scheme, but the Swedish project made a sudden and
radical change in our plans. You see, Jean's health has made no real
and [substan]tial progress in the past [?3 ye]ars. [N]one whatever.
We had tried the bath[s, and the do]ctors and everything—all no
good. [What s]hould we do? For one, I was [willing to] try anything that might turn [?the tide—] except Christian Science.

Just then Poultney Bigelow stepped up, [a]live and well: in fact
very robust and lively. I was aware that dysentery and the doctors
had been hard at work at him 7½ months, and that in the first days
of May his case had been given up as hopeless. I knew these things
to be strictly true. I knew that in the early part of May he had then
been for weeks in his bed, and was no longer able to turn over. I
had written him in February that he *must* find a ripe watermelon or
die—but he was not able to travel to the tropics, nor make a long
journey at all. As I don't believe a doctor can cure *any* really serious
disease except by ac[ciden]t, and that he can't *touch* dysentery
[whe]n it is bad, I suppose[d that he] was going to die, for certain.
[I was] very much astonished to se[e him] come thundering into
our p[lace, and in] his old-time boisterous [way ask] me to go with
him to a mi[dnight] supper and dance at an artist's s[tudio.]

He explained that his wife had hea[rd] of Kellgren and his
Swedish Movement C[ure] and had sent for him. Kellgren had
him out of bed in a day, without the use of medicines, and he
hadn't been in bed since, except for rest. He said he had gathered
strength fast, and was now as well as any one. I didn't go with him
to that party, but met him at a dinner party and dance a night or

two afterward, and at 2 in the morning he was still the livest dancer left in the gang. He writes me now from France that he is sound and well and can do 18 miles on his bicycle over indifferent ground without fatigue.

So I went down to Kellgren's London gymnasium and tried the treatment, and saw that it would prop a person up physically, whether it could cure disease or not. We decided to come here to the summer establishment and take the treatment 3 months. Jean and her mother and I have been at it 3 weeks, now and are quite reconciled to continue. I like it. It is vigorous exercise, and *other people do it for you.* Isn't that nice?

We take 20 minutes of it every morning. For the rest of the day I feel vigorous and frisky. If you lose your sleep it is no matter, the exercises set you up for the day in great style.

If I can believe these patients here, they get cured of all sorts of devilish diseases without the use of medicines. I have watched one case with much interest. It's a Frenchman. He arrived 3 weeks ago. For a year this wreck had not been able to sit or stand. His arms and legs were twisted and stiff, and mainly useless. I saw them begin work on him. The most they could force his ⟨le⟩ knees apart was 4 inches; they spread them 8, now. In ten days they had him standing on his feet, with the support of two canes. Day before yesterday (we all went on a trip to an island up the lake) he walked with his canes a good quarter of a mile, 300 yards of it up hill; drove from that point a couple of hours through the country with the rest; and then walked up [a] hill a hundred yards, and after dinner walked to the boat, a matter of 300 yards. I saw all this myself. ⟨He arrived here full of⟩

The patients tell such wonderful things that you half believe you have wandered into an asylum of Christian Science idiots. In some cases there's confirmation—the confirmation of one's eyes. We have it in the case of an old lady who came here when we did, with her port side paralysed. With a person to hold up that side she could creep along, but she couldn't stand alone. She's walking, now, by herself. I saw her at it yesterday. She passed along the road by our house—at a gravel-train gait, it is true, but she was *going,* anyway.

They claim to cure *any* disease that is not ⟨of⟩ cancer or other incurable malady.

I got them a chance to see what they could do with one of my old long-lasting bronchial coughs. They relieve it in ten minutes every morning, and I hea[r] no more of it until I get up with [a] loose and free bark next morning. This has been going on about a week, and I am obliged to confess that no medicine has ever given me a week of anything approaching such comfort. I got the cold by getting badly chilled in the lake and by repeating the chill by a similar bath the very next morning. The head-cold which followed was of a sort to insure me a month's hard coughing, under the old regime. I do not know how long the present ⟨cold⟩ cough will last, but it is not a matter of consequence, for they dispose of it in ten minutes every morning, and then for the rest of the day I am not aware that it is in me.[3]

This curative system is seldom heard of, even in London, where Kellgren its inventor has practiced it 25 years. Nothing about it has been in print, and the only way to hear of it is to run across one of the patients. It has not been advertised in any way. You have probably heard of *a* Swedish Movement Cure. [This is not that] one, and but little resembles it. There are families in London whose doctoring has been done exclusively by Kellgren for many years. I know one of them. They call him for any and all diseases.

I will keep watch as long as the [thi]ng looks promising, and if I get convinced that it is sound and safe I will let you know and you can send over any friends who have tried all other ways to get well of stubborn diseases, and we'll put them through the mill.

The fact is I *want* the thing to succeed, for I don't like medicines —and moreover I have but a pale and feeble confidence in them. There's an old Denver pox-patient here who is loaded to the eyes with mercury, and is a poisoned hulk. As between mercury and pox, which would you prefer? I guess there's no choice.

[I've sent my Christian Science] article to the Cosmopolitan and told Walker to send it to you if he doesn't want it.[4] I shan't print the rest of the series till I issue a book. The first article merely makes fun of Christian Science and Mrs. Eddy and her book, and stops there.

I have marked part of th[is] letter "private," because we do not want it known that Jean is ailing. If this treatment should definitely help her we shall continue it in London when we return thither the 28th of Sept. No doctor will ever do her any good; that is perfectly plain. The best in the world have had charge of her for 3 years and haven't made an inch of progress toward a cure.

I forgot my other experiment. No physician has ever helped my semi-annual itching piles with even a moment's relief; but I have a rather deadly quack medicine that can do it. These manipulations here relieved it promptly every day for a week. Promptly and thoroughly. It seems to have disappeared, now, but I am waiting to see.

God be wi' you!

SLC.

[P].S. I [several words missing] y to me, care of Chatto, as it will come very good.

---

¹ The margins of this letter have been partly destroyed. The editor has supplied appropriate conjectures based on the size of the missing fragments as well as the sense of what survives.

² Rogers, although he was a member of the New York Yacht Club, at this time "contented himself with chartering steam yachts for cruising purposes" (New York *Times,* 24 April 1901); later he purchased a cruising yacht of his own.

³ Clemens was not initially so enthusiastic about the Swedish treatment. Shortly after their arrival, he wrote on 12 July to Clara, who had remained in London, as from "Hell . . . (Sanna Branch)":

This is the daily itinerary:

8 to 10 a.m.	Inferior London coffee for the damned.
10 to 12 a.m.	"Treatment" for the damned.
12 to 2.	Pant and gasp and fight the flies.
2.	Dinner for the damned.
3, till 8, p.m.	Pant and gasp and fight the flies.
8	Supper and flies for the damned.
9 till 11.	Flies, fans and profanity.
11 p.m.	Bed. Tallow candles. Flies. No night—dim, pale-blue daylight all night (lat. 58 N.) Cool, and might be pleasant, but the flies stand watch-and-watch, and persecute the damned all night.

To Richard Watson Gilder, however, he wrote on 23 July 1899: "Damn all the other cures, including the baths and Christian Science and the doctors of the several schools—*this* is the satisfactory one! Every day, in 15 minutes it takes all the old age out of you and sends you forth feeling like a bottle of champagne that's just been uncorked" (Yale). He was especially pleased at what it had done for Jean:

> Jean has taken a week of Kellgren's Movement Cure and the improvement is so astonishing that we hardly venture to talk together about it lest it presently turn out to be only a transient flurry with nothing substantial about it. For two years, now, she has been obliged to take from one to three doses of bromide daily to conquer the daily absent-mindnessess. With her first treatment here she left off the bromide, and meantime has been absent-minded only twice, instead of 15 or 20 times, as formerly. Kellgren says bad attacks are in store, but that she must weather them without resorting to drugs (Notebook 32, TS pp. 57–58).

He recommended to the wives of Sir Henry Stanley and Alfred Dreyfus that they put their husbands under Kellgren's care.

[4] Clemens had already written John Brisben Walker on 30 July 1899: "Do you want this Christian Science article? If so, please send check to me. . . . But if you don't want it, will you please send it to H. H. Rogers, Esq / 26 Broadway, New York, and greatly oblige me." "Christian Science and the Book of Mrs. Eddy" appeared in the *Cosmopolitan* for October 1899.

234. CLEMENS TO ROGERS

Sanna
22 August 1899

Dear Mr. Rogers—

I have looked over the originals of the Dream Sweetheart and Wapping Alice, and perceive that the first does not convey my idea clearly at all; and so, for me it has no value and must remain unpublished. And I perceive that a part of Alice needs re-writing —so *she* isn't publishable ⟨till that happens⟩ as she stands. She'll never get that re-writing. She should have applied while I was interested in her—and she didn't. I wash *my* hands of the business.

⟨I wish I could afford to⟩

We shall reach London 9 days after Harry has sailed. I don't know what has gone with our luck. We miss fire on Harry at both ends of his trip, and the same with Joe Twichell and his wife. [They] arrived in London the night before we left; gave us no notice, and we missed them; and they are to sail for America about a fortnight before we return to England. Of course *this* is Providence's affair, Joe being a parson; but I don't know who is running Harry. Goodness knows I hope it is not the other firm, though deep down I have my shudders when I think.

Jean's health booms along here ⟨for⟩ ⟨and⟩ in the most surprising and gratifying way. For the first time in 3 years we go to bed untroubled, and get up the same. We comprehend that trouble must come, and several times before her cure is perfect, but we do not bother about that—she is on the safe road. I hope we can go home before spring. It looks like that, but of course predictions are not in order yet.

I have a very good time here ⟨prac⟩ experimenting with the system in my own person and watching the patients. I wish you were here and had about a hundred diseases to experiment on, so that I could keep the record. They would knock them out of you as fast as you could call game.

It would be splendid to be yachting around with you these days; but you wait till I come. It will be cold, then, but that is nothing, we'll go South; I know where there's some warm weather.

I am very glad my financial affairs are in such good shape. By George they were ill enough when you took hold of them, doctor. I think you and Kellgren stand at the head of the profession: you for a sick bank account and he for a sick body; it is the strongest team I know.

I've found a stunning unknown artist here, and I mean to ask the Century to boom him.[1] And I'll help. His pictures ought to sell. They are water-color peasant-heads, true to a hair, and just delicious for their humor, *I* think.

With best regards to all of you—

SLC

---

[1] That same day Clemens wrote to Richard Watson Gilder of the *Century,* urging that Gilder arrange an exhibition of the artist's work in New York. His "discovery," Kapten O. Brander of Vesteras, Sweden, was being treated by Kellgren: "One of the patients here whose left arm had become useless from gout and who has had its functions restored here (it has taken two seasons, but it is

accomplished), is a retired military officer of 50, who teaches drawing in a public school in an obscure Swedish town. Now *I* think he is a find! I think that when he makes a water-color peasant-head he gets a something or other into the countenance that is just delicious. And true?—true to the last detail" (22 August 1899, Yale).

235. Clemens to Rogers

Sanna
3 September 1899

Dear Mr. Rogers:

I wonder what it is you've got your financial eye on now—for I guessed from a remark you made that you are watching another combination. Don't leave me out; I want to be in, with the other capitalists. I was forgetting that I am a capitalist, and I think Mrs. Clemens is in danger of never thoroughly realising it, for I found she was neglecting a part of this treatment here because she had to pay extra for it if she took it on an emergency in her own house.

I have been under a wrong impression this long time, and she has been correcting me this morning. I thought it was held that Jean could be cured in six months, but she says no, it was to be six months *possibly,* but it might take 9 and even 12. It puts off America a good while, and makes me tired to think of it.

An outsider would think Jean is already cured. Her health has blossomed out in the most extraordinary way, and she is full of life and go and energy and activity. Her disease still slightly manifests itself for a minute or two, mornings, this past week, but she has not had an "attack" for 35 days, which is an amazing thing. She *has* to have them, and *will* have them, but maybe the intervals will be wide between—I hope so. This morning the promise of an attack was strong, but it passed off soon and then she was in as fine condition as ever. It is 54 days since she took a dose of any kind of medicine (it was the morning after we arrived here.)

The Official Records of the Joan of Arc Trials (in Rouen and the Rehabilitation) have at last been translated ⟨well⟩ *in full* into English, and I was asked to write an Introduction, and have just

finished it after a long and painstaking siege of work. I am to help
edit it, and my name will go on the title page with those of the two
translators. I expect it to be ever so readable and interesting a book.
I am offering it to Bliss as a subscription book, and then to be added
to the Uniform Edition later.[1]

Canon Wilberforce wants to start a Joan of Arc cult in England,
and of course his great position will enable him to do it. He wants
to start the boom with a lecture on Joan in the winter, at St. James's
Hall, with all the [gr]eat and influential people present; [(he
would] contract to have them there), and he wanted me to do the
lecture, but *that* wouldn't do; the subject is too grave. If *he* will do
the lecture I will play second fiddle and talk 15 minutes.

This is a grand place to build up a person's muscle. I can lick
you, now. Anyway I can lick Harry, and I mean to do it when I get
my hands on him.

P'raps I have bothered you enough for this time.

Sincerely Yours

SLC

Well, I missed seeing Laurence Hutton, too—⟨They all⟩ along
with Harry and the Twichells. Talcott is coming, now; and *he* will
be gone from London a couple of days before we get there.

[1] On 26 September 1899 Bliss responded to Clemens:
I have just received your letter of Sept. 3rd in regard to the JOAN OF ARC
scheme, and I should judge that it might result in considerable of a boom. It
seems to me that while the trial book would be a very attractive one to the
reader, it would be for *your* best interest to have a regular edition of the book
go through the Harpers' hands; inasmuch as they issued your first JOAN OF
ARC book, it is natural that this should run with greater ease through the
same mill, and it would also avoid confusion in the minds of buyers as to
where to buy both books, if they wanted to, and would result in helping along
the sale for both. You should, however, reserve the entire rights for us to use
the book in the Uniform set without having to pay the Harpers any royalty
or their having any rights in the plates which we should make; for, as I have
written you before, the royalties that we are paying on the present Harper
books cut into the profits altogether too much. They will be satisfied to take
the book for their own sales if the condition is made to them. The above is
my honest opinion about the proposed book, but of course we could do it by
subscription, and make a good sale of it. . . .
Neither Harper & Brothers nor the American Publishing Company published the
Official Records of the Joan of Arc Trial which appeared in 1902 as *Jeanne*

d'Arc: Maid of Orleans, Deliverer of France. Clemens's introduction was printed as "Saint Joan of Arc," *Harper's Magazine,* December 1904. For a full account of the project, see *MTHL,* pp. 708–711.

236. KATHARINE HARRISON TO CLEMENS

New York
3 October 1899

Dear Mr. Clemens:

The enclosed letter [1] came this morning addressed to you in my care, and Mr. Rogers suggested that I open it. For your better understanding of the manuscript, he suggested that I translate it, and I enclose same herewith.

With kindest regards, I am,

Yours truly,

K. I. Harrison

[1] The enclosure was a typed copy of a letter of 30 September 1899 to Clemens from J. Henry Wiggin of Roxbury, Massachusetts, who was grateful for Clemens's articles on Christian Science. He had been one of the "salaried . . . polisher[s] of Mrs. Eddy's Bible, the polisher to whom you do such ample justice." He described "wading through" Mrs. Eddy's "extraordinary sentences" which he, as polisher had had to "lick into shape"; but he declined to bore Clemens, he said, with extensive descriptions of "behind the scenes in Christian Science."

237. CLEMENS TO ROGERS

London
4 October 1899

Dear Mr. Rogers—

Yours of Sept. 22 has arrived, and was very welcome, for I did not know but that you were ill. I am sorry your mother is not well, and glad you have her in your own house where she can have your personal care. I often think of her, and I beg to be remembered to

her, with my sincerest regards and homage. You can assure her that
I consider myself quite competent to defend Satan, for I have
known him ever since I was a boy, and have transacted much
business with him. I think I am his pet—though I know this
sounds like bragging.

I am glad you settled that copyright business—I think, myself,
that the Harpers had no stake in it.[1]

If you will manage to spread it around quietly that Clemens,
Rogers & Co. are solvent, it may have a good effect on the market. It
has a blamed good effect on *me,* and makes me proud and overbearing.

I shall be glad if you will order a study to be coopered up on the
yacht, so that I can take up my regular quarters on board next
season. I wish Mrs. Clemens and I could have been there to
complete your party. We should have enjoyed the excursions very
thoroughly. It was pretty dull for the madam at Sanna, but not for
me: I was at work. It was a nice quiet place for scribbling.

We arrived from Sweden Saturday, but found the birds flown—
Miss Mai and Harry. I feared it, for I had written Miss Mai from
Sanna in answer to her letter, and as I didn't hear from her again I
guessed they were gone. Harry was afraid to wait for me.

We may have to continue Jean's cure ⟨several⟩ 6 or 9 months,
and so we are hunting for comfortable ⟨and⟩ quarters which shall
not overstrain the purse; and they are not easy to find, for we need
to be near Kellgren's place and that is in a high-priced region.

As I am deep in my work and shan't want to be disturbed, I am
planning to keep out of society and out of the newspapers. I am the
burnt child—I don't want to get into the society-fire any more.

To-day you are out in the yacht viewing the first great cup-race.
By gracious, I should like to be along![2]

We both join in kindest regards to you and Mrs. Rogers and in
thanks for the good times you would have given us if we had been
home in the yachting season.

Yrs Ever

SLC

I think I *will* let Harper issue a new volume of short things on the usual royalty (15% up to 5,000 and then 20%) if he says Bliss won't be hampered in using the vol. in the Uniform edition. I have hinted that, in answer to Alden's letter, but haven't *promised*.

Alden didn't say *when* they wanted to issue the new vol.[3] If for the Xmas trade, the time is rather short, I guess. If they should apply to you, and say there is hurry, and that they will satisfy Bliss, authorize them to go ahead with the book if that is your judgment. A new book gives new life to the old ones. I don't see that it could interfere with Bliss's Uniform and de luxe.

P.S. Oct. 4. '99. As I said yesterday [4] (and also in my letter to Harper) I don't want Harper to hamper Bliss in adding the new short-story book to the Uniform. I think, also, that Harper should have no ownership in the plates made for the new book for the Uniform, and receive no royalty from Bliss on the book. I have the instinct that *I* pay part of the present royalty which goes from Bliss to Harper. In any case I want Harper to have no interest of any kind in the book when added to the Uniform. Ain't that your judgment?

What unspeakable sharks those Harpers are! Bliss intimates that they will expect me to pay them a royalty on the English sets of my Uniform.[5] When they charge Bliss a royalty it is merely robbery; but when they charge me, it is robbery and fornication combined.

You are watching the yacht race again to-day—lucky man!

SLC

[1] Frank Bliss had written Clemens on 15 September 1899:
Regarding the English edition, there seems to be a delay in getting the matter of the copyright with Harper settled. I do not know yet how it is coming out, although Rogers told me the last time I saw him that he thought it would be fixed satisfactorily. It is in his hands and has been for some considerable time, and I suppose that he will get it fixed just as soon as he can. I don't like to annoy him by crowding too hard. I have just written Chatto & Windus that we would proceed to get the books out, and do our utmost to get them over there at the earliest possible moment. . . . There is one change which they have asked, however, which is quite serious. They want all our copyright marks taken off, and our lawyer here tells us it will not do; that we shall imperil our copyrights here if we issue the books that way. He says notwithstanding the books are made for the English market, that we are really

the publishers of the books, and they are virtually issued from us in this country, and we shall lose our copyrights if we take the marks off. Harper & Brothers insisted to Bliss on 19 September 1899 (Salm) that the "copyright notice is essential for the protection of the books." Bliss assured Harper & Brothers on 20 September 1899 (Salm): "Proper notices will . . . appear in all copies of the English Edition."

[2] The America's Cup yacht races were being run in the waters off Sandy Hook, New Jersey.

[3] H. M. Alden had written Clemens on 14 September 1899 to suggest the publication by Harper & Brothers of two volumes: a book of stories, with "The Man That Corrupted Hadleyburg" as its "splendid *pièce de résistance,*" and a book of articles.

[4] Clemens mistakenly gave both parts of this letter the same date.

[5] On 17 October 1899 Harper & Brothers would inform the American Publishing Company: "We have just learned from Mr. Clemens that there is some misunderstanding in your mind in regard to royalty upon the copies of the Uniform Edition of Mark Twain's works supplied to England. . . . We understand that the copies of the Uniform Edition supplied by you to Messrs. Chatto & Windus are sold at cost of manufacture, and therefore, as a matter of course, we would not expect to receive royalty upon them."

238. CLEMENS TO ROGERS

London
9 November 1899

Dear Mr. Rogers:

My temper is under a heavy strain this morning, for I find that the Kellgren system (under the new name of "Osteopathy,") is being ⟨succ⟩ practiced all over America! If I had only found this out in September, instead of yesterday, we should all have been located in New York the 1st of October—and we should have had that Fairhaven visit into the bargain. We are here *only* to have the Kellgren treatment for Jean, yet we could get it in several places in New York; and now we are tied here till April or May, because we have taken the flat for 7½ months and have paid half of the rent in advance.

I happened to write my nephew about the treatment, and now I find that his mother has been taking it several months in Buffalo. She sends me circulars and pamphlets which show that Osteopathy is exactly the Kellgren treatment.

There are establishments at 156 Fifth avenue; 107 East 23d;

and 136 Madison avenue, corner 31st street. I beg you to go in at one of those places and take the treatment for a month, whether there is anything the matter with you or not. It will set you up and make you gay. I wish you would take it *two* months. It will cost you but a trifle of time—15 or 20 minutes two or three times a week—3 times is best.

And when there *is* anything the matter with you, send for those people. You can't possibly regret it. From Miss Harrison's last I am hoping you are well again, now—but go to those people and get yourself set up in good shape. They will take the lassitude and fatigue out of you and enable you to work double tides if you want to.

I took the treatment daily during 2 months. I began again 3 days ago because I was not sleeping well and was seedy and needed freshening up for work. I am all right again, now, and shall stop after a few days.

Go and freshen up—please don't say no.

Agreey etc

SLC

239. Clemens to Rogers

London

17 November 1899

Dear Mr. Rogers:

We have a notion that it will be best to put the money into a safe thing which stands a chance to rise in value,—according to one of your suggestions—and so, when you find one I hope you will empty it in.

I am in accord with you on the Mt. Morris suggestion. When I get home I will proceed in that way.

I am very glad to hear that your mother is up and about again, and I beg to be kindly remembered to her. I am not expecting her to lose courage; I am the same age that she is—when I am not 25 years older—and I am keeping up *my* courage, these days.

You are keeping up yours, too. Putting yourself into that old poker-sharp's hands!—a man embittered by his billiard-defeats and poker-defeats, and in all sorts of ways. Rice is going to get even with you this time—he holds all the cards.

I am going out and walk home, now and enjoy the fog. You couldn't cut it with an axe.

Sincerely Yours

SLC

240. CLEMENS TO ROGERS

London
20 November 1899

Dear Mr. Rogers:

I know that that which was to come has come, and that your first friend is gone; a release for her—for death is always that, whether it come early or late—but an affliction for you.[1] She was good and fine in her nature, and beautiful in her life, and this is your best comfort in your loss—no words of mine or another can add to it. I am sorry I could not see her once more before she was called to her rest, for she was always good to me, and I think she had a friendly place in her heart for me. I wish you would give yourself a rest, now, for your anxieties have worn upon you and you need it. There will be no competent recuperative rest for you there in the crush of business—come away from it; come abroad with Mrs. Rogers and forget and put behind you the wear and tear of life for a while. The profit will be great and sure, and neither of you can regret it. Come to London. Will you? Won't you? Write and say you will.

In the deepest and sincerest sympathy,

S. L. Clemens

---

[1] Rogers's mother, Mary Eldredge Huttleston Rogers, had died in Fairhaven on 9 November 1899. She was 88.

241. CLEMENS TO ROGERS

London
7 December 1899

Dear Mr. Rogers:

If I remember rightly, my Harper book-contracts provide that the Harpers can cancel them at the end of 10 years, if they wish, but that I cannot cancel them at all.[1]

If this is so, won't you ask them to add a clause extending to me the privilege which they enjoy, so that I can cancel the contracts ⟨of existing⟩ at the end of 10 years from the day they were originally entered into if I like.

There can be nothing unfair about this.

Sincerely Yours

SLC

Dear Mr. Rogers: [2]

If you find that my memory in this matter is correct, won't you send the foregoing letter to the Harpers, or communicate its prayer to them in your own way?

And if they refuse my request, won't you ask them to let me withdraw my proposed new book of short things from their hands?

If I had stuck to my original purpose of signing no contract except the usual Houghton & Mifflin contract which allows the author to cancel at the end of 5 years, I would hand ⟨my⟩ the Harper books to Doubleday & McClure, now, for the Harpers can't sell books and have proved it.

I only gave them the proposed volume of short stories [3] because Robert McClure told me it was the same as giving it to Doubleday & McClure—otherwise I should not have given it to Harper. Now that the Harper-McClure combination has fallen through I think I am morally entitled to withdraw the book if I like. And that is what

I want to do if the Harpers decline to amend my contracts and make them fair and just to both parties.

Sincerely Yours

SLC

[1] Clemens was correct about this; when the contracts were drawn, Harper & Brothers insisted on the ten-year cancellation clause for itself, but no such privilege was granted to Clemens (see Appendix A).

[2] Clemens continued this 7 December letter on another page of stationery, which he numbered at the top, "2."

[3] *The Man That Corrupted Hadleyburg and Other Stories and Essays* was published by Harper & Brothers in 1900.

242. CLEMENS TO ROGERS

London
11 December 1899

Dear Mr. Rogers:

I didn't really want to write for the World, but I was loafing for a few days, and they furnished me a Text and asked for only 2,000 words and offered $500, and I thought I might as well put in an afternoon on it.[1]

But in any case if I had sent it to the Harpers they wouldn't have wanted it enough to pay the half of that. They only offered $300 (through Robert McClure, here) for the thing I wrote about "Boyhood's Dreams" and I should have withheld it, only Robert increased the offer to $400, and I let him take it. It was written for the "Round Table"; but Robert said that the R. T. had been suspended; so I told him to ship it and let the Harper-McClure combination put it where they pleased.[2]

The cablegrams say the Harpers are straightening up and going on with their business.[3] I wish them success—though they advertise everybody's books but mine. I don't see why they should select me for a victim in preference to the others. So far as I know, I have done nothing to earn or justify this treatment. They urge all books upon Christmas buyers but mine.

I am wishing you all the happiness and prosperity due at Christmas to the best man I know except one. Modesty does not allow me to name that one, and I suppose you couldn't guess in a year.

Yrs Ever

SLC

[1] On 30 October 1899 Clemens had written H. M. Alden:

The N.Y. World asked for a sketch of 2,000 words on Lying, for $500. And I wrote it day before yesterday, and if I still like it after examining it in type-copy to-morrow, I will let them have it. I think it will be 3,000 words before I get done fussing at it and injecting nonsense. Maybe the World may object to letting it go in the book; I don't know; I have never written anything for the World before, except a cablegram (TS in MTP).

"My First Lie and How I Got Out of It" appeared in the *World*, 10 December 1899.

[2] After "My Boyhood Dreams" appeared in *McClure's Magazine,* January 1900, Clemens was delighted to receive from S. S. McClure on 11 January an extra $100 for the sketch, bringing its price up to the $500 which Clemens had considered proper.

[3] Harper & Brothers was being reorganized; Col. George Harvey became president of the firm and remained in that position for the rest of Clemens's life.

243. CLEMENS TO KATHARINE HARRISON

London

21–22 December 1899

Dear Miss Harrison:

The "World" wants an article per week—1,000 to 2,000 words —for a year—any subject, serious or otherwise. I declined, of course—no sane man would do that. But I was already engaged, anyway—as far as I ever mortgage myself—that is, I was engaged to offer all articles *first* in another quarter—in case I write any. I'm not going to write any that will be declined in that quarter. I finished a couple lately which I much like—to-wit, "How the Chimney-Sweep got his Message to the Emperor"—and "The Death-Disk." [1]

It's awful here!—half of our friends are in mourning, and the hearts of the other half stop beating when they see a newsboy.[2] And the fogs and the day-long darkness! and my dreary attempts to feel cheerful, and the people's attempts—on the street—to *look* so—it's dismal times!

I am very glad you have not written me about Mrs. Rogers—you said it would mean that she was better. I hope she is well by this time, and that Mr. Rogers is over his anxiety.

If any of you or all of you *want* a Merry Christmas, I wish it you. I don't—I couldn't stand it; it would make me shudder. This is no place for merriment.

Sincerely Yours

SLC

P.S. I've answered Harry Harper's letter about the 2 new-proposed vols.

It is most kind of Mr. Lancaster,[3] but I am never going to lecture again, I hope.

Dec. 22/99.

P.S. to yesterday's letter.

I've withheld the Harper letter, and ⟨will⟩ hereby enclose it to you, as his letter was to you, and as I don't know what may have been happening in the Harper affairs since Harper wrote his letter (Dec. 4.)[4] You will know whether Mr. Rogers thinks it best to forward my letter to Harry Harper or to withhold it and send him the substance of it.

It is probably best for me to keep in the background until I hear how the Harpers are going to answer my proposition lately sent through Mr. Rogers, that they ⟨reduce⟩ put a five-year limit into all my contracts (from date of that proposition).

I wish I had not given them this book. If I had it back I would give it to them only on concession of the five-year limit on all the books. They are a tough lot, with their shabby one-sided contracts, and I wish I had kept out of their shop.

Yrs sincerely

SLC

¹ "How the Chimney-Sweep Got the Ear of the Emperor" and "The Man with a Message for the Director-General" were printed as "Two Little Tales," *Century Magazine,* November 1901; "The Death-Disk" appeared in *Harper's Magazine,* December 1901.

² The British were suffering severe reversals in the Boer War.

³ Probably Charles Lancaster of Liverpool, a old friend of Rogers's.

⁴ Clemens annotated the copy of the letter from J. Henry Harper (Salm) before he returned it to New York:

Dec. 4th, 1899.

Dear Sir:

We beg leave to enclose herewith our plan for dividing the two volumes of Mr. Clemens' articles, stories, etc., which we are proposing to publish in the Spring. You will note that, among the stories, we include the two from the COSMOPOLITAN of 1893, "Is he Living; or Is He Dead?" and "An Eskimo Maiden's Romance." Mr. Alden referred to these two stories in his first letter to Mr. Clemens on the subject (September 14th, a copy of which we sent you) but Mr. Clemens made no direct reference to them in his replies, although his general permission, by cable and letter, *seemed to include them.* [Written at the bottom, with a line drawn to above underlined phrase: *"Correct. Use them. SL. Clemens."*] Before doing anything further, we should be glad to know positively whether in your judgment they are available for book publication by us in this way. We should be grateful for any suggestion which you may make to us as to the order of the material, etc., etc.

Very truly yours,
J. Henry Harper.

H. H. Rogers, Esq.

Christian Science, three papers	16,500		
In Memoriam 1 page [added by Clemens: "—put this on *last* page of the book. SLC."]			
About Play Acting	5,000		
Concerning the Jews	9,000		
Diplomatic Pay and Clothes	4,650		
Stirring Times in Austrian Parliam't	12,000		
Austrian Edison [Clemens's "—a *Postscript*"]	1,000	50,150	
Great Republic's Peanut Stand		8,000	58,150.
The Man that Corrupted Hadleyburg (illustrated)	22,000		
My Debut as a Literary Person	13,500		
Private Hist. of a Campaign that failed	7,000		
London Times of 1904	4,000		
Appetite Cure	4,300	50,800	
The First Lie		3,250	
Is He Living, or Is He Dead?		3,500	
Eskimo Maiden's Romance		4,000	61,550.

Clemens labeled "Austrian Edison" as "2" and "London Times of 1904" as "1" and wrote in the left margin between them: "Add No. 2 to No. 1 as a postscript. SLC."

244. CLEMENS TO ROGERS

London
26 December 1899

Dear Mr. Rogers:

If you approve, won't you please send the enclosed to Harry Harper and see what comes of it?

In withdrawing these books [1] I am not inventing a precedent, but following one invented by the Harpers. I entered into a detailed agreement with them whereby they were to take my Webster & Co books and add to them the Bliss books from time to time as the old copyrights fell in and restored the books to me. The contract was written out in accordance with the agreement; then after reflection, and consultation with their wonderful lawyer, they blandly withdrew and declined to sign. I am withdrawing now, in my turn.

If they are willing to reorganize that old contract and make the fairnesses equal and just and Christianlike all around, I am satisfied —otherwise I must go elsewhere with the proposed new volumes of short things, for I will not publish any more books under that old arrangement.

The amendments which I claim and ask for are these:

1. Their control of these new books and the old ones to continue 5 years from Jan 1, 1900; after that, either party to be privileged to cancel the contract at any time by giving 6 months' previous notice in writing.

2. The Harpers to have no property in translations and dramatisations of my books.

3. They to pay 6 per cent interest on moneys due me from the date when it becomes due until payment 4 months later.

Will you be generous, as usual, and let me put this new burden on your shoulders?

If there is anything unfair about this proposition I do not see where it is.

If they decline I would like the 2 new volumes to be put into Doubleday & McClure's hands.

———

I hope Mrs. Rogers is well again, and that you are having a cheerfuler Christmas over there than we are having here. Mrs. Clemens is in bed with influenza—this is the 6th day—a bad attack; and there is fog, and mud, and everybody in mourning for friends dead or wounded in South Africa.

As ever and always

Sincerely Yours

SL Clemens

[1] Clemens apparently wanted to withdraw his books from Harper & Brothers if they refused to grant him the five-year cancellation clause, as well as other privileges, in a revised contract. Subsequently he either recognized the hopelessness or the unreasonableness of his demands, or perhaps he took heart on hearing of Col. Harvey's reorganization of the company; at any rate, after his next note to Miss Harrison (letter 245), he does not mention it again.

245. CLEMENS TO KATHARINE HARRISON

London

8 January 1900

Dear Miss Harrison:

I feel quite sure that this [1] is from my contract with <i>Bliss</i>. I think you will find that the Harper contract does not afford me these protections, nor indeed any protections at all.

I don't care to have a copy of the Harper contract, but I hope you will examine it and see if there is any way for me to get hold of my Harper books—which there <i>isn't,</i> I guess.

Yrs Ever

SLC

Bliss paid me $10,000 in advance on "Following the Equator," but I had no advance-money from Harper.

---

[1] This note is written at the top and bottom and in the margin of a sheet which reproduced Section XIV of the agreement of 31 December 1896 between Livy and Clemens and the American Publishing Company (see Appendix C) and Sections V and VI of the agreement of 31 December 1896 between Harper & Brothers and the American Publishing Company and Mrs. Clemens (see Appendix B).

246. CLEMENS TO ROGERS

London
8 January 1900

Dear Mr. Rogers:

It was splendid to get that good long letter—it was the next best thing to seeing you in person and having a handshake. I should like *that* mighty well.

When I arrive, Mrs. Rogers and I will arrange a scheme. There won't be any competition, for I am not going to read or lecture for any other agency. I don't suppose I am competent to talk in a big theatre, any more, but there is voice enough for the largest drawing room we can find; and we will invite the rich and charge war prices for tickets.[1] Something swell, is the idea.

I am strongly hoping we may get home the middle of May; and yet there is this objection: that we should have to hunt summer quarters at once; therefore we may end by remaining here till next God knows when! I can't endure the thought of it. I am tired to death of this everlasting exile. We have this flat until the middle of May, and must pay for it, and therefore stick it out.

That is very nice news from Miss Mai. We wish her all possible happiness, and shall keep her secret.[2] Harry next, I suppose. Very well, let him have his way; I am coming to take his place in the office anyway; I see that he is too indolent—it injures the business. Energy is what is wanted in that position.

If we come in May, all right—charter the yacht; it is my intention to pay the whole expense. I shall keep you and the family in good style, and only charge you enough to level up. Some people would want to get a profit out of a guest, but I am not that sort. We must make a long trip; it is the best of all ways to build up mental and bodily health.

I trust I am properly sorry for people who get hit by a panic and have to sacrifice their good stocks, but if you have been buying them in for me it would be sinful in me to be too much sorry. Your account of the depression in the Xmas traffic tallies with the condition of things here, where the war has taken all gaiety out of the people and a smile is a forgotten aspect. For one instance, as a reflection of Tiffany's experience: Whiteley has not booked a single order for February in the matter of feasts, balls and blow-outs. Last year he booked 400 of that kind of orders for February. I am sorry you have had a hard time the past weeks, but glad you were able to tide-over your friends and save them; and they are pretty glad themselves, I reckon.

The thing that beguiled me with the "World" was the fact that a year ago they captured some mighty big writers for Xmas. I jumped to the conclusion that the paper had become respectable. I don't intend to get caught again.

Last night I was trying to guess the size of the Rice children, and your letter comes to-day and posts me.

Two weeks ago Mrs. Clemens was guilty of an incredible imprudence, for a grown-up person, and by consequence was promptly taken down with a heavy triple attack—influenza, bronchitis, and an affected lung. She weakened, and wanted a doctor called, but I dissuaded her; it seemed to me that the case was too serious for any risk-running of that sort. She is up and around and all right, now, (and has taken no medicine); but if I had allowed her to have her way she would be like some other influenza-patients I am acquainted with—booked for the season or the grave. Here, this winter, the influenza is just deadly. I am not afraid of doctors in ordinary or trifling ailments, but in a serious case I should not allow any one to persuade me to call one. Our Susy died of cerebro-spinal menengitis—and as soon as it manifested itself, her physicians gave her up. It was assassination through ignorance.

Kellgren would have cured her without any difficulty. The menengitis manifested itself on a Friday at noon; her doctors immediately
told her friends that the case was now hopeless, and they made no
further effort—which was quite right, for they could only have
done damage, which is their main trade. She lived until noon the
following Tuesday. I have seen Kellgren's performances daily for
six months, and I know that what he cannot do for a patient, those
licensed quacks need not attempt. It is my conviction that outside
of certain rather restricted limitations they are all quacks without
an exception.

Best luck and best wishes to you all.

Sincerely Yours,

SLC

[1] Clemens did, however, often speak publicly after his return to New York on
15 October 1900; which of these occasions was for the charity in which Mrs.
Rogers was interested has not been determined.

[2] Mai Huttleston Rogers, Rogers's youngest daughter, was to marry William
Robertson Coe, a New York insurance broker on 4 June 1900.

247. CLEMENS TO ROGERS

London
13 January 1900 [1]

Dear Mr. Rogers:

S. S. McClure is here and has made me a proposition.[2] As I
wanted to ask your advice, I have postponed my answer to the 1st of
March.

He is going to start a new magazine next fall, whose complexion
is to be peculiarly American; its writers to be nearly all of that
nationality; and one of its projects is to help hatch out and develop
the rising young American literature.

He wants me to be its editor, with my name on the cover. After
the matter for a number of the mag. has been selected by a staff of
sub-editors, I am to go over it and veto any of it that I do not

approve. This would occupy me one or two days per month. I am not required to do any other work.

When I sign the contract I am to receive a tenth part of the stock, fully paid up and non-assessable.

At the beginning of the second year I am to receive a twentieth of the stock; and at the beginning of the third year I am to receive another twentieth—these twentieths also to be paid up and non-assessable. First and last, one-fifth of the stock.

I am to receive $5,000 a year (paid monthly) for 5 years—not as salary, but guaranty. That is, I am to have that, anyway, even if my profits fail to reach that sum. *He* thinks my profit will reach $20,000 a year by the third year.

Whatever I write for the magazine is to be paid for, extra, at the rate of $150 per magazine-page of 1000 words, whether the article be long or short. But I am not required to write, except when I choose. And I am to be free and independent in my movements, live where I please, and go and come as I choose, arranging the duration of my absences to suit myself.

If I retire in the first year, I have only my permanent tenth share; if I retire in my second year, I keep that year's twentieth share also; if I retire in the third year I carry with me the whole accumulation—a permanent one-fifth of the stock, non-assessable.

I am very much in love with the idea. The American writers of highest repute are to be secured for me as contributors. *Now* then, Uncle Henry, give me your very best judgment on this matter, for I greatly value it, and am depending on you.

Yours Sincerely,

SL Clemens

---

¹ Clemens miswrote the year as "1990." The letter is on stationery headed "30, Wellington Court, / Albert Gate."

² After a personal conference with Clemens, McClure on 11 January 1900 put his propositions in writing. He wanted, first, to obtain control of Clemens's books published by Harper & Brothers. Then he would (1) publish all of Clemens's future works, for which he was willing to arrange a five-year contract at a royalty to Clemens of 20 per cent of the published price; (2) pay $150 per thousand words for sketches and stories of whatever length; (3) appoint Clemens editor of a department of miscellaneous contributions in the proposed magazine and allow Clemens 20 per cent of the annual profits of the magazine for a guaranteed profit

of $25,000 over a period of five years. These terms were later revised to those mentioned above.

Clemens responded enthusiastically (see *MTB*, pp. 1099–1101), but McClure later modified some of his expectations, particularly about the amount of editorial labor to be expected of Clemens. (See Peter Lyon, *Success Story: The Life and Times of S. S. McClure* [New York, 1963], pp. 182–185.) On 28 February 1900, McClure wrote: "When I came to think the matter over, there is practically no instance where the editors-in-chief of a magazine are out of practically physical contact with their business"; thereafter, Clemens, advised by Rogers, lost interest.

248. ROGERS TO CLEMENS

New York
26 January 1900

My Dear Clemens:

I have your favor of the 8th, also the one of the 13th inst. I informed Mrs. Rogers what you said in regard to that grand Entertainment, and you may consider yourself booked. You certainly must come home in the Spring. We cannot have you away any longer. I am seriously contemplating the chartering of a yacht, in the expectation that you will look after the commissary department. It was not run to my satisfaction last year, and I want a skilful man at the head, if I follow the business.

I have read with interest your complimentary opinion of Doctors, and when I have the courage, I shall read it to our mutual friend.[1] At present it would be dangerous.

Now the important letter concerning which you ask my advice: If the scheme is to be just as you express it, I believe it would be well for you to make an arrangement with McClure, but I cannot consent to your making the trade without having a hand in it myself. I am going to have a copy made of your letter, and send it back with this, so that you may know just what you have written me, and what I have consented to. I do all this, because I know I shall have most of the work to do in editing the Magazine, and I am sure you will not object to that, in view of the many duties you will be called upon to perform at my office. I would not advise your spending that twenty thousand dollars that he thinks you will get at the end of the third year. I know you have a lot of sporting blood in your veins, and so suggest that you sell that twenty thousand at a discount of 25 or 50%, if you can find a purchaser on the spot. Joking aside, I think it would be a nice business for you. It would keep you occupied, and I am sure you would make a success of it. One thing that I shall insist upon, however, if I have anything to do in the matter, and it is this: that when you have made up your mind on the subject, you will stick to it. I have not found in your composition that element of stubbornness, which is a constant source of embarrassment to me in all friendly and social ways, but which, when applied to certain lines of business, brings in the dollars and fifty cent pieces. If you accept the position, of course that means that you have got to come to this country. If you do, the yachting business will be a success.

We are all well at home. Our new grandson is getting along in great shape.[2] I understand he has told his first lie, and promises to place himself on an equality with the older hands at the business.

Regards to the family

Yours sincerely

HH Rogers [3]

[1] Dr. Rice.
[2] Henry Rogers Broughton was born on 1 January 1900.
[3] The letter is typewritten, except for the last eleven words, the closing, and the signature, which are in Rogers's hand.

249. CLEMENS TO ROGERS

London
5 February 1900

30 Wellington Court
Knightsbridge

Private

Dear Mr. Rogers:

I mark it private because I want to explain what keeps us over here so long—the reason being one which a family conceals from even its friends as long as it can, let alone the world. Jean's head got a bad knock when she [was] 8 or 9, by a fall. Seven years ago she showed capricious changes of disposition which we could not account for; and four years ago the New York experts pronounced her case *epilepsy*. This we learned when we got back from around the world. We put her into the hands of the world's head expert in Vienna, who said that in some cases this disease had been outgrown, but that he knew of no authentic instance of its cure by physicians.

Here in London we heard of Kellgren. He said he could cure Jean; it might take a longer time than our patience could stand—a year, two years, three years—he could make no guess—but he could certainly cure her. He had cured several cases that were as bad, and some that were worse. Two were English ladies, and we now know them quite well. One of these was cured 24 years ago, and there has been no return. The cure occupied 2½ years. It was an unusually bad case, and in 5 years had practically extinguished the mental functions. She has remained perfectly healthy in body and mind ever since the cure. The cure of the other lady occupied 5 years; it was finished 5 years ago. She has had no return.

⟨And so it amounts to this.⟩ Kellgren has treated Jean 7½ months. She has made great improvement. Her natural disposition —lost during 7 years—has returned. Her physical condition is good. Her mind is sound and capable—however, it was that all the time; the disease did not attack it.

And so, this is the situation. We are obliged to believe that in time ⟨indefinite,⟩ Kellgren can accomplish the cure. Nobody else can do it, except, possibly, an osteopathist. If the osteopathist can do it, we can go home; otherwise we must stay here, and stick it out. Osteopathy greatly resembles Kellgren's system, but it is not just the same. I have tried privately through several friends to find out if any osteopathist has cured this disease, and if so, to get for me a close description of the *cases,* length of time absorbed, etc; but as I did not wish to reveal *why* I wanted to know, those friends did not go to osteopathists for information, but to physicians! It was as sane as going to Satan to find out about the Christian religion. By consequence I am rich in knowledge of what the doctors think of osteopathy, but poorer than poverty in any valuable information concerning that art.

At last, however, I have gone at the matter in a square way. I have sent a relative to a New York osteopath to ask what *he* can say, and what he can promise.[1] I am hoping that when I get that report it will determine us to go home a few months hence. Don't tell Rice anything. He does not believe in osteopaths.

————

I meant to ask you to pull McClure in and have a talk about the half-proposed magazine before forming an opinion, but I forgot it—no, I believed you would do it anyhow. But there is time yet; I don't have to decide till March 1st. I want you to analyze the *man*; I want you to measure his *talk*. He has made a great magazine-success without any money to do it with, but his very success might be a damage to him by making him recklessly enterprising. I think he is safe if he doesn't spread out *too* much; for this time he has money to work with; also a plant; also experience; also an organised circulating-system; also an organised advertising-department. His peril is not in his magazines, but in his book department. That is where a big spread can overwhelm him. He cleared $150,000 on his magazine this last year; with the same magazine in London, Harmsworth,[2] (who hadn't a cent twelve years ago) would have cleared a million. Harmsworth spreads wider and wider every year, but it is not *books* but cheap periodicals (and the "Daily Mail"); and the more he spreads the more difficulty the Bank of England has to find room to stow his swag in.

Of course I can't afford to go into a concern that is unsafe; and therefore, since with your usual worldly sagacity you perceive that you have got to do the work, it will be worth your while to look very closely into this venture before you commit yourself and me too far. Send for McClure and have a talk; look him well over; *weigh* him; and then tell me just what in your opinion is wisest for me to do in the matter.

I doubt if I should remain in the editorship any more than a year, for I do not like slavery and work; but I am *prepared* for a year—

stuff lately written, and laid away ⟨till⟩ for use in that magazine in case the cat jumps that way. My "element of stubbornness" is not increasing, you see. I should expect to do my whole duty by the magazine for that year, and try to put it on the best footing I could, with an impulse that should keep it going; but this exacting labor and attention could fatigue a person constructed as I am, and cause him to withdraw and take a holiday, perhaps.

If McClure decides to start the Mag., he will write me a letter putting into a detailed statement all that my office will require of me, so that there can be no mistake. Ask him to give you a copy of that, so that you will be fully informed of everything. I don't know but I will cable you to talk with McClure. I will see.

————

Never mind the commissariat, it is a detail; I am going to run the whole yacht, and of course that part will be taken care of. Fetch the yacht over, when I am ready to go home. It will save expense.

Hey! How would you like to try Norway and the fiords with the yacht? Now *that* is the excursion of excursions. I haven't made it, but I know it's so; and the minute the yacht is ready I will point her stem for that region.

Kindest regards to you all, ⟨and⟩ including the new grandson. Poor boy, they will always make him believe he was born in the next century. My father was of the crop of 1800, and he lived and died in the belief that he belonged in this century.

Yrs Ever

SLC

————

[1] On 23 April 1900 Clemens would write his nephew, Samuel E. Moffett, disclosing the nature of Jean's illness, explaining that it had been revealed to only two others (Livy's sister, Mrs. Crane, and Dr. George J. Helmer, a New York osteopath with whom Clemens had been corresponding) (CWB). Clemens sent his nephew detailed questions to ask the osteopath and requested that Helmer's answers be taken down in shorthand and sent on to him: "I have worn my soul out trying to get hold of *somebody* who had sense enough to ask straight questions and send me *informing* answers, but I have struck nothing but fools and incapables."

[2] Alfred C. Harmsworth, later Viscount Northcliffe, was at this time proprietor of the London *Daily Mail*.

250. Clemens to Rogers

London
27 February–4 March 1900

Wellington Court

Dear Mr. Rogers:

No, somehow I am not willing to believe we shall be kept here after May or June. I keep on inquiring into Osteopathy, in the hope that we may venture to go home and let Jean try that. There are some differences between that system and Kellgren's, but I feel sure that they are not serious ones. Kellgren can certainly cure Jean in time, for he *has* cured cases like hers—I know the people.

My faith in him is so strong and so well based upon experience that I can take the chances on recommending him to any desperate patient I come across. When I heard, in the second week of this month that Henry M. Stanley was nearing death with his twelfth heavy attack of gastralgia in 17 years, I did not hesitate to urge Lady Stanley to send for Kellgren and throw the medicine bottles out of the window. He had been in bed since Jan. 12, keeping himself alive with white of egg and other spoon victuals, and allaying the pains with ½-grain hypodermic injections of morphia administered by his wife whenever the pains were severe beyond endurance. He had no physician. He had tried 16 of the best in 17 years, and they had with difficulty pulled him through 11 attacks —in bed each time from two to four months. They pulled him through a four-months siege last year, and then told him physicians could not help him again, and that his next attack would kill him. And so he sent for no doctor this time. He was in very bad case when Kellgren called on the ⟨21st⟩ 15th of this month. K. manipulated the pains out of him at once and showed Lady Stanley how to do it. Stanley had a comfortable night, she removing the pains whenever they came. I kept track of his progress, and called on him two days later. (Privately I will remark that Lady Stanley kissed me

on both cheeks and made me feel a good deal like a benefactor.)
Stanley sat up and ate bacon and eggs and smoked a pipe and
talked an hour and a half. Two days afterward he drove out, and
also walked a few minutes in the park. To-day he resumes his seat
in the House of Commons a well man. If he had had a doctor he
would be under a slab in Westminster Abbey now. The Stanleys
have another patient—but no doctor; Kellgren is the man.[1]

Good! You did the very thing I hoped you would do, in the
McClure matter, and I am ever ever ever so much obliged to you. I
know that when you superintend a contract it will be definite and
clear, and a proper thing for a sane person to sign. By George, I
wish I had you over here to pilot me over a crossing or two. You
would do the job in an hour, and do it right; but as likely as not I
shall overlook a detail or so.

———

⟨*March 4.*⟩

⟨The Harper statement payable May 1, for the last 6 months of
'99 (as perhaps you already know) is $3,000, and double the
previous 6 months. This is a handsome and business-like improvement. 8 old books.

Bliss's 7 old books have paid in the neighborhood of $3,000 for
the whole year, and that is well enough.⟩

March 4.

In all her life England has never seen such a tremendous change
of mood as these recent victories [2] has caused. The heavy gloom of
the past 5 months disappeared in an hour, and everybody went
quietly mad for joy. ⟨Many⟩ Some went boisterously mad, but that
was only the young and giddy—students, street Arabs, and members of the Stock Exchange. We are all affected in spirits by the
change; the cheerfulness is catching. I should not want to live
those 5 months over again, even at an advance of wages.

It's a funny house—Harpers. They cable over here to ask "What
is Professor Ferguson's [3] Hartford address?" As if there were 500
colleges in the village of Hartford and a Prof. Ferguson in each of

them. They need an Intelligence Department—presided over by a cat.

Welcome to the new Broughton! I am hoping you are going to have a considerable family in the course of time if you'll only have patience and wait.

Yrs Ever

SLC

¹ Lady Stanley wrote Clemens on 15 February 1900:
My dear Mr. Clemens—I think and Stanley thinks we have been Divinely guided. . . . My Stanley had been *oh so very ill!* for a long drawn month. Two years ago he had this Gastralgia of the stomach and only just *didn't* die—last year he was 4 months in bed—and I saw seven leading doctors. They none of them did any good—but somehow we battled through. This time I said—and Stanley said—"What will doctors do!—they are powerless to stop these fearful spasms"—so we did nothing. When the pain passed bearing, I injected hypodermically ½ a grain of Morphia—it only allayed the pain for a time, and invariably brought distressing nausea. Last week Mrs. Myers . . . wrote to urge me to try a certain Dr. Kellgren. I called and saw a Swedish maid at the door—who said in bad English that the *"Herr Direktor cured by gymnastics!"* I came home determined not to ask his help. What could gymnastics do for Stanley! lying faint with pain—in bed. So Saturday-Sunday-Monday-Tuesday and Wednesday passed—yesterday I feared the worst. This morning came another letter from Evelene Myers explaining more—and *imploring* me to go to Dr. Kellgren. So I took a long written account, in case he was out, and saw him this morning. . . . Already he has somehow "helped" and eased Stanley. He is coming back tonight—in a few minutes—for it is now past nine—and he will calm Stanley off. Now, I am full of joyous hope—the burden alone to bear was so awful—feeling there was no one who could alleviate—much less cure. So I thank you—as well as my sister—you were *chosen* to help Stanley.
² Boer General Piet Arnoldus Cronjé had surrendered at Paardeberg to British General Frederick Sleigh Roberts.
³ The Reverend Henry Ferguson was a professor at Trinity College, Hartford. Clemens had made extensive use of the diaries kept by him and his brother, Samuel Ferguson, in writing his narrative of the sinking of the *Hornet* in 1866 and the survival of fifteen of its men, who spent forty-six agonizing days in an open boat. The story had first been published in the Sacramento *Union,* in 1866. It had appeared again as part of "My Debut as a Literary Person," in the *Century Magazine* (November 1899). Ferguson had written Clemens on 8 December 1899 to protest Clemens's revival of the long-forgotten tragedy, specifically objecting to the inclusion of proper names in passages uncomplimentary to the men in the lifeboats. He was mollified by Clemens's offer to donate his proceeds from the article "to a church in Stamford," the Fergusons's hometown. Furthermore, Clemens meticulously complied with his requests for textual changes before the story was included in *The Man That Corrupted Hadleyburg and Other Stories and Essays* in 1900. Harper & Brothers's request for Ferguson's address

indicates that they were planning to ask his permission to use quotations from the Ferguson diaries in the forthcoming volume.

251. CLEMENS TO ROGERS

London
11 March 1900

Dear Mr. Rogers:

In bank here------		$5,000
Due from Harper, May 1----		3,000
" " Edinburg, April 1,--		3,000
" " Chatto (de luxe ed.)--		10,000

(but not all payable till Sept.)
Prospectively due from Bliss,
    Harper, Chatto (old books) and
    Edinburg by next October, say-- 12,000
                                    $33,000

And Charley Langdon has recently blown life into some coal-stock of my wife's which has lain dead for 13 years, and it is now worth—$100,000. In addition, old 5 per cent stocks in Langdon's hands—75,000.

In view of these facts it has seemed to me that it ⟨is⟩ was about time for me to look around and buy something. So I looked around and bought.[1] Therefore please send me $12,500, so that it will reach me by mid-April. Pretty soon I will tell you what it is I have bought; then you will see that I am thoughtful and wise.

Mind—don't you sacrifice any good securities. No, keep them as security and lend me the money if you can't get it without making sacrifices. This conduct will please God, and He will not allow the interest to default, nor the principal. (No, it will be better for you to take care of those details yourself; it is not well to trust too much to strangers whom you have had no dealings with.)

I've accepted the Lotos complimentary dinner,[2] and shall hope to get home in time—before the dinner season is over. I don't know, though—I suppose it is doubtful. I was not able to say to Mr. Lord [3] when we were coming, but I said you would know, some weeks beforehand and would telephone him.

Yrs Ever

SLC

[1] Clemens was becoming involved with Plasmon, a health food, the promotion of which would beguile him for the next eight years. On 19 April 1900 he would be elected a director of the Plasmon Syndicate; and he was later prominent in promoting the product in the United States. He recorded now in his notebook (Notebook 32b, TS p. 60):

> *Mailed March 14,* letter to Mr. Rogers asking him to send me $12,500 so that it will reach here (London), Apl. 15. It is for Plasmon-syndicate and is 50% of my purchase. The other 50% to be paid later.
> March 24 it arrived.

Clemens could not interest Rogers in this enterprise, although once he thought he might (SLC to J. Y. W. MacAlister, 27 October 1900, CWB):

> I took Mr. Rogers out of his sick-bed with plasmon. He is a convert.
> The first time I see Mr. Rockefeller I will tell him how to beat his indigestion.

Finally, however, he admitted (SLC to MacAlister, 27 August 1901, CWB): "Mr. Rogers is so headstrong I can't do anything with him. He *will* stick to his own schemes and won't look at mine."

[2] The Lotos Club dinner in Clemens's honor would be given in New York on 10 November 1900 (see *MTS* [1923], p. 197).

[3] Chester S. Lord was managing editor of the New York *Sun* and secretary of the Lotos Club.

252. CLEMENS TO ROGERS

London
25 March 1900

Dear Mr. Rogers:

Another job for you! I am doing my best to keep you busy. ⟨I hav⟩ I am trying to save you a part of it by asking Mr. Howells to ⟨settle⟩ determine for me what share I am to have, for he has produced several plays, whereas your experience and mine is not so wide; but if he backs down, Mr. Kester [1] is to make terms with *you* —your decision to be final. I will say privately to you, that if he offers 25% of his receipts from the play, take him up. Mayo gave

20%, which was plenty, in his case. Tell him to draw the contracts and you will sign them for me.

I have suggested that he leave a copy of the play with you, but this is not important.

———

Now I will turn out and look up another job for you. Do not get discouraged—I am watching out for your interests all the time.

Ever yours

SL Clemens

¹ On 11 April 1900 (Salm) Paul Kester would write Clemens:
We descended upon Mr. Howells at ten o'clock Sunday night, our first chance, and broke up a gathering of Miss Mildred's and exhibited your letter in triumph. Mr. Howells seemed quite willing to umpire the arrangement, and as soon as we have gone over the matter with him we will submit our ideas to Mr. Rogers for his opinion and send you the figures at once. My idea would be that a percent of the gross receipts would be the best arrangement, say five percent on the first four thousand, seven-and-a-half percent on the fifth thousand, and ten percent of everything above that amount. . . . We have visions of three or four Tom Sawyer companies passing in triumph over the land and bringing in barrels of money. We think it may prove another Uncle Tom's Cabin if the play has half the charm and delight of the book.
Clemens was pleased by this proposition and wrote in the margin of Kester's letter: "These seem very fair terms." Through Rogers's intervention, however, the final terms were considerably more favorable to Clemens. On 28 May 1900 an agreement was signed which gave Paul and Vaughan Kester the sole right to dramatize *Tom Sawyer* in the United States, Canada, Great Britain, and Australia, provided that the play was ready for production between 1 September 1900 and 1 June 1901. Clemens was to be paid weekly on a sliding scale: he was to receive 6 per cent on full gross receipts up to $2,000, 7 per cent on gross receipts from $2,000 to $3,000, 8 per cent from $3,000 to $4,000, 9 per cent from $4,000 to $5,000, 10 per cent from 5,000 to $6,000, and 12 per cent on receipts exceeding $6,000 (CWB).

253. CLEMENS TO ROGERS

London
8–9 April 1900

Dear Mr. Rogers:

McClure wrote, some weeks ago, that there was nothing lacking but an understanding in written detail of what my duties were to be—then he would lay the contract before you. I said go ahead, there's no hurry, and when his contract was ready, carry it to you.

In truth there is not the least hurry, I am getting along comfortably enough.

Oh, now, look at you! Trying to smuggle details into the partnership that are not in it. It has *always* been understood that you are to have the losses and I the profits—it makes a perfectly equal distribution on both sides, and no chance for anybody to find fault. And yet the Standard Oil pans out a $20,000,000 dividend, I go into a lot of extravagances on account of it, and presently along comes your statement and my share overlooked. You mustn't act like that —it impairs business confidence.

Now as to this speculation of mine over here, I put £5,000 into it (half down, the rest in a month or two),[1] and I am going to do my level best to save you from loss; but if I don't succeed, you must bear it like a man. Then God will not punish you.

It is "Plasmon." Plasmon is pure albumen, extracted at an expense of sixpence a pound, out of the waste milk of the dairies—the milk that is usually given to the pigs. The pound of powder contains the nutriment of 16 pounds of the best beef, and will do the same nourishing that the 16 pounds would do, besides being no trouble to digest. The pound of Plasmon retails at 62½ cents. It has neither taste nor smell.

It has not been advertised, and will not be until the English company has been formed and capitalised (two or three months hence), but meantime it is making its way. All the great physicians and the hospitals nourish their sick upon it, for it is not only pure albumen but it dissolves without the aid of an alkali, and 99.4 per cent of it digests. We get it from the Berlin Company, but they are crowded, and cannot furnish as much as we need, but we have now let a contract to a man out in the country who agrees to furnish us half a ton a week as a beginning, (at 11 cents a pound) and increase the output speedily. He furnishes the plant himself, it being simple and not costly. The Berlin Co can only let us have a ton a week at present, and the doctors already require more than that; for when their patients get well they go on putting Plasmon into their food and the food of their families, because they find that it is not only very nourishing but drives out indigestion and keeps it out.

I tried to get a chance in Plasmon when it was invented in Vienna two years ago, but failed; but I have been keeping track of it since, and I got in here, through finding out that a special friend of mine was in it. He is secretary to the Royal Medical and Chirurgical Society and is an educated physician. There is a small syndicate, and he is a director.[2]

The syndicate owns the patents for everywhere except Germany and Austria-Hungary; but we have to give the Berlin Company one-fourth of whatever we get out of any country (including England.) I own a sixth of the syndicate for the £5,000, but will have to sell a part of it to influential friends of the enterprise. The others will have to do the same. "The others" are rich business men, and not sentimental. About ten days ago we sold the American rights to a New Yorker named Butters[3] who has been here two or three months trying to get it. We made the trade through the "Exploration Company" (Lord Rothschilds's), and they have had large contracts with him before and they believe in him. He pays no money, but must spend $50,000 in a year in pushing the thing; then retire and lose it at the end of the year if he doesn't establish a competent company in the meantime. The syndicate are to have one-third of the American stock, fully paid.

I think it would be well for the Standard Oil to keep an eye on Butters, and if he makes a success of it, buy control of the company. "Plasmon" is a trade-mark and can eternalise the business after the patents expire.

I must send you some pamphlets containing the reports on Plasmon made to the German government by ⟨the⟩ ⟨its⟩ their official experts, the two greatest authorities in Europe, Virchow and Hoffman.[4] Virchow has spent half his life seeking a cheap food for the people. Bovril and Liebig are only stimulants, not *food*, and are very expensive. Bovril costs six shillings a pound, retail. Virchow says "Plasmon is not only more digestible than all other albumen preparations, but also *more than meat*, (and in the experiment the best fillet steak was used").

Now you get some Plasmon of Butters, and give it to Mrs. Rogers and her father, and you will find good results. In any case it will do away with indigestions, and that is something.

Why did you send Mr. Randel [5] to Georgia? There was no use in it. You should have sent him to Dr. Helmer, corner of 36th and Madison avenue—osteopath. Can't I beat it into your head that physicians are only useful up to a certain point? There their art fails, and then one osteopath is worth two of them. And Mrs. Rogers needs the osteopath—I see it perfectly well. It is time I was getting home; you don't half take care of your family.

Don't you hurry to California—you wait. If I find I can't come, *then* you can go.

You misunderstood. It isn't coal properties, it is Company *stock*. It has always paid dividends these forty years; but for the past 13 the dividends were eaten up by interest on a debt made by a purchased mine which produced debt *only*. The stock is freed, now, and the dividends will come to Mrs. Clemens's pocket, as in the old times. It was always gilt-edged stock, and has never passed a dividend since the beginning.

With best regards to all of you

Yours sincerely

SLC

P.S., *April 9.* Mrs. Clemens is greatly troubled about that Plasmon-cure, and wants me to write you and tell you to *boil* it before using—thus:

Stir several teaspoonsful of Plasmon in *lukewarm* water until it is a *thin paste,* with no lumps in it; then thin it still a little more with water, then *boil* it, *stirring* it all the time. As soon as it boils, take it off the fire. Cover it and keep it on the ice. It is now Plasmon *stock.* Mix it in the food in that form.

Oh, hell, I says, he won't ever take all that trouble, I says. But she said:

"Nobody ever takes it raw but yourself. The fact that it cured you in 2 months of a fiendish dyspepsia of 8 years' standing 3 years ago and still keeps you sound, is no proof that another person can take it raw and have the same results. All the London physicians boil it—there's 20,000 of them and only one of you. Ask him to follow them, in medical matters, and ask you for advice in matters of finance only."

As the genii say in the Arabian Nights, "I hear and I obey."

Rice says he is going to join you. Lucky rascal!

SL C

¹ Clemens wrote in the margin at this point: "Mrs. Clemens hopes we shan't have to send to you for the second half—at least not all of it."
² The London director was Samuel Bergheim.
³ Henry A. Butters would later be subjected to Clemens's virulent attack (see *MTE*, pp. 349–351) for his alleged theft of funds from the American branch of the company.
⁴ Dr. C. Virchow of Berlin had written a report on the nutrient value of Plasmon. His endorsement was published on the Plasmon labels. Dr. Hofman, Medical Privy Councillor and president of the Hygienic Institute of Leipzig University, had also praised the food.
⁵ Mrs. Rogers's father, Henry Randel.

254. CLEMENS TO ROGERS

London
20 April 1900

Dear Mr. Rogers:

By a letter received yesterday from Mr. Kester I am aware that he has been to see you, with good results. Whether he makes a good play or not, I like his enthusiasm. Doubtful people are handicapped to start with.

And yesterday I received a couple of belated letters from McClure. They were delayed in his agency here. The putting off of the magazine is a good deal of a relief to me. It will give me time in which to write some things for the first year's issue without feeling crowded for time.

You will perceive that he has mapped out an excursion for me. It won't take place. It is too circusy for my tastes; and too much work.¹ I don't like work.

Don't sign any contracts with him *until the wages begin.* However, you wouldn't, anyway. Whenever I *definitely* commit myself, either orally or in writing, the wages will begin on that day. No postponement on account of the weather.

He is due here soon, and if he doesn't take a course of Kellgren he is booked for the cemetery; and I shall consider it bad politics to have commercial relations with a man whose business-office is so soon to be transferred to a better world.[2]

My letter—referred to by him—was to impress upon him the necessity of arranging with you, in detail, and in black and white, exactly what would be required of me if I took the editorship.

He *must* go to Kellgren; otherwise he may just as well give up, and call the undertaker. We have been spending several days at Stanley's country place. Stanley is well and hearty now, but he quite realizes that he was beyond the help of doctors when Kellgren took hold of his case.

We are still hoping to leave for home within two months, but thus far we get no information of a clear and definite sort concerning the osteopaths, and we cannot venture to take Jean away from Kellgren until we can transfer her to reasonably competent hands. We are still digging for information and hoping to get it. I hope Miss Harrison is well again and that she will remain well—otherwise I hope she will try an osteopath, next time, and observe the result. Kellgren would have had her back at her desk in twelve hours. No—he wouldn't have allowed her to leave her desk at all for a disorder so swiftly and easily removable as tonsilitis.

No fires in the house to-day, for the first time since this tedious winter began.

Aloha haori!

SLC

P.S. Mrs. Clemens has just come in, and says she has about made up her mind (the Fates not intervening) that we shall sail in the American liner leaving on the 16th June. I'm glad.

I suppose we shall stop in a hotel—possibly the San Remo—till we can hunt up a flat for the winter (to be furnished from the Hartford house); then go out of town for the rest of the summer.

¹ On 30 March 1900 McClure had written Clemens about "some notions that would be splendid" for the proposed new magazine: "I think if we could arrange to have a special train made up for you to take you over the American continent under the most luxurious conditions, and have you write a series of articles reporting the United States, it would be immense. . . . You could be the guest of the principal railroads and we could have the whole country placed under our eyes."

² McClure's illness may have been one reason why he did not press Clemens further about the editorship of the new magazine. An extended collaboration between McClure and Clemens, each as erratic as the other, would have led almost inevitably to spectacular success or impressive disaster.

255. Clemens to Rogers

London
17 May 1900

Dear Mr. Rogers:

Program re-organized once more. We shall probably not start home until October. The reason is, that a fortnight ago Jean passed the main crisis and turned a corner—an event which we have been anxiously watching for for 6 or 7 months: several times thinking it had arrived, but Kellgren always said "No," until now. However, she has scored the main one, for sure. There may be others to follow—he cannot tell—but she is over the worst, and eventual cure is not doubtful. Since then, she is quite another person—the change is very marked, and exceedingly gratifying.¹

Necessarily we shall stay, now, and give Kellgren the fairest chance we can. We go to Sanna, Sweden, before the middle of July and spend the summer as before. Sanna suits me—the others don't like it.

It is my duty to report to you the secrets of the Plasmon Syndicate, Limited, so that you can interfere in case I get to going wrong. At a meeting of the Directors day before yesterday I asked for a statement of the business. (We buy our plasmon from Berlin at cost.) This is the ⟨statement: We gave the Medical⟩ statement:

Our purchases of Berlin plasmon have cost us $3,000 cash.

Out of this we have given 2 tons to the War Department of the

British Government (Medical Section) and it has gone to the hospitals in South Africa; the sick soldiers prefer it to the other food.

Also, we have given plasmon-packages to the London hospitals and to 4,000 physicians.

To hospitals and physicians and their patients we have *sold* $4,500, and collected the money—

And we've got exactly half of our Berlin purchase *left.* That is to say, we've cleared $1,500 and got $10,000 worth remaining and salable for the money. Isn't that good enough on an outlay of $3,000? $11,500 profit—it's as good as railroading.

Necessarily this work is done privately. The public advertising will begin after the company is floated. The company will be floated in the autumn—October, probably. The capital will be £250,000. Such of it as is not subscribed for by the public will be taken by the Exploration Company, as they guarantee the thing. Its members have already subscribed for £240,000 of it; I don't think they will need to put up very much of it, unless they want to.

John Hays Hammond is a member of Butters's American syndicate. There are a dozen or more; I do not know the others personally.

In this family we eat very little meat—Jean has tasted none for several weeks. Plasmon takes the place of it, and is no trouble to digest. Among us we eat about a quarter of a pound of it per day—the equivalent of 4 pounds of steak. The result is improved health. All the big doctors boom plasmon outspokenly.

In July the Managing Director (S. Bergheim) has to go to New York—a fine man. I want you to have a talk with him. Will you telephone the Lotos boys that the family's health ⟨of our youngest daughter⟩ delays our home-coming until October?

Yours ever

SLC

[1] On 4 May 1900 Clemens had recorded (Notebook 33, TS p. 9): "Director Kellgren discovered that Jean has turned a corner and will get well."

256. CLEMENS TO ROGERS

London
13 June 1900

Dear Mr. Rogers:

Well, you have certainly put the Kester matter through in first-class style. I am ever so much obliged to you. I hope there's a play in Tom Sawyer and that those boys will dig it out and make it go.

If we can get a comfortable country house with 4 or 5 acres of garden and grove and grass close to London—within 30 minutes of it—we shall remain until October, and continue Jean's treatment without going to Sweden. Thus far we have found only one place that comes near to being satisfactory, although we have been scurrying around for some days. To-morrow we shall look at it again and see if we can make it answer. Doubtful. The house is large, but wretchedly furnished; all the other details are perfect, and the distance only 17 minutes from London by slow train, with ten minutes' walk at the end of it.

I came near seeing Marcus [1] at Anaconda in '95, but he escaped. I was ready to compromise with him for stock.

Punch up the firm! Brooklyn Gas is the right model. Get yourself ready and go to speculating. I'm afraid you think Plasmon is a speculative thing, but really it isn't. I am not running any risk. I get back my £5,000 in the autumn, and also 5,000 paid-up shares. The guaranteeing-company is well able to carry out its contract.

The biggest of the bakers offers us 2 shillings a pound for plasmon if we will give him a monopoly of plasmon bread for London. We expect to take him up. We can make the plasmon for less than sixpence a pound; our own factory is beginning work now. Why don't you take £1,000 of this Syndicate stock—and Rice £200 and Miss Harrison £200? You can't lose a penny. You can pay Rice and Miss Harrison back any time they please and charge to my account. But I don't need to protect you—⟨go⟩ you are getting able to do that yourself.

Come—save up some of that junketing and excursioning till we get home—you make my mouth water. And ask Mrs. Rogers not to give up the Reading—I shall be along in the autumn.

———

Here is this troublesome cuss, Will M. Clemens,[2] turning up again. I won't have it. The enclosed letters will explain the situation. I have mailed copies to his publisher. Won't you enclose copies to Col. Harvey and ask him to watch for advertisements of these books and keep you posted, so that you can set Wilder or some other brisk lawyer to work squshing them at the right time? Bliss and Harvey ought to pay some of the cost, I think. Clemens can't write books—he is a mere maggot who tries to feed on people while they are still alive.

Yrs ever

SLC

[1] Marcus Daly, president of Amalgamated Copper.

[2] Will M. Clemens, not a relative, had in 1892 published *Mark Twain, His Life and Work,* a book of which Clemens did not approve; now he wrote for permission to publish three further manuscripts: "The Mark Twain Story Book," "The Homes and Haunts of Mark Twain," and a biographical sketch. Clemens replied on 6 June:

I am sorry to object, but really I must. Such books as you propose are not proper to publish during my lifetime. A man's history is his own property until the grave extinguishes his ownership in it. I am strenuously opposed to having books of a biographical character published about me while I am still alive (Berg).

But Will Clemens was persistent; he wrote again on 10 July 1900:

in no instance have I or would I copy a single line of your copyrighted work. But your public spoken utterances become public property once they are spoken and there is no law against writing truthful facts concerning a man's life. The book is shelved for the moment much to my regret and loss—I can wait—I've waited now forty years for other things—and I can add you to the collection now in storage. It was not my doing in the first instance. I was asked to write a book and I wrote it. One thing remember—I possess more material concerning your life and work than any other man living, dead or still unborn —and the material is far too valuable to the world to throw away. I can then only wait for a change in the weather.

257. CLEMENS TO ROGERS

London
31 July 1900

Dear Mr. Rogers:

It is too bad about Rice. Is he going to come out all right, do you think? I think it strange he did not take your advice before making his ventures, you being right there at his elbow.

We have had a time of it getting settled in this farm-house 300 yards from London;[1] but we are settled at last, Mrs. Clemens has gotten herself reconciled to housekeeping, the servants are first-rate, and things are going smoothly. There are 6 acres of hay and sheep, the lawn is spacious and there are plenty of old forest trees for shade. Jean and ⟨the⟩ her maid drive in, every day, 45 minutes from here to Kellgren's. There is a railway station 2 miles from our house, with trains every 2 or 3 minutes which take you to Baker street—3½ miles—in 17 minutes. We could not be more secluded nor more thoroughly in the country, if we were fifty miles from London. It was a lucky strike, finding this place. When Miss Harrison comes over on her vacation there's a plate and bed for her, if she's willing. I like it here; I haven't been to town for three weeks.

We go home in October or November, we can't tell which, yet. Pond offers me $10,000 for 10 nights, but I do not feel strongly tempted, and Mrs. Clemens ditto. It could help Bliss's sales, but I would rather settle down and go on with the tale I am writing. It looks as if we shall go to Hartford, but we can't make up our minds. Half of the friends there are dead, and we sort of shudder at the prospect.

Hilf Dich Gottesmütterchen!

SLC

[1] This and the next three letters are written at Dollis Hill House, Kilburn, N.W.

258. Clemens to Rogers

London
17 August 1900

Dollis Hill House
Dollis Hill, N.W.

Dear Mr. Rogers:

I wish I could live on offers. Here is this one,[1] which offers to raise my rate $50 a page above McClure's—which was $50 above previous rates. "Puck" offers me $10,000 a year for "one hour per week" to be devoted to editorship, and if that isn't enough will pay considerably more. Pond offers me $10,000 for ten nights. I have declined all these offers, and others. For I know you will not be able to do without my advice in financial matters, and I must keep my talents unembarrassed and ready.

On Jean's account we need promenade-deck quarters at sea, and we came very near not finding any that we could afford, for the month of October. There is a suite still vacant in the St. Paul (Oct. 6), but if we filled it it would transfer the vacancy to our purse. I went from there to the Atlantic Transport Line, over the way, with a good recommendation from the American Line manager, and secured promenade quarters in the "Minnehaha" for Oct. 6, due in New York the 15th or 16th. I think we shall stop at the Everett House a week or so while we look up a flat or a dwelling-house for the winter. Brander Matthews has been here, and thinks we can get what we want, unfurnished (and possibly furnished) in his neighborhood, which is 93d street and West Avenue.

Even with coal fires we have been having trouble to keep warm, evenings; but we are out of that difficulty these past 4 days.

Sincerely Yours

SLC.

¹ Clemens wrote this letter to Rogers at the bottom of a letter from Richard Watson Gilder, who had written on 17 July to repeat an earlier request for a manuscript for the *Century*. "At the risk of seeming too persistent, I want to say that the publishers are willing to pay very high rates for something of yours. For as little as fifteen thousand words they would pay as much as $3000., if they could divide it and make a novelette in that way."

259. CLEMENS TO ROGERS

London
20 August 1900
Kilburn

Dear Mr. Rogers:

And now if you will send me five thousand dollars I shall be glad —not that it is needed immediately, but on the 29th of September, when the second half of the Plasmon payment is due.

⟨Perhaps⟩ I didn't tell you the name of the ship we sail in. This was partly because I didn't know. But I can tell you now: it is the Minnehaha or the Minneapolis—the former, I think—and sails on the 6th of October, reaching New York 9 or 10 days later. Which will surprise this family; for they have gathered from remarks of mine that she is the new 4-day boat.

Yours ever

SLC

VI

"This Odious Swindle"

(OCTOBER 1900-JUNE 1904)

"Ah, this odious swindle, human life"
Notebook 37, TS p. 13, 20 June 1904

RETURNING to New York on 15 October 1900, Clemens was caught in wave upon wave of public and private greeting. His days and his evenings were filled with visitors, luncheons, dinners, speeches. He and his family moved into a furnished house at 14 West Tenth Street, where they remained until 21 June 1901, when they went for the summer to a cabin on Saranac Lake in upper New York State. Upon their return to the city in the autumn, they rented a large house at Riverdale-on-the-Hudson. On 24 June 1902 Rogers took the Clemenses by yacht to York Harbor, Maine, where the Clemenses planned to spend the summer. There in August Mrs. Clemens, who had fallen ill in the late spring of 1902, became alarmingly worse, and Rogers kept his yacht ready, said Clemens, "to fly here and take us to Riverdale on telegraphic notice" (Notebook 35, TS p. 25).

451

When they did return to New York in October, however, it was by rail, in a special car which took them directly to the little station at Riverdale. They remained in Riverdale through the spring of 1903, the house hushed with illness. "I see Howells at wide intervals; the Rogerses every week or two, but I hardly ever have a sight of the other friends," Clemens wrote Laurence Hutton (18 March 1903, Princeton).

Mrs. Clemens's health continued to decline; and when her doctors decided that a more moderate climate was necessary for her recuperation, the Clemenses began preparations for a trip to Italy. On 1 July 1903 Rogers took the family in the *Kanawha* from Riverdale to the Lackawanna pier in Hoboken, New Jersey, where they boarded a train for a farewell visit to Quarry Farm, their old summer home near Elmira, New York. On 3 October, Clemens placed flowers—for the last time, he thought—on Susy's grave. Two days later the family left for New York, to await their departure for Italy, where they expected to take up permanent residence in Florence.

The last days before sailing were occupied with business matters. Rogers saw to the drawing up of a contract with Harper & Brothers which gave that firm first refusal of everything which Mark Twain wrote and which promised Clemens substantial income for life. Trips to Fairhaven on the *Kanawha* were necessary for the arrangement of final details. The Harpers gave an elaborate farewell dinner. At last, on 24 October 1903 the Clemenses sailed on the *Princess Irene,* their cabins filled with Mrs. Rogers's gifts of fruit and flowers.

In Florence, Mrs. Clemens lingered for months, now better, now worse. When on 8 April 1904 Clara made her debut there as a concert singer, her mother roused briefly in affectionate response, but the next day she was again desperately ill. Clemens filled the lonely hours with intermittent writing, with sittings for a portrait which was to be exhibited at the St. Louis Fair, and with almost constant promptings to Rogers to come and join him in Italy. He quarreled with the person from whom the Clemenses rented their villa; he quarreled with doctors who, he was sure, were overcharg-

ing him; he was worried and lonely and often ill himself. He looked
for another villa, where they might settle permanently, and on 4
June 1904 took an option on two, so that Mrs. Clemens might
choose between them. But on the next day she died—"after 22
months," Clemens wrote, "of unjust and unearned suffering"
(Notebook 37, TS p. 11). He and his daughters returned sorrow-
fully to Elmira, where on 14 July 1904 his old friend Joseph
Twichell read a funeral service in the same house in which the
Clemenses had been married thirty-four years before. Life, now
more than ever, seemed to Clemens an "odious swindle."

260. CLEMENS TO EMILIE ROGERS

New York
31 October 1900

8.30 p.m.

Dear Mrs. Rogers:

Mrs. Clemens took my statistics and discovered what I hadn't
thought of: that there would be no study for me and no sewing-
room; and so, to our sorrow we had to give up Madison avenue.

I don't think we are to have a house at all; but Mrs. Clemens is
going hunting again to-morrow.[1] That bars her going to your house
for luncheon; so I will "expedite" this, to let you know.

She wants Rose; she has a cook and two maids, but she wouldn't
take that colored butler. We are all fixed for housekeeping—lacking the butler—but we are short of one minor detail—a house.

Sincerely Yours

SL. Clemens

[1] The Clemenses were staying at the Hotel Earlington; from there Clemens had
written Thomas Bailey Aldrich, 27 October 1900, "We are here in New York
looking for a house."

261. Clemens to Emilie Rogers

New York
4 November 1900
'lection Day.

Dear Mrs. Rogers:

Mrs. Clemens sends thanks and salutation, and will go to lunch with you on Friday and bring a daughter along.

I shall come ⟨then⟩ before that and look over the ground with you anent the children-charity.[1]

Yours very sincerely

SL Clemens

[1] When Clemens gave a reading on 10 January 1901 at the Rogerses's residence (presumably for the charity in which Mrs. Rogers was interested) he began with their favorite watermelon story (Notebook 34, TS pp. 2–3).

262. Clemens to Emilie Rogers

New York
13 November 1900

14 W. 10th st.
Tuesday.

Dear Mrs. Rogers:

I am coming up ⟨alone⟩ to dine with you and the Rices to-morrow evening at 6.45 and go to the theatre—*in case* it's all right.[1] This is the arrangement entered into with your husband, with the clear understanding that it is subject to your veto without prejudice, and he to be held harmless.

Mrs. Clemens begs to send you her love, and is very sorry she cannot be in this scheme, but she is booked for Henry V with the children to-morrow evening, (and is disgusted with her luck, as I know.)

She is distressed because she was in a turmoil of interruptions this morning and could not send back a reply to your kind note; otherwise she would have explained to you that I am engaged to dine here with company and entertain them this evening and couldn't have gone to play billiards, notwithstanding I said I was free and *could*.

Well, that is true, but I didn't know it. That is, I forgot it, which is the same thing.

I suppose women have a good deal of trouble rectifying their husbands. It is what they are *for*.

Sincerely Yours

SL. Clemens

[1] It was all right. Clemens recorded in his notebook for 14 November 1900: "Mrs. Clemens and not the Rice's—dinner 6.45 Dine with Mr. Rogers" (Notebook 33, TS p. 29).

263. CLEMENS TO ROGERS

New York
16 November 1900

Dear Mr. Rogers: [1]

Please look these over and I'll sign next Monday when I return from Princeton.

I notice but one doubtful point: it seems to put no time-limit upon Huck, but only on Sawyer.[2]

Yrs Ever

SLC.

[1] Clemens wrote letter 263 on the back of a letter from William Gillette, who had written him from Baltimore on 15 November 1900 (CWB):

Mr. Frohman wrote me regarding royalties to be paid you for dramatic use of "Tom Sawyer," saying that it had been agreed to leave it to me. He made the

proposition that he pay the same for the dramatization of "Sawyer" that he
does for "Richard Carvell,"—viz—5 per cent on first $5000. taken in on each
week, 10 percent on next $2000. and 15 percent of all above. (That is, 15
percent of all over $7000. on each weeks receipts.) This royalty it would be
necessary to divide equally between you and the dramatizer, making your share
2½ percent on $5000. 5 on next $2000. and 7½ percent on what was over
$7000. I wrote him that I would much prefer, if he could arrange it, to have
the terms so adjusted that you received for yourself 4 percent of the gross on
all receipts, straight through—that I thought this would be preferable to the
sliding scale—and not put you at the very low rate of 2½ percent in case business was not much more than $5000. (which it might not be, and still be very
good business) I think this arrangement would be fair and right.
The play was not produced in Clemens's lifetime (cf. *MTHL*, p. 762, note 1).
² See letter 252, note 1.

264. CLEMENS TO ROGERS

New York
21 November 1900

night.

Dear Mr. Rogers:

I find a lunch and a tea on my invoice for Saturday afternoon,
but as you said I could come that *night* and billiardise with you and
Rice, I'll do it unless I hear from you more differently. If Saturday
night "goes," you don't need to answer this.[1]

Yrs Ever

SLC

[1] Rogers scrawled "All right" across the top of the letter.

265. ROGERS TO CLEMENS

New York
19 January 1901

My Dear Clemens:

I have received a letter from Mr. Bliss,[1] and will not answer it
until I have seen you. My general method of doing business is to get

all the money in hand. I think we should keep the account up as close as possible with Bliss.

> Yours truly,
>
> H H Rogers
>
> [per] KIH

[1] Frank Bliss had written Rogers, 18 January 1901, to ask whether Clemens would be willing to leave some of the money due him as royalties from the American Publishing Company in that company's hands: "I told Mr. Clemens that if he didn't need the money we could make good use of it and pay him interest." On the envelope of the letter from Rogers, Clemens wrote: "Preceding proposed Scribner deal."

266. CLEMENS TO ROGERS (postcard)

> New York
> 21 January 1901
>
> Monday evening.

I shall be at Helmer's [1]—corner of Madison Ave and 31st st tomorrow (Tuesday) after 5. Remember?

> SLC

[1] Helmer was the osteopath whom Clemens wished Rogers would also visit.

267. CLEMENS TO EMILIE ROGERS

> New York
> 22 January 1901
>
> Tuesday:

Dear Mrs. Rogers:

Oh, thank you ever so much for my dear old patriarch's picture —it is in safe and appreciative hands, you may be sure of that.

This family—by special request of Mr. Major, author of the play —are booked for the Criterion Theatre to-morrow night [1]—the Madam and Clara will arrive from Washington at 3 p.m.

Can you hold the two places at your table for 2 of us—that is, for me and one other in case Jean should be ailing? Or me alone—then I could join the family at the theatre after dinner.

Don't answer this—*I'll* come, anyway, and shall expect to bring another Clemens if I'm not enough.

Sincerely Yours

SL. Clemens

[1] Clemens had a box at the Criterion Theatre (Notebook 34, **TS** p. 4) for Paul Kester's dramatization of Charles Major's novel, *When Knighthood Was in Flower.*

268. CLEMENS TO ROGERS

New York
[11] March 1901

Dear Mr. Rogers:

Whitmore thinks as within.[1]

I sent the Pratt & Whitney letter back to Pratt & Whitney Co, and told them to send their bill to you and you would give it your personal attention.[2] I haven't heard any more from them.

SLC

[1] This letter is written on the back of a letter from Franklin G. Whitmore to Clemens (9 March 1901, CWB). Pratt & Whitney had just renewed their request for payment of $1,744.20—their fee for an estimate of the cost of building the Paige typesetter. As early as 10 January 1891 (CWB), and as recently as June 1898 (Whitmore to SLC, 28 June), they had tried to collect from Clemens. "Wasn't this matter disposed of, long ago?" Clemens asked Whitmore (8 March 1901). "I certainly got the impression that Henry Robinson showed the Company that by the terms of the contract this indebtedness was wiped out by the fact that a portion of the Webster plant (Chicago) was ordered of Pratt & Whitney and constructed by them." Whitmore's letter confirmed this:

after talking with Mr. Pratt, Whitmore had "supposed that the account had been closed up and ruled off" (9 March 1901).

² Rogers did give the bill his personal attention and seems to have resisted the claim with every available resource. On 12 March 1901 he wrote Pratt & Whitney asking for an "itemized bill" of their account with Clemens (see Pratt & Whitney to HHR, 13 March 1901, CWB). Though at least two such bills were sent, neither managed to convince Rogers that the claim was legitimate; and by 24 April the company had again appealed to Clemens, saying they had not "thus far been favored with a reply" from Rogers (CWB).

269. CLEMENS TO EMILIE ROGERS

New York
11 April 1901

Dear Mrs. Rogers:

I am bedridden again.¹ Please read the letter of the Czar Tom Reed ²—also the purple pamphlet.³ Now add this additional advantage: If you will buy $5 worth of soap of this boy (and really you must!) you will get one more acre and one more "row of vegetables."

Ever Yours

SL. Clemens

¹ Clemens would write Rudyard Kipling, 23 May 1901 (TS in MTP): "Between Jan. 3 and May 1 I had 3 gout attacks and spent among them 21 days in bed."

² This note was written on a letter which Thomas B. Reed had written Clemens, 6 April 1901. Reed's letter concerns "what seems to me," Reed said, "the finest proposition yet made to an earnest world."

You will see that the Company is organized under the laws of Maine, which is a guaranty that there will be nothing but pure water in the stock, with no stimulants even in the prospectus.

The capital stock is only $2,250,000, with ten per cent. off for cash, which makes the price of the whole only $2,025,000, a sum now, thank heaven, in these prosperous days, within the reach of the laboring poor. The acres in the concession amount to 77,441. The prospectus is a document wherein the promoters have evidently carefully restrained themselves. Now, each twenty acres will make a man in five years worth ten thousand dollars ($10,000) and also give him board and lodging, and the cigars and wines of the country, including climate, and a chance at the minerals. . . . Now, why cannot you and Mr. Rogers and I take this whole thing? He is eager for money, and you and I want safety. Now, he could furnish the first four figures (so as to give him a controlling interest) and we furnish the last three figures (,000) and share alike. *We two* could go there and take in as much of the climate as we wanted, and make arrangements for canning the rest and sending it on to the other partner, or pipe it through to New York in the winter.

Now, think this thing over, dress it up in your severely logical manner, and we can make it go. Your influence with Mr. Rogers will be compensated for by suitable commissions (to be paid out of ⟨your⟩ his share) and you and I can live happily ever afterwards, while Mr. Rogers will start in on his third (or fourth?) hundred million, with a consciousness that he has aided the deserving poor (that's us). . . .

[3] Frank Fuller's Health Food Company was producing a vegetable oil and wheat gluten soap which "does more good things than any other soap and does all good things better than any other"; it would do away with all "the dreadful soap of which you have perforce endured, or evaded when to endure would have been fatal to peace and conducive to profanity" (Fuller to SLC, 27 January 1902). It can be presumed that the "purple pamphlet" told of this product, or one like it.

270. CLEMENS TO EMILIE ROGERS

New York
[16] April 1901
Tuesday.

Dear Mrs. Rogers:

Mrs. Clemens thanks you very much, and wishes she could go with me, but she has a freshet of country cousins due to break on her Wednesday evening; but *I* shall come and feed and play.

Ever yours

SL. Clemens

P.S. I did not send the soap-boy [1]—it was Mr. Rogers. I strongly advised against it.

[1] Author of the pamphlet mentioned in the preceding letter.

271. CLEMENS TO KATHARINE HARRISON

New York
1 May 1901
(Night)

Dear Miss Harrison:

Mr. Rogers approves of Chicago & Alton pref. to the extent of
$10,000.[1] Therefore I am prepared to send you the check at any
moment you require it.

Sincerely Yours

SL. Clemens

[1] By August the investment had paid a dividend of $200 (SLC to OLC, 2
August 1901).

272. CLEMENS TO ROGERS

New York
3 June 1901

Dear Mr. Rogers: [1]

These have come from Whitmore, ⟨and I⟩ but not the big check=
book.[2]

I have been hard at work ever since the time you didn't turn up
at Mr. Broughton's,[3] but I am coming down soon.

Yrs Ever

SLC

[1] This letter is written on the envelope of a letter from Whitmore to Clemens.
[2] Clemens probably enclosed Whitmore's long letter to him (23 May 1901,

CWB) which had in turn enclosed documents related to the original Pratt & Whitney bill: the 1891 bill itself, a letter from Paige requesting payment, and a draft of Clemens's letter to Paige refusing the same. Whitmore, apparently at Rogers's suggestion, had "spent three hours looking through all the papers, receipts, memoranda correspondence of every character relating to the machine" in order to find some record of payment. Rogers was apparently somewhat confused because he had paid another bill of $6,562.69 to Pratt & Whitney when he had formed the Paige Compositor Manufacturing Company in 1894, a fact which he took the trouble to confirm (Urban H. Broughton to KIH, 13 May 1901, CWB). Whitmore had not sent the checkbook, insisting it would "be of no service to Mr. Rogers in this matter, [since] as I said before I am positive that you have never paid this bill." A final letter from Pratt & Whitney to Clemens (17 June 1901, CWB) offered to take his note, payable in six months with 5 per cent interest. But they also reported that "Mr. Rogers [had] declined to make any appointment" about the matter.

[3] Clemens had spent the evening of 29 May 1901 with the Broughtons at their home on 230 West 72nd Street (Notebook 34, TS p. 12).

273. CLEMENS TO ROGERS

New York
19 June 1901

Dear Mr. Rogers:

I don't know which to do—take no notice of P & W's New York letter, or send them the enclosed invitation. And so I'll just get you, as head of the firm, to decide for me. I'll never pay that bill till I'm forced.

I stood on the front steps of the Holland [1] yesterday from 4.50 till Mr. Broughton finally came along and relieved guard. He said I was in the way, and attracting too much attention, and that it was all being wasted, as you would not be along for a day or two yet.

I shall [send] this, with our good-byes, to you all, to 26 Broadway to await your return next Monday, there being nothing very urgent about P. & W's affairs except their desire to collect. Mr. Broughton said the good news (Amalgamated) would content your spirit and satisfy you to stay out the week at Fairhaven and finish your rest.

Put me in deep, in the Monoline combination [2]—and do me a line and tell me about it when you've accomplished the cinch.

We shall finish packing to-morrow, and leave for our summer

shanty at Saranac Lake, N.Y., Friday morning at 7.50, arriving there at 7 p. m—through without breaking bulk.

With our love to Mrs. Rogers (and not a word about soap),

Yrs Ever

SLC

---

[1] The Holland House was at Fifth Avenue and 30th Street.

[2] Clemens probably refers to the J. P. Morgan–E. H. Harriman consolidation of most major railroads west of Chicago, reported in the New York *Times,* 17 June 1901. This composite agreement had divided eleven roads among Harriman, Morgan, Jay Gould, the Rockefellers, and several other interests, but "J. Pierpont Morgan and E. H. Harriman . . . will be the real dictators and direct the policy to be pursued by these combinations, thus establishing the 'community of interest' which has been the dream of Mr. Morgan." The significance of this agreement was a topic for the *Times's* financial page: a total of 55,592 miles of railroad lines now possess "a community of interest which, by the removal of all disturbing and destructive rate wars, assures substantial and stable earnings to the various Northwestern roads and . . . places these systems on a much firmer foundation, dividendwise."

---

274. CLEMENS TO ROGERS

Ampersand
28 June 1901
Saranac Lake, N.Y.

Dear Mr. Rogers:

We are sweating away, here at the "Liar(s)" [1]—which should be plural, for there are several of us. This weather is not from Heaven.

We are very sorry to hear of Mrs. Rogers's bad state of health, and sorry too that she must not go where she could be better. It has been a wearing year for her.

We are having a time with our letters and freight. There are 75 Saranacs in this (cussed) region and our stuff gets distributed amongst them all—for each is a P. O.

Mrs. Clemens thinks you are kind and considerate, and so she is willing to spare me for that fortnight whenever you notify me to come.

Yours ever

SLC

---

¹ The Clemens family spent the summer in a cabin named "The Lair," at Ampersand, New York.

275. CLEMENS TO ROGERS

Ampersand
5 July 1901

Dear Mr. Rogers:

How would Ex-President Cleveland do? or Judge Howland? or both? Tom Reid ¹ and Cleveland would make a grand team—if they are friendly, and I don't see why they shouldn't be. Both have fought to victory and covered the field with the slain; both have retired to the paths of peace, and they should not mind smoking its pipe and burying the tomahawk. Shall I write and invite them? Will Reid be willing? Would you mind asking him? No use for Cleveland without Reid; *we* couldn't bait him and make him roar; we couldn't draw him out and make him ⟨call⟩ do music, but Reid could.

Yours ever

SLC

---

¹ Clemens is suggesting guests for a cruise on Rogers's recently acquired steam yacht. Henry E. Howland could not go; Grover Cleveland was probably not asked; Clemens was careless in spelling Thomas B. Reed's name. On 17 April 1901 Rogers had purchased the two-year-old *Kanawha*, the fastest cruising steam yacht in American waters, capable of a speed of twenty-two knots an hour and "easily the superior of J. Pierpont Morgan's noted Corsair" (New York *Times*, 18 April 1901). The *Kanawha*, first owned by John P. Duncan, was 227 feet overall, 192 feet on the water, with a "high, sharp clipper bow, a fine sheer, and

a long overhand aft" (New York *Times,* 28 May 1899). The vessel had two engines, and its forward deck house contained a large dining saloon.

276. CLEMENS TO ROGERS

Ampersand
9 July 1901
Monday.

Dear Mr. Rogers:

Your telegram hasn't reached the Ampersand Hotel yet (5 p. m), but I shall send over there again this evening.

I take it Judge Howland is going. If he backs out we can write Sloane.[1]

Sailing-day is Saturday, Aug. 3,—is that it? I shall go to New York one or two days before that, and do errands [2]—for we have taken Mr. Appleton's furnished house [3] ⟨for⟩ at Riverdale on the Hudson, 25 minutes out of town by rail—for a year, beginning Oct. 1, with ⟨privilege⟩ option of a second year at the same rate—$3,000.

Bliss's check for the past half-year is just received—nearly $6,000. Eight or nine thousand still owing, but not due yet, because it isn't yet due from Newbegin.

Newbegin's backer, Mr. Underwood, has asked me to give a circular letter for canvassers' use, to modify Harper's big advertisement of "Mark Twain's Best Books," and I feel pretty willing, for in using that heading Col. Harvey has gone back on an agreement made with me months ago. He was going to use a heading "Mark Twain's Choicest Books," and I protested.[4]

If you approve the circular, please mail it to Mr. Underwood, for he is uneasy; and the Newbegin business is large, the Harpers' trifling. *Their* July statement for past 6 months foots up $2,000— and I get it next November.

Yrs Ever

SLC

The address is
F. L. Underwood, Esq
   % Newbegin Co.
      66 and 68 Reade st.,
         New York

[1] William Milligan Sloane (1850–1928) was Seth Low Professor of History at Columbia University.

[2] Something of Clemens's increasing dependence on Rogers is indicated in a letter which he hurriedly wrote Livy on 2 August from "Mr. Rogers's Office" on the eve of his departure on this cruise:

Livy darling, please send a check on the Guaranty Trust Co to Miss K. I. Harrison for twenty thousand dollars payable to her order. She is going to put it in Union Pacific preferred. Date the check Aug. (4—which is day after tomorrow, Monday) 3—or Aug. 5—and rush *it straight along!* She will buy on Monday.

The Chicago & Alton paid a dividend of $200 July 2d—it is in Mr. Rogers's hands.

The U. S. Steel pf. will pay one of $175 four days hence.

Those coupons are on the International Navigation and were due yesterday —$1,000. . . .

I got down here to the Standard Oil in time for late luncheon with young Rockefeller—it is the best homemade table in the North.

I will cut off those coupons when I come back.

Miss Harrison sends her kindest regards.

I have seen not a single flannel suit—everybody wears gray and gray only—and black. I will discuss with Benjamin and Mr. Rogers before buying that suit (TS in MTP).

[3] The residence of William Henry Appleton (1814–1899) fronted the Hudson River between 248th and 252nd streets.

[4] The R. G. Newbegin Company handled distribution of the uniform edition for the American Publishing Company, advertising themselves as "sole agents in the United States for the complete works of Mark Twain." Clemens would suggest to Bliss on 13 July 1901: "the Harpers don't say *I* call theirs the latest and best—they say it themselves. Therefore why doesn't Newbegin say the very same thing? Harper has set the example, and could not complain" (TS in MTP).

277. CLEMENS TO ROGERS

Ampersand
17 July 1901

Saranac Lake, N.Y.

Dear Mr. Rogers:

Judge Howland can't go—friends due at his house Aug. 5.

There's Professor Wm. Sloane [1] of Columbia, a perfectly delight-

ful man—would you like to have him? If so, will you write him
(time being short), or shall I? At this time of the year he will be
living in his house at

Princeton, N.J.

I think you couldn't possibly help liking Sloane. Perhaps you know
him; if so, you *do* like him. He wrote the big History of Napoleon
that appeared in the Century.

Yours ever

SLC

[1] On 29 July 1901, however, Sloane wrote Clemens apparently declining the
invitation. Sloane mentioned his illness and continued: "Do thank Mr. Rogers
properly for me." On the back of the first page of Sloane's letter Clemens wrote a
note to Rogers dated 31 July: "I shall be in New York and abed by 11 o'clock
tomorrow night" (Parke-Bernet Galleries catalog, 28–29 April 1959, item 89).

278. CLEMENS TO ROGERS

Ampersand
23 August 1901
Noon, Friday

Dear Mr. Rogers:

I am just out of bed for the first time since I left the ship.[1] The
first time we came here there was an interruption near this point
which halted the train four hours; this time, at the same place there
was another break-down which caused a still longer halt, and
turned an 11-hour trip into a 17-hour journey—and so I reached
home at half past 1 in the morning instead of at 7 the previous
evening. But that was not the worst of it. The weather was
roasting hot, and close and humid, and I arrived with a cold in the
head. But it is gone, now, after a couple of days in bed.

The chief steward delivered me in good order and well conditioned on board the train and thus put the finishing and perfecting
touch upon the most contenting and comfortable and satisfactory
pleasure-excursion I have ever made. Profitable in health, too—for

I have picked up enough of that to last me a good while. For all of these benefits I owe you more thanks than I can express. I found the family well, but sitting up and expecting to hear that my train was destroyed.

I hope you found Mrs. Rogers well, and that Richfield Springs will furnish rest and peace for her and her mother. Mrs. Clemens sends love to her and kindest regards to you.

Sincerely Yours

SLC

[1] The cruise had been a great success. Leaving New York on 3 August 1901, the *Kanawha* carried the Benjamins, the Coes, the Harry Rogerses (Harry had married William Evarts Benjamin's niece, Mary Benjamin, on 7 November 1900), Colonel Augustus G. Paine (a New York businessman), Dr. Rice, Clemens, and Rogers. The company stopped at Fairhaven for the laying of the cornerstone of the Unitarian Memorial Church, which Rogers was donating to the town in memory of his mother. On 6 August Paine, Rice, Harry, Clemens, and Rogers sailed to Portland, Maine, where former Speaker of the House Thomas B. Reed came aboard to complete the "permanent garrison." The next twelve days were filled with sailing from port to port, excursions ashore, light-hearted horseplay, and poker. After cruising to Boothbay and then to Bar Harbor, Maine, they advanced to New Brunswick and Nova Scotia and returned along the Maine coast to stop at Rockland, Bath, Boothbay, and finally (on 17 August), Portland, where Reed disembarked. The *Kanawha* then sailed directly to New York. (See *MTB*, pp. 1139–1140; Clemens's log of the cruise exists in a draft in MTP [DV 242]; a fair copy of this log, "Summer Excursion to the Nutherd," with illustrations by Harry Rogers, is in the Salm Collection.)

Clemens was in high spirits when he wrote Livy from St. John, New Brunswick, on 9 August:

At breakfast, an hour ago, I ventured, for the first time, to throw out a feeler, for all these days' silence made me a little uneasy and suspicious. I intimated that *at home,* I sometimes snored—not often, and not much, but a little—but it might be possible that at sea, I—though I hoped—that is to say—

But I was most pleasantly interrupted at that point by a universal outburst of compliment and praise, with assurances that I made the nights enjoyable for everybody, and that they often lay awake hours to listen, and Mr. Rogers said it infused him so with comfortableness that he tried to keep himself awake by turning over and over in bed so as to get more of it; Rice said it was not a coarse and ignorant snore, like some people's, but was a perfectly gentlemanly snore; Colonel Payne said he was always sorry when night was over and he knew he had to wait all day before he could have some more; and Tom Reed said the reason he moved down into the coal bunkers was because it was even sweeter, there, where he could get a perspective on it. This is very different from the way I am treated at home, where there is no appreciation of what a person does.

279. CLEMENS TO ROGERS

Ampersand
29 August–6 September 1901

Dear Mr. Rogers:

I carried off Mr. Coe's sponge, but I seem to have left a set of my underwear in place of it. I'll trade back if he will. He mustn't think ill of me. I give you my word I didn't intend to take the sponge; I did it while thinking of something else; I was only intending to take his dressing gown; he can send it to me here.

⟨Aug.⟩ *Sept.* 6. I broke off, there, Aug. 29, because I happened upon a text for a story. Up to yesterday evening I had written 108 pages like this upon it; an average of 18 pages a day—20,000 words altogether—magazinable at 20 cents a word. Am getting wealthy. I have been revising and correcting all day, and shall add a final chapter to-morrow, then take a rest.[1]

"Yes, I know, but what's *on* it." You will know when you come to take a whiff of it. It is a burlesque of Sherlock Holmes.

Oh, I say! Won't you send Fred (with the cash—$1) to the General Postoffice for these cussed books, and *keep them till I come?* And charge to me.

I think Payne has missed his vocation. His foreign-English letter is first-rate literature, and hard to beat—let the experts try; they'll find it so.

I've got a subject for a parody—

> The old broken Mugwump,
> The iron-bound Mugwump,
> The moss-covered Mugwum
> That's pointed for . . . . Well—

(and so-on.)

Do you remember the words of the Old Oaken Bucket? If you

do, and I were near you, I'd milk you. By and by I will send to Harper for it.

Yrs Ever

SLC

---

[1] "The Double-Barrelled Detective Story" would appear in *Harper's Magazine,* January and February 1902.

280. CLEMENS TO ROGERS

Ampersand
7 September 1901

I don't know the date.

Dear Mr. Rogers—

I have finished the story, and it makes somewhere between 22 and 25,000 words. I am going to take a day off, to-morrow.

There was a report last night that the President has been shot.[1] But there are no newspapers, and no one knows whether it is true or not. It may be only talk; I will hope so.

Yrs

SLC

---

[1] McKinley had been shot on 6 September; he died on 14 September 1901. Clemens wrote Twichell, 8 September 1901, Yale; TS in MTP):
This news of the President! We never got it until yesterday evening, when a N. Y. paper wandered into the camp. I doubt if it is serious. Otherwise they would not have moved him. Doctors (and politicians) always get all the advertising they can out of a case; making it desperate, and then fetching it out all right, after they've sucked the profit out of it. I was never able to feel alarmed about Mrs. McKinley when she was ostensibly so sick. Once when she was apparently dying in San F., the President (as usual) wasn't able to make up his mind as to whether he would keep a junketing-engagement next morning! (He kept it.) Considering the unbulky size of his mind it is odd that

he has such difficulty making it up. (If he dies, I desire to withdraw these remarks.)

281. CLEMENS TO ROGERS

> Ampersand
> 12 September 1901

Dear Mr. Rogers:

How can you be so unfeeling? You know very well it *wasn't* "by request"—I only hinted it. But I'm glad to get the song, anyway.[1] I am singing it every day, and it gives a new aspect to the woods, which are gladder and more inflamed than ever an autumn here saw before.

O, pile-in the Salvation Army!—you'll have a good time; and send Rice a detachment.

I have been trying to think up something for you to put in your idle time on, and I've got it.:

I have made you and 26 B'way my mail-matter address for the present. There'll be nothing to do but re-direct the stuff, which is fun.

We leave here for Elmira Sept. 18 or 19; remain there a week; then a few days at the Grosvenor in 5th ave; then go to housekeeping at Riverdale, above Spuyten Dyvel Oct. 1.

Can you remember all that?

To-day I am busy, but to-morrow I will think up some more things for you to do. Depend on me. I am your friend.

> Yrs
>
> SLC

[1] "The Old Oaken Bucket"? See letter 279.

282. Clemens to Rogers

Ampersand
18 September 1901

Dear Mr. Rogers:

We are packed; and we leave to-morrow morning for Elmira.

For days I have been in despair about something for you to do in your idle hours, and at night I have not slept well, for worrying over it. But I have it now. Last night 3 of the enclosed things reached me from Chicago—returned ⟨⟨to *me*⟩⟩ because unclaimed; returned to *me* because the "S. L. Clemens, U. S. A" in the corner of the envelop erroneously indicated me as the sender.[1]

This is a mighty cold-blooded piece of rascality. The Newbegin Co wanted me to give them something just about like this, (they applied first through Bliss and he brought me the draft of it) but of course I didn't consent. But I sent them something through you (which you approved) and never got even a thank-you. I didn't suit, I guess.

So now they resort to plain forgery. They forge my signature, and then they put into my mouth a shameless personal letter no word of which ever had its source in either my mouth or my head, and then they add sacrilege to impudence and counterfeit my *style!*

Now then, am I not right? *Sue these rascals at once.* I suppose that no action for damages is ever worth bringing when you can't prove the actual amount of the damage suffered, but surely there ought to be a good safe *criminal* action here, for these people have not done this forging for fun, but to get money out of it.

I have yet the pencil-draft of the *first* circular-letter which I framed for them, but which didn't suit them; but I kept no copy of the one I sent through you and which also didn't suit, apparently; but I remember the purport of it, and also have a pretty good idea of its phrasing.

Do you approve of a suit? If so, can you appoint a lawyer?—a tip-top one—no Colby, no Whitford, no Stern and Rushford. Do you think Tom Reed would take it? [2]

Ever Yours

SL. Clemens

Shall fetch up in New York about Sept. 26.

[1] Clemens had received, through the return address, letters advertising his books. These letters and, he assumed, hundreds like them, had been sent to families all over the United States, in envelopes bearing the return address "S. L. Clemens, U.S.A.," making it appear that he had made a personal appeal for sales. When confronted with the letters, Newbegin insisted that W. I. Squire (another agent) was responsible. Squire had just purchased 500 sets of the Popular Edition. (See R. G. Newbegin to SLC, 7 October 1901).

[2] Reed did apparently take the case, though Clemens did not prosecute very energetically. The suit was abandoned when Squire died (Thomas B. Reed to SLC, 28 October 1901).

283. Clemens to Rogers

Elmira
25 September 1901

Dear Mr. Rogers:

The trouble with Tom Reed is, that he don't belong to no church and ain't got no sympathy with suffering.

How much would they allow us on an umbrella-display at the Pan-American? You can have half. [1]

Yrs,

SLC

[1] Private jokes became very much a part of the public friendship between Clemens and Rogers. The umbrella alluded to here must have become a theme for Clemens's raillery after the "Summer Excursion to the Nutherd" (see letter 278, note 1). Shortly after embarkation on 3 August, Clemens noted in his log, "A valuable umbrella missing." He proceeded to ring endless changes on this "missing" (that is, stolen) item, noting on 7 August that "it is thought by some

that the reform of the Reformed Pirate is not complete" and concluding on 18 August that "A final search for the umbrella produced nothing, except regret."

A cryptic and probably spurious postcard in the Coe Collection may represent still another example of these private jokes. Postmarked in Boston, 27 September 1901, the card reads: "Dear Hen. Simply had to leave. I was making your illness a joke. Twain." Although the card was evidently received by Rogers in Fairhaven, it is doubtful that Clemens could have mailed it from Boston; it is certainly not in his hand, and was evidently first printed in an unidentified journal as part of a series: "Never Sent Postcards.—No. 10." This last suggests that the document represents a public joke at Rogers's expense. For a month Rogers had been dodging subpoenas to appear for hearings in the suit of J. Edward Addicks against the Boston Gas Company. "Mr. Rogers spends much of his time on his yacht in the summer, and . . . is hard to reach" the New York *World* reported on 4 October 1901.

284. CLEMENS TO ROGERS (postcard)

New York
26 September 1901

Grosvenor, midnight

Langdon hopes to be able to come. Yesterday evening I wrote and invited Twichell.

SLC

I'm coming.[1]

[1] The *Kanawha* would cruise off Sandy Hook on Thursday, 3 October 1901, to watch the third heat of the America's Cup race between the American yacht *Columbia* and Sir Thomas Lipton's *Shamrock*.

285. CLEMENS TO ROGERS

New York[1]
29 September 1901

Sunday.

Dear Mr. Rogers:

I shall try to get in, to-morrow or Tuesday and telegraph Twichell what day to come, and what hour in the morning, and whether at

West 35th st, or where. He can't report to me at this hotel,[2] because we remove to Riverdale Tuesday morning; whereas No. 3 will come off Thursday, I guess.

[no signature]

---

[1] This letter is written in the margins of a letter Twichell had written to Clemens on 27 September 1901, saying that he would be happy to join the yachting party and asking the exact date of the race.
[2] Clemens was still at the Grosvenor Hotel.

286. CLEMENS TO ROGERS (postcard)

New York
21 November 1901

The Baker letter [1] hasn't its match in literature anywhere. It can't be approached—it stands alone. I've sent it to Howells—but only lent it. If he loses it I must have another copy. I think Twichell ought to be allowed a sight of it when he comes.

SLC

---

[1] Rogers had sent Clemens a long and rambling, ungrammatical and misspelled letter from William H. Baker of Fairhaven (copy in MTP). Baker began by praising Rogers's benefactions, which "have made the town of Fairhaven a town of beauty and joy forever, as long as times last." Then, recalling the laying of the cornerstone for the Unitarian Memorial Church on 5 August 1901, he wrote:
. . . Your Friend, Mr. Clemons, (Called Mark Twain for short) that you ortherised to speak for you or in your stead, He told the People of Fairhaven, you remember, if there was any thing more thay wanted, any more buildings or anything else, he was impowed to grant it. After thinking over the many buildings that I could not count on the fingers of one hand, I was ungreatfull enough to think of one more, yet I had not the courage to name it that is not there, for fear the people of the Town would do me the bodyly harm for my rank ingratude. Perhaps you may feal different about it, so I will tell you what it is. It is an Old Peoples Home. It seams to me that it would be a great blessing. Some would say Have we not got a good Alms House for the Old People to go to whare thay will be taken care of. Yes that may be so, but you know dear Mister Rogers, that there is many little comforts that old people (especly when thay are feeble) require, that they cant always get to the Almshouse.

Clemens immediately sent the copy to William Dean Howells, writing in the margin:

Read this, Howells.

Mark.

P.S. And return it to me. I think it perfect.

"Read the Baker letter *several* times," he told Howells a few days later:

it is one of those supreme & unapproachable masterpieces which one must read & re-read in order to get all the juice of it. If one were writing a novel & had this poor rotten old Christian in it, what a nugget that letter would be! No genius & no training can equip one to successfully imitate that phrasing (*MTHL*, pp. 733–734).

Howells agreed:

That Baker letter is indeed precious: he could use an old people's home all by himself. The spelling, spirit and expression all go together. I wish Keats could have lived to hear of "a town of beauty and a joy forever" (*MTHL*, p. 734).

287. CLEMENS TO ROGERS

Riverdale
12 December 1901

Dear Mr. Rogers:

I found a note from Mr. Rockefeller when I got back home yesterday, and I answered accepting his invitation and saying I would read or talk, whichever he might prefer—I named "Two Little Tales" as the reading.[1]

If he should choose the reading, here's ammunition for comment! —a text to glaringly illustrate the futility of trying to write *any*-thing that a born idiot can be made to understand.

The Madam says——but as I told you yesterday, we *can't* word it, we can only *feel* it. You are just too dear and lovely for anything!

Yours ever

SLC

P.S. If I *read*, you must be there. If I *talk*, stay by your hearth-stone and don't waste your time.

An' ye'll plaze me if ye'll sind me the idiot's letters back. I'll always inthrojuce them whin I publicly read the "Two Little Tales."

[1] John D. Rockefeller, Jr., had invited Clemens to read before the young men's Bible Class of the Fifth Avenue Baptist Church in New York at its meeting on 27 December 1901 (Notebook 34, TS p. 20; Rockefeller to SLC, 10 and 19 December 1901). The reading was postponed, however, until 28 January 1902, when Mark Twain spoke as part of a program that also featured a speech by Robert C. Ogden, the manager of John Wanamaker's New York department store since 1896 (New York *Times*, 29 January 1902). "Two Little Tales," which incorporated practical advice on how to gain access to powerful people, had appeared in the *Century Magazine* for November 1901.

288. CLEMENS TO ROGERS

Riverdale
12 December 1901

Dear Mr. Rogers:

For 20 years I have owned $5,000 of this stock.[1] It has paid one dividend; that was 19 years ago.[2]

I know no one connected with the concern now. Shall I send a proxy? And shall I make it to this President—Flandreau?

SLC

[1] Clemens wrote this message at the top of a form letter in which Charles E. Flandrau, president of the St. Paul Roller Mill Company, announced a special meeting of stockholders to consider liquidation of the company's assets. The next day Clemens noted at the bottom of the same letter: "Sent no proxy. SLC. Riverdale, Dec. 13/01."
[2] Clemens was slightly in error about the dividends, for two had been paid: 2 per cent on 30 March 1891, and 1½ per cent on 7 November 1891.

289. CLEMENS TO ROGERS

Riverdale
21 December 1901

Dear Mr. Rogers:

"Wally" Bliss was here yesterday, and I guess there are going to be some developments. I have kept out of the Harper-Newbegin fight [1] up till now, but I believe the time has come to take a side in it. So I will drop in on you and get your advice before I do anything in the matter.

Yours alle wile

SLC

[1] Harper & Brothers claimed that the printing of the Popular Edition of the works of Mark Twain, which the American Publishing Company provided to the R. G. Newbegin Company, was not covered by the agreement of 31 December 1896 between Harper & Brothers and the American Publishing Company (Appendix B).

290. ROGERS TO CLEMENS

New York

26 December 1901 [1]

My dear Clemens:

I send you a clipping from the "World" relating to the much advertised history of the Standard Oil Company now being prepared for Mc Clure's Magazine by Ida M. Tarbell.[2] It would naturally be supposed that any person desiring to write a veritable history, would seek for information as near original sources as possible. Miss Tarbell has not applied to the Standard Oil Company, nor to anyone connected with it, for information on any subject. On the contrary, I have reason to believe, she is seeking all her information from those not disinterested enemies of the "Standard" who have for years invented and published falsehoods concerning it. She may in this way make her work more striking and spectacular, but a reputable magazine should have some assurance that what purports to be history is truthful as well as interesting. I do not know whether you can be of any service in the matter, but it would be a kindness to Mr. Mc Clure as well as myself if you could suggest to him that some care should be taken to verify statements which may be made through his magazine, whether affecting corporations or individuals.

Yours truly,

H H Rogers

I got a stocking full of water. I hope you fared better. Harry got his filled with oil. R [3]

[1] At the top of Rogers's letter, Clemens made two notes for the letter he would write on 27 December 1901 (letter 291): "63 points above what it cost us" and "Monday Tuesday or Thursday."

[2] In her autobiographical *All in the Day's Work* (New York, 1939), pp. 211–212, Ida M. Tarbell reveals that Clemens had inquired of McClure "what kind of history" his magazine proposed to publish and had suggested that Miss Tarbell talk to Rogers himself before proceeding. The first interview between the two took place at Rogers's New York home, and a series of subsequent "frank" discussions were held at 26 Broadway. "The History of the Standard Oil Company" was serialized in *McClure's Magazine* from October 1902 to October 1904; it was published as a book by McClure, Phillips & Company in 1904.

[3] In this instance Rogers has added the postscript in his own hand.

291. CLEMENS TO ROGERS

Riverdale
27 December 1901

Dear Mr. Rogers:

Ah, the luck is with Harry and me!—a just reward of virtue. There's no water in *my* Xmas presents. ⟨Both⟩ There is a profit of 27 per cent on my U.S. Steel—I don't remember what I paid for it; do you? And my Amalgamated is nearly 70 points above what it cost me. These things make me thankful.

I am writing Jaccaci [1] of McClure's to come out and dine with us Monday next, or Tuesday or Thursday, and talk over a private matter—Monday preferablest.

Yrs Ever

SLC

[1] Auguste F. Jaccaci was art director for *McClure's Magazine* and a fellow member of The Players.

292. CLEMENS TO ROGERS

Riverdale
2 January 1902

Dear Mr. Rogers:

Jaccaci, of McClure's came up yesterday, and said Miss Tarbell would be only too glad to have both sides, and I told him she could have free access to the Standard Oil's archives.

I paid a New Year call at your house yesterday, but found only one little chappy on deck.

Happy New Year to you all!

SLC

293. CLEMENS TO ROGERS

Riverdale
31 January 1902

Dear Mr. Rogers:

Enclosed is the summons.[1] If you can't get me released, take my place—the court will prefer that, anyway.

Please let me have your hen-composition.[2] I promise not to let it get out of my hands, and I won't print it unless I put it into Huck's or Tom Sawyer's mouth one of these days when I transfer your school-jubilee to the banks of the Mississippi.

I'm expecting to leave for Hartford at 4 p. m. and be Twichell's guest for 24 hours, then return.

Jean is bad again. It is a continuous distress—without a break these 5 years.

Sincerely Yours

SL. Clemens

¹ This may refer to one of two things: Clemens records (Notebook 35, TS p. 4) that he appeared on 1 March to "testify before Commissioner Dulon (for Prussia)." An MS note in MTP, dated 20 June 1902, states, "Lately, by order of a German court, I appeared before the Prussian Commissioner in the city of New York and gave testimony in the case of ⟨Robert⟩ Lutz vs. Jacobsthul. I now appear of my own free will and desire before His Imperial Majesty's Consul in the same city to correct an error made by me in that testimony." The error concerned his statement of where "Tom Sawyer Abroad" and "Tom Sawyer Detective" had first been published. Perhaps more likely, the summons was for jury duty: Isabel Lyon in her notebook (4 January 1908) recorded that Clemens remembered later with gratitude that Rogers had got him off jury duty.

² As part of a reunion celebration for the Fairhaven High School, a mock school session was held in which "an original composition [was] read by Mr. Rogers, the subject of which was 'The Hen Roasted, or Truth Fricasseed.'" Although Rogers "would not part with his manuscript and as he read it rather fast, some of his points will never be recorded," the Fairhaven *Star* reported as many as it could, concluding that the "absurdity of the theme and the manner in which he treated it completely surprised the gathering" (Fairhaven *Star* Supplement, 1 February 1902).

294. CLEMENS TO ROGERS

Riverdale
7 February 1902

Dear Mr. Rogers:

Very many thanks for the Fairhaven Highschool jubilee reports. (I will squeeze that hen-composition out of you on the yacht-trip.)

Last night a neighbor—Mr. Kingsley of the New York Life—was in, and said he would not be positive but *believed* Mr. Perkins (*the* Perkins)¹ got the Woods place, which is next to us, for $70,000 last week, furniture and all, and 10 acres. Says the house must have cost $100,000 to build.

Yrs Ever

SLC

Feb. 7.

P.S. Don't you think it would be a good scheme to invite Laurence Hutton to go in the yatch?

Yrs

SLC

¹ George W. Perkins, of J. P. Morgan & Company.

295. KATHARINE HARRISON TO CLEMENS

New York
3 March 1902

Dear Mr. Clemens:

Please send me check for $10425, to pay for the Bordens stock. It was a trifle higher than I expected but you get the dividend due March 15th of $150, so it makes the stock about 102½ which is a good price. I also have a bottle of ink all ready for you next time you come to 26. I would send it to you only I hav'nt the facilities for packing here.

With kindest regards, I am

Yours sincerely

Katharine I. Harrison ¹

¹ Clemens apparently received notes like this often from Miss Harrison, who, acting for Rogers, managed the details of Clemens's financial accounts. On 20 May 1902, for example, she would write: "To date 10% has been paid on the Steel investment which Mr. Rogers made for your account some time since. As you owe Mr. Rogers $5000, I am taking this to offset your indebtedness. I suppose this will be all right. The $5000 has been credited to your account to-day."

296. CLEMENS TO ROGERS (telegram)

Riverdale
[? 8] March 1902

½ rate
Night telegram ¹

H. H. Rogers
Fairhaven, Mass.

Can't get away this week I have company here from tonight till

middle of next week will Kanawha be sailing after that and can I go
as Sundayschool Supt at half rate Answer and prepay.

Dr. Clemens

¹ The text for this telegram is a draft. The telegram itself does not survive and
may not have been sent.

297. CLEMENS TO ROGERS

[Miami]
[? 18] March [1902] ¹

Dear Mr. Rogers:

Nassau; That's the trip to take—all sunshine and summer seas
below Hatteras.² Look it up, in that Cyclopedia; and I will go and
interview somebody acquainted with the trip, to-morrow evening.

Yrs Ever

SLC

¹ The dating of this letter is problematic. Clemens headed it simply "March
28," and most of the evidence indicates that the year was 1902. In 1902,
however, the *Kanawha* had already visited Nassau on 20 and 21 March. On 14
March 1902, Clemens had reported to Livy: "There is no itinerary, thus far." On
the other hand, Clemens wrote Laurence Hutton on 2 March 1902, indicating
that the decision to "escape the storms of Hatteras and the cold weather" had
already been made. It is possible that Clemens miswrote "28" for "18" March,
when they were still in Miami and preparing to sail for Nassau on the 19th.
² The itinerary finally decided upon took the company from Palm Beach to
Miami by rail where they joined the yacht; then to Nassau, back to Key West,
and westward to Havana on 23 March. Turning the western end of Cuba on 25
March, the yacht headed for Kingston, Jamaica, arriving on 27 March. They
touched at Santiago, Cuba, and then headed northward by way of Rum Cay;
Nassau; Jacksonville, Florida; and finally Charleston, Norfolk, and New York
City. Rogers, Clemens, Rice, Colonel Paine, Laurence Hutton, and W. T. Foote
made up the party, which undertook numerous expeditions inland at these ports.
Clemens's log of this "Winter-end Excursion to the Sutherd" is in the Salm
Collection.
  On the return trip, Reed had to leave the *Kanawha* at Old Point Comfort,
Virginia, in order to hurry north by rail to argue a law case. After he left, the
yacht struck a storm, violent squalls of wind, a downpour of rain, and a "mellow"

thunderclap (Notebook 35, TS p. 9). Rogers subsequently framed and hung in his office a letter which Reed wrote on 17 April 1902. A copy (all in Clemens's hand) survives in the Salm Collection:

Dear Mr. Rogers:

I still think we had a most lovely trip, and I am still grateful; I am told, however, that you had trouble immediately after I left. Which leads me to counsel you not to take the yacht out unless you have on board persons of such weight with the community that they can keep the boat level. The Colonel, Hutton, Foote and Mr. Twain are all well enough in their way: quite interesting people, but they lack gravity.

Very truly yours
T. B. Reed

This is well meant, but not well reasoned: for a yacht needs virtue as well as ballast.

Mark

298. CLEMENS TO ROGERS

Riverdale
14 April 1902

Monday

Dear Mr. Rogers:

Mrs. Clemens bought the Casey house, near Tarrytown, while we ⟨are⟩ were away, for what the Caseys paid for the land the house stands on—$45,000. There are 19 acres, and everything in good shape. We are very well satisfied.[1] Mrs. C. paid $2,500 down, and we must pay the rest ten or fifteen days hence.

There's $21,000 in the Guaranty Trust; so we must sell 200 shares of Union Pacific or of U.S. Steel. Will you decide which it shall be?—and ask Miss Harrison to sell for me. Both are selling at what we paid for them, I think; so the dividends have been a gain, and there'll be no loss on the sales. There's enough money in the Lincoln bank to piece out the rest of the bill.

We shall need some more cash, but I'll borrow that of you when the necessity arrives. I will also hunt up some other investments for you.

I wrote the Funston article yesterday, for the North American (May number.)[2] It is short, and worth only $600. But last month's article brought $1,000, and I put it up on a letter of credit for Clara, who sails in the Kaiser Wilhelm der Grosse, April 22.

We have offered our Hartford house for sale at $75,000—bottom price $60,000. Mrs. Clemens puts her foot down, there.

There's an applicant for this Riverdale house for the summer months. We are willing. The agent has taken charge of the matter, and hopes to get more than the summer is worth. We are willing.

It was a grand trip in the yacht—it couldn't be improved on. I am expecting to look in on you as soon as I get the letters cleared off.

Yrs ever

SLC

[1] The Clemens family never lived in the Tarrytown house. They went to York Harbor, Maine, for the summer; and later Livy's health made a visit to Italy seem advisable. While they were away, the house was rented; after Livy's death, it was sold in December 1904.
[2] "A Defence of General Funston," *North American Review*, May 1902.

299. ROGERS TO CLEMENS

New York
28 April 1902

My dear Clemens:—

I want you to read the enclosed story, because it has been in my mind all these years as one of the great mysteries.[1] The finding of the vessel as described is true. The Captain and his wife were from Marion, near Fairhaven.

Yours truly,

H H Rogers

[1] Rogers enclosed a clipping from the London *Illustrated News* which recounted "A Riddle of the Sea"—the strange voyage of the brig *Marie Celeste*

which in the 1860's sailed from Boston for Mediterranean ports, but arrived in Spain without any of its passengers or crew. Clemens wrote on the envelope: "Wonderful sea-tale."

300. ROGERS TO CLEMENS

New York
5 May 1902

My dear Clemens:

I have answered one letter as requested.[1] Will tackle the other to-morrow.

Yours truly,

H H Rogers

[1] James F. Strang, of Invercargill, New Zealand, had written "Samuel Clemence Esq (Mark Twain)" on 31 March 1902 to ask whether he would not "send over a message, anything, a few lines," which Strang could read in response to a toast to Mark Twain at a forthcoming meeting of the First Church Literary Society. Clemens noted on Strang's letter: "*You* send him a line." Rogers, as "P. Huttleston," answered the New Zealander:

My son-in-law, Samuel Clemence, has asked me to acknowledge receipt of your letter of March 31st, and say that he regrets exceedingly that he is unable to write you at this time, because of a serious attack of lapsipall. He begs me to thank you very heartily for your kindly expressions, and feels complimented that you and your people should think so well of his literary efforts. He has told me charming and astounding stories of his visit to New Zealand, and it has created in me a great desire to visit your country. My age is ninety-three, and my family think the journey too much for one of my years, but as I am a man of the strictest habits, never having tasted spirituous liquors, tea or coffee, and never having smoked a cigar or lost my temper, I feel sure that I am likely to live to above the century mark.

Mr. Clemence has been in good health until recently, but a trip to the West Indies with a party of riotous gentlemen has laid him low, and we are quite doubtful as to his recovery. He has lost his sense of humor entirely, and is now writing on metaphysical and religious subjects. His latest, and to my mind his best production is in the form of a sermon which has been published in the "Christian Pulpit." His text is "Why will ye doubting stand?" He has also just published in the "National Register" an article entitled: "Do calves need water?" The article has produced much discussion and criticism, and the general feeling in the community is that he is "getting religion."

301. CLEMENS TO ROGERS

Riverdale
16 May 1902

Great Scott!—why *didn't* I stay and tend to that business myself. Pull him in again, and send for me.

We expect to leave for York Harbor in the last half of June, in the Kanawha.[1] I told Mrs. Clemens I invited you and Mrs. Rogers and all the friends you please, and she said it was an impudent speech after your generosity. That is what I get for trying to do the handsome thing by you.

I rushed home yesterday to do some work—and didn't do it.

Mrs. Clemens had a bad time with her heart last night, and for a while could only breathe when sitting up; but she is in much better shape, now, and has gone to the osteopath. She wouldn't allow him to come here—double rates and the Hartford house not sold.

Yours ever

SLC

[1] Rogers did put the *Kanawha* at their disposal when the Clemens family left on 24 June 1902 for York Harbor, Maine.

302. CLEMENS TO ROGERS

Riverdale
17 May 1902

Dear Mr. Rogers:

I believe the enclosed [1] is calculated to deceive. If it has that luck it will load that island onto Tom Reed for *one* while. His free-handed purse will be in for many an assault; and as for his name, it will be given to all the male babies for a generation or so to come. If he lives up to his opportunities, Rum Cay will disappear from the charts by and by, and "Tom Reed's Sand-Pile" will take its place.

Yrs

SLC

Some time Harry must go with me to see those organs. I mean to get one myself. I didn't know they were so inexpensive.

---

[1] Clemens enclosed a copy of a letter dated 17 May 1902 from Reed to the Rev. M. M. J. Cooper, Rector of St. Christopher's, Rum Cay, Bahamas:

Rev. and Dear Sir: Having learned indirectly that an organ is needed for St. Christopher's Church, I have taken the liberty and allowed myself the very real pleasure of buying and shipping one to you by way of Nassau, as a small token of my appreciation of the courtesies and kindnesses extended to the Kanawha's party during our recent visit to Rum Cay. Trusting that this act will be received in the same spirit of good will which prompted it, I remain, dear sir, . . .

303. CLEMENS TO ROGERS

Riverdale

26 May 1902

Dear Mr. Rogers:

I leave to-morrow night for the West,[1] to return by June 12th. Take care of the business the best you can, and telegraph me if you get stuck. Good-bye.

Yrs Ever

SLC

---

[1] He received on 4 June 1902 the honorary degree of LL.D. from the University of Missouri.

304. CLEMENS TO ROGERS (telegram)

York Harbor
27 June 1902

Housed and at home by noon had a perfectly lovely voyage

SLC

305. CLEMENS TO ROGERS

York Harbor
7 July 1902

Dear Mr. Rogers:

It was a shame that I did not speak to you and ask your consent,[1] and you must have been properly and righteously offended; but I thought Miss Harrison had, and naturally she thought I had, and so it never once occurred to me to inquire. Mrs. Clemens was pretty hard on me, and I couldn't think of any defensive thing to say, because heedlessness and carelessness seem poor excuses to people who are not used to dealing in them, and besides they left me just as much to blame, with them as without them. But I will ask you, next time, sure; I shan't forget again. It is awful good of you to hold still and not blow me up; wait till I see you—that's the Christian way; and I need a restful interval in between, anyway.

Jean is all right, now—for another three weeks, no doubt. But if we had been in a train instead of on board the yacht and private and secluded, it would have been equivalent to being in hell. The scare and the anxiety would have been unendurable: Mrs. Clemens was alert, and up the most of the time two nights—and I helped, after a man's fashion—and so the convulsion was staved off; a close fit, but it produced a valuable interval, which lasted clear till yesterday. Then I saw it; I have seen it only three times before, in all these five fiendish years. It comes near to killing Mrs. Clemens every time, and there is not much left of her for a day or two afterward. Every three weeks it comes. It will break her down yet. Some people pray at such times. Yesterday—I didn't.

We are going to squeeze ourselves into the little Tarrytown house next October. It seems to be settled. And we mean to *stay* squeezed till the Hartford house is sold, whether the squeezing is comfortable or not.

I am at work, and progressing first-rate.

With just no end of thanks—*and* apologies—

Yours ever

SL. C

---

[1] Clemens may refer to the tribute to Rogers which he had written on 25 April 1902 and which Rogers refused to allow him to publish. See Appendix G for the text of this tribute, first published by Paine (*MTB*, pp. 1658–1659).

306. CLEMENS TO ROGERS

York Harbor
11 July 1902

July(?) Friday(?) 11th(?) '02.

Dear Mr. Rogers:

I know what year it is, but am not certain about the rest. *Do* come! Choose any date you please, and *see* if you can annoy me. It can't be done. You will be the welcomest man in the universe. And we'll feed you the best we can, too, though not up to Kanawha standard. Come the earliest you can, and the oftenest. We hope you will come now, on your way back from Fairhaven. Our cigar-box (house) is equidistant from York Harbor and from Kittery Point— or thereabouts: 15 minutes by trolley from York Harbor and a little more from Kittery Point. The latter is a snug harbor, shut in, and plenty of water, but York Harbor is exposed and shallow.

Baker is just a darling! And he so wonderfully and clearly and sanely and unerringly differentiates the two personalities that are in him. When he is ⟨glorifying you⟩ admiring you and your goodness to him he is the very model and perfect representative of the gentle and thankful Christian with his happy eyes uplifted to the Throne; and when he is admiring himself and his benignant exploits among the poor and ornery you think it is God that is telling about it, until you notice the spelling. He has the style, the manner, the serene self-complacency, the innocent self-admiration—he has the whole thing down fine; nothing to betray him but his Satanic orthography. But leave him just so; don't send him a spelling-book; for we should lose him: it would elect him to the Holy Family. I think his letters are the gemmiest things I ever saw. Without your testimony to their genuineness, one would be obliged to regard them as extravagant and gross inventions. I have never seen their match; and in only one case (Capt. Ned Wakeman's) have I seen them approached. I think Twichell would say the same. Some time you must let him see one of them.

Why, I thought Rice sailed long ago. I hope there is nothing serious. It is a pity and loss that he can't ⟨enjoy⟩ stand the sea; even when sea-sick he is an excellent addition to a yacht-crowd. He'll have to be converted and reorganized, for he can't properly be spared.

Thanks to goodness I haven't missed a day yet. I believe I can finish this book by the middle of August; a good summer's work, and satisfactory thus far; but I already had a fifth of it (22,000 words) written when I came here.[1]

We'll be looking for you right along, now.

Yrs

SLC

Cuss those Fairchild bonds and stuff![2] Keeps me awake nights.

---

[1] Clemens was working on "Was it Heaven? Or Hell?" (*Harper's Magazine*, December 1902). He had completed it by 11 September; and on 15 September,

in response to an urgent telegram from Frederick A. Duneka of Harper &
Brothers, he sent it on to New York: "Said I would send 'Russian Passport'
tomorrow" (Notebook 35, TS p. 27). Later that day he had second thoughts and
wrote Duneka:

> I tried that Hell or Heaven on Howells [who summered at nearby Kittery
> Point, and who had suggested the story to him], and he left me with the
> impression that it was all right—whereas, it wasn't.
>   I was full of doubts, but when your telegram came to-day I started the story
> along. Half an hour later my eldest daughter remarked that she had carried the
> thing to her room and examined it, and it had a couple of large merits, but that
> they belonged apart, to *be* merits: joined together, they destroyed each other.
> She was right—I saw it in a moment. Too much sermon: it is a millstone
> around the story's neck.
>   Return it to me, and if I can't weed enough of the sermon out at one quick
> sitting to properly and artistically subordinate it, I will at once mail you a brisk
> yarn to take its place: "The Belated Russian Passport." It is short—about 7
> pages of the Monthly I think. I wrote it yesterday and day before, because I
> couldn't get rid of my doubts about that Hell or Heaven (Berg).

2 On the advice of Charles Fairchild, a Wall Street broker, Clemens had
invested $16,000 in the American Mechanical Cashier Company, receiving bonds
and 400 shares of stock which Fairchild had assured him "will be worth $40,000
cash within a reasonable time—and much more later" (Fairchild to SLC, 26
December 1901). Fairchild had formed the corporation in 1901 to market an
automatic money-changing and registering device. By this time it must have
seemed to Clemens a repetition in smaller scale of his Paige typesetter fiasco:
Fairchild wrote occasionally complaining of continuous difficulties in the mass
manufacture of a machine which had won "unlimited praise" as a hand-made
model, but always promising eventual total success. On 11 August 1902 he wrote
Clemens: "The machine is as yet one of promise rather than performance. The
delay has been greater than I expected but the promise is as great as you could
ask. . . . Two hundred machines are building and the shop where the work is
going on is being organized to turn them out in much larger quantities." Yet two
years later, on 12 February 1904, he would again report: "There have been delays
beyond reason and they still continue. . . . As soon as actual deliveries are being
made I will write you again." No additional correspondence between Fairchild
and Clemens has been found, and Clemens later rejected proposals that he invest
still further in the enterprise (see letter 423, note 1).

307. CLEMENS TO ROGERS

York Harbor
28 July 1902

Dear Mr. Rogers:

I'm enclosing the check but not the interest. I don't ever pay
interest until I have examined into a thing and ascertained whether

there is a legal way of avoiding it or not. I have ⟨always⟩ generally found this to be a good business method.

Yesterday Dillingham brought up the dramatist of "Huck Finn," with the MS.[1] It promises to be a pretty good play, and Klaws and Erlanger are so satisfied with it that they are spending $60,000 on it. It will be staged (in the country) in November.

Mr. Witherbee[2] is gone to hell or Mexico, but Whitmore expects to hear from him from there.

The blessing of God rest upon you and Mrs. Rogers.

Yrs ever

SLC

[1] Charles Bancroft Dillingham represented the theatrical managers Marc Klaw and Abraham Erlanger. Clemens had recorded in his notebook on 27 July 1902 (Notebook 35, TS p. 22):

Gave Erlanger a note thro Dillingham approving Lee Arthur's "Huck Finn" and promising no "Tom Sawyer" shall be dramatized before Finn is staged (Nov. 2 '02) and not then until talking with Erlanger first.

Kester's "Tom Sawyer" privilege has lapsed by time limit.

[2] Sidney A. Witherbee of Detroit, Michigan, was negotiating to buy the Hartford house. He had made a preliminary offer early in July (Notebook 35, TS p. 1).

308. Clemens to Rogers

York Harbor
3 August 1902
Sunday.

Dear Mr. Rogers:

I am mailing you a letter containing a proposition to buy the Hartford house for $50,000 worth of 5% railroad bonds; and I am telegraphing Whitmore to ask for an appointment and go down and get your judgment as to whether the bonds are safe and sound or not. The price ($50,000) is eminently satisfactory.[1]

Won't you please tell Whitmore what you think, and whether

the *cash-down* part of W.'s proposition should be $5,000 or double that?

The proposer wants possession Oct. 5. We can give it, possibly, by dreadful work and crowding, but would much rather it should be a fortnight (yes, a *month* later,) if possible, for the emptying of the house will be a good deal of a job for Mrs. Clemens.

If those bonds should happen to be satisfactory it would much gratify

Yrs ever

SLC

---

[1] Witherbee had made this offer to Franklin G. Whitmore on 29 July 1902: "Let Mr. Clemens put, say, a $10,000.00 mortgage on his place, and subject to this mortgage, deed it to me putting deed in escrow, and I put in escrow in same bank, an assignment of $40,000.00 of Kansas City, Mexico and Orient R. R. 5% bonds, upon which I agree to pay 4% until delivered, and further agree to dispose of for him at par within 3 years."

On 1 August Whitmore passed Witherbee's letter on to Clemens, suggesting: "Possibly you may want to refer it to Mr. Rogers and get his opinion. It is quite evident that we shall lose him if we insist upon his making a cash payment as his money seems to be tied up at present."

Clemens wrote this note over the top of Whitmore's letter, when he sent it and Witherbee's to Rogers:

York Harbor, Aug. 2—midnight.
Dear Mr. Rogers: I can't tell, for the life of me, whether this is first-rate or second-rate or what. It is too deep for me. Won't you arrive at a decision for me and tell Whitmore or me whether to take it [or] decline it? By Jackson, I'll be everlastingly obliged if you will.

Yrs ever
SL Clemens

309. ROGERS TO CLEMENS

New York
5 August 1902

My dear Clemens:—

I have read Mr. Whitmore's letter, also Mr. Witherbee's. In the first place, it would seem quite natural to inquire as to the Kansas City, Mexico & Orient Railroad. In view of the fact that Poor's

Manual makes no reference to the railroad, it is reasonably fair to assume that it is not of any great prominence. I certainly would never undertake to enter into the arrangement for myself. In the first place, if you put a ten thousand dollar mortgage on your property, that is a nuisance. In the second place, if you put up the deed of your property subject to that mortgage against forty thousand dollars in bonds of a Railway that has no existence in the investment world, you might as well put your deed up against so much brown paper. Then you surrender your property and the party moves in. The improvements that Mr. Whitmore refers to, might prove in the end to be injurious.

If Mr. Witherbee can sell those bonds within three years, and will guarantee to do so at par, it would be pretty good financial business for him to sell them now at 90, and pay you the cash.

I may be too conservative in this matter, but I have always felt that it is a good deal safer to deal with the devil I know than it is to have business with the devil I don't know.

I judge from Mr. Whitmore's letter that he has told Mr. Witherbee that some cash must be paid down, and Witherbee suggests that you raise it by mortgage. Don't let me influence you too much, but do be careful. It is much easier to keep out of trouble than it is to get out. You and I know that of old.

With best wishes. and kindest regards to the family, I am, as ever,

> Yours truly,
>
> H H Rogers

P.S. I return the letters herewith.[1]

---

[1] On 6 August 1902 Clemens sent Rogers's letter to Whitmore, with this annotation at the top:

Dear Brer: The following shows that Mr. Rogers disapproves. So do I, then, for I have the greatest confidence in his judgment.

> Yours ever
>
> K

On the envelope of Rogers's letter he wrote to Whitmore:

P.S. I understand the enclosed to disapprove of the *renting*-proposition suggested, also. It has some grave objections.

310. CLEMENS TO ROGERS

York Harbor
7 August 1902

Dear Mr. Rogers:

Your letter entirely settled the thing; and as it confirmed Mrs. Clemens's judgment she is pleased and flattered; and as it hoists me out of a fog and into clear air I am pleased, too—flattered, also, I reckon, tho I am unclear as to that. I am always expecting to be flattered, and sometimes it may be that I discover it where it was not intended.

Tom Re⟨i⟩ed was here to the celebration,[1] and was the same delightful and irresistible old bullfrog as ever.

Confound those editors, they emasculated Baker.[2] They've taken his 22 carats of gold out of him and left nothing but his 1 carat of alloy. All the same, his suggestion that if rich men would concentrate their attention on laying *out* their treasures *here below,* the Lord would take care of the transfer Himself, was mighty good.

The thing is happening which was to be expected. Mrs. Clemens's five years of constant anxiety and periodical shocks and frights on Jean's account are bringing a break-down. I am alarmed about her, and she suspects it, tho I lie the best I can in the circumstances, and so does the doctor. In order to be able to breathe, she had to sit upright in bed last night from 9 o'clock almost all the time until 4 this morning. This is becoming a nightly experience. In the daytime she feels fairly well, but has to be watched all the time to keep her from making exertions herself which others could make for her. She has always had good staying power, but good staying power has its limits.

Yours ever

SL. Clemens

Mrs. Clemens has no opinion of Witherbee and instructs Whitmore to withhold his project to propose to him a scheme for taking the house two years on a rental, with privilege of making improvements.

---

[1] Both Clemens and ex-Speaker Thomas B. Reed (from Maine) had spoken briefly at the 250th anniversary celebration of York Harbor, Maine, on 5 August 1902.

[2] The publication of one of William H. Baker's letters in a New Bedford newspaper apparently intimidated the Fairhaven resident into stopping his flow of letters to Rogers; a letter written on 5 October 1904 to thank Rogers for his recent gift to the town—the Unitarian church—explains the lapse:

Perhapes you may wonder why I have wated so long in not bothering you with my comuneacations no doubt you will smile when I tell you the principale reason is when I read in the N B Standard about that wonderfull sectuary of yours and that she read all the Letters that I sent you it allmost took my breath away when I thought of the many foolish things I had wrote it come to my mind that she must have thought that if I claimed to be your frind you wer not very choist of your Friends well you can feel thankfull that their is something to hold me in check no doubt you have enough to take up your valuable time with out my bothering of you.

311. CLEMENS TO ROGERS

York Harbor
13 August 1902

Dear Mr. Rogers:

Matters reached a culminating point at 7 a.m., yesterday, when Mrs. Clemens said she was dying and I was not able to doubt it. But by 7.30 we had the doctor, and he took heroic measures. Before noon the case had ceased to be immediately alarming, though the danger was not past, and will not be past until we know ⟨there is not⟩ the attack is not merely suspended but is *over*.

We have a pair of excellent physicians. One is an osteopath with an allopathic diploma and training, and the other is a New York M.D. They work together. One comes several times a day and the other stays all night.

Clara arrived from Europe last night, and the doctors decided that she could see her mother a moment. They thought it might be good medicine. It proved so.

Yrs Ever

SLC

312. Rogers to Clemens (telegram)

New York

14 August 1902

Your letter of yesterday rec'd. I have been very anxious since your last letter. Mrs Rogers, who is with me, joins in earnest sympathy and we are both desirous of serving you if we can   Dont fail to command us because we are to be classed among your warmest friends

H H Rogers

313. Clemens to Rogers

York Harbor

21 August 1902

Aug. 21 or 22.

Dear Mr. Rogers:

As soon as you had been gone 2 hours and I had sent off an urgent letter to Boston for an air bed, *then* somebody mentioned that you had air beds on the yacht!

It is just my luck. I believed Mrs. Clemens had lost a whole day by that accident. Up to now she has lost *several.* Of all the impossible places for the meeting of emergencies promptly and successfully, this is the impossiblest.

The illness drags along. Part of each day, now, we feel fine and cheerful—the other part of it we feel discouraged. But the worst of all is, that Mrs. Clemens feels doubtful all the time. She was never like this before, in her life.

I strongly want to write Whitmore to get rid of the house—sell it for a song. So that I can tell Mrs. Clemens that that burden upon her spirits is gone. For she secretly reproaches herself for buying the new house before selling the old one. I *shall* write him substantially that, now.

Yrs Ever

SLC

314. CLEMENS TO ROGERS

York Harbor

22 August 1902

Dear Mr. Rogers:

The air bed is on its way from Boston and will arrive to-morrow. And the same is good news.

Mrs. Clemens is doing so well that at last she was able to partially quit plasmon this morning and take to solid food. She slept well last night and is sleeping a good deal to-day.

Yours ever

SLC

315. CLEMENS TO ROGERS

York Harbor

27 August 1902

Dear Mr. Rogers:

We are scheming on a most difficult problem: how to move Mrs. Clemens to Elmira—say a week from now or a few days later. It is not expected that she will be strong enough by that time to sit up in a train, but the idea is to move her from Boston by Albany and Binghamton in a sleeping-stateroom.

The gap between here and Boston is not coverable by land, in any thinkable way. Could you cruise around to York Harbor about that time, do you think, and take us to Boston in the yacht? It was the doctor's idea, but Mrs. Clemens does not want me to put it before you. I said there could be no indelicacy in putting it before you, for the reason that you do not dodge around stumps, but are a frank man, and will say no, if the project would be inconvenient— as indeed it may, for you may be going away on a summer excursion.

She is tired of the bed, and longing to get away—go somewhere —anywhere, for a change—and there is but one place where she will be entirely at home, and that is at "Quarry Farm," our summer home in the early days, on the hill-top 1300 feet above sea-level. The doctor recognizes the wisdom—and maybe the necessity—of moving her.

She was getting along fairly well—so much so that during the past three days I have hardly been a sick-nurse at all,[1] but have written a story—8,000 words, which is more than 4 days' work.[2] But in the house, of course, and close at hand. Mrs. Crane occupies my study, in Mr. Sewall's house.[3] No work now for a while, I suppose. It looks that way. She had a bad night, and has lost ground a little. She will pick it up, though, I believe.

I am sending my love to Mrs. Rogers.

Yours ever

SLC

[1] On 25 August 1902 Clemens, however, had recorded (Notebook 35, TS p. 24): "Livy's illness hangs on, and on, from day to day, and there is never any *great* improvement; never anything to rouse us and make us jubilant."

[2] Among other things, Clemens was revising "Was it Heaven? Or Hell?"

[3] Millard Sewall was a neighbor; when things were difficult at home, Clemens sometimes spent the night at his house (see Notebook 35, TS p. 28).

316. CLEMENS TO ROGERS (telegram)

York Harbor
28 August 1902

Thank you without limit will write you my later scheme [1]

Clemens

[1] On 3 September 1902 Clemens would set down a grateful entry (Notebook 35, TS p. 25): "Always Mr. Rogers keeps his yacht (Kanawha) in commission and ready to fly here and take us to Riverdale on telegraphic notice."

317. CLEMENS TO ROGERS

York Harbor
28–29 August 1902

Aug. 28/02.

Dear Mr. Rogers:

To-day I've struck it!

I have found that I can get a special car, with a bed in it and various accommodations, which will take us aboard at York Harbor station and land us in Elmira without change.

It will travel over various roads, and it may be that

Aug. 29, 1 p.m.

But the doctors are not so confident about that scheme: too much rattle and clash, and wear and tear ⟨and delay⟩ of land-travel, and too long a stretch, too much tension. They say if she could sail to Hoboken and be carried into a stateroom on a daylight train it would cut the railroading down to 6 or 7 hours and deliver her in Elmira in much better condition. (I perceive that this is more yachting than you've been called upon to consider—but that is all right, I would provide the cigars myself.)

This evening I am to get some of the time-and-distance details of the all-rail journey, and the rest of them to-morrow afternoon.

Aug. 29 again—20 minutes later.

Your generous letter of yesterday has just arrived—only 2 minutes after I had committed myself for the cigars; which is just some people's luck, you see. I showed Mrs. Clemens your telegram and it broke her all up. It will happen again when I show her your letter. I think the telegram is the only piece of writing she has been allowed to see during this sickness. She wanted to keep it, so I left it with her. She is improving—very slowly, but *actually*, I think, the past day or two. To-day she has sat up 10 minutes in a chair.

We shan't be able to move her until she can sit up one or two hours in a day. We can't tell when that will be, because she has had so many backsets that every prophecy we make scores a failure. But it will be days yet; then I will let you know as soon as we can safely guess a date.

I suppose this letter will not reach you before Sunday. I will put a hurry-stamp on it, so that the post-office will deliver it on the Sabbath.

With the kindest regards of us all to you all.

SLC

We only know for sure that it won't be next week that she can travel, but later.

318. CLEMENS TO ROGERS

York Harbor
1 September 1902

Dear Mr. Rogers:

It is lovely of you. We could not have shown your telegram to Mrs. Clemens yesterday, but she can see it (this evening or to-morrow) before night, I think, for she shows much improvement to-day. It continues to be a case of down-and-up, up-and-down. Yesterday I thought her chances were bad, she was so weak and exhausted and discouraged; but to-day it is handsomely different. When she is "up" she thinks she is going to start in a week—always that. But if it isn't the double of that I shall be very much surprised indeed.

I will give lots of notice—of date, number of persons, etc—

If she were able to talk, I would try to persuade her to go to Riverdale and avoid *all* railroading. But I don't know that I should succeed.

There's 200 Union Pacific pf. left. It cost 88½ and is selling at 94¼. Wouldn't it be good commerce for Miss Harrison to put in an order to sell at 100—if it gets there? If it shouldn't get there—well, that's another matter.

------

3 *p.m.* Mrs. Clemens has seen the telegram and sends her love and grateful thanks. In which joins

SLC

That $2,230.48 raises the credit in Guaranty Trust to a good figure—for which, a thousand thanks. I think there's $15,000 there now. Mrs. C. will be sure to begin building the addition at Tarry-town. I shan't oppose it any longer, if her heart is set on it.

319. CLEMENS TO ROGERS

York Harbor

[3] September 1902

Sept. 3(?) 02.

Dear Mr. Rogers:

Mrs. Clemens began to sit up yesterday once more, and did it twenty minutes. Therefore she was feeling better. Feeling better, she began to plan, of course. It was plain enough that she was not likely to be strong enough to travel in any way for as much as ten days yet, even if her recovery gets no check. Then of course she was at once troubled about the yacht and in dread lest you might be delaying a cruise on her account. So she urged me to write and beg you not to think of such a thing, but to make your cruise and if you didn't get back by the time she was strong you must not curtail your holiday by a day but let her take to the rail.

I promised to write the letter last night but I got no chance, so I am writing it now and sponging off my conscience. She is perfectly right about it—head and heart both—and so even I join with her and endorse. But if you should get back in time, I'll be on the lookout and will set up a hail!

She has sat up another 20 minutes to-day, and is thin and has lost color—much more than I thought for—in fact I was astonished, for these things are not so apparent when she is in bed. But all the same she is improving immensely.

Now I'll start this straight to the post by the doctor.

Yours Ever

SLC

320. CLEMENS TO ROGERS

York Harbor
11 September 1902

Dear Mr. Rogers:

Mrs. Clemens said this morning that the number to go in the yacht would be the family, the doctor, and a maid—6 persons.

Provided all are well. But if Jean should be on the sick list she will remain behind and go home with Katy [1] and the cook by rail when in condition.

That would make the number for the yacht, 5.

———

Mrs. Clemens is almost counting on Wednesday Sept. 17—*but!* We don't discuss anything with her—she would get excited—but we have doubts about that date. Whenever a date can be named I will at once telegraph you, as long a time in advance as possible— three or four days in advance, if possible.

Mrs. Clemens detests plasmon, yet she has to live on it, as far as keeping up her strength goes. She can take solid food, but not enough of it to nourish her.

She has had two bad turns in the last 48 hours, through experimenting with foods. One was an egg, and the other a half-teacupful of malted milk. They acted like poisons—numbed her arms and distributed pains over a large nerve-surface.

We can't oppose the patient, nor discuss any matter with her; otherwise we would say, *drop all idea of a railway journey*, and go to Riverdale. We are hoping she may see the wisdom of that herself, yet, and propose it.

Yours ever

SLC

---

[1] Katy Leary came to work as Livy's personal maid in 1880 and remained with the Clemens family until Clemens's death in 1910.

321. CLEMENS TO ROGERS

York Harbor

18–19 September 1902

Dear Mr. Rogers:

Confound it, the doctors have reversed their opinion to-night, and decide that Mrs. Clemens must give up the idea of going by sea. And we had just got your kind telegram last night. The *doctor,* I mean—there is only one, now. I cannot help thinking it is a mistake, but I can't say anything, because I mustn't venture the responsibility. In the morning I will telegraph you. I am very grateful to you for being so generous and patient and keeping the yacht so long at our disposal. I would thank you to the full, if I knew how—but you will understand.

I wish I could have had old Kellgren here from Sweden when Mrs. Clemens was taken, the 12th of August. With his two hands he is worth fifty osteopaths and fifty million doctors.[1] He would have had the madam on her feet and as sound as a nut in three days. I wonder she is alive at all. It has been one continual guess, guess, guess, change, change, change, from one incompetent drug to another, and from one indigestible food to another. It seems a stupid idea to keep a student 4 years in a medical college to merely learn how to guess—and guess wrong. If ever I am deadly ill I hope you will stand by me and bar out the doctors and let me die a natural death.

We have had three doctors, and I implored them all to feed the madam solely on plasmon for three days; but only two-thirds of a day would they ever stand—then they got scared and went to guessing again and raised some more hell. At last, having tried everything else and failed, this one consented yesterday to a 24-hour trial; the time is up, now, and the results are so good that the madam is herself almost convinced, and is willing to chance another 24. The only strength she has she got from the plasmon that was mixed with the failures—as the doctor has to admit.

Yrs ever

SLC

P.S. *19th.*

I was so counting upon the yacht, and now it is all spoiled.

---

[1] On 21 September 1902 Clemens would note: "Dr. Helmer was telegraphed for yesterday and came to-day and treated the patient." It was "a severe treatment" which "left Livy sore and lame and she slept but little, the night." When her physician suggested two days later that Dr. Helmer be telegraphed not to come again "for a few days," in order to "give the patient time to gather strength to bear the treatment," Clemens wrote, "*It was his treatment that enabled her to take food.*" But, he continued, "I stand alone in this opinion. We are a drifting ship without a captain" (Notebook 35, TS pp. 27–28). Clemens's old suspicions of the medical profession emerged again as he prescribed for Livy the Plasmon diet and strenuous massage, and made plans for sending her (a poor sailor) home by sea. However inept his attempts to care for her were, they reveal something of the depth of his concern and angry desperation.

322. CLEMENS TO ROGERS

York Harbor
20 September 1902

Dear Mr. Rogers:

It was pretty hard for Mrs. Clemens to give up the yacht, but she is not a good sailor, and the doctor says that if her stomach should refuse work for three or four hours she would be exhausted. Therefore Charley Langdon is going to attend to engaging a Pullman to take us through from York Harbor station to Riverdale without change, and I am writing Mr. Daniels of the N.Y.C.[1] to ask him to have us hitched to an Express from Boston by Albany and discharge us at Riverdale in the daytime; or detach us at Yonkers and snatch us down with dispatch behind a locomotive or a local train.

When, I don't know. Not for days yet—and maybe other days.

It is still a case of up and down, and down and up—has been, for 40 days. She had a bad time yesterday afternoon late. Then was better. Bad again this morning, with heavy sweating from weakness. This afternoon she is better again, and is sleeping.

Jean prospers here. It is 7½ weeks, now, since she has had a faint. It is the longest interval by a week and a half, in four years.

Yrs ever

SLC

[1] George H. Daniels was general passenger agent for the New York Central Railroad.

323. CLEMENS TO ROGERS

York Harbor
23 September 1902

Sept 23—night.

Dear Mr. Rogers:

We have been profoundly alarmed about Mrs. Clemens for several days, and particularly to-day. But to-night we are easier, as we are assured that there is no immediate danger.

Sincerely

SLC

324. CLEMENS TO ROGERS

York Harbor
24 September 1902 [1]

Dear Mr. Rogers:

Your letter is infinitely touching, and I am grateful beyond any words. I wrote you a note last night which was gloomy, and there was cause. We believed that the end was very close at hand. Mrs. Clemens is only a shadow now, and she seemed past the rallying point. Nothing escapes her, even when there is apparently no light in her eyes, and she discovered our alarm and hunted it home, questioning the witnesses one at a time; and out of their tangle of lies extracting the truth, to the last detail. She saw that there was no one about her with any real courage left, except Katy. She lay and meditated long upon the situation—two or three hours—then her mind was made up, and she said *"I intend to get well,"* and dismissed the subject. Meantime I had been flying about York Harbor, and caught one New York physician of note and started him out, and telephoned Boston for another. The New York doctor raised the chances and did good.[2] This morning the Boston one [3] said (I privately asked him to tell me the square truth and not spare me) "I at present see no reason at all that she should not build up and get as well as she was before."

I improved on this report a little, and the effect upon the patient was (imme) fine.

A professional nurse has arrived from Boston, and the impossible has happened: Mrs. Clemens has received her with favor.[4] We have been banished, and Mrs. Clemens accepts it.

Our difficulty has been, that Mrs. Clemens has remained what she always was: boss. Her long-headed intelligence and wisdom (and strong character) have kept the place for her in spite of her physical helplessness, and we weaklings have done as was our life-long habit—succumbed; we were never taught anything else. She has bossed the 4 doctors just the same, and made them do her way. But not the two new ones—the specialists: they have character, they have reputation, they require obedience, and she has promised it. She is able to recognize merit and masculinity when she sees them, and defer to their authority.

We shall be here weeks yet.

Yes, a considerable factor in this heart-attack and its allies, was worry. But when I found it was about the Tarrytown house I modified it a good deal, I think. I showed her an offer of $50,000 for it, and told her I had replied that we preferred to keep the place and were not in the market. Fortunately she has not worried very much over the disastrous and unexpected detail that the Hartford house doesn't sell—no, I do *that* worrying myself. The Tarrytown place will hold its value—but the Hartford one doesn't seem to have any to hold.

I hope I can soon get permission to show Mrs. Clemens your letter—it should be good for heart disease, I think.

I will send this to New York and Miss Harrison will know whether to forward it or retain it.

Yours Ever

SLC

¹ Clemens dated this letter "Sept. 23/02." Both notebook entries and a letter to Mrs. James Ross Clemens (26 September 1902) indicate that the letter actually was written on 24 September.
² "Dr. Allen came yesterday and raised our spirits. A marked change followed" (Notebook 35, TS p. 27).
³ Dr. Putnam, according to Notebook 35.
⁴ The new nurse, Miss Gourangé, did not last long: Clara discharged her six days later. The next nurse, Margaret Garrety, took charge on 29 September 1902 and seemed better at first: "If we had had her in the beginning Livy would be well, now," wrote Clemens; but less than a month later he discharged her also as "vain, silly, self-important, untrustworthy, a most thorough fool, and a liar by instinct and training" (Notebook 35, TS pp. 29–30).

325. CLEMENS TO ROGERS

York Harbor
26 September 1902

Dear Mr⟨s⟩. Rogers:

Mrs. Clemens has read the letter, and it moved her deeply, as I knew it would. Among other things, she said, "In sharp stress you would go [to] Mr. Rogers, and I would consent; but you would not go to any other friend in the world; and if you should be willing, I should not consent."

Now, you see, you are protected, for I can't make out a case of sharp stress which would come up to her standard.

The improvement goes on. I sleep out of the house, and the family keep away from her room and leave her to the trained nurse —which is solitude and quiet and rest.

The doctors have been babies in her hands—and the rest of us. If we had had a *man* on deck, she would have had a nurse and tranquillity and been on her feet 4 weeks ago, and she would have saved her summer and I mine.

She asked me to send her kindest regards to you and emphasize it.

Yrs ever

SLC

326. CLEMENS TO ROGERS

York Harbor
11 October 1902
Saturday

Dear Mr. Rogers:

We expect to attempt the flight next Wednesday, 15th, leaving here at 8.45 a.m., and reaching Riverdale 9 hours later—*about* 6. p.m. The physicians agree that Mrs. Clemens can venture it.

We have cut the trip down 2 hours at each end by hiring special locomotives. We've got an invalid car, and it goes through without breaking bulk—whole expense, $340. Cheaper to go by yacht. I mean for *us,* not for you.

It is a long time since I have seen the patient, but the reports are pretty fair. But she is no stronger than she was when I saw her.

Jean's case is miraculous—no attack in upwards of 10 weeks.

Yrs Ever

SLC

Clara does all the generalship of breaking up here and unloading at Riverdale and is doing it like an expert—same as her mother.

327. ROGERS TO CLEMENS

New York
24 December 1902

My dear Clemens: [1]

For many years your friends have been complaining of your use of tobacco, both as to quantity and quality. Complaints are now coming in of your use of time. Most of your friends think you are using your supply somewhat lavishly, but the chief complaint is in regard to the quality.

I have been appealed to in the matter, and have concluded that it is impossible to get the right kind of time from a blacking-box.

Therefore, I take the liberty of sending you herewith a machine [2] that will furnish only the best. Please use it with the kind wishes of

Yours truly,

H H Rogers

P.S. Complaint has also been made in regard to the furrows you make in your trowsers in scratching matches. You will find a furrow on the bottom of the article enclosed. Please use it, Compliments of the Season to the family.

[1] This letter was copied by an amanuensis and signed by Rogers. On the envelope Clemens has written: "Livy Dear, this has just arrived by special messenger."

[2] On the same day Miss Harrison wrote Clemens: "After the holidays if you will please bring me your watch, I will see that the proper inscription is put on it."

328. CLEMENS TO ROGERS

Riverdale
25 December 1902

Xmas,/02.

Dear Mr. Rogers:

I am right down glad my friends did not approve the quality of the time I was exploiting and had no cordial confidence in the blacking-box, for now I have my reward. It is just a daisy, this new watch! and if I had old Baker's flow and gift of language I could thank you as I *want* to; but as it is, I only feel it and can't say it. You know there *was* something inadequate about the blacking-box, although I dissembled concerning it. It never called me at eight exactly; it couldn't seem to hit the bull's eye, but knocked the splinters off all around it, five and ten points out, sometimes to the east, sometimes to the west—but this one drove the centre this morning, a fine and impressive novelty.

The furrow-preventer is lovely—it was dear and good of you to think of that protector. Mrs. Clemens took the care of the silver one years ago, lest I should lose it (that was her way of smoothing-over robbery with violence), and her friend the Jesuit priest got away with it. She will want to protect this one when she gets well. I wonder when that will be; she had a bad time day before yesterday, but is doing well, now, and sent down her Xmas greetings for you and Mrs. Rogers this morning, but you were away from home and the telephone. Clara is lying to her with an expertness and ability born of sick-room practice, and making her believe Jean is having pleasant times out-doors; if she knew Jean's temperature of yesterday (103⅖) and to-day (103⅘) and that the doctor cannot determine what the disease is, she would go out of her mind.[1]

I'm coming in, in a few days. Thank you ever so much about that contract, I must call Harvey's attention to that clause.[2]

Your chances are good for a Merry Xmas, and here is hoping you and yours ⟨will⟩ are hav⟨e⟩ing it in full measure.

Yours ever

SL. Clemens

---

[1] On 23 December 1902, while Clemens was staying overnight at Rogers's house in New York, Jean had come down with a severe fever. On 28 December Clemens would record: "It was pneumonia," adding later that evening:

For 6 days, now, my story in the Xmas Harper ("Was it Heaven? or Hell?") has been enacted in this house: every day Clara and the nurses have lied about Jean to her mother—describing the fine time she is having out of doors in winter sports! (Notebook 35, TS p. 35.)

[2] In November 1900 Clemens had given Harper & Brothers exclusive rights to all Mark Twain books and articles until January 1902 (George Harvey to SLC, 14 November 1900); negotiations must now have been under way for the extension of that agreement which in October 1903 became a contract between them (see Appendix E).

329. Clemens to Emilie Rogers

Riverdale
25 December 1902

Xmas/02

Dear Mrs. Rogers:

It is lovely of you to remember my vices, not to rebuke them but to condone them. It is the right spirit, and I thank you. If there was more of it in the world we could have more vices and be happier.

(That pension is collected. *He* doesn't believe there's any Lewis, but it's all right, I've got the money.) [1]

1.45 p.m. The doctor has just been in. He is still uncertain as to Jean's malady, but fears it is pneumonia. I was privately suspecting it myself.

The very best of Christmases to you, dear Mrs. Rogers.

Sincerely Yours

S. L. Clemens

[1] Rogers joined Clemens in contributing to the pension of John T. Lewis, a retired servant of the Langdon family who years before, in 1877, had saved Mrs. Charles Langdon and her small daughter from possible death or serious injury when a horse ran away with the carriage she was driving (see *MTB*, pp. 599–600).

330. Clemens to Rogers

Riverdale
1 January 1903

Dear Mr. Rogers:
Here is what he says. [1]

SLC

Happy New Year to you all! (Jean improves.)

¹ This note is written across the top of a letter of 31 December 1902 from George Harvey to Clemens, which said: "I cannot tell you how sorry I am to hear of your daughter's illness, and I sincerely hope that by this time the worst is over. Regarding the contracts, I shall hold myself fully at Mr. Rogers's convenience."

331. CLEMENS TO EMILIE ROGERS

Riverdale
2 January 1903

Dear Mrs. Rogers:

I hasten to put into your hands part of a letter from Mrs. Crane (Mrs. Clemens's sister) which can be used on Mr. Rogers, not as proof that there is such a person as John T. Lewis, but as presumptive evidence. I shall accumulate other evidence of a plausible sort from time to time, and pass it through your hands—not to be used suddenly and breed suspicion, but applied warily and with the most cautious judacity.¹ I think a photograph will be a persuasive thing —a nice smart dark-complected photograph, ostensibly of Lewis. Also a receipt in a dark-complected orthography purporting to come from Lewis. In this way we can eventually convince Mr. Rogers; and then we can get the money every time, and spend it. I think he is more than half convinced ⟨no⟩ already.

Think of Providence putting off a debt to Lewis 18 years, and then ⟨paying it⟩ smouching it out of Mr. Rogers's pocket, a perfect stranger. It was 18 years ago that he was executor. The ways of Providence are past finding out. I'm sorry, too; for some of them are economical.

I saw Mrs. Clemens again yesterday for 5 minutes, and she was in great spirits, and sent her love to you, and the same in a properly qualified form to Mr. Rogers.

Jean is doing finely, *very* finely.

Sincerely Yours

SL. Clemens

¹ It must have been at this time, or soon after, that Clemens sent the following undated burlesque note (Salm) to Rogers:

Mister roggers dear sir i left a cain in that crockery jug in yore offis it has a
sollid gold hed on it but looks like puter on accounts of wether and hard usidge
and is wuth ninety fore dolers send me the mony if she is lost or took by yore
son hairey or eny of those others which hangs eround thair they probly took
her before this time send it to jon t louis he will see i git it and goddlemighthty
will bless you dear mister roggers so no more at preasant from yore true freind
in jesus

archible askins
care jon t louis

And, perhaps a little later, he sent this note (now in CWB) to Rogers:
(*Night telegram.*)
Henry Rogers, 26 Broadway, N. Y.
    Party here name of Lewis addicted to simple Christian life is busted pleas
send releaf send it awful quick or too late to help yours truly
Baker of Fairhaven

(Operator please follow both spelling and punctuation.)
Charge to ac of
SL. Clemens
I was going to telegraph you this, but on second thoughts it seemed to lack
gravity. SLC

332. CLEMENS TO KATHARINE HARRISON

Riverdale
12 January 1903

Dear Miss Harrison [1]

I keep forgetting. Do remind me the next time I come, to
mention to Mr. Rogers two or three very important details that
should go into the Harper contract.

1, that the original price of the book cannot be reduced without
my consent in writing;

2, Bliss shall be allowed to add the book to his collection after a
named interval, say six months or a year;

3, that I being Bliss's partner want the threatening letters to
cease, as they injure my pocket.

Mrs. Clemens is progressing splendidly; she is buoyant and
cheerful; I see her fifteen minutes every day now; I believe she will
be creeping about the house before the summer comes.

Jean sits up in bed, and reads and plays games, eats well, sleeps
well and has a good time. She has not looked so fresh and healthy

in five years. But both lungs had hard usage, and the Doctor has ordered her south. We are in a condition of consternation, for Mrs. Clemens would be sure to find out she was gone, and the shock would prostrate her again. Providence is after me with a Gatling.

My watch keeps perfect time now that it is marked.

Send Lewis's check to me the first of the month; don't send it to Lewis it might get lost. Draw it to my order too, Lewis does not write a very good hand.

Please tell Mr. Rogers not to forget that we are to raid the families. I am ready any time.

Sincerely Yours.

SL. Clemens

Bliss has sent me $7000.00 and will send the rest soon.[2]

[1] This letter, signed by Clemens, is in the hand of Isabel V. Lyon, his private secretary.

[2] Clemens had noted that "cash income from my books for 1902 was $60,000 (both publishers). Cash from all sources, something over $100,000" (Notebook 36, TS p. 3).

333. CLEMENS TO EMILIE ROGERS

Riverdale
1 February 1903

Dear Mr. Rogers:[1]

Mrs. Clemens's delight in those magnificent roses reached standard. I knew it would when I saw them down stairs. I promised to thank you for them the first thing in the morning, and send you her love.

And I made her envious of the birth-day evening at your house,[2] and told her how handsome each member of the family was, and yet how stunningly and conspicuously beautiful Mr. Rogers was, in the midst of even that formidable competition; and how splendidly competent Mr. Broughton was at table with his pawnshop reminiscences; in a word, what an all-round charming and satisfactory a birth-day it was, and how she might have been there herself if she had taken better care of her health when she had a chance.

Mr. Rogers promised to come here to luncheon with you on a Sunday, and Clara and I want you to make it ⟨next⟩ Sunday after next if you can. (I first wrote "next," but Clara has some idiots here that day.) By that time we mean to get the weather in good shape for you, and will have that old ambulance chartered and waiting at the station if we hear favorably from you.

I have a ten-dollar check for that John T. Lewis whom Mr. Rogers has so many doubts about.

Sincerely Yours

SL. Clemens

---

[1] Clemens miswrote. The context and the envelope address clearly indicate that he meant "Mrs." Rogers.
[2] Clemens noted in his appointment book under 29 January 1903: "Mr. Rogers's birth-day 7.30 p.m." Rogers was sixty-three.

334. CLEMENS TO EMILIE ROGERS

Riverdale

6 February 1903

Yes, dear Mrs. Rogers, Sunday the 15th, that is the date. If you will be good enough to telephone me an hour before you leave home I will roust out the Riverdale ambulance so that you won't have to walk up from the station.

With my love

Sincerely Yours

SL. Clemens

335. ROGERS TO CLEMENS

New York
24 February 1903

My dear Clemens:

I have your letters, and will make the appointment for the review of the article in the "Cosmopolitan." [1]

I note what you say in regard to jury duty, and will endeavor to get you relieved.

I hand you herewith copy of letter received from Mr. Bliss, which will explain itself. Please read carefully. I think you had better get permission from Harper & Bros. in regard to the publication of the Russian Passport story,[2] and remember about copyrighting hereafter.

Sorry to hear that Mrs. Clemens is not progressing favorably.

Yours truly,

HH Rogers

[1] The reference is unclear. The *Cosmopolitan* had been running a series of biographical sketches called "Captains of Industry" since May 1902, and Samuel E. Moffett had already written a sketch of Rogers for the September 1902 issue (XXXIII, 532–534). Rogers may have wanted to "review" a similar article about one of his business associates. But another possibility is suggested by John Brisben Walker's promise in the January 1903 *Cosmopolitan* ("Pierpont Morgan, His Advisers and His Organization"), that in a future issue "Mr. Rockefeller, his chiefs of staff, and his organization will be treated" (p. 244). No article on the Standard Oil appeared in *Cosmopolitan* for 1903 or 1904.

[2] Bliss was not sure that he would be allowed to publish "The Belated Russian Passport" in Volume 23 of the autograph edition; Clemens sent him Rogers's letter on 25 February with the following note (in Isabel Lyon's hand, signed by Clemens) written on it: "I have this moment telephoned Mr. Duneka and asked him to send you an authorization to use the "Russian Passport" in your forthcoming volume, and he said he would attend to it at once. Go ahead and put it in" (Yale). It was included in *My Début as a Literary Person with Other Essays and Stories* (April 1903).

336. Clemens to Rogers

Riverdale
28 February 1903

Dear Mr. Rogers—

Consound it, Clara tells me the Rices are coming here to dinner Tuesday Evening March 3, an engagement 2 weeks old, and swears she told me of it at the time—which is mere sick-room veracity; she never told me till to-day.

I am sorry to miss going with you to see the General,[1] and so is Mrs. Clemens.

I thank you ever so much for getting me out of that jury business —I can not *stand* jurying.

Yrs ever

SLC

[1] Clemens had been scheduled to attend a dinner at which Rogers and Salvation Army General William Booth were to be present.

337. Clemens to Rogers

New York
13 March 1903

Friday, 13th.

Dear Mr. Rogers:

I gather that you are likely to be down Monday or Tuesday. In that case could you see Mr. Doubleday [1] a moment, and let him get your judgment on the Bliss-Collier-Harper matter? [2] He has been working at it about a fortnight and I think he has got it in promising shape.

If you will telephone him he will come down at any time.

Collier is getting restive, but I hope he won't fly the track.

The cussed business is full of complications, but nearly all of them have been side-tracked.

By the latest word from the office I am glad to know that Mrs. Broughton is doing as well as the surgeons could expect.

Yours sincerely

SL. Clemens

[1] This letter is written on the letterhead of Doubleday, Page & Company, 34 Union Square, New York.

[2] Clemens wanted the Collier Publishing Company to issue a ten-volume edition of selected writings of Mark Twain, which would include books published by Harper & Brothers and by the American Publishing Company (SLC to Frank Doubleday, 26 April 1903). Bliss had explained in a letter of 7 March 1902 to Clemens:

> Collier's ideas were to pay $1. per set for the use of the American Co.'s books and 50 Cts. per set for the Harper books, which arrangement with the Harpers he would undertake to make himself, in that way getting around the difficulty in our contract with the Harpers. The $1. to be paid us was to be divided between you and us, Collier guaranteeing 25,000 sets per year for three years, amounting to $75,000. Of course there was nothing attractive in that; but I felt that he would make better figures than those and that if he would pay $2. per set there was some chance to do something, and so we spent several days in chewing over and discussing the subject. I labored pretty hard trying to bring him to the point; but all I could succeed in doing up to last night was that he advanced his guarantee to 35,000 sets per year for three years, on the basis of $1. per set; giving $105,000. to be divided up. Now, I hate to give a thing up after I get at it, and so I ran up home here today to think the matter over a little further and to see whether the folks here thought there was anything worth considering in the last offer; but after going all over the question, we have come to the conclusion that there is no advantage for anybody in taking up the Collier offer. His principle is all right, but his figures are too close.

338. CLEMENS TO ROGERS

Riverdale
7 April 1903

Dear Mr. Rogers:

By George, if I had known! For this good while I have been afraid to go near you lest I shed a blue cloud over you. I had a pretty large one on hand. I supposed our expenses were away beyond what we could stand.

It was all a mistake. I have examined the check-books several times, and it always came disastrously out the same way. It was because, for some reason not known to me, I always multiplied the totals by 2. I have got it right, at last, and am not blue any more, now. I find that since Mrs. Clemens was taken sick our expenses are only $8,000 or $9,000 a year more than we can afford. I do not mind that—at least I don't mind it enough to be blue about it. If you were back now,[1] I wouldn't be afraid to infest you.

We had a conspiracy of physicians the day you sailed, and they decided that Mrs. Clemens must spend next winter in a moderate climate—Italy. That looks as if they expect her to be able to stand the voyage by fall. I believe she is making actual progress at last. The idea of going abroad has cheered her up and is good for her, for she is not deceived about our expenses here, in spite of all our lying. She says I will not be satisfied unless I can take you along, but I have told her the same doctors that send her can send you, and I will attend to it. Clara is writing to a friend in Florence to find a villa for us 3 miles outside the city, and I will tell her to get two—one for you. A whole restful winter there will set you up and restore your youth; and we can dine together back and forth, and lumber around and lampoon the Old Masters and have a time. I'll have it all arranged pretty soon.

I have been attending one of the exhibitions of Hutchison's electrical invention for making the deaf hear,[2] and I wished I could pull up Mary Stover out of my long-vanished boyhood and have her tested. She had the reputation among us schoolmates of being very "deef"—as we called it. But John Buckner, who was well enough, maybe, in the commonplaces of fact, but didn't know any more about auricular science than God knows about astronomy, came to me excited over a wonderful discovery, one day, and said Mary Stover could hear as well as anybody. I dissembled my astonishment and said it was a lie—(this to encourage him to explain)—and he said:

"I was standing by the window with her at recess, and a bee

stung me and I slipped a little small fart—the weeniest teeniest little small fart, only just a kind of a chirp, you know—and said to myself 'I'm thankful to God she's deaf,' but felt pretty sick and uncertain, just the same, and held my breath and watched her. She stood solid as a much as a minute, then she sort of gasped, and turned her head away and said to herself very soft like a whisper, '*Phe*-e-u'—so then I knew she'd heard it. She ain't any deefer'n you are."

Oh, give my love to the boys and have a good time! I wish I was there, buried under apple dumplings and nobody to help dig me out.

> Ever yours
>
> SLC

---

[1] "Mr. Rogers is off yachting for 5 or 6 weeks," wrote Clemens on 7 April 1903 to J. Y. W. MacAlister (CWB). He was in the West Indies.

[2] Miller Reese Hutchison, an inventor who later became associated with Thomas A. Edison, established the Hutchison Laboratories in New York in 1899. There, among other electrical and mechanical products, he produced his "Acousticon."

339. CLEMENS TO EMILIE ROGERS

> Riverdale
> 20 April 1903
> Monday, 10.30 AM

Dear Mrs. Rogers:

Your kind letter has just arrived, and I am speechless! I never imagined this—I thought that the press report of an attack of appendicitis had turned out to be false.[1]

If I had known! I would have slipped out of bed yesterday, and escaped the sentry and run down to your house. I wish I had known. I wish I had known.

I must wait two hours, now, to hear—long ones to me, and what *will* they be to you and the family! I do hope you will telephone this house the moment you can—I must not intrude upon you to-day to ask tidings.

Mrs. Clemens has just sent me a note to urge me to let the doctor try to do something for me—it is Mrs. Clemens and her anxiety that have kept me here shut up these past days.

I wish I had known. I would have raised the blockade.

With the love of us both (Mrs. Clemens thinks Mr. Rogers is getting along well) to you and Mr. Rogers—

SL. Clemens

---

[1] The New York *Tribune* of 11 April 1903 had reported that Rogers had been taken ill on a cruise to the West Indies, but that he had seemed better on his arrival home; the New York *Times* on 21 April announced that he had been operated on for appendicitis the previous day.

340. CLEMENS TO ROGERS

Riverdale
20 April 1903
Monday.

Dear Mr. Rogers:

This is dreadful! I have stopped all papers except the Evening Post—therefore I did not hear of your illness and return until this minute. Mrs. Rogers telephones that you are doing well; I am unspeakably glad to know that. I worked without a fire, yesterday afternoon, and caught a very severe cold, and that means a bronchial attack to-morrow, unless Helmer stops it to-day, which I don't doubt he will do. He stopped the last one with a single treatment when it had had 5 days' start. He is coming out this afternoon or to-night. As soon as they let me out of bed I shall go down, and shall hope to find you out of bed, too. Good-bye. I am very very glad you are at home, and not tossing about at sea.

Yrs ever

SLC

341. CLEMENS TO EMILIE ROGERS

Riverdale
28 April 1903

Dear Mrs. Rogers:

Thank you for your kind letter. I'm up and about my room to-day, at last, and I am hoping to be allowed to resume life on the old terms in a day or two.[1] Doctor and osteopath have failed with me, but I am curing myself by a scheme of my own invention. Maybe it won't succeed, but I know one thing, for sure: it will either cure me or kill me.

To-day I'm in awful need of business-advice,[2] and neither of my Captains of Industry is get-atable—Mr. Rogers[3] and Mrs. Clemens. But I had to act, and I've acted. I thought it all out, first, and did what I thought Mr. Rogers would admire.

I'm coming down as soon as permitted. To be admired.

Mrs. Clemens continues to do better and better, *I* think.

And with her love and mine

Sincerely Yours

SL. Clemens

[1] But he was less optimistic in phrasing a reply to another correspondent on this same date: "I haven't been out of my bed for 3 weeks (bronchitis) and am likely to be in it a good while yet. Mrs. Clemens has not been out of hers for 8½ months. None of the family is robustly well" (SLC to William Winter, 28 April 1903, Folger Shakespeare Library).

[2] On 29 April 1903 Clemens recorded (Notebook 36, TS p. 15):

Mr. Robert J. Collier of Collier's Weekly was anxious to have the handling of one set of my books—a cheap set—and offered to guarantee me $40,000 a year for 2 years, and Scribner wanted a $50 set to handle and offered a royalty of $7.50 a set.

Collier also offered to allow Clemens to buy back the plates after two years, and he suggested a royalty of approximately $50,000 to the American Publishing Company (Bliss to SLC, 27 June 1903, CWB, and Bliss to F. N. Doubleday, 13 August 1903, Yale). On 30 April Clemens continued in his notebook:

Collier and Scribner together would have earned $100,000 a year for me in the subscription trade, leaving to Harper the entire bookstore and mail-order trade —but the old Harper contracts had full command of the situation—I was a Harper slave and couldn't get free. I had to accept whatever terms the Harper corporation were willing to grant. So they forced the American Publishing Co out and took the whole thing, merely giving me a small 5-year guaranty . . . and paying me 30 cents a word for magazine articles. If Collier were in their place the books would pay me $200,000 a year. However, after a 2-year tuition the Harpers will do well enough with them.

Apparently Harper & Brothers and the American Publishing Company did not approve of Collier's or Scribner's offer; instead, in October 1903, Harper & Brothers became Clemens's exclusive publisher.

[3] On the same day Clemens had written Frank Bliss: "As soon as I can I'll go and talk with Mr. Rogers. I can't write him about business, he isn't well enough for that. You will hear from me as soon as I have seen him" (TS in MTP).

342. CLEMENS TO ROGERS

Riverdale
11 May 1903

Dear Mr. Rogers:

It's fine, that you are able to sit up and write a firm strong hand. It looks as if you are getting along exceedingly well. I've been up to-day and down stairs to breakfast, with my clothes all on.[1] But then Whitmore arrived, in the midst, and brought a deed to sign—for we have sold the Hartford house [2]—and we talked 4 hours while waiting for a notary from Kingsbridge; then I was tuckered out and went back to bed, leaving him to do the waiting. Which was not long. The deed was executed, then Mr. Collier arrived from New York in his mobile and we have talked 2 hours. He is just gone—6 p.m. He wants the handling of a cheap edition of the books, and when Harvey gets back from Europe and you get back from Fairhaven I think it can be managed. Duneka came up the other day, and I talked plain. Duneka finally said he was willing, and the Colonel would be willing, to destroy the existing contracts and start fresh, the Harpers to have the whole retail-handling of my books and Bliss to have the monopoly of all sets and charge for them any price he might choose, the Harpers to have no dictation in the matter.

We've rented the Tarrytown house for 5 months, with option to buy within that time at $52,000 cash. It's the same man that's been snooping around for 4 years, and who wanted it some months ago on $20,000 cash and $32,000 secured by mortgage.[3]

We've built a deck-room, with awnings on top of the porch, and Mrs. Clemens sits or lies there a good part of each day, now, and is making good progress, though she cannot yet walk alone.

To-day, of her own accord, she proposed to let me go up and spend a night at Fairhaven some time when the yacht is going. *That* shows she is getting healthy—it's the surest sign I've seen. Heretofore she has not been willing to have me outside the house a night lest her anxieties give her a nervous setback.

I think I'll get up again, now, for an hour. I live on spoon-victuals altogether—I can't bite anything. The dentist came out here and performed the surgical operation for Riggs's disease [4]—performed it on all my teeth in 2 or 3 hours. It will be a week or so yet before I can bite. But they are mighty good teeth, and sound as a nut.

The madam and I are sending our love to you both.

SLC

[1] On 8 May 1903 Clemens had written J. Y. W. MacAlister (CWB) that Rogers "has returned and been operated on for appendicitis 2 or 3 weeks ago, and his wife telephones that he has been sitting up a little the last 2 or 3 days, and will sail for his summer home on his yacht to-morrow morning—and so, I shan't see him for weeks to come." As for himself, Clemens said, on 7 April "I . . . rushed up to my bed quaking with a chill. I've never been out of the bed since—oh, bronchitis, rheumatism, two sets of teeth aching, land, I've had a randy time for 4 weeks. And to-day—great guns, one of the very worst!"

[2] The Hartford house was sold to Richard M. Bissell.

[3] The Tarrytown house was rented to Charles A. Gardiner, who purchased the property in December 1904.

[4] Clemens fully described the treatment for this problem in a letter to Howells in 1884 (*MTHL*, pp. 495–496).

343. CLEMENS TO ROGERS

Riverdale
20 May 1903

Dear Mr. Rogers:

I believe it would have been a good scheme for you to make that trip yesterday and return without going ashore. Well, no—it wouldn't. Because there was no insurance on the weather. As it turned out, the weather was perfect—cool without being cold, and the water as slick as glass. We came through like a wireless dispatch —9 hours from anchorage to anchorage. I came within 2 minutes of catching the 4.31 train. *Could* have caught it if there had been occasion to hurry.[1]

Clara had a desperate day Monday, with intolerable pains in the chest and throat, but they had to be endured—alleviating drugs could not be given because of the measles. Temperature 104. She was better yesterday and is still better this morning—temperature normal. Calomel is in fashion again in the best measles circles, and Clara's teeth are all loose, in consequence.

Jean is up and out again, and Mrs. Clemens is proceeding satisfactorily.

I suppose you are watching the Harriman case with interest. The evening papers will tell us about the operation, no doubt.[2] I should think they would take him to the hospital, as there is scarlet fever in his house.

The difference between this air and that of Fairhaven is extraordinary. I tell you this heat and humidity are oppressive—you will certainly find your profit in staying where you are. My trip did me a lot of good—the air, the billiards, the driving, the yacht trip, the social cussing and discussing, and the spiritual healing conferred by immersion in that simple Christian tank all contributed; my back is straight again, and I am what the English call "fit."

I am sending my love and the madam's. I do not know what to do with the enclosed application. I do not know these persons; still, for the Company's sake I would not let a chance like this go by if I were you.

                                                              SLC

---

[1] Clemens had been visiting Rogers in Fairhaven and apparently had made part of the trip home on the *Kanawha*. On 17 May 1903 he had written Livy: "Yesterday Mr. Rogers played one game of billiards too many—then we shut him off; after dinner Benjamin and I sent him to bed earlier than he wanted to go."

[2] Edward H. Harriman was operated on for appendicitis on 20 May 1903.

344. ROGERS TO CLEMENS

Fairhaven
26 May 1903 [1]

My dear Clemens

I received your letter of the 20th and since that time have seen in the papers accounts of the condition of your patients.[2] I hope they are still improving.

I made application for a position in the S. O. Co for one Mark Twain twice but got nothing—something agin him. Let him try again.—at Sing Sing if he has a good will.

The Broughtons came on Friday and left this morning.

We have had lovely weather and I am leading a simple Christian life, trying to get strong and fit. I wish you were young enough to be influenced religiously. It would I am sure be the making of you.

The enclosed being news may interest you. The picture of the young woman surely will if all else fails.

Much obliged for "Flood tide" I have enjoyed it but——. "Captain Simon's Stove" still has my vote. I have been there, yes! staid five years. My salts lied about whales instead of mackerel.

I had expected to go up to New York with the Broughtons but the doctor said No! not until next week. The Coes came on Friday and I hope to go up on Sunday.

Trust this will find you well   Best love to everybody

Yours sincerely

HH Rogers

---

[1] This letter is in Rogers's hand, not typewritten.

[2] The New York *Tribune* on 24 May 1903 had reported that Clemens was convalescing from an ulcerated tooth, Clara and Jean from the measles, and Livy from an unnamed illness.

345. Clemens to Rogers

Hartford
4 June 1903

Dear Mr. Rogers:

I destroyed it. In fact, I knew your verdict when you returned from reading it. It is the right verdict; the work was crudely done—and in fact such things cannot be inoffensively worded while a man is still alive: there are loving reverences and gratitudes which we can pay the dead without offence—but these are forbidden in the case of the living, and their absence make a lack which cannot be supplied. You are the last man I should ever select to pay with printed acknowledgments for a service done for affection's sake. But now and then the newspapers mention the kindnesses you have done me, and I have often been troubled by the thought that I was wrong in leaving these kindnesses unendorsed and unconfirmed. But I shan't degrade our friendship again, but keep it up in the high place where it belongs; and I want you to forget this mistake which I have made—made reluctantly and against my judgment.[1]

I am here to put a stopper on the Bliss pair, if it can be done. I have seen two of the 5 directors, and shall see those 2 and a third one this afternoon. The Blisses are the other two that complete the Board. I am glad I came. So are these 3 directors. They were getting very uneasy about their Company. There was reason for that apprehension. I probably return home to-morrow, but shall return and help them talk to the Blisses if they desire it.[2]

You will be sailing to-morrow, and I am glad of that, for you will surely be a gainer by each day spent in the repose and charm of Fairhaven.

With my love to you both if I may,

SLC

¹ If Clemens is speaking, as he seems to be, of the tribute to Rogers which he had written the year before and which he apparently had just revised, he did not destroy it. The MS survives in MTP. It is published in this volume as Appendix G.

² The American Publishing Company had been threatened with a suit by Harper & Brothers which claimed violation by the American Publishing Company of the contract of November 1898; the suit apparently was dropped when Harper & Brothers bought out the American Publishing Company in October 1903.

346. CLEMENS TO ROGERS

Riverdale
25 June 1903
Noon.

Dear Mr. Rogers:

Frank Bliss and Mr. Jacobs arrived here 2 hours ago by appointment, and I made the American Publishing Co. this offer, which Mr. Jacobs took down in writing:

1. The Co. to go on and market the "Hillcrest" edition of 2,500 sets, paying neither the Harpers nor me any royalty thereon.

*2. They must not sell at a price *below* $36.50 per set.

3. They to destroy all the old sheets, books, and old plates.

4. They may finish supplying Vol. 23 to old subscribers to the Uniform editions.

(Necessarily they must do this, whether they pay me anything on it or not.)

5. They may fill *existing* orders for the old single volumes, but take no new ones.

(On all business *except* the Hillcrest (and possibly Vol. 23 as above) I shall expect them to pay me my share as of June 30 (Aug. 1.)

I pay them $10,000 cash upon the signing of the contract.

Of course they must return my contracts to me or cancel them.

They have gone home to consider the matter with the stockholders.

They tried to argue that I was not offering enough, considering how many years, etc., etc., but I said it would be best to carry all that to you, next Monday; but set it down in *figures,* not in sentiment.[1]

I arranged with Collier and with the Harpers yesterday.

No change, except that Collier proposed a *royalty* of 10 per cent instead of $2 per set. I liked that, and said all right. (It is not to reduce the $40,000 guaranty a year for 2 years: that *remains.* But it gives us a chance to issue very cheap editions if we like, without needing to reform the contract.)

Collier is to sell in sets only, and by subscription.

Harper is to sell to the trade only, and not in sets nor by subscription. He must retail no volume at less than $1.50.

(I forgot to say to Duneka that he must contract to advertise the *full list* of my books EVERY MONTH—say in Harper's Monthly.)

The contracts, both with Collier and with Harper to be limited to 5 years.

I did not understand Mr. Duneka to object to this. I *must* have this kind of command over my books if it can be achieved. There is nothing unreasonable about it. The Col. has conceded that, long ago, but thought he ought to uphold a contract made before his time. All right, but this is an entirely *new* contract.

While I was arranging with Mr. Duneka, his lawyer telephoned from Hartford to say he should open the case against the Am. Pub. Co. to-day. He was ordered by telephone to hold on for a week.

I had a perfectly gaudy time in Fairhaven—I wouldn't have missed that orgy for anything.

With love to you all

Billy's friend
"Dr. Rice." [2]

[Written in pencil at the head of the letter:] What they will owe me for the half year ending June 30 must form a part of the $10,000, in case it shall be less than that sum. (I guess it won't be $3,000.) [3]

Footnote.

* I forgot this condition, but have sent it to them by mail.

¹ In an undated statement left among his papers Clemens summarized his experiences with the Blisses as publishers:

AS REGARDS THE COMPANY'S BENEVOLENCES.

"It (50,000) is rather a small sum for us to name (for the Co.'s plant, and rights in my books) for thus abandoning a business which has taken several years to lead up to this point, neglecting other lines of business for the sake of developing yours. Having accomplished what we have to your benefit rather than to our own, as we have had to pay for the plant, we cannot be expected to step one side for a trifle."—(Mr. Bliss's letter, June 27 [1903].)

If Mr. Bliss neglected other *profitable* lines of business to develop mine *to the pecuniary injury of the Company*, (which is what he plainly intimates), and as a benevolence to me, (which he also intimates), he was a distinctly unfit person to trust with the management. It is a hardy confession which he makes.

"As we have had to pay for the plant." I must modify that statement a little. For 34 years the Company has never had to put its hand in its pocket to pay a penny toward plant, rent, salaries or any other expense connected with its business. All the money was furnished by my books—with a profit besides.

There is history for this.

In the Summer of 1869 the stock of the Company was not saleable at 25 cents on the dollar—so the late Elisha Bliss told me. In August of that year, the Company having during 13 months tried all kinds of ways to get out of publishing "The Innocents Abroad," (the late Mr. Drake begging me, as a charity, to take the book away, because it was not serious enough and could finish the destruction of the Company), I telegraphed from Elmira that I would bring suit if the book was not on sale in 24 hours. So it was issued, without a canvasser under engagement, a year after the subject of it had passed out of public interest, and had to be revived—if possible—by the book itself. Thus it was published, not willingly, but under compulsion.

By the following February or March it had sold 65,000 copies, and I was paid my 5% royalty on that.

At the same time Elisha Bliss told me it had paid off the Company's debts ($20,000) and cleared $70,000 besides. He was probably right. All bindings considered, the book's average price was about $4. Cost of manufacture about 60 cents a copy—average. Agent 45% off—there was no General Agent with his 60% off in those days, and no outgo for collections—the canvasser collected the money when he delivered the book.

Agent's commission on 65,000 copies,	$117,000.
Cost of manufacture, at 60 cents a copy,	39,000.
Royalty of 5% to me,	13,000.
	$169,000.
Received for 65,000 copies,	$260,000.
Costs,	169,000.
Profit to the Company,	$91,000.

In that day benevolent sacrifices in my interest, to the pecuniary injury of the Company, had not yet been born. It is a late, a recent, a fire-new growth—and wonderful!

The Harpers bought the novel "Trilby" out and out, and paid $7,500 for it. But when it had sold 100,000 copies they voluntarily paid Du Maurier a

handsome royalty thenceforth—and they are still paying it. No member of the
American Publishing Company has ever had the bowels of his compassion
strained, out of pity for me, with my $13,000 to the Company's $91,000. They
never even offered me a chromo for taking them out of the poorhouse and
making them rich.

"The Innocents Abroad" had sold 170,000 copies before 1878—so Elisha
Bliss told me.

I had never received anything but my 5% on that book until 7 years ago.

Has the Company cleared less than $200,000 on single volumes on that
book?

I haven't had $35,000 out of it—on single volumes.

Elisha Bliss told me, several years before his death, that "Roughing It" had
sold 150,000 copies. That book was published on half-profits to me over and
above cost of manufacture. Did I get my half? No. The Company got
$100,000 of it—through a shameless crime perpetrated by the late Elisha Bliss.
The Company still owes me this money, with interest beginning 30 years ago.
No part of it has ever been paid. I can say this for Elisha Bliss, to-wit: he did
not have his son's passion for "neglecting other lines of business" to develop
mine. No, he was not that kind of a developer; he looked after the "other lines
of business" first—just as any other thoughtful burglar would. If I had that
money now, it would go far toward making pleasant to me the reflection that
out of my books has come all the Company's plant, rent, profits and salaries for
34 years, and that today—notwithstanding—I am blandly set down as an
object of that Company's BENEVOLENCE! And by a Bliss!

[2] Rogers's two-year-old grandson, William Rogers Coe, seems to have confused
Clemens with Dr. Rice.

[3] Clemens's notebook entries for the next four months suggest some of his
activities as he, then Robert Collier, and finally Harper & Brothers moved toward
purchasing the American Publishing Company, thereby gaining exclusive rights
to publish the writings of Mark Twain. On 31 May: "Go to Mr. Rogers and show
him the Collier proposal"; on 8 June: "Visit and ask Duneka if he has *proof* that
(Bliss) has transgressed. Show MS to Mr. Rogers"; on 28 June: "Probably laid
Bliss's letter before Mr. R. on Monday June 29"; and on 4 July: "Wrote Mr.
Rogers, outlining the proposal." On 9 July: "Wrote details to Mr. Rogers of my
project to have Colliers buy out Am. Pub. Co."; and on 15 July: "Collier has
secured a purchase-option from Am. Pub. Co." On 4 September he sailed from
New York on the *Kanawha* for another conference with Rogers in Fairhaven
(Notebook 36, TS pp. 18–23). Clemens continued to be suspicious of all
publishers:

Monday, Sept. 28/03. Talk with Duneka (Harper & Brothers). If ever a
publisher gets a non-terminable contract with an author, that author can never
buy his freedom from that slavery on *any* terms. A publisher is by nature so
low and vile that he—that he—well from the bottom of my heart I wish all
publishers were in hell (Notebook 36, TS pp. 23–24).

But Robert Collier tempted him by proposing:

1. I to write exclusively for him; (magazine stuff).
2. At 30 cents a word;
3. And get $10,000 a year;
4. Even if I write *nothing*.
5. If I write *more* than $10,000 worth, the surplus to be paid at 30¢ per word
(Notebook 36, TS pg. 25).

347. Olivia Clemens to Emilie Rogers

Elmira
30 July 1903

Dear Mrs Rogers:

It was four weeks yesterday since we had the delightful trip down the river in the yacht.[1] It seems to have been my first entering into the world after my long seclusion. It was so great a pleasure to see you and Mr Rogers once more that it makes the memory of the day a pleasant one. The rest of the trip was very tiresome—the heat and dust of the train seemed unendurable after the yacht. I tried to turn and send a waving greeting back to you as we left the yacht but it seemed almost impossible to turn as the men carried me away.

During my illness I have thought so often of your mother and of your anxiety and care for her. I do hope she is gaining in the summer weather.

I want to thank you with my own pen, dear Mrs Rogers, for the beautiful flowers sent by you to brighten my sick room last winter.

Did ever such a wealth of flowers delight the eye of an invalid as the ones that you brought to me when you came out to lunch with the family at Riverdale. They hailed me with the fact that spring had come.

Will you give my most cordial greeting to Mr Rogers and believe me

very sincerely yours
Olivia L. Clemens

---

[1] On 1 July 1903 the *Kanawha* had taken the Clemens family from Riverdale to the Lackawanna pier in Hoboken; from there they had gone by train to Elmira, reaching Quarry Farm that evening (see *MTB*, p. 1205).

348. CLEMENS TO ROGERS

Elmira
14 September 1903

10 a. m
Monday.

Dear Mr. Rogers:

Your telegram from Boston conveying Harvey's acceptance at nine dollars [1] has just been telephoned up here to the hilltop from town, and has made me immensely comfortable. Things do certainly point to a pull-off, and I guess it will happen; but there isn't anybody that could make it happen but you.

I took the telephone myself, and no one knows about it but me—and won't, for the present. I am superstitious, and shan't make a noise till we are out of the woods. I told Mrs. Clemens night before last that you were handling the matter, and that that was particulars enough for the present. She was quite satisfied with that, and will shut down the inquiry-mill until the business is finished.

She is getting along pretty well, and is as grateful to you as I am.

Evers yours

SL. C

Dear Mrs. Rogers:

Ask him what message he sent to them (coming down in the elevator.)

SLC

---

[1] In the 23 October 1903 contract between Harper & Brothers, Clemens, and the American Publishing Company, Harper & Brothers agreed to purchase from the

American Publishing Company a maximum of 1,800 sets of the Hillcrest Edition at $9.00 per set (see Appendix F).

349. Rogers to Clemens

New York
15 September 1903

My dear Clemens:

I sent you the following telegrams to-day:

"Duneka and Bliss are in the other room and are going to agree "before they come out."

"P. S. Duneka and Bliss have come out, and have agreed on all "points of mutual interest. I am holding out for the royalties "from the first of July to go to you. Am sending letter of ex- "planation by mail."

In addition I beg to hand you herewith the conditions agreed upon between Mr. Duneka and Mr. Bliss.[1] In order to have a clear understanding of the matter, and no more misunderstandings, I had both Duneka and Bliss initial the paper and leave it with me. I told Bliss as emphatically as I could that we would never consent to yielding the royalties from the first of July, and he pretends that he has got to take it back and have it considered by his Directors. As he went out of the door, he said: "I don't know what will happen when I present this to the Directors." I told him that I was a mind-reader, and that they would yield at once. We are simply waiting for them to do so. I expect they will do it.

Sorry to know that you are ill, but trust you are steadily improving.

I arrived from Fairhaven this morning; left everybody well.

Rice and Colonel Paine are to spend to-morrow night with me on the boat.

Yours truly

H H Rogers

¹ These conditions were enclosed:

SOME CONDITIONS YET TO BE AGREED UPON.

September 15, 1903.

That the $50,000 be paid as follows: $2,000 per month for twelve months, the balance at the rate of $3,000 per month; one half to be provided for by Mr. and Mrs. Clemens; the other half, $25,000, to be paid by Harper & Brothers.

That in case of failure of Harper & Bros. at any time to make payment of what may come due, the subscription rights of Harper & Bros. and plates, and the publication of the entire list of Mark Twain's writings shall revert to the American Publishing Company, free from any restrictions as to selling prices, and without royalty to the said Harper & Bros; also free from all claims that may exist by reason of other interests. This arrangement to have the consent and approval of Mr. and Mrs. Clemens, whose present contract with the American Publishing Co. shall be suspended till the completion of the payments, but to be in full force and effect at any time when a reversion of the Publication rights may come to the American Publishing Co.

That the evidence of indebtedness from Clemens shall be given jointly by Mr. and Mrs. Clemens.

That releases shall be obtained and furnished to the A. P. Co. from existing general agents before papers are passed between the several parties hereto.

That the sales of all books from July 1st to the time of transfer shall be free from all royalties.

F. A. D.

F. E. B.

350. CLEMENS TO ROGERS

Elmira

18 September 1903

Dear Mr. Rogers:

I am ashamed, that I am still dawdling here, when I ought to have been in New York days ago. I can't get rid of the bronchial trouble, and I telegraphed yesterday, hoping to go down last night. But I got a fresh cold, and was afraid of the night journey.

Lord, I know you are out of patience with me—it couldn't be otherwise. If I could have caught yesterday's train—but I couldn't, there wasn't time. ⟨I have⟩ [rest of page torn off.]

But perhaps that was just as well, anyway, for as this is your last day in your office for the present you will need all your time in your own affairs, and you have placed mine in a position where a few days' delay cannot hurt them.

But dead or alive I shall be in New York when you get back, and

I will stay there. I know I did not need to tell you how to protect me from Bliss, but I just thought of that, and so I put it in without stopping to reflect that it would be superfluous.

Ever yours

S. L. Clemens

351. Rogers to Clemens

New York
18 September 1903

My dear Clemens:—

I have just sent you the following despatch:

"I am compelled to go Fairhaven to-night, and hope to "be back not later than Tuesday, although I may be detained "because of law suit. I conclude to send you Bliss's letter "by mail to-day. I have taken no further steps in the "matter. Will write you."

Herewith please find the letter from Mr. Bliss. Of course he is endeavoring now to get all that he can. The suggestion you make as to acquiring the business in the event of Harpers' failure does not connect itself with the royalties under discussion. We can undoubtedly arrange that feature without paying much for it. The only ground that Bliss has for claiming that you waive royalties from July 1st lies in the fact that that was what you contemplated when the Collier arrangement was under consideration. We have made him a concession from the Collier plan by shortening the time of payments to practically eighteen months instead of twenty-four. However, I think all this can be left until we meet again. I think you had better plan to be here on Tuesday.[1]

I trust that Mrs. Clemens is improving, and that you are quite recovered from your bronchitis.

Rice has been with me for two nights. We had Colonel Paine on

Wednesday night, and Lancaster, of Liverpool, last night. Booker Washington is going down to Fairhaven to-morrow on the yacht with Mr. and Mrs. Benjamin.

Yours truly,

H H Rogers

P.S. Since writing the above, Mr. Bliss has been calling us up, but I told him there was nothing further to say at present. Evidently he is a little uneasy.

---

[1] Clemens has written on the envelope for this letter: "The final (and accepted) terms." More than a month later, on the eve of the departure of the Clemens family for Italy, the contract with Harper & Brothers was signed. Clemens remembered then:

In 1895 Cheiro the palmist examined my hand and said that in my 68th year (1903) I would become suddenly rich. I was a bankrupt and $94,000 in debt at the time, through the failure of Chas. L. Webster & Co. Two years later—in London—Cheiro repeated this long-distance prediction, and added that the riches would come from a quite unexpected source.

I am superstitious. I kept the prediction in mind and often thought of it. When at last it came true, Oct. 22,/03, there was but a month and 9 days to spare.

The contract signed that day concentrates all my books in Harper's hands, and now at last they are valuable: in fact they are a fortune. They *guarantee* me $25,000 a year for 5 years, but they will yield twice as much [as] that for many a year, if intelligently handled. Four months ago I could not have believed that I could ever get rid of my 30-years' slavery to the pauper American Publishing Co—a worthless concern which always kept a blight upon the books (Notebook 36, TS p. 15).

352. OLIVIA CLEMENS TO EMILIE ROGERS

Riverdale

22 October 1903

Dear Mrs Rogers:

What a delicious mass of flowers followed in your wake this afternoon.[1] You had scarcely left our door when my maid brought them in. When I saw the box I knew they were from you. They are a great delight to us all. Thank you more than I can express for all your kind thoughts and expressions toward us.

I was so very sorry to have so short a visit with you today. If our "palace" proves to be one that we can make you and Mr Rogers comfortable in, I do hope that you will come over there. Toward spring you and Mr Rogers will need a rest and I shall hope to be entirely well.

May I send through you my greetings and good byes to Mr and Mrs Broughton, Mr and Mrs Benjamin and Mr and Mrs Coe? I should also like to include in my messages our future boarders Mr and Mrs Harry Rogers.

Believe me dear Mrs Rogers

Affectionately yours

Olivia L. Clemens

[1] On 24 October the Clemens family left for Italy on the *Princess Irene.* "Flowers and fruit" awaited them on board, Clemens recorded (Notebook 36, TS p. 28), "from Mrs. Rogers and Mrs. Coe." They arrived in Naples on 5 November, went from there to Genoa, then to Florence, where they settled into the Villa Reale di Quarto, in Castello.

353. CLEMENS TO ROGERS

Florence
12–15 November 1903

P.S. Next day—Nov. 12.[1]

The fact is, the place improves. This is a brilliant late-September morning, with a prodigality of sunshine and stimulating air not findable elsewhere outside of heaven. And certainly the grounds would satisfy Adam himself. Which is well; for Mrs. Clemens was sent to Italy that she might live out-doors.

Nov. 15. Just in the edge of the evening of that day (the 12th) Mrs. Clemens got a bad and disabling burn, and is keeping her bed ever since. It was an accident, and not her fault. It will not be well soon.

. She had one of those (breathless) bad turns day before yesterday —the first for 2 or 3 months—and was very despondent for a while, but she has cheered up and resumed hope again.

. I hope Mr. Gardiner will buy the Tarrytown house. If he does, I shall want to apply some of the money to paying Bliss off in cash and ridding myself of that debt. He would probably knock off some of it for the sake of getting a lump sum to use in his business.

And I shall want to keep the rest of the money in bank and ready for use in case the Harpers should at any time fail to "put up" on their monthly instalment.

We hope you are all well and satisfied with life and Tammany, and I hope Harry is not over-working himself.

Yours ever

SLC

[1] The body of this letter has not been found.

354. CLEMENS TO ROGERS

Florence
28 November 1903

Villa di Quarto
Costello [1]

Dear Mr. Rogers:

Yes, I am very glad Mr. Benjamin is looking into that matter.[2] Whitmore, speaking as a professional real-estate agent, said it was a proper procedure for Reeves [3] to sell to Gardiner a year's extension of his option for a thousand dollars and charge *commission* for it at once, but not gobble half of it at the present time on the plea that he was going to let it be part of the commission on the *sale* of the house, since the house *isn't* sold yet. This latter was Reeves's latest explanation. Reeves was worried, and said he wanted to do "anything in the world that would satisfy" me. I ought to have had wit enough to say, "Very well, then, return the $500 and wait till you have earned it."

I reckon the stocks must be nearly ready to hit bottom by this time, so I sent the cable thinking you might find it wise to put $10,000 on the cards for me. Thank you very much for the Sun. The first copy arrived yesterday and came very handy, for I was knocked down with gout and needed mental reinforcement.[4] I am over the attack, now, and shall get up before night.

Harper is advertising 6 vols of my "funniest books" in McClure's mag. All right, but I thought the contract did not allow "incomplete sets" to be sold. I'm not objecting, but I doubt the wisdom of issuing selected volumes and suggesting to the public that the others are inferior. But I would surely have to object [if] they advertised to sell a broken set *by subscription*—which they don't.

No, I had not heard of the Bennet-Cup June race. The deep-sea course will give the victory to Harry and the Kanawha, I guess. I feel certain of it; still, if I can be there to superintend Harry it will be all the certainer, I reckon.

We are getting along pretty smoothly, now, and Mrs. Clemens feels sure a trained nurse is no longer necessary, and is sending her back to America next week. I wish I could feel as sure about it myself.

With our warmest regards to all of the households,

> Yours ever
>
> SLC

[1] Clemens meant "Castello."

[2] William Evarts Benjamin, who lived in neighboring Ardsley, was helping with the sale of the Tarrytown house.

[3] George W. Reeves was a realtor with extensive listings in Westchester County.

[4] The New York *Sun* from the death of Charles A. Dana in 1897 until July 1903 had been under control of Dana's son Paul, a friend and Long Island neighbor of Theodore Roosevelt, whom Clemens did not consistently admire. Now under the editorship of Edward P. Mitchell, the newspaper apparently pleased him.

355. KATHARINE HARRISON TO CLEMENS

New York
10 December 1903

Dear Mr. Clemens:

I have your favor of the 19th ult., and am very sorry to hear that Mrs. Clemens has had a bad burn. I hope she is feeling much better ere this.

I had the Power of Attorney acknowledged before a Notary, and sent to the Steel Company, so that matter is all right.

I received, a week or two ago, 400 shares of Plasmon for your account, also 20 shares each for Miss Clara and Miss Jean of the Tabard Inn stock.

Mr. Rogers received last week a draft for £350 from Mr. MacAlister, of London,[1] which has been placed to your credit. I think Mr. Rogers will write you in a few days.

Wishing you all a very Merry Christmas and a Happy New Year, I am,

Yours truly,

K. I. Harrison

[1] J. Y. W. MacAlister, editor of the *Library* in London, was a fellow investor in Plasmon.

356. CLEMENS TO ROGERS

Florence
16–18 December 1903

Villa di Quarto
Castello

Dear Mr. Rogers:

I am not at all sure that I wasn't a little premature in wanting ten thousand invested, but I hope not. It's all right, if I pull $10,000 out of the Harpers in 1904 on magazine articles—and that I most certainly mean to do. I've already written $7,500-worth of it—so there is plenty of time left in which to do the rest.

I was afraid to tell them to send this magazine-money to me, because they are *always* tardy and have to be stirred up; you are there close by and can remind them by telephone, you know. The money is due as soon as the article is received, but I have always had to send them a reminder. I will post you whenever I ship them a MS. I shipped them a brief one a few days ago; 2,000 words exactly—I had them counted, word by word. Due, $600—30 cents a word. Title of the article, "Italian Without a Dictionary."[1] Read it—it will make you cultivated and wise. Like me.

First 5 weeks expenses here—up to last night—$2100. This does not include gas, fuel for the winter, nor doctor-bills nor specialist-bills. They're not in, yet. It includes many extras which are one-timers and will not repeat—but it's an even bet that there will be new ones to take their place. Servants' wages are lower here by two-thirds than in the States. That is the one solitary economy; if there is another one I haven't run across it.

Meantime I have found a villa for you, and a mighty choice one and well furnished. It stands in solitary state on a hill, and looks down upon the roofs of Florence, and out over wide expanses of hill and valley bordered on one side with a distant vast upheavel and tumult of snowy alps. One can drive down the hill and be in Florence in 7 minutes. Possession can be had when Lord Salisbury vacates it next summer. *Do* come over and take it. Shall I speak for it? Ask Mrs. Rogers.

I am glad Mr. Benjamin has taken hold of that thing. Reeves has had more than a year in which to find out that the house needs shingling; perhaps he finds it out now for spite, since he got caught "doing" me for $500 unearned money.

I am exceedingly glad to have the Sun. It seems to me that it has very greatly improved.

Daniel Hanks at 150 is not a bad picture by any means.[2] I don't remember when it was taken, nor where.

I have a letter from Mrs. Crane all about the alleged John T. Lewis. I will have it typed and sent to you.[3]

Dec. ⟨*17*⟩ *18.* Mrs. Clemens was very ill all yesterday afternoon and last night, with white spots in her throat and high fever, mind wandering at intervals. She is better this morning, but very weak. She has no strength wherewith to withstand such attacks. She is far from being as strong as she was when you took her down the Hudson in the yacht. The 14-day sea-voyage was a terrible strain on her, the first-cabin savages kept her awake night and day. We shall travel in a *real* cattle-boat next time; I want no more contact with ladies and gentlemen and other ⟨s[ons] of bitches.⟩

I will go down now and see her a moment. Only a moment is allowed. I wish we had stayed at home.

Good-bye and warmest regards to you all.

SLC

[1] "Italian Without a Master" appeared in *Harper's Weekly* (January 1904) and "Italian With Grammar" in *Harper's Magazine* (August 1904).

[2] The reference is apparently to Harry Rogers. Clemens adopted the name "Daniel Hanks" from a poem, "The Village Oracle," by Joseph C. Lincoln, collected in 1902 in *Cape Cod Ballads and Other Verse*. Lincoln's "Dan'l Hanks" is characterized as an aging, opinionated New England villager, with a streak of stubbornness which perhaps reminded Clemens of Harry:

> The Lord knows all things, great or small,
>   With doubt he's never vexed;
> He, in his wisdom, knows it all,—
>   But Dan'l Hanks comes next.
>
> Says I, "How d'yer know you're right?"
>   "How do I *know*?" says he;
> "Well, now, I vum! I know, by gum!
>   I'm right because I be!"

Sometime in 1903 Clemens copied the first stanza quoted above and the title of Lincoln's book into his notebook (Notebook 36, TS p. 33).

[3] Clemens sent a typed copy of Mrs. Crane's letter (Salm), with this note added:

> Dear Mr. Rogers: It is about the alleged John T. I wanted to send it to you, but Mrs. Crane's writing isn't always easy to read, so I made Jean copy it. SLC

Apparently Rogers's contributions to Lewis's pensions had been discontinued for a time, but were then resumed. Mrs. Crane described Lewis's gratitude on a "porch-visit" the month before: "As it drew to a close, I brought to Lewis your offering and mine, for the month, and said 'I do not know whether the gift will be continued from Mr. Clemens' friend or not, it is doubtful as he has met with some losses.' . . . He thought a few minutes, as if to put down any selfish consideration, then said, 'I wish you would ask Mr. Clemens to thank his friend for what he has done for me, and tell him I am very sorry he has lost money, and not just because I shall miss his gift to me.'" In the margin at this point, Clemens wrote: "Now then, this ought to touch you, Mr. R.!"

357. ROGERS TO CLEMENS

New York
18 December 1903

My dear Clemens:

I intended writing you earlier in the week, so that the letter would reach you soon enough to wish you a Merry Christmas at the appropriate time.

Miss Harrison and Mr. Benjamin have been looking into your affairs at Tarrytown, and Miss Harrison will write you in reference, so that you will understand it. Mr. Benjamin I believe is of the opinion that your property is in pretty good condition, and should sell when the Springtime comes.

Things are going along much after the usual fashion. There is nothing of special importance to report. The financial situation does not materially improve, although prices have advanced a little. There is so much timidity, however, that we are inclined to think that lower prices will again prevail. I note your desire for investment, and we will endeavor to do the best we can.

Miss Harrison has forwarded to you the notice about the increase of capital of the Brooklyn Union Gas Company stock.[1] We will undertake to protect your interests in the matter. The bonds referred to will be first class in every respect, and the privilege of conversion within three years will be a very valuable right.

I expect to see Harvey this afternoon, when I shall take the liberty of asking him about your matters, and if I get anything of special interest, will add a post-script to this.

We are all well, as usual, excepting Mrs. Broughton, who has had quite a serious set back and been confined to her bed now for about a week,—the result, I think, of overwork in connection with Christmas duties. The ear specialists say that the trouble does not come from the operation, and we hear from the family physician that she is probably tired out.

Dr. Rice is on deck as usual. He and Durant,[2] I think, are coming

to our house on Saturday for a week or ten days. I may be mistaken
in this, but Mrs. Rogers says so, and I judge we will have them for
at least part of the time.

The children are excited over the expected arrival of Santa
Claus, and we sympathize accordingly.

With best wishes to Mrs. Clemens and the young ladies, and
pious regards to yourself, I am,

> Yours truly,
>
> H H Rogers

P.S. I have had a talk with Colonel Harvey this afternoon, and
he says the book business is pretty good this Fall. He reported to me
that he had received a cablegram from you, telling him to deposit
money with me.[3] I will undertake to get it.

> HHR

---

[1] On 15 December 1903 the Brooklyn Union Gas Company had sent a form
letter to Clemens in care of Miss Harrison, notifying him that a special meeting
of company stockholders would be held on 30 December 1903 to decide whether
to increase the capital stock of the company from fifteen million to twenty million
dollars. If approved, the transaction would produce 50,000 additional shares of
stock at $100 each. Clemens noted on the envelope of Rogers's letter: "Brooklyn
Gas etc Ans. Dec. 30/'03."

[2] Rice's son and oldest child.

[3] Harper & Brothers had written Clemens on 1 December 1903, asking where
they should send the vouchers for the amount due him and Mrs. Clemens. On
the envelope of their letter Clemens recorded his cabled reply: "Make all
payments to Rogers. Clemens."

358. CLEMENS TO ROGERS

> Florence
> 30 December 1903
>
> Villa di Quarto
> Castello

Dear Mr. Rogers:

I am very glad indeed that Mr. Benjamin has Reeves in charge
and has "pinned him down," for he needs a strong grip on him

(and more sense than I keep in stock) for his proper management. (I think I've already paid his firm the rent-commission, but Miss Lyon is sick at her home and I shan't know till to-morrow morning where the check-books are. Then I will see.) [Preceding two sentences lightly crossed out.] (Found the check-book—rent-commission hasn't been paid.)

I can't find the Brooklyn-Gas document; I am sure it is on this big table somewhere among the wreckage and literature, but I can't get on its track. Will hire a detective. I think it entitles me to one or two thousand dollars of the issue, and I hope you will capture it for me.

I am sorry to hear that Mrs. Broughton is tired out. *That* is a malady which makes me shudder,—the very suggestion! Once I took it quite easy when Mrs. Clemens was tired, for I did not know what it was prophecying. Send the Broughtons over here; and you and Mrs. Rogers come along with them. I have instructed a real estate man to let me know if a roomy and attractive villa comes his way. It will be well for you to have a rest, if you can get away; your evidence is all in, at Boston, if I read the news aright, and I hope I do.

We were uneasy about Mrs. Clemens, but she is picking up nicely these last 3 days.

Merry Xmas and happy New Years to you all, in which Mrs. Clemens joins me. And to that good bachelor, Rice.

SLC

359. ROGERS TO CLEMENS

New York
8 January 1904

My dear Clemens:—

I have neglected answering your esteemed letter of the 16th ultimo, and I trust this will find Mrs. Clemens in much better health and you in better spirits in consequence.

The "Italian Without a Dictionary" has been published and the

Harpers have sent us here about ten thousand dollars which Miss Harrison will give you full particulars about later. We have had a week of confusion. Broughton has been ill, and subjected to a surgical operation from which he is now recovering. Their baby has been ill in bed with some throat trouble, and Mrs. Coe's baby has been at death's door because of some poisoning, but I am thankful to say that they are all improving, and I trust will soon be on their feet.

I have nothing particular to write about. I don't think I have been quite so busy for a year as I am at present. I do not know what keeps me so occupied, but everything seems to pile in so I have but little time to think of anything but care and worry.

Dr. Rice we see a great deal of. I am going to the Opera this evening and expect a good nap. I will try and write you more next week. Please excuse haste and a bad pen.[1]

Yours truly,

H H Rogers

[per] KIH

[1] Like most of Rogers's letters from New York, this one was typed by Miss Harrison. Rogers's reference to a "bad pen" however, suggests that he may have supplied an autograph draft to his secretary.

360. KATHARINE HARRISON TO CLEMENS

New York
[11 January 1904][1]

Dear Mr. Clemens:

Harper & Brothers have sent for account of Mrs. Clemens $1663.77 (regular books,) and $6516 (six volume editions), making $8179.77. This amount was sent the first of January,[2] although the vouchers are dated November 1, 1903. On your account as of December 1st, $1083.33 on account of contract dated October 23d, and January 1st $1083.33, second payment on account of contract dated October 23, 1903. As yet I have not signed the vouchers, as I do not know whether these are the correct amounts you should receive, and from the contract I cannot reach these figures. Possibly you will understand them. The total amount received is $10,346.43.

I hope Mrs. Clemens is feeling better, and that you are also better than when you were here. With kindest regards, I am,

Yours truly,

K. I. Harrison

I asked Mr. Lauterbach to learn for me if possible the exact amount you should receive, and I enclose herewith Harper's letter to Mr. Lauterbach, and his reply to me.[3]

[1] Although Miss Harrison dated this letter 11 December 1903, the topics it discusses and the enclosures it mentions indicate clearly that the letter was written approximately a month later.

[2] Harper & Brothers had sent the vouchers and the checks on 4 January 1904, with a letter requesting that the vouchers be signed and returned to them.

[3] A letter dated 6 January 1904 from Harper & Brothers to Edward Lauterbach, Clemens's attorney, sought to assure him that all provisions of existing contracts had been carried out by their recent payments; Lauterbach had sent this letter with his 7 January 1904 letter to Miss Harrison, in which he verified that the terms of the contracts had been fulfilled. Clemens relied on Lauterbach's advice with confidence, at least for the time: "If I had had him 30 yrs ago I shd not have been swindled so often" (Notebook 36, TS p. 24).

361. ROGERS TO CLEMENS

New York

12 January 1904

My dear Clemens:

I have your favor of the 30th ult. Miss Harrison is sending you statements of account showing receipts from Harper,[1] which I trust will be satisfactory. The explanations will go forward with her letter, so I need not refer to them here.

Miss Harrison has sent you a paper concerning the Brooklyn Union Gas.² That is merely an announcement. When the subscriptions are made, we can attend to it here through my Power of Attorney. You need not bother your head about it.

I wish I could follow out your suggestion in regard to going to Italy. I am about fagged out again, having been at work since last October. My Boston law suit is not yet settled, and I go on the rack again on Saturday next.

Broughton has been quite ill and confined to his house. He is now, however, recovering. We had a scare at the Coe house the other night, because of the serious illness of Billy Coe, the oldest baby. After careful attention for twenty-four hours he rallied, and is now himself again.

We are delighted to hear that Mrs. Clemens is improving. Perhaps the turn has come now for the better, and she will benefit by the mild weather and change of air.

It is pretty hard to write you anything new, for the reason that you take the "Sun." You will see through the columns that Laffan is gradually getting around to a position that will justify his opposing the re-nomination of Roosevelt. John Hay is still in the minds and mouths of all the people as the most desirable man for the Presidency. If he only had a little more physical strength he would be forced to take the nomination, I am sure. I only regret that he is not physically able.

Rice is still a bachelor. He had his boy down for the holidays, and seemed to enjoy his visit. We went with him to the Minstrels Saturday night, and had a good time. I wish you could see the "County Chairman." There is the best bit of negro acting in it that I have seen for years. I have been twice and laughed all the evening.

With kindest regards to all, I am,

Yours truly,

H H Rogers

P.S. You have 57 shares of Brooklyn-Union, which will entitle you to one $1000 bond for the 50 shares at par, or $1000. The rights on the seven shares we will sell for your account.

---

[1] On the envelope in which these statements were sent Clemens noted: "Harper Statement. Jan. 1, 1904. Settles up to Nov. 1, 1903 and closes out the old contract, which was replaced by the new one of Oct. 23. Next statement not due till Nov. 1, 1904."

[2] Clemens has identified this letter on its envelope as "Brooklyn gas. and family news," but has added; "(Second thought) Latest word consult Rogers of Standard Oil do as he directs."

362. Clemens to Rogers

Florence
25 January 1904

Dear Mr. Rogers:

Mrs. Clemens says she is *not* "in better health and spirits in consequence" of your not writing me; that your letters haven't any such effect. But I tell you what! she finds these last 6 weeks in bed a pretty hard trial; she got knocked back just as she was beginning to get out-doors. But Professor Grocco [1] says she will certainly begin to make some progress soon.

It is sorrowful news you send about the Broughtons and the Coes. You have been having an anxious time, but I judge that you are feeling much less anxious now. I do hope everything is all right by this time, and recovery complete. But your own condition is not satisfactory at all—confound that Boston rack that you have been stretched on so long; you have enough of wear and tear of body and spirit without that addition. Mrs. Clemens is worried about you, and thinks you and Mrs. Rogers could be persuaded to come here, but I tell her *I* couldn't be persuaded unless I could bring my work with me, a person's industries being a very essential part of his life; and the idea of your being contented with folded hands and an idle mind being a thing not imaginable. A month or two of it you might endure—and with profit, too—but not more; more could make the remedy a harm rather than a help. Maybe I can find a villa with more bedrooms in it than this one. I shall try. Then I hope you and Mrs. Rogers will come over and take a rest with us. I don't want to stay in this house 6 months longer, anway, and I foresee that Mrs. Clemens has got to stay in Italy a good while yet. I dictate autobiography from 11 till 12.30, daily, and can have all my afternoons free to skirmish with you.

Next month and its sunny weather will do great things for Mrs. Clemens; I live in a strong conviction of that.

I venture affectionate congratulations to the Broughtons and the Coes, and hope they will not be mistimed.

Yours ever

SLC

Love to Rice, and I hope his bachelor days will soon be over.

---

[1] Professor Pietro Grocco, a Florentine physician apparently recommended to Clemens a year earlier (cf. Notebook 36, TS p. 3). He and an associate had arrived to begin Livy's treatment the first of January; Clemens recorded in his notebook that the pair "changed Livy's regime" (Notebook 37, TS p. 2).

363. Rogers to Clemens

New York
8 February 1904 [1]

My dear Clemens:

I am in receipt of your favor of the 25th inst., together with the pictures of your Hotel and one of its guests. The guest really looks under-fed. Don't get the reputation of starving people. In the dim distance I see a lady in white. Perhaps the lady has been saying things to the gentleman.

Sorry to hear that Mrs. Clemens does not improve as rapidly as you would wish. I trust, however, the warmer weather will be most beneficial.

I am head over heels in trouble. We have been reasonably successful in our Montana decisions,[2] but the Boston trouble is still on, and I am to go over on Wednesday for an indefinite visit. The case is in Court, and I expect we are going to have a long, troublesome siege.

Mrs. Broughton has quite recovered, and we are very happy in consequence. Broughton is confined to his house, but will be out before many days. Mrs. Rogers is well, as also the rest of the flock.

There is a terrible fire to-day in Baltimore, of which of course you have a full description by this time.[3] The stock market is unsettled because of it and the news concerning the Japanese War.

J. B. Stanchfield of Elmira wrote me last week, asking for an appointment later in the week. I replied that as soon as he arrived in town, if he would call me on the telephone I would endeavor to see him. It was on some affair of yours. I assume that whatever service I render, you will compensate me for at a later time.

Rice is still a bachelor; he came up to our house last Saturday evening and deliberately walked away with thirty dollars. No need of his charging a fee as he usually does for coming up, but I assume that it will be in the bill just the same.

I would be most delighted if I could get away from business long enough to go to Italy and know you for a couple of months, but it is out of the question, and while I am sure Mrs. Rogers would be delighted to join me if I were to make such a suggestion, I am afraid it is a thing that cannot be done. Our Montana troubles are in such a condition that I expect to go there as soon as I am released from the Boston case. You will have seen in the columns of the "Sun" ere this reaches you, the resignation of Mr. Scallon, President of the Anaconda Company, and a few remarks by your obedient in reference.[5] We are, I think, gaining slowly.

The death of Mr. William C. Whitney has been a great shock to the community, and I have been congratulated fifty times upon my escape last Spring.[6]

Roosevelt seems to be in the lead on the Republican side. John Hay has been in Georgia for a long time, ostensibly on the sick list; rumor says that he is unhappy in his relations with the President. I only wish it were possible for him to get the nomination. Your friend Grover Cleveland came up from Princeton to attend the funeral of Mr. Whitney. I never saw him look better. He has lost a lot of flesh; his complexion was clear; his eyes as bright as possible. It is astonishing the hold he has on the American people, but I notice this singular thing: Even among Cleveland's friends, they say "Yes, Mr. Cleveland is a good man, but he is thoroughly impracticable." Against that, everybody says that Mr. Roosevelt will be the man, but nobody wants him.

Give my love to all, and believe me, as ever,

Yours sincerely,

H H Rogers

"Daniel Hanks" is tottering about and wants to be remembered.

---

[1] Clemens identified this letter on the back of its envelope: "Mr. Rogers writes concerning Roosevelt, Cleveland, Baltimore fire etc Feb 1904."

[2] The Supreme Court of Montana on 1 February 1904 had reversed the decision of a lower court which had ruled that one corporation (Amalgamated Copper) could not hold stock in another; this judgment secured for Amalgamated Copper the legal right to exist in Montana. The New York *Sun*, reporting the decision on 2 February 1904, said that the "real plaintiff" was Frederick A. Heinze, owner of rival copper mines in Montana. After the adverse lower court opinion, according to the *Sun*, there had been a general shutdown of the Amalgamated mines, because if that decision had been upheld, "the Amalgamated Copper Company would have had to dispose of its stocks in subsidiary companies and would have been wiped out."

[3] Insurance losses were expected to be exceedingly high in the Baltimore fire, which had already gutted twenty blocks of the business district. Baltimore firemen were even dynamiting buildings in the path of the flames; the conflagration was not extinguished until men and fire-fighting equipment were brought in from Washington, Philadelphia, and New York.

[4] Relations between Russia and Japan had been severed on 6 February 1904, and newspapers were reporting Japanese troop movements toward Korea and Manchuria. During the night of 8 February the Japanese would torpedo Russian cruisers in the harbor of Port Arthur without a declaration of war.

[5] On 2 February 1904 William Scallon had announced his resignation as president of the Anaconda Copper Company and manager of the Amalgamated properties in Montana. Rogers's comments, as reported in the New York *Sun* (3 February 1904), had been polite and perfunctory: Scallon's decision to retire came at an opportune time, he said, because "the recent decisions of the Supreme Court of Montana (on the cases which Mr. Scallon had under his immediate care) have been favorable to the Amalgamated." As chief legal adviser for the

Amalgamated company, said Rogers, he "has rendered most valuable service to the interests he represented, and our severance of relations is a matter of great personal regret, because of his fine qualities as a man and associate."

⁶ William C. Whitney, former Secretary of the Navy, street-railway financier, and sportsman, had died on 2 February 1904 of blood poisoning and peritonitis following an operation for appendicitis.

364. CLEMENS TO ROGERS

Florence
25–26 February 1904

Dear Mr. Rogers:

I wish you could get through with that wearisome Boston matter and have a rest. If you were not such a fighter—but you are, and you cannot be changed. It wouldn't be best anyway, I reckon. I was glad to gather from the Sun that you were getting the best of the Montana crowd at last, but I did not see what you said, and I *would* like to—we have been in such a sweat here for a month that I have sometimes been obliged to let the papers go unread. First I cabled Stanchfield to decline Butters's offer,¹ but then I began to think maybe you might not approve—so I cabled him to do as you should direct. It is one of those investments of mine that I am ashamed of, and would like to forget. Damn!

Well, we *have* been in a sweat for a month! The Countess Massiglia (the American bitch who owns this ⟨pla⟩ Villa) ² found that she could afflict me with all sorts of trivial and exasperating annoyances because I couldn't raise a row lest it get to Mrs. Clemens and give her a fatal backset; and couldn't leave the place because Mrs. Clemens cannot be moved from her bed—but at last when the Countess ordered the telephone company to remove my telephone (I had just got it in and needed it to send hurry-calls to doctors with), it was one feather more than I could stand. I got the weightiest lawyer in Italy, and game was called.

The Countess is doing the sweating, now. She "hollered" yesterday—but it is too late. She has made my life a burden to me for 3 months.

Meantime, on top of this we have several times been extremely
uneasy about Mrs. Clemens. The past week has been awful—she
has had bad nights, and been obliged to sit up in bed for hours, in
order to get her breath—and she is only a shadow. Three nights ago
her pulse went up to *192,* and nothing but a subcutaneous injec-
tion⟨s⟩ of brandy brought her back to life. Her pulse usually
oscillates between 115 and 140. But she is doing fairly well yesterday and to-day.

I am in bed a week (bronchitis, as usual), but hope to be out
again in a fortnight.

I expect to drive the Countess off this place (she lives over her
own stable, 50 yards from one end of the Villa.) Her presence
poisons the whole region. I am backing some peasant-suits against
her—2 civil and one criminal—and when those are through I have
some more up my sleeve. She appealed to the priest, yesterday, to
placate me and call me off—which he declined. He and I are good
friends. She hasn't any.

I expect to move out of this Villa as soon as Mrs. Clemens can be
moved. I have examined 2 and 3 a day for 2 weeks, and have found
the right one I think. I shall soon know, when I get out of bed. I
shall leave Quarto, but I expect to drive the Countess off the place
first. She ⟨told the pr⟩ knows that if I leave it she will have a [one
word canceled: illegible] difficult time trying to rent it again—for
she knows I will prove to any applicant that he will be an ass to
take it on any terms.

                                    With the love of
                                    SLC

Feb. 26, 8 a.m. News comes that Mrs. Clemens slept a little
while *lying down.* The first time for many weeks.

                    P.S.[3]
Mister Rodjers dear sir I will now tell you what it was which was
this and probly in the Sunday-school—

Teacher. Wen the first Walking Delegate (or maybe Second)
step out on the Sea his foot slip from under, and he cry out "Help
me or I sink," for he is being too cocky and need a lesson. Also wen

that Schwab scheme is examine by the stockholders they detect a fault.[4]

Now then, I will explain you the moral hid in the two histories —it is this, to-wit, thus: The Walking Delegate put too much trust in the water, the other put too much water in the Trust.

[1] Henry A. Butters, an associate in promoting Plasmon, had written that he would restore some 250 shares of stock in the company, which Clemens insisted had been stolen from him, if Clemens would make a further investment (SLC to Stanchfield, 29 January 1904); Clemens declined: he considered what he had already invested to be "totally lost" (SLC to MacAlister, 21 March 1904). In an autobiographical dictation of 1908 Clemens would call Butters "easily the meanest white man, and the most degraded in spirit and contemptible in character I have ever known" (DV 356).

[2] Clemens made extensive notes on the countess and her shortcomings (DV 350), apparently planning to expose her to the world in print. She was "male in everything but sex"; she was "excitable, malicious, malignant, vengeful, unforgiving, selfish, stingy, avaricious, coarse, vulgar, profane, obscene, a furious blusterer on the outside and at heart a coward." Isabel Lyon in her journal used fewer adjectives, but agreed with Clemens's estimate of their landlady.

[3] Clemens scrawled "P.S." (in pencil) across the top of this page and probably enclosed it with this letter: both are in an unusual, bright blue ink which he used briefly in early 1904 to send short notes to Livy. The postscript is a further testimony to Clemens's enduring admiration for William H. Baker's prose.

[4] Charles M. Schwab had been accused of (and in early February 1904 had admitted) an illegal move to merge the United States Shipbuilding Company with the Bethlehem Steel Company. Although the details of the deal are complex, Clemens refers here to the falsification of the assets of Bethelehem Steel. When the shipbuilding company was forced into receivership, they sued Schwab and charged, among other things, that "the issues of $10,000,000 preferred stock and $10,000,000 of common stock were fraudulent and void." At the time of the suit, Schwab was former president of the United States Steel Corporation and "still the largest stockholder in the Steel Trust" (New York *Times*, 5 and 8 January, 5 February 1904).

365. CLEMENS TO ROGERS

Florence
21–22 March 1904

Dear Mr. Rogers:

I have been waiting and waiting for that McClure—and yesterday I found it in one of the daughters' rooms; it had been there a fortnight, I judge. They carry off anything that is addressed to me, if it looks interesting. Miss Tarbell always gives you a good character, as a man,[1] and this time she does it again, but she gives you no rank as a conspirator—does not even let you say any dark things; does not even let you sit mute and awful in a Buffalo Court like John D., and lower the temperature of justice. Henry H., the woman has been *bought!* There are people who will do anything for distinction, and to rob another person of it—even a friend. I say nothing, I make no charges, but my thoughts are upon a person the principal letters of whose name spell Archbold. When you see him again, look at his eye. It is the eye that tells what a man is. It would be a mercy if some people had but one; it suppresses half the testimony for the prosecution. Do you know if Archbold has ever tried a green patch? It has been known to work.

Will you kindly hand the enclosed to Danl. Hanks? It is my latest, and is much admired.[2] There is nothing like this climate to restore vanished youth.

To-day is the first time I have been cheerful for some weeks. Day before yesterday we took the madam out of her bed for the first time in 3 months and she sat in a chair 25 minutes. There was great jubilation. But she was up too long, and the results were bad, and for some hours she was threatened with one of those alarming turns. But she escaped it, and this morning we are feeling easy again. This has been an awful 3 months, with these periodical frights. I have worked all the time; it was the only way to get respite from the blues. I have not taken enough interest in business to remind Duneka that he has fallen back into his old habit of never paying for magazine matter until I stir him up. I guess I've sent him about $10,000 worth, maybe more—all I expect to furnish this year. By and by I will remind him; he mustn't be allowed to get his habit so solidified that he can't break it.

I was not able to take a sharp interest in the Plasmon matter. I think it wasn't worth it. I had an instinct that you would consider an additional purchase an additional insanity. That is what it would have been, I think.

A month ago I was knocked down with bronchitis and remained in bed until 3 days ago.

I do hope your Boston troubles are over by now, and that you have come out on top; and that all your home patients are safely out of the doctor's hands, and that your fearful winter is over and that you and Mrs. Rogers are perfectly well.

As ever

SL. C

March 22/04

P.S. I have a third dividend (this one is an interim) from the English Plasmon Co. It is three 7% dividends in eleven months on the £5,000 I put in there. If I had kept out of American Plasmon I would now be a good business man; but as it is, I am only half a good business man.

SLC

Mrs. Clemens sat up 15 minutes to-day without damage.

---

[1] In her history of the Standard Oil Company, which was still running serially in *McClure's Magazine,* Ida M. Tarbell described Rogers as one of the "ablest and frankest" of the "candid" members of the company.

[2] Probably the enclosure was a recent photograph.

366. CLEMENS TO ROGERS

Florence
12 April 1904

Dear Mr. Rogers:

Clara made a *debut* on the concert stage here last Friday evening, and astonished the house—including me—with the richness and volume of her voice, and with her trained ability to handle it. It was a lone hand quite triumphantly played. The congratulations have been abundant and cordial.

Two nights later, when I was just beginning to get over my ⟨several⟩ fortnight's preliminary nervous strain on Clara's account, Mrs. Clemens had another of those frightful attacks of breathlessness and strugglings, and we believed she would not come out of it. I am not quite recovered from *that,* yet.

However, things are looking cheerfuller this afternoon. We have had a consultation of physicians, and they say there is no occasion for alarm, and that [there] is going to be improvement, and that it is really beginning.[1]

The Boston sketch has just arrived and I thank that ten-thousand-dollar secretary of yours for sending it: the one I have read so much about, recently as being as unpumpable as the Sphynx, and the only secretary of her sex that either earns that salary or gets it.[2] That sketch is fine, superfine, gilt-edged; you will live *one* while before you see it bettered. It is a portrait to the life—in it I see you and I hear you, the same as if I were present; and by help of its vivid suggestiveness my fancy can fill in a lot of things the writer had to leave out for lack of room. Five days of fencing was a heavy strain on an ailing man, but if you didn't enjoy it it is unlikely that anybody found it out—and now you've got a reputation that's worth its cost: you can command your own terms as a witness after this.[3] Well, I am glad you are free again and can take a rest, and I hope everything came out to your satisfaction. Things seem to be going your way—I suppose Heinze thinks so, too, now that they have cut his comb at last.[4]

I am sorry to hear of Mrs. Randal's illness, and that Mrs. Broughton must suffer another operation—I hope it will succeed perfectly this time; much of Mr. Broughton's own illness is probably due to anxiety on her account. Now that you are hoping for an opportunity to see me "soon," [5] I'll take that to mean that you are coming over. Do—and the quicker the better. Come, and bring the household—I'll furnish the weather, and warrant it.

Yours ever

SL. C.

¹ Clemens began this letter on stationery imprinted with a Villa di Quarto letterhead; the remainder is written on larger-sized pages, but seems to continue the same letter.

² Miss Harrison had been similarly characterized by W. R. Givens, a former New York *Times* financial reporter and editor, in an article entitled "Interviewing Wall Street Leaders" (*The Independent,* 24 December 1903, p. 3042). He identified her as the chief reason that Rogers was "always difficult" for a newsman to approach:

> Before one could see him one had to run the gauntlet first of an attendant, then of an acolyte higher up in the scale, and, finally, of a woman private secretary—the only female secretary, to my knowledge, in the office of a Wall Street leader, and one who by her sphinx-like demeanor and policy, if nothing else, earns the $10,000 yearly salary she is understood to draw. If any editor or reporter, past, present or future, has been, is or will be able to get any information from this secretary he ought to chronicle it as among the modern miracles.

³ The "Boston sketch" has survived in MTP. It is a feature article from the Boston *Sunday Post* of 27 March 1904, in which Rogers's courtroom appearance and behavior at one hearing during the Addicks case were described admiringly. Illustrated with line drawings of Rogers on the witness stand, the article related how, despite "an incessant volley of questions by one of the ablest lawyers in the Commonwealth," he had remained "as calm and serene and unruffled, as fresh and vigorous, as though he were two score of years younger than he is, and as though he had just finished a pleasure trip on his yacht, instead of having passed through what to most men would be an extremely trying ordeal." The report concluded that "as for verbal fencing," Rogers "is entitled to wear a crown of superiority over any witness examined in Massachusetts for many a day. When he had finished, the court had gleaned precious little about the case."

⁴ Frederick A. Heinze was a Montana copper magnate who had recently suffered severe reverses in a long battle with Rogers's Amalgamated Copper Company over rights to the rich Butte copper deposits. The bribing of judges, one of Heinze's chief tactics, had been rendered ineffectual when a special session of the Montana legislature, called in December 1903 at the instigation of Amalgamated Copper, passed a "Fair Trial Law," which enabled a party to request a change of court if he suspected judicial partiality. After this, Heinze, "though he lingered in Montana for awhile, was through. He had lost the courts, and Amalgamated had demonstrated its overwhelming power" (Merrill G. Burlingame and K. Ross Toole, *A History of Montana* [New York, 1957], I, 215).

The impact of the new law was soon evident: on 31 March 1904 the New York *Times* reported that Heinze had been convicted of contempt of court for entering the Michael Davitt lode claim and extracting valuable ore, thereby violating an 1899 court injunction forbidding such action. The Michael Davitt mine at Butte had long been a point of contention between Amalgamated, whose Pennsylvania Mine bordered it on one side, and Heinze, whose Rarus Mine was adjacent to it on the other. Heinze was fined $20,000.

⁵ Apparently an intervening letter from Rogers, enclosing the "Boston sketch," had promised that he would visit Europe "soon"; the letter itself has not been found.

367. Rogers to Clemens

New York
22 April 1904

My dear Clemens:

I am so confused that I do not recall whether I wrote you a letter or not.

We are having a great cotillion over the Boston case. Some of those fellows over there having in the past ten years made a lot of money by following me, are now turning "state's evidence" as it were, and seeking to drag me down because of their misfortunes, but I will try and keep my powder dry, and with a stout heart and a steady head, I am quite willing to take the chance.

Mrs. Randel [1] is in a very low condition. She has been gradually failing for the past two months; her sufferings in the past two weeks have been something awful, but to-day she has dropped into a comatose state, and we are hourly expecting the end. I do not know what will happen to Mrs. Rogers, as she has been so devoted, and so much of her time has been spent with her mother that I am afraid the reaction will be serious. I think she will have to go abroad.

I hope Mrs. Clemens is improving, and that you are thinking of coming home. We are getting the "Kanawha" ready for the June Races, which are already attracting some attention. Daniel Hanks, Jr., is in command, and is doing the work very satisfactorily. We have a new sailing master, Captain Geer, who is far more attractive in appearance than our old Captain Miller. [2] By the way, the latter gentleman finds it a little difficult to get a situation without a recommendation from me. I think it is about time I took an inning. Evidently a man who has been on the "Kanawha" for three years and is laid off without a recommendation from the owner, is in a rather mysterious position. I don't bear malice, but I don't feel like doing much for such a man.

Rice was up to dinner last night and spent the evening. He is the same old sixpence. He has a new card story, and I wish I could put it on paper. It seems a sharp was teaching a fellow to play draw poker. When they were showing down the hands, the victim said: "I have three kings"; Said the sharp: "I have three kings, what else have you got?" "I have another king," said the victim; "Well," said the sharp "I have an ace" and grabbed the pot. That seemed to close the game, and the victim said: "I have some chips in my pocket; what shall I do with them?" "Well," said the sharp, "You won them, didn't you?" "Yes," said the fellow. "Just keep them, and say nothing about it" said the sharp.

I told Miss Harrison to put in one of the articles that has appeared in the paper about her recently.[3] Remember, she does it entirely at my instance, and not of her own volition.

> With kindest regards, I am,
>
> Yours truly,
>
> H H Rogers
>
> [per] KIH

[1] Mrs. Rogers's mother.
[2] Captain W. A. Miller had been the master of the *Kanawha* when the yacht was first launched in 1899.
[3] Miss Harrison was attracting increasing attention in the popular press; two days after Rogers wrote this letter, the Sunday edition of the New York *World* would publish a full-page article on "the one woman in the world who knows everything that goes on in Standard Oil," replete with photographs of Miss Harrison and her home in Brooklyn. It was her $10,000 annual income that particularly interested the reporter: "You might count on your fingers the women in the United States who receive this salary."

368. Clemens to Rogers

> Florence
> 9 May 1904
> Villa di Quarto

Dear Mr. Rogers:

I wish I could find a pulpit that could rationally excuse and justify Nature's atrocities—such as persecuting and harassing and torturing unoffending people like Mrs. Randel and Mrs. Clemens months and years to no valuable end. I cannot keep my temper when I think of these wanton and unforgivable malignities; and as I think of them several times a day I lose my temper pretty often. I have not told Mrs. Clemens of Mrs. Rogers's bereavement; it will be weeks yet, no doubt, before we can begin again to tell her things that can touch her feelings. If the doctor allows me to see her to-day she will be sure to ask me if I have heard from you, for she knows by instinct when a letter from you is due, although we never let her see any letters nowadays; I shall have to say I have a letter—and then go on and invent, saying you wrote only to say you and New York are getting along about as usual and no news to report.

I keep on hunting for villas, for it looks as if I was sure she would be able to be moved by and by, and so it helps to keep her courage up. Also I hired a summer-villa 20 miles from here for the same reason. It doesn't look as if we could ever move her there, but Clara and I *pretend* with all our might.

I shan't tell any one you and Mrs. Rogers are coming over, but I tell you it's splendid news! for I do long for the faces of old friends. I stick close to the house except when obliged to go to town—which does not often happen—and it does get deadly lonesome on the days when the pen refuses to go and I can't work. It's a whole-day thing, too; for the girls are as busy as bees, and far away in their corners of this barrack, and so we are not likely to meet, except at dinner—for we all breakfast in bed, and I take no luncheon. I go to bed as soon as dinner is over, for my back remains about as bad as it was in Fairhaven, and I get horribly tired. Now then, don't you give up the European trip, but keep it in mind and come along; let Dan'l take care of the shop—it will develop him.

> With benedictions on you all
>
> Yrs Ever
>
> **SLC**

369. KATHARINE HARRISON TO CLEMENS

New York
26 May 1904

My dear Mr. Clemens:—

I have your favor of the 3rd inst. and am pleased to know Mrs. Clemens is progressing once more. I only hope the improvement will continue. I have meant several times to write you regarding your affairs but many things have come up which keep me busy all the time. I enclose a statement of your account to date which will show exactly the money paid out and the money received, and the balance in the Bank to-day is $24,808.80.[1]

On the 29th of January, you will notice that we paid out $1,000. for a Brooklyn Union bond. You were entitled to subscribe for the same at par; 50 shares entitling you to one bond at $1,000. The rights on the fractional shares were sold as you will see under date of February 24th, 1904 (in money received). Your bond to-day for which you paid $1,000. is worth $1,850.; they have been as high as 193. As it pays 6% it is well to hold it for investment.

Regarding the articles on which you said Harper was to send money, the only thing we have received payment for is January 13, "Italian Without a Dictionary." We expect to see Col. Harvey the 1st of the week when I will take up the matter and ask why the money is not forwarded on "Saint Joan of Arc," "Sold to Satan," "You're a Jackass, Mary,"[2] "Italian with Grammar," and the "Thirty Thousand Dollar Bequest."

Since writing the above I have been looking over the contract with Harper Bros. but I see no mention of magazine articles mentioned in it. I will ask Col. Harvey in the beginning of the week about them. I enclose an article which I think will interest you regarding Miss Mayo.

With kindest regards to you all, I am, as ever

Yours truly,
K. I. Harrison [3]

¹ Miss Harrison enclosed the following:

SAMUEL L. CLEMENS' STATEMENT.
MONEY PAID OUT.

Oct.	29/03	By Cash	W/M. H. Aldridge Col. Real Est. Tax	$ 227.61
"	30/03	" "	Standard Oil Company draft	1,200.00
Nov.	30/03	" "	Standard Oil Company draft	1,200.00
Jany.	4/04	" "	Standard Oil Company draft	1,200.00
"	14/04	" "	Joseph Blouin (Carpenter's bill)	61.50
"	14/04	" "	C. H. Curtiss & Co. (Plumber's bill)	73.52
"	14/04	" "	Alfred Blouin (Carpenter's bill)	306.66
"	15/04	" "	Philip Ruprecht (Int. Plasmon Ltd.)	12.70
"	29/04	" "	Guaranty Trust (Bklyn. Union Gas Bond)	1,000.00
Feby.	8/04	" "	Standard Oil Company draft	1,200.00
"	18/04	" "	Hoadley, Lauterbach & Johnson (drawing up Harper Agreements)	1,020.34
Mch.	3/04	" "	Standard Oil Company draft	1,200.00
"	31/04	" "	S. Buckhout, Receiver of Taxes,	214.63
Apr.	2/04	" "	Standard Oil Company draft	1,200.00
May	3/04	" "	Standard Oil Company draft	1,200.00
			Deduct two checks which were out at the time the book was balanced last	1,495.83
		"	Balance in bank May 26, 1904	24,808.80
				$37,621.59

SAMUEL L. CLEMENS' STATEMENT.
MONEY RECEIVED.

Oct.	26/03	To Balance in Bank		$15,471.44
Oct.	30/03	" Cash	U. S. Steel Pref. Dividend	350.00
Dec.	1/03	" "	Brooklyn Union Gas Dividend	114.00
"	7/03	" "	J. Y. W. McAllister draft £350	1,688.75
"	14/03	" "	Geo. W. Reeves, Rent	200.00
"	15/03	" "	Borden's Con. Milk dividend	150.00
Jany.	2/04	" "	Chicago & Alton Pref. Dividend	200.00
Jany.	6/04	" "	Harper & Brothers	10,346.43
"	13/04	" "	Harper & Bros. (The Italian without a Dictionary)	627.00
"	14/04	" "	Geo. W. Reeves, Rent.	200.00
Feby.	2/04	" "	Bklyn. Union Gas Co. Bond Acct. Int.	4.83
"	3/04	" "	Harper & Brothers	1,083.33
"	15/04	" "	Geo. W. Reeves, Rent.	200.00
"	16/04	" "	U. S. Steel Pref. Dividend	350.00
"	19/04	" "	Bklyn. Union Gas Rights 2 at $13.50	27.00
"	19/04	" "	International Navigation Co. Coupons	500.00
"	24/04	" "	Bklyn. Union Gas Rights 5 at $13.50	67.50
March	1/04	" "	Brooklyn Union Gas Dividend	114.00
"	2/04	" "	Harper & Brothers	1,083.33
"	10/04	" "	C. J. Langdon	1,000.00
"	15/04	" "	Borden's Con. Milk, Pref. Dividend	150.00
"	28/04	" "	Geo. W. Reeves, Rent	200.00

April	2/04	"	"	Union Pacific Pref. Dividend	200.00
"	2/04	"	"	Harper & Brothers	1,083.33
"	14/04	"	"	Geo. W. Reeves, Rent	200.00
"	15/04	"	"	Henry C. Griffin (re-tax O. L. Clemens)	70.85
"	26/04	"	"	Jewell Pin Company Dividend	44.90
May	3/04	"	"	Harper & Brothers	1,083.33
"	10/04	"	"	Geo. W. Reeves, Rent	200.00
"	13/04	"	"	Interest from Guaranty Trust Co. to Dec.	261.57
"	16/04	"	"	U. S. Steel Pref. Dividend	350.00
					$37,621.59

[2] "Sold to Satan" would not be published until its inclusion in *Europe and Elsewhere*, 1923; "You're a Jackass, Mary" is an unpublished manuscript in MTP (DV 373) entitled "You've Been a Dam Fool, Mary. You Always Was!" It was also called "The Honest Rebel."

[3] On the envelope in which this letter and its enclosures were sent, Clemens directed: "Please write and thank Miss Harrison."

370. CLEMENS TO ROGERS

Florence
6 June 1904

3 a.m.

You have received my cablegram, dear Mr. Rogers, and you know that a desolation has come upon this household which nothing can repair. Mrs. Clemens died at a little past 9 last night—no one suspecting that the end was near. It was heart-failure, and instantaneous. She had been talking cheerfully and happily a moment before.

Our life is wrecked; we have no plans for the future; she always made the plans, none of us was capable. We shall carry her home and bury her with her dead, at Elmira. Beyond that, we have no plans. The children must decide. I have no head, I am stunned; I was not expecting this. In these last days I was beginning to hope, and half-believe, she would get well. It is a thunder-stroke.

With my love—and hers—to you all,

SLC.

371. CLEMENS TO ROGERS

Florence
8 June 1904

Wednesday
Clara's Birthday
June 8/04, afternoon.

Dear Mr. Rogers:

I am very grateful for your cablegram, and for Mr. and Mrs. Coe's. I must write you a line about our plans, if I can make myself coherent—my head is stunned and muddled, I cannot think clearly. Clara is prostrate, ever since Sunday night, and seldom speaks, seldom eats anything. I am not yet alarmed about her, only troubled. Jean slept none Sunday night, and this brought on an attack —the first she had had in 13 months; but it cleared her up, and she is the executive head and manager, now.

I expect to cable you to-morrow, that our sad journey homeward will begin June 28—from Naples, steamer Prince Oscar—(Hamburg line, I think).

The Consul is writing a private letter (he volunteered this) to the Collector of the Port of New York, asking him to make our way as easy and swift as he can, through the Custom House. I hope you will make the like request of him. I think we have nothing with us that we did not bring from America except a pair of side-saddles. Our silver all came from home, by American Express from the Lincoln National Bank last winter.

I have cabled Gilder of the Century that I want one of his up-country cottages for the summer and am expecting his answer.[1] The girls are anxious to go there, as the Gilders are specially intimate friends of theirs. I hope there will be no disappointment. We shall stay in Elmira only a few days after the funeral, because of the associations.

We are taking a small ship because there was no large and fast one except the Princess Irene—and we came out in her.

Death came in an instant—no one was dreaming of danger. Mrs. Clemens was chatting cheerfully a minute before. She had been dead some seconds before we suspected it. It was 9.20, and I was just going to say good-night to her. It was a most merciful death and I was and am full of gratitude that it came without warning and was preceded by no fear.

We are planning, now, *we* are superintending the packing, *we* are doing the thinking. We have never done any of these things before.

Ever yours

SLC

P.S. By telephone I learn that our passages are taken in the Prince Oscar.

---

[1] On 7 June 1904 Clemens wrote Richard Watson Gilder (PH in MTP): "I have been worrying and worrying to know what to do; at last I went to the girls with an idea: to ask the Gilders to get us shelter near their summer home. It was the first time they have not shaken their heads. So to-morrow I will cable you and shall hope to be in time." The cable, sent on 8 June 1904 (PH in MTP) to the "Century Magazine / NY," said: "Gilder we want your cottage next your house for the summer."

372. CLEMENS TO ROGERS

Florence
13 June 1904

Villa di Quarto

Dear Mr. Rogers:

The "Prince Oscar" is due to arrive Sunday July 9—so Jean says; my head is muddled, and I do not know anything myself. The Consul has written the Collector asking him to see that we are delayed as little as possible, but I hope you will add your influence, too. (I seem to have written this to you before—I don't know; I have written you 50 letters in my head, and this may be one of them.)

I am not allowed to see Clara to-day. She was strongly threatened with a nervous breakdown, and we are still troubled about her. We hope to persuade her not to go to Elmira—at least we can try. If she goes, we shall make the strain upon her as brief as possible, going up the day before the funeral and returning the day after. We must go to a strange hotel in New York—a house with no associations. We have chosen the St. Denis. If she does not go to Elmira, she will stop in that hotel with Miss Lyon and her mother till we return.

Then we go at once to the woods in Massachusetts, where I have secured a house for the summer by cable. It is next door to Gilder's, of the "Century," and belongs to him.

It is an awful blow and wholly unexpected, and we do not rally very well.

Ever yours

SL. C

Will you telephone Harvey our ship's name and date?

VII

"Nothing Agrees with Me"

(JULY 1904–MARCH 1908)

"Nothing agrees with me. If I drink coffee it gives me dispepsia; if I drink wine it gives me the gout; if I go to church it gives me dysentery. A vacation seems necessary."

SLC to HHR, 7 August 1905

AFTER THE funeral in Elmira, Clemens and his daughters spent the remainder of the summer of 1904 in a cottage on Richard Watson Gilder's "Four Brooks Farm" in the Berkshire Mountains near Lee, Massachusetts. "Mark, in our cottage next door," wrote Gilder, "is most grim and unhappy, but full of life and abounding in scorn of a mismanaged universe" (*Letters of Richard Watson Gilder*, ed. Rosamond Gilder [Boston and New York, 1916], p. 362). After a brief visit to Elmira in the autumn, Clemens returned to New York, where he stayed at the Hotel Grosvenor while a house at 21 Fifth Avenue, on the corner of Ninth Street, was prepared for occupancy. Clara, still suffering from the shock of her mother's death, was placed in a "rest-cure," first in New York City and later in Norfolk, Connecticut. It had become clear that Jean would never be completely well again—nor would Clemens himself.

During the unhappy winter of 1904/05, Clemens saw few people. Mrs. Rogers gave him a birthday dinner—but on 2 December rather than 30 November: "I don't want my *real* birthday noticed," he wrote Jean (25 November 1904). As he was about to be interrupted by an unwanted visitor, Clemens told his daughter in the same letter: "I wish I could stay in bed. 'Dam!' as Mr. Rogers says when his cards don't suit him." Rogers himself dropped in occasionally, as did Andrew Carnegie, but Clemens customarily spent a good portion of each day playing cards with Miss Lyon, listening to her Orchestrelle recitals, and writing. "Saint Joan of Arc" appeared in the Christmas issue of *Harper's Magazine;* "Concerning Copyright" was published in the *North American Review* in January of 1905. Clemens worked over *Eve's Diary,* which celebrated the loveliness and loyalty of woman, and *King Leopold's Soliloquy,* which exposed the cruel cupidity of man. He was out of sorts from grief and bronchitis and remorse, and the world seemed disordered also: "Damn such a world anyway," he wrote to Twichell, whom he affectionately regarded as his "equilibrium-restorer." He would have given that position to Rogers "and," he told Twichell, "he is plenty good-natured enough, but it wouldn't be fair to keep him rescuing me from my leather-headed business snarls and make him read interminable bile-irruptions besides" (*MTB,* pp. 1235–1236).

Early in May 1905 Clemens went with Rogers to Fairhaven and then settled for the summer in a house at the foot of Mount Monadnock in Dublin, New Hampshire. Gout, dyspepsia, bronchitis, and the state of the world continued to plague him, but he finished *Eve's Diary,* revised *Adam's Diary,* and worked on "A Horse's Tale" and on the unfinished "3,000 Years Among the Microbes." He was back in New York in time for a gala seventieth-birthday dinner, which Colonel Harvey had arranged for him at Delmonico's on 5

December rather than on Clemens's birthday in order not to conflict with the Thanksgiving holiday. In January 1906 Clemens
began dictating "Chapters from My Autobiography," which would
begin appearing in the *North American Review* the following
September. He spoke frequently that winter from what he termed
the "gratis-platform" and often attended banquets at which his
after-dinner remarks were in great demand. On 19 April 1906 he
delivered what was advertised as his "farewell lecture" on behalf of
the Robert Fulton Memorial Association, and although this was
formally a "pay-platform" speech, he insisted on contributing his
thousand-dollar fee to the Fulton Association. It was only a week
later that Clemens expressed his weariness of the New York routine
in a letter to Thomas Bailey Aldrich: "I am leaving for Dublin,
N.H., for a long summer, and am impatient to start, for I have led a
turmoilsome life this winter, and am tired to the bone" (26 April
1906, TS in MTP). He was back in Dublin by the middle of May,
but he soon grew lonely there and spent much time with the
Rogers family that summer, in New York fussing over the fate of
his *Library of Humor*, at Fairhaven, or cruising on the *Kanawha*.
Miss Lyon recorded in her journal that one morning when he
wanted to send Rogers a telegram she had to explain: "It is Sunday,
Mr. Clemens, and the telegraph office isn't open," at which
Clemens exploded, "It *isn't?* And the churches *are?* What a hell of
an idea!" (IVL Journal, 26 August 1906).

He continued also to keep up with other members of the Rogers
family. On 29 August 1906 he sent Mrs. William Evarts Benjamin
three copies of a series of pictures taken of him on his veranda in
Dublin:

> Mrs. Rogers senior as good as said you would accept my series of
> moral photographs, so I send them. Let Beatrice [Mrs. Benjamin's
> daughter] paste them up in a row in her room and you can't imagine
> the change that will happen.
>
> Will you kindly pass the other two sets along, for me? One is for
> Mrs. Rogers senior, the other is for my pal [Mrs. Harry Rogers].
> Both are under contract and cannot escape. I take it Mrs. Senior is

with you by now, as I sent her an urgent and (un)important telegram to the mountains when I returned from Fairhaven, and as she didn't answer it I knew she didn't get it.

He added in a postscript: "I am doing my very *very* best to expect Harry and Mary to-morrow—I think there's going to be some fun —*I think so*" (TS in MTP).

Clemens returned to New York in the middle of October of 1906. His winter there was gladdened by the billiard table which Mrs. Rogers gave him as an early Christmas present. Visits from Rogers during this period were described by Albert Bigelow Paine:

> H. H. Rogers came in with a good deal of frequency, seldom making very long calls, but never seeming to have that air of being hurried which one might expect to find in a man whose day was only twenty-four hours long, and whose interests were so vast and innumerable. He would come in where we were playing, and sit down and watch the game, or perhaps would pick up a book and read, exchanging a remark now and then. More often, however, he sat in the bedroom, for his visits were likely to be in the morning. They were seldom business calls, or if they were, the business was quickly settled, and then followed gossip, humorous incident, or perhaps Clemens would read aloud something he had written. But once, after greetings, he began:
> "Well, Rogers, I don't know what you think of it, but I think I have had about enough of this world, and I wish I were out of it."
> Mr. Rogers replied, "I don't say much about it, but that expresses my view" (*MTB*, p. 1337).

Although a part of Clemens's despair was due to his persistent illness, he could also appreciate the usefulness of his infirmities. He came to think of his "permanent bronchitis" as "one of the very best assets I've got, for it excuses me from *every* public function this winter—and all other winters that may come" (SLC to MacAlister, 29 November 1906, CWB). There were some functions, however, public as well as private, which Clemens didn't wish to avoid. Early in December of 1906 he traveled to Washington to lobby for a new copyright bill; he had Christmas dinner with the Rogerses and gave a New Year's Eve party at 21 Fifth Avenue. On 2 January 1907 Clemens and Twichell left for a week in Bermuda. Back in New York again, Clemens dined out occasionally with friends, was several times an overnight guest at Rogers's house, and on 16 January had a small party for Helen Keller. But the winter dragged on slowly: his loneliness, wrote Miss Lyon, "is too dreadful . . . Dr. Rice is busy—The Coes are in Florida—The Benjamins in Lake Placid—The Broughtons en route for some southern place—and the rest of the world can't play" (IVL Journal, 26 February 1907). Clemens went to Bermuda again in March; in April he accompanied Rogers to a ceremonial dinner given to honor the new German ambassador and later in that month went on a cruise in the *Kanawha* to Jamestown, Virginia, to watch a naval review. In May he moved to Tuxedo Park, New York, to spend the summer there near Mary and Harry Rogers. It was delightful, said Miss Lyon, to see Clemens with Harry's young wife (IVL Journal, 4 May 1907).

Clemens saw the elder Rogerses briefly in England in June when he went to Oxford to receive an honorary degree. The young Rogerses went with him to Jamestown again on the *Kanawha*, this time to celebrate Robert Fulton Day on 23 September 1907. It soon became clear that H. H. Rogers, who had suffered a stroke during the summer, was still seriously ill. From 24 February to 11 April 1908 Clemens was with him in Bermuda, resting and playing. The long holiday was good for both of them; on his return to New York Clemens stood up well under a strenuous round of dinners and speeches—including a luncheon at the Aldine Club where he and Rogers joined John D. Rockefeller, Senior and Junior, in facing and charming a meeting of magazine publishers. Among the publishers, said Clemens, "there was probably not one whose magazine had not had the habit for the past few years of abusing the Rockefellers, Henry Rogers, and the other chiefs of the Standard Oil" (*MTE*, pp. 96–103). Meanwhile, he waited with forbearance for the new house which John Mead Howells had designed for him in Redding, Connecticut.

373. Emilie Rogers to Clemens

Fairhaven [1]
17 July 1904

My dear Mr Clemens.

I enclose a letter which Helen Keller sent to me and asked me to give to you when you should return.[2] I have not written more promptly because I could not find words to tell you how I sympathize with you and your daughters. I know something of what they are feeling for I too, am bereft of a loving mother. For you to lose the companionship of one so lovely as Mrs Clemens must be sorrow indeed—I send you all my warm love and sympathy

Very sincerely

Emilie R. Rogers

[1] Clemens has written on the envelope: "Mrs. Rogers Ans."
[2] Helen Keller's letter of condolence is dated 14 June 1904. "Do try," she concluded, "to reach through grief and feel the pressure of her hand, as I reach through darkness, and feel the smile on my friends' lips and the light in their eyes, though mine are closed." Clemens wrote at the bottom of her letter: "Helen was graduated from Ratcliff College, Harvard University, last month (June, 1904). I think she is 26. She has been stone-blind and deaf ever since she was 19 months old. Note the beauty and pathos of her closing sentence."

374. Clemens to Emilie Rogers

Lee, Massachusetts [1]
26 July 1904

Dear Mrs. Rogers:

Your kind word of July 17 has reached me this morning, and I and mine thank you deeply for your love and sympathy.

I suppose you are far at sea, now, and I hope you and Mr. Rogers are already the better for the holiday and the change. I need to run down to New York, but I have not been able to do so, being until the past few days a good deal concerned about the daughters, particularly Clara. But there is an improvement, now, and I feel less uneasy.

Very soon I shall go house-hunting down there.

With affectionate regards and best wishes to both of you, who are our best friends,

SL. Clemens

[1] Clemens and his daughters spent the remainder of the summer at a cottage in the Berkshires belonging to Richard Watson Gilder.

375. CLEMENS TO ROGERS

Great Neck, Long Island
18 August 1904

Dear Mr. Rogers:

I have been house-hunting and house-negociating for 9 days; and for the last 3 days I have been almost too tired to sleep. But Mr. Broughton brought me down to this quiet and beautiful place and I have put in a couple of nights in sleep of a most solid kind. To-day I am taking the whole day for a holiday. It is noon, and I am not dressed yet. But I finished the house-business yesterday, and signed the lease—3 years.[1] It is the quietest place I could find; and Clara is going to need the quietest kind of quiet for many months to come, I think. She is not perceptibly better or stronger than she was when we arrived on this side. Katy says she is thinner than her mother was.

Jean and her horse were knocked 50 feet by a trolley-car lately.[2] The horse was killed, but Jean escaped with a torn tendon, and with 4 wounds on her back and neck, one at the base of her skull, and 5 on her forehead, eyes, nose, and mouth. She is getting along much better than Clara, however, and is beginning to get out on crutches, now.

I send my love, and I hope you and Mrs. Rogers are having pleasant times and will come back to the consecration-ceremonies well rested and refreshed.

To-day it is 12 weeks since I lost the life of my life, it is 8 years to-day since we lost Susy.

SLC.

¹ For the house at 21 Fifth Avenue.
² In Lee, Massachusetts, on 31 July (see *MTB*, p. 1224).

376. CLEMENS TO ROGERS

Elmira
[?15 September 1904]

Dear Mr. Rogers:

Could you have this ad. put in the paper one time down in the corner in a cheap place, and charge. Rice or Harry has the umbrella and this will make them ashamed and they will give it up.

SLC

[Typed enclosure.]

LOST. On Broadway or stolen, a comparatively new umbrella showing some wear, cost 97 cents at Sterne's fore part of January. Finder will be suitably rewarded by leaving the property at Dr. Rice's in Irving Place, where owner will call for same.

377. CLEMENS TO ROGERS

Elmira
24 September [1904]

Dear Mr. Rogers:

We shall reach town Thursday Evening—Grosvenor hotel.

If you get the umbrella, don't send it there, let the Guaranty Trust take care of it for a day or two—get a check for it.

⟨Does your butler know of a butler out of a place?⟩

We are arriving with neither *cook nor butler.*

Yrs

SLC

378. CLEMENS TO KATHARINE HARRISON

New York
17 November 1904

Dear Miss Harrison:

Please place 3,500 lire for me with the *Manhattan Trust Co.,* Wall st., cor. Nassau for the credit of

Haskard & Co., Ltd., Florence.[1]

Sincerely Yours

SL. Clemens

In future when I have to pay money on Florentine account I will ask you to place it as above.

SLC

[1] Clemens must have wanted money deposited in Italy because he was involved in legal proceedings with the physician who, he thought, had overcharged for the

care of his wife. In addition, Clemens had instituted a suit against the countess who had rented the Clemens family a villa outside of Florence.

379. CLEMENS TO KATHARINE HARRISON

New York
22 November 1904 [1]

Dear Miss Harrison:
    This Aeolian bill is correct. Will you please send a check for it to the Co. for me,[2] and greatly oblige

Yours sincerely

SL. Clemens

    A week from to-day I expect to move into the house,[3] and shall expect to have Jean with me two days later. Then I shall be glad!

[1] This letter is written on stationery of the Grosvenor Hotel, Fifth Avenue and Tenth Street.
[2] Three days later Miss Harrison sent a check for $2,607.25 to the Aeolian Music Company in payment for Clemens's Orchestrelle (an elaborate player organ).
[3] On 30 November, however, Miss Lyon would write in her journal that Clemens was still at the Grosvenor, since the house at 21 Fifth Avenue was not ready.

380. ROGERS TO CLEMENS

New York
27 March 1905

My dear Clemens:
    I have thought the matter over very carefully, and conclude that I do not want anything published.[1] I don't see how I can get around to it. There does not seem to be any occasion for it in the first place,

and then I don't see how I could quite talk to you as freely as you would want.

> Yours truly,
>
> H H Rogers

[1] F. N. Doubleday wanted a biographical sketch of Rogers for the *World's Work* (Doubleday to SLC, 23 March 1905). Miss Lyon wrote at the bottom of this letter: "Mr. Rogers made no appointment with Mr. Doubleday. Mr. D. thinks that Mr. R does not understand the point that they wish to make."

381. KATHARINE HARRISON TO CLEMENS

> New York
> 6 April 1905

Dear Mr. Clemens:—

At Miss Lyon's request we have transferred the one thousand dollars from the Guaranty Trust Company to the Lincoln National Bank. This was done this morning. We also deposited Harper & Brothers' check for $583.33.[1]

> With kindest regards,
>
> Yours truly,
>
> K I Harrison

[1] A few more brief notes (in MTP) from Miss Harrison to Clemens represent all that has been discovered of communications to him from 26 Broadway during the spring of 1905. On 19 April she wrote:

Kindly send me check for $43,125.00 payable to the order of Chase & Barstow. Please direct the letter containing above to Miss Watson, so that she can attend to this, as I may not be at the office to-morrow. I will have the stock made out in your name and send it to you as soon as I receive it.

On 1 May:

In buying your Utah, Mr. Chase, the broker in Boston had to carry it two or three days before the money was sent him, and to-day he has sent me a statement for $8.75 interest.

Will you send me a check for this amount or shall I draw a check from your book here?

On 3 May:

    I deposited to-day for your account in the Lincoln National Bank the following checks:

Harper & Brothers	$583.33
Guaranty Trust Co. (as per tel. mes.)	500.00
	$1,083.33

On 5 June she reported again on what seems to have been a regular monthly transaction:

    As requested in Miss Lyons' letter of the 3rd inst. I have deposited to-day in the Lincoln National Bank, Guaranty Trust Company's check for $1,000.00 also Harper & Brothers' check for $583.33.

Like the others, this note was typewritten, perhaps dictated; at the bottom Miss Harrison added in her own hand: "I hope you keep well these days." When on 13 June Miss Lyon wrote Miss Harrison again to tell her that "Mr. Clemens directs me to ask you to transfer $2000.00 (two thousand dollars) from the Guaranty Trust to the Lincoln National Bank," she replied for him in a postscript, "Mr. Clemens is well." Miss Lyon made similar requests for the transfer of funds in July, August, and October.

382. Clemens to Rogers

New York

21 April 1905

Dear H.H.

    I was going to wait, that day, but the sky, up the river, began to loom so black that I rushed away to escape the storm. It wasn't much of a success. I got 40% of it.

    Baker beats the band!—thus far. Each of the band has inspected the case—and decided it—from one or another of 13 points of view, but Baker's battery works the whole 13. It is my opinion that there is nothing quite so delightful ⟨in⟩ elsewhere in all the literature of dialectics as his naïve picture of the repentant harlot cleansing the American Board's unsanitary feet with Standard Oil and tears, and wiping them with the hair which he hasn't got.

    I believe it would not be improper for Mr. Rockefeller to kill Baker—certainly not immoral. In fact this is a corrective which ought always to be applied to one's over-zealous friends, wherever caught.[1] I think it is St. Paul who says, "Oh, damn the over-zealous friend."

Presently I will send the Baker clipping to Joe, but not yet—I want to study it.

I am making note of the fact that the yacht goes into commission May 1. Also, that you will drop in, when well and strong, and assault a 451. Good—then I will arrange so that you can get a box for $4—(a bottle of champagne goes with every box.)

I'm getting well and strong in my crippled back—my man can beat all the osteopaths and all the masseurs, and give them odds in the game.

Yours (not much tainted but not wholly disinfected)

SLC

¹ Various Congregational Church ministers had denounced the American Board of Foreign Missions for accepting a gift of $100,000 from John D. Rockefeller. Led by the Reverend Washington Gladden, the clergymen protested that Rockefeller's money was "tainted" by the "flagitious" methods by which he had acquired it. The American Board had defended its decision in a statement issued through a subcommittee: "Before the gifts are received the responsibility is not ours, but is that of the donors . . . it is a matter between them and their God" (*Outlook* [8 April 1905], p. 867).

Rogers had issued a statement on 31 March 1905 justifying the means by which Rockefeller had obtained much of his wealth. The New York *Times* (1 April 1905) reported that he had complained that "ministers say queer things. . . . Slavery in certain sections of the United States was legal until President Lincoln's Emancipation Proclamation. Rebates on railroads were just as legal until the passage of the Interstate Commerce Commission Act." On the night before Clemens wrote this letter, Rogers had assailed the protesting ministers in a speech at the Board of Trade in New Bedford, Massachusetts. According to the New York *Times* (21 April 1905), he had asked rhetorically: "Why do so many foolish people go into the ministry?" His reply to the objectors was scarcely designed to pacify their misgivings: "Now, Mr. Rockefeller is just as nice a man as I am. . . . I have known him thirty years and can vouch for him."

Rockefeller answered his critics by making several gifts to other churches in the following weeks. Evidence in MTP indicates that it is extremely unlikely the "over-zealous friend" Clemens mentions was W. H. Baker of Fairhaven, but no relevant comment by anyone named Baker has been found in contemporary periodicals.

383. ROGERS TO CLEMENS

New York
16 June 1905

My dear Mr. Clemens:

I cannot understand why you have not answered my letter of May 26. Are you sick?

We go to Fairhaven to-night for a few days.

I have not overlooked the matter of the Amalgamated stock, but the market has not been favorable to selling, so I have deferred it. It will come out right in the end, I am sure.

Mr. Broughton has quite recovered from his operation, and we are all, generally speaking, in good health. Rice comes around and sees us occasionally. We are hoping to take him to Fairhaven again very soon.

I am just loaded down with care this afternoon, because of everything coming together.

I hope to hear from you very soon.

Yours truly,

H H Rogers.

384. CLEMENS TO ROGERS

Dublin
19 June 1905

Dublin, ⟨Sunday⟩ Monday

Dear Mr. Rogers:

Why, I *must* have answered it. It may be that I merely worded the answer in my mind and then thought I had written and sent it. I am aware that that does happen to me sometimes. It's like *intending* to wind a watch; the intention gets registered as an act, and the watch runs down.

No, indeedy, I'm not sick—I'm trying to work myself to death—and not succeeding, but I keep up the rush just the same. I am enjoying it.

We were fortunate, to find this place. It is perfectly satisfactory. Jean is outdoors all the time; I am indoors all the time, and both of us are content. Clara has lost some of her voice again—thinks the cause is bronchial. But she says she is having delightful times, and drives out every day, over very pretty country roads.

We are hoping and expecting that before very long we shall be allowed to go to Norfolk and see Clara. Twichell is to see her soon. His duties will carry him to Norfolk to disseminate some of his trade-superstitions.

I am exceedingly glad to hear that Broughton is all right again, and this time I hope it is a permanency.

If you can make Rice believe he owes me money, collect it and we will divide. Don't strike him high—it would start his suspicions —hit him moderate, and get what you can.

You might try it with Mrs. Rogers, too. You can hit her harder, she has confidence in good people and is not suspicious.

With love to you both

SLC

385. Clemens to Rogers

Dublin
28 June 1905

Dear Mr. Rogers:

This is a line to say there's a report in Norfolk, Conn. (which we are doing what we can to keep out of the papers) that Clara's horse has been running away with her. It isn't so. It was her horse, but she wasn't in the carriage.

Jean and I expect to go and see Clara in a few days—as soon as we get a permit from the doctor, which may come any day, now.

It is pretty cold weather here, but we don't mind it.

With warm regards to both of you.

SLC

386. EMILIE ROGERS TO CLEMENS

Fairhaven

2 July 1905

Dear Mr Clemens

Mr Rogers received your note last evening and he has asked me to send you a line in reply—We came from Boston yesterday and we shall return there this afternoon, as Mr Rogers has to go on the witness stand again to-morrow—We may have to remain there all the week, it is uncertain how long they intend to question and worry the poor man—We stay at the Hotel Lorraine and if you have to stop ⟨at⟩ in Boston on your way to Norfolk you will find us there. We shall of course come here for Sunday even if the case continue into next week—Please let us know just how and when you are planning your visit to Norfolk as we hope to have a visit from you at Fairhaven while you are on the way for, if you get back to Dublin we know it will be hard to induce you to start out again —Mr Rogers joins me in kindest messages to Jean and to you—

Very cordially yours

Emilie R. Rogers

387. CLEMENS TO ROGERS

Dublin

9 July 1905

Sunday.

Dear Mr. Rogers:

If the news is correct, things have turned the other way in Kansas,[1] by direction of Providence, and I wish to congratulate

[you] upon this evidence of your continued popularity in that quarter. I wish I had your secret. It isn't righteousness, for I've tried that myself, and there's nothing in it.

It is warm weather at last, and it weakens me. I lose no day, but my output grows smaller daily. It has dwindled from high-water mark—32 pages a fortnight ago, one day—to 12 day before yesterday, 10 yesterday, and 8 to-day.

Clara and Jean are having delightful times in Norfolk, and I've told Jean to take her time and not hurry.

With love to you both

SLC

[1] During the winter of 1905 the Kansas legislature had enacted several measures to restrict the operations of the Standard Oil Company within that state. Their most ambitious act had appropriated $400,000 for the construction of an independent, state-owned oil refinery at Peru, Kansas. On 8 July 1905, the newspapers had reported that the Kansas Supreme Court had ruled that construction of this plant would be unconstitutional, inasmuch as it would violate a clause of the state constitution which declared that "The State shall never be a party in carrying on any works of internal improvement" (New York *Times,* 8 July 1905).

388. ROGERS TO CLEMENS

New York
11 July 1905

My dear Clemens:

I have your favor of Sunday, and am glad that you have interpreted the Kansas matter aright. I have always told you that I was in communication with righteousness, and I have been sorry for you that you were not.

I should suppose that about the best thing that you could do would be to sail down to Fairhaven and build yourself up. I am very sorry that you are not able to do more work than you state, but the truth is that you are like Lawson,—you are played out; he has lost his voice because he has nothing further to say.[1] You need inspiration. Come down to the factory and get it.

I send you herewith a check for \$4731.25. I think you ought to give about a quarter of it to the man whom I am reminded of when I think of that old Negro song: "Ole Joe kickin up ahind and afore; Yaller Gal kickin' up ahind Ole Joe," etc., etc.[2]

Rice was with us last night, as cheerful and as disagreeable as ever. He has an opinion of you which I would not dare to express in a letter.

We are all well with the exception of Mrs. Rogers, who is poorly. I don't know what we are to do. I think she would like to go abroad, but I cannot see the way to go with her. I have been over in Boston for two or three weeks, participating in the delights of the witness stand. I am but a shadow of my old self.

I think it is about time for you to get out of bed and get the fresh air. Shall I send you a ticket to Fairhaven? We are going there on Thursday. I hope to stay a long time when I go, but am unable to tell now.

Yours truly,

H H Rogers

[1] Thomas W. Lawson's "Frenzied Finance: The Story of Amalgamated," had been running serially in *Everybody's Magazine* since July 1904; it continued through 1905. The first installments had been particularly vehement in denouncing Rogers, "the big brain, the big body, the Master of 'Standard Oil'" (XI [August 1904], 158). By the summer of 1905, however, Rogers was less often the center of attack, and the exposé itself seemed less vigorous. Rogers's allusion to Lawson's voice is still more topical: encouraged by the success of his revelations about stock manipulations, Lawson had embarked on a speaking tour in the western United States. In Kansas City he had declared, "It's a new holy war that we're making, and I'm the leader of it, and our Jerusalem is Wall Street" (New York *World*, 8 July 1905). It must have amused Rogers to read, on 10 July 1905, that after only two platform appearances Lawson, a novice at public speaking, had utterly lost his voice and had conceded that he might be forced to cancel the remainder of his western crusade (New York *Times*, 10 July 1905).

[2] When Rogers heard that Joseph Twichell was having financial difficulties, he agreed to send him \$1,500 if Clemens would take credit for the gift (see *MTB*, pp. 1241–1242). On 13 July 1905 Clemens wrote Twichell (Yale):

I want you to accept this \$1500 conscience-money if you will, as it marks the turning of a reform-corner for me: I've been into Wall Street again in a small way and am out again with a profit of \$4,700 and am not going in any more. This profit is tainted money; and lies heavy on my conscience; but I remember with a spiritual uplift that other new convert who found that her jewelry was dragging her down to hell, so she gave it to her sister Mary.

389. CLEMENS TO ROGERS

Dublin
13 July 1905

Dear Mr. Rogers:

That check comes mighty handy, and I am exceedingly obliged, I do assure you. I am communicating with that ole Joe who is given to kickin' up behine and befo'.

Don't you tempt me! You make me want to come to ⟨Fairhaven,⟩ "the factory," in spite of the fact that I am busy writing two books and a booklet—"Eve's Diary." When the weather gets cooler, I'm coming. Jean is with Clara at Norfolk; her account of the heat of the journey fairly exhausts me. I was to have gone with her, but the thermometer appalled me and I dropped out of the game at the last moment. This is an easy summer for me but a tough one for you, and I haven't a doubt that you are "but a shadow" of what you were. Well, we must go to Nantucket—maybe that would help Mrs. Rogers as much as Europe.

Jessus! but I had a narrow escape. Suppose you had gone into humor instead of oil—where would I be?

Yrs Ever

SLC

390. CLEMENS TO ROGERS

Dublin
26–27 July 1905

Dear Mr. Rogers—

I ought to be clear out of patience with Clara, but I'm not, for I find she is sick and cannot attend to things. I sent to her the letters which came from Joe and Harmony Twichell,[1] telling her to return them immediately—oh, many days ago! I wanted her to see what a generous father she's got, and what grateful praises people whom he has saved from dire distress can pour out on him. I didn't tell her it was you, but by and by I want to tell her, when I have your consent; then I shall want her to remember the letters. I want a record there, as she is to prepare my Life and Letters when I am dead, and must be able to furnish the facts about the Relief-of-Lucknow-Twichell, in case I fall suddenly, before I get those facts with your consent before the Twichells themselves.

I read those letters with immense pride! I recognized that I had scored *one* good deed for sure on my halo-account. I hope the letters will come very soon, for I want to send them to you. I haven't had anything that tasted so good, since stolen watermelon.

Love to you both

SLC

Dear Mr. Rogers:
P.S.—July 27/05
Here the letters are, at last! Clara thought she had sent them to me. I am hurrying them off to you, because I dasn't read them again, I should blush to my heels to fill up with this unearned gratitude again, pouring out of the thankful hearts of these poor swindled people, who do not suspect you, but honestly believe *I* gave that money!

SLC

---

[1] Both Twichells were fervent in their thanks: "Mark—dear fellow how came you ever to do it?" wrote Mrs. Twichell on 14 July 1905:
I say to myself that it is his own big heart that prompted it. Then I seem to feel Livy's presence in it and the sound of that sweetest voice is so clear to me that the tears run down like rain.
Oh! bless you bless you! I can not thank you for there are no words.
And on 15 July, Joe Twichell told Clemens:
You have paid every earthly cent we owe, leaving us with a handsome, big balance on which to begin a new celestial life of *forehandedness.* Yes, Mark,

you have put us financially where we never were before, and where we are going to be able to stay. The comfort of it—the sweet peace, deep, inward—is past all telling. We feel ourselves permanently better off, and in a vital respect happier than we were two days ago.

391. ROGERS TO CLEMENS

New York
27 July 1905

My dear Clemens:—

I wish you would improve your spelling or get other people to.[1] Either you are right and everybody else wrong, or everybody else is right in the present case and you are wrong.

The offensive remarks about being in the oil business and my changing places with you will be kept in mind until we meet.

If you do not want to come to Fairhaven, why don't you say so? Why this indefinite talk? Why this feigned sickness? Rice has been to Fairhaven with Calomel and leeches for two weeks, hoping to get relief himself by experimenting with you.

Mrs. Rogers and I together with Harry's family have been to Fairhaven this week and the Broughtons are going down to-morrow.

Mr. and Mrs. Benjamin have gone to Europe and Beatrice and Roger[2] are visiting at Fisher's Island and the Coes, big and little, are in the Adirondacks, so you can imagine we have been having quiet times.

Winsor[3] came up with me on the boat this week and Rice spent the night with us. You need not waste any sympathy on Rice any more. He has graduated as a professional at poker.

The weather is hot and everybody is cross and I think that if you were here your amiability would be drawn on.

I cannot imagine what you are writing unless it is that you are apologizing for what you have done in all these years. I knew your conscience would be touched up some time but hardly felt that you would do yourself justice. When the watermelons are ripe send us some. We are saving some cantaloups for you.

With best wishes, I am,

Yours truly,

H H Rogers

[per] KIH

[1] Probably a reference to Clemens's emphatic spelling, "Jessus," in letter 389.
[2] Rogers's grandchildren, the children of Mr. and Mrs. William Evarts Benjamin.
[3] Probably Robert Winsor, of Kidder, Peabody, & Company in Boston, a co-defendant with Rogers in the Boston gas suit.

392. ROGERS TO CLEMENS

Fairhaven
1 August 1905

My dear Clemens

The letters are lovely. Don't breathe. They are so happy! It would be a crime to let them think that you have in any-way deceived them. I can keep still. You must. I am sending you all traces of the crime so that you may look innocent and tell the truth *as you usually do* when you think you can escape detection. Don't get rattled.

Seriously. You have done a kindness. You are proud of it I know. You have made your friends happy and you ought to be so glad as to cheerfully accept reproof from your conscience. Joe Wadsworth and I once stole a goose and gave it to a poor widow as a Christmas present. No crime in that. I always put my counterfeit money on the plate. "The passer of the sasser" always smiles at me and I get credit for doing generous things. But seriously again. **If you do feel** a little uncomfortable wait until I see you before you tell anybody. *Avoid cultivating misery.* I am trying to loaf ten solid days.

We do hope to see you soon

Yours truly

H H Rogers

393. CLEMENS TO ROGERS

Dublin
7 August 1905
Monday.

Dear Mr. Rogers:

I am keeping the secret and collecting the revenue all right.

I hope you are noticing that it is Lawson's turn, now—a thing which was sure to happen. If he likes skinning, there's good times ahead.[1]

I've knocked off work and Clara's doctor has given me permission to go and see her. I start day after to-morrow and hope to stay a week or ten days. Then I am coming back to Boston and get aboard the yacht and run over to Nantucket, if you would like to go; or down to Fairhaven and play billiards.

I am having a time. Nothing agrees with me. If I drink coffee it gives me dispepsia; if I drink wine it gives me the gout; if I go to church it gives me dysentery. A vacation seems necessary.

Along with my love

SLC

---

[1] Clemens's certainty of Lawson's failing fortunes met with caution from his friends, who were perhaps more alert than he in recognizing the power of the muckraker's antagonism. He had attempted to publish the following as a letter to the editor in *Harper's Weekly* (undated proof in MTP):

THE AMERICAN LEAGUE OF HONEST MEN

Sir,—It will be a favor to me if you will contradict the report that I am getting up an organization to bear the above title. It is true that until recently I was trying to get it up, but circumstances interfered. It was my ambition to have it consist of two members, but was obliged to give it up.

Very truly yours,

MARK TWAIN

But George Harvey had written him (in a letter which Miss Lyon noted as received at Dublin on 22 July 1905):

The abundance of moral turpitude now existing makes this very pat and of course it would be widely quoted.

But isn't it *possible*—not probable, only possible—that in view of your well-known relationship to Mr. Rogers, the keen-scented Lawson might seize upon it as a subtle dig on your part and exploit it as corroborative of his tirade.

394. CLEMENS TO ROGERS

Norfolk, Connecticut
14 August 1905

Immediate.

Dear Mr. Rogers:

I am stranded here with gout. Pray for me.

Yours ever

SLC

P.S. No—never mind, never mind. Get somebody who knows the game.

395. CLEMENS TO ROGERS

Norfolk, Connecticut
21 August 1905

Monday noon

Dear Mr. Rogers:

I am going to venture the trip to Boston to-day and the trip to Dublin to-morrow morning. I am still crippled, but I believe I am competent—competent to *start,* anyway. But I've had so many backsets, and had my plans smashed so often in the last week or ten days that I've stopped betting on *any* plan.

For a little while I thought the gout had retired; so I wrote Dublin and said I was expecting to start for Fairhaven in a day or two—but next day I was bedridden again. That was days ago; since then, no letters have come here—is it possible that Miss Lyon has sent them to Fairhaven? What the nation could I do with them *there?* Answer them myself? Not by an Amsterdamn sight! Here Clara was answering them for me.

Clara is surprisingly well, and has been able to take first-rate care of me and not overhear me when I was blaspheming.

With love to you all

SLC.

396. CLEMENS TO ROGERS

Dublin
7 September 1905

Dear Mr. Rogers:

I want to send you Twichell's letter,[1] but it is lost—not permanently, I merely can't find it. I was going to carry it to you when I thought I was going to Fairhaven from Norfolk, and so I must have put it away too carefully. I will find it between now and next time I see you.

I do not get entirely over my lameness, and the gout has never kept up its threatenings so long before. Certainly the righteous do have a rough time of it in this world, I wish I was like Rice.

I haven't any news: this letter hasn't any office to perform except to let you know I am still existent, so that you can sleep easy.

Yrs ever

Mark L. C.

[1] Twichell on 14 August 1905 had written another letter of gratitude, which said in part:

> You have commanded Harmony and me to spare you any further expression of our feelings about the great thing you did for us last month—it is just a month to-day since the convoy arrived—but really, old fellow, we can't quite make up our minds to let you off so easily.

397. CLEMENS TO ROGERS

Dublin
16 September 1905

Dear Mr. Rogers—

Read and destroy the enclosed, and don't blame me, I'm not doing anything. It is from Mrs. Tom Bailey Aldrich, and I *had* to give her an answer, of course. I have told her your private mail goes to you, not to an intermediary. ⟨It is possible that I was expected to take hold of you myself.⟩ [1]

I am still doing the rest-cure in bed—nearly ever since the journey to Clara in the hot weather broke me down. The worst of it was, that I was *not* obliged to go at that time—as I supposed, by grace of misinformation—Clara was not expecting [me] until October. The journey from here to Boston in hot weather is murderous, and I *expected* it to knock me out, and it did.

I've got dyspepsia, now, and have had a disagreeable time with it —and gruel, all by itself—but I am getting over it.

I have lost a straight two months from my work; but I did 4 months' work in the preceding 2, so I am not behind.

Yours ever

SLC.

[1] Mrs. Thomas Bailey Aldrich had written Clemens on 15 September 1905:

> Do you know the name of Mr. H. H. Rogers confidential advisor in money matters? I am in sore distress to get some money to enlarge a Hospital which now for want of space is much curtailed in the splendid work it is doing for the sick and suffering. Knowing that all ultra millionaires have an almoner through whose hands all correspondence of this nature passes, I want to write to this

person by name, asking him to please allow my letter ITSELF to reach Mr. Rogers instead of simply the abstract of the request. I shall be grateful if you know this person's name and can give it to me.

Clemens replied that, although Rogers never read his business mail, which was handled by secretaries, he always read his personal mail. Meanwhile, he wrote Mrs. Aldrich into *What Is Man?*, deleting her name in the manuscript (DV 378, MS p. 108):

When Mrs. ⟨Aldrich⟩ W. asks how can a millionaire give a single dollar to colleges and museums while one human being is destitute of bread? She has answered her question herself. Her feeling for the poor shows that she has a standard of benevolence; therefore she has conceded the millionaire's privilege of having a standard; since she evidently requires him to adopt her standard she is by that act requiring herself to adopt his. The human being always looks down when he is examining another person's standard, he never finds one that he has to examine by looking up. ⟨The human being is an ass; this explains many things.⟩

398. CLEMENS TO ROGERS

Dublin
[?22] September 1905

Dear Mr. Rogers—

I have just received yours of the 18th—which is several days ago, I suppose, but I am in bed and don't know either the day of the week or the day of the month.

I have made an improvement—I have slept 3 nights out of 4, counting last night. I have hardly any dyspepsia left. I am safest in bed, for the present, but I am at work again this last 2 days.

My plan is, to return to New York in the first week of November, arriving last of my tribe. Clara was to be in Boston yesterday, and I was to meet her there, but I was not able to go. She returns to-day. I am hoping to find her installed at 21 Fifth avenue when I arrive in November, but it isn't sure yet.

I didn't suppose you ever stayed at Fairhaven after August. You were not there when you had the attack; but you ought to have been; then you would have escaped it.

I am glad Mrs. Rogers has had such good fortune. I missed my good fortune by that injudicious trip to Norfolk. I was in great form, until then; I have been in bad form ever since.

I tried to go to Boston on the enclosed ticket, to hear you testify, but they said it went the other way.

Yours ever

SLC

399. ROGERS TO CLEMENS

New York

26 September 1905

My dear Clemens:

Mrs. Rogers came up with me on the boat last Sunday from Fairhaven. She was not well, but is now much better.

Our plans are to go east on Thursday afternoon, stop at Fairhaven Friday morning, and then go to Nantucket to spend the day. I wish you were able to go along. If so, please let me hear from you by telegraph to-morrow. I assume it is quite as easy for you to come to New York as it is to Fairhaven, but if you should elect to join us, I am sure you will have a pleasant time. Of course you understand the season is getting late and the weather doubtful, but I have no reason to think that we should not have good weather for this trip, since we will make the usual application for it.

We baptized Henry Rogers, Jr. a week ago last Sunday at the Church in Fairhaven. Millicent (Harry's little girl) ran through the house before the occasion, and told the people that the baby was to be *atomized* on Sunday.

I shall try to get Rice to go to Nantucket, but I imagine he will decline.

Yours truly,

H H Rogers

400. Rogers to Clemens

New York
27 September 1905

My dear Clemens:

I return herewith the letter of Mrs. Aldrich. I received her letter in reference to the Hospital, and was obliged to say in reply that I could not undertake the matter because of my obligations in other directions.

We are waiting to hear from [you] about going to Fairhaven.

Yours truly,

H H Rogers

401. Clemens to Rogers

Dublin
5 October 1905

Dear Mr. Rogers—

At 3 p.m. to-day I finished the fifth and last revising of "A Horse's Tale" and am going to bed and stay there 2 weeks, for I am a free person once more. I have worked like a slave, from morning till—well, all day—for I don't know how many consecutive days, and have enjoyed it ever so much—thoroughly, in fact—but I'm as tired as a dog.

I believe I've got through in time to crowd it into the Jan and Feb numbers of Harper,[1] and that is what I have been rushing to accomplish. (Don't pray for me, I can get along without that—I only want congratulations. I'm not legging for influence.)

Clara and Katy are keeping house at 21-5th ave, I think—and I woke up scared, last night, and wondering if the place is warm enough with its new furnaces to be safe. I do hope so. Last year I sent to hell for an expert, but he was defeated, and went away ashamed.

With love to you all,

SLC

1 "A Horse's Tale" did not appear in *Harper's Magazine* until the issues of August and September 1906.

402. CLEMENS TO ROGERS

Dublin
20 October 1905

Dear Uncle Henry:

I suppose you are about arriving back from raiding the South [1] by this time, and I hope you have had a good time and that there are some survivors down there—some for Roosevelt to finish up. I am leaving for Boston, to fill various social engagements (with my jaw) and I will finish up *that* end of the country—if the weapon holds out; she used to be pretty effective when Samson had her. I shall be there a week; possibly a couple, though I hope not, for Clara will have the house ready for me the 25th, and I certainly would like to get home as soon as possible.

I've done lots of work here, and could have doubled it if I hadn't got knocked out by going to Norfolk in the hot weather. As it turned out, it was a misunderstanding and I didn't need to go. I broke up all of Clara's plans, and my own into the bargain. I've got back the most of my health, and I don't greatly miss what is still lacking.

I have secured a house here for next year, with an option for the 2 years following. This is the best atmosphere outside of Fairhaven. Physically regarded, I mean. The moral atmosphere wasn't much to speak of, before I came.

I am anxious about the new game, if it is one where the righteous have precedence. But it ought to be understood that Rice must play his cards, and make up his mind after he goes home. Procrastination paralyzes trade.

With affectionate regards to Mrs. ⟨Rice⟩ Rogers, ever yours

SLC.

[1] "Mr. Rogers has for many years been acquiring some of the most valuable coal lands in West Virginia" (New York *World*, 12 March 1907).

403. Clemens to Emilie Rogers

New York
[?December 1905] [1]

Thursday night.

Dear Mrs. Rogers:

I walked out to your house ⟨and⟩ this afternoon, hoping and expecting to see you, and was sorry to learn that you were not feeling well, and not seeing people. The footman offered to report my name and see if you would make an exception in my favor, but I was afraid your goodheartedness might ⟨be⟩ overreach your judgment, so I wouldn't let him do it.

My walk extended to the Broughtons and the Coes, but the day was so fine that they were all out. I meant to call on the Benjamins, but was interrupted by a friend, ⟨but⟩ and before I could extricate myself from him I was clear down to 12th street again.

I met H.H. below the Park, flying toward 78th street, but he wouldn't halt. B'goshtlmighty, I walked 74 blocks, twice over, and caught nobody.

With love,
SLC

[1] The dating of this letter is somewhat arbitrary; it is placed here because December 1905 is apparently the only month in which both Clemens's health and the locations of the Rogers, Broughton, Coe, and Benjamin residences would have made his marathon walk possible.

404. CLEMENS TO ROGERS

New York
30 December 1905

Dear Mr. Rogers:

I had already telegraphed Booker "All right, but don't commit me to talk upon any particular subject." [1]

Are you going to spend Saturday afternoon at home, tomorrow? If so chalk your cue and expect me right after luncheon.

Yrs Ever

SLC

[1] On 22 January 1906 Clemens planned to speak at Carnegie Hall on the twenty-fifth anniversary of the founding of Tuskegee Institute by Booker T. Washington.

405. CLEMENS TO ROGERS

New York
9 April 1906

Dear Mr. Rogers:

When you come by for me at 5 this afternoon [1] won't you please bring me

　　　　1—$500-banknote;
　　　　4— 100- 　" 　　"
　　　　10— 10- 　" 　　"

and please ask Miss Harrison to draw this $1000 from my balance at the Guaranty trust.

Yours ever

SL. Clemens

Miss Lyon doesn't know about this. [This sentence is circled.]

---

[1] Clemens and Rogers were to go that evening to see a champion billiard match at Madison Square Garden. They had been conspicuous there, Clemens told Miss Lyon the next day, because they were "about the only men in evening clothes, and because of our old white heads." As they had started to leave the match at ten o'clock, she reported in her journal (10 April 1906), "there was a great wave of applause, and Mr. Clemens turned instinctively to see the shot that had been made, only to find the billiardists surprised at applause for what wasn't anything to applaud, and then Mr. Clemens knew that he 'was the shot' they were celebrating."

406. Isabel Lyon to Rogers

New York

30 April 1906

Dear Mr. Rogers.

Mr. Clemens directs me to hand you herewith his check for $50,000.00. Will you kindly have an acknowledgment of its receipt returned by bearer.

Very Truly Yours

I. V. Lyon, Secy.[1]

---

[1] Written across the letter is: "Received check/K I Harrison/Apr 30, 1906."

Not many indications of the state of Clemens's financial affairs during this period are found in the correspondence with Rogers or his office; they seem to have been in good condition. On 15 December 1905 Miss Harrison had written Clemens: "I deposited this morning for your account in the Guaranty Trust Company check for $150.00, being dividend on Borden's Condensed Milk Company Preferred stock."

Again on 16 January 1906 she wrote:

Miss Lyon wrote me this morning about closing your account with the Guaranty Trust Company. You only receive from 1½ to 2% interest and if you think it wise I will close the account with the Guaranty Trust Company and send the money to the Knickerbocker Trust Company.

I enclose herewith check for $34,700.00 for 500 shares of Utah Consolidated Mining Company stock as per statement attached. There will be a charge for expressage, the amount of which I will send you later.

At the bottom of this letter, paraphrasing Andrew Carnegie, Miss Lyon wrote: "Leave that egg in another basket and leave the basket where it is" (see *MTB*, p. 964). Clemens did not close his account with the Guaranty Trust Company until November 1906 (see W. C. Edwards, treasurer, to SLC, 3 November 1906).

407. ROGERS TO CLEMENS

New York
18 May 1906

My dear Clemens:

I sent you yesterday a statement of the Directors of the Standard Oil Co. to its Stockholders, which I hope you will read when you have time, between now and the 1st. of January.

I am reminded to write you because I have just had an interview with Charles Fairchild, a gentleman of pleasant memory, whom you will recall. He is trying to sell me some property in Boston. I did not "catch on." He looked somewhat depressed and dilapidated. I told him I would not buy the City of Boston if I could get it for $5,000. He thought it an amazing remark, and I told him I thought it would have your endorsement.

Mrs. Rogers, Dr. Rice and I are going to Fairhaven to-night. It is needless to say we would like to have you along, but that is impossible. I hope you reached Dublin in safety. The stock I had advised you to buy did not work as well as I thought it would, and so I have done nothing in the matter.

With kindest regards,
Believe me,

Yours truly,

H H Rogers

P.S. I cannot lie. I did not use your name with Fairchild. That remark crawled in.

408. CLEMENS TO ROGERS

Dublin
18 May 1906

Dear Mr. Rogers:

I am lying fallow here, all these days, and drowsing and resting. Life begins to stir in me at last, but I've no use for it yet, for my stenographer is delayed and I can't begin work until 3 days hence.[1]

I do prodigiously like this air, this altitude, this deep silence, this unneighbored solitude. By the end of the month we shall be entirely settled and wonted and smoothly going, and ready for you and Mrs. Rogers to come to us and get a breath of brisk unsalted back-country air. We are 80 miles from Boston, by excellent 'mobile roads.

If you sent for that check your order went to Dublin, Ireland. Do it again, and do it right.

Brer Duneka is slippery beyond imagination! I must tell you about it when you come. I remember, now, that he played slippery once before. I had forgotten it. In minor ways he is slippery a good 3 times out of 5.

I want to get my Christian Science book out of his hands without raising a coolness.[2] I must think of a way.

I'm sending you my love.

SLC

[1] On 6 January 1906 Clemens had begun a series of "Autobiographical Dictations" which were to continue regularly throughout 1906 and 1907, with intermittent additions as late as 29 December 1909. Miss Josephine Hobby acted as Clemens's stenographer and typist. Paine notes that the dictations at Dublin began on 21 May when Miss Hobby arrived (*MTB*, p. 1308).
[2] *Christian Science* was nevertheless published by Harper & Brothers in 1907.

409. ROGERS TO CLEMENS

New York
4 June 1906

My dear Clemens:

I received your letter in due time and note that the automobiling is good to Dublin. Mrs. Rogers has a new machine of which she is very proud, and it is barely possible that you will see us in New Hampshire before many moons have passed.

Col. Harvey was in here to-day for a chat about matters in general, and particularly because he is going back to Europe to-morrow on the Baltic. Your friend Duneka remained in the hall, and I only saw him at the parting. I wanted to ask Duneka for the money due on the manuscript you have at Harper's; but hardly dared take the liberty. The Colonel said business was not very good, and he could go away as well as not, which leads me to say that I am of the opinion that they are not particularly prosperous.

You will recall that we talked a little about "a dollar a word" business some time ago. Don't allow yourself to think of anything that will vitiate the Harper contract. I am of the opinion that the property may fall into your hands in a natural sort of a way after a short time, and all other business will surely keep. Please excuse me for referring to this at all, or other business, for I look upon the contract with Harper as being so valuable that they would seize the opportunity of breaking the arrangement if it were possible, and then you know you promised me you would not do anything in that line without consulting me.

Yours truly,
H H Rogers

P.S. Are you still an investor? [1]

R

---

[1] Rogers added the postcript in his own hand; the letter itself is typed.

410. CLEMENS TO ROGERS (telegram)

Dublin
6 June 1906

Yes still am investor to amount formaly [1] mentioned Come up here both of you and I will return with you if properly invested.

S. L. Clemens

---

[1] The telegraph operator apparently garbled the message in transmission.

411. CLEMENS TO ROGERS

Dublin
6 June 1906

Dear Mr. Rogers:

I've been sending you a line by telegraph.

Harvey was due here on a visit—any time between June 4 and 10—and I was going to talk "Library of Humor" with him. But I shall now have to do the talking with Duneka. Duneka must arrange a satisfactory compromise with me or I will enjoin that book and sue for damages for unauthorized use of my name for the acquiring of money under false pretenses. I wrote him a letter the other day (first to be submitted to your judgment),—I will enclose a copy of it in this.[1]

Now then, jump into the 'bile, the both of you, and come! We are all ready, and waiting, and wanting you. Telegraph me.

This is country here—real country. Yesterday at 6 p.m., I was standing alone on the front porch looking out on the distant valley and the frame of mountains, when a buff and beautiful creature—a doe—came loafing as unconcernedly across the grounds as if she owned the property. ⟨Co⟩ There—aren't we in the country? Isn't that a sign of it? I was quite unarmed, there was no help near, yet I was not afraid. I got under the porch, but that was because it was going to rain.

Yes, the $10,000 is waiting there for investment—tuck it in for me.

I was going to offer Harvey $50,000 worth of Autobiography for the Weekly, (162,000 words at 30 cents); he would decline; then he would concede (in writing) my *right* to take it elsewhere.

With love to you all—

SLC

<hr/>

[1] Harper & Brothers had contracted to publish *Mark Twain's Library of Humor,* with a 3 per cent royalty to Clemens, explicitly not for profit but to prevent piracy of the book by other publishers (Duneka to SLC, 6 October 1905). Clemens enclosed with his letter to Rogers a copy in Miss Lyon's hand of the letter of protest, dated 4 June 1906, which he planned to send to Duneka. In it he complained that "this 'Library of Humor' is not the one which was compiled by me," that "it is not a cheap book, 'with no money in it for either of us,' but is cloth-bound and higher priced than my own book." This seemed to him an "astounding violation" of his agreement with Harper & Brothers: "I must ask you —in fact I must require you—to take this book out of print immediately, and destroy the plates."

412. CLEMENS TO ROGERS

Dublin
13 June 1906

Dear Mr. Rogers:

Please get my Christian Science book from the Harpers, and put it in your safe until I come.

Sincerely yours,

SL. Clemens [1]

<hr/>

[1] The signature is Clemens's; the rest of the letter is in Miss Lyon's hand.

413. CLEMENS TO ROGERS

Dublin
[?17] June 1906
Sunday

Dear Uncle Henry:

Certainly I retain you; and—as you suggest—I mean to go to you and begin operations at the source.

First, I want McClure to see you and explain his scheme—I think he clearly understands that no scheme can be arranged with me until it has secured your approval *first*. He wants 50,000 words of my Autobiography for his syndicate, for $50,000 cash, or for 80% of the gross receipts. I have now about 250,000 words for him to choose from.[1]

I'd like to see a lot of this stuff in print before I die—but not the *bulk* of it, oh no! I am not desiring to be crucified yet. Howells *thinks* the Auto will outlive the Innocents Abroad a thousand years, and I *know* it will. I would like the literary world to see (as Howells says) that the *form* of this book is one of the most memorable literary inventions of the ages. And so it is. It ranks with the steam engine, the printing press and the electric telegraph. I'm the only person who has ever found out the right way to build an autobiography.

I've had a secret enemy at Harpers from the very beginning. I suppose it is Duneka, that Jesuit. With a sleeping partner, Major Leigh.[2] Duneka has defeated several legitimate projects of mine. Unless he is a fool, he knows there's more advertising for Harper and my books in McClure's project than we could buy for the whole Harper income; but if Duneka can defeat it he'll do it.

His conduct in the "Library of Humor" matter convicts him of being not merely a thief, but a particularly low-down sneak-thief. I desire his scalp.

My project is this: go to New York a couple of weeks from now or a shade later, and have some talks with you and Lauterbach, and perhaps a talk with Duneka. Then I propose to get out the yacht and take you up to Fairhaven and play billiards until you have to return to New York; then take you down in the yacht and look over the ground again. Then back to Dublin via Boston.[3]

How does it strike you?

This is the Sabbath day. Try to keep it holy.

Yrs ever

SLC

[1] S. S. McClure had written Clemens, 8 June 1906, offering to syndicate "a series of short articles, made up of parts of your autobiography." Clemens dictated to Miss Lyon notes for a reply: "It may be that I can accept your offer, but I can't tell about that yet." On 9 June McClure wrote again, suggesting the syndication of *Roughing It* and *Tom Sawyer:* "I drop this out as a mere hint, thinking you might like me to call and see Mr. H. H. Rogers about it." Clemens dictated a reply on 12 June indicating that he favored the plan and suggesting that McClure discuss it with Rogers (IVL Notebook 1). On 13 June McClure offered to travel to Dublin to look through the autobiography for publishable portions. Clemens expressed his approval of the proposed visit, but Rogers was slow to reply, and McClure wrote Miss Lyon on 18 June:

I have written to Mr. Rogers but have received no word from him. I shall make my arrangements to go up to Dublin at such time as will best suit Mr. Clemens. There is a rumor that he is coming back to town soon. Is there anything in the rumor?

Despite these intricate preliminaries, Clemens eventually refused McClure's offer.

[2] Frederick T. Leigh was treasurer of Harper & Brothers.

[3] Miss Lyon wrote in her journal on 23 June that "Mr. Clemens has been harassed ever since we arrived here by what he calls 'the Harper treacheries,'" in the publication of the new *Library of Humor.* She continued:

we are negotiating with Mr. Rogers by long distance telephone to make a plan for Mr. Clemens to go to NY. next week and begin operations against the Harpers, by making them withdraw the Library of Humor from the trade, and destroy the plates—at the same time publishing Mr. Clemens's repudiation of the book. He grows so angry, so indignant—and every day he makes a fresh plan; every day he outlines a fresh attack on those publishers.

All publishers are "scamps," she reports his having said, though "Duneka is more fool than knave." Yet, said Miss Lyon, "he loves all these men."

Clemens depended heavily on Rogers to deal with the "scamps." On 1 July he wrote Clara from Fairhaven:

I spent Wednesday and Thursday in New York, then slept on board the yacht and sailed for here early Friday morn.

I was expecting to return in the yacht to-night and be in New York a fortnight—till Col. Harvey's return from England—but it isn't necessary. On the way here Mr. Rogers and I discussed my matter, and concluded that he could perhaps take care of it better without me than with me.

And so I expect to stay here a day or two longer, then go home to Dublin direct, by rail. I think I shall leave for home the 4th or 5th, when the Rogerses sail for New York.

But soon plans changed again: "Mr. Rogers decided as follows: I must return to New York in the yacht on the 4th; have some talks with Duneka for several days and get an understanding arranged, to be ratified or opposed by Harvey when he gets back from England the middle of the month; then return to Fairhaven in the yacht next Friday or Saturday and go thence to Dublin by rail." To Jean he reported on 10 July: "I spend the days in the Standard Oil and the lawyer's office, and my nights on board the yacht where it is cool and noiseless. At 6 p.m. (or 5) we go aboard and drop down about ten miles and anchor out in the open. We come up to East 23d Street in the morning and go ashore right after breakfast. This evening I shall dine with the Coes, and sleep at home."

The "fight with Harpers," Miss Lyon recorded in her journal on 11 July 1906, kept Clemens "on and on in the city." On 13 July she wrote that she had received a note from him, telling her that "He was just off for Fairhaven, to spend Sunday there—and then on to N. Y. for another week of controversy, and with Col. Harvey newly arrived from Europe to settle the matter." Clemens returned to Dublin on 25 July, just in time for Jean's birthday, tired, but exhilarated. "I never had a delightfuler holiday in my life," he wrote Clara two days later, "and I did hate to leave Fairhaven. Big Mrs. Rogers is too lovely for anything, and so is little Mrs. Rogers; and as for old Henry himself, he is the finest they make."

414. Clemens to Emilie Rogers

New York
[Summer 1906]
Tuesday.

Dear Mrs. Rogers:

In packing my things in your house yesterday morning I inadvertently put in some articles that was laying around, I thinking about theollogy and not noticing, the way this family does in similar circumstances like these. Two books, Mr. Rogers brown slippers and a ham. I thought it was ourn it looks like one we used to have. I am very sorry it happened but it shant occur again and don't you worry He will temper the wind to the shorn lammb and I will send some of the things back anyway if there is some that wont keep.

Yores in jesus
SLC

415. ROGERS TO CLEMENS

New York
8 August 1906

My dear Clemens:

I have been hesitating a couple of days as to whether I should tell a lie or confess the truth. Of course, you know what would happen if you were in such a dilemma. You would simply lie out of it and ease your conscience. I cannot reach such a conclusion.

The letter which you sent me to copy and send to Dr. Twichell, I really intended doing; but, the fact was, I went home on Monday night and left my desk in rather a disordered condition, and as a consequence Miss Harrison supposed that the letter was intended for Dr. Twichell and sent it forward to his address. I do not think I care if Miss Harrison should be found out, because she had no right to do anything of the kind; but I wanted the pleasure of keeping the letter and sending it out just as you requested, because I know that Dr. Twichell would have appreciated it on account of his high regard for my standing as a Theologian. What in Hell am I to do? And, what will happen to you when Twichell gets you by the throat? And, what will Harmony say?

I don't agree with you in your conclusions, either as to color or age, and that is what I should tell you if you were to ask me. I am sure to get a letter from him, and when I do, it will be my duty to send it to your address.

Col. Harvey was in this afternoon and told me that you had a Gospel Meeting at Dublin when he was there, and that he had arranged for an hundred thousand words of the autobiography.[1] He was in great spirits, and it seemed to me that he was rather gloating over some great victory.

Since writing the above, I have had a call from friend Stone. He, I think, is feeling somewhat depressed because of a letter he has received from you which does not carry out his idea of what ought to be done in the matter he has on with you.[2] I know enough of it from somewhere (perhaps you have talked with me in reference) so that I want to have something to say about it. In other words, let me "butt in" and make a suggestion, and I have not a doubt at all but that Mrs. Rogers will approve of what I say, because she never does approve of what you say, and if so, we may be able to influence you. At any rate, Mrs. Rogers is quite angry with you about various matters, and I am sure you will feel influenced when she gets near you.

Yours truly,

H H Rogers

[1] Clemens identified this letter on its envelope as: "100,000 words of my Autobiography sold to Harvey." Twenty-five installments of the *Autobiography* appeared in Harvey's *North American Review* from 7 September 1906 to December 1907.

[2] Melville Stone, general manager of the Associated Press, was making arrangements for Clemens to speak at that organization's annual dinner at the Waldorf Astoria Hotel on 19 September 1906 (see *MTS* [1923], pp. 315–322). Clemens sent an invitation to Rogers with this note: "Dear Mr. Rogers: I'm accepting . . . tell me if you can go and if it will pay you to go" (quoted in AAA-Anderson Galleries Sale, No. 4098, 4–5 April 1934, item 116).

416. CLEMENS TO EMILIE ROGERS (telegram)

Dublin
27 August 1906

Mrs. H. H. Rogers
White Mountain House [1]
I brought away a trunk for a memento and I had to put some of the admiral's things in it for ballast because it was light and down by the head and wouldn't steer but God will make it up to him. They were all sorry to see me go, and most of them said so.

S. L. C.[2]

¹ The text for this telegram is a draft in Clemens's hand. Miss Lyon corrected "White Mountain" House to "Mount Washington" House; Albert Bigelow Paine corrected them both by adding "Bretton Woods."

² Clemens had been on another cruise with "Admiral" Rogers on board the *Kanawha,* having left Miss Lyon (in Dublin) "a drowsy little note . . . to say that the dictating is a burden to him, and so he is flying away down to Fairhaven and pretty Mrs. Harry Rogers and the yacht and he is so glad to have the holiday" (IVL Journal, 17 August 1906). He returned to Dublin on 24 August, "gay and jolly and darling; and full of his yachting trip to Bar Harbor, and Mrs. Harry, and the joy of living. Sly, he was; and like a boy fresh from his wild oats" (Journal, 24 August 1906; see also *MTLM,* pp. 44–46). Clemens boasted to Howells: "I have been dissipating on the yacht and at Fairhaven for ten days" (*MTHL,* p. 819).

417. Rogers to Clemens

New York
31 August 1906

My dear Clemens:

First, before I forget it, let me remind you that I shall want the trunk and the things you took away from my house, as soon as possible. I learn that, instead of taking old things, you took my best. Mrs. Rogers is at the White Mountains and I am going to Fairhaven this afternoon. I hope you will not be there.

I rather think I have made a great mess of Mr. Stone's matter. You will remember, I talked with you a little about the Banquet that he was going to have here, and that I thought I could influence you to attend. You got so angry when I talked with you on the subject, that it rather went out of my mind since. To-day, Mr. Stone called on me and I was reminded of the Banquet, and so had to lie to straighten myself. I know you won't mind that, because you can back me up without any trouble to your conscience. But, seriously, the Banquet is to be on the 19th. and Mr. Stone is anxious for you to be there. I told him that I thought the best thing for you to do was to let you ramble on anything you wanted to say. I believe this carries out your suggestion to me, and Mr. Stone would like to know if you are coming to New York soon. If not, he will run over to see you at Dublin from some place he is near there.

Please telegraph me where you will see Mr. Stone, or telegraph to him direct, as you please.

By the way, I have been using a pair of your gloves in the Mountains, and they don't seem to be much of an attraction.

Yours truly,

H H Rogers

418. CLEMENS TO ROGERS (telegram)

Dublin
3 September 1906

God be thanked have found some of the things send another trunk this one leaked.[1]

Clemens.[2]

[1] A copy of this telegram (in Clemens's hand) is pinned to letter 415. Clemens's copy varies only in the last word: he wrote "leaks."

[2] Clemens obviously understood the comic potential of telegraphic, unpunctuated prose. A series of consecutively numbered but undated fragments in Clemens's hand (probably drafts, possibly not sent) forms the following cryptic barrage. First,
"I am afraid I cannot go, I have lost my father."
Then,
"He was all I had."
And then,
"Family prostrate."
And finally,
"Do not send flowers send the money family will select flowers."
And it may have been about this time that he sent the following note (dated "summer of 1906 or 7" by Miss Lyon) to "H. H. Rogers, Fairhaven, Mass" (Berg):
"Well if I were as obtuse about perceiving a hint as you are, I would go and drown myself. Why don't you take something for it?
Clemens"
Clemens spent more time at Fairhaven and on the *Kanawha* that fall. On 2 October 1906 he would write Aldrich: "I have just returned from another 3 weeks' junketing—and still with a good conscience, for 'wasted time' is no longer a matter of concern to me . . . I have worked pretty steadily for 65 years, and

don't care what I do with the 2 or 3 that remain to me so that I get pleasure out of them." On the same day he would write Clara: "perhaps you thought I couldn't leave my niece, Mary Rogers, but I did it. I came away from Fairhaven yesterday."

419. CLEMENS TO EMILIE ROGERS

New York
24 October 1906

Dear Mrs. Rogers, it is lovely of you! Yes, Mr. Coe is the very man. He will know the exact size of the Fairhaven table, and can duplicate it. When he examines this room I think he will say it is large enough: it is 15 feet wide by 18 long, and the 18 can be increased to 18.6 if necessary, by removing a book case.[1]

The long railway journey from Dublin last Wednesday *destroyed* me for 7 whole days!—both mentally and physically; and there's been heart-burn enough to almost move me to take out a fire-policy. Indeed, to use Uncle Henry's phrase, I've had a hll of a week. At last, the week culminated last night with an assault of a disease I am not much subject to—depression of spirits. But I am all right, this morning, in *all* ways, and your letter comes at a happy time, and I thank you very sincerely.

I played billiards with Mr. Broughton last Sunday and had a quite high and holy time.[2]

Clara has been in here to shake her engagements in my face and prove to me that her time is already worth a thousand dollars a month.[3] That doesn't disgruntle me. I am tired working, anyway, and will knock off and be supported. Her illustrious master, Leschititzki, is dying in Vienna,[4] and her conscience is urging her to go over and be at the funeral, but I am persuading her that she would feel very funny if she attended his and missed mine. I guess that that settled it and she won't go; for naturally she wouldn't miss mine for anything.

I did not know Miss Lyon was going to write you, but if I had known it I would have said "go right ahead, Mrs. Rogers will not be offended."

I was at 26 B'way yesterday and learned that you are expected to-day. When you are rested I will come and gamble-off that quarter I won of you.

With love to you both

SLC

---

¹ Mrs. Rogers had promised Clemens a billiard table as a Christmas present, but was persuaded that he could not wait that long; on 30 October 1906 Miss Lyon noted in her journal that the new table "has been put into place today" (see also *MTLM*, pp. 36–37, 83, and *MTB*, pp. 1324–1327).

² Miss Lyon wrote in her journal on Sunday, 21 October 1906: "All day it has rained hard and Mr. Clemens went out to the Broughtons to play billiards. He is restless and finds a great emptiness in life. He doesn't like this house—and finds no comfort outside of his own room."

³ Clara had sung at Norfolk, Connecticut, on 22 September 1906 and was now arranging a recital tour.

⁴ Theodor Leschetizky did not die until 1915.

420. CLEMENS TO EMILIE ROGERS

New York
[?5] November 1906

Monday.

Dear Mrs. Rogers:

The billiard table is better than the doctors. It is driving out the heartburn in a most promising way. I have a billiardist ¹ on the premises, and I walk not less than ten miles every day with the cue in my hand. And the walking is not the whole of the exercise, nor the most health-giving part of it, I think. Through the multitude of the positions and attitudes it brings into play every muscle in the body and exercises them all.

The games begin right after luncheon, daily, and continue until midnight, with 2 hours' intermission for dinner and music. And so it is 9 hours' exercise per day, and 10 or 12 for Sunday. Yesterday and last night it was 12—and I slept until 8 this morning without waking. The billiard table, as a Sabbath-breaker can beat any coal-breaker in Pennsylvania, and give it 30 in the game. If Mr. Rogers will take to daily billiards he can do without the doctors and the massageur, I think.

I was meditating a descent upon the Coes yesterday afternoon, but learned by telephone that they were not at home. However, the weather was not auspicious for gout, and I am threatened with that, these days. The billiards will knock it out.

We are really going to build a house on my farm,[2] an hour and a half from New York. It is decided. It is to be built by contract and is to come within $25,000. I have been up to see Jean,[3] and it is a pathetic exile and captivity; I must have a country home for her.

With love and many thanks,

SLC.

Clara is in the sanitarium—till January 28, when her western concert-tour will begin. She is getting to be a mighty competent singer. You must know Clara better; she is one of the very finest and completest and most satisfactory characters I have ever met. Others knew it before, but I have always been busy with other matters.

I shan't forget the 29th—*sure.*

---

[1] Albert Bigelow Paine.

[2] Clemens commissioned John Mead Howells to design and supervise the building of his house at Redding, Connecticut.

[3] Jean Clemens was in a sanitarium in Katonah, New York. At this time, Clemens wrote to her that "Mr. Rogers stops in every morning and furnish[es] advice and abuse."

421. CLEMENS TO EMILIE ROGERS

Washington[1]
8 December 1906
Saturday.

Dear Mrs. Rogers:

Oh, dear me I *am* ashamed! I forgot to telephone you (in my hurry) that I must rush off to Washington in the interest of the new copyright bill and couldn't keep my engagement for 5 p.m. yesterday with you. I am dreadfully sorry, and I apologise.

I came down to do a few days' or a week's lobbying, leaving to the others the speech-making before the committee; but yesterday afternoon when I was tired out and asleep in the Speaker's private room in the Capitol, I was ordered to go before the Committee and speak; which I did; then I resumed my lobbying again, and shall now go on with it from day to day. I tried to persuade Uncle Joe Cannon to smuggle me in on the floor of the House, for lobbying purposes, but he dasn't. However, he has compromised by doing for me what he has not done for a lobbyist before, probably: he gives me his private room for as long as I want it, and a servant to invite members to come in and talk copyright; and so I shall stay here and conduct a strenuous private canvass of the House.

Clara invited you and Uncle Henry, but I didn't know, when I left home, whether you had accepted or not. I hope I'll be there when you come, but I may be disappointed, for I must abide here and keep on striking while the iron is hot—for this [is] a very important bill. Lobbying, man by man, buttonhole by buttonhole, is the only possible way to get it through, and there is no one to help me in this. It carried the bill of 22 years ago, and I am fully as shameless a lobbyist as I was then.

With love to you both,

SLC.

[1] Clemens was staying at the New Willard Hotel. He was in Washington with William Dean Howells and other members of the Copyright League (see *MTHL*, pp. 821–822; *MMT*, p. 96; the New York *Times*, 8 December 1906). Congress ultimately passed the Act of 4 March 1909 which, in almost all its essentials, is the present copyright law of the United States.

422. CLEMENS TO EMILIE ROGERS

New York
22 December 1906
Saturday.

Dear Mrs. Rogers:

I thank you ever so much [for] those Xmas cigars and for the kind remembrance which they betoken. I'm wishing you a merry Christmas, but I am coming up pretty soon to attend to it in person[1] as soon as I have worked off the several-days' engagements which Clara has piled upon me.

Sincerely Yours

SL. Clemens

[1] Clemens had Christmas dinner with the Rogerses. Miss Lyon notes in her journal for that day that he was waiting to see "what kind of an indigestion" he would get from all "the mince pie and plum pudding mixed together he had eaten."

423. CLEMENS TO ROGERS

New York
1 January 1907
New Year's, /07.

Dear Mr. Rogers:

After you were here, this morning, Miss Lyon took an account of stock, and I am able to report as follows:

We lived on $32,000 this past year—$12,000 less than the year before.

The books paid $40,000 for the year—which is distinctly better than either of the two previous years.

The Autobiography has paid about $12,000 or $15,000 thus far.

There is about $40,000 in the bank to invest when I get back, and money due from Harper in addition not collectable until April.[1]

Twichell is due to arrive, now.

With Happy New Year and love to you both.

SLC.

[1] Miss Harrison, whose responsibility in Clemens's financial affairs was such that she kept a key to his safety deposit box, continued to send reports on investments which Rogers had made or approved for Clemens. On 4 March 1907 she wrote:

Enclosed please find check for $350.00, Preferred Stock Dividend from U. S. Steel Corporation. Would it not be a good idea to put this in your own name, now that you have all the stock?

On 27 May 1907, she reported:

I have bought the 400 Anaconda, as you requested—200 at 60 and 200 at 59, as per enclosed bills. I am returning you the balance of your money, namely, $6,150., having no further order. I will hold the stock here until I hear from you.

On 31 May 1907, she admonished:

I think the enclosed check from the United States Steel Corporation for $350., Preferred stock dividend, belongs to you. Will you kindly have your Certificate made in your own name, so that your check will be sent direct to you.

But Clemens also made investments of his own, most of which, like the Plasmon venture, did not do well. In 1902 he had purchased 200 shares of stock in the Tabard Inn Corporation (which was financing the Booklovers Library); by 1905, when the company was in grave financial difficulties, he was trying to get rid of his shares, but could find no buyers (Notebook 35, TS p. 2; SLC to Seymour Eaton, 28 March 1905). In 1904 J. Y. W. MacAlister had persuaded him to trade three Plasmon Founders' shares for £1,000 stock in the Formaline Company, an enterprise which seems to have met with little success (SLC to MacAlister, 7 April 1904, CWB). In that same year Clemens purchased fifty Koy-lo Company and sixty International Spiral Pin Company shares for $4,500. This investment was solicited by Ralph W. Ashcroft, whose uncle in Australia was interested in the products—hairpins and locking safety pins (Ashcroft to SLC, 19 September 1904).

By August 1904 he had accumulated $16,000 in bonds in Charles Fairchild's American Mechanical Cashier Company. For some time that company, a competitor of the National Cash Register Company, was involved in lawsuits with the machinery firm that had produced its first one hundred change-making devices, so that further production was pretty much at a standstill. In October 1906 Ashcroft advised Clemens to invest $30,000 more in the company, because it now seemed to have brighter prospects; but Clemens resisted, and Ashcroft later advised Fairchild to sell the bonds (Ashcroft to SLC, 4 November 1904, 10 and 25 October 1906).

In 1905 Clemens had considered investing in the Insole Company, in which Ashcroft had such confidence that he persuaded servants in the houses of his friends to test insoles in their shoes (Ashcroft to SLC, 23 June 1905).

And in 1907 he invested $5,000 in the Hope-Jones Organ Company, of New York and Elmira, of which his nephew, Jervis Langdon, was president and treasurer, and for which Langdon also solicited, apparently without success, additional capital investment (Langdon to SLC, 9 September 1907).

424. ROGERS TO CLEMENS (telegram)

On board the SS *Baltic*
8 May 1907

Have just started by land Mrs Rogers prefers it [1] tell the girls

Rogers

[1] About an hour after Rogers and his wife had set out for Europe, the captain of the White Star steamship *Baltic*, mistaking an anchored Standard Oil Company tank steamship for an oncoming vessel, took such drastic evasive action that the *Baltic* went aground in the mud within New York Bay. It was twenty-four hours before the undamaged ship was hauled off the shoal by a fleet of tugboats. Jocular passengers lined the deck rails, shouting messages to reporters and encouragement to the towboats struggling with their stranded vessel. "I'm getting a rest," called a man whom the New York *World* (10 May 1907) identified as the vacationing Andrew Carnegie: "Mr. Rogers will pour oil on the troubled waters."

More than levity may have inspired the cryptic form of this telegram, since the embarrassed captain of the *Baltic* had imposed a ban on wireless messages from the ship telling about the accident.

425. CLEMENS TO ROGERS

Tuxedo Park
29 May 1907

Dear Admiral:

Why hang it, I am not going to see you and Mrs. Rogers at all in England! It is a great disappointment. I leave there a month from now—June 29. No, I *shall* see you; for by your itinerary you are most likely to come to London June 21st or along there. So that is very good and satisfactory. I have declined all engagements but two —Whitelaw Reid (dinner) June 21, and the Pilgrims (lunch), June 25. The Oxford ceremony is June 26. I have paid my return passage in the Minne-something, but it is just possible that I may want to stay in England a week or two longer—I can't tell, yet.[1] I do very much want to meet-up with the boys for the last time.

Harry is getting along all right; I was there three or four days ago and saw him.

Mr. Vanderbilt is back in New York and doubtless has invited Mr. Cleveland in behalf of the Fulton Association. I have already invited him on behalf of the Kanawha.[2]

I have signed the contract for the building of the house on my Connecticut farm and specified the cost-limit, and work has been begun. The cost has to all come out of a year's instalments of Autobiography in the N. A. Review.

Clara is winning her way to success and distinction with sure and steady strides. By all accounts she is singing like a bird, and is not afraid on the concert-stage any more.

Jean will never be well, but is contented and happy where she is and does not want to see the city again.

Miss Lyon runs Clara, and Jean, and me, and the servants, and the housekeeping, and the house-building, and the secretary-work, and remains as extraordinarily competent as ever. Mr. Broughton

—after his characteristically engaging and Broughtonian fashion— was elaborately courteous and courtly to her on sight (there at his office) and said he was intemperately eager to help her run my stock-affairs, and even threatened to take her out to lunch at his club some day. I think Miss Lyon is a flirt—and Broughton the same.

Tuxedo is a charming place; I think it hasn't its equal anywhere.

Very best wishes to you both.

SLC

[1] Clemens would leave New York 8 June 1907 on the SS *Minnesota* to receive an honorary Litt.D. from Oxford University; he left England on 13 July on the SS *Minnetonka*, arriving in New York nine days later. In London, Ambassador and Mrs. Whitelaw Reid entertained him at an elaborate dinner at Dorchester House (see *MTB*, p. 1384), and Clemens spoke at a Pilgrims Club luncheon at the Savoy Hotel (*MTS* [1923], pp. 335–343); he did not, however, restrict his social and public life to these two engagements (see *MTB*, pp. 1380–1403).

[2] Cornelius Vanderbilt was president and Clemens vice-president of the Robert Fulton Monument Association; they were planning a program for the Robert Fulton Day celebration on 23 September 1907 at the Jamestown Exposition in Virginia. Rogers had offered Clemens the use of his yacht for the trip (see *MTLM*, pp. 103–106).

426. EMILIE ROGERS TO CLEMENS

Vichy [1]
12 June 1907
Hotel du Parc

Dear Mr Clemens

Mr Rogers received your letter and he has asked me to tell you that we shall be so very glad to see you, even if it be for a short time, in London—We expect to be there on the evening of the twenty third—We shall stay at Claridge's where we shall hope to hear from you, as well as to see you. We are booked to sail for home

on the Baltic on the 27th inst—Mr Rogers joins me in affectionate
greetings

Very sincerely

Emilie R. Rogers

[1] Rogers and his wife had arrived in Vichy on 28 May 1907. Interviewed on 2
June by a reporter for the New York *World*, he explained that they were there
"for the benefit of Mrs. Rogers's health," and that "until they went to Vichy they
had been automobiling, and . . . they had enjoyed the scenery and altogether
had had a splendid time" (New York *World*, 8 June 1907).

427. ROGERS TO CLEMENS

Vichy

12 June 1907

Dear Parson,

We have your letter written at Tuxedo Park. It of course was
intended to let us know where you are to stay in London but
inasmuch as we are to be housed at Claridges it is d—n little we
care where you sleep. Never mind, we will probably see you as I am
invited to the Pilgrim's Luncheon, and shall try and go. I don't
know who is so polite to me but Lancaster of Liverpool sends the
invitation.

We go to Paris on the 19th and to London on Sunday the 23d.
We then go to Liverpool on the 27th and sail in the evening or
from Queenstown next day the 28th. If you want or need good
company you can catch us anywhere. The White Star Company
and Atlantic Transport Co are all one and tickets can be made
interchangeable if you apply to Chas Lancaster 20 Water St Liverpool. We will be delighted to have you on our ship. The only
essentials this time will be drunkenness, profanity and sodomy. The
"Crown Jewels" and "preachers pride" will be found there.

That Jamestown show will come off as arranged. You and Cleveland and Harry are welcome to everything but if you take on board that fakir from Washington I'll have him dumped from a Water Closet. Where better dung is made. You remember Rice's yarn about the Cheese and what was on it.

Mrs R would join in regards if she thought I was writing properly

Yours truly

Your Uncle Henry

428. ROGERS TO CLEMENS

Vichy

13 June 1907

My dear Clemens

I wrote you yesterday and mailed to Liverpool Care Hughes & Lancaster 20 Water street to learn later that your ship went to London not Liverpool. I wanted to let you know that I intended going to the Pilgrims luncheon and so will be on hand to keep you in lines of truth and righteousness.

We will be at Claridges on Sunday the 23d instant (from Paris that afternoon). We leave London on the 27th, Queenstown the 28th and if you want or need good Christian companionship you can get it (two for a shilling) as Mrs Rogers and I will be on the ship.

I have good cigars. I bought them in France. They cost 1 franc a dozen—six in a dozen. The mixture is grape-leaf and goat-dung strong and searching. One draws, the other drives. Come along and try them. I believe there is a possible President to be hatched from the mixture. We can try it on the cat—Mrs Anthony instead of setting her again.

We leave here on the 19th. Arrive Paris evening 20th and stay until Sunday morning.

Hope you came over comfortably with all sorts of good passages.

I forgot in this to tell you that I received your letter written at Tuxedo Park

So long

Admiral

429. ROGERS TO CLEMENS

London

26 June 1907

Wednesday

My dear Clemens

The enclosed cablegram has just come in and I forward for your decision. You know that Reick is now on the Times.[1]

Sorry not to see you after the luncheon but I could not get around in time for your telephone call. Suppose you will have great times at Oxford and we congratulate you in advance. You made me prouder than ever yesterday, and I had as good a time as you did.

We are off at noon to-morrow, and I am glad enough to go.

Mrs R. joins me in best regards,

Yours sincerely

H H Rogers

If you want to answer Reick you can cable Harrison Standard Oil New York Tell Reick ******—anything you damn please.

R

[1] William C. Reick formerly had been city editor of the New York *Herald*. Rogers enclosed his cable, dated 27 June 1907. It read:
Hope pleasant voyage ask uncle mark if he will give us characteristic interview his experiences in england he is creating great sensation

430. ROGERS TO CLEMENS

London
27 June 1907
Thursday

My dear Clemens.

The N.Y. Times man called me up last night to learn if I had received a cable from Reick. I told him that I had sent the same to you. I suppose that lets me out. At any rate Mrs Rogers and I are leaving in 5 minutes. You look well in your gown, and I am proud to see you in the front row as I had expected that W. R.[1] would ⟨hog⟩ have the show.

Mrs R. joins in love and blessings,

HHR

[1] Whitelaw Reid had received an honorary degree (Doctor of Civil Laws) from Oxford University the day before.

431. CLEMENS TO ROGERS

Tuxedo Park
29 July 1907
Monday p.m.

Dear Uncle Henry—

I am in bed again and out of temper. Bronchitis. It is from the slightest of slight colds, caught at sea on the 17th and now a dozen days old. It almost disappeared when I reached Tuxedo, but it hit me hard Thursday evening, and by Friday evening I was in Dr. Rushmore's[1] hands. He has modified it—the first time a doctor has performed that miracle.

Be it prudent or *im*prudent, I mean to get up to-morrow: there's company coming Wednesday, and Friday, and next Tuesday, and I wish to resume life.

Miss Lyon has been to town to-day and brings news from No. 26 that confirms Mrs. Rogers's telegram and discredits the exaggerations of the newspapers regarding your attack.[2] Good. I was pretty uneasy at first.

Will you please tell Mary and Harry the Clevelands can't go, on account of Mr. Cleveland's half-wrecked health. And so the Choates [3] will probably be our guests. Choate promised to fill the breach if Mr. Cleveland should fail us.

The enclosed note from the Lady Mayoress [4] will prove to you—which my unassisted word could not do—that I obeyed your commands and went to Liverpool. I did most profoundly dread the journey and the banquet and the reception, but it came out all right, and I was very glad I went. Mr. Lancaster sat opposite me at table and was very pleasant and friendly, and I was glad of a chance to foregather with him.

Monday.

Harvey is coming this evening. He and I were going to Bermuda to-morrow for a couple of weeks, but it turns out that he can't. He thinks Deal Beach will set me up, and so I am to go there, 7 or 8 days from now and stay a week or ten days.

With love to all the lovely tribe

Yrs ever

SLC

[1] Dr. Edward C. Rushmore of Tuxedo Park.

[2] On 27 July 1907 the New York *Tribune* reported that although Rogers had been "a little indisposed on account of the heat," early rumors of serious illness had been "greatly exaggerated." In reality, he had suffered a stroke on 22 July, of which Clemens at this time knew nothing. When Miss Lyon made inquiry of Mrs. Rogers on 17 September, she was told that the stroke had "muffled his speech so that he could not be understood at all for a week, and his left arm and leg were affected." At the same time, Miss Lyon continued in her journal (17 September 1907): "A rumor ran out into the world that Mr. Rogers was dead, a few weeks ago, and there was nearly a panic in Wall Street. That was denied, and then came the great demand I mean the law suits of the Standard Oil which

demanded Mr. Rogers's presence as a witness. The Doctors say it would kill him to go on the witness stand and they have to hedge one way or another continually."

[3] Joseph A. Choate was at this time a delegate to the Second Peace Conference at the Hague.

[4] Clemens enclosed a letter from Margaret C. Japp, wife of Lord Mayor John Japp, thanking the author for having spoken at Liverpool: "I cannot tell you how much we have been congratulated on the success of that evening, and of the pleasure your presence gave" (see also *MTB,* p. 1401).

432. EMILIE ROGERS TO CLEMENS

Fairhaven
12 August 1907

Dear Mr Clemens

You have been a little neglected but not intentionally, I assure you, for I am sure you have no warmer friends than these at Fairhaven. Mr Rogers came back here on the third of August, a week ago Saturday. He had really been in worse shape than we have cared to acknowledge to anybody. The rest, of the past week, has done a lot for him and he is much improved. He will remain here this week and I hope longer—He has spoken of you many times and, if you care to come, we should all be glad to welcome you to Fairhaven—The Kanawha is ⟨in⟩ at New York and if you can communicate with Harry he will tell you when she is likely to return. I presume the last of the week—The family send kindest messages and Mr Rogers says he would like to see "Old Mark"—

Yours very sincerely
Emilie R. Rogers

433. EMILIE ROGERS TO CLEMENS

Fairhaven
15 August 1907

Dear Mr Clemens

I have just received your letter and we are all disappointed that you will not favor us. I read the letter to Mr Rogers and he could not quite understand as to what you call your colossal blunder. He bids me say that, as he recalls the matter of Ex President Cleveland's visit to Jamestown, it was understood that you were to have the Kanawha to invite Mr Cleveland for the trip, and the boat was to be in Harry's command. He understands that now Mr Cleveland is unable to make the trip, and you have invited Mr Choate instead. That arrangement has his entire sanction, on one condition, and that is that you will understand that Mr Choate will accept. Of course the people of Jamestown understood that you were going to invite Mr Cleveland, and it would be proper to confer with them as to the substitution of Mr Choate. That is the primal thing. Following it must be the acceptance by Mr Choate without any reservation or qualification. Between us Mr Rogers is of opinion that Mr Choate might hesitate about going on Mr Rogers' boat.[1] *That* settled the whole thing is very clear. You are at liberty to go on and make the arrangements. Mr Rogers joins me in love and the family all unite in kindest messages.

Yours very sincerely

Emilie R. Rogers

[1] Clemens had not realized that Choate and Rogers were not on good terms. The difficulty was settled when on 19 August 1907 Choate wrote from The Hague to express regrets that he could not be present at the Robert Fulton Day celebration (Salm).

434. CLEMENS TO EMILIE ROGERS

Tuxedo Park
18 August 1907
Sunday.

Dear Mrs. Rogers:

Then ⟨I⟩ it is all right, and I am relieved. I must have had some groping dull instinct that I had been making a blunder, for when I did not get an answer at once from the Admiral I was distinctly uneasy, without knowing why. Very well, there's one thing sure: I shall not make *another* blunder. Until next time.

I should have gone with Harry but for engagements. Particularly a dinner one—the others could have been canceled; but for the chief guest to fail of a dinner-engagement, even when dead, is apparently not permissible. However, as it turns out, there wasn't any such engagement: it was a tea. The dinner is Tuesday night. ⟨By George, if⟩

I thought I would have my surgical operation [1] *now,* and get it done over again when the time should come to use it as a pretext— for Col. Harvey said he had tried it, and it was a trifling matter. So I asked Dr. Rushmore to proceed with it. But he declined. He said that at my time of life it could land me in the graveyard. So *that's* off. It is a world of disappointments.

Clara is prospering in Boston, where she is studying. She has gained 7 pounds in two months, and is proud and fat. Also, she has ⟨had a tonsil cut out, and thinks God arranged it for the summer season, so that she wouldn't lose any time from concerting in the fall.⟩ Mebbe so. One can't most always sometimes tell what His game is.

Somebody sent that picture to me, but I could not have it around, because it was indelicate. So I sent it to the Admiral. In this I am plagiarising the attitude of

[The remainder of this letter is missing.]

---

[1] Perhaps for a hernia suffered in 1893.

435. ISABEL LYON TO EMILIE ROGERS

Tuxedo Park
27 August 1907

Dear Mrs. Rogers:

Mr. Clemens would write this letter to you himself, but what with doing too heavy a day's work in a literary way, and with fretting over the complications of securing the right orator, for the Fulton Memorial Day at Jamestown, he is very tired and has deputed me to explain everything to you.[1] There seems no question now about the possibility of having Mr. Choate; for according to last reports he will be kept at the Hague for at least a month. Such being the case, I telephoned in today to one of the managers of the Jamestown affair, and told him that since, without doubt, Mr. Choate would be unable to be present, that Mr. Clemens now felt that he would withdraw ⟨as well⟩ and take no further part in the celebration. But it seems that they count so much on having Mr. Clemens there; they feel so that without him they might as well give up all idea of having the celebration, as he is their great card, and their disappointment is so keen, that Mr. Clemens will reconsider his decision to withdraw. If they can secure Dr. Nicholas Murray Butler as orator for the day, Mr. Clemens would like to know if he would be acceptable to Mr. Rogers, as a guest for the Kanawha. All these things Mr. Clemens would have liked to thrash out with Mr. Rogers at Fair Haven, and would have done so, but he has been very much tied up here, trying to finish his dictation of the ⟨auto⟩ trip to England. If he stops once to go away for a day or so, he says that he knows he will be unable to resume work again, and so he dares not break in on what he feels is a very great duty. He has been working very steadily; in fact, today he has done too much, and has gone to bed very tired. Then he has fretted a good deal over the trip to Jamestown; or rather, about the uncertainties of it; but otherwise he is well, and is enjoying being here. He sends a great deal of love to you and to Mr. Rogers, and would like to see you both very much indeed, and hopes you can answer this question about Dr. Butler without troubling yourselves.

Very Sincerely Yours,

I. V. Lyon. Secy

[1] Miss Lyon had reported in her journal only four days before (23 August 1907) that Clemens "cannot bear to write letters. He looks at a pen with a shudder in these days."

436. Rogers to Clemens

Fairhaven
30 August 1907

My Dear Clemens:—

Mrs. Rogers received your letter of the 28th inst. and has handed same to me. I note that you are getting into trouble in that Jamestown matter. I think you make a mistake in trying to advertise a man like Butler. People of Virginia don't want to see him. They want Mark Twain. If you cannot see that, I can. Why not make short work of the whole matter by saying that Mr. Rogers writes you that he would be very glad to send you and your friends down to Virginia, and now since Mr. Cleveland is unable to attend, why not make it a "Clemens" Day? If you do not want to speak, just get into the background, and take along with you such good fellows as W. J. Howells, Peter Dunne and Geo. Harvey. What is the matter with Max Reach,[1] Geo. Ade, and Hop. Smith, and a lot more good fellows whom we know, and would make it an interesting occasion?

If your modesty prevents you from making a suggestion in the matter, just send this letter along to Mr. Tucker, chairman of the Committee. I don't think since you have been in Europe you know as much as you used to. I am sure that this is right because I am always so. You had better consider yourself under orders at once. However, if you and your stupidity have a different idea, why let us have that, but you will never make any success unless you do what people want you to do.

I am hoping to see you here in Fairhaven. I have been on the loaf for seven or eight weeks, and think I will stay. Am due in New York after a time for law suits, but what is the need of being in a hurry?

The house is full, or will be on Sunday, with the entire family, including the last Coe baby.[2]

If you would like to get in good company after your recent experience, it would do you good to look in on us. Sometimes I think that the Pilgrim Dinner came near spoiling you. What they said about you I will explain later on.

Just call in a few friends, and see if they do not think that I am right in regard to the Jamestown matter. That's the thing to do.

Yours truly,

H H Rogers

[1] This letter, typed at Fairhaven and probably from dictation, contains a number of obvious errors. Rogers certainly knew Howells's name; it is possible that, having recently suffered a stroke, his pronunciation of "Rex Beach" could have been heard as "Max Reach."

[2] Henry Huttleston Rogers Coe had been born on 30 June 1907.

437. ROGERS TO CLEMENS (telegram)

New Bedford
3 September 1907

Letter received we can never settle matters by coresspondance the kanawaha will be coming to Fair Haven the latter part of this week Broughton can give you details at his office please come here and arrange the virginan matter please advise.

H H Rogers.

438. CLEMENS TO ROGERS

Tuxedo Park
20 September 1907

Friday.

Dear Mr. Rogers:

I hope you are ever so much better to-day, and I do also hope that it was not the billiards that sent you to bed with that pain—though I very much fear it was, and I am so sorry.

Harry sails tomorrow night—I shall go on board in the afternoon.[1] We shall hurry through, at Jamestown, as quickly as possible, so that we can return the yacht to you. Mary [2] thinks we can sail homeward at midnight, Monday—so that is what we shall do.

It may interest Mrs. Broughton to have the latest news from that cricket. After I left for Fairhaven Monday,[3] Miss Lyon instituted a search for him and kept it up, off and on till midnight—no success. Then she went to bed there, and he kept her awake until 3, then he drove her out.

The entire household continued the search on Tuesday and Wednesday and Thursday, and on each of these nights the butler tried to sleep in the room, but was driven out. I suppose I shall be driven out to-night.

Now *that* news is all for Mrs. Broughton—there isn't any for you, at all, for not a thing has happened here since I went away, except that cricket.

So I send my love

SLC

[1] The younger Rogerses and Clemens were leaving for Jamestown.
[2] Mary Benjamin Rogers.
[3] Clemens had left New York for Fairhaven, according to Miss Lyon's journal entry of 16 September 1907, on the New Bedford boat, the *Maine*, "to see Mr. Rogers, who has been a very ill man."

439. CLEMENS TO ROGERS

Tuxedo Park
26 September 1907

Dear Admiral:

This is my official report. In the first place I was the yacht's guest, and therefore yours; therefore, also, I was the guest of your deputies, Harry and Mary. No guest has ever fared better; in truth your deputies very much exceeded the due hospitalities devolved upon them by their official position. It would have been no breach of hospitality if they had remained on board on that stormy 23d, but they didn't; they saw me ashore themselves. It was a shame to allow them to do it—I realized that—but I hadn't the grit to say "stay aboard," for the R.F. Day was bound to be a failure and a fiasco, and I greatly needed the countenance and presence and support of friends, otherwise my share of the fiasco could easily be disastrous. They saved the day for me; then they came back and saved the night, too—the most welcome faces, and the most unexpected, I ever saw! I had not dreamed that they would take all that trouble and come back, after all the trouble they had taken to help me through in the day. And so I was not surprised when I saw that the seats which they were to occupy with Mrs. Miller and me had been given away. I judged that they had sent word they were not coming. I am grateful to your deputies for another good service: their presence forbade me to shame them with certain vicious and ungracious public utterances which longed for an outlet, but were much better unsaid than said. I was discreet and proper and parliamentary, but the credit was not mine.

I would like to run up to Fairhaven soon, for a day or two, if I can be of any use to you.

I wish you could have been there that day; it was the completest and perfectest fiasco in history, and worth going a thousand miles to see. But all the same I had a good time, notwithstanding the conditions were so ridiculous.

With love to you and all.

SLC

440. ROGERS TO CLEMENS (telegram)

New Bedford
3 October 1907

Delighted to have you come to Fair Haven Yacht Leaving on Friday communicate with 26 Broadway regarding hour.

H H Rogers.

441. Clemens to Rogers

New York
4 October 1907

Friday, p.m.

Dear Admiral—

Didn't Mary promise to write me a line (before Oct. 3) and tell me if the yacht would be sailing to-day or to-morrow?—so that I wouldn't be making obstructing engagements.[1] Yes, I think she did, if I didn't dream it. I'd have postponed Clara, which would have been just as well, for I think she has postponed herself. She was due here hours ago and isn't here yet, and hasn't telegraphed.

Will you please examine the enclosed and correct the spelling and then mail it to the N.Y. Times.[2] I believe it will help Howells with worldly people.

Now as to this Bumpkin Club.[3] If you will draw the check to my order and send it here, I will endorse it over to Mr. Steele and see that he gets it. I will see to it personally. Please send it right away, because as you see by his letter that you cannot get in after he closes the list, at any price at all, and he is liable to close it any minute. He evidently has great power in the Club. Would you like to be an officer? I believe I can fix it for you for $3. Send the money right now, or it may be too late. Harry has been accepted; I proposed him. I should wish to have the money soon. Could you speak to Winsor about this—and Broughton and Benjamin? I will get them in if I can. Let them send the money now. Would they like to be officers, think? $9.

Love to all.

SLC

⟨Say—⟩ P.S. Hurry!

P.P.S. He will call on you, if you wish further particulars. But hurry!

[1] Clemens evidently had changed his mind about the visit to Fairhaven, and preceded this letter with a telegram. He dictated a draft for this to Isabel Lyon:

H.H.R.   Oct. 3. 1907
Very much disappointed cannot go. Visitors/Clara
expected here Saturday.   S.L.C.

or could I say Clara expected Saturday. I expect her Saturday as much as any time.

[2] "The enclosed" was most likely a version of a note addressed to the editor of the New York *Times* (*MTHL*, p. 827):

Sir to you, I would like to know what kind of a goddam govment this is that discriminates between two common carriers & makes a goddam railroad charge everybody equal & lets a goddam man charge any goddam price he wants to for his goddam opera box

W D Howels
Tuxedo Park   Oct 4
(goddam it)

Howells it is an outrage the way the govment is acting so I sent this complaint to N.Y. Times with your name signed because it would have more weight.

Mark

[3] Clemens enclosed a letter (2 October 1907, Salm) from David P. Steele, a retired insurance agent turned vaudeville actor. Steele invited Clemens to join his newly formed Bumpkin Club: "Its sole object is to be recreation and pleasure, to drive the cobwebs from the brain wearied by business cares. . . . Please reply immediately and I will call at your convenience and give you further particulars, or if you can have sufficient confidence in me, mail to me your check for Five dollars and leave it to me to give you value received. When I choose to close the list of membership no one can get in for love or money, as a full fledged member." Clemens noted in the margin: "I don't know Steele, and he may be doubtful. Send the money to me."

442. CLEMENS TO ROGERS

New York
8 October 1907

Dear Mr. Rogers—

I'm coming up next Friday per New Bedford boat or Kanawha —or maybe Saturday or Sunday per Kanawha, I can't tell which till I find out dates and terms. Will you telegraph me when you get this? [1]

Oh, well, there's different kinds of postcards, they're not all like the one you sent, thanks be! Mary wrote that one, I recognized her hand through the disguise, without any trouble.[2] Another thing: you told her to return my scurrilous literature, along with your indignation. Very well, she sent the indignation, but kept the literature for her scrapbook. I knew she would admire it. I will ask you to give her my love, and thereto my thanks for her appreciation of that literature. And it *is* good, you know. Mighty good.

Do you know, wonderful are the ways of Providence. I mean, in smoothing the path of His own. For the enclosed postcard came yesterday, to soothe the sorrows to be caused by the one that comes from you to-day, and to soothe some that arrived day before yesterday—which was like this:

Some ladies called, and told an anecdote, all upside down and *wrong*—oh, altogether incorrect—and said it was drifting around Tuxedo and being believed—thus:

That a lady called me on the telephone and said:

"Will you come and dine with us to-night?"

"Oh, I am unspeakably sorry, but I have an imperative engagement."

"It's too bad. Can you come to-morrow night?"

"I do *wish* I could, but I have to be in New York."

"Well, then, make it Thursday."

After a reflective pause:

"Oh hell, I'll come tonight!"

It is all wrong, I give you my word. It didn't happen in Tuxedo at all; it was New York. And more than a year ago, at that. And it wasn't a lady, it was a man. A man whom I detest.

Yrs Ever

SL C

---

[1] Cara Broughton would telegraph Clemens from Great Neck, New York, on 11 October 1907: "The yacht left for FairHaven today to bring all the family home on sunday" (MTP). By that time Clemens had already decided not to make the trip, for he wrote Mary Rogers on the same day: "It was my purpose to thank you for your letter in person, but the court had a more different idea about it, and it forbade Fairhaven, and furnished me a couple of days' testifying to do" (*MTLM*, p. 110).

² On 7 October 1907 Mary Benjamin Rogers had written Clemens:

Father Rogers has asked me to return your scurrilous literature, and to say, that as for him, he will have nothing to do with persons who indulge in anonymous postcards, however much he might feel himself in sympathy with their sentiments.

He hopes that having enjoyed yourself, by taking away your own character, so openly you are ready to suffer the penalty, with meekness, which the law inflicts on those who are caught sending opprobrious remarks through the mail. . . . Father Rogers says the aforementioned "penalty" is waiting for you down here and he wants you to come and get it (*MTLM,* p. 109).

443. CLEMENS TO EMILIE ROGERS

New York
2 December 1907

Dear Mrs. Rogers:

It helps to reconcile me to my antiquity [1] to have it recognized and approved in this lovely way. I thank you for the roses, and for the remembrance, dear Mrs. Rogers.

Sincerely Yours

SL. Clemens

[1] Clemens had become 72 on 30 November 1907.

444. ROGERS TO CLEMENS

New York
16 January 1908 [1]

Dear Mr. Clemens:

The enclosed letters will explain themselves.

Lest you do not understand, I beg to inform you that Henry Watterson evidently is going to attend the Booker T. Washington Meeting on Friday evening, and you are invited to the platform or a box.[2] If you want my company, I will go in a box with you, provided I can wear a veil. I think, however, that Mrs. Rogers is going to ask you and Stone to dinner Friday night. If you want to go to the Washington Meeting, we can take Stone along with us and have cards at another time.

Please let me hear from you by telephone or messenger what you will do.

Yours truly,

H H Rogers

KIH [3]

<hr>

[1] At the bottom of this letter Miss Lyon has written: "5360—Spring/1820 Rector/Mr. Auerbach."

[2] Washington had written Clemens on 8 January 1908 to ask him to sit on the platform at the Tuskegee Institute dinner at Carnegie Hall. Clemens dictated to Miss Lyon a draft reply which she copied in the margin of Washington's letter:

> Oh, I'd jut as soon sit on the platform and be looked at, as not. But it would mean a speech—and I don't want to make one. But I could sit there and be a target for bouquets. It might be a chance to heave in a word for the durned blue laws. But I don't decline and I don't accept. I leave it open.

[3] Rogers was by this time back in New York and at work; when he and Mrs. Rogers had called on Clemens on 5 January, Miss Lyon had noted in her journal (5 January 1908): "I tried to find a change in Mr. Rogers since his stroke last July, but there are no effects of it visible now."

445. CLEMENS TO EMILIE ROGERS

Bermuda
2 March 1908

Princess Hotel

Dear Mrs. Rogers:

He is getting along splendidly! This was the very place for him. He enjoys himself and is as quarrelsome as a cat.[1]

But he will get a backset if Benjamin goes home. Benjamin is the brightest man in these regions, and the best company. Bright? He is much more than that, he is brilliant. He keeps the crowd intensely alive.

With love and all good wishes,

SLC

[1] When Clemens and Rogers sailed for Bermuda on 22 February 1908, "Mr. Rogers came feebly onto the boat, a sick sick man," wrote Miss Lyon in her journal; on 28 February she recorded that "Mr. Rogers is improving every day now, and he isn't the grey feeble man he was less than a week ago." Clemens seemed to her "gay and young and full of a new and splendid life"; she liked to hear him and Rogers "abuse each other with an earnestness entirely deceptive to the uninitiated," but which was a "blessedness to us" (2 March 1908). Mrs. Rogers would join them on 16 March; they would sail for New York on 11 April.

VIII

"I Wish Henry Rogers Would Come Here"

(JUNE 1908–MAY 1909)

> "I wish Henry Rogers would come here, and I wish you would come with him."
>
> SLC to ERR, 12 August 1908

THE NEW house in Redding was exactly right: Clemens wrote in the guest book which Mary Rogers had given him that he had come there only "to spend the summer, but I shan't go away any more." After seventeen footloose years, he had a place to stay and to entertain people. By the time he had been there a year, almost two hundred guests had come and gone, including two burglars. Many of the guests were young. The Harry Rogerses motored up, as did the Coes; Beatrice Benjamin came with her father to present her financé, Alexander D. B. Pratt, for Clemens's approval. The Twichells came to visit, and William Dean Howells came, but the elder Rogerses never did, in spite of repeated invitations. Nor did

Clemens visit them again at Fairhaven, though he was often asked. His fondness for Stormfield, as well as his poor health, usually kept him in Connecticut. "I get homesick," he wrote Beatrice Benjamin, "the minute I get out of sight of the house" (11 February 1909, Pratt).

He did miss his old friends, however, and his audiences. He wrote Howells:

> Dictating Autobiography has certan irremovable drawbacks.
>
> 1. A stenographer is a lecture-audience; you are always conscious of him; he is a restraint, because there is only one of him, and one alien auditor can seldom be an inspiration . . . If it's a she person, there are *so* many thousands and thousands of things you are suffering to say, every day, but mustn't, because they are indecent. . . . If it's a religious person, your jaw is locked again, several times a day: profane times and theological times. . . . Often you are burning to pour out a sluice of intimately personal, and particularly private things—and there you are again! You can't make your mouth say them. It won't say them to any but a very close personal friend, like Howells, or Twichell, or Henry Rogers.

If he had his way, he would inaugurate a new scheme, an "all-comforting, all-satisfying, all-competent scheme," which would blow "these obstructing and irritating difficulties to the winds!" He would "fire the profanities at Rogers, the indecencies at Howells, the theologies at Twichell" (*MTHL,* pp. 844–845).

When he did go occasionally to New York, he stayed with or dined with the Rogers family. He was there on 29 January 1909 when Rogers's sixty-ninth birthday was celebrated—"a family dinner-party—a pretty large one, for it is a big family when they all get together." Clemens thought his friend doubly fortunate in being able to celebrate in the capacity of businessman as well as family man:

> He was a happy man, for the last rail of his railroad was laid down and spiked that morning—a road just twice as long (lacking 6 miles) as the distance from New York to Boston; and he has built the bulk of it since the panic began and all large enterprises were hampered, crippled, and thrown into confusion. A stately achievement for a

man of his age. The first through train will leave Norfolk to-morrow for the terminus, 446 miles west'ard (SLC to Dorothy Sturgis, 31 January 1909).

Clemens went with Rogers to Norfolk to speak on 3 April at a banquet which the businessmen of that city gave to celebrate the opening of the Virginian Railway. He told them of Rogers's generosity to Helen Keller and of his helpfulness as financial adviser. But even such a pleasant duty as this was tiring now. In a letter to a young friend, Clemens had explained the special arrangements made for his appearance at the Norfolk banquet:

> I am allowed to stay away until the banquet is over and the speeches begin: 10 p.m. and am not required to come in black clothes. I cannot endure long banquets—the fatigue is too great, and as for black clothes, my aversion for them is incurable (SLC to Frances Nunnally, 28 March 1909, TS in MTP).

On 19 May 1909 he came again to New York to see Rogers, but was met at Grand Central Station by Clara with news that his friend had died that morning. "The expression of grief on Father's face," she said, "was pitiful to behold. . . . he looked so delicate, enveloped in this shadow of sorrow" (*My Father Mark Twain* [New York, 1931], p. 278). Newsmen were on hand to report Clemens's reactions, so his grief became a public thing. "Tears filled his eyes and his hands were trembling," reported the New York *Times* on 20 May 1909:

> "This is terrible, terrible, and I cannot talk about it," Mr. Clemens said to the reporters. "I am inexpressibly shocked and grieved. I do not know just where I will go. . . ."
>
> Mr. Clemens and his daughter lingered in the waiting room of the main station for a few minutes. Then Mark Twain, still leaning on his daughter's arm and looking toward the ground, walked slowly to the street through the Forty-second Street exit. Together they proceeded to the Subway station and boarded an uptown express.
>
> Later in the day Mr. Clemens went to the home of Urban H. Broughton, son-in-law of Mr. Rogers, where they were joined by other friends of the family. After spending a few minutes there he reappeared and went away in a carriage.

The following day he joined Melville Stone, E. H. Harriman, and William Rockefeller among the pallbearers at the funeral in the Church of the Messiah at Park Avenue and 34th Street. He did not go with the burial party to Fairhaven because, explained Paine, he "could not undertake to travel that distance among those whom he knew so well, and with whom he must of necessity join in conversation" (*MTB*, pp. 1491–1492).

446. CLEMENS TO ROGERS

Redding [1]
26 June 1908

Dear Mr. Rogers:

Will you and Mrs. Rogers come and pay me a visit? I hope you can, and that you will give me that pleasure. I have been in the house a week, now, and am nearly wonted.[2] I am sending this note to New York, as you were still there and making preparations for Bermuda when I last heard of you, which was a week ago.

This is a good house, and a very comfortable one—however, it is better that you judge of that when you come.

Yours ever

SLC

[1] The letterhead on which this and the next letter from Clemens are written reads "Innocence at Home/Redding/Connecticut."
[2] Clemens had moved into his new house on 18 June 1908.

447. EMILIE ROGERS TO CLEMENS

Fairhaven
3 August 1908

Dear Mr Clemens

Mr Rogers asked me to send you the enclosed note and he says, if you will care to come on he will be delighted to have you and to go with you to the clam-bake. I have been hoping that you would find your way to Fairhaven before this but I presume you are so delighted with the new home that you cannot tear yourself away. I am leaving for the mountains to-day where I hope to find some rest and to get strong again. Mr Rogers joins me in most affectionate messages—Kind regards to Miss Lyon—

Very sincerely

Emilie R. Rogers

448. CLEMENS TO EMILIE ROGERS

Redding

6 August 1908

Dear Mrs. Rogers:

Yes, it is as you say: I am perfectly contented with my new home, perfectly delighted with it; and I realize that I haven't had a real home, until now, since we left the Hartford one 17 years ago. It is a long, long time to be homeless. I can hardly bear to go a mile from this one; that is the reason I haven't been to Fairhaven, though I have longed to go there. It was always lonesome and home-sicky in New York, with Clara and Jean seldom in sight and no guests but 2-hour and 3-hour luncheonites and dinnerites, but [it] is not lonesome here. The friends come, and bring a trunk, and stay from two days to eight. Already we have had 21 in the 7 weeks that I have been here, and the guestrooms are fast being taken for August and September. The distance from New York is so easy that the friends do not mind the journey. I wish you and Mr. Rogers had elected to come here for a few weeks' rest, for this is the very quietest place outside the dungeon of St. Peter and St. Paul; no strangers, no crowds, no fashion, ⟨no⟩ only one neighbor⟨s⟩ within three-quarters of a mile—Miss Lyon's mother. Whereas it ain't so where you are, in the mountains, and of course you *can't* rest *there*. ⟨Guests⟩ I guess the clam-bake would be a very pleasant thing, with uncle Henry for company, but I shan't be able to go, because friends will arrive on the 26th and 28th to stay several days, and the clam-bake is to take place on the 28th.

I saw Will Coe at 26 Broadway yesterday, and he has engaged to come with his wife later in the season; and Miss Harrison promised also. I was down there to attend the funeral of my nephew, Samuel E. Moffett, who was drowned in the sight of his little son, and almost in sight of his wife.[1] It is the most heart-broken family I have seen in years. Sam left $30,000 or $40,000 accident insurance, but no other property of consequence; and as the body had no water in the lungs, it is claimed that he died not by accident but by apoplexy, a natural disease, brought on by fright caused ⟨by the violent⟩ by the turbulent seas. Robert Collier and I took measures to do what can be done to contest that curious view.

Col. Harvey and David Munro[2] came up with me yesterday to stay over night, but they like it here and are not going back until to-morrow.

This was the place for you; still I am aware that Poland Spring is next best, and I hope you will soon be as well and strong as ever you were.

With love to you both and best wishes,

SLC

[1] Moffett was "drowned in the surf off the Jersey beach" (*MTL,* p. 816); at the time of his death he was an editor of *Collier's Weekly.*
[2] David Munro was associate editor of the *North American Review.*

449. CLEMENS TO EMILIE ROGERS

Redding
12 August 1908[1]

Dear Mrs. Rogers:

I believe I am the wellest man on the planet to-day, and good for a trip to Fair Haven (which I discussed with the Captain of the New Bedford boat, who pleasantly accosted me in the Grand Cen-

tral August 5) but the doctor came up from New York day before
yesterday, and gave positive orders that I must not stir from here
before frost. It is because I was threatened with a swoon, 10 or 12
days ago, and went to New York a day or two later to attend my
nephew's funeral and got horribly exhausted by the heat and came
back here and had a bilious collapse. In 24 hours I was as sound as a
nut again, but nobody believes it but me.

This is a prodigiously satisfactory place, and I am so glad I don't
have to go back to the turmoil and rush of New York. The house
stands high and the horizons are wide, yet the seclusion is perfect.
The nearest *public* road is half a mile away, so there is nobody to
look in, and I don't have to wear clothes if I don't want to. I have
been down stairs in night-gown and slippers a couple of hours, and
have been photographed in that costume; but I will dress, now, and
behave myself.

That doctor had half an idea that there is something the matter
with my brain . . . Doctors do know so little and they do charge so
much for it. I wish Henry Rogers would come here, and I wish you
would come with him. You can't rest in that crowded place, but you
could rest here, for sure! I would learn bridge, and entertain you,
and rob you.

With love to you both,

Ever yours,

S. L. C.

---

[1] The manuscript for this letter has been lost. The present text is quoted from
MTL, pp. 815–816. The ellipsis appears in Paine's text.

450. CLEMENS TO EMILIE ROGERS

Redding
7 October 1908

Dear Mrs. Rogers:

The letter was an urgent one from Clara; and as she knew I was
going to Fairhaven she rushed it thither. Dear me, I wish you two

would come here, and right away! and look at the foliage. Can't you? Won't you? *Will* you?

> With love to you both,
>
> SLC.

451. CLEMENS TO EMILIE ROGERS

> Redding
> 12 October 1908
> Monday

Dear Mrs. Rogers:

Yes, I was coming, and my arrangements were all made; but on the evening of the day that I telephoned you about it some guests arrived and broke it up. My idea was to fly over there and get a one-day glimpse of you before the next guests were due to arrive, and put in the said day persuading you and Henry H. to come out of your seclusion and pay us a visit.

I'll try again, the first chance. By my calculation that may occur about Tuesday or Wednesday of next week, but it may possibly fail, because 3 guests who are booked to come have not given us their dates yet.

The reason we have company in the house all the time now, is because we never had *any* in New York during four winters, and I got nearly starved for human society, and am trying to catch up. I don't ever want to be so lonesome and dreary again. I've grown young in these past three months of dissipation here. And I have left off drinking—it isn't necessary now. Society and theology are sufficient for me.

Jean has arrived in Germany.[1] Off the coast of Holland her ship sunk another ship in a fog. Clara was in collision fifteen months ago; I was in collision a month ⟨ago.⟩ later. The family record is complete now.

The burglars scared off every servant we had.[2] We brought up our two Italians from the New York house and are getting along plenty well enough, by help of a native or two, from the farmhouses around. We think we shan't need city servants at all. I don't like them anyway: they have to have facilities all the week for going to hell, and facilities every Sunday for grafting their way into the other place.

I am sending my love to you both and would desperately like to see you.

SLC

---

[1] Jean had sailed for Europe on 26 September 1908 to consult again with specialists (IVL Journal, 26 September 1908).

[2] Stormfield was burglarized on 18 September 1908, and the event was widely publicized. After a brief but dramatic pursuit climaxed by a gunfight, the thieves were apprehended early that morning (see *MTB*, pp. 1462–1463).

452. EMILIE ROGERS TO CLEMENS

Fairhaven
17 October 1908

Dear Mr Clemens

We just got home last evening and now Mr Rogers says we must go to town again to-morrow night. Can you not come to us the last of the week? We shall surely be back here by Friday—We want very much to see you and we must find our way to Redding sooner or later—Send me a little telegram to 3 East 78th st and let me know—Your letter reassures my mind as to your habits—I am so glad. With kind regards to Miss Lyon

Very sincerely

Emilie R. Rogers

453. CLEMENS TO EMILIE ROGERS

Redding
24 October 1908

Dear Mrs. Rogers:

Thank you very much, and I hope to take advantage of the invitation.

I want Mr. Rogers to ⟨try⟩ buy and try the Arnold electric vibrating machine—for sale cor. 38th and 5th ave.,—and you must try it too. It seems to do all that the human massageur does with his hands—and more, and better, and pleasanter, and simpler, and more effectively. It stops headaches for Miss Lyon and cures and limbers lame and stiff backs for me. It claims to ease all sorts of pains, and I judge it can do it, for it stirs up the circulation quite competently and tones up the nerves—and that is really *the* essential function of osteopathy and kindred treatments.

It costs but little, and I am convinced you will like it, and prosper by it.

Yours as always

SLC

454. CLEMENS TO EMILIE ROGERS

Redding
23 November 1908

Dear Mrs. Rogers:

I'm a-coming just as soon [as] I can find a vacancy—some day next week, I hope. I wish I could camp with the tribe at the Thanksgiving orgy, but there will be company and profligacies here on that day and for a day or two after. I wish you and the Admiral were going to be here and were no better than you ought to be—we would have a scandalous good time. Miss Wallace and another member of the I.C.[1] are coming.

Yes'm, I thank you very much, and I shall give you notice before long.

With my love to you and the Admiral—

SLC

---

[1] Elizabeth Wallace, whom Clemens had met in Bermuda and who later would write *Mark Twain and the Happy Island* (Chicago, 1913), was a member of his Juggernaut Club, which was made up of girls and women with whom Clemens corresponded. The reason Clemens wrote "I.C." is not clear.

455. ROGERS TO CLEMENS

New York
18 December 1908

Revered Doctor:

I knew you many years ago, before you got piety and the balance of your vices, and I suppose you may have a remembrance of me because of my distinction as an evangelist.

There is going to be a conference at Norfolk in the course of two or three weeks, to open up our religious work in Virginia and West Virginia. There will probably be a great many people there; but the more distinguished ones will be the Rev. Doctor Broughton, perhaps Deacon Coe and that budding bundle of hopefulness, Mr. Harry Rogers. In other words, they are going to open up the railroad by a few choice spirits, and if you would like to join the saintly party, perhaps we will include Elder Benjamin. I don't suppose you really want to; but then it is my Christian duty to invite you. Do you think that you could endure the company of such choice people for a day or two, or long enough to make the trip? If so, formal invitation will be sent you, together with your railroad fares and the other perquisites that will follow. Dr. Rice may be included, although that is yet in doubt.[1]

Now, to get down to worldly things:—I have to say that Mrs. Benjamin has quite fully recovered from her illness and we are breathing freely again. Mrs. Rogers is fairly well, as are all the others of the flock. Why don't you come down and make us a visit? We have had that promise for a long time. Mrs. Rogers is inclined to fit up a hen house for you at Fairhaven because you are getting so secluded. I think I have said about all I want to say at the present time, and so will hope to meet you face to face in the near future, when we will either discuss this case or fight it out.

I was sorry to have missed our beloved Betsy [2] when she called about ten days ago; but I heard that she had been in your company for three or four days, and while that was to be regretted, I was glad to know that she had the opportunity of exercising her moral influence on your saintly home. Goodbye!

Yours truly,

H H Rogers

[1] Clemens wrote at the top of this letter "Dr. Rice."
[2] Elizabeth Wallace.

456. CLEMENS TO ROGERS

Redding [1]
19 December 1908

Dear Admiral:

That trip would just suit me, and I should ever so much like to make it with a real holy crowd such as you have mentioned, but as the doctor has vetoed all projected trips of any considerable size since I was knocked out for several days by something akin to a sunstroke acquired by heat and over-fatigue at Sam Moffett's funeral last August, he will say no again, now, sure. But I am myself aware that I couldn't stand it. I am as brisk and active a young thing as there is in any country—on a brief strain; but it has to be pretty brief. My flying trip to New York a week or two ago, with its unaccustomed industries, live interests, and activities, kept me tired out and played out for several days afterward. My health is so fine, so perfect, so splendid that it stands every test and holds its own against every assault except over-fatigue. You will have a grand time down at Norfolk. And you will deserve it, too. You have carried that giant enterprise through as patiently and quietly and unostentatiously as a geologic period overlays a continent with a new crust—well, it's just great! That majestic achievement is the triumph of your life, and will be and remain your eulogy and your monument in the far by-and-bye.

I hope Mrs. Rogers will soon get well, so that you and she can come up here. It is always peaceful here, always still, always restful; and in all these 6 months there has never been any weather that couldn't take the chromo in an international weather-show. Can't you come in January or February? I hope so.

Betsy and we had a good time here. She is coming by and by to stay a month, in the spring or the summer.

Mrs. Benjamin has my heartiest congratulations; and so have you all.

Get nearer to God. It is the best investment there is. Tell Rice, too.

SLC

[1] The letterhead now reads "Stormfield/Redding/Connecticut."

457. CLEMENS TO ROGERS

Redding
25 February 1909

Dear Mr. Rogers:

I love you, and I love Frank Lawrence, and I love St. Andrew; [1] and so I would strain many points to Yes a proposition from you, when I believe God to be on your side, as in the present instance. (And, I may add, as *usual.*) But I can't come, because I am keeping hotel, and no train comes or goes without bringing me a guest or robbing me of one—and so I am always on deck. All my beds—as usual—will be full on St. Patrick's Day, and I shall be here to collect the tips. You must thank Lawrence for me, and give him my love.

I note what you say: That you and Mrs. Rogers are coming as soon as there's good automobiling. I am very glad and shall watch the roads.

With love to you both,

S. L. C.

[1] Frank R. Lawrence, president of the Lotos Club had written on 23 February 1909 to ask Clemens to speak at a dinner honoring Andrew Carnegie ("St. Andrew") on 17 March 1909.

458. CLEMENS TO ROGERS

Redding
4 March 1909

Dear H. H.

I think it likely that I shall go to the Lotos-Carnegie banquet, 17th of March, after all. It was getting so difficult to keep on declining and explaining, that night before last I suspended payment in that kind, and said I would go, and would very much *like* to go, if I could be privileged to feed elsewhere and arrive at 10 p.m; and if also I might stipulate that my name be left out of the list of pledged speakers, so that I would not have to prepare a speech, and needn't speak at all unless moved by the spirit so to do.

The terms seem to me to be fair, and so if I get word that they are accepted, I'll go down on the 17th by the 10.30 express, arriving at the Grand Central at noon. In which case, am I going to find eatables, drinkables and lodging at your tavern at reduced rates?—

on account of the country having lost the creator and propagator and promoter of its prosperities to-day.[1]

With love to you both,

SLC

[1] Theodore Roosevelt's term as President expired on 4 March 1909, when William Howard Taft was inaugurated.

459. ROGERS TO CLEMENS

New York
8 March 1909

Dear Mr. Clemens:

I received in due time your letter of the 4th. of March. A proper time for you to crawl back into politics by way of the Lotos Club.

I have communicated with Mr. Lawrence through his Secretary, and he replies that he can speak for Mr. Lawrence and, in fact, for all the Lotos Club, in saying that they would obey Mr. Clemens' commands to the letter, and that they would be very glad to reserve a room for you in the new Club; but think you would prefer to stay at my house while you are in town, all of which I herewith approve.[1]

They are very glad that you have changed your mind, and I imagine that you will receive some communication, either from Mr. Lawrence or his Secretary, concerning the truthfulness of my statement.

I notice that you are to come down on the 17th. on the 10:30 express, arriving at the Grand Central at noon, and also that you expect to find eatables, drinkables and a bed at our Tavern, subject to such changes as it seems pleasant to me. I am going to ask Mrs. Rogers to answer this letter, in order to have it correct.

Yours truly,

H H Rogers

¹ "I shall arrive at H. H. Rogers's house, 3 East 78th at 12.30 next Wednesay, 17th, and stay a couple of days" (SLC to Mrs. Helen Kerr Blackmer, 13 March 1909). On the evening of 17 March Carnegie was a guest of honor at the first dinner given by the Lotos Club at its new quarters at 110 West 57th Street. Clemens was introduced as "St. Mark"; in response, he said, "I am glad I have got my due. At last I am ranked with the saints, where I belong" (New York *Times*, 18 March 1909). Carnegie in a letter of 28 April 1909 expressed his appreciation of Clemens's presence: "Awfully good of you to come to Lotos dinner. You never made a happier speech—great—and oh so funny—" (see *MTS* [1910], pp. 345–346).

460. CLEMENS TO ROGERS (telegram)

Redding
26 April 1909

I will spend tomorrow night with you.

SL Clemens.

461. CLEMENS TO EMILIE ROGERS

Redding
2 May 1909

Sunday

Dear Mrs. Rogers:

I shall arrive at noon next Friday, and go at once down town on business, and back to No. 3 for dinner,¹ provided there will be a bed for me and no extra charge. I return home next day. I'm due at the Jerome banquet Friday evening at 10.²

If there's no vacant bed, or if you are to be away Fairhavenward, will you please telephone me here when you receive this?

My telephone address is

"*774 Danbury.*" [3]

⟨(I'll get that No. in the morning—I'm in bed now.)⟩

Yours ever

SL Clemens

Please don't tell Mr. Rogers. He would try to raise the limit.

[1] Rogers's New York residence was now 3 East 78th Street.
[2] Clemens was a member of the committee which arranged a testimonial dinner for District Attorney William Travers Jerome at Delmonico's on 7 May 1909; on that occasion Clemens was introduced to speak as "the last word on all public questions and public men" (New York *Times,* 8 May 1909).
[3] Clemens noted on the outside of the envelope: "Opened to furnish address (telephone)"; after he had supplied "774" to complete the number he had originally given as ". . . . *Danbury,*" he then deleted the next sentence of the letter with a pencil.

462. CLEMENS TO ROGERS

Redding
4 May 1909

Dear Mr. Rogers:

The check-books and vouchers which Ashcroft will have to place before your expert are my property, and I would be glad if you will keep possession of them for me, when the inquiry is finished. I don't want them to go back into Ashcroft's hands.[1]

I shall spend Thursday and Friday in New York, with Robert Collier, for I think you are all in Fairhaven and your city house closed for the season.

Good night. I am praying for all of you.

SLC

[1] Clemens had asked Rogers to investigate his financial dealings with Isabel Lyon and Ashcroft, who had married on 18 March and whom Clemens suspected of having misused his funds. After Rogers's death on 19 May 1909, Harry Rogers, Albert Bigelow Paine, and Clara Clemens aided Clemens in continuing the investigation.

463. Clemens to Rogers

Redding
9 May 1909
Sunday

Dear Mr. Rogers:

Lounsbury[1] says the Ashcrofts have borrowed $1500 on the house and land I gave to Miss Lyon—this $1500 to be used in "squaring up with Mr. Clemens" and leaving them "free of indebtedness to him."

It will hardly "square," for the rehabilitations cost Miss Lyon more than $3,100.

If Ashcroft brings me the money he will probably want a receipt "in full of all claims" to date. In that case I will tell him to go and ask you for it, (and get it if he can), since this matter is in your hands, with full authority to act for me.

I'm coming down Tuesday to stay over night. If your tavern is closed I'll break in somewhere else.

Wednesday I go to Deal Beach to discuss with the Colonel the proposition to let Collier have a cheap edition ($19) for 5 years, Collier to guarantee to sell so-many sets in that time. We began the discussion last Thursday. Collier exhibited telegrams (on a 5-year estimate) from all his general agents but ten, and the Colonel was visibly impressed. I am offering the Harpers *half* of the swag, but I want them to restore my guaranty of $25,000-per-annum for another 5 years. If we make the Collier-trade they can't decline, I think.

I left four dollars laying around. Will Mrs. Rogers send part of it to me now and the rest when I come?

Yrs ever
SLC

Telephone addr:
"774 *Danbury*"

¹ Harry A. Lounsbury was a Redding neighbor who acted as agent for much of Clemens's business there.

464. KATHARINE HARRISON TO CLEMENS

New York
11 May 1909

Dear Mr. Clemens:

Just a line to let you know that I have the signatures to both certificates of the Mark Twain Company,¹ so your mind can be easy on this point.

Yours truly,

K. I. Harrison

Sec'y

¹ On 24 December 1908, the New York *Times* had reported that the Mark Twain Company was recently incorporated "in order to keep the earnings of Mr. Clemens's books continually in the family, even after the copyright on the books themselves expires." In addition to Clemens as president, the officers of the company were Ralph W. Ashcroft, secretary and treasurer, and Clara and Jean Clemens and Isabel V. Lyon, directors. Clemens later replaced Isabel Lyon and Ashcroft with Albert Bigelow Paine.

Afterword

How to memorialize Henry Rogers and his goodness remained for Clemens a conscience-rending problem. Andrew Carnegie wrote from Italy on 22 May that, upon hearing of Rogers's death, "my heart went out to you knowing that of all his friends you would miss him most—I have admired him for what he did for you and you for your devotion to him. . . . his memory will be kept green in your heart and I doubt not history will do him justice because you will take care to record him as your friend in need, showing the real man" (TS in MTP).

When word came that Rogers's English friend, Charles Lancaster, criticized Clemens for not having publicly eulogized his benefactor, Clemens wrote William R. Coe on 16 June 1909 to attest

> that I wrote a part of the Eulogy three years ago and Mr. Rogers would not let me publish it; that I finished it a year later; was not satisfied with that finish, and destroyed it: re-framed it once more, two days after Mr. Rogers's funeral, and again destroyed the product; that it will never be published until it is worded to suit *me,* if I have to wait seven years. The most of my books have had to wait several years until I could finish them to suit me. Whenever I have had anything of real importance to do, these waits have always occurred.

Perhaps Lancaster could "sit down and knock off a Eulogy in an hour—*any* hour, any day—without any difficulty. But I am not built in that way. I was never in a hurry yet, on a piece of work that I wanted to do well." And, he continued,

> *Eulogy?* In the 6 unpublished volumes of my Autobiography Mr. Rogers is *pervasive;* the references to him and to his goodness, his greatness, his nobility, his charm, are scattered all through those books, and *they* are his best Eulogy—affectionate, grateful, spontaneous, unaffected; and they will still be read, and in them his kindly face and his lovable nature will still shine, a hundred years after all the hasty Eulogies of to-day shall have been forgotten (Coe).

Brighter times briefly followed. Jean was now with her father at Stormfield. Clara performed at a concert in Redding on 21 September for the benefit of the Mark Twain Library there. On 6 October she was married by the Reverend Joseph Twichell to the pianist Ossip Gabrilowitsch. Jean was her sister's only attendant; Jervis Langdon came down from Elmira to be groomsman. The father of the bride wore his splendid Oxford gown and proudly saw to it that every guest signed the guest book which Mary Rogers had given him the Christmas before.

But then, seven months after Henry Rogers died, on the morning of the day before Christmas, 1909 Jean was discovered dead. Mrs. Rogers, Harry and Mary Rogers, the Coes, the Broughtons, the Benjamins, Katharine Harrison, and William Rockefeller were among those who sent condolences. Clemens was not strong enough to follow Jean's body to Elmira, where she was buried beside her mother and Susy. Early in January of 1910 he set out on what was to be his last trip to Bermuda. "My health is blemishless," he wrote Mary Rogers on 21 February 1910, "except for the pain in my breast. That is permanent, I suppose" (*MTLM*, p. 133). When, late in March, he complained of "having a most uncomfortable time . . . with that breast pain," Paine hurried to Bermuda to bring Clemens home (*MTB*, p. 1563). They left the island on 12 April, and two days later Clemens was carried to his bedroom at Stormfield. There he died on 21 April 1910.

APPENDIXES

APPENDIXES

APPENDIX A

Agreement of 23 May 1895 between Mrs. Olivia L. Clemens and Harper & Brothers.

APPENDIX B

Agreement of 31 December 1896 between Harper & Brothers, the American Publishing Company, and Mrs. Olivia L. Clemens.

APPENDIX C

Agreement of 31 December 1896 between Olivia L. Clemens and Samuel L. Clemens, the American Publishing Company, Samuel L. Clemens, and Charles Dudley Warner.

APPENDIX D

Supplement of 11 November 1898 to agreement of 31 December 1896 between Harper & Brothers, the American Publishing Company, and Mrs. Olivia L. Clemens.

APPENDIX E

Agreement of 22 October 1903 between Harper & Brothers, and Samuel L. Clemens and Olivia L. Clemens.

APPENDIX F

Agreement of 23 October 1903 between the American Publishing Company, Harper & Brothers, and Samuel L. Clemens and Olivia L. Clemens.

APPENDIX G

A Tribute to Henry H. Rogers (1902) by Samuel L. Clemens.

APPENDIX A

Agreement of 23 May 1895 between
Mrs. Olivia L. Clemens and Harper & Brothers

THIS AGREEMENT, made the twenty-third day of May, 1895, between MRS. OLIVIA L. CLEMENS, of Hartford, Connecticut, and HARPER & BROTHERS, of the City of New York, Publishers, WITNESSETH:—

Copyrights and guarantee.   1. Samuel L. Clemens, of Hartford, Connecticut, the author of various works published under the *nom de plume* of "MARK TWAIN," having on the 9th day of March, 1894, sold, assigned, transferred, and set over to Mrs. Olivia L. Clemens, all his right, title, and interest in the copyrights (and stereotype plates) of the aforesaid books, the said Mrs. Olivia L. Clemens, as the legal representative of the said Samuel L. Clemens, does hereby, in consideration of the premises, grant and assign to the said Harper & Brothers the exclusive rights of publication in book-form in the United States of the said works of the said Samuel L. Clemens during the respective unexpired terms of the copyrights of said works and the renewals thereof, guaranteeing and agreeing with them that she is the sole proprietor of said works and has full power to make this agreement and grant; that said works contain no

matter which is a violation of the copyright of any
other works, or which is scandalous or libellous; and
that she and her legal representatives will hold
harmless and defend said Harper & Brothers against
any claim, demand, or recovery, by reason of any
such violation of another copyright, or any scandalous or libellous matter in said works.

Publication.   2. Harper & Brothers agree that they will publish a uniform edition of said works at their own expense, at such time and in such style as they deem
best suited to their sale; and will pay to said Mrs.
Olivia L. Clemens, or her representatives or assigns, fifteen (15) per cent. on their respective
trade-list (retail) prices for each copy of such books
by them sold up to five thousand (5000) copies and
twenty (20) per cent. on their trade-list (retail)
prices for each copy of such books sold by them over
and above five thousand (5000) copies. The trade-
list (retail) price, on which percentage shall be
Statements of   paid, shall be that of the cloth binding. And Harper
account and   & Brothers shall render always, on application there-
payment.   for, semi-annual statements of account, in the
months of January and July and make settlement in
cash four months after date of each statement. But
for copies sold to canvassers or otherwise, for the
purpose of introducing said books, at a discount
greater than that customarily allowed by them to the
largest buyers in the regular trade in the United
States, Harper & Brothers shall pay the said fifteen
or twenty per cent. only on the actual price received
for each copy. Said Harper & Brothers hereby agree
that work upon the said series is to begin within a
month after the signing of this agreement.

Selections,   3. Harper & Brothers may publish, or permit
Translations, others to publish, such selections from said works
abridg-   as they think proper to benefit their sale, without
ments, etc.   compensation to the grantor herein; but the compensation for translations and dramatizations shall
be subject to agreement between the parties hereto.

If Harper & Brothers sell the right to publish selections or abridgments, the revenue or payment therefor shall be divided equally between the parties hereto.

Alterations by author.

4. Alterations made by the author or by the said Mrs. Olivia L. Clemens in type, plates, or otherwise in any of the works published under this contract, after delivery of copy to Harper & Brothers, which exceed fifty (50) dollars in cost, shall be at the expense of said Mrs. Olivia L. Clemens.

Insurance.

5. No insurance on the works, plates, or printed copies shall be effected for joint account, or for account of said Mrs. Olivia L. Clemens by said Harper & Brothers.

Destruction of plates.

6. If the plates or type forms of any of the said works be rendered valueless by fire or otherwise, Harper & Brothers shall have the option of reproducing them or not; and if they decline to reproduce them, then, after the sale of all copies of such work or works remaining on hand, they shall reconvey to said Mrs. Olivia L. Clemens or her heirs or assigns, all rights in said work or works herein granted on her or their request in writing, and this contract shall terminate so far as it relates to the publication of such work or works.

Disposition of plates, etc., on discontinuance of publication.

7. If, at any time after ten years from the date of publication, Harper & Brothers shall be satisfied that the public demand does not justify the continued publication of any or all of the works published under this contract, or if for any other cause they shall deem its or their further publication improper or inexpedient, then they may offer, in writing, to said Mrs. Olivia L. Clemens or her heirs or assigns, the plates and any original engravings or illustrations to said works at half cost, and all copies then on hand at cost; and said Mrs. Olivia L. Clemens or her heirs or assigns, shall have the right within sixty days to take and pay for the same; but if said offer be not accepted, and if such payment

be not made, within sixty days, then Harper & Brothers may, without further communication with said Mrs. Olivia L. Clemens or her heirs or assigns, destroy the plates, and dispose of all copies then on hand, and this agreement shall thereupon terminate so far as it relates to the publication of said work or works. No royalty shall be paid to the said Mrs. Olivia L. Clemens, or her heirs or assigns, upon copies sold as above provided, unless said copies shall have been sold as *books,* in which case the royalty to be paid to the said Mrs. Olivia L. Clemens, or her heirs or assigns, shall be the same percentage upon the price actually received by Harper & Brothers as would have been paid upon the retail price, if the books had been sold in the ordinary course of trade.

Infringement of copyright.

8. In case of any infringement on the copyright of the works herein contracted for and published under this contract, Harper & Brothers are authorized, in their discretion, to sue for or otherwise seek such remedy as they may be advised; and all such suits or proceedings brought against infringers of the copyrights hereby ceded to Harper & Brothers shall be at the joint expense and cost of the two parties to this agreement, and any surplus of damages, or recovery, or settlement, above the expense, shall be divided equally between the parties hereto.

Engravings, etc., which do not belong to the copyright.

9. If, under the provisions of this agreement, the plates become the property of said Mrs. Olivia L. Clemens, or her heirs or assigns, and if in the books there are any engravings or illustrations not made originally for said books nor furnished therefor by said Mrs. Olivia L. Clemens, it is expressly stipulated that said Mrs. Olivia L. Clemens or her heirs or assigns, shall then take, with the plates or copyright, the right to use casts or electrotypes of such engravings or illustrations for editions of this work or these works only; but shall take no right, copyright, or property in them, either to duplicate or

reproduce them, or for any other use, transfer, or disposition whatever.

If used as a school-book.

10. Should any of these works be sold in a special edition, at a reduced price, for use in schools, the royalty to be paid to said Mrs. Olivia L. Clemens or her heirs or assigns, upon the first five thousand (5000) copies of such work sold, shall be fifteen (15) per cent. upon the price actually received by said Harper & Brothers, and for all copies of said work sold over and above five thousand (5000) the royalty shall be twenty (20) per cent. upon the price actually received.

Assignment.

11. The interest in this contract which belongs to each party respectively may be assigned, but only as a whole, and no part of such interest shall be assigned by either party; but no assignment by said Mrs. Olivia L. Clemens or her heirs or assigns, shall be valid, as against Harper & Brothers, unless and until said Harper & Brothers shall have been notified, in writing, of such assignment; and all payments or advances upon this contract, made by Harper & Brothers prior to notification of assignment as above provided for, and any lien or obligation incurred thereon, in favor of Harper & Brothers, prior to such notification, shall stand and be binding prior to and hold as against such assignment, and shall have the same force and effect as if such assignment had not been made.

12. It is hereby understood and agreed that "Personal Recollections of Joan of Arc" and "Tom Sawyer Detective," by the said Samuel L. Clemens, will be exclusively published by said Harper & Brothers in book-form under the terms and conditions of this contract.

It is hereby understood and agreed that this agreement embraces the following books by said Samuel L. Clemens, the exclusive publication of which at the date of this agreement is hereby conveyed to the said Harper & Brothers, viz.:

"The Adventures of Huckleberry Finn"
"A Connecticut Yankee in King Arthur's Court"
"Tom Sawyer Abroad"
"The Prince and the Pauper"
"Life on the Mississippi"
"The White Elephant, etc."
"The American Claimant"
"£1,000,000 Bank Note"
"Library of Wit and Humor," and
"A Californian's Tale" (originally published in
the volume issued by The Author's Club.)

And it is further understood and agreed that the
publication of the following books by the said Samuel L. Clemens, which cannot at the date of this
agreement be conveyed to said Harper & Brothers,
will be so conveyed at the earliest practicable date,
viz.:

"Pudd'nhead Wilson"
"Innocents Abroad"
"The Gilded Age"
"Roughing It"
"The Tramp Abroad"
"Tom Sawyer"

It is also understood and agreed that said Harper
& Brothers, if they deem it advisable to include, in
the proposed uniform edition, any short stories by
the said Samuel L. Clemens, already published,
may make any combination or combinations of such
stories for publication in said uniform edition as
they may see fit excepting those stories contained
in a volume entitled "Sketches New and Old," published by the American Publishing Company.

Olivia L. Clemens
by Henry H Rogers Att'y
Harper & Brothers.

[Addendum to contract]

Section 1, Line 4, "6" changed to "9";

same section, Lines 6 and 7, the words "and stereotype plates" stricken out;

both before delivery of contract, which was July 26, 1895.

J.F.P. July 26, 1895.

APPENDIX B

Agreement of 31 December 1896 between Harper & Brothers, the American Publishing Company, and Mrs. Olivia L. Clemens

THIS AGREEMENT, made this thirty first day of December 1896, between the Corporation of Harper & Brothers, of the city, county, and state of New York, party of the first part; The American Publishing Company, of the city and county of Hartford, state of Connecticut, as party of the second part; and Mrs. Olivia L. Clemens, of the said city of Hartford, as party of the third part, WITNESSETH:

WHEREAS, the party of the first part are now publishing, by virtue of a contract with the party of the third part, certain books and writings of which Samuel L. Clemens is the author, viz.:

"The Adventures of Huckleberry Finn"
"Life on the Mississippi"
"A Connecticut Yankee in King Arthur's Court"
"Joan of Arc"
"The Prince and the Pauper"
"Tom Sawyer Abroad, Tom Sawyer, Detective, and Other Stories and Sketches"
"The American Claimant, and Other Stories," etc.

WHEREAS, the party of the second part are desirous of publishing

678

the aforesaid books and writings in a uniform edition, together with other books by the said Samuel L. Clemens now published by them,

WHEREAS, the party of the third part is willing and hereby assents that the party of the second part may publish, as proposed above, the aforesaid books and writings by Samuel L. Clemens, and any others which they may now have the right to publish.

THEREFORE, in consideration of the conditions and covenants hereinafter contained, it is mutually agreed by the parties hereto, as follows:

I. The party of the first part, whenever it is practicable to do so, are to loan to the party of the second part, upon their application, the electro-type plates of not more than two volumes at a time of the aforesaid books and writings by Samuel L. Clemens published by them, hereinafter called the Harper Volumes, from which the party of the second part may print copies to be published in their uniform edition of books by Samuel L. Clemens, as described above. Said copies are to be published by said party of the second part in handsome library style, not inferior in quality to the edition of the aforesaid Harper Volumes published by said party of the first part. They are to bear the proper copyright notices belonging to the respective books, and are to contain a note to the effect that they are printed from the plates belonging to the party of the first part. Editions of not less than five hundred (500) copies of any one book shall ⟨not⟩ be printed by said party of the second part unless otherwise agreed upon by the said parties of the first and second parts. Said party of the second part shall bear the expense of the freight upon said plates between New York and the place of printing, and also upon their return to New York; they shall also bear the expense of proper boxing of the said plates; they shall keep them insured at their full value while in their possession or at the printing office and while in transit back and forth; and they shall be responsible to the said party of the first part for any loss or damage received by said plates while absent from the office of the said party of the first part. Said party of the second part shall return the said plates to the said party of the first part in good condition within twenty (20) days after their shipment by the party of the first part, unless otherwise agreed by said parties of the first and second parts.

II. The party of the second part are not to sell the Harper Volumes singly, but only in complete sets, that is, together with the volumes now published by them. The retail price of the said Harper Volumes, published and sold by said party of the second part under this agreement, is not to be lower than the present price of the Harper editions of the same books, and the said party of the second part are not to sell said books at a lower price than eighty (80) cents per volume at their greatest discount.

III. The party of the second part are to pay to the party of the first part, in consideration of the use of the plates of the aforesaid Harper Volumes for the purpose before described, for each and every copy sold by them of the said Harper Volumes a royalty of eight (8) per cent., based upon the retail price of the cloth-bound copies of the edition of said volumes published by the party of the first part. Statements of the number of copies sold shall be made by the said party of the second part, semi-annually, on the 30th day of June and the 31st day of December in each year, and settlement shall be made in thirty days thereafter by payments in cash. Copies of said books given away for editorial notice, are to be exempt from royalty to the party of the first part.

IV. Said party of the third part hereby approves, so far as her approval may be necessary, of the terms and conditions of the aforesaid agreement, and she hereby releases the party of the first part from any obligation to pay her anything upon copies of said Harper Volumes sold by the party of the second part under this agreement.

V. This agreement shall continue and be binding upon the parties hereto during the life of a certain contract dated and executed contemporaneously, between the said parties of the second and third parts and Samuel L. Clemens and Charles D. Warner. It is understood, however, that the termination of this contract shall in no wise interfere with the said party of the second part continuing the sale of said books, to the extent of disposing of any stock they may have on hand at the time of said termination, and of continuing to account to said party of the first part for all copies sold of said Harper Volumes under the provisions and stipulations herein contained.

VI. If the party of the second part becomes, from insolvency or any other cause, unable to fulfill their part of this contract, the party of the first part shall then be at liberty to terminate the same.

In witness whereof the parties hereto have hereunto and to quadru-

plicate copies hereof set their hands and seals this the day and year first
above written.

Olivia L. Clemens   L. S.

Corrections made before signature.
Clause I, 18th line [here, 14th line], the word "not" scratched out.
Clause III, word "to" interlined.

HHR

Added before signature by Harper & Brothers and the American
Publishing Company.
Page 1, line 2 [here, p. 678, line 2], the words "the Corporation of"
inserted betwen the words "between" and "Harper & Brothers."
It is hereby understood and agreed that the insurance by the party of
the second part of the plates of the Harper Volumes as stipulated in
Section I. of this contract, shall be in accordance with the methods of
insurance pursued by the said Corporation of Harper & Brothers.
It is further understood and agreed that, if any of the provisions of a
certain agreement between Olivia L. Clemens, The American Publishing Company, Samuel L. Clemens, and Charles Dudley Warner, referred to in Section V. of this contract, conflict in any way with this
contract, such provisions of that agreement shall be null and inoperative
as against the said Corporation of Harper & Brothers, or their successors
or assigns.

Signed Feb. 26, 1897. Harper & Brothers.   Olivia L. Clemens LS
                       by J. Henry Harper,   by Henry H Rogers
                       V. Pres't.   Att'y
Signed March 4, 1897 The American Publishing Co Hartford Ct
                     FE Bliss Pres't L.S.

APPENDIX C

Agreement of 31 December 1896 between
Olivia L. Clemens and Samuel L. Clemens, the
American Publishing Company, Samuel L.
Clemens, and Charles Dudley Warner

THIS AGREEMENT BETWEEN

Olivia L. Clemens of the City and County of Hartford and State of Connecticut, and Samuel L. Clemens her husband, (the said Samuel L. Clemens joining with his said wife for the purpose of capacitating her to make this contract) as party of the first part, and The American Publishing Company a corporation organized under the laws of the State of Connecticut and located in said Hartford, Conn., as party of the second part, and said Samuel L. Clemens, individually as party of the third part, and Charles Dudley Warner of said Hartford, as party of the fourth part, WITNESSETH:

WHEREAS the party of the first part is the owner of the author's rights in certain writings written by Samuel L. Clemens, entitled "The Innocents Abroad," "Roughing It," "The Gilded Age," "Tramp Abroad," "Tom Sawyer," "Sketches," and "Pudd'nhead Wilson," all of which have heretofore been published by the said party of the second part; also the owner of the manuscript of a new work which is now being completed by the same writer, Samuel L. Clemens, relating to his

682

late journey around the world, and also of the author's rights in several books, which are now published by Harper & Brothers of the City of New York, and written by the said Samuel L. Clemens, and

WHEREAS the party of the second part has made an arrangement and entered into a contract with Harper & Brothers whereby the party of the second part has obtained the consent of the said Harper & Brothers to the publication by the said party of the second part, of all of those books written by Samuel L. Clemens which the said Harper & Brothers now have the right to publish.

WHEREAS the party of the second part is desirous of publishing a new book now being written by said Samuel L. Clemens relating to his recent trip around the world, and also to issue a "uniform edition" of all of this author's works, and also to continue the regular sale of the books already published by them.

NOW, THEREFORE, in consideration of the premises and the conditions and covenants hereinafter contained, it is mutually agreed by the parties hereto as follows:

I. It is agreed by the parties hereto that all existing contracts now held by said parties of the first and second parts with each other, shall be suspended by the signing of this agreement; and remain suspended so long as this contract continues in force and the provisions thereof are duly fulfilled by the party of the first part and the party of the third part.

II. The party of the first part gives to the party of the second part the exclusive right to manufacture, publish and sell in such ways as shall seem best to the said party of the second part, all the books before mentioned during the life of the copyrights, and any renewals thereof; and agrees to protect the said party of the second part from all liabilities arising from any contracts relating to S. L. Clemens's writings, that may exist either between S. L. Clemens or Olivia L. Clemens and any other party or parties, excepting that the books published by Harper & Brothers shall be subject to a contract existing between said Harper & Brothers and the party of the second part, a copy of which is hereto annexed. And said parties of the first and fourth parts further agree that they or their representatives will duly make application for and take out or cause to be taken out any renewal of any copyright to which she or they or said party of the third part may be entitled by law to take out.

III. The party of the second part agrees to publish the separate volume edition of the afore-mentioned books and also the uniform edition as early as practicable after the execution of this contract, assuming all costs of publication, and placing them on the market in good style, and to use all their best efforts to secure a large and satisfactory sale of the same. The quality of paper for the uniform volume edition shall be equal to that used by Messrs. Harper & Brothers in their [edition of] Clemens's books, but may be changed on approval of the party of the first part.

IV. The party of the second part agrees to pay the said Olivia L. Clemens, party of the first part, a royalty of 12½ per cent of the retail price, of all copies sold of the various books, (those copies given to editors and others for advertising purposes, to be exempt from royalty), except in the cases of the cheap 12mo editions of "Tom Sawyer," "Sketches," "Pudd'nhead Wilson," and any other that may hereafter be mutually agreed upon, which shall be settled for on a one-half (½) profit basis as provided for hereafter and excepting also "The Gilded Age" upon which the royalty shall be as follows: All of the said royalties to be computed on the 30th day of June and December 31st respectively, and a statement thereof with payment of amounts due to be given and made to the party of the first part within thirty (30) days thereafter. The party of the second part agrees to pay to the parties of the first and fourth parts, a royalty of 12½ per cent of the retail price of all copies sold of said "Gilded Age"; one-half of which shall be paid to said party of the first part, and one-half to said party of the fourth part.

V. The party of the second part further agrees to keep an accurate account of the sales and expenses incident to the publication of the said books, and to render unto the party of the first part, a statement, as hereinafter mentioned, giving an account of the number of copies of each publication sold during the period between the previous statement and the one rendered, and shall exhibit, on request, to the party of the first part or her agent, all accounts relating to the manufacture and sale of the various books.

VI. And the party of the second part further agrees that if at the end of each calendar year, it shall appear that one-half (½) of the gross profits of the sales of single volumes of the said books which have hitherto been published, shall exceed the 12½ per cent royalty which has been earned on the sales of the year past, then the said party of the second part will pay to the said Olivia L. Clemens, party of the first part, and in the case of the "Gilded Age," to the said parties of the first and fourth parts equally, the amount of such excess over said royalty; and in the case of the new book to be published, if at the end of five years from the date of its first publication, it shall be found that one-half of its gross profits of the sales of single volumes thereof shall exceed the said royalty thereon during the said five years, then said party of the second part will pay to the party of the first part such excess, and thereafter, such excess over the royalty, if any excess there be, shall be computed and paid yearly; and in the case of the "uniform edition," any excess of one-half of the gross profits over said royalty shall be computed and paid at the end of two (2) years from the issue of each volume in said edition, and thereafter yearly.

VII. IT IS FURTHER AGREED that the gross profits shall include the entire difference between the price which the party of the second part shall realize on the sale of said books and the cost of manufacture.

The cost of manufacture is to include only the cost of plates, use of plates, and repairs thereof, paper, printing, binding, and boxes for shipment, together with insurance on the plates, sheets and finished copies of said book. Any portion of the printing or binding, which may be done by the party of the second part, shall be charged for at a fair and reasonable rate for such work, to be approved by the party of the first part; or in case of disagreement as to any charge, the matter shall be referred to an impartial arbitrator to be selected by the parties hereto.

VIII. The party of the second part agrees to pay to the party of the first part, Ten Thousand ($10,000.00) Dollars in cash as an advance on the royalties to arise from the sales of the new book to be published, on acceptance by it of a satisfactory manuscript of original matter written by the afore-mentioned S. L. Clemens, sufficient to make an octavo volume of at least 550 pages, relating to his late journey around the world; and the said party of the second part further agrees that the royalties on the sale of the said book shall amount during the first five (5) years after publication, to at least Ten Thousand ($10,000.00) Dollars, (which is to be paid her in advance as aforesaid).

IX. And the said party of the first part further agrees with said party of the second part in relation to the said new book, that the party of the second part shall have the exclusive use of said book and the right to publish the same, and that the said S. L. Clemens will not write or furnish any portion of the same subject matter that might come in competition with the said book or any part thereof, to any other printer or publisher, nor do anything that will interfere with the sale of the said work by said party of the second part.

X. The said party of the third part hereby acknowledges that the said party of the first part is the owner of the manuscript already prepared for said new book, and that which is to be prepared therefor in the future. And he agrees that he will not write for or furnish to any person or party other than said party of the first part, any portion of the same subject matter that might come in competition with said book or any part thereof, and he also agrees that he will do nothing to prevent said parties of the first and second parts from fully executing this agreement between them.

XI. Said party of the fourth part agrees that so far as he has any interest in the Book entitled "The Gilded Age," and the royalties therefor that he will accept of one-half of the royalties therefor as herein provided, and that he will to the same extent be bound by the provisions hereof.

XII. For the purpose of settlement on this contract the retail price of the several books shall not be less than one and one-half (1^{50}\!/_{100}$) dollars per copy respectively, except in the cases of "Tom Sawyer," "Sketches," and "Pudd'nhead Wilson," which shall not be less than one ($1.00) dollar.

XIII. Changes of the minimum prices may be a matter of subsequent contract between the parties of the first and second part.

XIV. If the party of the second part becomes from insolvency or other cause, unable to fulfill its part of this contract, the party of the first part shall then be at liberty to terminate the same. Provided however, that in case said party of the first part shall so terminate this contract after the execution hereof and before five (5) years from and after the first publication of said new book have elapsed and before said party of the second part shall have received back the said sum of Ten Thousand ($10,000.00) Dollars from the royalties on said new book as above provided, then and in such case, said party of the second part or its successors or representatives, shall have the right to continue the said publication and sale of said new book for and during so much of said period of five (5) years, as will enable said party of the second part, its successors or representatives, to reimburse itself for the balance of said royalties so advanced as aforesaid.

XV. Any assignment of this contract by the party of the second part without the consent of said party of the first part, shall at the option of the said party of the first part, render the same null and void.

XVI. It is further agreed that in case of the termination of this contract from any cause, that the said party of the second part shall have the right to continue the sales of all the books, under the provisions of this contract, to the extent of disposing of any stock they may have on hand at the time of said termination.

In witness whereof the parties hereto have hereunto and to quadruplicate copies set their hands and seals this 31st day of December, 1896.

                 Olivia L. Clemens   L. S.
                 Samuel L. Clemens   L. S.
                 The American Publishing Co. L. S.
                 F. E. Bliss Pres't
                 Charles D. Warner   L. S.

Correction made before signature.
    Clause III the word "the" interlined.
       Olivia L. Clemens LS
          by HH Rogers Att'y
       Samuel L. Clemens LS
          by HH Rogers Atty
       The American Publishing Company Hartford Ct
       FE Bliss Prest L.S.

APPENDIX D

*Supplement of 11 November 1898 to Agreement
of 31 December 1896 between Harper & Brothers,
the American Publishing Company, and
Mrs. Olivia L. Clemens*

SUPPLEMENT to Agreement of December 31, 1896, between the Corporation of Harper & Brothers, of the City of New York, the American Publishing Company, of Hartford, Connecticut, and Mrs. Olivia L. Clemens, also of Hartford, in regard to the publication by the American Publishing Company in their uniform edition of Samuel L. Clemens's works of the books by the said Samuel L. Clemens published by Harper & Brothers, which books are mentioned by name in the said Agreement of December 31, 1896, and are therein collectively designated as the "HARPER VOLUMES." It is mutually agreed as follows:

1. To the HARPER VOLUMES mentioned in said agreement another volume will be added, including the contents of "How to Tell a Story, and Other Essays," published by Harper & Brothers; the article on the Austrian Parliament, published in Harper's *Magazine* of March, 1898; and the poem entitled "In Memoriam," published in Harper's *Magazine* of November 1897.

2. The American Publishing Company, instead of printing the HARPER VOLUMES from the present plates of Harper & Brothers, as provided in Section 1 of aforesaid Agreement, will set up and

688

electrotype the said VOLUMES at its own expense, making one single set of said plates thereof, and will print its edition of said VOLUMES from the plates so made. The said plates, however, as soon as made are to be the property of Harper & Brothers, but are to be used only by said American Publishing Company. The American Publishing Company is to have the right to hold the said plates and use them only for the purpose mentioned in this Supplementary Agreement. It is to handle them with great care and to keep them in good condition, and also to repair at its own expense any injury received by them. In case of the failure of the American Publishing Company to carry out any or all of the provisions of this agreement, it shall deliver said plates at once to Harper & Brothers. Harper & Brothers agree that, at the expiration of the copyright of the volume entitled "Joan of Arc," or of any renewals of said copyright, provided all the provisions of this Agreement have been duly complied with by the American Publishing Company, they will assign to said American Publishing Company all their interest in said plates.

3. The said HARPER VOLUMES are to bear the proper copyright notices belonging to the respective books, and are to contain a note to the effect that they are printed from plates belonging to said Harper & Brothers.

4. The size and style in which the American Publishing Company shall set the HARPER VOLUMES for its uniform edition of Samuel L. Clemens's works shall be in accordance with the specimen pages submitted to Harper & Brothers and approved by them.

5. The American Publishing Company agrees to pay to Harper & Brothers a royalty of eight per cent. upon $1.75 for each and every copy sold by it of each of the said HARPER VOLUMES printed from the plates made by said American Publishing Company under the provisions of this Supplementary Agreement, whether in the Popular Edition, Edition de Luxe, or Autograph Edition. This is upon the understanding that each of said HARPER VOLUMES shall make one volume in the proposed uniform edition; but if for any reason not now foreseen it should be thought advisable by the American Publishing Company that "Joan of Arc," "Life on the Mississippi," or any other of the said works should be divided into two volumes, the American Publishing Company must first arrange with Harper & Brothers as to the royalty to be paid upon the copies in two volumes sold of such works.

6. The manufacture of editions from said plates of said HARPER VOLUMES is to be done by the American Publishing Company in first class manner and style and entirely at the cost of the American Publishing Company.

7. The HARPER VOLUMES included in the uniform edition of Samuel L. Clemens's works are not to be sold separately by the American Publishing Company, but only as portions of the said complete uniform edition, bound in cloth or better material, and not in sheets, and only to its accredited agents. The retail price of said HARPER VOLUMES in said Popular Uniform Edition shall be $2.50 per volume, unless mutually agreed otherwise, and no sales to agents shall be at less than $1.00 per volume. Orders from trade agents duly appointed shall be accepted only for complete sets of the work as specified herein, and shall be subject to the regular canvassing or general agents' discounts established by the American Publishing Company.

8. All the other provisions of the aforesaid Agreement of December 31, 1896, not covered in this Supplement, are to remain in force.

Signed New York   Harper & Brothers.
    Nov. 11, 1898.   by J. Henry Harper, V. Pres't.

                                   The American Pub Co
                                     by Walter Bliss Sec'y

                                   Olivia L. Clemens
                                   by HH Rogers Attorney

APPENDIX E

Agreement of 22 October 1903 between
Harper & Brothers, and Samuel L. Clemens
and Olivia L. Clemens

THIS AGREEMENT made and entered into this 22nd day of October, 1903, by and between HARPER & BROTHERS, a corporation created by and existing under the laws of the State of New York, party of the first part, and SAMUEL L. CLEMENS and OLIVIA L. CLEMENS, both of the City of New York, and hereinafter referred to as the parties of the second part:

WHEREAS, Olivia L. Clemens, one of the parties of the second part hereto, by agreement made with Harper & Brothers, dated the twenty-third day of May, 1895, did grant and assign to the said Harper & Brothers the exclusive rights of publication in book form in the United States of the following works of the said Samuel L. Clemens, one of the parties of the second part, to wit:

"The Adventures of Huckleberry Finn,"
"A Connecticut Yankee in King Arthur's Court,"
"Tom Sawyer Abroad,"
"The Prince and the Pauper,"
"Life on the Mississippi,"
"The White Elephant" &c.,
"The American Claimant,"
"£1,000,000 Bank Note,"

"Library of Wit and Humor,"
"A Californian's Tale,"

during the respective unexpired terms of the copyrights of said works and the renewals thereof, a copy of which said agreement is hereunto annexed, marked "A" and hereinafter designated as agreement Exhibit "A"; and

WHEREAS, the parties of the second part and Charles Dudley Warner conferred upon the American Publishing Company, a corporation organized under the laws of the State of Connecticut, by agreement dated the 31st day of December, 1896, the right to manufacture, publish and sell certain other works of the said Samuel L. Clemens, to wit:

"Pudd'nhead Wilson,"
"Innocents Abroad,"
"The Gilded Age,"
"Roughing It,"
"The Tramp Abroad,"
"Tom Sawyer,"

during the unexpired terms of the copyrights of the said works and the renewal thereof, in accordance with the terms of said contract, a copy of which is hereunto annexed, marked "B" and hereinafter designated as agreement Exhibit "B"; and

WHEREAS, Harper & Brothers and the parties of the second part hereto and the said American Publishing Company entered into an agreement, dated the 31st day of December, 1896, and which said agreement was supplemented by an additional agreement, dated November 11th, 1898, whereby the American Publishing Company acquired certain rights, as appears by said agreement, copies of which are hereto annexed and marked "C" and are hereinafter designated as agreement Exhibit "C"; and

WHEREAS, the party of the first part hereto has purchased from the American Publishing Company all its right, title and interest in and to all its contracts made with the parties of the second part or the party of the first part, relating to the works of the said Samuel L. Clemens, with the consent of the parties of the second part, and which said agreement is hereunto annexed and is hereinafter designated as agreement "Exhibit D"; and

WHEREAS, the parties of the second part, by agreements variously dated, did grant and assign to the party of the first part the exclusive rights of publication in book form of the following works of Samuel L. Clemens, to wit:

"Volume of Short Stories,"
"Life on Mississippi,"
"How to Tell a Story,"
"A Double Barrelled Detective Story,"
"The Man That Corrupted Hadleyburg,"

and

WHEREAS, it is the intent of the parties hereto that the exclusive right of publication in the United States, its insular possessions, and Canada, of all the works, present and future, of said Samuel L. Clemens, shall become vested in the party of the first part hereto; and

WHEREAS, the parties hereto have agreed to contribute towards the purchase price of the interest of the American Publishing Company in said contract:

NOW, THEREFORE, for the purpose of determining the interests of the respective parties hereto and of more fully formulating the relations of the parties for the present and for the future, and in consideration of One Dollar by each of the parties hereto to the other paid, and other valuable and sufficient consideration, the receipt whereof is hereby acknowledged, the parties hereto have covenanted and agreed and do hereby covenant and agree as follows:

FIRST: The parties of the second part do hereby grant and assign to the said party of the first part the exclusive rights of publication in the United States, its insular possessions and Canada, of all the said works and writings of the said Samuel L. Clemens, to wit:

"The Adventures of Huckleberry Finn,"
"A Connecticut Yankee in King Arthur's Court,"
"Tom Sawyer Abroad,"
"The Prince and the Pauper,"
"Life on the Mississippi,"
"The White Elephant" &c,
"The American Claimant,"
"£1,000,000 Bank Note,"
"Library of Wit and Humor,"
"A Californian's Tale,"

"Pudd'nhead Wilson,"
"Innocents Abroad,"
"The Gilded Age,"
"Roughing It,"
"The Tramp Abroad,"
"Tom Sawyer,"
"Volume of Short Stories,"
"Life on Mississippi,"
"How to Tell a Story,"
"A Double Barrelled Detective Story,"
"The Man That Corrupted Hadleyburg,"
"Following the Equator,"

and any other of his works and writings which may have been omitted from said list during the respective unexpired terms of the copyrights of the said works and the renewals thereof, guaranteeing and agreeing with the said party of the first part that she, the said Olivia L. Clemens, is the sole owner of said works and the copyrights thereof and has full power to make this agreement and grant; that said works contain no matter which is a violation of the copyright of any other works, or which is scandalous or libelous; and that she and her legal representatives will hold harmless and defend Harper & Brothers against any claim, demand or recovery, by reason of any such violation of another copyright, or any scandalous or libelous matter in said works.

The party of the first part agrees that it will publish the said works and will pay the parties of the second part, or their representatives or assigns, twenty per cent on their respective retail prices for each copy of such books by them sold, except

(a) that when books are sold in combination with a periodical, the custom heretofore and now existing between the parties shall be adopted and the royalty shall be paid only on the price received for such combination, less seventy-five per cent. of the retail price of the periodical, this provision shall not apply to complete sets which may be published at $12 or less;

(b) that the parties of the second part shall receive as a royalty on any complete edition of said books which may be published and sold for twenty-five dollars or under but not less than twelve dollars, a royalty of seventeen per cent. instead of twenty per cent. The said party of the first part agrees and guarantees that the minimum royalty upon all books to be paid each year during the first five years of this contract shall be not less than twenty-five thousand dollars.

It is agreed, however, by the parties of the second part that the party of the first part shall have the right to publish in book form not more than twenty thousand words, certain of the short stories and writings of the said Samuel L. Clemens on which the royalty shall be and is hereby fixed at ten per cent. of the retail price for each copy of such books by them sold. But for copies sold to canvassers or otherwise for the purpose of introducing said books at a discount greater than that customarily allowed buyers in the regular trade in the United States, the party of the first part shall pay the regular afore-mentioned royalties only on the actual price received for each copy.

In respect to certain books purchased from the said publishing company by the party of the first part hereto under the terms of the agreement, Exhibit "D" afore-said, the party of the first part hereto agrees to pay the same royalties to the parties of the second part hereto as herein provided, but the payment of said royalties shall be credited therefor as fast only as the books purchased by the party of the first part shall be actually sold by it.

It is further agreed between the parties hereto that for the period of five years from the date hereof the party of the first part shall pay to the parties of the second part the said minimum guaranteed royalty of twenty-five thousand dollars per annum in equal monthly payments for and on account of all the royalties to become due to the parties of the second part annually, and the party of the first part will furnish to the parties of the second part, at the end of each year, for a term of five years, statements of the sales of the books referred to in this agreement, and should the royalties earned be a greater sum than twenty-five thousand dollars per annum, make settlement in cash four months after the date of each statement; and the party of the first part is hereby authorized to apply as much of the monthly payments just referred to as may be necessary from time to time in the payment of the instalments provided by the agreement known as Exhibit "D" to be paid by the parties hereto of the second part and charge the same against the said parties of the second part.

And the said party of the first part shall after the expiration of five years and for each and every year thereafter pay to the parties of the second part in like manner a minimum guaranteed royalty, the amount of which shall for each year after the fifth be equal to forty per cent. of the earned royalties of the parties of the second part for the immediately preceding year.

Selections,   Harper & Brothers may publish, or permit others
Translations,   to publish, such selections from said works as they
Abridgments, &c.   think proper to benefit their sale, without com-
                       pensation to the grantors herein; but the compen-
sation for translations and dramatizations shall be subject to agreement between the parties hereto. If Harper & Brothers sell the right to publish selections or abridgments, the revenue or payment therefor shall be divided equally between the parties hereto.

Insurance.   All plates shall be insured, and continued to be
                       insured by the party of the first part, and all mon-
eys received on account of any policies issued shall be applied to the restoration of such plates.

Infringement   In case of any infringement on the copyright of
of Copyright.   the works herein contracted for and published
                       under this contract, Harper & Brothers are author-
ized in their discretion to sue for or otherwise seek such remedy as they may be advised; and all such suits or proceedings brought against in-fringers of the copyrights hereby ceded to Harper & Brothers shall be at the joint expense and cost of the two parties to this agreement, and any surplus of damages, or recovery or settlement, above the expense, shall be divided equally between the parties hereto.

Assignment.   The interest in this contract which belongs to each
                       party respectively may be assigned but only as a
whole, and no part of such interest shall be assigned by either party; but no assignment by said Mrs. Olivia L. Clemens or her heirs or as-signs, shall be valid, as against Harper & Brothers, unless and until said Harper & Brothers shall have been notified, in writing, of such assign-ments; and all payments or advances upon this contract made by Harper & Brothers prior to notification of assignment as above provided for, and any lien or obligation incurred thereon in favor of Harper & Brothers, prior to such notification, shall stand and be binding prior to and hold as against such assignment, and shall have the same force and effect as if such assignment had not been made.

Advertising.   Harper & Brothers will during the continuance
                       of this agreement publish an advertisement of the

works of the said Samuel L. Clemens in every number of Harper's Magazine, and failing to do so the party of the first part shall forfeit to the parties of the second part Two Hundred Dollars for each failure.

SECOND: In the event that the party of the first part shall fail to make the payments required of it under the terms of the agreement Exhibit "D" after notice given as provided by said agreement, then the parties of the second part shall be and are hereby authorized to make the payments of any instalments in lieu of the party of the first part in manner provided by said agreement Exhibit "D" and the default of the party of the first part having continued for a period of three months and the parties of the second part having completed and made the balance of any payments remaining due to the American Publishing Company under the agreement Exhibit "D" the parties of the second part shall be entitled to the possession of the said plates and other property transferred to the party of the first part by agreement Exhibit "D" and shall be entitled as against the party of the first part to the exclusive right of publication of all of the said works and writings of the said Samuel L. Clemens specified in this agreement and all rights of the party of the first part herein shall cease and determine.

THIRD: The parties of the second part hereto agree with the party of the first part that the exclusive right to publish any works or writings of which the said Samuel L. Clemens shall be or hereafter become the author during the life of this agreement or of agreement Exhibit "D", shall belong to and is hereby granted to the party of the first part upon the same terms and conditions as to books as are specified in paragraph first hereof and as to serials or miscellaneous writings as hereinafter provided, and neither of the parties of the second part nor their executors, administrators or assigns shall publish through any publisher or persons other than the party of the first part, any books, writings or works now existing or which may hereafter be created. All books shall be published under the terms and provisions specified in paragraph first and miscellaneous articles accepted for magazines or periodicals shall be paid for at the rate of thirty cents a word.

FOURTH: The parties of the second part will take out copyrights on all articles and writings before the same or any parts of the same shall be published and will from time to time renew such copyrights as may be about to expire within the time limited by the statutes in such case made and provided, and will join with the party of the first part in any action which it may bring to restrain the infringement of any of the rights of either of the parties to this agreement.

And the parties of the second part and each of them hereby constitute and appoint the party of the first part the attorney in fact of them and each of them irrevocable with full power and authority to take any and all proceedings at law or otherwise or do any and all acts in the name of the parties of the second part or either of them or otherwise as may be necessary or requisite to carry into effect the objects and intent of this agreement hereby ratifying and confirming all that the party of the first part or its substitute, agents or attorneys, may do hereunder.

And as the party of the first part has an interest in the subject matter of this agreement and as additional security this power is conferred upon it and is coupled with said interest and is hereby declared to be irrevocable.

FIFTH: Upon the execution and delivery of this agreement all other contracts between the parties hereto for the publication of the books, works and writings of the said Samuel L. Clemens are terminated as of the date hereof.

SIXTH: Any and all payments required to be made by the party of the first part may be made to either of the parties of the second part with the same force, effect and satisfaction as if made to both and in the event of the death of either of the parties of the second part the party of the first part may make any and all payments herein provided to be made to the survivor and when so made shall be free and clear of any claim or demand by or on behalf of the executors or administrators of the party so deceased.

SEVENTH: This agreement shall bind the executors administrators, assigns and successors of the respective parties hereto.

IN WITNESS WHEREOF, the party of the first part has caused its seal to be hereunto affixed and these presents to be executed by its president and the parties of the second part have hereunto set their respective hands and seals the day and year first above written.

Signed, sealed and delivered
  in the presence of:
  Geo. T. Van Valkenburgh.

                                              S. L. Clemens. (Seal)

                                            Olivia L. Clemens (Seal)

State of New York, ⎫
County of New York, ⎬ ss.:

On this 22d day of October, 1903, before me personally came SAM-
UEL L. CLEMENS and OLIVIA L. CLEMENS, to me personally
known to be the individual described in, and who executed the foregoing instrument, and acknowledged to me that he executed the same.

Geo. T. Van Valkenburgh,

Notary Public,

New York Co.

(Notary Seal.)

APPENDIX F

Agreement of 23 October 1903 between the
American Publishing Company, Harper & Brothers
and Samuel L. Clemens and Olivia L. Clemens

THIS AGREEMENT, made and entered into this 23d day of
October 1903, by and between THE AMERICAN PUBLISHING
COMPANY, a corporation created by and existing under the laws of
the State of Connecticut and having its principal place of business at
Hartford in said State, party of the first part, HARPER & BROTHERS,
a corporation created by and existing under the laws of the State of New
York and having its principal place of business in the City of New York,
party of the second part, and SAMUEL L. CLEMENS and OLIVIA L.
CLEMENS, his wife, both of the City of New York, acting jointly and
severally, parties of the third part, WITNESSETH:

WHEREAS, the party of the first part, by an agreement between it
and the parties of the third part and Charles Dudley Warner of said
Hartford, dated the 31st day of December, 1896, did acquire the right to
manufacture, publish and sell certain works of the said Samuel L.
Clemens, published under the *nom de plume* of Mark Twain, said
works being specified in said contract, during the unexpired terms of
the copyrights of the said works and the renewals thereof, in accordance
with the terms of said contract; and

WHEREAS, the party of the second part heretofore obtained by agreement, dated May 23rd, 1895, by and between Olivia L. Clemens and Harper & Brothers, the right of publication in book form in the United States of others of the said works of the said Samuel L. Clemens, and in said agreement specified, and which were published under said *nom de plume,* during the unexpired terms of the copyrights of said works and the renewals thereof, and in accordance with the terms of said last mentioned agreement; and

WHEREAS, such rights of publication granted to the parties of the first and second parts covered all of the books and works at any time copyrighted by the parties of the third part, or either of them, or by any one on their behalf; and

WHEREAS, by agreement between the party of the first part, the party of the second part, and said parties of the third part, dated December 31st, 1896, and an agreement between the same parties supplemental to said agreement, dated November 11, 1898, the party of the first part acquired the right to publish as part of a uniform edition of Samuel L. Clemens's works certain books and writings of his specified in said last named agreement, under the terms, conditions and limitations set forth in said agreement and the supplement thereto; and

WHEREAS, the party of the second part desires to acquire the sole and exclusive right to publish all the works of the said Samuel L. Clemens, as well the complete editions as in separate volumes and in all other forms, for the unexpired terms of copyright and the renewals thereof;

NOW, IN CONSIDERATION of the premises and of the sum of One Dollar by each of the parties hereto to the other paid, the receipt whereof is hereby acknowledged, and of the covenants and agreements on the part of each other herein contained, and other valuable considerations, the parties hereto have covenanted and agreed, and do hereby covenant and agree, to and with each other as follows:

FIRST: There is to be paid to the party of the first part the sum of Fifty thousand Dollars, Twenty-five thousand Dollars thereof to be paid by the party of the second part, and Twenty-five Thousand Dollars thereof to be paid by the parties of the third part. This payment shall be made at the rate of one thousand dollars per month by or on account of each of the parties of the second and third parts on the first day of each month, beginning on the first day of December 1903, for a period of twelve months, until the full sum of twenty-four thousand dollars shall have been paid to the party of the first part. The balance shall be paid at the rate of fifteen hundred dollars per month by or on account of each of the parties of the second and third parts, the payment of the first installment of said balance to be made on the first day of December 1904, and to continue until the full amount of said balance, that is, twenty-six thousand dollars, shall have been paid to the party of the first part. And the party of the second part and the parties of the third part do hereby severally covenant and agree to make said payments, severally to be made by them as aforesaid, as above specified. Any and all of the payments herein provided to be made may be anticipated and paid before the time above specified.

SECOND: The party of the first part hereby sells, assigns, transfers and sets over to the party of the second part all its right, title and interest in and to the copyrights of any books, works or writings of which the said Samuel L. Clemens was the author, either solely or jointly with another, and also all its right to manufacture, publish and sell any of the books, works or writings aforesaid and all its right, title and interest in, to and under the agreement made between it, the parties of the third part and Charles Dudley Warner, dated December 31st, 1896, and the agreement made between it and the parties of the third part and the party of the second part, dated December 31st, 1896 and the supplement thereto dated November 11th, 1898, and in, to or under any other agreement which may exist between the party of the first part and any of the parties hereto, and further agrees to deliver to the party of the second part on or before the 23rd day of November 1903, all plates from which the said works and their various editions have been printed or published, or were intended to be printed or published, and further agrees that it will, except in the event of default of the payments hereinbefore provided for, forever refrain and desist from printing or publishing, or causing to be printed or published, any of the books, works or writings aforesaid, until the right to print, publish or sell the same shall by the expiration of the copyrights thereof, or otherwise, have become common property.

And the party of the first part further covenants and agrees that it has not granted, bargained or sold to any person or persons any right, title or interest in or to the said contracts, or either of them, or in any of the copyrights, works or writings aforesaid, nor has it granted, bargained or sold any right to manufacture, publish or sell any of the said books, works or writings, or any part thereof, to any person or persons whomsoever, except certain rights of sale which have been granted to four certain general agents hereinafter referred to, expiring not later than September 1, 1904, whose forms of contracts are hereunto attached, and except the right granted to general agents or customers to sell volumes or editions of said works heretofore manufactured, published and sold by the party of the first part, as explained in letter of George H. Gilman hereunto annexed.

It is understood, however, that permission has heretofore been granted by the party of the first part to certain parties mainly without compensation therefor, and as a matter of courtesy to use temporarily certain disconnected chapters and short separate articles or short stories, as explained by letter of George H. Gilman hereto attached.

THIRD: In the event that the party of the second part shall have made default as herein provided in any of the payments to be made by it, as hereinbefore specified, and the parties of the third part shall have paid the defaulted payment, then the said parties of the third part shall have the right to assume and carry out all the then unfulfilled provisions of this contract and of receiving the full benefit thereof, and the party of the second part shall be excluded from any further right, title or interest herein, and the rights to publish the volumes described in the agreement aforesaid of December 31st, 1896, and the supplement thereto of November 11, 1898, as the Harper Volumes by subscription, and the plates for said subscription or uniform editions including all plates made by the party of the second part for any new subscription or uniform edition, and also any new volumes or writings of Samuel L. Clemens that may be published by subscription in the meantime and the full rights of publication of the books, volumes and writings hereinafter referred to and plates therefor, including any plates made by the party of the second part for any future addition thereof, to wit, the books or works referred to in the contract between the party of the first part and the parties of the third part, and Charles Dudley Warner, dated December 31, 1896, shall revert to and become the property of the parties of the third part without royalties to the party of the second part, and free from all restrictions except as to the Harper volumes which shall be sold as before by subscription only, subject nevertheless to be divested and to become the property of the party of the first part on the further default of the parties of the third part in the manner hereinafter specified.

And the parties of the third part hereby expressly authorize and empower the party of the second part to make any and all of the payments herein provided to be made by the parties of the third part to the party of the first part under this agreement and charge the same against the parties of the third part as payments on account of any and all royalties or other sums of money which may then be or hereafter become due to them or either of them under any contract or contracts with the party of the second part.

FOURTH: Whenever either of the parties of the second or third parts shall fail to make the payments of any of the installments hereinbefore provided for within five days after the same shall have become due, notice of such default shall be mailed by the party of the first part by registered letters, addressed both to the party of the second part and the parties of the third part at their present place of business or residence in the City of New York, or other place in the City of New York previously designated by them, or either of them, in writing, to the party of the first part that such default has taken place.

FIFTH: If within thirty days after the notice of default shall have been given in manner above provided, payment shall not have been made either by the defaulting party or by the other of the parties so notified, the rights of publication as the same existed at the time of the execution of this agreement and all plates, including those made by the parties of the second or third parts for the volumes known as the American Publishing Company's volumes whether made for the trade or for subscription edition and also all plates made for the subscription or uniform edition and any other additional volume or writings that may be published in the meantime shall revert to and become the property of the party of the first part without the payment of royalties to the party of the second part, and free from all restrictions and free from all prior liens or interest in any other person or persons, except that the said Harper volumes and additional volumes shall be published and sold only by subscription as in existing contracts therefor, and thereupon all the existing contracts between the party of the first part and the parties of the third part or party of the second part, and herein referred to, shall thereupon become operative and effectual as though this contract had not been made, provided nevertheless that the party of the first part shall have the right to publish and sell said works without the payment of any royalties to said party of the second part, and free from all restrictions as to selling price, or otherwise, except that the so-called Harper volumes and additional volumes shall be published and sold by subscription only as in existing contracts, anything in said contracts to the contrary notwithstanding.

SIXTH: The party of the second part agrees to keep and maintain in good condition all the plates transferred to it under the terms of this agreement until all the payments hereinbefore provided for shall have been fully made, and the parties of the third part agree, in case said plates shall be acquired by the parties of the third part in manner as hereinbefore provided for, to keep and maintain the same in good condition until said payments shall have been fully made, and in case the party of the first part shall become entitled to the re-delivery of said plates as hereinbefore specified, then the party of the second part or the parties of the third part, if they shall theretofore have acquired possession of said plates under the provisions of this contract, agree to deliver the same upon demand to the party of the first part.

SEVENTH: A schedule is hereto annexed of all the books sold by the party of the first part since the first day of July, 1903, and up to the day of the date hereof, in which the party of the second part or the parties of the third part had any interest, or on which they or either of them were entitled to any royalties, and upon such books to the extent of the actual sales thereof, not exceeding, however, the quantity named in said schedule, neither the party of the second part nor the parties of the third part shall be entitled to receive any royalty or royalties from the party of the first part. Said schedule also shows the number of volumes which have been printed of the works of said Samuel L. Clemens known as "My Debut as a Literary Person" and intended to make volume 23 of Mark Twain's complete works, and the party of the third part shall not be entitled to receive any royalties from the party of the first part on said volumes, and the party of the first part shall have the right to sell without the payment of royalty the volumes of said work it already has printed and now has on hand, consisting of not more than 2923 volumes, of which all but 200 have been sold to purchasers. The balance not sold to customers on the first day of April 1904 shall be delivered to the party of the second part who shall pay therefor at the price of fifty per cent off the list prices.

EIGHTH: The party of the second part hereby purchases from the party of the first part, and the party of the first part agrees to sell and deliver to the party of the second part, not exceeding 1800 bound sets of the Hillcrest edition of the works of Samuel L. Clemens, at the price of nine dollars per set, and its stock of single volumes, bound or unbound, of the works of Samuel L. Clemens, not exceeding 5000 volumes, at the price of an advance of forty cents per volume above the cost of production; neither the party of the second part nor the parties of the third part are to be entitled to any royalties on account of this sale.

NINTH: All the books bound or unbound so purchased by the party of the second part are to be paid for by two non-negotiable notes of the party of the second part, payable to the party of the first part, one for one-half of the amount, payable January 25th, 1904, and one for the other half of the amount, payable March 25th, 1904, said notes to be made, dated, and delivered within five days after the books aforesaid are delivered to the party of the second part.

TENTH: Contracts in form hereunto annexed, marked Exhibit I, having been made with certain general agents by the party of the first part for the sale by the said agents of the works of said Samuel L. Clemens, and the said contracts not having expired, the party of the second part agrees to perform the terms and provisions of said contracts in all respects in lieu and instead of the party of the first part, and agrees to keep the party of the first part indemnified and saved harmless from all loss, cost or damage for or by reason of any claim, demand or causes of action which may arise in favor of the said agents, or either of them, by reason of the execution of this contract, or by reason of any claim, demand or cause of action that may arise in favor of the said agents, or any of them, by reason of any act or transaction or neglect by the party of the second part hereafter. No claim or demand shall arise under this clause unless the party of the first part shall within ten days after notice of any claim or demand made against it notify the party of the second part in writing and upon action brought thereon forward at once to the party of the second part the summons or other process, and it hereby permits and authorizes the party of the second part to appear and defend and represent it in any such action or proceeding. But all the expenses of such appearance or defence are to be borne entirely by the party of the second part.

ELEVENTH: The party of the first part and the party of the second part will unite in an endeavor to obtain the release of the party of the first part from all such general agents' contracts or the cancellation thereof, and when obtained the same shall be delivered to the party of the first part, but if such releases or cancellations cannot be obtained, this agreement shall not be affected thereby, the party of the second part to pay reasonable travelling expenses incurred by the party of the first part in obtaining or endeavoring to obtain said releases and cancellations.

TWELFTH: All legal proceedings heretofore instituted by the party of the second part against the party of the first part shall be withdrawn and discontinued without cost to either party against the other, and the parties of the second and third parts hereby release the party of the first part, and the party of the first part hereby releases the parties of the second and third parts of and from all claims, demands and causes of action whatsoever, except such as are preserved or may arise under this agreement.

THIRTEENTH: Mrs. Charles Dudley Warner of Hartford, Connecticut, having an interest with the parties of the third part, or one of them, in the royalties to be derived from a certain book entitled "The Gilded Age," the party of the second part assumes and agrees to pay to her, or to such persons as may become entitled to receive the same, all such royalties to the extent of her or their interests therein and to keep and save the party of the first part harmless and fully indemnified from all loss, cost or damage by reason of the execution of this contract or of any claim or demand which may arise in her or their favor by reason of any sales, or the failure to sell said book hereafter.

FOURTEENTH: No claim or demand shall arise under the last clause unless the party of the first part shall within ten days after notice of any claim or demand made against it notify the party of the second part in writing and upon action brought thereon forward at once to the party of the second part the summons or other process; and permits and authorizes the party of the second part to appear for, defend and represent it in any action or proceeding. But all the expenses of such appearance or defence are to be borne entirely by the party of the second part.

IN WITNESS WHEREOF, the parties of the first and second parts have caused these presents to be signed by their presidents respectively, and their respective seals to be hereto affixed, attested by their respective secretaries, and the parties of the third part have hereunto set their hands and seals the day and the year first above written.

> SL. Clemens (L.S.)
>
> Olivia L. Clemens (L.S.)
>
> Harper & Brothers
>   by George BM Harvey Prest (L.S.)
>
> The American Publishing Company
>   by FE Bliss prest. (L.S.)
>
>   [Seal]

Attest

FA Duneka Secretary.

State of New York,   } ss.

County of New York {

On this 23d day of October 1903 before me personally came S. L. Clemens and Olivia L Clemens to me personally known to be the individuals described in, and who executed the foregoing instrument, and severally acknowledged to me that they executed the same.

Mark J Katz	Attest
Notary Public	Walter Bliss
N Y Co.	Secretary

State of New York,   } ss.

County of New York {

On the 23d day of October in the year 1903 before me personally came Geo B.M. Harvey to me known, who being by me duly sworn, did depose and say that he resided in the City of New York that he is the president of Harper & Brothers the corporation described in and which executed the above instrument; that he knew the seal of said corporation; that the seal affixed to said instrument was such corporate seal that it was so affixed by order of the board of directors of said corporation, and that he signed his name thereto by like order.

Philip J. Fox.

Notary Public.

N.Y. County. NY

APPENDIX G

A Tribute to Henry H. Rogers (1902) by
Samuel L. Clemens

April 25, 1902. I owe more to Henry Rogers than to any other man whom I have known. He was born in Fairhaven, Conn., in 1839, and is my junior by four years. He was graduated from the High School there in 1853 when he was fourteen years old, and from that time forward he earned his own living, beginning at first as the bottom-subordinate in the village store with hard-work privileges and a low salary. When he was twenty-four he went out to the newly-discovered petroleum fields in Pennsylvania and got work; then returned home, with enough money to pay passage, married a school-mate, and took her to the oil regions. He prospered, and by and by established the Standard Oil Trust with Mr. Rockefeller and others, and is still one of its managers and directors.

In 1893 we fell together by accident one evening in the Murray Hill hotel, and our friendship began on the spot and at once. Ever since then he has added my business affairs to his own and carried them through, and I have had no further trouble with them. Obstructions and perplexities which would have driven me mad were simplicities to his master mind and furnished him no difficulties. He released me from my entanglements with the scoundrel Paige and stopped that expensive outgo; when Charles L. Webster & Co. failed he saved my copyrights for Mrs. Clemens when she would have sacrificed them to the creditors although they were in no way entitled to them; he offered to lend me money wherewith to save the life of that worthless firm; when I started lecturing around the world to make the money to pay off the Webster debts he spent more than a year trying to reconcile the differences between Harper & Brothers and the American Publishing Co and patch up a working-contract between them, and succeeded where any other man would have failed; as fast [as] I earned money and sent it to him he banked it at interest and held on to it, refusing to pay any creditor until he could pay all ⟨alike;⟩ of the 96 alike; when, after two years, I had earned enough to pay dollar for dollar, he swept off the indebtedness and sent me the whole batch of complimentary letters which the creditors wrote in return; when I had earned $28,500 more, 18,500 of which was in his hands, I ⟨cabled⟩ wrote him from Vienna to put the latter into Federal Steel and *leave* it there, he obeyed to the extent of $17,500, but sold it in two months at $25,000 profit, and said it would go ten points higher, but that it was his custom to "give the other man a chance"—⟨and that was a true word—there was never a truer one spoken.⟩ That was at the end of '99 and beginning of 1900; and from that day to this he has continued to break up my bad schemes and put better ones in their place, to my great advantage. I do things which ought to try any man's patience, but they never seem to try his; he always finds a colorable excuse for what I have done. His soul was born superhumanly sweet, and I do not think anything can sour it. I have not known his equal among men, for lovable qualities. But for his cool head and wise guidance I should never have come out of the Webster difficulties on top; it was his good steering that enabled me to work out my salvation and pay a hundred cents on the dollar—the most valuable service any man ever did me.

His character is full of fine graces, but the finest is this: that he can load you down with crushing obligations, and then so conduct himself that you never feel their weight. If he would only require something in return—but that is not in his nature; it would not occur to him. With the Harpers and the American Co at war, those copyrights were worth but little; he engineered a peace, and made them valuable; together, $60,000 this past twelvemonth. He invests $100,000 for me here, and in a few months returns a profit of $31,000. I invest ⟨in London and here⟩ $66,000, and must wait considerably for results; ⟨in case there shall ever be any⟩; I tell him about it and he finds no fault, utters not a sarcasm. He was born serene, ⟨tranquil,⟩ patient, all-enduring, where a friend is concerned, and nothing can extinguish that great quality in him. Such a man is entitled to the high gift of humor: he has it, at its very best.

He is not only the best friend I have ever had, but is the best man I have known.

[On the manuscript envelope Clemens wrote: "H. H. Rogers. Add to it the Judge's verdict in the Boston Gas Case—'nothing illegal or dishonest.' "]

A Calendar of Letters

THE LOCATION of the authority for each text is listed after the date, using the abbreviations listed below. All texts are based on manuscript of the original letter, except when the abbreviations TS (typescript), PH (photocopy) or OC (office copy) indicate that the location of the original letter is unknown. In addition, two letters (174 and 449) have been based on printed texts, as specified in the Calendar.

Benjamin	The Henry Rogers Benjamin Fund New York City
Berg	Henry W. and Albert A. Berg Collection New York Public Library
Coe	The Collection of William Rogers Coe New York City
Cushman	The Collection of Bigelow Paine Cushman Newark, Delaware
CWB	Clifton Waller Barrett Library University of Virginia Charlottesville
Fairhaven	The Millicent Library Fairhaven, Massachusetts
MTP	Mark Twain Papers University of California Library Berkeley

712

Salm   The Collection of Peter A. Salm
                    New York City

Yale   Mark Twain Collections
                    Yale University Library

I. 13 December 1893–12 February 1895

No.	To	Location	Date	Authority
1.	SLC to HHR	New York	13 December 1893	MTP
2.	HHR to SLC	New York	19 December 1893	MTP
3.	HHR to SLC	New York	28 December 1893	MTP
4.	SLC to HHR	New York	29 December 1893	MTP
5.	SLC to HHR	New York	30 December 1893	Fairhaven
6.	SLC to HHR	New York	1 January 1894	MTP
7.	SLC to HHR	New York	3 January 1894	Salm
8.	HHR to SLC	New York	5 January 1894	MTP
9.	SLC to HHR	New York	27 January 1894	MTP
10.	HHR to SLC	New York	3 March 1894	Cushman
11.	SLC to HHR	New York	4 March 1894	Salm
12.	OLC to HHR	Paris	14 February 1894	Salm
13.	SLC to HHR	New York	4 March 1894	Berg
14.	SLC to HHR	At Sea	8 March 1894	Salm
15.	HHR to SLC	New York	8 March 1894	MTP
16.	HHR to SLC	New York	13 March 1894	MTP
17.	SLC to HHR	Paris	19 March 1894	Salm

No.	To	Location	Date	Authority
18.	HHR to SLC	New York	20 March 1894	MTP
19.	SLC to HHR	Paris	22 March 1894	MTP
20.	SLC to HHR	Paris	26 March 1894	MTP
21.	SLC to HHR	Paris	30 March 1894	MTP
22.	SLC to HHR	New York	8 May 1894	MTP
23.	SLC to HHR	At Sea	16 May 1894	MTP
24.	SLC to HHR	Paris	22 May 1894	Salm
25.	SLC to HHR	Paris	25 May 1894	MTP
26.	SLC to HHR	Paris	31 May 1894	Berg
27.	HHR to SLC	New York	1 June 1894	MTP
28.	KIH to SLC	New York	1 June 1894	MTP
29.	HHR to SLC	New York	2 June 1894	MTP
30.	SLC to HHR	Paris	16 June 1894	Salm
31.	SLC to HHR	La Bourboule	25 June 1894	MTP
32.	SLC to HHR	La Bourboule	29 June 1894	Coe
33.	SLC to HHR	La Bourboule	29–30 June 1894	MTP
34.	SLC to HHR	Étretat	25 August 1894	Berg
35.	SLC to HHR	Étretat	2–3 September 1894	MTP
36.	SLC to HHR	Étretat	9 September 1894	Berg
37.	SLC to HHR	Étretat	14 September 1894	MTP
38.	SLC to HHR	Étretat	16 September 1894	MTP
39.	SLC to HHR	Étretat	24 September 1894	Salm
40.	SLC to HHR	Étretat	30 September 1894	MTP
41.	SLC to HHR	Rouen	5 October 1894	MTP
42.	SLC to HHR	Rouen	7 October 1894	Berg

No.	To	Location	Date	Authority
43.	SLC to HHR	Rouen	11 October 1894	MTP
44.	SLC to HHR	Rouen	13 October 1894	MTP
45.	SLC to HHR	Rouen	19 October 1894	Salm
46.	SLC to HHR	Rouen	28 October 1894	Salm
47.	SLC to HHR	Paris	2 November 1894	Salm
48.	SLC to HHR	Paris	6 November 1894	MTP
49.	SLC to HHR	Paris	7 November 1894	Salm
50.	SLC to HHR	Paris	11 November 1894	Salm
51.	SLC to HHR	Paris	15 November 1894	MTP
52.	SLC to HHR	Paris	21 November 1894	Salm
53.	SLC to HHR	Paris	28 November 1894	Salm
54.	SLC to HHR	Paris	29–30 November 1894	MTP
55.	SLC to HHR	Paris	7 December 1894	MTP
56.	SLC to HHR	Paris	9 December 1894	MTP
57.	SLC to HHR	Paris	16–17 December 1894	MTP
58.	SLC to HHR	Paris	21 December 1894	Coe
59.	SLC to HHR	Paris	22 December 1894	Berg
60.	SLC to HHR	Paris	27 December 1894	Berg
61.	SLC to HHR	Paris	2 January 1895	MTP

No.	To	Location	Date	Authority
62.	SLC to HHR	Paris	3 January 1895	MTP
63.	SLC to HHR	Paris	8 January 1895	MTP
64.	SLC to HHR	Paris	21 January 1895	Salm
65.	SLC to HHR	Paris	23 January 1895	Berg
66.	SLC to HHR	Paris	29 January 1895	Berg
67.	SLC to HHR	Paris	3 February 1895	Salm
68.	SLC to HHR	Paris	8–9 February 1895	MS, TS, MTP
69.	SLC to HHR	Paris	12 February 1895	Salm

II. 28 March 1895–12 August 1896

No.	To	Location	Date	Authority
70.	OLC to HHR	Paris	28 March 1895	Salm
71.	SLC to HHR	At Sea	3 April 1895	Salm
72.	SLC to HHR	At Sea	3 April 1895	Salm
73.	SLC to HHR	Paris	7 April 1895	Salm
74.	SLC to HHR	Paris	9 April 1895	Salm
75.	SLC to HHR	Paris	14 April 1895	MTP
76.	SLC to HHR	Paris	28 April 1895	Salm
77.	SLC to HHR	Paris	29 April 1895	Berg
78.	SLC to HHR	Paris	1 May 1895	MTP
79.	OLC to HHR	At Sea	15 May 1895	Salm
80.	SLC to HHR	Elmira	26 May 1895	MTP
81.	SLC to HHR	Elmira	4 June 1895	MTP
82.	SLC to HHR	Elmira	11 June 1895	MTP
83.	SLC to HHR	Elmira	15 June 1895	Salm
84.	SLC to HHR	Elmira	19 June 1895	Berg
85.	SLC to HHR	Elmira	22 June 1895	MTP
86.	SLC to HHR	Elmira	[?22] June 1895	Salm

No.	To	Location	Date	Authority
87.	SLC to HHR	Elmira	25–26 June 1895	Salm
88.	SLC to HHR	Elmira	26 June 1895	Coe
89.	OLC to HHR	Elmira	27 June 1895	Salm
90.	SLC to HHR	Elmira	29 June 1895	Salm
91.	SLC to HHR	Elmira	30 June 1895	Salm
92.	OLC to HHR	Elmira	1 July 1895	Salm
93.	SLC to HHR	Elmira	5 July 1895	Salm
94.	SLC to HHR	Elmira	6 July 1895	Salm
95.	SLC to HHR	Elmira	8 July 1895	MTP
96.	SLC to HHR	Elmira	14 July 1895	MTP
96a.	HHR to SLC	New York	16 July 1895	Cushman
97.	SLC to HHR	Cleveland	16 July 1895	Salm
98.	SLC to HHR	Mackinac, Mich.	20–22 July 1895	MTP & Salm
99.	SLC to HHR	Minneapolis	24 July 1895	Salm
99a.	HHR to SLC	New York	25 July 1895	Cushman
100.	SLC to HHR	Crookston, Minn.	29 July 1895	MTP
100a.	HHR to OLC	New York	2 August 1895	Cushman
101.	SLC to HHR	Spokane	7 August 1895	Coe
102.	SLC to HHR	Vancouver	15 August 1895	Coe
103.	SLC to HHR	Vancouver	17 August 1895	Salm
104.	SLC & OLC to HHR	Vancouver	17 August 1895	Salm
105.	SLC to HHR	Vancouver	19 August 1895	Salm
106.	SLC to HHR	At Sea	13–15 September 1895	Salm
107.	SLC to HHR	Sydney	25 September 1895	Salm
108.	SLC to HHR	At Sea	1 January 1896	Salm
109.	SLC to HHR	At Sea	12 January 1896	Salm

No.	To	Location	Date	Authority
110.	SLC to HHR	Bombay	5 February 1896	Salm
111.	SLC to HHR	Calcutta	8 February 1896	Salm
112.	SLC to HHR	Calcutta	17 February 1896	Salm
113.	SLC to HHR	Jeypoor	6 March 1896	Salm
114.	HHR to SLC	New York	6 March 1896	OC, CWB
115.	SLC to HHR	Jeypoor	15 March 1896	Salm
116.	HHR to SLC	New York	20 March 1896	OC, CWB
117.	SLC to HHR	At Sea	2 April 1896	Salm
118.	HHR to SLC	New York	10 April 1896	OC, CWB
119.	HHR to SLC	New York	13 April 1896	OC, CWB
120.	SLC to HHR	Curepipe	24 April 1896	Coe
121.	HHR to SLC	New York	29 April 1896	OC, CWB
122.	SLC to HHR	Durban	8 May 1896	Salm
123.	HHR to SLC	New York	22 May 1896	OC, CWB
124.	SLC to HHR	Pretoria	26 May 1896	Coe
125.	SLC to HHR	Queenstown	6 June 1896	Coe
126.	SLC to HHR	Port Elizabeth	18 June 1896	Benjamin
127.	HHR to SLC	New York	18 June 1896	OC, CWB
128.	SLC to HHR	Port Elizabeth	19 June 1896	Coe
129.	SLC to HHR	Port Elizabeth	22 June 1896	Benjamin
130.	HHR to SLC	New York	22 June 1896	OC, CWB
131.	HHR to SLC	New York	9 July 1896	OC, CWB
132.	SLC to HHR	At Sea	[22] July 1896	Coe
133.	SLC to HHR	Southampton	31 July 1896	Coe
134.	SLC to HHR	Guildford	12 August 1896	Coe

III. 14 August 1896–12 July 1897

| 135. | SLC to HHR | Guildford | 14 August 1896 | Salm |

No.	To	Location	Date	Authority
136.	SLC to HHR	Guildford	10 September 1896	Salm
137.	SLC to HHR	London	20 September 1896	Salm
138.	SLC to HHR	London	27 September 1896	Salm
139.	SLC to HHR	London	6 October 1896	Salm
140.	SLC to HHR	London	13 October 1896	Salm
141.	SLC to HHR	London	20 October 1896	Salm
142.	SLC to HHR	London	1 November 1896	Salm
143.	SLC to HHR	London	6 November 1896	Benjamin
144.	HHR to OLC	New York	10 November 1896	MTP
145.	HHR to OLC	New York	10 November 1896	MTP
146.	HHR to SLC	New York	10 November 1896	MTP
147.	SLC to HHR	London	[?20] November 1896	MTP
148.	SLC to HHR	London	24 November 1896	Salm
149.	SLC to ERR	London	26 November 1896	Benjamin
150.	SLC to HHR & ERR	London	18 December 1896	Benjamin
151.	SLC to ERR	London	22 December 1896	Benjamin
151a.	HHR to SLC	New York	24 December 1896	Cushman
152.	SLC to HHR	London	4 January 1897	Salm
153.	SLC to HHR	London	15 January 1897	Salm

No.	To	Location	Date	Authority
154.	SLC to HHR	London	19 January 1897	Salm
155.	SLC to HHR	London	2 February 1897	Salm
156.	SLC to HHR	London	8 February 1897	Salm
157.	SLC to HHR	London	26 February 1897	Salm
158.	SLC to HHR	London	5 March 1897	Salm
159.	SLC to HHR	London	19 March 1897	Salm
160.	SLC to HHR	London	26 March 1897	Salm
161.	SLC to HHR	London	8 April 1897	Salm
162.	SLC to HHR	London	14 April 1897	Salm
163.	SLC to HHR	London	16 April 1897	Salm
164.	SLC to HHR	London	26–28 April 1897	Salm
165.	SLC to HHR	London	18 May 1897	Salm
166.	SLC to HHR	London	3 June 1897	Salm
167.	HHR to SLC	New York	16 June 1897	MTP
168.	SLC to HHR	London	16 June 1897	Salm
169.	HHR to SLC	New York	21 June 1897	MTP
170.	SLC to HHR	London	23 June 1897	Salm
171.	SLC to HHR	London	25 June 1897	Salm
172.	SLC to HHR	London	7 July 1897	Salm
173.	SLC to HHR	London	12 July 1897	Salm

IV. 23 July 1897–10 May 1899

174.	SLC to HHR	Lucerne	23 July 1897	Feldman Catalog; (May 1956); City Book Auction (Dec. 1954).

No.	To	Location	Date	Authority
175.	KIH to SLC	New York	30 July 1897	CWB
176.	SLC to HHR	Lucerne	6 August 1897	Salm
177.	SLC to HHR	Lucerne	[?13] August 1897	PH, MTP
178.	SLC to HHR	Weggis	13 September 1897	Salm
179.	SLC to HHR	Weggis	18 September 1897	Salm
180.	SLC to HHR	Vienna	8 October 1897	Salm
181.	SLC to HHR	Vienna	10–11 November 1897	Salm
182.	OLC & SLC to HHR	Vienna	17 November 1897	Salm
183.	HHR to SLC	New York	10 December 1897	MTP
184.	SLC to HHR	Vienna	16 December 1897	Salm
185.	SLC to HHR	Vienna	21 December 1897	Salm
186.	SLC to HHR	Vienna	29 December 1897	Salm
187.	HHR to SLC	New York	6 January 1898	PH, MTP
188.	KIH to SLC	New York	7 January 1898	MTP
189.	SLC to HHR	Vienna	20 January 1898	Salm
190.	SLC to HHR	Vienna	5–6 February 1898	Salm
191.	SLC to HHR	Vienna	7 February 1898	Salm
192.	HHR to SLC	New York	9 February 1898	CWB
193.	KIH to SLC	New York	11 February 1898	MTP

No.	To	Location	Date	Authority
194.	KIH to SLC	New York	25 February 1898	MTP
195.	SLC to HHR	Vienna	7 March 1898	Salm
196.	SLC to HHR	Vienna	15 March 1898	Salm
197.	SLC to HHR	Vienna	17–20 March 1898	Salm
198.	SLC to HHR	Vienna	22 March 1898	Salm
199.	SLC to HHR	Vienna	23 March 1898	Salm
200.	SLC to HHR	Vienna	24 March 1898	Salm
201.	SLC to HHR	Vienna	12 April 1898	Salm
202.	SLC to HHR	Vienna	21 April 1898	Salm
203.	SLC to HHR	Vienna	29 April 1898	Salm
204.	SLC to HHR	Vienna	13 May 1898	Salm
205.	SLC to HHR	Kaltenleutgeben	31 May 1898	Salm
206.	SLC to HHR	Kaltenleutgeben	10 June 1898	Salm
207.	SLC to HHR	Kaltenleutgeben	10 July 1898	Salm
208.	SLC to HHR	Kaltenleutgeben	26 July 1898	Salm
209.	SLC to HHR	Kaltenleutgeben	3 August 1898	Salm
210.	SLC to HHR	Ischl	19 August 1898	Salm
211.	SLC to HHR	Kaltenleutgeben	28 August 1898	Salm
212.	SLC to HHR	Kaltenleutgeben	14 September 1898	Salm
213.	SLC to HHR	Kaltenleutgeben	21 September 1898	Salm
214.	SLC to HHR	Kaltenleutgeben	26 September 1898	Salm
215.	SLC to HHR	Kaltenleutgeben	1 October 1898	Salm
216.	SLC to HHR	Vienna	18 October 1898	Salm
217.	SLC to HHR	Vienna	2 November 1898	MTP

No.	To	Location	Date	Authority
218.	SLC to HHR	Vienna	6–7 November 1898	Salm
219.	SLC to HHR	Vienna	12 November 1898	Salm
220.	SLC to HHR	Vienna	17 November 1898	Salm
221.	SLC to HHR	Vienna	8–13 December 1898	Salm
222.	SLC to HHR	Vienna	27 December 1898	Salm
223.	SLC to HHR	Vienna	3 January 1899	Salm
224.	SLC to HHR	Vienna	24 January 1899	Salm
225.	SLC to HHR	Vienna	2 February 1899	MTP
226.	SLC to HHR	Vienna	19 February 1899	Salm
227.	SLC to HHR	Vienna	14 March 1899	Salm
228.	SLC to HHR	Vienna	18 April 1899	Salm
229.	SLC to HHR	Vienna	10 May 1899	Salm

V. 6 June 1899–20 August 1900

No.	To	Location	Date	Authority
230.	SLC to HHR	Broadstairs	6 June 1899	Salm
231.	SLC to HHR	London	25 June 1899	Salm
232.	SLC to HHR	London	3 July 1899	Salm
233.	SLC to HHR	Sanna	3 August 1899	Salm
234.	SLC to HHR	Sanna	22 August 1899	Salm
235.	SLC to HHR	Sanna	3 September 1899	Salm
236.	KIH to SLC	New York	3 October 1899	MTP
237.	SLC to HHR	London	4 October 1899	Salm

No.	To	Location	Date	Authority
238.	SLC to HHR	London	9 November 1899	Salm
239.	SLC to HHR	London	17 November 1899	Salm
240.	SLC to HHR	London	20 November 1899	MTP
241.	SLC to HHR	London	7 December 1899	Salm
242.	SLC to HHR	London	11 December 1899	Salm
243.	SLC to KIH	London	21–22 December 1899	Salm
244.	SLC to HHR	London	26 December 1899	Salm
245.	SLC to KIH	London	8 January 1900	MTP
246.	SLC to HHR	London	8 January 1900	Salm
247.	SLC to HHR	London	13 January 1900	MTP
248.	HHR to SLC	New York	26 January 1900	MTP
249.	SLC to HHR	London	5 February 1900	Salm
250.	SLC to HHR	London	27 February–4 March 1900	Salm
251.	SLC to HHR	London	11 March 1900	Salm
252.	SLC to HHR	London	25 March 1900	MTP
253.	SLC to HHR	London	8–9 April 1900	Salm
254.	SLC to HHR	London	20 April 1900	Salm
255.	SLC to HHR	London	17 May 1900	Salm
256.	SLC to HHR	London	13 June 1900	Salm
257.	SLC to HHR	London	31 July 1900	Salm

No.	To	*Location*	*Date*	*Authority*
258.	SLC to HHR	London	17 August 1900	MTP
259.	SLC to HHR	London	20 August 1900	Salm

VI. 31 October 1900–13 June 1904

260.	SLC to ERR	New York	31 October 1900	Benjamin
261.	SLC to ERR	New York	4 November 1900	Benjamin
262.	SLC to ERR	New York	13 November 1900	Benjamin
263.	SLC to HHR	New York	16 November 1900	CWB
264.	SLC to HHR	New York	21 November 1900	Coe
265.	HHR to SLC	New York	19 January 1901	MTP
266.	SLC to HHR	New York	21 January 1901	MTP
267.	SLC to ERR	New York	22 January 1901	Benjamin
268.	SLC to HHR	New York	[11] March 1901	CWB
269.	SLC to ERR	New York	11 April 1901	MTP
270.	SLC to ERR	New York	[16] April 1901	Benjamin
271.	SLC to KIH	New York	1 May 1901	PH, MTP
272.	SLC to HHR	New York	3 June 1901	CWB
273.	SLC to HHR	New York	19 June 1901	MTP
274.	SLC to HHR	Ampersand	28 June 1901	MTP
275.	SLC to HHR	Ampersand	5 July 1901	PH, MTP
276.	SLC to HHR	Ampersand	9 July 1901	MTP
277.	SLC to HHR	Ampersand	17 July 1901	MTP
278.	SLC to HHR	Ampersand	23 August 1901	MTP

No.	To	Location	Date	Authority
279.	SLC to HHR	Ampersand	29 August–6 September 1901	MTP
280.	SLC to HHR	Ampersand	7 September 1901	MTP
281.	SLC to HHR	Ampersand	12 September 1901	Salm
282.	SLC to HHR	Ampersand	18 September 1901	MTP
283.	SLC to HHR	Elmira	25 September 1901	MTP
284.	SLC to HHR	New York	26 September 1901	MTP
285.	SLC to HHR	New York	29 September 1901	Salm
286.	SLC to HHR	New York	21 November 1901	MTP
287.	SLC to HHR	Riverdale	12 December 1901	MTP
288.	SLC to HHR	Riverdale	12 December 1901	MTP
289.	SLC to HHR	Riverdale	21 December 1901	MTP
290.	HHR to SLC	New York	26 December 1901	MTP
291.	SLC to HHR	Riverdale	27 December 1901	Salm
292.	SLC to HHR	Riverdale	2 January 1902	Salm
293.	SLC to HHR	Riverdale	31 January 1902	MTP
294.	SLC to HHR	Riverdale	7 February 1902	Salm
295.	KIH to SLC	New York	3 March 1902	MTP
296.	SLC to HHR	Riverdale	[?8] March 1902	MTP
297.	SLC to HHR	[Miami]	[?18] March [1902]	MTP

No.	To	Location	Date	Authority
298.	SLC to HHR	Riverdale	14 April 1902	Salm
299.	HHR to SLC	New York	28 April 1902	MTP
300.	HHR to SLC	New York	5 May 1902	MTP
301.	SLC to HHR	Riverdale	16 May 1902	Coe
302.	SLC to HHR	Riverdale	17 May 1902	Salm
303.	SLC to HHR	Riverdale	26 May 1902	MTP
304.	SLC to HHR	York Harbor	27 June 1902	Coe
305.	SLC to HHR	York Harbor	7 July 1902	Salm
306.	SLC to HHR	York Harbor	11 July 1902	Salm
307.	SLC to HHR	York Harbor	28 July 1902	Salm
308.	SLC to HHR	York Harbor	3 August 1902	MTP
309.	HHR to SLC	New York	5 August 1902	MTP
310.	SLC to HHR	York Harbor	7 August 1902	MTP
311.	SLC to HHR	York Harbor	13 August 1902	Salm
312.	HHR to SLC	New York	14 August 1902	MTP
313.	SLC to HHR	York Harbor	21 August 1902	Salm
314.	SLC to HHR	York Harbor	22 August 1902	Salm
315.	SLC to HHR	York Harbor	27 August 1902	Salm
316.	SLC to HHR	York Harbor	28 August 1902	Coe
317.	SLC to HHR	York Harbor	28–29 August 1902	Salm
318.	SLC to HHR	York Harbor	1 September 1902	Salm
319.	SLC to HHR	York Harbor	[3] September 1902	Salm
320.	SLC to HHR	York Harbor	11 September 1902	Salm
321.	SLC to HHR	York Harbor	18–19 September 1902	Salm

No.	To	Location	Date	Authority
322.	SLC to HHR	York Harbor	20 September 1902	Salm
323.	SLC to HHR	York Harbor	23 September 1902	Salm
324.	SLC to HHR	York Harbor	24 September 1902	Salm
325.	SLC to HHR	York Harbor	26 September 1902	Salm
326.	SLC to HHR	York Harbor	11 October 1902	Salm
327.	HHR to SLC	New York	24 December 1902	MTP
328.	SLC to HHR	Riverdale	25 December 1902	MTP
329.	SLC to ERR	Riverdale	25 December 1902	Benjamin
330.	SLC to HHR	Riverdale	1 January 1903	Coe
331.	SLC to ERR	Riverdale	2 January 1903	Benjamin
332.	SLC to KIH	Riverdale	12 January 1903	MTP
333.	SLC to ERR	Riverdale	1 February 1903	Benjamin
334.	SLC to ERR	Riverdale	6 February 1903	Benjamin
335.	HHR to SLC	New York	24 February 1903	Yale
336.	SLC to HHR	Riverdale	28 February 1903	Salm
337.	SLC to HHR	New York	13 March 1903	MTP
338.	SLC to HHR	Riverdale	7 April 1903	Salm
339.	SLC to ERR	Riverdale	20 April 1903	Benjamin
340.	SLC to HHR	Riverdale	20 April 1903	MTP
341.	SLC to ERR	Riverdale	28 April 1903	Benjamin
342.	SLC to HHR	Riverdale	11 May 1903	Salm
343.	SLC to HHR	Riverdale	20 May 1903	MTP

No.	To	Location	Date	Authority
344.	HHR to SLC	Fairhaven	26 May 1903	MTP
345.	SLC to HHR	Hartford	4 June 1903	Salm
346.	SLC to HHR	Riverdale	25 June 1903	CWB
347.	OLC to ERR	Elmira	30 July 1903	Benjamin
348.	SLC to HHR	Elmira	14 September 1903	MTP
349.	HHR to SLC	New York	15 September 1903	MTP
350.	SLC to HHR	Elmira	18 September 1903	Salm
351.	HHR to SLC	New York	18 September 1903	MTP
352.	OLC to ERR	Riverdale	22 October 1903	Benjamin
353.	SLC to HHR	Florence	12–15 November 1903	Salm
354.	SLC to HHR	Florence	28 November 1903	Salm
355.	KIH to SLC	New York	10 December 1903	MTP
356.	SLC to HHR	Florence	16–18 December 1903	Salm
357.	HHR to SLC	New York	18 December 1903	MTP
358.	SLC to HHR	Florence	30 December 1903	Salm
359.	HHR to SLC	New York	8 January 1904	MTP
360.	KIH to SLC	New York	[11 January 1904]	MTP
361.	HHR to SLC	New York	12 January 1904	MTP
362.	SLC to HHR	Florence	25 January 1904	Salm
363.	HHR to SLC	New York	8 February 1904	MTP

No.	To	Location	Date	Authority
364.	SLC to HHR	Florence	25–26 February 1904	Salm
365.	SLC to HHR	Florence	21–22 March 1904	Salm
366.	SLC to HHR	Florence	12 April 1904	Salm
367.	HHR to SLC	New York	22 April 1904	MTP
368.	SLC to HHR	Florence	9 May 1904	Salm
369.	KIH to SLC	New York	26 May 1904	MTP
370.	SLC to HHR	Florence	6 June 1904	Salm
371.	SLC to HHR	Florence	8 June 1904	Salm
372.	SLC to HHR	Florence	13 June 1904	Salm

VII. 17 July 1904–2 March 1908

No.	To	Location	Date	Authority
373.	ERR to SLC	Fairhaven	17 July 1904	MTP
374.	SLC to ERR	Lee	26 July 1904	Benjamin
375.	SLC to HHR	Great Neck	18 August 1904	Salm
376.	SLC to HHR	Elmira	[?15 September 1904]	Salm
377.	SLC to HHR	Elmira	24 September [1904]	Salm
378.	SLC to KIH	New York	17 November 1904	MTP
379.	SLC to KIH	New York	22 November 1904	PH, MTP
380.	HHR to SLC	New York	27 March 1905	MTP
381.	KIH to SLC	New York	6 April 1905	MTP
382.	SLC to HHR	New York	21 April 1905	Salm
383.	HHR to SLC	New York	16 June 1905	MTP
384.	SLC to HHR	Dublin	19 June 1905	Salm
385.	SLC to HHR	Dublin	28 June 1905	Salm
386.	ERR to SLC	Fairhaven	2 July 1905	MTP
387.	SLC to HHR	Dublin	9 July 1905	Salm
388.	HHR to SLC	New York	11 July 1905	MTP
389.	SLC to HHR	Dublin	13 July 1905	Salm

No.	To	Location	Date	Authority
390.	SLC to HHR	Dublin	26–27 July 1905	MTP
391.	HHR to SLC	New York	27 July 1905	MTP
392.	HHR to SLC	Fairhaven	1 August 1905	MTP
393.	SLC to HHR	Dublin	7 August 1905	Salm
394.	SLC to HHR	Norfolk	14 August 1905	MTP
395.	SLC to HHR	Norfolk	21 August 1905	Salm
396.	SLC to HHR	Dublin	7 September 1905	Coe
397.	SLC to HHR	Dublin	16 September 1905	Salm
398.	SLC to HHR	Dublin	[?22] September 1905	Salm
399.	HHR to SLC	New York	26 September 1905	MTP
400.	HHR to SLC	New York	27 September 1905	MTP
401.	SLC to HHR	Dublin	5 October 1905	Salm
402.	SLC to HHR	Dublin	20 October 1905	Salm
403.	SLC to ERR	New York	[? December 1905]	Benjamin
404.	SLC to HHR	New York	30 December 1905	MTP
405.	SLC to HHR	New York	9 April 1906	Salm
406.	IVL to HHR	New York	30 April 1906	MTP
407.	HHR to SLC	New York	18 May 1906	MTP
408.	SLC to HHR	Dublin	18 May 1906	Salm
409.	HHR to SLC	New York	4 June 1906	MTP
410.	SLC to HHR	Dublin	6 June 1906	Coe
411.	SLC to HHR	Dublin	6 June 1906	Salm
412.	SLC to HHR	Dublin	13 June 1906	Coe

No.	To	Location	Date	Authority
413.	SLC to HHR	Dublin	[?17] June 1906	Salm
414.	SLC to ERR	New York	[Summer 1906]	Benjamin
415.	HHR to SLC	New York	8 August 1906	MTP
416.	SLC to ERR	Dublin	27 August 1906	MTP
417.	HHR to SLC	New York	31 August 1906	MTP
418.	SLC to HHR	Dublin	3 September 1906	Coe
419.	SLC to ERR	New York	24 October 1906	Benjamin
420.	SLC to ERR	New York	[?5] November 1906	Benjamin
421.	SLC to ERR	Washington	8 December 1906	Benjamin
422.	SLC to ERR	New York	22 December 1906	Benjamin
423.	SLC to HHR	New York	1 January 1907	Salm
424.	HHR to SLC	SS *Baltic*	8 May 1907	MTP
425.	SLC to HHR	Tuxedo Park	29 May 1907	Benjamin
426.	ERR to SLC	Vichy	12 June 1907	MTP
427.	HHR to SLC	Vichy	12 June 1907	MTP
428.	HHR to SLC	Vichy	13 June 1907	MTP
429.	HHR to SLC	London	26 June 1907	MTP
430.	HHR to SLC	London	27 June 1907	MTP
431.	SLC to HHR	Tuxedo Park	29 July 1907	Coe
432.	ERR to SLC	Fairhaven	12 August 1907	MTP
433.	ERR to SLC	Fairhaven	15 August 1907	MTP
434.	SLC to ERR	Tuxedo Park	18 August 1907	Benjamin
435.	IVL to ERR	Tuxedo Park	27 August 1907	Salm

No.	To	Location	Date	Authority
436.	HHR to SLC	Fairhaven	30 August 1907	MTP
437.	HHR to SLC	New Bedford	3 September 1907	MTP
438.	SLC to HHR	Tuxedo Park	20 September 1907	Salm
439.	SLC to HHR	Tuxedo Park	26 September 1907	Salm
440.	HHR to SLC	New Bedford	3 October 1907	MTP
441.	SLC to HHR	New York	4 October 1907	Salm
442.	SLC to HHR	New York	8 October 1907	Salm
443.	SLC to ERR	New York	2 December 1907	Benjamin
444.	HHR to SLC	New York	16 January 1908	MTP
445.	SLC to ERR	Bermuda	2 March 1908	Benjamin

VIII. 26 June 1908–11 May 1909

No.	To	Location	Date	Authority
446.	SLC to HHR	Redding	26 June 1908	Salm
447.	ERR to SLC	Fairhaven	3 August 1908	MTP
448.	SLC to ERR	Redding	6 August 1908	Salm
449.	SLC to ERR	Redding	12 August 1908	*MTL*, pp. 815–816
450.	SLC to ERR	Redding	7 October 1908	Benjamin
451.	SLC to ERR	Redding	12 October 1908	Benjamin
452.	ERR to SLC	Fairhaven	17 October 1908	MTP

No.	To	Location	Date	Authority
453.	SLC to ERR	Redding	24 October 1908	Benjamin
454.	SLC to ERR	Redding	23 November 1908	Benjamin
455.	HHR to SLC	New York	18 December 1908	MTP
456.	SLC to HHR	Redding	19 December 1908	Salm
457.	SLC to HHR	Redding	25 February 1909	TS, MTP
458.	SLC to HHR	Redding	4 March 1909	Benjamin
459.	HHR to SLC	New York	8 March 1909	MTP
460.	SLC to HHR	Redding	26 April 1909	Coe
461.	SLC to ERR	Redding	2 May 1909	Benjamin
462.	SLC to HHR	Redding	4 May 1909	Salm
463.	SLC to HHR	Redding	9 May 1909	MTP
464.	KIH to SLC	New York	11 May 1909	MTP

Biographical Directory

THE FOLLOWING selective directory of persons who figure in the Mark Twain-H. H. Rogers correspondence is intended only to help place the person in the context of the present volume or to supply information that is not given in such standard sources as Webster's *Biographical Dictionary, The Oxford Companion to American Literature,* or the readily available volumes of Mark Twain scholarship. Genealogical charts of the immediate members of the Clemens and Rogers families appear at the end of this directory.

ALDEN, HENRY MILLS (1836–1919). Editor of *Harper's Magazine* for fifty years, beginning in 1869. A graduate of Williams College and the Andover Theological Seminary, he began to work for the Harper publishing house at the age of twenty-seven. He wrote several theological works, as well as a volume of literary criticism, but he was mainly occupied with editorial advice concerning the manuscripts of others, including Clemens. He was given increasing control by the Harper family over the content of their journal, and by 1885 his understanding of reader interest had at least partly accounted for a rise to a monthly circulation of 200,000 in America.

ASHCROFT, RALPH W. (1875–1947). Secretary and treasurer of the Plasmon Company of America in 1905 when Clemens considered instituting legal action against the company's directing agent Henry A. Butters for mismanagement of investments. Ashcroft's sympathetic approach to Clemens's interests led to his being hired to accompany

Clemens to England for the awarding of Clemens's Oxford degree in June 1907. He was retained to handle Clemens's business affairs until 1909. At that time he and his bride, Isabel Lyon (Clemens's confidential secretary), were charged with financial mismanagement and abruptly dismissed. Ashcroft subsequently worked as advertising director for various Canadian business firms.

BENJAMIN, WILLIAM EVARTS (1859–1940). The husband of H. H. Rogers's eldest daughter, Anne Engle Rogers. The youngest son of poet and editor Park Benjamin, he attended Union College in Schenectady. He was employed by Dodd, Mead & Company until 1884, when he entered the rare-book and autograph business with his brother, Walter Romeyn Benjamin. Although he was a director of the Virginian Railway Company after his marriage in 1886, his chief interest continued to be in rare books and manuscripts. The Library of Congress and Columbia University were recipients of valuable contributions from his collections. For several years beginning in 1887, he was a publisher; one of his principal publications was the Stedman and Hutchinson *Library of American Literature* (1894), which he had taken over from Charles L. Webster & Company.

BLISS, FRANCIS EDWARD (1843–1915). He succeeded his father, Elisha, as president of the American Publishing Company in 1880. His half-brother, Walter (1860–1917), served as secretary of the company, which under their management published Clemens's *Following the Equator* and a twenty-three-volume uniform edition of Clemens's collected works (1899–1903).

BROUGHTON, URBAN HANLON (1857–1929). Husband of Cara Leland Rogers, he was an English civil engineer, who had been educated at the University of London and several other British schools. Shortly after his immigration to the United States, he supervised a drainage project in Fairhaven, where he met and married Cara (12 November 1895). Thereafter he became an officer in numerous American engineering, mining, financial, and railway companies, most of them affiliated with Rogers. Broughton was made president of the consolidated Paige Compositor Manufacturing Company, formed under Rogers's direction. In 1912 the Broughtons moved to England, where he was elected to Parliament (1915–1918). He was a dedicated supporter of the Conservative party. He died shortly before he was to be elevated to the peerage as Baron Fairhaven, but his sons—first, Urban Huttleston Rogers Broughton (1896–1966) and then Henry Rogers Broughton (b. 1900)—have retained the title.

COE, WILLIAM ROBERTSON (1869–1955). Husband of Mai Huttleston Rogers. Born in Worcestershire, England, and educated at Albion Academy, Cardiff, Wales, he moved with his family to Philadelphia in 1883 and was naturalized in 1890. In 1893 he went to New York as an insurance broker in the firm of Johnson & Higgins. After the death of his first wife in 1898, he married Rogers's youngest daughter on 4 June 1900. He became a director of Johnson & Higgins in 1902 and was named president in 1910. He was a director of the Virginian Railway Company and an investor in coal and real estate. In his later years he was a sportsman who maintained a large racing stable, and he was well known for his philanthropy.

CRANE, SUSAN LANGDON (Mrs. Theodore) (1836–1924). Olivia Clemens's foster-sister, an investor in Paige typesetter stock, made substantial sympathetic but ineffective efforts to help Clemens forestall the failure of that doomed enterprise as well as that of the Charles L. Webster publishing company. She owned Quarry Farm, in Elmira, New York, where the Clemens family spent many summers.

DOUBLEDAY, FRANK NELSON (1862–1934). Joined S. S. McClure to found the publishing firm of Doubleday & McClure in 1897. In 1900 he founded Doubleday, Page & Company.

DUNEKA, FREDERICK A. (d. 1919). Became general manager and secretary of the board of directors of Harper & Brothers in 1900 when George Harvey became president of the company. Formerly city editor for Pulitzer's New York *World,* he was instructed by Harvey to use new promotional techniques to bolster Harper's declining advertising and subscription revenue. He was largely responsible for editing Clemens's "Chapters from My Autobiography" for serial publication in *North American Review* (1906/07) and assisted Albert Bigelow Paine in assembling a text of *The Mysterious Stranger* for posthumous publication.

FROHMAN, CHARLES (1860–1915). Theatrical impresario and manager of various New York theaters, including the Lyceum. His brother Daniel (1851–1940), also a theater manager, an author, and a playwright, was financially involved in the Lyceum.

GILDER, RICHARD WATSON (1844–1909). Editor of *Century* magazine, which published many of Clemens's writings over a period of twenty years, including the 1893/94 serialization of *Pudd'nhead Wilson*. Clemens and his daughters stayed with the Gilder family in the summer of 1904 following Livy's death.

GRANT, FREDERICK DENT (1850–1912). A military and political figure, he became involved in the settlement of the Charles L. Webster publishing company's affairs when, as U. S. Grant's eldest son, he advanced claims for payment of additional royalties on his father's memoirs. Lincoln Steffens, recalling this period in his Autobiography, compared Colonel Fred Grant to the daily report of the Chicago hog market—"dull but firm."

HALL, FREDERICK J. He succeeded Charles L. Webster as manager of Clemens's publishing company in 1888. Although Clemens later attacked Hall bitterly, it is evident that the inexperienced young man was earnest in trying to prevent the company's collapse under its overexpanded publication schedule and the disastrous Panic of 1893.

HARRISON, KATHARINE I. (1867?–1935). Rogers's private secretary and administrative assistant. A graduate of Wright's Business College in Brooklyn, she was employed by the Standard Oil Company as a stenographer, probably in 1888. According to Clemens (*MTA*, I, 252), Rogers called her in an emergency from among a pool of seven hundred and fifty typewriting clerks and was so impressed by the young woman that he retained her as his personal aide until his death in 1909. She became "a cyclopaedia in whose head is written down the multitudinous details of Mr. Rogers's business." She was characterized in Wall Street as "the Sphinx," the woman who knew all there was to know about Standard Oil. Newspaper and magazine reporters were intrigued by this privileged and inscrutable figure, who made it a lifetime rule never to grant personal interviews and who was "harder to approach than some of the giants of finance of the day" (New York *Times*, 17 January 1935). Despite her desire for privacy, her astounding $10,000 yearly salary kept her in the public eye; at the turn of the century she was a pioneer among high-salaried women executives in business.

Seated within the inner sanctum at 26 Broadway, she was the last hope and the final barrier for the many callers seeking interviews with Rogers. It was well known that "there [was] no appeal to Mr. Rogers

over her head" (New York *World,* 24 April 1904). Indeed, few suppli-
cants were even permitted to state their cases to Miss Harrison; her own
secretary, stationed some distance down the corridor, was rumored to
turn back thirty-five of every forty men who sent in their cards. Those
few who were allowed behind the ground-glass doors encountered an
imposing woman who was tall (nearly six feet, according to contemporary accounts), bespectacled, and rather severely dressed; Ida Tarbell
described her as a woman who "radiated efficiency—business competency," but "with her competency went that gleam of hardness which
efficient business women rarely escape" (*All in the Day's Work,* New
York, 1939, p. 216).

After Rogers's death she retired from business and remained for some
time at her three-story brick home on Dean Street in Brooklyn with her
mother and two sisters. In 1913, however, when the Pujo Committee of
the House of Representatives tried to subpoena her for hearings in
Washington during the "Money Trust" investigations (they sought
information about Rogers's 1902 Amalgamated Copper transactions),
private detectives could not find her, so it was concluded that she had
left the country. She later moved to Fifth Avenue in New York,
continuing to refuse all interviews with a firm "I am sorry, I'd rather be
excused." On 16 January 1935 she died of a cerebral hemorrhage at a
hotel in Palm Beach, Florida, where she was staying with her sister.

HARVEY, GEORGE (1864–1928). From 1899 he was editor of the *North
American Review,* which published extensive "Chapters from My Autobiography" in 1906 and 1907, as well as other writings by Clemens.
Harvey, formerly the managing editor of the New York World, became
president of the financially pressed firm of Harper & Brothers in 1900 at
the request of J. P. Morgan, the company's principal creditor. With
Rogers he negotiated long-range contracts for that company's publication of Clemens's works. He had received his title of "Colonel" when, at
the age of twenty-one, he was appointed aide-de-camp on the staff of the
governor of New Jersey.

HOWELLS, JOHN MEAD (1868–1959). Son of William Dean Howells,
he studied architecture at *École des Beaux Arts* in Paris and won several
architectural competitions. He was a founder of the architectural firm of
Howells, Stokes & Hornbostel. Clemens hired him in 1906 to design
and build "Stormfield," which Clemens described as an "American-Ital-
ian villa . . . the ideal house, the ideal home."

HUTTON, LAURENCE (1843–1904). Editor, essayist, drama critic, and author of numerous books about the theater, he was a charter member of The Players Club. From 1886 to 1898 he was literary editor of *Harper's Magazine.* From 1901 to 1904 he was a lecturer in English literature at Princeton University.

KELLGREN, JONAS HENRIK (1837–1916). A Swedish therapist, his "mechano-therapeutics" method of treatment was widely publicized at the turn of the century. He founded Kellgren Institutes in London (1875), Baden-Baden (1883), and Paris (1884); and in 1886 he established a health sanitorium near Jonkoping, Sweden, on Lake Vettern. At these centers Kellgren, assisted by his son Harry and a number of devoted disciples, undertook the cure of patients who included Sir Henry M. Stanley and Queen Sophia of Sweden. Kellgren took pride in the "simplicity and rationality" of his treatment, which was designed to affect the nerves "by vibrations and frictions of a special nature, by means of the touch . . . combined with muscular exercises." His disdain for the use of drugs dismayed many doctors. Clemens was enthusiastic about the Kellgren Treatment, as it was called, and Jean Clemens, suffering from epilepsy, was a Kellgren patient at least until 1900. The clinic in Sweden, open only in summer, closed in 1904.

LAFFAN, WILLIAM MACKAY (1848–1909). He joined the staff of the New York *Sun* under the editorship of Charles A. Dana in 1877 as a drama and art critic; and he subsequently directed the business affairs of the paper. An amateur artist, Laffan served as consultant in the development of J. P. Morgan's art collection, and he was a trustee of the Metropolitan Museum of Art.

LANGDON, CHARLES JERVIS (1849–1916). Olivia Clemens's brother, he succeeded their father in the management of the J. Langdon Coal Company in Elmira. And he exercised considerable responsibility for his sister's inherited investments. The governor of New York made him a commissary general in 1880. His children were Jervis, Julia, and Ida.

LYON, ISABEL V. (1868–1958). She became Clemens's secretary in 1903 and took increasing responsibility in his business and social affairs until 1909 when she and Ralph Ashcroft, whom she had recently married, were accused of attempting to defraud Clemens. Although the episode was widely publicized, Clemens's charges were never tested in court.

McCLURE, SAMUEL S. (1857–1949). Volatile and enthusiastic founder of McClure's Syndicate and *McClure's Magazine*. Despite repeated attempts to interest Clemens in publications and editorial ventures, only two minor pieces by Clemens were ever published in *McClure's Magazine*.

MAYO, FRANK (Frank McGuire) (1839–1896). An American character actor, he was most famous for his performance of *Davy Crockett*, which he toured through the United States and England. He successfully dramatized *Pudd'nhead Wilson* and was performing the title role in a traveling company when he died. His son Edwin's attempts to continue the production were not successful.

MOFFETT, SAMUEL ERASMUS (1860–1908). The son of Clemens's sister Pamela, he attended the University of California and received a Ph.D. from Columbia University. He worked as a reporter, a political correspondent, and an editorial writer for such newspapers as the *Examiner* and the *Evening Post* in San Francisco and the *Journal* and the *World* in New York. When he died, while swimming off the coast of New Jersey, Moffett had been conducting a column titled "What the World Is Doing" in *Collier's* magazine for three years. Later, the editors of that journal stated that "his humor was unfailing; he was so gentle and lovable; it was a surprise to find every line he wrote vigorous and militant for human progress." After his nephew's death, Clemens wrote that Moffett "lived and died unsordid . . . he lived and died a gentleman."

PAIGE, JAMES W. An inventor in the Yankee tradition, he arrived in Hartford from Rochester, New York, with a design for a machine "for distributing, setting, and justifying type." The idea had occurred to him in 1872, and when he moved to Hartford in 1876 to supervise construction of the first model, he confidently listed himself in the city directory as "James W. Paige, Patentee." Clemens described him as "an extraordinary compound of business thrift and commercial insanity" because of his continual tinkerings to perfect the machine, just when it seemed that huge sums of money were within the grasp of its financiers. The companies formed to develop the compositor required frequent financial assistance: Rogers advanced them more than $78,000, and, according to Albert Bigelow Paine, Clemens eventually invested $190,000 in Paige's models. Only two of the machines were actually completed (both were soon relegated to museums; one is now on display at the Mark Twain Memorial in Hartford). The machine had eighteen thousand parts and it was rumored that during the eight years in which the patents were pending, one suicide and two cases of insanity were recorded among the examiners of the hundreds of drawings and specifications.

Even after hope for the typesetter collapsed, Paige stayed on in Chicago, and apparently remained convinced of his future as an inventor. The man Clemens wished he could catch in a steel trap so that he could "shut out all human succor and watch that trap till he died" went on to other ventures. In 1896 he was granted the patent for a "pneumatic tire" which featured an inner tube with internal compartments separated by flaps which unfolded when the tire was inflated. In 1905, and again in 1907, he was granted a patent for innovations in "corn husking and shredding machines"; these inventions were subsidized by several individuals and firms, but were never commerically manufactured.

POND, JAMES B. (1838–1903). A prominent lecture agent, he managed Clemens's 1884/85 tour of public readings with George Washington Cable. Pond also made the arrangements for Clemens's 1895/96 lecture trip around the world, and he and his wife accompanied the Clemens family across the United States during the initial phase of the tour.

RICE, CLARENCE CHARLES, M.D. (1853–1935). As Rogers's friend and physician and Clemens's fellow member of The Players Club, it was he who introduced the two men. Rice was a nose-and-throat specialist whose patients included many operatic and stage performers such as E. H. Sothern, Julia Marlowe, Enrico Caruso, Edwin Booth, and Lillian Russell. In addition, Rice served as the house physician for the Metropolitan Opera and held several distinguished appointments on the faculty and administrative staffs of the New York Post-Graduate Medical School and Hospital and a wide variety of other institutions and professional organizations. Clemens once characterized him as "a physician of great reputation, and one of the choicest human beings in the world. I go bail for him."

ROGERS, ABBIE PALMER GIFFORD (1841–1894). The first wife of H. H. Rogers (m. 1862) and the mother of his five children: Anne, Cara, Millicent (1873–1890), Mai, and Harry. A schoolmate of her husband in Fairhaven, Massachusetts, she shared with him many early privations in the oil fields of Pennsylvania. She later became a quiet but gracious hostess in his handsome New York town house and in his country home at Fairhaven. She seems to have been the initiator of many of the early Rogers benefactions, including the presentation of the Fairhaven Town Hall. At the time of her death she was a director on the board of the New York Post-Graduate Medical School and Hospital.

ROGERS, ANNE ENGLE (1865–1924). Rogers's eldest daughter, she married William Evarts Benjamin in 1886. Her daughter Beatrice (1889–1956) married Alexander D. P. Pratt in 1909; her son Henry Rogers Benjamin (1892–1967) contributed generously to this volume from his collection of Mark Twain letters.

ROGERS, CARA LELAND (Lady Fairhaven) (1867–1939). Rogers's second daughter. In 1890 she married Bradford F. Duff, who died of "lung disease" at the age of twenty-four on 6 September 1893. She was married again on 12 November 1895, to Urban Hanlon Broughton. In 1912 they and their two sons returned to his native England. She was permitted to use the title Lady Fairhaven, although her husband died shortly before he was to have been elevated to the peerage by George V. Their first son, Urban Huttleston Rogers Broughton (b. 1896), was created Baron Fairhaven in 1929; his brother, Henry Rogers Broughton (b. 1900), was given a warrant of precedence. In that same year Lady Fairhaven donated to the British nation the historic meadow of Runnymede on the Thames. In 1936 she presented Fort Phoenix in Fairhaven to the town as a park in memory of her father.

ROGERS, EMILIE AUGUSTA RANDEL HART (1847–1912). Rogers's second wife (m. 3 June 1896). She had previously been married to Lucius R. Hart, who was in the metal business in New York. She survived Rogers and was bequeathed an annual income of $100,000 at his death.

ROGERS, HENRY (HARRY) HUDDLESTON (1879–1935). He was the only son of Rogers, educated at private schools in New York and, briefly, at Columbia University. He married Mary Benjamin on 7 November 1900. A lieutenant colonel in the New York National Guard, he served on the Mexican border in 1916 and in World War I received the Distinguished Service Medal and the Croix de Guerre with Palm for service in the French offensives. His financial interests were varied, particularly after his father's death in 1909; he was successively vice-president and general manager of the Atlantic Coast Electric

Railroad and the Staten Island Midland Railroad, president of the Richmond Light and Railroad Company, and vice-president of the Virginian Railway. Divorced in 1929, he married Mrs. Marguerite von Braun Savelle Basil Miles in the same year. He married again, Mrs. Pauline Van Der Voort Dresser, in 1933. He had two children by his first wife, the younger of whom was Henry Huddleston Rogers, Jr. (1905–1948); his daughter, Mary Millicent (1902–1953), was the mother of Peter A. Salm, from whose collection many of the letters in this volume derive.

ROGERS, MAI (MARY) HUTTLESTON (1875–1924). Rogers's youngest daughter, she married William R. Coe on 4 June 1900, after the annulment of her early marriage to Joseph C. Mott. The Coes had four children: William Rogers Coe (b. 1901); Robert Douglas Coe (b. 1902); Henry Huttleston Rogers Coe (1907–1966); and Natalie Mai Coe (b. 1910). In later years Mrs. Coe was known as a cultivator of flowers, particularly prize-winning camellias.

ROGERS, MARY BENJAMIN (1879–1956). Daughter of George Hillard Benjamin and niece of William Evarts Benjamin, who had married Anne E. Rogers in 1886. She was the first wife of Rogers's only son, Harry, whom she married on 7 November 1900; they had two children, Mary Millicent Rogers (b. 1902) and Henry Huddleston Rogers, Jr. (b. 1905). She was a great favorite of Clemens's; her correspondence with him and an account of their friendship has been published as *Mark Twain's Letters to Mary*. She never remarried after her divorce from Rogers in 1929. In later years she became a serious artist; her work was exhibited in New York and California. She engaged in Red Cross activities and welfare work for the armed forces in both World Wars. At the time of her death she maintained residences in Bennington, Vermont, and Boca Grande, Florida.

STANLEY, HENRY M. (1841–1904). The success of this renowned newspaperman and explorer as a public lecturer was at least partially responsible for Clemens's decision to undertake his 1895/96 lecture tour.

STOKER, BRAM (Abraham) (1847–1912). He was an Irish civil servant until he became the manager of Sir Henry Irving's Lyceum Theatre in London in 1878. He was associated with Irving until the latter's death in 1905, when he wrote *Personal Reminiscences of Henry Irving*. The author of several novels (including *Dracula,* 1897) and a good companion, he listed as his recreations in *Who's Who,* 1901, "pretty much the same as those of the other children of Adam." Encouraged by Clemens's friendship, he made small investments in Paige typesetter stock.

TWICHELL, JOSEPH HOPKINS (1838–1918). Pastor of the Asylum Hill Congregational Church in Hartford, he was one of Clemens's most intimate friends after 1869. He officiated at Clemens's marriage, at Livy's funeral, at the funerals of various members of the Clemens family, and finally at Clemens's own funeral. In 1905 he and his wife, Harmony, received a much-needed anonymous gift of $1500 from Rogers, which Rogers never acknowledged—an example of the financial czar's frequent private generosities.

WEBSTER, CHARLES L. (1851–1891). A partner and manager of the Charles L. Webster & Company publishing house, which was largely owned by Clemens. The firm's initial success in 1885 with U. S. Grant's *Memoirs,* the reminiscences of other Civil War figures and Twain's own books gave way to bankruptcy in 1894, six years after Webster's retirement in 1888. Assessment of responsibility for the failure can be found in *Mark Twain's Letters to His Publishers, 1867–1894.*

WHITMORE, FRANKLIN GRAY (1846–1926). A Hartford dealer in real estate and insurance, Whitmore began serving as Clemens's business agent at least as early as 1887. Their sustained, if uneven, business relationship virtually drew to a close after Whitmore finally sold the Clemenses's Hartford house in 1903.

HENRY HUTTLESTON ROGERS'S IMMEDIATE FAMILY

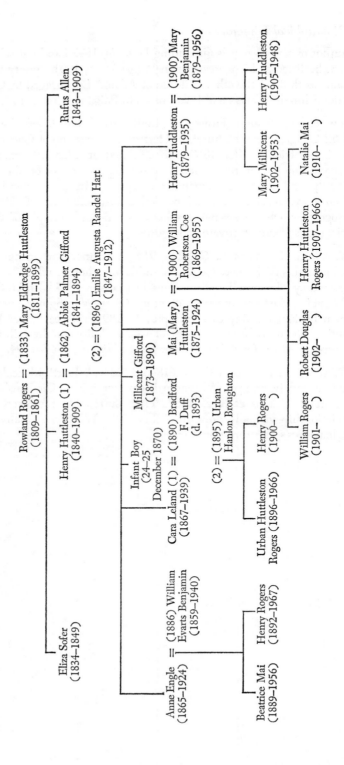

Samuel L. Clemens's Immediate Family

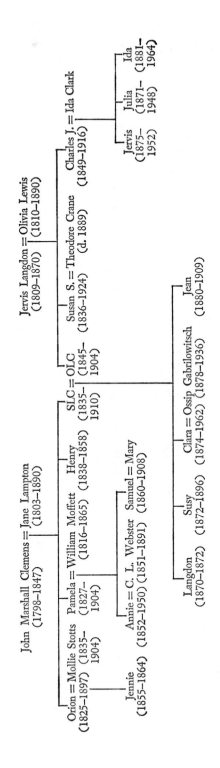

Index

This is a selective index. Persons mentioned in the text are recorded here only when the information given about them is substantive. Only those business firms in which Rogers or Clemens had an important interest are listed, and newspapers and periodicals which are merely cited in the editorial material are not. Material in the appendixes is not indexed. Mark Twain's writings are listed by title.